Handbook of Research on Digital Marketing Innovations in Social Entrepreneurship and Solidarity Economics

Jose Manuel Saiz-Alvarez
Tecnologico de Monterrey, Mexico

A volume in the Advances in Marketing, Customer Relationship Management, and E-Services (AMCRMES) Book Series

IGI Global
DISSEMINATOR OF KNOWLEDGE

Published in the United States of America by
IGI Global
Business Science Reference (an imprint of IGI Global)
701 E. Chocolate Avenue
Hershey PA, USA 17033
Tel: 717-533-8845
Fax: 717-533-8661
E-mail: cust@igi-global.com
Web site: http://www.igi-global.com

Library of Congress Cataloging-in-Publication Data

Names: Saiz Alvarez, Jose Manuel, editor.
Title: Handbook of research on digital marketing innovations in social entrepreneurship and solidarity economics / Jose Manuel Saiz-Alvarez, editor.
Description: Hershey, PA : Business Science Reference, [2019]
Identifiers: LCCN 2018061677| ISBN 9781522589396 (hardcover) | ISBN 9781522589402 (ebook)
Subjects: LCSH: Social entrepreneurship. | Internet marketing. | Social marketing.
Classification: LCC HD60 .H3348 2019 | DDC 658.8/72--dc23 LC record available at https://lccn.loc.gov/2018061677

This book is published in the IGI Global book series Advances in Marketing, Customer Relationship Management, and E-Services (AMCRMES) (ISSN: 2327-5502; eISSN: 2327-5529)

British Cataloguing in Publication Data
A Cataloguing in Publication record for this book is available from the British Library.

For electronic access to this publication, please contact: eresources@igi-global.com.

Advances in Marketing, Customer Relationship Management, and E-Services (AMCRMES) Book Series

Eldon Y. Li
National Chengchi University, Taiwan & California Polytechnic State University, USA

ISSN:2327-5502
EISSN:2327-5529

Mission

Business processes, services, and communications are important factors in the management of good customer relationship, which is the foundation of any well organized business. Technology continues to play a vital role in the organization and automation of business processes for marketing, sales, and customer service. These features aid in the attraction of new clients and maintaining existing relationships.

The Advances in Marketing, Customer Relationship Management, and E-Services (AMCRMES) Book Series addresses success factors for customer relationship management, marketing, and electronic services and its performance outcomes. This collection of reference source covers aspects of consumer behavior and marketing business strategies aiming towards researchers, scholars, and practitioners in the fields of marketing management.

Coverage

- Data mining and marketing
- Ethical Considerations in E-Marketing
- Social Networking and Marketing
- Legal Considerations in E-Marketing
- CRM in financial services
- Online Community Management and Behavior
- Cases on CRM Implementation
- E-Service Innovation
- Cases on Electronic Services
- Relationship Marketing

IGI Global is currently accepting manuscripts for publication within this series. To submit a proposal for a volume in this series, please contact our Acquisition Editors at Acquisitions@igi-global.com or visit: http://www.igi-global.com/publish/.

The Advances in Marketing, Customer Relationship Management, and E-Services (AMCRMES) Book Series (ISSN 2327-5502) is published by IGI Global, 701 E. Chocolate Avenue, Hershey, PA 17033-1240, USA, www.igi-global.com. This series is composed of titles available for purchase individually; each title is edited to be contextually exclusive from any other title within the series. For pricing and ordering information please visit http://www.igi-global.com/book-series/advances-marketing-customer-relationship-management/37150. Postmaster: Send all address changes to above address.

Titles in this Series

For a list of additional titles in this series, please visit: www.igi-global.com/book-series

Leveraging Computer-Mediated Marketing Environments
Gordon Bowen (Regent's University London, UK) and Wilson Ozuem (University of Cumbria, UK)
Business Science Reference • copyright 2019 • 473pp • H/C (ISBN: 9781522573449) • US $205.00 (our price)

Integrated Marketing Communications, Strategies, and Tactical Operations in Sports Organizations
Manuel Alonso Dos Santos (Universidad Católica de la Santísima Concepción, Chile)
Business Science Reference • copyright 2019 • 325pp • H/C (ISBN: 9781522576174) • US $215.00 (our price)

Exploring the Dynamics of Consumerism in Developing Nations
Ayantunji Gbadamosi (University of East London, UK)
Business Science Reference • copyright 2019 • 428pp • H/C (ISBN: 9781522579069) • US $225.00 (our price)

Evaluating the Gaps and Intersections Between Marketing Education and the Marketing Profession
Margarida M. Pinheiro (University of Aveiro, Portugal) Ana Estima (University of Aveiro, Portugal) and Susana Marques (University of Aveiro, Portugal)
Business Science Reference • copyright 2019 • 252pp • H/C (ISBN: 9781522562955) • US $190.00 (our price)

Advanced Methodologies and Technologies in Digital Marketing and Entrepreneurship
Mehdi Khosrow-Pour, D.B.A. (Information Resources Management Association, USA)
Business Science Reference • copyright 2019 • 818pp • H/C (ISBN: 9781522577669) • US $315.00 (our price)

Multifaceted Explorations of Consumer Culture and Its Impact on Individuals and Society
David J. Burns (Kennesaw State University, USA)
Business Science Reference • copyright 2019 • 318pp • H/C (ISBN: 9781522561200) • US $215.00 (our price)

The Role of Language and Symbols in Promotional Strategies and Marketing Schemes
Manuela Epure (Spiru Haret University, Romania) and Lorena Clara Mihăeş (University of Bucharest, Romania)
Business Science Reference • copyright 2019 • 333pp • H/C (ISBN: 9781522557784) • US $205.00 (our price)

Application of Gaming in New Media Marketing
Pratika Mishra (Presidency University Bangalore, India) and Swati Oberoi Dham (New Delhi Institute of Management, India)
Business Science Reference • copyright 2019 • 312pp • H/C (ISBN: 9781522560647) • US $215.00 (our price)

IGI Global
DISSEMINATOR OF KNOWLEDGE

701 East Chocolate Avenue, Hershey, PA 17033, USA
Tel: 717-533-8845 x100 • Fax: 717-533-8661
E-Mail: cust@igi-global.com • www.igi-global.com

Editorial Advisory Board

List of Reviewers

List of Contributors

Table of Contents

Detailed Table of Contents

Capitalism has required the function of the entrepreneurs, people who use creativity, understood as the ability to solve problems and put innovation into practice. Firms can be social, public, and private; in this last case, the creation of an enterprising company involves new products, new production methods, the opening of new markets, the development of new sources of raw materials and inputs, and the creation of new market structures in the industry. This chapter is a bibliographical review of the theories of entrepreneurship from economics, sociology, psychology, and management aiming to contribute to the construction of a definition of entrepreneurship and entrepreneur that can be accepted by scholars in this field.

This chapter deals with how the socioeconomics of solidarity inserted in the Industry 4.0 can bring about solidarity and the creation of social and economic wealth based on the guiding principles of subsidiarity, the search for the common good, and solidarity based on social justice. After having grounded these principles, the author develops different solidarity-based public policies, mainly focused on the European Union, by including principles, objectives, and stages of the European ODA (Official Development Aid), the European Development Fund, the Common Framework for Joint Multiannual Programming and Efficiency, and the European Consensus on Development "Our World, Our Dignity, Our Future." Some ideas complement this analysis linked to the socioeconomics of solidarity that focuses on solidarity and justice to search for a more balanced business world defined by social welfare and economic wealth.

Management concepts have evolved as a separate discipline after the industrial revolution. In connection with this development, this discipline has combined so many different theories from different disciplines and approaches from different researchers and applications from different managers and other professionals. This amazing development of management has reached its peak in today's global business environment. Strategy concepts like vision, mission, SWOT, and competition on war footing for markets were influence of military science. Different contemporary management techniques, approaches, and implications are applicable in this unstable, dynamic, and knowledge-intensive environment. Among the various approaches, competitiveness, competitive strategies, and competitive advantage are at the core of organizational growth, development, and sustainability. Adopting a grounded theory approach with in-depth literature review, this study aims to discuss and deliberate on factors creating competitive advantage for organizations, especially family-owned SMEs, irrespective of their stage of development.

This chapter studies family micro business in Chile and economic development generated around them, specifically in the commerce sector. Firstly, it introduces the micro, small, and medium enterprises context. Then, through a mixed methodology, narrative, and descriptive based on information from secondary sources such as legal bodies, reports, and databases generated by various Chilean State entities, it determines what is the micro family business in Chile and enterprises that are concentrated in the grocery stores. And finally, obtaining as main conclusions, the experience of these microentrepreneurs in opting to establish themselves as companies through an exceptional legal regime, based on the benefits gained from participating in the public technical cooperation program Grocery Stores of Chile is presented.

This chapter reviews the factors that are relevant to promote an entrepreneurial attitude, identifying education as an element of vital importance that influences the disposition to start a venture and its results. This is particularly important in the case of social entrepreneurship projects, in which good intentions frequently overcome sound business realities. To deepen the understanding of the relationship between education and social entrepreneurship, the authors develop the model "pyramid of catalysts for entrepreneurship," which helps to understand the mechanism by which the educational process affects the quantity and quality of social entrepreneurship. This chapter also presents several elements of paramount importance in designing a program of social entrepreneurial education.

Entrepreneurship needs a vision and leadership skills to accomplish it and a motivation to build something new, which will develop and sustain it. And society needs social entrepreneurs, contributing to a new organization of the welfare system, while making a difference and helping each other. The central theme in the existing social entrepreneurship literature is the pursuit of a social mission or objective. Thus, social entrepreneurs play a role as reformers and revolutionaries, who are intending to solve social problems, and not being answered by governmental policies. Entrepreneurial thinking and acting as well as innovation driving managers is a need for society. However, it is not the organization but the people, united by a proactive and market-driven culture, that are innovative and which combine to populate and to equip the organization with the required competencies. The chapter proposes a methodology to analyze the competencies that should be fostered by higher education programs to provide graduates with the desired competencies for entrepreneurship and driving innovation.

This chapter aims to analyze the relationship between business models and dynamic capabilities in firms of the systems development sector of Bogota (Colombia). Based on the theoretical framework of business models, the author applies an analysis based on principal categorical components and categorical regression. Results show a correlation between the elements of the business model (strategy and dynamic capabilities) and business performance. In conclusion, the author proposes a business model endowed with efficiency, effectiveness, and efficacy for newly created micro, small, and medium-sized family firms that highly correlates with business performance.

Scarce research was identified regarding the academic entrepreneur as a critical agent of change and its relation within the process of academic entrepreneurship, as well as the dynamics of different factors in the decision to become an entrepreneur. The study of academicians' entrepreneurial intention is of special relevance due to their roles as teachers and researchers, and because entrepreneurs are part of innovation ecosystems, entrepreneurial universities, entrepreneurship, and innovation itself. Accordingly, academic entrepreneurs have become the focus and strategic orientation of decision makers in the higher education system. Consequently, the purpose of this descriptive study is to contribute to the knowledge of the characteristics of academicians in Mexico and the way these characteristics influence the entrepreneurial intention. In this chapter, a sample of 209 scholars was obtained. The results show significant differences for entrepreneurial intention depending on previous work experience and formation.

As a predominant form of business organization, family firms have attracted increasing attention by scholars, and especially by those researching entrepreneurial orientation with the aim of better understanding of entrepreneurial activities pursued by enterprises. However, the literature on the confluence of entrepreneurial orientation and family firms has paid scant attention to the influence of affective and emotional factors. To cover this research gap, the authors analyze the impact of affective commitment and concern for socioemotional wealth preservation on entrepreneurial orientation. To do so, they performed an empirical study using the data collected from 342 small and mid-sized family firms from Portugal, a country where family firms are under-researched even though they make up the backbone of the economy. Results show that both affective commitment and socioemotional wealth positively impact entrepreneurial orientation, pointing to the need to further research the relationships between such factors and strategic behaviors in the family business context.

This chapter gives an account of how the orange economy begins to penetrate the traditional economy of Latin American countries, which are oriented towards the export of generic products and low commercial value. For this, the authors have analyzed the experiences of 18 Latin American creative companies identified by the Inter-American Development Bank. Cases selected concentrates in the media and software platforms sectors of the orange economy, with a qualitative approach and a narrative design through the analysis of the information of these 18 extreme cases of business success describes the possibilities that in the Latin American reality can be visualized. As a result, this chapter allows us to understand the opportunities of entrepreneurship, through the orange economy in Latin America, and to distinguish how this economic, social, and cultural phenomenon is observed, starting from the Latin American academic discourse, contributing to the construction of a definition that tries to achieve a greater conceptual precision concerning Orange economy.

The chapter contains the concepts of social entrepreneurship, planned and perceived obsolescence, corporate social responsibility, the legal framework for electrical and electronic equipment (EEE) waste, and reverse logistics, as theoretical support from different authors. Applied to Manizales, Colombia, the study was conducted with a quantitative and qualitative approach. The information was collected through surveys and interviews with 26 entrepreneurs and 331 households' consumers to know the type of appliances, how they buy, change, and use them, and the chain of intermediaries. With planned and perceived obsolescence, products lose their life in a short time, are dumped as waste of electrical and electronic equipment (WEEE), and collected by people of a low educational and economic level that survive in precarious conditions. Due to these results and conclusions, the authors offer in the chapter the opportunity to generate proposals for their inclusion and social development.

The purpose of this chapter is to examine the effect of joint liability lending on micro businesses in Madina municipality. Joint liability lending has become a popular and fashionable word in financial and development circles. It is a cross-sectional survey study and used both primary and secondary data on joint liability lending. The study reveals that joint liability lending improves entrepreneurship and reduces poverty. There exists a significant relationship between joint liability lending and a high repayment rate. The implications are that individual within the group are encouraged to continue saving and microfinance institutions should continue investing in educating and training clients to improve upon their micro businesses.

A redirection towards wellbeing with a view to produce lasting social and economic vitality for the global civilization necessitates moving from conventional economic methods towards innovative solutions, which are necessary to face challenges of today and the future to foster sustainable growth. Social innovation and its agents can be considered as a toolbox which may facilitate a transition by positively influencing wellbeing, developing ways of integrating it into policy, and promoting it as an alternative measure of progress. Social innovation may increase the role of civil society in solving social problems, while sustaining and improving people's wellbeing beyond increasing their welfare in monetary term. By providing up-to-date solutions to challenges ranging from global warming to fair income distribution, and from social innovative entrepreneurs to grass-rooted innovation, social innovation seems to be capable of transforming the society in a way to tackle with a new kind of societal problems, and of exploring new ways to create added value for the economy.

Section 2
Digital Marketing

Given the rise of new technologies and the resultant changes in consumer behavior, marketing practices need to evolve, which requires organizations to rethink their strategies. Having a digital marketing strategy can establish a direct dialog with customers, thereby increasing knowledge about customers, suppliers, and partners, as well as building, consolidating, and maintaining brand awareness. However, little is known about the attitudes and perceptions of consumers toward popular digital marketing tools that can strategically be used in an integrated digital marketing strategy. Therefore, the objective of this research is to understand the perceptions of digital moms toward technology and digital marketing strategies. Following a qualitative and interpretative approach, the results contribute to the literature by (1) addressing the symbolic meanings that technological tools have in the lives of this group of consumers and (2) providing insights on how different digital marketing strategies commonly implemented by brands are perceived by digital moms.

The digital world is changing at an extraordinary phase. The never-ending advances in new information and communication technologies (ICT) have more than ever changed the way in which we live, communicate, and process information. This has reshaped our habits to cope with a world constantly demanding new daily virtual experiences. People of all ages are in need to grip these experiences in one way or another. Regarding the advances in ICT, the internet alongside digital and social media have created whole new possibilities to gather real-time data and store valuable information while being virtually connected at all times. This postulates an evident challenge for companies to capitalize on the possibilities of digital marketing media and an opportunity to reach customers effectively using metadata and other resources virtually available. In this chapter, the authors used OLS regressions using Google Trends query data from 2008 to 2016 to measure the growing interest in digital marketing and other related topics and the monetization of such interest in the Spanish media sector.

The purpose of this chapter is to make a combination of two concepts CSR and digital marketing and to find out the various challenges faced by practitioners for effective CSR communication. A total of 15 in-depth interviews were conducted in a leading automobile company. The interview transcripts were

Preface

Nations endowed with high rates of entrepreneurship are usually the most dynamic economies on the planet. Added to this fact, companies operate in intensely competitive and globalized environments where the information and communication technologies are of growing importance. Hence, making appropriate digital marketing policies are essential for business success. As a result, this Handbook of Research is born in this context aiming to study the relationships between entrepreneurship, digital marketing, and the solidarity economics with the ultimate goal of creating employment and wealth for society.

The target audience of this Handbook of Research is composed of professionals and researchers working in the field of topics related to entrepreneurship, digital marketing, and social and solidarity economics in various disciplines, e.g., economics, business administration, administrative sciences and management, education, sociology, among others. Moreover, the Handbook of Research provides insights and support executives and policy-makers concerned with strategic management and planning, knowledge, information and organizational development related to entrepreneurship, digital marketing, and solidarity economics in different types of work communities and environments.

This Handbook of Research is divided into two sections. The first section (Chapters 1-13) deals with entrepreneurship and the second one (Chapters 14-20) relates to digital marketing. Regarding entrepreneurship, Chapter 1 titled "A Brief Theoretical Approach to the Definition of Entrepreneurship," and written by Dr. Jorge Gamez-Gutierrez, from Universitaria Agustianiana (Colombia), and Mr. Nicolas Gamez Abril, from Corporación Universitaria Minuto de Dios (Colombia), aims to construct a definition of both entrepreneurship and entrepreneur that can be accepted by scholars of this area of knowledge. To cope with this goal, this chapter is a comprehensive bibliographical review of the theories and definitions of entrepreneurship from a multiple economic, sociologic, psychologic, and managerial perspectives.

This theoretical approach is complemented with Chapter 2 titled "Solidarity Economics, Entrepreneurship, and Social Wealth," written by Dr. José Manuel Saiz-Álvarez, from EGADE Business School-Tecnologico de Monterrey (Mexico), where the Socioeconomics of Solidarity inserted in the Industry 4.0 can impulse solidarity and the creation of social and economic wealth based on the guiding principles of subsidiarity, the search for the Common Good, and solidarity based on social justice. After having grounded these principles, the author develops different solidarity-based public policies, mainly focused on the European Union, by including principles, objectives, and stages of the European ODA (Official Development Aid), the European Development Fund, the Common Framework for Joint Multiannual Programming and Efficiency, and the European Consensus on Development "Our World, Our Dignity, Our Future." Some ideas complement this analysis linked to the Socioeconomics of Solidarity that focuses on solidarity and justice to search for a more balanced business world defined by social welfare and economic wealth.

Entrepreneurship in general and especially social entrepreneurship has a remarkable impact on family business and entrepreneurship education. At this respect, Chapters 3 and 4 deal with family firms by following a complementary perspective, while Chapters 5 and 6 focus on entrepreneurship education. So, in Chapter 3 named "Factors Creating Competitive Advantage for Family-Owned Business," and written by Dr. Neeta Baporikar, from Namibia University of Science and Technology (Namibia) and University of Pune (India), the author analyzes how management has evolved as a separate discipline after the Industrial Revolution, and now is reaching its peak in today's' global business environment. Strategy concepts like vision, mission, SWOT and competition on a war footing for markets are the influence of military science. Different contemporary management techniques, approaches, and implications are applicable in this unstable, dynamic and knowledge-intensive environment. Among the various approaches, competitiveness, competitive strategies, and competitive advantage are at the core of organizational growth, development, and sustainability. Adopting a grounded theory approach with in-depth literature review this chapter aims to discuss and deliberate on factors creating a competitive advantage for organizations, especially SMEs, irrespective of their stage of development.

These good management practices foster business growth, mainly in micro family businesses, as studied in Chapter 4 named "Micro Family Business and Socioeconomic Development: Chilean Grocery Store" and written by Dr. Alejandro Vega-Muñoz, Universidad Autónoma de Chile (Chile), and Prof. Guido Salazar-Sepúlveda, Universidad Católica de la Santísima Concepción (Chile). Based on secondary data resources, the authors study the organization of the micro family business in Chile as a tool for economic development in the public technical cooperation program 'Grocery stores of Chile'.

Complementary to micro, small and medium firms, which constitutes the bulk of the business network in developing countries, entrepreneurship education is key for GDP growth. This relationship is studied in Chapters 5 and 6. In Chapter 5 named "A Model for Social Entrepreneurship Education," and written by Dr. Carlos Cuervo-Arango Martínez, and Dr. Carlos Torrejón Martín, both from Nebrija University (Spain), these authors review the relevant factors to promote an entrepreneurial attitude, identifying education as a crucial element for entrepreneurship. This fact is particularly important in the case of social entrepreneurship projects, in which good intentions frequently overcome sound business realities. To deepen the understanding of the relationship between education and social entrepreneurship, the authors develop the model entitled "Pyramid of catalysts for entrepreneurship," which helps to understand the mechanism by which the educational process affects the quantity and quality of social entrepreneurship. This chapter also presents several elements of paramount importance in designing a program of entrepreneurial social education.

These pages related to entrepreneurship education are complemented with the ideas expressed in Chapter 6 titled "Social Entrepreneurship and its Competences. Implications for Higher Education," and signed by Dr. Sue Rossano, Münster University of Applied Sciences (Germany), Prof. Thomas Baaken, Münster University of Applied Sciences (Germany), Miss Balzhan Orazbayeva, Münster University of Applied Sciences (Germany), Miss Marieke C. Baaken, Georg-August-Universität Göttingen, Germany & RUG Rijksuniversiteit Groningen (The Netherlands), Prof. Bert Kiel, Münster University of Applied Sciences (Germany), and Prof. Gideon Maas, Coventry University (UK). In this chapter, the authors affirm that entrepreneurship needs a vision, some leadership skills to accomplish, and a motivation to build something new, which will develop and sustain. And, according to these authors, societies need social entrepreneurs with a shared social mission or objective. Entrepreneurial thinking and acting, as well as innovation driving managers, is a need for society. Given these premises, this chapter proposes a methodology to analyze the competencies that should be fostered by higher education programs to provide graduates with the desired competencies for entrepreneurship and innovation.

Besides entrepreneurship, a second key factor to impact directly on business success is the adoption of dynamic capabilities in the firm. The analyses of these business-related capabilities are made in Chapter 7 titled "Proposal of a Business Model Based on the Triple Business Performance-E," and written by Dr. Carlos Ricardo Rey-Campero, Universidad Externado de Colombia (Colombia). In this chapter, the author studies the relationship between business models and dynamic capabilities in Colombian firms. Based on the theoretical framework of business models, the author applies an analysis based on principal categorical components and categorical regression. Results show a correlation between the elements of the business model (strategy and dynamic capabilities) and business performance defined by efficiency, effectiveness, and efficacy for newly created micro, small and medium-sized family firms that highly correlates with good business performance.

Using a sample of 209 Mexican academicians, the perspective described from the company is complemented in Chapter 8 titled "Entrepreneurial Intention Among Academicians in Mexico: A Descriptive Approach," and written by Dr. Cynthia L Franco-Rodriguez, and Dr. Patricia Esther Alonso-Galicia, both from Tecnologico de Monterrey (Mexico). In this chapter, the authors the scarce research available on the study of academic entrepreneurship, as these entrepreneurs are critical agents of change depending on their entrepreneurial intention. Academic entrepreneurs are part of the innovation ecosystems in entrepreneurial universities. Consequently, the purpose of this descriptive study is to contribute to the knowledge of the characteristics of academics in Mexico and the way these characteristics influence the entrepreneurial intention, given their previous work experience and academic formation.

Heavily rooted in entrepreneurship, family firms are key to sustain the industrial network of nations and to create social wealth and economic development. As a predominant form of business organization, family firms have attracted increasing attention by scholars, and especially by those researching entrepreneurial orientation with the aim of better understanding of entrepreneurial activities pursued by enterprises. However, the literature on the confluence of entrepreneurial orientation and family firms has paid scant attention to the influence of affective and emotional factors. At this respect, Chapter 9 titled "Affective and Emotional Determinants of Entrepreneurial Orientation Within Family Firms," and written by Prof. Remedios Hernández-Linares, Universidad de Extremadura (Spain), Prof. María Concepción López-Fernández, Universidad de Cantabria (Spain), Ms. María José Naranjo-Sánchez, Universidad de Extremadura (Spain), and Dr. Laura Victoria Fielden, Universidad de Extremadura (Spain), covers this research gap, as these authors analyze the impact of affective commitment and concern for socioemotional wealth preservation on entrepreneurial orientation. To do so, they perform an empirical study using the data collected from 342 small and mid-sized family firms from Portugal, a country where family firms are under-researched even though they make up the backbone of the economy. Results show that both affective commitment and socioemotional wealth positively impact entrepreneurial orientation, pointing to the need to further research the relationships between such factors and strategic behaviors in the family business context.

The last chapters of Section 1 of this Handbook of Research deal with technology and finance. Given globalization, the crucial role played by technology is analyzed in Chapters 10 and 11. In Chapter 10 titled "Orange Economy and Digital Entrepreneurship in Latin America: Creative Sparkles Among Raw Materials," and written by Dr. Alejandro Vega-Muñoz, Universidad Autónoma de Chile (Chile), Prof. Guillermo Bustamante-Pavez, Universidad Finis Terrae (Chile), and Prof. Guido Salazar-Sepúlveda,

Universidad Católica de la Santísima Concepción (Chile), these authors 18 Latin American creative companies to explain how the orange economy is penetrating in Latin American, a continent oriented towards the exportation of generic products with low commercial value. An orange economy where avoiding technical obsolescence is key for business success, although obsolescence can be transformed into an opportunity for social entrepreneurship, as it is analyzed in Chapter 11 titled "The Electronic Obsolescence as an Opportunity for Social Entrepreneurship: The Case of EEE in Manizales, Colombia," and written by Dr. Diego Lopez Cardona, and Rocío del S. Tabares Hoyos, both from the University of Manizales (Colombia). The chapter contains the concepts of Social Entrepreneurship, Planned and Perceived Obsolescence, Corporate Social Responsibility, the legal framework for Electrical and Electronic Equipment (EEE) waste, and Reverse Logistics, as theoretical support from different authors. Applied to Manizales, Colombia, the author uses a quantitative and qualitative approach by applying surveys and interviews with 26 entrepreneurs and 331 households' consumers to know the type of appliances, how they buy, change and use them, and the chain of intermediaries. With planned and perceived obsolescence, products lose their life in a short time, are dumped as Waste of Electrical and Electronic Equipment (WEEE), and collected by people of a low educational and economic level that survive in precarious conditions. Due to these results and conclusions, the author offers a proposal in these pages for their social inclusion to foster economic development.

The last pages of this section deal with how to finance social entrepreneurship is a tool to create wealth. This analysis is made in Chapter 12 titled "Joint Liability Lending, Entrepreneurial Development, and Poverty Reduction," and written by Christopher Boachie, from the Central University (Ghana), who examines, by using a cross-sectional survey study and both primary and secondary data on joint liability lending, the effect of joint liability lending on micro businesses in Madina municipality as a tool for economic growth. The study reveals that joint liability lending improves entrepreneurship and reduces poverty, as there exists a significant relationship between joint liability lending and a high repayment rate. The implications are that individual within the group are encouraged to continue saving and microfinance institutions should continue investing in educating and training clients to improve upon their micro businesses.

Finally, Chapter 13 titled "Going Beyond GDP: The Role of Social Innovation in Building a Welfare State," and written by Dr. Seyithan Ahmet Ates, Ankara University of Social Sciences (Turkey), Dr. Muradiye Ateş, Konya Necmettin Erbakan University (Turkey), and Prof. Murat Ali Yülek, Istanbul Commerce University (Turkey) deals with how social innovation and its agents can be considered as a toolbox which may facilitate a transition by positively influencing well-being, developing ways of integrating it into policy, and promoting it as an alternative measure of progress. These authors affirm that social innovation may increase the role of civil society in solving social problems while sustaining and improving people's well-being beyond increasing their welfare in monetary terms. By providing up-to-date solutions to challenges ranging from global warming to fair income distribution, and from innovative social entrepreneurs to grass-rooted innovation, social innovation seems to be capable of transforming the society in a way to tackle with a new kind of societal problems, and of exploring new ways to create added value for the economy.

Along with entrepreneurship, digital marketing is becoming increasingly important nowadays. This importance is studied in Section 2 of this Handbook of Research. At this respect, in Chapter 14 titled "Digital Moms: Devices, Social Networking Sites, and Perceptions Towards Digital Marketing Strategies," and written by Dr. Teresa Treviño, Universidad de Monterrey (Mexico), this author analyzes how given the rise of new technologies and the resultant changes in consumer behavior, marketing practices need to evolve, which requires organizations to rethink their strategies. Having a digital marketing strategy can establish a direct dialog with customers, thereby increasing knowledge about customers, suppliers, and partners as well as building, consolidating, and maintaining brand awareness. However, little is known about the attitudes and perceptions of consumers toward popular digital marketing tools that can strategically be used in an integrated digital marketing strategy. Therefore, the objective of this chapter is to understand the perceptions of digital moms toward technology and digital marketing strategies. Following a qualitative and interpretative approach, the results contribute to the literature by (1) addressing the symbolic meanings that technological tools have in the lives of this group of consumers, and (2) providing insights on how digital moms perceive different digital marketing strategies commonly implemented by brands.

Applied technology through the use of ICTs (Information and Communication Technologies) is playing a fundamental role in this transformation process. At this respect, Chapter 15 titled "Google Trends Metadata as a Revenue Indicator for Digital Marketing Activities in Spanish Businesses" and written by Dr. Jesús Manuel Palma-Ruiz, from the Universidad Autónoma de Chihuahua (Mexico), and Dr. Raúl Gómez-Martínez, from the Universidad Rey Juan Carlos (Spain) studies how the digital world is changing the way firms communicate and process information to reshape consumers' habits to cope with a world constantly demanding new daily virtual experiences. People of all ages are in need to grip these experiences in one way or another. Regarding the ICTs advances, the combination of the Internet and social media has created new possibilities to gather real-time data and store valuable information while being virtually connected permanently. In this chapter, the authors apply OLS regressions by using Google Trends query data from 2008 to 2016 to measure the growing interest in digital marketing and other related topics, and the monetization of such interest in the Spanish media sector.

When companies present policies based on CSR complemented by digital marketing, the impact caused is even greater than if they use traditional marketing. At this respect, in Chapter 16 titled "Corporate Social Responsibility and Digital Marketing" and written by Usha Chauhan, Dr. Ritu Garg, and Dr. Ritu Chhikara, all from BML Munjal University (India), this relationship is analyzed. The purpose of this chapter is to make a combination of two concepts CSR and digital marketing and to find out the various challenges faced by practitioners for effective CSR communication. To cope with this goal, the author's transcript a total of 15 in-depth interviews conducted in a leading automobile company to propose different themes derived from the perceptions of the respondents related to corporate reputation, public awareness, CSR efforts, profitability, CSR commitment, and public image. These results are useful to make effective CSR communication campaigns to enhance corporate reputation.

Fundraising and NGOs (non-governmental organizations) can play a crucial role in this digital process of transformation, especially if they are focused on people at risk of social exclusion. At this respect, in Chapter 17 titled "Fundraising and Its Impact on Digital Marketing for NGOs" and developed by Prof. Ruth Sabrina Rojas Dávila, The Catholic University of Santiago de Guayaquil (Ecuador), the author describes how NGO use fundraising as a strategy for generating resources to sustain themselves through time, and how human resources can help to achieve this goal.

The combination of digital marketing and social networks is a powerful tool to attract prospective clients and to retain existing customers. This relationship is studied in Chapter 18 named "The Use of Geolocalized Social Networks Information to Guide and Enhance the Design of Local Cultural and Tourist Policies" and written by Dr. Víctor Temprano-García, and Dr. Rebeca San José-Cabezudo, both from the University of Valladolid (Spain). In recent years, the upsurge in the use of social networks by companies with the application of diverse execution formats and the multiplicative effects caused after it, have changed the way how organizations communicate with their users. This chapter aims to understand the behavior of residents and tourists in a Spanish city to provide local decision-makers insights and pioneer tools to help them for designing more effective action policies, which may have a positive impact on their cities. The methodological design used is based on the observation and collection of geolocalized data, provided spontaneously by residents and visitors in a real context. Based on the analysis of the photographs that the subjects share about the city and the interactions taking place between the members of the social networks under study, these authors propose some strategies to decision-makers.

The last two chapters of the Handbook of Research deal with how digital marketing affects the firm, both in the brand and in the communication of the company with customers. So, in Chapter 19 titled "Evolving Faster Than Lightning: How Is Digital Marketing Changing the Brand? The Future for Digital Marketing Tools" and written by Prof. Danny C. Barbery-Montoya, Universidad de Especialidades Espíritu Santo (Ecuador), the author shows how digital marketing is creating the interaction between the company, customers, and stakeholders to propose a model to show the stages of eBehavior connected with digital marketing tools backed with security, which creates a new value digital string to benefit the firm.

Finally, in Chapter 20 named "Digital Marketing as a Communication Tool in Emerging Businesses," and written by Dr. Carlos Luis Torres Briones, Universidad de Guayaquil (Ecuador), the author studies how startups compete against major brands. As a result, startups should be more intelligent to compete better by using the theory of digital marketing as a communication tool. As a result, the author proposes an EComPymes model, where the appropriate basic tools for these type of companies are shown and grounded on content generation through social media, mobile marketing, and email, not only for startups but also to compete with low budgets.

The relationship analyzed from different perspectives in this Handbook of Research between entrepreneurship, digital marketing, and the economy of solidarity fills a gap in the existing literature. I wish you all the best while reading this Handbook of Research, and I hope that it will be very useful and fruitful for you.

Jose Manuel Saiz-Alvarez
Tecnologico de Monterrey, Mexico

Acknowledgment

To my family and friends for their encouragement while preparing this book, and to all those who have made the publication of this book possible. I extend this gratitude to the prestigious publishing house IGI Global, and especially to the IGI Global Book Development Team.

Also, I warmly thank all 38 authors who have accepted to participate in this book for their excellent work and collaboration. Researchers and professors located in universities and research centers in Africa (Ghana and Namibia), America (Chile, Colombia, Ecuador, and Mexico), Asia (India and Turkey), and Europe (Germany, Spain, The Netherlands, and United Kingdom).

I acknowledge both the Editorial Advisory Board and the referees who have participated in this Handbook of Research for their dedication.

Finally, I thank the financial support received from the National Council of Science and Technology (CONACYT) in Mexico, and the Mexican Academy of Sciences. Thanks to this financial support, academicians working in Mexico are being incentive to help other colleagues, as well as the society as a whole.

Section 1
Entrepreneurship

Chapter 1
A Theoretical Approach to the Definition of Entrepreneurship From a Multidisciplinary Perspective

Jorge Gamez-Gutierrez
Universitaria Agustiniana, Colombia

Nicolas Gamez Abril
Corporación Universitaria Minuto de Dios, Colombia

ABSTRACT

Capitalism has required the function of the entrepreneurs, people who use creativity, understood as the ability to solve problems and put innovation into practice. Firms can be social, public, and private; in this last case, the creation of an enterprising company involves new products, new production methods, the opening of new markets, the development of new sources of raw materials and inputs, and the creation of new market structures in the industry. This chapter is a bibliographical review of the theories of entrepreneurship from economics, sociology, psychology, and management aiming to contribute to the construction of a definition of entrepreneurship and entrepreneur that can be accepted by scholars in this field.

INTRODUCTION

Capitalism would be different without the adoption of new ideas and their adaptation to companies, a process carried out by the entrepreneurs (Schumpeter, 1947), as these individuals use creativity and innovation to solve business problems. The research field of entrepreneurship shows theoretical developments and breakthroughs in the analysis of its features and functions, though it lacks the construction of a consensus on an accepted definition of entrepreneurship. With several types of entrepreneurs, environments, and conditions, there are diverse ways to be an entrepreneur, so firms vary and can use multivariate models that attempt to capture the complexity of their reality.

DOI: 10.4018/978-1-5225-8939-6.ch001

Theoretical advances on entrepreneurship allow us to see a general panorama of this field of knowledge, but from separate visions. As a result, entrepreneurship can be grouped in Economics, Psychology, Sociology, and Management (see table 1). Having approached entrepreneurship and startup creation from a systemic view, some factors can be identified that influence a startup process formed by the business project, its launch, and the initial development of the company. The Economic School offers an understanding of the entrepreneurial phenomenon from individual action -*homo economicus*- that achieve their welfare through profit maximization; the Psychological School includes the influence of the individual within the entrepreneurial model; from the Sociological approach, individuals and their relationships in the pursuit of development are studied from the creation of economic value. Finally, the vision from Management and Strategy shows how the company and the entrepreneur fit to the market conditions.

The birth of entrepreneurial centers at the end of the XX century in Latin-America impulsed the analysis of the formation, performance, and socioeconomic prominence of the Latin-American entrepreneur to foster economic and social development, along with the participation of the state and the institutions in the economy. Nowadays, entrepreneurship and firm creation are being analyzed in Europe, North America, and some Asian nations; and the analysis is not aware of the own characteristics of the Latin-American culture and environment. According to Kantis (2002), formal Latin American firms are created with low salaries and bad quality jobs; besides, these startups are far more complex in the informal economy. Latin-American entrepreneurs are young, with the high formation in higher education institutions (HEIs), have previous experience, and are oriented to domestic markets. Their families, HEIs, and previous jobs have a strong influence on them, and they already participate in networks to formulate their projects and strategies.

Latin American countries are in a vicious circle: many laws and regulations are generated to control uncertainty and the unforeseeable. But strong regulations damage firms, as it is higher the possibility of breaking these rules, so increases the possibility of later conscious or unconscious transgression. The informality augments the probabilities of the existence of several forms of informal entrepreneurship in the provision of public goods and forms of government (Hernández, 2008).

Table 1. Some current approaches of entrepreneurship

Economy	Sociology
• Risk • Benefit • Costs • Innovation • Leadership • Maximization of profit	• Context • Attributes • Networks • Values • Routines • Competence
Psychology	**Management**
• Creativity • Challenges • Motivation • Incentives • Mass media • Independence need • Locus of control	• Strategies • Risk • Proactivity • Management • Innovation • Advantages

Source: Author

Startups' founders must bear in mind, especially in Latin America, that they will face corruption practices, sometimes linked to financing. Financial problems are concealed with a limiting factor in the creation: to grow and develop startups. Although financing is a problem for SMEs, a sort of venture capital has emerged on the continent which has reduced this imbalance. As a result, startups have grown and disposed of a complete portfolio. Despite this fact, entrepreneurs and people in business have difficulties in reaching resources because of the lack of guarantees, risk and credit history (GEM, 2006).

Third World economies need more entrepreneurs and new firms to promote economic and social development. To stimulate startup growth, education has been focused, at least partially, to encourage entrepreneurship (Guzmán, 2005), endowed with some rules and laws.

It is necessary to know who and why to use entrepreneurship and be an entrepreneur and define its characteristics to approach a deep analysis of the particularities of the entrepreneurial process within its time and context. A list of characteristics of the entrepreneur must give a new dynamic conception of the entrepreneur as an object of study, with theories and models that can be shared with other sciences for analyzing and explaining entrepreneurship. This chapter aims to contribute theoretically with some basic entrepreneurial elements to describe entrepreneurs for generating policies that give sustainable business strategies for the benefit of next generations. Business strategies linked to better management tools, higher access to R&D and innovation, and opportunities for social development. Entrepreneurial proposals can be made to solve the problems linked to social cohesion that influence entrepreneurship and startup creation, just like in case of institutions and network collaboration to confront new scenarios for both social and economic integration.

The literature on entrepreneurial epistemology of the last twenty-five years lacks unified paradigms and theories, as there is an important research gap in understanding the companies' internationalization process (Javalgi & Martin, 2018). Entrepreneurship has been established as a discipline, but it is a term immersed in many topics and areas of knowledge. Therefore, for the researchers, it is difficult to show their work results because the entrepreneurial activity is tackled from different approaches, and different angles, which makes difficult the debate and the academic construction of the topic (Berglund & Johansson, 2007), as the history of science establishes links between subjects and disciplines of science and other fields of knowledge (Uribe, 2017). In the case of entrepreneurship, it is not evident the confirmation of a scientific field that has reached maturity over the years, that shows solid theoretical advances and epistemological reflection, that exhibits high degrees of convergence and has clarified doubts about its progress and legitimacy (Grègoire, Noël, Dèry, & Béchard, 2006). It is expected that a theoretical field has solid foundations based on ontology -how the nature of reality is defined-, epistemology -the type of relationships between knowledge and researchers, and the implemented methodology -the way knowledge is discovered- (Martínez, 2018).

ENTREPRENEUR AND FIRM: CONCEPTUAL APPROACH

Entrepreneurship and firms are topics that are taken in a scattered way, which contributes to some people speaking about *pretheories* of entrepreneurship, formed by ideas from previous researches that do not -still- link themselves in a solid corpus. Is entrepreneurship advancing or just expanding in size? (Pereira, 2007). In this chapter, these approaches are shown from economic, psychological, sociological, and management-related definitions, theories, types, models, and entrepreneurial profiles.

Who Is an Entrepreneur

Entrepreneurs in the XVIII century were architects, and based their performance on the construction of great works by order, starting from design and when the work value was defined. An entrepreneur was the warrior who undertook a fight or a battle, while the king or the head of state reflects and plans strategies and means for achieving goals. Today, entrepreneurs execute actions that imply adventure, uncertainty, and risk (Verin quoted by Pereira, 2007; Tarapuez y Botero, 2007).

According to the Dictionary of the Royal Spanish Academy of Language, entrepreneurship involves an entrepreneur that assumes a constant process of innovation without being an inventor, nor a scientist, nor an owner of resources; he is an innovator (Schumpeter, 1947) who carries out social changes processes and has a multidimensional character. He is a person who takes risks that contains the creation of enterprise and sees and capitalizes the profitable efforts or business (Ecotec, 2007).

The term "entrepreneurship" refers to a way of thinking, reasoning, and acting, obsessed with finding opportunities, with an approach both holistic and balanced by leadership (Belausteguigoitia, 2007), including now-existing businesses and the conservation of the entrepreneurial spirit that gave birth to the origin, the capacity to innovate, and the vulnerabilities in the face of other organizations. It has also been called *intrapreneurship* and *organizational entrepreneurship* –analysis of the entrepreneurial spirit in the organizations- for recovering their entrepreneurial spirit.

Other ways of contributing to definitions have been made up based on the questions What happens when entrepreneurs do not act? Why do their act? And how do they behave? Entrepreneurs do not live the present moment only; entrepreneurs and their firms exist today, but always with a contextual view towards the future (Fontela et al., 2006). As a result, the consequences of today's decisions will be held tomorrow according to what it is thought to be more complicated and less reasonable (See table 2).

For economists, entrepreneurs are analyzed on the results of their actions only, more than being entrepreneurs, their effects on the economic system, and their role played in market development. Schumpeter is the person who associates the entrepreneur with the businessman. The second approach is studied in Social sciences (e.g., Psychology and Sociology) where entrepreneurs are individuals, so the analysis is centered on human behavior and its background, social environment, goals, values, and motivations. In the third type of definitions, entrepreneurs are analyzed by following managerial characteristics and the settlement of goals without studying personal reasons for being in pursuit of their interests, the environment, and the effects of their actions (Steven & Jarillo, 1990).

Table 2. The term "entrepreneur" in different languages

Spanish	Emprendedor	Empresa	Empresario
German	Unternehmer	Unternehmen	Arbeitgeber
French	Entrepreneur	Entreprise	Employeur
English	Entrepreneur	Enterprise Company	Employer

Source: Adapted from Moriano (2005).

What Characterizes Entrepreneurs?

The term "entrepreneur" refers to the producer, the individual who makes, manufactures, fabricates, processes or creates a good or service. In the United Kingdom is the one who directs an enterprise or is a businessman, but in the United States or Canada he or she negotiates, finances, directs or organizes firms. Another definition relates as an individual who makes himself through independent activities, trusts in himself, is self-sufficient, and uses entrepreneurship. This vision includes entrepreneurial strength, security, quickness, determination, stability, permanence, and prosperity. Entrepreneurs are rare and scarce.

Entrepreneurs are defined by finding problems and solving them, setting objectives, controlling their destiny, searching prestige and recognition, though their main goal is not to obtain an economic profit. They are worried more about their present and future, and their plans, organization, efficiency, and technology. According to Smelser (quoted by Mc Clelland, 1989), values can be modified by the educational system, religion, family, and society. Goals set by entrepreneurs are moderated, and their achievement asks for feedback.

According to Fontela et al. (2006), an entrepreneur is a dreamer when the firm with dreams cannot exist yet; the future is not available and is open to the sole imagination. Although being a part of this future, it is constructed by decisions based on the present, and the proper actions and interpretations made by the entrepreneur in reasonable contexts which requires aesthetic competences. The person who uses entrepreneurship is a user of predictions as, in most cases, he or she resembles art and requires intuition and common sense. Consequently, these future explorations are based in three methodologies: a) Consulting with experts to collect structured knowledge; b) Trends and extrapolations on including models for identifying past regularities; and c) Tools of thinking for individual use (Fontela et al., 2006). As a result, creativity is understood as a process and capacity, with uncertain results that arise from experience, intuition, and expectations. What an entrepreneur expects of his work is very much alike to the tension artists feel when creating works.

Creativity and Innovation, Activities of Entrepreneurs

From the 20th century, creativity can be seen in all people, and not just belonging to God and artists, as creativity refers to the attitude or ability of individuals and groups "to form combinations, to relate or restructure elements of their reality, obtaining products, ideas or results, both original and valuable" (Lopez, 1995, p. 18). All human beings are creative, and creativity can be developed. The levels of creativity are a) Expressive, spontaneous; b) Productive, with a purpose; c) Inventiveness, to discover and invent; d) Innovative, to modify principles, and e) Emerging, to create new principles (Taylor quoted by Lopez, 1995).

Creativity is essential in entrepreneurial activity, as it is understood as a mental activity (Gámir, 2007), a process and a capacity with uncertain results that arise from experience, intuition, and expectations (see Table 3). Being creative is to see things that others do not see, and suggests two phases: *Divergent creativity* that opens the spirit to play and combine, and *Convergent creativity* that selects the strengths and weaknesses of each idea (Ponti, 2008).

Table 3. Competencies and skills of a creative persona

Psychological	To have the belief of being creative
	Introspection
	Mental curiosity
	Logical thinking plus lateral thinking
Behaviors	The constant search of ideas
	Transgressor attitude
	Naïve thinking
Techniques	Knowledge of creative methods

Source: Adapted from Franc Ponti (2008, p. 25)

The result of the implementation of creativity is innovation, and its loss affects the weakness of the company. The innovation, according to Schumpeter (1978), is reflected in new combinations of productive factors that are palpable in a new good or quality of good, a new method of production, the opening of a new market, the conquest of a new source of raw material, and the launch of new types of organization. There are strictly innovative companies, innovative companies in a broad sense, potentially innovative companies, and non-innovative companies (Turriago, 2002). Society supports innovation through technology centers, technology parks, business and innovation centers, universities and transfer offices; in Europe's leading innovation countries are Switzerland, Finland, Sweden, Denmark, and Germany (Gámir, 2007).

Entrepreneurial Types

Entrepreneurs stay alert to opportunities to discover unmade up needs and select appropriate formulas for meeting them. They imagine and put into practice new answers to social problems along time, as they take opportunities, and bear the reputational, emotional and financial risks to maintain actions with uncertain outcomes.

The first type of entrepreneurship is related to the public sector, where they are agents of change in social settings that encourage institutional innovation (Chamber of Commerce, 2003). They propose public reforms to shift the corporate culture to the state sector, have a social service orientation, seek the public's association with civil society, and pretend to be made up with the unmade-up needs of the population (Moriano, 2005).

The second sort of entrepreneurship is social. In this case, they aim to promote and sustain social values, look for new opportunities, follow innovation-related processes and have a high sense of responsibility in social work (Moriano, 2005). Today, social enterprise is assumed by companies with philanthropic and social entrepreneurship-related strategies integrated into the business (Gutierrez, 2007).

The third type is the private entrepreneur who creates startups (table 4). They can be a *pushing entrepreneur* -push- defined by being unsatisfied with his or her current job and decides to start a business or a *pulling entrepreneur* –pull- when a startup is created by attraction, as they are fascinated by the startup launched (Moriano, 2005).

Table 4. Types of entrepreneurs

Moriano & Palací (2006)	Hernández (2008)		Amit (1993)	Lee & Chan (1998)	Pinchot (1985) Manuel (2006)
Vocation	Opportunity	Formal Sector	Attraction	Ambition	*Intraentrepreneur*
Needs	Needs	Informal Sector	Pushing	Network worker	e-entrepreneur
				Hard worker	

Source: Adapted from Moriano (2005) and Hernández (2008)

Entrepreneurs can also be classified by vocation, who are individuals having the momentum, illusions and dreams of launching startups; and necessity-based entrepreneurs when startups improve founders' financial and social status or are driven by their circumstances (Moriano, 2005). In Latin America, entrepreneurs can be distinguished by how they act in the formal and informal sectors. In the first case, they desire to exit unemployment and informality; while in the second, the access to financial resources and knowledge prevent them from entering the formal sector.

Necessity-based entrepreneurs can be described as impersonal businesspeople with family responsibilities with incomplete secondary school level, working in the tertiary sector, with an income smaller to two minimum wages, without any affiliation to social security. A vast majority of them do not subscribe to labor contracts in a written form and work in their houses (Hernandez, 2008: p 287).

Entrepreneurial Stages

Entrepreneurial abilities can be harnessed through education; so in HEIs, it is possible to identify entrepreneurs. In this case, three stages are distinguished: (a) potential startups; (b) rising startups, and (c) dynamic startups. In each case, education can sensitize, support and contribute to the profit of the firm's quality (Guzmán, 2005).

At this respect, Kantis (2002) identifies three stages in the firm entrepreneurship: the gestation of the project, the running of the company, and the initial development of the project. The gestation stage includes the motivation and the competences of the entrepreneur, the identification of the opportunity and the elaboration of the project. The running contemplates the decision of starting the enterprise activity and the access to the resources to begin. Finally, the initial development of the project includes the introduction of goods and services to the market and the management of the first years.

The Firm: To Take Advantage of the Opportunities at Each Space

What do the entrepreneurs do when they create a company? To create or to take an opportunity that other people do not see, to use resources most efficiently, to construct a value, to generate and to distribute benefits for an individual, group and society. Therefore, the company is the result of a complex activity that is developed within the community and has effects within itself and in its surroundings; therefore, it is assessed by his creators, managers, and groups interested in it, as in the case of *stakeholders*. The company is located in a sector, and the generation of results benefits it, like to the group of companies and the society generally.

Each company has diverse degrees of creativity depending on the human beings that create it, and the innovation used in the firm reflects it. Innovation, according to Schumpeter (1947a), is a new combination of productive factors reflected in a new and a higher-quality good, or a new method of production – it is not necessary yet ideal, that it might be the result of scientific research-, the opening of a new market, the conquest of a new source of raw materials, and the running of new types of organization - monopoly. The industrialist is the one who introduces innovation and decides when to do it, and as soon as he does it, to increase productivity and competitiveness. Innovation can also exist in the machinery and equipment or the administrative processes.

The industrialist is different to the capitalist and the leader of the company; as Cantillon (1755) affirms that industrialists buy means of production for a price, they combine them and sell to another non-foreseeable price after having combined these factors. According to Say (1821), industrialists are productive agents who buy services of the other agents and combine them in the production process to generate products that have more value compared to the sum of the used services that are necessary for production. From their perspective, they do not include innovation. The arrival of the steam motor impelled the creation of big corporations requiring capital and forced the appearance of shares with the historical support of the Royal House that guaranteed monopolies to protect their growth (Herrerias, 2006).

Companies' founders decide their size and objectives with the little information they have and therefore take risks. They maximize short-term benefits and create a structure to match up the lowest point of the average costs curve with the price of the product, and in the long-term, they optimize size and structure to move down their cost curve to maximize profits.

When growing urbanization and the development of new transportation routes, entrepreneurs generate basic needs of housing, feeding, and clothing, and made firms grow to achieve the number of the companies focused on direct consumer goods' production. Some SMEs form industrial empires, while management creates big conglomerates of companies. This phase of capitalism includes the production on a large scale with a great concentration of machines and people, which made arise new forms of a labor organization to face different atmospheres of economic competition. Thus, the decision making can be distributed today between the entrepreneur, who takes the initiative to create the company; the capitalist, who contributes with the physical means to carry it out; and the administrator that manages it. In small companies, a person can play the three roles, whereas in big organizations these roles are distributed between many individuals. Big companies with many shareholders separate the interests of owners and administrators. The division between property and management of those big firms generates the problem of moral risk and the agency costs.

Stages of the Firm

Startups are generally connected to ICTs (Information and Communication Technologies) which can impulse business growth when attractive web pages are designed. The company's creative process includes the phases of gestation, creation, launch, and consolidation (table 5). The *gestation phase* includes the childhood and professional preparation of the entrepreneur, the experience of having a favorable event, and the positive surrounding conditions to create the startup; the *creation phase* includes the search and identification of business opportunities, the creation of a possible solution, the enlargement of social networks, and the assessment of opportunities linked to the necessary steps to create it. Finally, the *launching phase*, with a duration of 1 or 2 years, implies creating the organization, searching resources, and promoting goods and services. Finally, the *consolidation phase*, which can last between two and five

Table 5. Stages in the creation of firms

	Veciana	Interamerican Development Bank (IDB)	Global Entrepreneurship Monitor (GEM)
Stages for creating a startup	Gestation *- Childhood and preparation* Creation *-Search and identification of opportunity* Launch *-The search for resources and good or services launch* Consolidation	Gestation Launch Initial development	New enterprises: • Recently born or less than 3-months startups • *New enterprises or baby business with a duration between 3 and 42 months* Established Enterprises: • *Established business with more than 42 months*

Source: Author

years, implies assuming success or failure (Veciana, 2001), where taking dynamic business decisions are critical for success (Guzmán, 2005).

Regarding, Kantis et al. (2002) identify three stages of the enterprising process that finishes in company creation: gestation, launch, and initial development. In the gestation process, motivation and entrepreneurial competences take part, close with opportunity identification and the elaboration of the project. During the launching process, the starting decision of a company is taken, and it can access the resources to begin. In the initial development stage, goods and services in the market are introduced, and the company is managed during the first years (Kantis, 2002).

Today, the study of the firm is assumed to be achieved from the evolutionist economy which affirms that the observed history to successfully collect information about how opponent entrepreneurs are expected to act, determines future business strategies and incorporates imitation processes as part of the learning (Leon, 2006). In other words, entrepreneurs establish "*induction forward and backward*" (Leon, 2006, p. 78) to incorporate notions of credibility and sequential rationality in the firm. As a result, the different stages of the evolution in the firm shows diverse entrance and exit rates of companies in the market, based on the sort of knowledge used by an entrepreneur to propose greater innovation levels. Consequently, companies compete by experimenting with new ideas that, being successful or not, are forced to prevail (Geroski et al., 2007)

EVOLUTION OF THE CONCEPT "ENTREPRENEURSHIP"

Regarding entrepreneurship, some of the synonyms founded in the literature on this topic written in Spanish include the terms *emprendedorismo, emprenderismo, emprendedurismo, emprendeduría, empresario*, and *empresarialismo*, among others. As a result, and for a Spanish perspective, by including Latin America and Spain, many Spanish theoreticians of entrepreneurship have set some questions like what happens when the entrepreneur's act? What are the causes that take the entrepreneur to look towards change? Why assume the risk of creating a firm?

At this respect, from articles published in *Frontiers of Entrepreneurship Research* between 1981 and 1999, Gregoire, Déry, and Béchard (2001) study the coincidences on the analysis of the enterprising spirit in 13.593 citations of 752 articles, and they gather five core ideas on this topic:

1. Factors affecting the decision of a person to initiate a new company.
2. Variables affecting the firm's performance.
3. Business practices of investors and their impact.
4. Influence of social networks.
5. Strategic perspectives based on resources.

From Economics: Initiatives in Pursuit of Profit

Entrepreneurs are methodical, tenacious and energetic individuals that invest money to generate value and perceive non-fixed and uncertain profit; they take risks that assume with the capital they have accumulated, turn their productive capacity, and look for their mobility to obtain better performance. Also, they alter and disorganize production factors, as a traditional or capitalist entrepreneur do, to maximize wealth. They are superior workers, egotistic, motivated by gain and vanity, with some spontaneous impulse for action or animal spirits to create and buy companies. They take care of consumers' needs and are different from managers who carry out routines. They distinguish between uncertainty and risk that especially in developed countries, they are constantly looking for opportunities. They are people who take new initiatives, create and provide creative answers to problems with new practices of innovation in new businesses performing permanent reorganizations in the economic system. It is clear that they have the forces of will, they value scientific progress, innovate and stay alert before achieving opportunities as they know how to use knowledge. Entrepreneurs are surrounded and are part of the social and economic institutions that influence their decisions to create firms. They are talented, lean on education to assure the sustainability of the company through innovation, and are influenced by social capital, civic virtues, and family networks. In each context, they adapt to the law and extralegal customs of the country they establish their firms. Entrepreneurs are active organizers of the production with the intention of gain and become capital owners while tending to perceive high income. They innovate to receive new gains, rely on society, universities and research centers, and improve their social and economic conditions in developing countries through salaries and corporate social responsibility.

In short, entrepreneurs can be defined by

Classical School (Economy)

1. **Cantillon:** Risk, uncertainty, to be intelligent, hired and entrepreneurial producer, and uncertain gains.
2. **Turgot:** Risk, and to be intelligent.
3. **Smith:** Superior worker, innovator, accumulation, and division of the work.
4. **Ricardo:** Capital and profitability.
5. **Say:** Risk, benefit, experience, good judgment, and innovation.

Neoclassical School (Economy)

6. **Weber:** Innovation, religion, capital, traditionalistic businessman, and capitalist businesspeople.
7. **Pareto:** Risk, assets, and imagination.
8. **Marshall:** Superior worker, *businessman*, egotistic, conceited, and uncertainty.

9. **Keynes:** Animal spirits, sanguineous temperament, the possibility of creating companies, and political and social environment.
10. **Mises:** Uncertainty, risk, and the possibility of obtaining a benefit.
11. **Knight:** Be methodical, tenacious, vigorous and trusting in his act, insurable risks, risk different from uncertainty, gains, benefit, dynamic activity, judgment for the businesses, and enterprise ability.
12. **Hayek:** Constant search of opportunities and advantage on others.

This author, considered as the theoretician who collects the characteristics of an entrepreneur and company in the XX century deserves special mention:

13. **Joseph Schumpeter (1883-1950):** The entrepreneurship was born in the economy, but his nature is sociological. In 1939, he foretold the influence of the entrepreneur in the economy, by affirming that his or her role to stimulate the investment and the innovation from the analysis of the economic cycles. The use of the enterprising word is attributed to Schumpeter is the possible conception of the word in German language *Unter* (taking) and *Nehmer* (under), as the action of the entrepreneur that looks for opportunities, creates fortunes, and generates an accumulation of wealth. Besides, entrepreneurs reorganize the economic system permanently and the layers of the society, while propelling the economic growth by using the physical environment and a social organization that includes contracts, property, inheritance, the system of credit, taxes, work relations, public regulations of the economic activity along freedom and security. There is a national spirit that denotes different systems of ideas, a religious set of beliefs, and current attitudes towards cash saving, economic progress, assumption of risks, physical and intellectual work, and social equality (Schumpeter, 1947, 1978).

The true function of an entrepreneur is to take initiatives and create, more than to execute, *management* or to reunite production factors to obtain products. To undertake a firm implies to execute the function of direction in the economic field; the routine works are for those individuals who cooperate in an automatic manner without leaders' participation. On the other hand, and according to Rodriguez and Jiménez (2007), when it is necessary to abandon a routine in case of the supply of new products to clients, leaders' intervention is necessary, since their role is to motivate. Many startups are created with a defined idea and purpose, but they die for different reasons, although they emphasize that some fail as their capacity for innovation decreases. Innovation is associated with the promotion of new leaders (Schumpeter 1939).

14. **Israel Kirzner:** He describes the propensity of the human beings to discover the useful knowledge and its limits, what he calls *enterprising propensity*. The enterprising propensity is responsible for the *entrepreneurial alertness* to search benefit opportunities and entrepreneurial discoveries by overcoming the limits of the existing knowledge. This entrepreneurial alertness can lead to errors that can be discovered, but there is a tendency to correct them (Kirzner, 1986). By using information, the improvement of the human condition is improved by matching up entrepreneurs, market, innovation, capital, and interest, with an emphasis on the dangers of a regulated economy and the importance of the individual's freedom, focused on creativity.

New Economic Institutionalist School

15. **North:** Individual decision, institutions, incentives for society, cultural learning, transaction costs, and political institutions.
16. **Galbraith:** Talented individual, education, human capital, competition, economic opportunity, innovation, research, and the use of technical resources.
17. **Coase:** Risk, flexible institutional environment, and knowledge networks,
18. **De Soto:** Same enterprise spirit worldwide, law, talent, enthusiasm, and abilities.
19. **Kalmanovitz:** Accumulation of capital to incorporate the unemployed or under-employed population.
20. **Kliksberg:** Social or share capital.

Other Economists

21. **Baumol:** Innovation, strategic decisions based on instinct, the supply of entrepreneurship, attitude against the risk, credit, differences from managers, stimulating entrepreneurial activity, and entrepreneurship promotion and training.
22. **Fontela:** Financial issues, management, education, art, intuition, inspiration, aesthetic (to improve what is imagined), emotions, efficiency, information and knowledge, availability of resources and its efficient use, and satisfaction.
23. **Guzmán:** Education, motivation, ambition, innovation, cooperation, and pro-activity.
24. **Saiz-Álvarez:** Ambition, intuition, hard-working, challenge, accuracy, and social responsibility.
25. **Furtado:** Income, time, chain production, profit, energy, intelligence, production problems, dynamism, regional development, income application, new techniques, and combinations of factors.
26. **Max-Neff:** Social companies and practices.

From Sociology: The Influence of the Context

Entrepreneurs create new organizations according to how much they are influenced by economic and social processes, and specific social structures and their influence. They also join the aim of their actions with their characteristics and come from the middle-class to earn money and social prestige. They can see themselves as influenced by religious beliefs and are interested in getting control over other people.

Entrepreneurs can be traditionalistic or capitalist businesspeople. Their last multiplier is how to maximize social wealth. They change and reorganize the existing pattern of production looking forward social compensations and prestige, by incorporating labor customs, knowledge and beliefs. Their vocation impels them, and intermediate between the groups with resources and work in networks. They have complex capacities, practical abilities, and experience to exploit opportunities. They are different in each country and region, and their activity may contribute to reducing unemployment.

The Sociological School

27. **Weber:** Individual characteristics, social origin, obsession for gaining money, profit, traditionalism, professionalism, innovation, ethical and religious values, capital, control over other people, consumers' needs, and rules.

28. **Smelser:** Prestige, social compensation, access to capital and new markets, personality, values, and reorganization of production patterns.
29. **Simmel:** Traditions, knowledge, beliefs, benefits from competition, and gains.
30. **Swedberg:** Values, habits, group initiatives, social exclusion, and networks.
31. **Thornton:** Personal attributes, social behavior, opportunities, complex capacities, practical abilities; intrapreneurship, venture capital, corporative acquisitions, dynamic space and time, and differentiation.
32. **Pinillos et al.:** Local, regional and national cultural and social differences in a country.

From Psychology: Personality and Motivations

In Psychology, entrepreneurship is described partially and affects creativity, desire for independence, capacity for leadership, opportunism, individualism, intuition, organization, capacity for being rational, planning, and professionalism. Besides, entrepreneurs have aptitudes and motivations and interrelate between the need for success, and the structure of opportunities, so different performance can be observed according to the industrialized or not industrialized country analyzed.

Entrepreneurs have a strong need for success, interests, strategies, dispose of a good chronological perspective, and some ways of perceiving people. An entrepreneur is influenced by other modeler forces like urbanization, mass media, and the factory. They need independence, work for results, persevere and control his or her destiny. It would be possible to characterize it as an ambitious entrepreneur, in a double sense of being in professional networks and being a hard worker; also, entrepreneurs can innovate and be dualist and returners, but in any case, they must be entrepreneurs by conviction and needs.

The Psychological School

33. **McClelland:** Personal characteristics, human geography, motivations, individual interest, perception, motivated atmospheres, family and business environment, financial and social incentives and stimuli, values and attitudes, skills and opportunities, profit as a thought, need of profit, perseverance, self-confidence, need for success, initial level of success, probability of success, and value of the incentives, moderate goals, feedback, personal responsibility in the solution of difficulties, initiative, exploratory conduct, chronological perspective, different degrees of entrepreneurship in groups of people in similar conditions. For McClelland, entrepreneurs dispose of a quite strong probability of success in a population with a high need for success and fear of failure.
34. **Inkeles:** Urbanization and mass media.
35. **Carland:** Personality, the locus of control, results, perseverance, information, risk, need of independence, representations of failure or success, expected results, perseverance, information perceived like important, and differences between entrepreneurs and non-entrepreneurs in startups.
36. **Gartner:** Need for independence, risk, a locus of control, fulfillment needs and dependency, the taste of risk, context, and many external influences, not only during the creation of the company.
37. **Virtanen:** Goals and achievements.
38. **Moriano:** Ambitious, working in networks, hard, innovation, dualism (work-family conciliation), returner (business creation with social and family creation of wealth), achievement, hedonism, self-direction, universalism, security, and collective values (benevolence, tradition, and conformity).

39. **Bono:** Creativity, vertical, and lateral thinking
40. **Bruyat:** Person in charge of the creation process of new values.
41. **Verstraete:** Mental and structural dimensions, and functions in the organization

From Management and Administrative Sciences: The Strategy

Entrepreneurs as creators and business managers look for the ways of assuring their permanence in the market through the use of methods, practices, and styles of taking decisions. Effectiveness, productivity, efficiency, and excellence guide their behavior and, as a result, achieving efficiency is crucial in their division of work and specialization. For such aim, Taylor mentions that stimuli, teamwork, the standards used in the firm, planning, and functional organization are vital for business success. Besides, Fayol proposes the separation of operations in the firm among hierarchy, order, and initiative. Drucker does not believe in the enterprising personality; but, in some features, in entrepreneurs surrounded by networks and institutions, assuming the role of innovator. Systematic innovations have greater importance than technology, risk, leadership, and what ought not to be done – so, be clever and innovate. At this respect, Porter emphasizes the importance of innovation, technological change and costs reduction to preserve a competitive advantage, and the importance of the employee who discovers and exploits social and economic interrelations (*intrapreneurship*). Finally, Peters and Waterman affirm that creativity without effects is sterile, in other words, innovation is how creativity is being put in practice.

The Managerial and Administrative Sciences School

42. **Taylor:** Stimuli, teamwork, functional organization, maximization of the production, the technical excellence with minimization of costs, optimal use of the resources and tasks' specialization.
43. **Fayol:** Tasks' separation in the firm, hierarchy, order, fairness, and workers' participation
44. **Drucker:** Individual features and conduct, non-personal enterprising, systematic innovation, innovation for the future, non-risk inventions, technology, and individual motivations (money, power, curiosity, and fame or recognition)
45. **Porter:** Competitiveness, technological change, costs reduction, value chain, and *intrapreneurship.*
46. **Peters and Waterman:** Creativity, innovation, and *intrapreneurship.*
47. **Busenitz:** Strategy, heurism, enterprising knowledge, and expert's knowledge.
48. **Minzberg, Lumpkin, and Dess:** Autonomy and abandonment of safe positions.
49. **Davila:** Personal characteristics, business opportunities, action-oriented, reasonable risk, and non-monetary incentives.

Other Contributors

50. **Venkataraman:** Lucrative opportunities.
51. **Varela:** Opportunity identification, creativity, innovation, attainment and resources allocation, design participation, assembly, and proposal operation, risk assumption, time reversal, knowledge, energy, rewards evidenced in monetary benefits and personal satisfaction and prestige, wealth creation, employment generation, freedom, and independence

Generally, from these approaches, it is possible to assume that entrepreneurs create companies, take advantage of business opportunities, use results from research, apply R&D and innovation as a competitive advantage, and has action capacity. Nonetheless, businesspeople can sometimes be entrepreneurs, but businesspeople are different from entrepreneurs regarding innovation, as entrepreneurs cease from being entrepreneurs if they stop innovating. Entrepreneurs, in certain places and endowed with specific conditions, create startups that renew societies.

From the detailed analysis of the theoretical references presented above entrepreneurs can be defined as people with the capacity of detecting and taking advantage of opportunities to devise, propose and put into practice creative and proactive solutions filled with imagination, which allows the possibility to innovate in specific contexts of places and time (table 6). To reach this aim, they reunite and combine business resources to generate value and recover the invested capital with an additional benefit, sustained in the use of technology, and without the fear of change, to be the business managers.

CONCLUSION: TOWARDS A MULTIDISCIPLINARY DEFINITION

In this chapter, we have analyzed the evolution and development of the terms "entrepreneur" and "entrepreneurship," and the different approaches emerged from Social Sciences. From *Economy*, entrepreneurs are mainly guided by risk and uncertainty to generate uncertain gains in a political, social and competitive market. In *Sociology*, they contribute to the purpose of their actions and characteristics to create new organizations. As a result, culture and the social context determine entrepreneurship as an individual decision, but it requires social groups to be accomplished because regions and countries are different in the forms of implementing entrepreneurship to launch startups. In particular, entrepreneurship is affected by culture, law, knowledge, and business activity valuation.

Table 6. Characteristics of an entrepreneur

High work capacity	Intuition
Assumes risks	Independence
Searches personal prestige	Competitive
With long-term horizons	With initiative
Achievement need	High level of self-confidence
Strategy	Teamwork
Likes power	Participates in knowledge-based networks
Looks forward controlling other people	Social and cultural context
Not always motivated by money	In a constant learning process
Motivated by need and by the opportunity	Fixes reachable goals
Creates new value	Optimist
Oriented to results	Context adaptation capacity
Perseverant	Aggressiveness
Inspiration	Works in inflexible institutional atmospheres
Knows how to inform	The capacity of organizing and using resources

Source: Author

In *Psychology*, entrepreneurs are being defined by their aptitudes, need for success, interests, strategies, experience, the ways of perceiving people, and psychological features (creativity, desire for independence, leadership, opportunism, individualism, intuition, organization, capacity for rationality, planning, and professionalism). Finally, from the *Management and Administrative Sciences*, entrepreneurs and entrepreneurship are defined by creators and business managers searching ways of assuring their permanence in the market by using methods, practices, and styles of decision-making. They look permanently for effectiveness, productivity, efficiency, and business excellence based on the division of work and specialization.

FUTURE LINES OF RESEARCH

Latin American reports and surveys from external organisms do not identify with certainty the characteristics of all entrepreneurs, their motivation, location, attitudes and abilities, values and beliefs, formation, context, family or friend support, and presence in small or big locations. It is also unknown the set of conditions in which the companies were created, how they identified the opportunity, their sources of resources, support, and presence of venture capital, models of management, strategies, innovation, use of R&D and innovation, and network participation. The great challenges of launching startups in Latin America are developed in complex circumstances, like the volatility of the economic cycles, increasing external debt in some countries, low insertion in international markets and macroeconomic and fiscal imbalances; while in the socio-political issue, a high degree of corruption is kept, a low citizen participation prevails, more than half of the population is under the line of poverty and misery, and an internal conflict of more than half of a century prevails (Hernández, 2008).

Therefore, it is possible to progress in an interdisciplinary manner to identify the specific features of the Latin-American entrepreneurs, their motivation, location, attitudes and abilities, values and beliefs, formation, context, the use of technology, and family support. Entrepreneurship sees human beings from the perspective of business, but it can be studied from the social dimensions where and for whom it acts. The research expressed in publications cited has been emphasized on the methodologies to prepare, formulate and evaluate projects and their management, and the uncritical approach of their technical components. However, aspects that have to do with social reality and with human problems are left aside (Orrego, 2009).

As a result, the theoretical definition of the terms "entrepreneur" and "entrepreneurship" must move forward to respond to the epistemological problem and the consolidation of conceptually rigorous methodologies to surpass the initial state as a field of knowledge (Forouharfar, Rowshan, & Salarzehi, 2018). This definition is a necessary condition for researchers to contribute to the real growth of the field of study (Berglund & Johansson, 2007) while answering to the Pereira's question (2007): As a research line, has entrepreneurship been advancing or just expanding in size?

REFERENCES

Aristotle. (1973). *Politics*. Grolier Jackson.

Baumol, W. J. (1968). Entrepreneurship in Economic Theory. *The American Economic Review*, *58*(2), 64–71.

Baumol, W. J. (1970). *Introducción a la dinámica económica*. Barcelona, Spain: Marcombo.

Belausteguigoitia, I. (2007). *¿Entrepre.... qué?* Available at cedef.itam.mx/PDF/Entrepreneurship.pdf

Berglund, K., & Johansson, A. W. (2007). Constructions of entrepreneurship: A discourse analysis of academic publications. *Journal of Enterprising Communities: People and Places in The Global Economy*, *1*(1), 77–102. doi:10.1108/17506200710736276

Beugelsdijk, S., & Noorderhaven, N. (2002). *Entrepreneurial attitude and economic growth; A cross-section of 54 regions*. Paper presented at the 2002 Conference of the European Regional Science Association (ERSA), Dortmund, Germany.

Busenitz, L., & Álvarez, A. (2001). The entrepreneurship of resource-based theory. *Journal of Management*, *27*(6), 755–775. doi:10.1177/014920630102700609

Cantillon, R. (1952). *Ensayo sobre la naturaleza del comercio en general*. D.F, Mexico: Fondo de Cultura Económica. (Original work published 1755)

Carland, J., Hoy, F., Boulton, W., & Carland, J. A. (1984). Differentiating Entrepreneurs from Small Business Owners: A Conceptualization. *Academy of Management Review*, *9*(2), 354–359. doi:10.5465/amr.1984.4277721

Chamber of Commerce. (2003). Bogotá – Cundinamarca. Bases del plan regional de competitividad. Bogota, Colombia: Author.

Commission of the European Communities. (2003). *Libro verde. El espíritu empresarial en Europa*. Brussels: Bruselas.

Commission of the European Communities. (2006a). *Report on the implementation of the Entrepreneurship Action Plan*. Commission Staff Working Paper. Brussels: Author.

Commission of the European Communities. (2006b). *Programas de Apoyo a las PYME de la Unión Europea. Presentación general de los principales planes comunitarios de financiación para PYME*. Brussels: Author.

Commission of the European Communities. (2007). *Communication from the Commission to the Council, the European Parliament, the European Economic and Social Committee, and the Committee of the Regions*. Brussels, Belgium: European Union.

Covarrubias, I. (2003). Emprendedores y empresarios: un enfoque institucional. *Revista CE. Contribuciones a la Economía*. Retrieved from www.eumed.net/ce/icm-emp.htm

Cuevas, H. (2007). *La empresa y los empresarios en la teoría económica*. Bogota, Colombia: Universidad Externado de Colombia.

Dávila, C. (1996). *Empresa e historia en América Latina. Un balance historiográfico*. Bogota, Colombia: TM Editores y Colciencias.

Dávila, C. (1997). Los comienzos de la historia empresarial en Colombia. *America Latina en la Historia Economica*, *7*(07), 73–101. doi:10.18232/alhe.v4i07.203

Davis, T. (2008). *The OECD-Eurostat Entrepreneurship Indicators Programme. Preliminary Indicators for Italy, Europe and Other OECD Countries*. Urbino, Italy: Urbino University.

De Bono, E. (1994). *El pensamiento lateral. El poder del pensamiento lateral para la creación de nuevas ideas*. Barcelona, Spain: Paidós Empresa.

De Soto, H. (2000). *El misterio del capital*. Bogota, Colombia: Planeta.

Drucker, P. (1984). *La innovación y el empresario innovador*. Bogota, Colombia: Editorial Norma.

ECOTEC. (2007). *Design and implementation of the pilot action ERASMUS for young entrepreneurs, enterprise and industry*. Working Paper, 2. Brussels: Author.

EIM. (2003). *Entrepreneurship in Europe Green Paper*. Zoetermeer, The Netherlands: EIM Business & Policy Research.

Fayol, H. (2003). *Administración industrial y general*. Bogota, Colombia: Stilo Impresores.

Fontela, E., Guzmán, J., Pérez, M., & Santos, F. (2006). The Art of Entrepreneurial Foresight. *Foresight*, *8*(6), 3–13. doi:10.1108/14636680610712496

Forouharfar, A., Rowshan, S.A., & Salarzehi, H. (2018). An epistemological critique of social entrepreneurship definitions. *Journal of Global Entrepreneurship Research*, 1-40.

Furtado, C. (1970). *Teoría y política del desarrollo económico*. México, D.F.: Siglo Veintiuno editores.

Galbraith, J. (2004). *La sociedad opulenta*. Barcelona, Spain: Ariel.

Gámir, L., & … . (2007). *Innovación y productividad*. Madrid, Spain: LID Editores.

Gartner, W. (1985). A Conceptual Framework for Describing the Phenomenon of New Venture Creation. *Academy of Management Review*, *10*(4), 696–706. doi:10.5465/amr.1985.4279094

Geroski, P., Mata, J., & Portugal, P. (2007). *Founding Conditions and the Survival of New Firms*. Copenhagen, Denmark: Danish Research Unit for Industrial Dynamics.

Global Entrepreneurship Monitor. (2006). *Global report summary*. London, UK: Author.

Guzmán, J., & Liñán, F. (2005). *Perspectives on Entrepreneurial Education: A US-Europe Comparison*. Madrid, Spain: Jean Monnet European Studies Center-Nebrija University.

Hayek, F. (2002). Competition as a discovery procedure. *The Quarterly Journal of Austrian Economics*, *5*(3), 9–23. doi:10.100712113-002-1029-0

Hernández, I. (2008). *Empresa, innovación y desarrollo*. Bogota, Colombia: Universidad Nacional de Colombia.

Herrerías, A. (2006). *Fundamentos para la historia del pensamiento económico*. D.F., Mexico: Limusa.

Javalgi, S. L., & Martin, R. (2018). Epistemological foundations of international entrepreneurship. *The International Entrepreneurship and Management Journal, 14*(3), 671–680. doi:10.100711365-018-0517-4

Kalmanovitz, S. (2001). *Las instituciones colombianas en el siglo XX*. Bogota, Colombia: Alfaomega y Cambio.

Kantis, H. (2002). *Desarrollo emprendedor: América Latina y la experiencia internacional*. Bogota, Colombia: Banco Interamericano de Desarrollo & Fundes Internacional.

Keynes, J. M. (1986). *Teoría general de la ocupación, el interés y el dinero*. D.F., Mexico: Fondo de Cultura Económica.

Kirzner, I. (1986). *The open-endedness of knowledge. Ideas on Liberty*. Academic Research Library.

Kirzner, I. (1997). Entrepreneurial Discovery and the Competitive Market Process: An Austrian Approach. *Journal of Economic Literature, 35*(1), 60–85.

Kirzner, I. (2000). *Entrepreneurial discovery and the law of supply and demand. In Ideas on Liberty*. Academic Research Library.

Knight, F. (1942). Profit and Entrepreneurial Functions. *The Journal of Economic History, 2*(S1), 126–132. doi:10.1017/S0022050700083479

León, N. (2006). *Mecanismos para la regulación ambiental*. Bogota, Colombia: Universidad Nacional de Colombia.

Lewin, A., & Minton, J. (1986). Determining Organizational Effectiveness: Another Look, and an Agenda for Research. *Management Science, 32*(5), 514–538. doi:10.1287/mnsc.32.5.514

Lipman, A. (1965). Social Backgrounds of the Bogota Entrepreneur. *Journal of Inter-American Studies, 7*(2), 227–235. doi:10.2307/165147

López, R. (1995). Desarrollos conceptuales y operacionales acerca de la creatividad. Cuadernos de trabajo, 1, 49-65.

Lumpkin, G. T., & Dess, G. (1996). Clarifying the Entrepreneurial Orientation Construct and Linking It to Performance. *Academy of Management Review, 21*(1), 135–172. doi:10.5465/amr.1996.9602161568

Mantzavinos, C., North, D., & Shariq, S. (2003). *Learning, Institutions, and Economic Performance*. Bonn, Germany: Max Plank Institute for Research on Collective Goods.

Marshall, A. (1890). *Principles of Economics: An introductory volume*. Academic Press.

Martínez, L. (2018). *Política pública de emprendimiento en Colombia 2006-2016: Un análisis cognitivo desde los instrumentos de la planificación* (Ph.D. Thesis). Bogota, Colombia: Universidad Externado de Colombia.

Max-Neef, M., Elizalde, A., & Hoppenhayn, M. (2006). *Desarrollo a Escala Humana*. Available at www.ecoportal.net

McClelland, D. (1989). *Estudio de la motivación humana*. Madrid, Spain: Narcea Ediciones.

McClelland, D., & Winter, D. (1970). *Cómo se motiva el éxito económico*. D.F., Mexico: Unión Tipográfica Editorial Hispanoamericana.

Mises, L. (1998). Monopoly prices. The characteristic features of monopoly prices. *The Quarterly Journal of Austrian Economics*, *1*(2), 1–28.

Moriano, J. (2005). El perfil psicosocial del emprendedor. *Consejo económico y social*, 263.

Moriano, J., Palací, F., & Morales, J. (2006). El perfil psicosocial del emprendedor universitario. *Revista de Psicología del Trabajo y de las Organizaciones*, *22*(1), 75–99.

North, D. (1993). Desempeño económico en el transcurso de los años. *Nobel Prize Conference*, Stockholm, Sweden.

North, D. (2003). The role of institutions in economic development. *United Nations Discussion Paper Series, 2003.2*.

OECD. (2002). *OECD Small and Medium Enterprise Outlook*. Paris, France: OECD.

OECD. (2004). *OECD Compendium II on SME and Entrepreneurship Related Activities Carried Out by International and Regional Bodies*. Paris, France: OECD.

Orrego, C. (2009). La fenomenología y el emprendimiento. *Pensamiento y gestión, 27*, 235-252.

Pereira, F. (2003). Reflexión sobre algunas características del espíritu emprendedor colombiano. *Revista Economía. Gestión y Desarrollo*, *1*, 9–26.

Pereira, F. (2007). *La evolución del espíritu empresarial como campo del conocimiento. Hacia una visión sistémica y humanista. Cuadernos de Administración*. Bogota, Colombia: Universidad Javeriana de Bogotá.

Peters, T., & Waterman, R. (1984). *En busca de la excelencia*. Bogota, Colombia: Editorial Norma.

Pinchot, G. (1985). Intrapreneuring. Bogota, Colombia: Norma.

Pinillos, M., Reyes, L., & Soriano, I. (2007). *Actividad emprendedora en países de alto desarrollo*. Madrid, Spain: Universidad Rey Juan Carlos.

Ponti, F., & Ferràs, X. (2008). Pasión por innovar. Un modelo novedoso que incentiva la creatividad empresarial. Bogota, Colombia: Norma.

Porter, M. (2002). *Ventaja competitiva. Creación y sostenimiento de un desempeño superior*. CECSA.

RAE. (1992). *Diccionario de la Lengua Española*. Espasa Calpe.

Ricardo, D. (1959). *Principios de Economía Política y Tributación*. Fondo de Cultura Económica.

Rodríguez, C., & Jiménez, M. (2007). Emprenderismo, acción gubernamental y academia. Revisión de la literatura. *Innovar (Universidad Nacional de Colombia)*, *15*(26), 73–89.

Say, J. B. (1821). *Letters to Thomas Robert Malthus on Political Economy and Stagnation of Commerce*. London, UK: Academic Press.

Schumpeter, J. A. (1939). *Ciclos económicos*. Buenos Aires, Argentina: Claridad.

Schumpeter, J. A. (1946). *Capitalismo, socialismo y democracia*. Buenos Aires, Argentina: Claridad.

Schumpeter, J. A. (1947). Theoretical Problems: Theoretical Problems of Economic Growth. *The Journal of Economic History*, *7*(S1), 1–9. doi:10.1017/S0022050700065189

Schumpeter, J. A. (1947a). The creative response in economic history. *The Journal of Economic History*, *7*(2), 149–159. doi:10.1017/S0022050700054279

Schumpeter, J.A. (1978). *Teoría del desenvolvimiento económico*. Fondo de cultura económica.

Senger, J. (1971). Managers' Perceptions of Subordinates' Competence as a Function of Personal Value. *Academy of Management Journal*, *14*(4), 415–423.

Shane, S., & Venkataraman, S. (2000). The Promise of Entrepreneurship as a Field of Research. *Academy of Management Review*, *25*(1), 217–226.

Simmel, G. (1900). A chapter in the Philosophy of value. *American Journal of Sociology, 5*, 16.

Simmel, G. (1910). How is society possible? *American Journal of Sociology*, *16*(3), 13–23. doi:10.1086/211904

Smelser, N. (1965). *Sociología de la vida económica*. Uteha.

Smelser, N., & Swedberg, R. (2005). *Introducing Economic Sociology*. Princeton University Press.

Smith, A. (1776). *La riqueza de las naciones*. Madrid, Spain: Alianza Editorial.

Stevenson, H., & Jarillo, C. (1990). A paradigm of entrepreneurship: Entrepreneurial management. *Strategic Management Journal*, *11*, 17–27.

Swedberg, R. (2003). *The economic sociology of capitalism: an introduction and agenda*. Cornell University.

Tarapuez, E., & Botero, J. (2007). Algunos aportes de los neoclásicos a la teoría del emprendedor. *Cuadernos Americanos*, *23*, 39–63.

Taylor, F. (2003). *Principios de la administración científica*. Bogota, Colombia: Stilo impresores.

Thornton, P. (1999). The Sociology of Entrepreneurship. *Annual Review of Sociology*, *25*(1), 19–46. doi:10.1146/annurev.soc.25.1.19

Turgot, J. (1776). *Reflections on the Formation and Distribution of Wealth*. London, UK: E. Spragg.

Turriago, Á. (2002). *Gerencia de la innovación tecnológica*. Bogota, Colombia: Alfaomega y Cambio.

Uribe, B. (2017). La enseñanza de la ciencia. *Perfiles Educativos*, *39*(158), 226–230.

Varela, R. (2001). *Innovación empresarial. Arte y ciencia en la creación de empresas*. Pearson.

Veciana, J. (2001). Creación de empresas como campo de estudio y salida profesional: Evolución, estado actual y tendencias de desarrollo. *RGE-Revista de Gestão e Economia*, *12*(3), 2–9.

Virtanen, M. (1997). The Role of Different Theories in Explaining Entrepreneurship. *Journal of Best Papers of the 42nd World Conference "International Council for Small Business 1997"*.

Weber, M. (1942). *Historia económica general*. Fondo de Cultura Económica.

Weber, M. (1964). *Economía y sociedad. Esbozo de sociología comprensiva*. Fondo de Cultura Económica.

Weber, M. (1984). *La ética protestante y el espíritu del capitalismo*. Madrid, Spain: Sarpe.

KEY TERMS AND DEFINITIONS

Collective Values: They are composed of benevolence, tradition, and conformity.

Convergent Creativity: A sort of creativity that selects the strengths and weaknesses of each idea.

Entrepreneurship-Related Psychological Features: They are formed by creativity, desire for independence, leadership, opportunism, individualism, intuition, organization, capacity for rationality, planning, and professionalism.

Necessity-Driven Entrepreneurship: It is defined when business decisions are mainly guided by economic necessity.

Opportunity-Driven Entrepreneurship: It appears when entrepreneurs take advantage of foreseen business opportunities.

Pulling Entrepreneur: It is defined when a startup is created by attraction or imitation.

Pushing Entrepreneur: It is defined by being unsatisfied with his or her current job and decides to start a business.

Returner: Applied to firms and entrepreneurs, this term refers to combining business creation and social wealth.

Chapter 2
Solidarity Economics, Entrepreneurship, and Social Wealth

Jose Manuel Saiz-Alvarez
https://orcid.org/0000-0001-6435-9600
Tecnologico de Monterrey, Mexico

ABSTRACT

This chapter deals with how the socioeconomics of solidarity inserted in the Industry 4.0 can bring about solidarity and the creation of social and economic wealth based on the guiding principles of subsidiarity, the search for the common good, and solidarity based on social justice. After having grounded these principles, the author develops different solidarity-based public policies, mainly focused on the European Union, by including principles, objectives, and stages of the European ODA (Official Development Aid), the European Development Fund, the Common Framework for Joint Multiannual Programming and Efficiency, and the European Consensus on Development "Our World, Our Dignity, Our Future." Some ideas complement this analysis linked to the socioeconomics of solidarity that focuses on solidarity and justice to search for a more balanced business world defined by social welfare and economic wealth.

INTRODUCTION[1]

Today, the business world is characterized by a strong "glocalization" (think globally, act locally), with a business policy development based on outsourcing. A business strategy complemented with the launching of public Official Development Assistance (ODA) and economic policy recipes to achieve higher levels of economic and social welfare. In this process, the Information and Communication Technologies (ICTs) have a key role in converting the world into a global village (McLuhan, 1964). Following Rifkin (2011), we are now facing the Fourth Industrial Revolution, after the Third Industrial Revolution, also called the Revolution of Intelligence or Knowledge Economy[2] (Marginean, 2009). A Fourth Industrial Revolution defined by the transmission of real-time information based on the Internet for a "smartization" of manufacturing industries (Diez-Olivan et al, 2019) to increase the quality of manufactured

DOI: 10.4018/978-1-5225-8939-6.ch002

goods and services to satisfy customers by using natural and technical resources more rationally, and by conducting secondary processing of all waste, resources, or energy (Digilina, Teslenko, & Abdullaev, 2019). Faced with the undeniable benefits associated with the Internet, most notably (a) real-time communication independently of the type of transmission used; (b) higher levels of productivity; (c) more efficient academic work; (d) networks rooted on personal and professional contacts; (e) less operating and supply costs; (f) further expansion of clients by opening new markets, and (g) the possibility of collaborative consumption, the combination of these advantages lead to a global social re-humanization.

As the world is immersed in a global village, economic crises have a deeper impact, as has happened in the First Global Crisis, beginning on 15 September 2008 after the Lehman Brothers'[3] bankruptcy. Given the negative effects arisen from this crisis, it is necessary to reintroduce values and guiding principles defining subsidiarity, solidarity and the common good, as well as a strengthening the ODA mechanisms to diminish the negative effects caused by unemployment of senior workers unable to be adapted to the Industry 4.0 (Stojanova, Lietavcova, & Raguž, 2019).

The Socioeconomics of Solidarity has emerged in Latin America and Spain to diminish the strong economic imbalances concerning unfair income and welfare distribution around the planet. Fostering social entrepreneurship and welfare generates positive externalities (Leadbeater, 1997; Dees, 2001; Drayton, 2002), Braunerhjelm & Stuart, 2012), to combat poverty by implementing business strategies to maximize profit, such as applying Corporate Social Responsibility and the Triple Bottom Line. Any initiative based on economic issues has a social impact (Certo & Miller, 2008; Mair & Schoen, 2007), whose intensity varies according to business and social characteristics in the country, being particularly important in the case of social entrepreneurship.

After having analyzed the entrepreneurial activity in 49 countries, Lepoutre et al. (2011) show that entrepreneurship-based countries are mostly defined by social firms focused on creating economic welfare with social value while stimulating social change by offering goods and services to meet consumer needs and create value to stakeholders. The global fight against poverty would be based on the Ashoka's 'hybrid value chain,' and the 'holistic approach to development' conceived by Bangladesh Rural Advancement Committee (BRAC). At this respect, Kim (2014) propose a global social entrepreneurship model both to fight poverty and to highlight how entrepreneurial efforts can create opportunities for launching ventures to satisfy social needs while balancing economic and social imperatives on a global scale.

Social entrepreneurship can be impulsed through solidarity focused on social needs. Good business practices are defined by implementing social entrepreneurship seeking to "catalyze social change and social needs" (Mair & Marti, 2006, p. 37) and "social value through the implementation of new business opportunities" (Weerawardena & Mort, 2006, p. 25). This social value is translated into a higher quality of life for society, as well as a growing sense of self-worth and self-assessment individual sentiments.

This sense of self-assessment is enhanced by the desire for continuous improvement in the pursuit of excellence through cooperation and self-competition. This fact is a constant search of happiness for entrepreneurs and their immediate environment, leading to a constant search for quality and needs' satisfaction, not only for their customers and suppliers but also for their happiness.

Given these premises, social entrepreneurship can be fostered through solidarity addressing a variety of social needs. Generated from entrepreneurship, well-done jobs are a mixture of motivation, courage, determination, ethics, continuous learning, intelligence, passion, and entrepreneurship seeking welfare to create a better society. Public-private initiatives are necessary to melt for achieving this social objective through social entrepreneurship. The combination of a good capacity for innovation, strong working skills, and the ability to develop new business ideas, guarantees socio-economic development by creating business opportunities and GDP growth impulsed by industrial processes defined in the Fourth Industrial revolution as endowed with higher levels of automation, greater production speed, and accuracy (Lele, 2019). As a result, entrepreneurs must be associated with values, prosperity, and happiness gained in the market, to develop business policies rooted in quality management strategies, good practices, and efficient management principles by linking an increased turnover, profits, productivity, and customer satisfaction. As a result, business excellence identifies improvement opportunities and areas of strength.

Social entrepreneurship is directly affected by entrepreneurial spirit, culture, and business policies carried out by strategic business plans for decreasing differences regarding GDP per capita (*Beta convergence*) (Dolado et al., 1994), through opportunity entrepreneurship (Block & Wagner, 2010), that is directly influenced by education — as demonstrated by Kets de Vries (1985), cited in Hisrich et al. (2007), and Páez and García (2011), emotional and behavioral family conditions in childhood and adolescence influence entrepreneurial behavior, as entrepreneurship can be taught and learned (Kuratko, 2003).

This chapter aims to analyze the Socioeconomics of Solidarity's guiding principles, and how solidarity impulses economic growth and wealth. To do this, and mainly focused on the private sector, we will begin analyzing how the guiding principles can optimize the efficient use of resources to achieving fair and caring societies. Then we will study public solidarity from a European perspective. Finally, the Socioeconomics of Solidarity will be analyzed, as a complementary driving source of solidarity from private and community initiatives. The chapter will be finalized with some conclusions.

BACKGROUND

First Guiding Principle: The Importance of Subsidiarity

From a sociological point of view, the term "Subsidiarity" (from Latin, *subsidiarius*) can be defined as "trend favorable to the subsidiary State involved in supporting private or community activities." Born in the EU law, the principle of Subsidiarity limits EU actions to only those cases in which the States alone are not effective for achieving an objective. Therefore, Subsidiarity creates and guarantees the space for personal responsibility and personal initiative, especially at the level of good governance (Horga, 2010). This level of responsibility is collective because it is performed at a multilevel scale, so the implementation of the economic policy is made in any of the four existing Governmental levels (European, national, regional and local). As a result, the principle of Subsidiarity optimizes the efficient use of resources due to coordinated processes (Guerin, 2002). Therefore, subsidiarity increases welfare and wealth (Chowdhury & Garonna, 2007).

Along with these advantages, the Subsidiarity principle is connected with a social economy

characterized by people focused on consuming and on producing goods or services, equipped with management autonomy and democratic organization (internal management and participatory decision-making power). This strategy gives services to the community, respects the environment, and favors labor in the distribution of surplus. (García et al., 2006, p. 217).

The aim of both the principle of Subsidiarity and the social economy is to maximize welfare through an efficient allocation of resources, taking into account a topic ignored by the modern competitive economy: the perpetuation of values, whether person-centered (humanistic values), spirituality (religious values) or both. The absence of these values dehumanizes people. Hence is valid the sentence was written by the Roman playwright, Plautus Titus Maccius (254-184 BC) who, in his *Asinaria*, established that: *Lupus est homo homini, non homo, quom qualis sit non novit*[4] to describe a reality of his time which continues even today. Sentence popularized by the English philosopher Thomas Hobbes of Malmesmury[5] (1588-1679) in his *Leviathan*, written in 1651[6], in which the author includes his *Theory of social contract*, where agreements are reached between the Government and the ruled. Social contracts continue today, implicitly, in modern democracies for seeking social harmony and the common good. When corruption, this social contract is violated, causing social unrest and, in extreme cases, anarchy.

The State must be guided by social justice, freedom, and equality (Gallegos, 2008; Olives, 2011). Social interest is internationally-conceived, thanks to the implementation of ODA policies intended to benefit the poorest, and

to ensure that values, such as solidarity, transparency, and brotherly love, remain within the social conscience to fight against corruption through consensus and dialogue, and never under coercion and violence. (Saiz-Alvarez, 2013a, p. 75).

As merit and well-used values guide the behavior of economic agents, they have a positive-negative polarity, unlike things that can only be positive. As a result, values can be classified as (a) *useful and pleasant-based values*, formed by convenience, comfort, pleasure and wealth; (b) *vital values*, comprising health, fitness and longevity; (c) *spiritual values*, subdivided in aesthetic (beauty), legal (justice), and intellectual (truth and goodness), and (d) *religious values* expressed by holiness.

Therefore, every human action is based on values. But recently, a strong dehumanization process has fragmented and severely beaten today's societies. To avoid this loss of values, it is necessary to harmonize «all forces directed towards the common good, driven in genuine respect for the supreme values of the spirit» (John Paul II, 1982, p. 3). This will make greater values-based countries to benefit citizens as a whole.

In implementing these objectives, education is of fundamental importance, both in the family and in the elementary school as the first educational nucleus, and in upper levels, once the student has matured to internalize the use of values and the deep thinking of axiology as a science. This human capital management, defined as a resource-based strategic management approach, leads to the management of structural, human, and relational capital to involve the partnership and external relations focused on learning personal development processes (Stachová, Papula, Stacho, & Kohnová, 2019).

Second Guiding Principle: The Search for the Common Good

As a complementary way to Subsidiarity, searching for the common good is a guide to channel economic activities towards solidarity and mutual aid. This fact explains why the Social Doctrine of the Catholic Church defines the common good as "the sum of social conditions which allow people, either individually or collectively, to easily reach its full objective" (Pontifical Council for Justice and Peace, 2004). Therefore, the common good is what founds and legitimizes social communities and, by extension, economic policies.

To be fully comprehensive and effective in exploring common goods, a double spiritual (Christ-centered) and human (anthropocentric) vision must be performed, both based on the integral concept of the person as a whole. As a result, a comprehensive development of individuals and families, respecting their fundamental rights and dignity, will be achieved. A Christ-centric vision gives meaning to life and sanctifies human actions and decisions in daily life. Without Christ, human life is impoverished of content, even reaching a spiritual void.

Values-based societies must be rooted in people guiding others always looking their well-being, which contradicts the traditional idea advocated by Neoliberalism, where individuals are selfish, as they seek their good, and only the "invisible hand" generate welfare through a self-regulating market process in which the anarchic behavior of private economic agents (producers and consumers), guided by their selfishness, maximize their highest level of satisfaction or utility, and by extension, it leads to social welfare maximization.

Faced with this social vision, the Aristotelian-Thomistic tradition on the notion of the common good concerns about the good of people (Argandoña, 2011) and, by extension, of society, because the common good is formed by "the integration of civic awareness, political virtues, the sense of right and freedom, and any activity, material prosperity and wealth of the spirit, active unconsciously inherited wisdom, moral righteousness, justice, friendship, happiness, virtue, and heroism in every individual are living on the community" (Maritain, 1951, p. 45). As a result, once the common good is achieved, both collective welfare and social justice are maximized. Without social justice, peace and social stability are threatened. A social peace needed to achieve stable levels of economic growth and to increase the degree of happiness for society as a whole.

For this reason, and only when justice and solidarity are pursued, economic management is not immune "to the fundamental principles of the Social Doctrine of the Catholic Church, which is: the centrality of the human person, solidarity, subsidiarity, and the common good" (Bertone, 2009, p. 1). Moreover, "in the era of globalization, economic activity cannot be done without gratuitousness, which fosters and disseminates solidarity and responsibility for justice and the common good among different economic players" (Benedict XVI, *Caritas in Veritate*, 38).

This economic democracy can be strengthened when companies strive for desiring common goods following a spirit of solidarity full of social justice and Christian charity. Working for the common good is dealing with love. When nations (*gentium*), cities (*polis*), institutions, and organizations are structured following a multiple juridical, social, political, and economic perspective, while fighting for social welfare and collective wealth, societies (*societas*) will be guided by empathy and mutual respect. When the source of love is Christ as a guide towards the common good, higher values are accomplished. So, "every Christian is called to practice this charity, according to their vocation and their abilities to influence the *polis*. [...] The commitment for the common good, when it is animated by charity, has a higher value than a merely secular and political promise" (Benedict XVI, *Caritas in Veritate*, 7)

Today's society, part of which is characterized by its social dismemberment and its strong social irresponsibility towards future generations, must be based on the respect for the human dignity supported on justice, temperance, and culture. Therefore, styles and models of life must substantially change to preserve and to improve the social and political environment for future generations.

Although the last search is the common good, social wealth and economic profit are generated while working to achieve it. But when only profit is pursued, social wealth is destroyed, and poverty is created. This socioeconomic reality characterizes much of the current economic world defined by their high levels of job insecurity, by the existence of strong social inequalities, and by the unfair and unsupportive distribution of goods produced and/or marketed in global markets.

It is necessary to build a new economic world in which people, and not material goods, have a central position. No holistic development and the universal common good can be reached unless the support of spirituality and moral welfare. *Anima et corpus* acting together, according to the principles of subsidiarity and solidarity, and are directly focused on the common good and, by extension, on their sanctification.

Searching the common good and social peace must constitute a priority in economic policy, with the social inclusion of the poor, and the need for social dialogue as a contribution to peace. The inclusion of subjects related to morality and ethics in Social Sciences and Law is a necessary step to re-humanize both economics and law. As an example of this dehumanization, among many other cases, is the so-called "zero-hour contracts" in the United Kingdom, based on the flexibility in the labor market where workers without a contract (hence the name) can be called at any time of any day of the week to cover peak-hours.

Without going to this extreme, in other countries labor flexibility is widely used what dehumanizes people, especially if they belong to low educational backgrounds, have family responsibilities, and dispose of insufficient work experience. As a result, labor rights are depleted, and the provision of decent work is not guaranteed (Ferrajoli, 2013), a situation that does not change, despite the poor results obtained with this labor strategy, in terms of creating low degrees of wealth and welfare, reducing consumption level, and the impossibility of creating savings and investment (Gallino, 2014).

This globalization of indifference must be avoided by introducing labor-based strategies for achieving inclusive economies, where disadvantaged people are not left out (*cf.* Pope Francesco, *Evangelii Gaudium*, 54), and economic development is rooted in peace, solidarity, and the common good (*cfr.* St. John Paul II, *Sollicitudo Rei Socialis*, 10).

Third Guiding Principle: A Necessary Solidarity Based on Justice

Along with the implementation of the principle of subsidiarity, a third guiding principle in the economy is given by solidarity with the goal of seeking market economies focused on the common good to achieve higher levels of economic welfare. In fact, "solidarity-based markets set the condition that family production units organized in community groups turn into federated social enterprises" (González et al., 2003, p. 32)

This process of economic development based on solidarity has been largely possible thanks to the building process of a united Europe, as we know it today, led by the launch of the Social Market Economy (in German, *Soziale Marktwirtschaft*) based on economic policy's recipes designed between the Market Economy and the Planned Economy. Alfred Müller-Armack (1901-1978), in his *Soziale Marktwirtschaft: Alternative Politische und Wirtschaftliche Ein Projekt* [Social Market Economy: an Alternative Economic and Political Project], affirms the Social Market Economy aims to maximize both social prosperity and economic welfare, to reach Pareto optimal situations for achieving values, such as economic freedom, individual initiative, and solidarity, always to think on the common good and social justice to favor the weakest and most vulnerable, teaching them to act successfully in adverse situations. Moreover, and since the early seminal works of this Economic School of Thought born at the University of Freiburg (Germany), the Social Market Economy has been founded on four general principles, and three operational principles. As general principles can be cited: [1] the promotion of private initiatives and responsibility to achieve economic and social skills; [2] the protection of private property, and the support of both legal security, free competition and economic freedom, with the establishment of control and supervision mechanisms to eliminate, or at least to reduce corruption practices and tax fraud; [3] the definition of the principle of solidarity and joint action for the common good; and [4] the creation of the principle of subsidiarity, as a tool to achieve social justice by achieving equity, equality and justice in the distribution of scarce resources.

Among the operational principles, should be noted (Olives, 2011): [1] the protection of consumers and/or producers by assuring clear information for proper and effective decision-making processes; [2] the implementation of the principle of individual responsibility to ensure free competition and regulated market prices; and [3] the design of an adequate and consensual labor policy agreed among governments, business organizations, and trade unions to achieve fair and decent wages.

These good economic and corporate earnings are even higher in cooperatives regardless of their economic productivity, commercial sectors they operate, and investment companies they socially interact and impact (Giovanelli, 2014). Thus, the mere utilitarianism is exceeded, which is gained in spiritual and moral values (Morelos, 2004). Throughout this process, the State has a major supervisory role, so that "their actions are geared towards promoting efficient competition without breaking, oversee undisturbed, without obstructing monitor and intervene without destroying. That is, intervention should be proportional and gradual in the exercise of the legal powers of control and monitoring legally granted" (Olives, 2011, p. 2).

The combination of good practices carried out by companies and the government paths the way to implement the so-called Socioeconomics of Solidarity, whose main driver is born from combining private and social initiatives. Conceived as a way of helping others on a worldwide scale, the EU's ODA is a must to foster richness and health in Third World countries, as seen in the next section.

SOLIDARITY FROM PUBLIC INSTITUTIONS: ODA AND THE EUROPEAN DEVELOPMENT FUND

More than half the money spent in the world to help the Third and Fourth Worlds comes from the EU, whose legal basis in terms of development cooperation are synthesized in (a) the Title III of the Maastricht Treaty, signed on February 7, 1992, with entry into force on November 1, 1993; (b) the general mandate and guiding principles referred in Article 21, paragraph 1 of the Treaty, and (c) the Article 4, paragraph 4 and Articles 208 to 211 of the Treaty on the Functioning of the EU or the Treaty of Lisbon, signed on December 13, 2007 and entered into force on December 1, 2009 after a lengthy process of ratification by the EU parliaments. In addition to ODA inserted into the Maastricht and Lisbon Treaties, aid assistance is supplemented by (a) *specific cooperation agreements*, like the Cotonou Agreement concerning the African, Caribbean, and Pacific (ACP countries); (b) *bilateral association agreements* referred to in Article 217 of the Treaty of Lisbon, and (c) some *additional budgetary aspects* synthesized in Articles 312 to 316 of the Treaty of Lisbon.

This EU's ODA policy complements the provisions donated by the United Nations through the promotion and strengthening of a collective global partnership for development reaffirmed in (a) the "Millennium Declaration" (Resolution 55/2 the United Nations General Assembly, on September 13, 2000); (b) the "Monterrey Consensus" issued by the International Conference on Financing for Development held in Monterrey (Mexico), 18 to March 22, 2002; (c) the World Summit Implementation Plan on Sustainable Development within the Report of the World Summit on Sustainable Development held in Johannesburg (South Africa), from August 26 to September 4, 2002; (d) the 2005 World Summit Final Document, and [5] the Doha Declaration on Financing for Development, as the final document issued from the International Conference on Financing for Development to Review the Implementation of the Monterrey Consensus (resolution 63/239, annex).

All this regulatory complexity aims to reduce poverty in the world. The main objective of the European ODA is to reduce gradually and to eradicate ideally, poverty in the long term. Poverty reduction achieved after having applied a general framework of development characterized by following a purely economic endowment of aid and cooperation capped by four groups of beneficiary countries: the ACP countries (Africa, Caribbean, Pacific), South Africa, Overseas Countries and Territories (OCTs), and the Least Developed Countries. Such sectorial development policies promote both the protection of human rights and migration control, as an incentive, through the implementation of sustainable development policies for environmental protection and rural development, thus ensuring food security, and the right management of natural resources.

This ODA had a strong revival in the EU after the signing on December 20, 2005, by the Presidents of the Commission, Parliament and Council, of the so-called 'European Council' by which, for the first time, was defined the framework of common principles on which the EU will implement complementary development policies. With this Consensus, the EU undertook to increase budgets for ODA to 0.7% of GDP by 2015, with an intermediate target of 0.56% in 2010, half of this increase is intended for Africa's development.

Since the enactment of the Communication from the Commission to the Council and the European Parliament of June 21, 2007 (COM (2007) 349 final, not published in the Official Journal), there have been important changes regarding EU management policies development, by adopting strategies for stronger control, both on the methodology to be followed in evaluating results, and on the simplification of instruments for external assistance with the creation of the Financing Instrument for Cooperation Development (Regulation (EC) 1905/2006 of the European Parliament and Council of December 19, Official Journal L 378 of December 27, 2006, as subsequently amended by Regulation (EC) 960/2009 of 18 October, Journal Official L 270 of October 15, 2009) and the Instrument for the Promotion of Democracy and Human Rights (Regulation (EC) 1889/2006 of the European Parliament and the Council of December 20, 2006).

The ODA Principles

The European ODA launch has a double economic and political aspect based on the "principle of aid effectiveness" based on the integration of the European ODA into the Millennium Development Goals (MDGs) of the United Nations Beneficiary States. This double involvement of European ODA is more than a mere "European Consensus on Development" (Official Journal C 46 of February 24, 2006), as the EU is really interested in accelerating the compliance of the MDGs following a spirit of complementarily, under the so-called "European Consensus", signed on December 20, 2005, to make the EU remain the greater solidarity region in the world, by representing more than 55 percent of the world's ODA.

The general framework of the European ODA is given from the joint declaration entitled "The European Consensus on Development" signed between the Council and the representatives of the Governments of the Member States meeting within the Council, the European Parliament and the Commission on the European ODA, with the aim of achieving the MDGs promulgated by the United Nations (Bourgignon et al, 2008), so that by 2015 the goal is (a) to eradicate extreme poverty, and hunger in the world; (b) to contribute to good governance and respect for human rights throughout the world; (c) to encourage the creation of a global partnership for development; (d) to ensure environmental sustainability with the implementation of clean development policies and the fight against environmental dumping; (e) to achieve universal primary education in the Third and Fourth World; (f) to fight Acquired Immune

Deficiency Syndrome (AIDS), malaria, malaria and yellow fever, among other endemic diseases; (g) to improve maternal health with decreased mortality rate of women during childbirth; (h) to promote gender equality and empower women; and (i) to reduce infant mortality.

The European ODA is founded on the principles of concentration, ownership, and alignment. According to "the concentration principle," based on a limited number of priority areas for action to achieve the best results, efforts have been centralized to increase quality. Thus, when greater national ownership of the partner country is achieved, coordination and harmonization between donors and aid improvement in the recipient country systems and guidance based on the results are aligned. And all of this, in coordination and complementarily among donors, to implement a mechanism for joint multiannual programming.

Complementary to this principle, *the ownership principle* unites EU partners to exercise effective leadership over their development policies and strategies while coordinating development actions, and *the principle of alienation* where EU donor countries base their overall support on strategies, institutions and procedures for EU partner countries' development. These principles were established in the Paris Declaration on the Effectiveness of Development Aid, signed on March 2, 2005.

An important solidarity-based aspect of the European ODA is mainly focused on Africa, having multiple targets: (a) to have a sustainable economic development throughout the continent, especially in sub-Saharan Africa; (b) to undertake governance reforms that are necessary to launch and fuel sustainable development processes (Paris Declaration, point 20); (c) to work together for EU donor countries to establish mutually agreed frameworks for providing reliable assessments based on performance, transparency and accountability of the national systems of African countries (Paris Declaration, paragraph 19), and (d) to achieve the MDGs in Africa by 2015 (Communication from the Commission to the European Parliament, the Council, the Economic Committee and Social and the Committee of the Regions, COM (2010) 159 final, April 21, 2010, not published in the Official Journal) most notably, the commitment to increase spending on ODA to 0.7% of Gross National Income by 2015, aiming to allocate at least half of this additional funding for Africa.

Objectives and Stages in ODA: Towards a Greater Efficiency?

The implementation of these principles has resulted in the launch of three objectives through which the European ODA is channeled. These objectives are given by [1] contributing to economic and social development of developing countries; [2] improving neighborly relations with Northern Africa, Eastern Europe, and the Middle East; and [3] reaching financial and trading agreements focused on trade cooperation, poverty reduction, respect for democracy and human rights, good governance, environmental protection, social services, and education and health development.

Initially, the European ODA was not part of any of the three founding treaties of the EU. Therefore, their incorporation into the European policy has been gradual over time, always seeking greater impacts derived from aid, as well as an increased presence of the EU in the world, as discussed below.

First Stage: Helping OCTs

European ODA began in the French colonies of Africa in the late 1950s seeking to encourage its development. Such assistance was channeled through donations, mainly carried out by the European Investment Bank, as well as the growing development of non-governmental organizations (NGOs) as part of the Third Sector. Being considered as donations, the EU action does not create foreign debt problems to avoid financial suffocation in much of the Third World. This sensibility contrasts to what is happening in other regions of the world financed by other means of support, mainly born in non-EU countries.

Second Stage: Food Aid and Generalized System of Preferences

Financed from the EU budget, food aid began in 1968 as a result of the obligations acquired by the European countries after having acceded to the International Grains Agreement signed in 1967. Food Aid that was definitively established in 1996 with the dual strategy formed by the combination of delivery of EU agricultural surpluses close with technical assistance for the production of local crops in the Third World. This food aid was complemented by reducing barriers to entry of manufactured goods from the Third World (mainly tariffs and quotas on imports), creating the Generalized System of Preferences. The system established for all developing countries after the 1972 Paris Summit.

Third Stage: Development Third European Non-Governmental Development Organizations and Lomé Conventions

It began in 1976 when European NGOs could be able to get EU funding. Until then, only NGOs in the Catholic and some Protestant branches had a strong development, so the involvement of the European ODA through civil society was a turnabout in policy because it was channeled through political channels.

The signature of the first Lomé Convention between the EU and 46 African, Caribbean and Pacific (ACP) countries changed this situation based on three pillars: (a) elimination of entry barriers (tariffs, and technical and legal barriers) for products exported to Europe by the ACP countries; (b) economic and technical cooperation, and (c) the establishment of STABEX (compensatory mechanism for avoiding loss of export earnings in ACP countries, as a result of changes in international prices, according to arts. 186-212 of IV Lomé Convention), and SYSMIN (helping system to keep mines engaged in export, according to arts. 214-219 of the Lomé IV Convention).

Fourth Stage: Decentralized Cooperation

Decentralized cooperation involves the ODA democratization by various economic and social actors (universities, associations, NGOs, foundations, unions, business organizations, municipalities, and autonomous regions, among others) with the aim of getting aid to the Third and Fourth Worlds more efficiently. Since the entry into force of the Treaty of Maastricht on November 1, 1993, the European ODA has been centered into pushing democracy and human rights, as an objective of the European Common Foreign and Security Policy (CFSP).

THE EUROPEAN DEVELOPMENT FUND: A PAN-EUROPEAN INSTRUMENT BASED ON SOLIDARITY

One of the main European ODA instruments includes the European Development Fund (EDF) whose importance, chronology, composition, and effects will be discussed below.

Importance of the EDF

Born in 1993, the EDF is one of the largest and oldest instruments of European ODA directed to ACP countries and OCTs. The EDF is not included in the budget of the EU, because its inclusion would add administrative arrangements for the disbursement of funds phases, which would threaten the ACP-EU long-term co-management arrangements by reducing allocations given by the EU Member States to the EDF. Therefore, the EDF has its own financial rules, and a specific committee, and presents a definite timeline over time (see Table 1).

The EDF is made up of grants, risk capital, and loans given to the private sector. During the duration of the Lomé Conventions (II to VII FED) highlighted two programs: STABEX (from French, *Système de Stabilisation des Recettes d'Exportation*) consisting of a system of agricultural support, and the SYSMIN instrument (from French, *Système de Stabilisation Minière*) which dealt with aids to the mining sector. In short, the EDF covers cooperation with ACP countries and OCTs, and its main areas are economic development, social and human development, and regional cooperation and integration.

Today, and alongside the EDF, the Development Cooperation Instrument is a major source of funding through thematic instruments (investment in human capital, non-State actors and local authorities, environment, food safety and cooperation with third countries, migration and asylum) aimed to support States, NGOs and civil society groups for development. For the 2014-2020 period, the so-called "differentiation" will apply, which means that Middle-income countries, representing more than 1 percent of global GDP, will be graduated, that is, will be ceased to be eligible for funding EU bilateral grant-based aid. As a result, direct aid from the Development Cooperation Instrument has been replaced in 19 developing countries by differentiated development partnerships based on specific needs.

Finally, the EDF provides additional financing, called Incentive Amounts, to developing countries with histories of improved governance following a co-decision process, which is defined by including the approval of the European Parliament to enhance the democratic control of EU aid. Also, and to ensure transparency in the granting of EU aid, the EDF is allocated according to a rotating schedule in which partner countries participate in setting priorities and cooperation projects.

Table 1. EDF chronology

Period	Convention
EDF I (1959-1964)	---
EDF II (1965-1970)	Yaoundé I Convention
EDF III (1971-1975)	Yaoundé II Convention
EDF IV (1976-1980)	Lomé I Convention
EDF V (1981-1985)	Lomé II Convention
EDF VI (1986-1990)	Lomé III Convention
EDF VII (1991-1995)	Lomé IV Convention
EDF VIII (1996-2000)	Lome IV bis Convention
EDF IX (2001-2007)	Cotonou Agreement
EDF X (2008-2013)	Revised Cotonou Agreement
EDF XI (2014-2020)	---

Source: Adapted from Eurostat

The Common Framework for Joint Multiannual Programming and Efficiency

After the reform of the procedure for granting aid by the European Commission in 2000, the EU adopted a new framework for programming national and regional strategies in all developing countries benefiting from EDF, including TACIS and CARDS programs. The TACIS program, in operation from 1991 to 2006, mainly benefited the Slavic countries of the former Soviet Union (Russia, Ukraine, and Belarus), and was replaced in 2007 by the European Neighborhood and Partnership for seeking a greater impact on the area[7]. These programs include the implementation of indicative multiannual programs defined by (a) relations between donors and partner countries; (b) measurable objectives to be achieved through the implementation of support mechanisms, and (c) the implementation of scheduled program executions.

Respecting the CARDS program, established by Regulation (EC) 2666/2000 (Official Journal L 306, of 7 December)[8], whose objective was the Assistance for Reconstruction, Development, and Stabilization of the Southeastern European countries (Albania and the former Yugoslavia countries) was replaced in 2007 by the Pre-Accession Instrument. Before the CARDS program, can be included in the PHARE program, created by Regulation (EC) 3906/89, and the OBNOVA program, established by Regulation (EC) 1628/96. These EU aid programs show a constant concern towards the Western Balkans since the breakup of the former Yugoslavia on May 4, 1980, and its continuous acceleration during the Balkan Wars, as follows: (a) The Ten-Day War or the Slovenian Liberation War (1991); (b) The Croatian War of Independence (1991-1995); (c) The Croatian-Bosnian War (1992-1994); (d) The Bosnian War (1992-1995); (e) The Kosovo War (1998-1999), and (f) Conflict in Southern Serbia (2001) and Macedonia (2001).

This EU strategic vision to economically and politically develop its Eastern and Southeastern European neighbors, is complemented by a threefold strategy: (a) the approval of an strategic document entitled "The EU Agenda for Change", signed in May 2012, which aims to increase the impact of the Official Aid in countries most in need; (b) the concession of financial aid following the "principle of differentiation" to take into account not only the economic results of the aid granted, but also the governmental performance done by each recipient country; and (c) the promotion of human rights, democracy, rule of law and good governance and achieving inclusive and sustainable growth, as the basic pillars of a sustainable development policy.

Having analyzed the complexity of the European ODA, such financial aid should have a greater economic and social impact to achieve a Socioeconomics of Solidarity, at least in countries receiving EU aid. The European Consensus on Development "Our World, Our Dignity, Our Future" complements these EU programs to establish a new set of principles for development cooperation as part of the EU's response to the United Nations' 2030 agenda for sustainable development. Building on the global strategy for the EU's foreign and security policy and the rules for external action in the Lisbon Treaty, the new consensus highlights important cross-cutting elements, such as democracy and the inclusion of human rights, gender equality, good governance, innovative engagement with more advanced developing countries, investment and trade, using of domestic resources, labor mobility and migration, sustainable energy and climate change, and youth. Objectives set with the implementation of a comprehensive approach as agreed in the Addis Ababa action agenda, combining aid with other resources and a strengthened approach to policy coherence for development (European Union, Joint statement by the Council and the representatives of the governments of the Member States meeting within the Council, the European Parliament and the Commission, Official Journal of the European Union 2017C 2010/1, June 30, 2017).

Table 2. Overview of the EU instruments for development policy (2014-2020 multiannual financial framework)

Program	EUR Million
Development Cooperation Instrument Latin America, East Asia and Central, South Africa	19,700
European Neighborhood and Partnership European Neighborhood and Russia (since 2014, European Neighborhood)	15,400
IPA Balkans and Turkey	11,700
Cooperation with Industrialized Countries Industrialized countries (from 2014, Partnership Instrument)	955
European Instrument for Democracy and Human Rights Promotion of Democracy and Human Rights in the World	1,300
The instrument for Stability and Peace Achieving and Maintaining Peace	2,300
The instrument for nuclear safety since 2014, Cooperation Instrument for Nuclear Safety	225
Instrument for Greenland	184
ACP Countries and territories EDF	29,100
TOTAL	**80,864**

Source: European Parliament (2015). A sheet on the EU.

SOCIOECONOMICS OF SOLIDARITY: A SOLUTION FROM PRIVATE AND SOCIAL INITIATIVES

Also called "Solidarity Economy", "*Humanoeconomía*"·(Loebl, 1978), "Popular Economy", "Economy Emancipated Work", "Solidarity Socioeconomics" (Arruda, 2005), "Social Economy", "Popular Solidarity Economy", "Social and Solidarity Economy", and "Economy of Reciprocity" (Carranza, 2013), the Socioeconomics of Solidarity can be defined as the kind of economy "complementary to the Green Economy" (Rosas-Baños, 2012, p. 91), mainly based on humanistic Christian-based (charity and fraternal love) and human-based (solidarity, not fraudulent or corrupt behavior, cooperation and mutual assistance) values, focused on producing sustainable goods and services benefitting people, and not only shareholders, and thus achieving fairer, more equitable, and more inclusive social groups (Saiz-Alvarez, 2013a).

Rooted on the sixteenth century's School of Salamanca[9], ethics and morality play a key role in the Socioeconomics of Solidarity, where "the value of a good depends on three factors: objective utility (*virtuositas*), scarcity (*raritas*) and consumer appeal (*complacibilitas*), i.e., the subjective utility" (Partridge, 2004, pp. 23-24). Within the rich set of theologians[10] who belonged to this Spanish School, mainly Jesuits and Dominicans, highlights the Dominican Francisco de Vitoria (1483-1546) who, more than two centuries before Adam Smith (1723-1790), founder of the Classical School in response to the so-called "the Paradox of Mandeville"[11], wrote in 1535 that:

Whoever does something good, or for the benefit of a particular, he/she also makes it for the common and public interest, but if he/she hurts a person, he/she harms the common good. Therefore, who favors an individual, the entire society must deserve praise and rewards him/her, although this person only thinks on his/her profit. (De Vitoria, 1535, pp. 1344-1345).

Adam Smith wrote the same idea in 1776 with other words:

When the [economic activity] is managed by maximizing products with the highest possible value, entrepreneurs just think on their gain; but in this, as in many other cases, these individuals are led by an invisible hand[12] that guides them towards a goal which is no part of their intentions. (Smith, 1958[1776], p. 402).

This social benefit is determined by solidarity, as the *homo economicus* is characterized for being social (*zoon politikon*, from Greek ζῷον πολιτικόν). In fact, the fifth Principle (*De Indis recenter Inventis, prior relectio*), enunciated by Francisco de Vitoria, affirms that: "It is good and lawful for man to have private property, but no one owns exclusively, as they should sometimes share things [...] and with extreme need, all things are common". This principle can be applicable today in the Socioeconomics of Solidarity.

The main difference between the Spanish theorists and the Classical economists is the ethical and moral behavior shown by the Spanish theorists (Santos del Cerro, 1998). As a result, Economics might be rooted in moral philosophy, a fact forgotten by the Classical School, as their authors condemned the ideas born in the School of Salamanca two centuries before, as the School of Salamanca condemned from a double moral and ethical perspective the use of interest rates on the exchange and, when interest rates are too high, usury-based economic transactions are created. Therefore, the Socioeconomics of Solidarity's precepts of moral philosophy is closely related to the Spanish School of Salamanca. As a result, the Socioeconomics of Solidarity goes well beyond the economic principles established in traditional and well-established Schools of Economic Thought, such as Neoliberalism, Social Market Economy, and Keynesianism in their different variants, which theoretically aims to reduce inequalities in income distribution by maximizing economic wealth of individuals seeking social justice, without taking into consideration any further moral issue.

An example of solidarity-based socioeconomic development is rooted on communal lands (*Tupambaé*), community work (*Minga*) and the practical application of the Principle of reciprocity made with the Jesuit Missions (1609-1629) in the Guaraní region of Guayrá, now situated in Paraguay (Ossanna, 2008). Solidarity-based practices that preceded in more than three centuries the Rochdale Society of Equitable Pioneers created in 1844, as the first successful cooperative retail store made by working class members (Guerra, 2006).

These humanistic and axiological values inserted into the Socioeconomics of Solidarity leads to individuals come together with Christian values, as shown [1] in the Encyclical Letter *Rerum Novarum*, written by Pope Leo XIII (1878-1903), in which the relations between capital and labor are studied; [2] the Encyclical Letter *Quadragesimo Anno*, written by Pope Pius XI (1922-1939), on the restoration of both economic and social order illuminated by Christian charity; [3] the Encyclical Letter *Mater et Magistra*, written by St. John XXIII (1958-1963), dealing with social issues; [4] the Encyclical Letter *Populorum Progressio,* written by Pope Paul VI (1963-1978), with the need for greater social progress through economic growth, and [5] the Encyclical Letter *Centesimus Annus*, written by St. John Paul II in 1991, to commemorate the centenary of *Rerum Novarum* and to build a Socioeconomics of Solidarity in his speech to the Economic Commission for Latin America and the Caribbean.

Table 3. Organizations in socioeconomics of solidarity

Special Employment Centers	Limited Partnerships	Labor Foundations
Cooperatives of Social Inclusion	Associations	Mutual Trade
Neighboring Communities	Street Vendors	Religious Organizations
Popular Economic Organizations (OEPs)	Social Emergency Care Solutions	

Source: Own elaboration

Introducing Christian values in economic thinking leads to the creation of a new economy based on solidarity and responsibility, leading to fair trade, ethical finance, responsible procurement, eco-villages, and networks based on Alternative and Solidarity Economy (REAS) (Roman & Loebl, 1979). Thus, love, empathy, and desire to help others lead to the birth of a Socioeconomics of Solidarity characterized by "another way of production, close with the basic principles based on collective property, capital and the right for achieving individual freedom. The application of these principles unites production in a class of workers who are equal capital owners in each cooperative or economic society. The natural result "is the combination of both solidarity and equality" (Singer, 2002, p. 10).

The term "solidarity" appears recurrently in the Socioeconomics of Solidarity with different meanings. In this sense, Razeto (1993) and Max-Neef (1997) with their "barefoot economy" and "human scale development", respectively, say that solidarity, love, mutual aid, brotherhood, family care, and neighborhood ties are ways to achieving higher levels of social justice, especially for small and popular solidarity firms, many of them informal ("the invisible world"), which creates a socioeconomic development based on a human scale for everyone, as "human needs, self-reliance and organic joints are the fundamental pillars of Human Scale Development" (Max-Neef, 1994, p. 30). A supportive behavior affected by the so-called "factor C" (companionship, community, cooperation, collaboration, communion, and coordination) (Razeto, 1998) determined by the letter "c" as the capital letter of Christ. When the factor C is fully developed, economic and business growth lead to a collective improvement.

FUTURE RESEARCH DIRECTIONS

The Socioeconomics of Solidarity is, in the background, a kind of internal democracy based on solidarity and the sharing of goods and services generated by individuals, in which there is "a collective identity aimed at a common goal" (Defourny, Favreau, & Laville, 1998, p. 31). In fact, it is a kind of "economy at the service of the people" (Garcia, Vialop, & Xirinachs, 2006: p. 167-178) where cooperative movements and solidarity-based firms are characterized by "in varying proportions, collective arrangements in possession of the means of production, in the process of work and enterprise management, minimizing the presence of salaried relations, occurring mainly in the economies of the popular sectors" (Gaiger, 2004, p. 231).

The insertion of values in the Socioeconomics of Solidarity will move economics from *homo economicus* to *homo reciprocans* (Gintis, 2000) defined by companies headed by solidarity, cooperation, and reciprocal trade. This process of exchange "structure social relations, links, and obligations within the movement of material, symbolic, and knowledge-based goods, through the triple obligation of giving, receiving, and returning, which describes other economic relations, which does not necessarily correspond to supply and demand, economic profit, balance, or market" (Carranza, 2013, p. 15).

Finally, the Socioeconomics of Solidarity is a complement to capitalism so that they can enrich countries. Economic systems work by both buildings horizontal and vertical production networks, as well as through exchange and consumption of goods guided by the principles of compensation and solidarity, close with the rules surged from the future Fifth Industrial Revolution (Feshina, Konovalova, & Sinyavsky, 2019). Given these characteristics, it is expected that future researchers will suggest future research opportunities within the domain of this topic.

CONCLUSION

The EU is facing a challenge both concerning ODA in the search for new models of development based on solidarity. While in the Central and Eastern European Countries, the EU's ODA has had their effect, Africa's extreme poverty continues to have entrenched in the economic and social fabric of the continent, so it can be a fertile ground for introducing community practices based on Socioeconomics of Solidarity that generate economic growth and social welfare. Aware of this fact, through the European External Action Service[13] inserted into the MFF 2007-2013, the EU simplified and rationalized its development portfolio by replacing the 30 programs and 90 budget lines in the previous frame for eight instruments development. Thus, the Directorate General for Development and Cooperation-EuropeAid (DG DEVCO-EuropeAid) of the Commission, created in January 2011 is, at present, the only body responsible for the programming and implementation of most of the instruments development of the EU, and its objectives: [1] the eradication of poverty and hunger; [2] the promotion of sustainable development; and [3] the support of democracy, peace and security.

The DG DEVCO-EuropeAid has adapted the European development policy to the current needs in the recent proposal "A dignified life for all by 2030", currently under review by the Council and Parliament. The Directorate General for Humanitarian Aid and Civil Protection (DG ECHO) is responsible for providing humanitarian aid, civil protection, and crisis management tasks that formally constitute a separate ODA portfolio. Other organs of the Commission to help coordinate development instruments of the EU are the Directorate General for Regional Policy, the Directorate General for Economic and Financial Affairs, and the Service for Foreign Policy Instruments.

European development policy promotes the harmonization of policies and better inclusion of the countries in the financial allocation process and scheduling through a "Code of Conduct on the division of labor in development policy" in 2007, and "Operational Framework on aid effectiveness" in 2011. In 2005, the EU also adopted the program "Policy coherence for development" to be applied into twelve different policy areas, including trade, migration, and transport. All this makes a re-launch of the European ODA, once community partners have improved their economic fundamentals, especially concerning higher employment rates, and lower inflation needed.

In short, although the Triple-C (combination of economic crisis, financial crisis, and the crisis of credibility on economic policy) (Saiz-Alvarez, 2013b) has hampered the MDGs achievement, the Socioeconomics of Solidarity can help to recover the lost path. This recovery is crucial to achieve because the Industry 4.0 "envisages full elimination of human from the production system, ensuring absolute automatization of the production process, simultaneous combination of formation of global industrial networks with elimination of negative social consequences, changes the essence of industrial patents and creates a possibility for quick change of direction of industrial production's specialization." (Popkova, Ragulina, & Bogoviz, 2019, p. 1). Therefore, and in conjunction with the private and community initiatives, efforts made on the European side to re-launch ODA are always welcome to reduce poverty gaps and to accelerate the formation of united economic blocks. Moreover, increasing social, demographic and economic problems derived from higher poverty rates will cause greater and negative imbalances. And in this sense, the world's most developed countries have a moral obligation to avoid it.

REFERENCES

Argandoña, A. (2011). *The Common Good.* Working Paper, 937, Barcelona: IESE.

Bourgignon, F. (2008). *Millennium Development Goals at Midpoint: Where do we stand and where do we need to go?* Brussels, Belgium: European Commission.

Braunerhjelm, P., & Stuart, U. (2012). *Social Entrepreneurship: A Survey of Current Research.* Swedish Entrepreneurship Forum Working Paper, 9.

Carranza, C. (2013). Economía de la Reciprocidad: Una aproximación a la Economía Social y Solidaria desde el concepto del don, *Otra Economía. Revista Latinoamericana de Economía Social y Solidaria, 7*(12), 14–25.

Certo, S. T., & Miller, T. (2008). Social Entrepreneurship: Key Issues and Concepts. *Business Horizons, 51*(4), 267–271. doi:10.1016/j.bushor.2008.02.009

Chowdhury, A., & Garonne, P. (2007). Effective Foreign Aid, Economic Integration and Subsidiarity: Lessons from Europe. In *CASE Network Studies and Analyses, 346.* Warsaw, Poland: CASE-Center for Social and Economic Research. doi:10.2139srn.1436909

Comisión Europea. (2002). *Desvincular la ayuda en aras de la eficacia.* Comunicación de la Comisión al Parlamento y al Consejo Europeo, 18 de noviembre, COM (2002) 639 final, no publicada en Diario Oficial.

Comisión Europea. (2005a). *Estrategia de la UE para África: Hacia un pacto euroafricano para acelerar el desarrollo en África.* Comunicación de la Comisión al Consejo, el Parlamento Europeo y el Comité Económico Social Europeo, COM (2005) 489 final, 12 de octubre, no publicada en Diario Oficial.

Comisión Europea. (2005b). *Coherencia de las políticas en favor del desarrollo. Acelerar el avance para cumplir los Objetivos de Desarrollo del Milenio.* Comunicación de la Comisión al Consejo, al Parlamento Europeo y al Comité Económico y Social, COM (2005) 134 final, de 12 de abril de 2005, no publicada en el Diario Oficial.

Comisión Europea. (2006a). *Ayuda de la UE: realizar más, mejor y más rápido*. Comunicación de la Comisión, de 2 de marzo, COM (2006) 87 final, no publicada en el Diario Oficial.

Comisión Europea. (2006b). *Financiación del desarrollo y eficacia de la ayuda-Retos que plantea el incremento de la ayuda de la UE durante el período 2006-2010*. Comunicación de la Comisión al Consejo y al Parlamento Europeo, de 2 de marzo, COM (2006) 85 final-Diario Oficial C 130 de 3 de junio de 2006.

Comisión Europea. (2006c). *Cómo hacer más productiva la ayuda europea: un marco común para la elaboración de los documentos estratégicos nacionales y la programación plurianual común*. Comunicación de la Comisión al Consejo y al Parlamento Europeo, de 2 de marzo, COM (2006) 88 final, Diario Oficial C 130 de 3 de junio de 2006.

Comisión Europea. (2006d). *Cómo hacer más productiva la ayuda europea: un marco común para la elaboración de los documentos estratégicos nacionales y la programación plurianual común*. Comunicación de la Comisión al Consejo y al Parlamento Europeo, de 2 de marzo, COM (2006) 88 final, Diario Oficial C 130 de 3 de junio de 2006.

Comisión Europea. (2008). *La UE como socio global para el desarrollo-Acelerar los avances hacia los Objetivos de Desarrollo del Milenio*. Comunicación de la Comisión al Parlamento Europeo, al Consejo, al Comité Económico y Social Europeo, y al Comité de las Regiones, COM(2008) 177 final, de 9 de abril, no publicada en el Diario Oficial.

De Vitoria, F. (1535). *De eo ad quod tenetur veniens ad usum rationis*. Universidad Pontificia de Salamanca.

Dees, J.G. (2001). *The Meaning of Social Entrepreneurship*. Retrieved from http://www.caseatduke.org/documents/dees_sedef.pdf

Defourny, J., Favreau, L., & Laville, J. L. (Eds.). (1998). Insertion et nouvelle économie sociale. Un bilan international. Paris: Desclée de Brouwer.

Diez-Olivan, A., Del Ser, J., Galar, D., & Sierra, B. (2019). Data fusion and machine learning for industrial prognosis: Trends and perspectives towards Industry 4.0. *Information Fusion*, *50*, 92–111. doi:10.1016/j.inffus.2018.10.005

Digilina, O. B., Teslenko, I. B., & Abdullaev, N. V. (2019). Industry 4.0: Contents, problems, and perspectives. *Advances in Intelligent Systems and Computing*, *726*, 32–38. doi:10.1007/978-3-319-90835-9_4

Dolado, J. J., González-Páramo, J. M., & Roldán, J. M. (1994). Convergencia económica entre las regiones españolas: Evidencia empírica (1955-1989). *Moneda y Crédito*, *198*, 81–119.

Drayton, B. (2002). The citizen sector: Becoming as entrepreneurial and competitive as a business. *California Management Review*, *44*(3), 120–132. doi:10.2307/41166136

Endemann, W. (1874). Studien in der romanisch-kanonistischen Wirtschafts und Rechtslehre bis gegen 16 Jahrhunderts [Studies Done in the Roman-Canonique Economics and Law until the Sixteenth Century]. Berlin: Academic Press.

Ferrajoli, L. (2013). *Dei diritti e delle garanzie. Conversazione con M. Barberis*. Il Mulino.

Feshina, S. S., Konovalova, O. V., & Sinyavsky, N. G. (2019). Industry 4.0—Transition to new economic reality. *Studies in Systems, Decision, and Control, 169*, 111–120. doi:10.1007/978-3-319-94310-7_11

H.H. Francisco. (2013). *Exhortación Apostólica "Evangelii Gaudium" sobre el anuncio del Evangelio en el mundo actual.* The Vatican City: Author.

Gaiger, L. I. (2004). Emprendimientos económicos solidarios. In A. Cattani (Ed.), *La Otra Economía.* Buenos Aires, Argentina: Altamira-UNGS.

Gallegos, L. (2008). *Economía Social de Mercado, Medio Ambiente y Responsabilidad Social Empresarial.* Lima, Peru: Impresiones de Tarea Asociación Gráfica Educativa.

Gallino, L. (2014). *Vita rinviate. Lo scandalo del lavoro precario.* Roma-Bari: Editori Laterza.

García, J., Vialop, J., & Xurinachs, L. M. (2006). *La dimensión cooperativa: economía solidaria y transformación social.* Barcelona, Spain: Icaria.

Gintis, H. (2000). Beyond *Homo economicus*: Evidence from Experimental Economics. *Ecological Economics, 35*(3), 311–322. doi:10.1016/S0921-8009(00)00216-0

Giovanelli, F. (2014, September). Economia sociale di mercato. Una risposta alla crisi? *XIV International Conference on the Role of the Catholic Church in a Process of the European Integration.*

Gómez, F., & Robledo, R. (Eds.). (1998). El pensamiento económico de la Escuela de Salamanca. Salamanca, Spain: University of Salamanca.

González, A. A., Linck, T., & Moguel, R. (2003). El comercio de valores éticos: Las reglas del juego de café solidario. *Revista Europea de Estudios Latinoamericanos y del Caribe, 75*(75), 31–45. doi:10.18352/erlacs.9692

Gorosquieta, J. (1941). El sistema de ideas tributarias en los teólogos y moralistas principales de la «Escuela de Salamanca» (siglos XVI y XVII). Madrid: Academic Press.

Grice-Hutchinson, M. (1952). *The School of Salamanca: Readings in Spanish Monetary Theory.* Oxford University Press.

Grice-Hutchinson, M. (1982). *El pensamiento económico en España (1117-1740).* Barcelona, Spain: Crítica.

Grice-Hutchinson, M. (1989). El concepto de la Escuela de Salamanca: Sus orígenes y su desarrollo. *Revista de Historia Económica, 2*, 22–26.

Guerin, K. (2002). *Subsidiarity. Implications for New Zealand.* Treasury Working Paper Series, 02/03. Wellington, New Zealand: New Zealand Treasury.

Guerra, L. (2006). La economía de la solidaridad. O la vuelta de los valores sociales a la economía. *Revista Umbrales, 168*, 1–7.

H.H. Benedicto XVI. (2009). *Carta Encíclica "Caritas in Veritate" sobre el desarrollo humano integral en la caridad y en la verdad.* The Vatican City: Author.

H.H. León XIII. (1891). *Carta Encíclica Rerum Novarum sobre la situación de los obreros*. The Vatican City: Author.

H.H. Pablo VI. (1967). *Carta Encíclica Populorum Progressio sobre la necesidad de promover el desarrollo de los pueblos*. The Vatican City: Author.

H.H. Pío XI. (1931). *Carta Encíclica Quadragesimo Anno, sobre la restauración del orden social en perfecta conformidad con la ley evangélica*. The Vatican City: Author.

Hisrich, R. (2007). Entrepreneurship: Research and Practice. A Call to Action for Psychology. *Journal of the American Psychoanalytic Association, 62*(65), 575–589.

Horga, I. (2010). The Multilevel Governance and the Request of the Subsidiarity Principle. *MPRA Paper, 44477*. Munich, Germany: University Library of Munich.

Hurtado, J. (2004). 'Vicios privados, beneficios públicos' o la diestra administración del legislador utilitarista. *Lecturas de Economía, 61*, 71–99.

Iparraguirre, D. (1954). Las fuentes del pensamiento económico en España de los siglos XIII al XVI. *Estudios de Deusto, 2*(3), 79–113.

Kets de Vries, M. F. R. (1985). Narcissism and Leadership: An Object Relations Perspective. *Human Relations, 38*(6), 583–601. doi:10.1177/001872678503800606

Kim, H. (2014). Exploring and Emerging Field: The Implications of Global Social Entrepreneurship. *Management and Marketing Journal, 1*, 14–30.

Kuratko, D. F. (2003). *Entrepreneurship Education: Emerging Trends and Challenges for the 21st Century*. 2003 Coleman Foundation White Paper Series for the U.S. Association of Small Business & Entrepreneurship.

Leadbeater, C. (Ed.). (1997). *The Rise of the Social Entrepreneur*. London, UK: Demos.

Lele, A. (2019). Industry 4.0., *Smart Innovation. Systems and Technologies, 132*, 205–215.

Lepoutre, J., Justo, R., Terjesen, S., & Bosma, N. (2011). Designing a Global Standardized Methodology for Measuring Social Entrepreneurship: The Global Entrepreneurship Monitor Social Entrepreneurship Study. *Small Business Economics, 40*(3), 693–714. doi:10.100711187-011-9398-4

Mair, J., & Martí, I. (2006). Social Entrepreneurship Research: A Source of Explanation, Prediction, and Delight. *Journal of World Business, 41*(1), 36–44. doi:10.1016/j.jwb.2005.09.002

Mair, J., & Schoen, O. (2007). Successful Social Entrepreneurial Business Models in the Context of Developing Economies: An Explorative Study. *International Journal of Emerging Markets, 2*(1), 54–68. doi:10.1108/17468800710718895

Marginean, S. (2009). Globalization, Technology, and Competitiveness: From Industrial Revolution to Knowledge Economy. *Revista Economica, 47*(4-5), 114–119.

Maritain, J. (1951). *La persona y el bien común*. Bilbao, Spain: Desclée de Brouwer.

Max-Neef, M. (1994). *Desarrollo a escala humana. Conceptos, aplicaciones y algunas reflexiones.* Montevideo, Uruguay: Nordan-Comunidad.

Max-Neef, M. (1997). *Economía Descalza. Señales desde el Mundo Invisible, Colección Pensamiento Descalzo, 1.* Montevideo, Uruguay: Nordan-Comunidad.

McLuhan, M. (1964). Understanding Media. In The Extensions of Man. Berkeley, CA: Gingko Press.

Morelos, C. (2004). La fe en la eucaristía: luces y sombras en Asia. *XLVIII Congreso Eucarístico Internacional*, Guadalajara, Mexico.

Ocaña, M. (1996). Francisco de Vitoria: vida, muerte y resurrección. *Anales del Seminario de Historia de la Filosofía, 1*, 297-317.

Ossanna, J. A. (2008). Las misiones jesuitas en la región del Guayrá en las primeras décadas del siglo XVII. *Mundo Agrario, 8*(16), 1–12.

Páez, S. (2011). Acercamiento a las características del universitario emprendedor en la unidad de emprendimiento empresarial en la Universidad Nacional de Colombia. *Revista EAN, 71*, 52–69.

Pena, M. A. (2009). *La Escuela de Salamanca. De la Monarquía hispánica al Orbe católico.* Madrid, Spain: Biblioteca de Autores Cristianos.

Popkova, E. G., Ragulina, Y. V., & Bogoviz, A. V. (2019). Fundamental differences of transition to industry 4.0 from previous industrial revolutions, *Studies in Systems. Decision and Control, 169*, 21–29.

Ramola, F. (1973). Economistas españoles de los siglos XVI y XVII. *Economics and Politics, 63*, 159–165.

Razeto, L. (1993). *Los caminos de la economía de solidaridad.* Santiago, Chile: Vivarium.

Razeto, L. (1998). El factor C y la economía de la solidaridad. In *Cuadernos de Educación, 1.* Montevideo, Uruguay: Cofac.

Rifkin, J. (2011). *The Third Industrial Revolution: How Lateral Power Is Transforming Energy, the Economy, and the World.* New York: Palgrave Macmillan.

Roman, S., & Loebl, E. (1979). *The Responsible Society. Alternative to Communism and Capitalism.* New Delhi, India: Abhinav Publications.

Rosas-Baños, M. (2012). Economía Ecológica y Solidaria: Rumbo a una propuesta teórica integrada que visualice las rutas hacia la transición. *Revista de la Red Iberoamericana de Economía Ecológica, 18*, 89–103.

Saiz-Álvarez, J. M. (2013a). Socioeconomía de la solidaridad, valores y justicia social: La necesidad de recristianizar la economía. *Revista Gestión y Sociedad, 6*(2), 69–80.

Saiz-Álvarez, J. M. (2013b). ¿Constituye el ordoliberalismo social un nuevo paradigma socioeconómico ante la triple-C para el emprendimiento? In Cultura Emprendedora y Economía Social. Ávila, Spain: Universidad Católica de Ávila.

San Juan XXIII. (1961). *Enciclical Letter Mater et Magistra, sobre el reciente desarrollo de la cuestión social*. The Vatican City: Author.

San Juan Pablo, I. I. (1989). Enciclical Letter Sollicitudo rei socialis. The Vatican City: Author.

San Juan Pablo II. (1991). *Enciclical Letter Centesimus Annus en el centenario de la Rerum Novarum*. The Vatican City: Author.

Santos del Cerro, J. (1998). El pensamiento económico de la Escuela de Salamanca. *VI Congreso de Economía Regional de Castilla y León*, 1829-1837.

Schumpeter, J. (2008). *Historia del Análisis Económico*. Barcelona: Ariel Economía. (Original work published 1954)

Singer, P. (2002). *Introdução à Economia Solidária*. São Paulo, Brasil: Fundação Perseu Abramo.

Smith, A. (1958). *Investigación sobre la naturaleza y causas de la riqueza de las naciones*. Fondo de Cultura Económica. (Original work published 1776)

Stachová, K., Papula, J., Stacho, Z., & Kohnová, L. (2019). External partnerships in employee education and development as the key to facing industry 4.0 challenges. *Sustainability*, *11*(2), 345. doi:10.3390u11020345

Stojanova, H., Lietavcova, B., & Raguž, I. V. (2019). The dependence of unemployment of the senior workforce upon explanatory variables in the European Union in the context of Industry 4.0. *Social Sciences*, *8*(1), 29. doi:10.3390ocsci8010029

Weerawardena, J., & Mort, G. S. (2006). Investigating Social Entrepreneurship: A Multidimensional Model. *Journal of World Business*, *41*(1), 21–35. doi:10.1016/j.jwb.2005.09.001

KEY TERMS AND DEFINITIONS

ACP Countries: They are made up of African, Caribbean, and Pacific countries receiving Official Development Aid from the European Union.

Common Good: It is a natural law that leads to the creation of a commonwealth that must be shared to achieve happiness and, in the case of believers, their holiness.

Millennium Development Goals (MDGs): Formed by eight goals for 2015, it is a global strategy driven by the United Nations to eradicate extreme poverty and hunger, achieve universal primary education, promote gender equality and empower women, reduce child mortality, improve maternal health, combat HIV/AIDS, malaria and other diseases, ensure environmental sustainability, and develop a global partnership for development.

Official Development Aid (ODA): It is the total amount of economic aid donated by the European Union to the economically weakest countries in the world.

Principle of Subsidiarity: Defined in Article 5 of the Treaty on the European Union, it ensures efficiency and effectiveness in decision taking as decisions are taken as close to citizens.

Social Market Economy: It is a form of market capitalism by combining social policy and coordinated market economy. This type of capitalism was used in Germany after World War II, and it was responsible for the Austrian and German economic miracles.

Socioeconomics of Solidarity: It is a kind of economy based on Christian-based (charity and fraternal love) and human-based (solidarity, not fraudulent or corrupt behavior, cooperation, and mutual assistance) values, focused on producing sustainable goods and services benefitting people.

ENDNOTES

1 A previous version of this chapter has been published in the *Handbook of Research on Social Entrepreneurship and Solidarity Economics* with the title "Socioeconomics of Solidarity: A Multilateral Perspective from the European Union", pp. 192-215 (doi: 10.4018/987-1-5225-0097-1.ch011).

2 The First Revolution was the Industrial Revolution of the eighteenth century, which began with the creation of the steam engine by James Watt (1736-1819), the formation of large intensive manufacturing processes in labor generally underpaid and exploited occupationally lacking of labor rights. The Second Revolution, or Mass Media Revolution, was initiated in the early twentieth century, with the popularization of press, cinema, radio and television.

3 This bankruptcy has followed the provisions of Chapter 11 of the Bankruptcy Code of the United States. Until that date, the Lehman Brothers Group, formed by Lehman Brothers Inc., Neuberger Berman Inc., Aurora Loan Services Inc. SIB Mortgage Corporation, Lehman Brothers Bank, FSB and the Crossroads Group, was the fourth largest investment bank in the world measured by market capitalization.

4 The translation is: "Man is a wolf to [his fellow] man, [and he is] not a man when he does not know who the other is."

5 In his early works, he signed as Thomas Hobbs of Malmsbury. Malesbury or Malmsbury his place of residence and studio, as the English philosopher was born on April 5, 1588 in Westport, a small town belonging to the county of Somerset. Such county, situated in Southwest England, is formed by the towns of Westport and Hambridge, jointly having a total of 526 people.

6 The complete title of the book is: Leviathan or the Matter, Form, and Power of a Common Wealth Ecclesiastical and Civil.

7 Blanc (2007) critics the TACIS program since its inception given the limited socioeconomic impact of the program in the former Soviet Union, as it is more a technical assistance program than a cooperation program. All Soviet Union's republics, except Estonia, Latvia and Lithuania, have been TACIS members after the fall of the Soviet Union. The Baltic Countries have become full members of the EU after the signing of the Accession Treaty on 1 May 2004.

8 This EU Regulation was after amended by Regulation (EC) 2415/2001 (Official Journal L 327 of 12 December, Regulation (EC) 2257/2004 (Official Journal L 389 of 30 December), and Regulation (EC) 2112/2005 (Official Journal L 344 of 27 December).

9 From the abundant economic literature written on the School of Salamanca, see Pena (2009), Gómez and Robledo (1998), and Partridge (2004), as well as the classicals Gorosquieta (1941), Iparraguirre (1954), Schumpeter (2008 [1954]), Grice-Hutchinson (1952, 1982, and 1989) and, above

all, Endemann (1874), the true discoverer of the School of Salamanca, and Ramola (1973[1885]) its popularizer in Spain. On the figure and the role of Francisco de Vitoria, see Ocaña (1996).

10 According to Grice-Hutchinson (1995) the complete list of authors is: among the Dominicans, Francisco de Vitoria, OP (c. 1483-1546), Domingo de Soto, O.P. (1494-1560), Martin de Azpilcueta (or Azpilicueta), OP (1493-1586), Diego de Covarrubias y Leiva, O.P. (1512-1570), Domingo Báñez, O.P. (1528-1604), and Tomás de Mercado, O.P. (1530-1576). Among the Jesuits, Luis Saravia de la Calle, SJ (? -1623), Francisco Garcia, SJ (1641-1685), Luis de Molina, SJ (1531-1601), Juan de Salas, SJ (1553-1612), Francisco Suarez, SJ (1548-1617), Juan de Lugo, SJ (1583-1660), and Antonio Escobar, SJ (1589-1669). They were complemented with the ideas of the Augustinian, Miguel Hall, O.S.A. (1539-1621), and the Franciscan Luis de Alcalá, OFM (1490? -1549). Outside these religious orders, we can mention Juan de Medina (c. 1490-1546) and Cristobal de Villalón (1500-1580).

11 Mandeville affirmed that market-based societies are not virtuous, because markets lead to the creation of private vices, though public benefits are generated. See Hurtado (2004) for a complete description of the evolutionary controversy arisen with this paradox.

12 The "invisible hand" was firstly used on the founder of the Classical School, Adam Smith (1723-1790), is a metaphor used in his work *The Theory of Moral Sentiments* written in 1759, and its most famous work, *An Inquiry into the Nature and Causes of the wealth of Nations*, begun in 1763 and published on March 9, 1776.

13 Created in 2009 under the Treaty of Lisbon, it aims to increase the ODA's external impact, mainly in Africa.

Chapter 3
Factors Creating Competitive Advantage for Family-Owned Business

Neeta Baporikar
https://orcid.org/0000-0003-0676-9913
Namibia University of Science and Technology, India & University of Pune, India

ABSTRACT

Management concepts have evolved as a separate discipline after the industrial revolution. In connection with this development, this discipline has combined so many different theories from different disciplines and approaches from different researchers and applications from different managers and other professionals. This amazing development of management has reached its peak in today's global business environment. Strategy concepts like vision, mission, SWOT, and competition on war footing for markets were influence of military science. Different contemporary management techniques, approaches, and implications are applicable in this unstable, dynamic, and knowledge-intensive environment. Among the various approaches, competitiveness, competitive strategies, and competitive advantage are at the core of organizational growth, development, and sustainability. Adopting a grounded theory approach with in-depth literature review, this study aims to discuss and deliberate on factors creating competitive advantage for organizations, especially family-owned SMEs, irrespective of their stage of development.

INTRODUCTION

An organization is a structure, which consists of two or more people who have a deliberate objective and intention to accomplish it. Therefore, about this definition, it is easily understandable that the organization concept has roots not only in our time but also in ancient times. Management concept is also derivable from an equation in which both people and their organization exist as vital variables. Both management and organization practices stem from ancient times and survive in today's global era. Business management concept has evolved as a separate discipline during and after the industrial revolution. In connection with this development, this discipline has combined many different theories born from diverse

DOI: 10.4018/978-1-5225-8939-6.ch003

disciplines and approaches from researchers and applications from managers and other professionals. This amazing development of management has reached its peak in today's global business environment. Today's dynamic, chaotic and complex environment makes it a must for managers to adapt contemporary approaches for maximizing both individual and organizational effectiveness. Different contemporary management techniques, approaches, and implications apply to this unstable, dynamic and knowledge-intensive environment. Among the various approaches to competitiveness, competitive strategies and competitive advantage are at the core of organizational growth, development, and sustainability.

Porter (1990) gave a first conceptual framework of competitiveness in the book *The Competitive Advantage of Nations*. Stajano (2010) argues that the prosperity of an economy stems from its ability to compete in the global market. The ability of businesses to survive and compete in increasingly global and sophisticated markets depends on a wide range of aspects such as the efficiency of public institutions, the excellence of infrastructure, health and quality of education as well as political and economic stability. Innovation has a massive defense as the key element for the creation of wealth from the countries (Gibson & Naquin, 2011). Innovation is the defining challenge for global competitiveness (Baporikar, 2014b). The increasing globalization of markets and the resulting increase in a competition associated with increased technological complexity, make innovation a key aspect of the competitiveness of companies, economies, and regions hosting them (Baporikar, 2018). Thus, there is a growing interest by governments to maintain the competitiveness of their economies with policies to stimulate advances in science and technology (Clark & Guy, 2010).

In industrialized countries, the promotion of networking among small manufacturers has resulted in enhancing the competitiveness of firms and economies, fostering new standards of business sophistication (Baporikar, 2015a). Porter, Schwab, and Sachs (2004) distinguished two broad categories: macro and microeconomic dimensions about drivers of competitiveness. Microeconomic foundations, identified as traditionally neglected by policymakers assume the foundations of macroeconomic reforms to achieve sustainable prosperity of economies. The drivers of competitiveness are many and complex. Adopting a grounded theory approach with in-depth literature review this study aims to discuss and deliberate on factors creating a competitive advantage for organizations especially SMEs irrespective of their stage of development.

BACKGROUND

Competition is a universal social process that exists in all types of societies either civilized or uncivilized. This may in the form of service or goods offered to their customers. Competitive advantage is a superiority that gives an organization an edge over its rivals and an ability to generate greater value for the firm and its shareholders. Organizations get a competitive advantage when it acquires or develops an element or a combination of elements, which are unique so that it can outperform its competitors. Firm's competitiveness is the ability and performance of a firm to sell and supply goods and services in a given market capturing the awareness of both the limitations and challenges posed by firm's competition for the scarce resources. A firm is competitive when it delivers products or services at a lower cost or higher quality than that of its competitors, or when it has unique characteristics that are not easily replicable elsewhere. Firm's competitiveness inspires firms to excel and exceed expectations. If a company is competing with another company, they will produce more quality products at unbeatable prices.

Family owned businesses are a unique type of organizations. Usually, the start of family-owned business is by an individual who is entrepreneurial, and as the business a extends other family members join in. The business when successful grows in size and turnover but the way of managing business continues to be in the sand manner that is more personal and maybe less professional. This results in factors which provide a competitive advantage.

How a firm is organized and how it uses its resources and capabilities to create unique, better or lower cost products or services determines its ability to develop a competitive advantage, become an industry leader and create excellent value for its customers and higher profits for itself. Competition can be health meaning it leads to growth and can be hazardous to business leading to their collapse. It is therefore important for the firms to carry out industry analysis to determine the degree of competition in place. Porter (1985) suggests that the degree of competition in an industry depends on the behavior of five forces analysis which includes threats of new entrants, threats of substitute products, bargaining power of customers, bargaining power of suppliers, and rivalry within the industry. SMEs as organizations, which are growing world over, is no exception.

Research Problem

Competitive advantage occurs when the customers get better value through lower prices or higher benefits that are commensurate with the price of the product or service. Thus, business success repetition and growth in customer base that is expandable over time is a requirement for competitive advantage. There are niche markets in which both individual and wholesale buyers are looking for products with very specific characteristics or special services. These characteristics often use strategies that do not focus on costs and volumes exclusively rather the product or service may be of premium quality, be differentiated from other products and services available in the market. Competitive advantage can come in one or a combination of the following factors: Price, service, quality, location, or embedded customer base. The better your business performs against one of these factors, the more likely you are to succeed. Traditionally, SMEs have been catering to the small and protected market segment. They have been local in their operations. Today, due to globalization they have to face the threats of new entrants and competition. The challenge in transformation is not in meeting the competition, but in realizing the factors, which create the competitive advantages and the related costs to deal with them. Most SMEs are not able to identify the factors and hence not able to compete. There are other challenges for SMEs like finance, market, quality of products and services but irrespective of these challenges, and most SMEs are not successfully competing and being profitable due to lack of keenness to ascertain of factors that influence these firms to remain competitive. There is a serious knowledge gap in this area of competitive advantage on the factors that influence the competitive advantage in SMEs. The main concern is, though, the SME sector growth is high irrespective of the challenges surrounding it, it would be beneficial to understand what the factors are influencing the competitive advantage of SMEs? What competitive advantages can SMEs revel in? Hence adopting a grounded theory approach with in-depth literature review this study aims to discuss and deliberate on factors creating a competitive advantage for organizations especially family-owned SMEs, henceforth referred as SMEs irrespective of their stage of development.

LITERATURE REVIEW

Competition in an industry is rooted in its underlying economic structure and goes beyond the existing competitor behavior. Environmental and competitive forces determine the nature and degree of any industry or business competition. Further, this fact in an industry depends on the collective strength of these forces. The collective strengths of these forces ultimately determine the attractiveness of the profit potential of the industry where the measure of profit potential is regarding long-run return on investment capital. The key structural features of industries, therefore, determine the strengths of competitive forces and hence industry profitability. Whatever their collective strength, the organizations' goal is to find a position in the industry where it can best defend itself against these forces or can influence them in its favor (Porter, 1980). To cope with them, the policy maker in the firm must evaluate the competition sources of competition and identify why the firm is at risk to those forces. This understanding and gen of causal sources of competitive pressure can provide a sound framework for strategic planning and set a more realistic and robust action plan.

Competition of course in any industry continually brings the rate of return on invested capital. In a way, competition creates only that rate of return, which the economists say a firm can earn in "perfectly competitive" industry. One of the environmental influences to a business arises from competition. Increased competition threatens the attractiveness of an industry by reducing the profitability of the players. It exerts pressure on firms to be pro-active and to formulate successful strategies that facilitate proactive resource to anticipated and actual changes in the competitive environment. By identifying their core competencies, firms can concentrate on areas that give them a lead over competitors and provide a competitive advantage. Porter (1985) notes that competition is the core of a firm's success or failure. For nearly two decades, the dominant research paradigm has been Porter's (1980) competitive forces model, which argues that the intensity of competition determines the profit potential for individual firms. Porter contends that a firm seeks a position in an attractive market that they can defend against both existing and potential competitors. There are a great increase in Micro Finance firms in the country, and this has brought about stiff competition. Competition has forced microfinance firms to become more innovative in the creation of their different products.

Competitive Advantage

Competitive advantage is the strategic advantage one business entity has over its rival entities within its competitive industry. Competitive advantage is what enables a business organization to thrive. The term competitive advantage is the ability gained through attributes and resources to perform at a higher level than others are in the same industry or market. The term competitive advantage is the ability gained through attributes and resources to perform at a higher level than others are in the same industry or market (Porter, 1980). Figure 1 gives a generic model of competitive advantage.

A firm gets a competitive advantage when it is implementing a value creating strategy not simultaneously with any current or potential competitors (Barney, 1991). Competitive advantage is a superiority that gives an organization an edge over its rivals and an ability to generate greater value for the firm and its shareholders. Thus, it arises when an organization acquires or develops an element or combination of elements that allows it to outperform its competitors, thereby enabling the creation of superior value for its customers leading to higher profits. Large firms have traditionally commanded a competitive advantage over small firms.

Figure 1. Generic model of competitive advantage
Source: Self-Developed

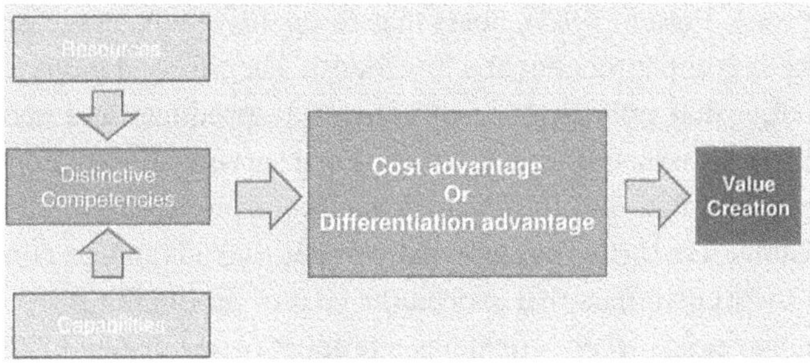

This is because large firms use substantial resources to conduct extensive market research, mount powerful advertising campaigns, place their products in readily accessible outlets and dominate selected markets with their products (Makhija, 2003; Teece, 2010). Firm-level competitiveness is the ability of the firm to design, produce and market products superior to those offered by competitors, considering the price and non-price qualities (Baporikar & Deshpande, 2017). Porter (1980) identified two basic forms of competitive advantage namely Cost advantage and differentiation advantage. A competitive advantage is when the firm can deliver the same benefits as competitors at a lower cost, which leads to a cost advantage. Alternatively, the competitive advantage also prevails when the firm can deliver the quality that must exceed those of competing products which leads to a differentiation advantage. These are two positional advantages since they describe the firm's position in the industry, as a leader in either cost or differentiation (Porter, 1990). Change Leadership as a core organizational competency is also a form of competitive advantage. The companies that survive in the coming decades will be those that can respond quickly and effectively to changing environmental conditions. This puts a premium on certain capabilities, adaptiveness, flexibility, and responsiveness. Another form of competitive advantage is Competitive Advantages for Pioneers where pioneering products have the first chance to become the trusted brand.

All competitive advantages are dynamic and dependent on a specific set of market and environmental conditions (Boulding & Christensen, 2001). Both internal factors and external factors influence a firm's competitive advantage. Internal factors include financial ability, human resources, research collaborations, marketing, product differentiation, and cost. External factors that influence a firm's competitive advantage include political factor, economic, social, and technical and culture. Other factors that can influence competitive advantage are quality and quantity of natural resources, the strength of country's currency, infrastructure in a country, research and development, workforce characteristics, entrepreneurship and government involvement (Baporikar, 2014a). Porter's (1985) states that a business can maximize competitiveness either by striving to be the low-cost producer in the industry and by differentiating its line of products or services from those businesses.

The competitive advantage concept refers to a set of factors or capabilities that allow firms to leave behind their rivals on a consistent basis. It is an upper hand over competitors gained by offering greater value. A company will have a competitive advantage whenever it has the edge over its rival in securing customers and facing competition. When a firm implements a value creating strategy not simultaneously implemented by any current or potential competitors, it will lead to competitive advantage (Barney, Ketchen, & Wright, 2011). For competitive advantage to have meaning, customers must perceive a difference between one firm's products or and those of competitors resulting from a capability gap between the firm and its competitors and theses aforementioned the difference in attributes and capability gap are expected to endure over time. Porter (1985), notes that competitive advantage exists where the firm can deliver the same benefits as competitors but at a lower cost. Therefore, it gains a competitive advantage or derives superior benefits that exceed those of competing products and hence gain differentiation advantage and focus on small market segment, which it can serve well than competitors can and hence acquire focus advantage. He noted that the primary factors of competitive advantage are innovation, reputation, and relationships. He further argues that competitive advantage comes from the value that organizations create for their customers that exceed the cost of producing it.

A competitive advantage exists when a firm has a product or service and is perceivable by its target market customers as better than that of its competitors. Hitt, Ireland and Hoskisson (1997) postulates the competitive advantage assumption that each firm is a collection of unique resources and capabilities according to resources based view. These resources and capabilities form the basis of organizations strategy and develop a competitive advantage. Moreover, earnings from superior value occur when an organization uses its core competencies to establish a competitive advantage over rivals. Sustainable competitive advantage is born out of the core competencies that yield long-term benefit to the company. Prahalad and Hamel (1990) defined core competencies as an area of specialized expertise that is the result of harmonizing complex streams of technology and work activity. They further explain that a core competency has three characteristics first it provides access to a wide variety of markets. Secondly it increases perceived customer benefits, and lastly, it is hard for competitors to imitate. To succeed in building a competitive advantage, a firm must try to provide what buyers will and perceive as superior value. This entails a good quality product, a lower price, or a better quality product that is worth paying more.

Sources of Competitive Advantage

According to Hitt, Ireland and Hoskisson (1997), a sustainable competitive advantage is achievable when firms implement a value creating-strategy that gets its root in their own unique resources, capabilities, and core competencies. This is on the resource-based model, which suggests that the unique resources and capabilities of a firm's internal environment are the critical link to strategic competitiveness (Wernerfelt, 1984). Figure 2 gives the elements that constitute the sources of competitive advantage from the resource-based view.

Firms achieve strategic competitiveness and earn above-average returns when leveraging of unique competencies is effective to take advantage of the opportunity of the external environment. If a firm lowers the cost of your product or service without compromising profitability, then you have a cost advantage over your competitors. In the cost reduction strategy, firms typically attempt to gain a competitive advantage by being the lowest cost producer. Porter (1985) argues that cost advantage will result in above average performance only if the firm can sustain it. Improving relative cost position in unsustainable ways may allow a firm to maintain cost parity or proximity, but a firm attempting to achieve cost leadership must also develop sustainable sources of cost advantage. A firm can gain a strong competitive advantage in its industry if it has strong research and development capabilities. Strong research and development reflect in the company products development processes. Firms with strong research capabilities often lead the market with innovation (Powell, Thomas, & McGee, 2004). Another source of competitive advantage, especially in this knowledge society, is intellectual rights in the form of trademarks, trade names, copyright, patents, reputation, brand names, etc. (Baporikar, 2016). These give a business a competitive edge.

Figure 2. Elements of competitive advantage from resource-based view
Source: Adapted from Ghemawat (1991).

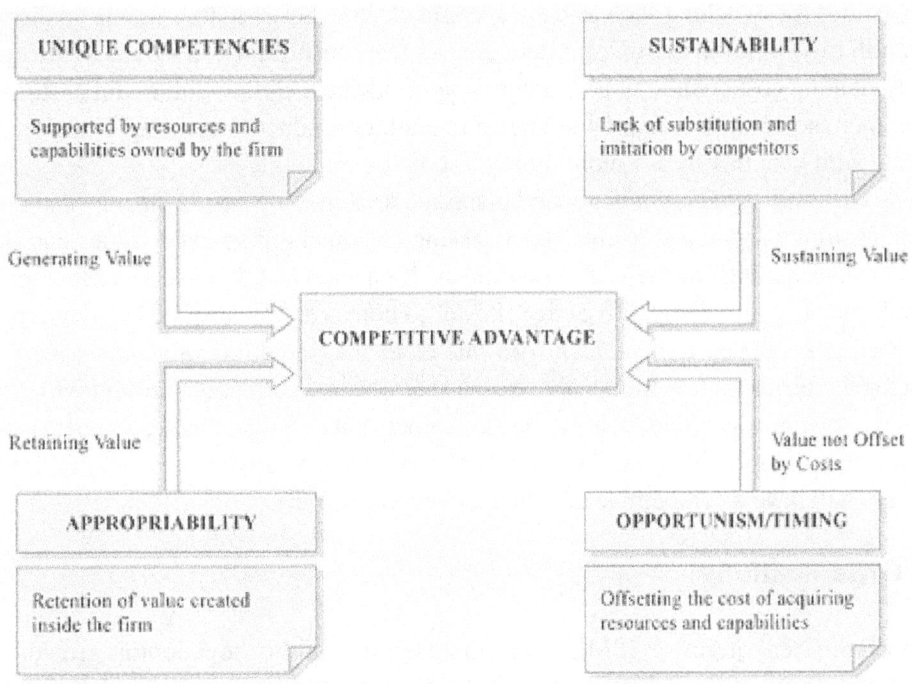

Network effects or network externality refers to how easy is it for new customers to adapt to your product or service (Porter, 2001). If a firm's product is good, easy to use or your service is excellent, then more customers will come to you. When Microsoft Windows came, out, it was so easy to use than the regular DOS or text-based programs. Therefore, people have grown a liking to it and have recommended it to more people, and those people recommended it to more people so on and so on. Another good example is Facebook. When many people use a particular product or service, the product or service becomes more valuable and thus increase in value thus creating a competitive advantage. Some businesses have gained a competitive advantage because surrounding circumstances have limited the entry in their industry. This is having barriers to entry or monopoly because there is government restriction on entry. This is achievable by having such as important attributes of the firm as rareness, value, inability to be imitated, and inability to be substituted (Barney, 1991). The competition to gain a stronger competitive advantage in the market place is the reason why giant corporations spend millions of money on marketing research and advertising annually. A firm can also use loyalty mechanisms for marketing through frequent flier miles, coupons, or other membership bonuses to lock customers.

Holding exclusive re-selling or distribution rights is a great source of competitive advantage. When a company holds exclusive rights to a product within a given territory, that product sourcing is only from the distributor or holder of such rights (Baporikar, 2017). This provides exclusivity leading to competitive advantage.

High Switching costs are the penalties a customer pays when they change from an existing product, supplier or brand to another. These penalties or negative utility are often monetary, but can also come in the form of time, effort, or social pressure. This dynamic is especially useful in competitive markets where there is little differentiation amongst options and creating incentives for customers to stay with you is essential for survival. A firm can create switching costs through transaction costs where the incumbents levy penalties for switching such as bank account closure fees. Another way is quality uncertainty where the familiarity with the existing product creates fear, uncertainty, or doubt in the quality of the new brand. Switching cost creates an advantage to your business so that you retain customers because it would cost them some time or money to switch to another product or service. Therefore, when your customers stay with you, this means more money is coming in.

Redefining customer value is going beyond planning, to delivering good customer satisfaction levels across all the customer segments. It involves assessing customers' perceived values and their relative importance and determining how best a firm should position itself to deliver services that match customers' perceived value to gain a competitive edge (Powell, Thomas & McGee, 2004). To redefine customer value, firm need to profile customers, identify value elements, spot high-value customers and develop delivery strategies. Firms that continuously realign their business strategies in line with the emerging customer needs may not only retain their existing customers but also gain unique competitive advantages in the industry. Any company that has the capital to respond to customer needs and provide subsequent support quickly will have a competitive advantage over competitors.

SMEs as Organizations

Small and medium-sized enterprises (SMEs) contribute significantly to the economic growth and development of a country (Taiwo et al., 2012). The fact that so many SMEs have been unsuccessful in promoting business growth and thus failed to contribute to the country development has raised serious concern globally (Banerjee, 2014); thus, this review covers constraints that hinder business growth. According to Omerzel and Antoncic (2008), entrepreneurs' knowledge has an impact on the firm's performance. Thus, for SMEs to succeed and attain growth, sound entrepreneurial knowledge of both the internal and external market in which they operate, such as attaining grants, shorter credits, targeting consumers and obtaining long-term liabilities such as loans, is eminent. SMEs tend to face a greater uncertainty toward the external environment than large firms do. As such, large firms are innovative with products and services to sustain continuous evolution and changes (Ha-Brookshire, 2009). While this is obviously advantageous to larger firms, SMEs lack these mechanisms (Marcotte, 2011).

Despite the global understanding on the role of SMEs in boosting the economy and the country development (Subhan et al., 2013), not much has been achieved especially in supporting SMEs to attain sustainable growth (Banerjee, 2014). To date, SMEs encounter some problems that hinder business growth. Globally, the belief is that SMEs are the engines of economic growth (Ayanda & Laraba, 2011). Over the years, there have been serious concerns globally on the inability of some SMEs in attaining business growth that is instrumental in boosting the economic growth through reduction of unemployment, job creation and diversification of business operations (Abor & Quartey, 2010; Ayanda & Laraba, 2011). To date, SMEs are facing serious internal or external factors that significantly affect and challenge their growth (Marcotte, 2012).

Figure 3 gives a simple diagrammatic representation as to what equals competitive advantage for SMEs from Resource-based view.

Figure 4 shows as to how SMEs can convert the environment to create competitive advantages.

Figure 3. Simple diagrammatic representation of competitive advantage for SMEs
Source: Self-Developed

Figure 4. How SMEs can convert the environment to create competitive advantage
Source: Self-Developed

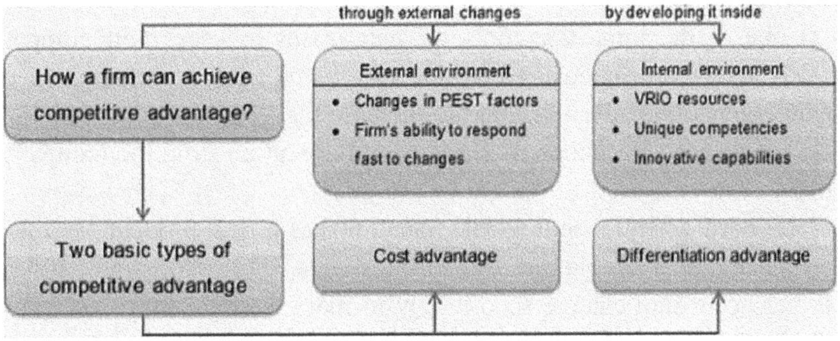

FACTORS INFLUENCING COMPETITIVE ADVANTAGE

SMEs all over the world have grown tremendously and are likely to continue to grow due to support from respective governments, and the rise in entrepreneurial orientation and networked global economy. Hence, it is resulting in fierce competition, and hence, all SMEs are changing and need to adapt their strategies to stay ahead of the game. Thus there is a need to analyze factors that influence the competitive advantage in SME organizations too. The factors analyzed below are price, service provision, quality, location, embedded customer base, product innovation, technology, risk management, knowledge of operations and leadership. The better your business performs against one of these factors, the more likely you are to succeed.

- A lower price for the product or service can be one of the quick paths to gain extra business or market share than competitors. Porter (1985) emphasized competitiveness at the level of a firm regarding competitive strategies such as low cost and/or product differentiation. To have a lower price certainly, a firm will need lower labor, materials or overhead cost. Even if that is possible the competitor firms will also tap that lower priced sources and do price-cutting as a response thereby the elimination of this competitive advantage.
- Service can also be a serious differentiator and competitive advantage for firms. In a study made on the pharmaceutical industry, findings reflected the primary sources of competitive advantage were their level of customer service, the ability to handle customer complaints effectively, and the quality of their products (McGee, 2002).

- Quality is another important characteristic of almost every industry. This can also be the primary source of competitive advantage as in the case of pharma products (Leask, & Parnell, 2005). People do not like to pay good money for work that has to needs replacement, repairs or purchase a new unit that fails prematurely. In certain instances, quality is not very important, and in other instances, quality is the only important consideration.
- Location is also a competitive differentiator as it provides convenience for your clients and customer. If your distant service competitors charge for travel time, other things being equal, you can charge more money but not so much more than it pays the customer to use your competitor.
- Entrenched customer base can also be a competitive advantage. This is because customers are willing to pay a little extra for the goodwill and the long relationship rather than reinvest time and energy to seek new suppliers.
- Innovation is one of the important tools for enterprises to keep their competitive advantage (Baporikar, 2015b). Due to intensified competition, companies search for emergent innovation models to gain competitive advantage and to increase their performance. The implementation of such new models requires decisions on strategy and execution from the company's management (Porter, 1980).
- New sectors are born when technological change makes a new product feasible (Porter, 1990). Technology is changing at a rapid rate, and businesses need to adapt to new ways of doing things due to customer needs and change accordingly to meet the demand to survive in the business industry and expand its operation, as technology assists to increase the productivity of the firm. An accompanying observation is that the growing predilection toward entrepreneurship in rural communities characterized by changing and uncertain contexts results in innovation getting constrained (Marcotte et al., 2010). Technology is a key factor that influences competitive advantage
- The risk is everywhere and is substantially unavoidable in all human activities involving uncertainty. Hence, all organizations need to prepare themselves to cope with uncertainty (Olson & Dash Wu, 2010a, p. 694). Shortreed (2010, p. 8) also states that all activities of an organization involve risk, not just those with negative outcomes but also with positive outcomes. Uncertainty presents both risk and opportunity, with the potential to erode or enhance value (Rao, 2007, p. 170; Ferkolj, 2010, p. 10). Olson and Dash Wu (2010b, p. 4919) report that uncertainty also creates opportunities for businesses to make a profit. Andersen (2006, p. 25) concur that risk-taking is necessary, and organizations need to understand the nature of the risks encountered.
- Comprehensive knowledge of business operations. According to Soini and Veseli (2011), the owner's business knowledge has an impact on business growth. This, in turn, has a multiplier effect on competitiveness thereby leading to sustainability and further growth.
- Last but not the least is leadership. Leadership from SME owners or managers is an important factor to create competitive advantage. Especially in SMEs it the visionary and motivational leadership that keep the enterprise on the path of excellence. This leads to innovation and most frugal innovations which, actually, have a multiplier effect on competitive advantage.

SOLUTIONS AND RECOMMENDATIONS

Given below is the model of how SMEs can adopt a building block approach to create and take benefits to gain competitive advantage. This approach helps SMEs to work on a tailor-made basis and to

Figure 5. Building blocks for SMEs completive advantage
Source: Self-Developed

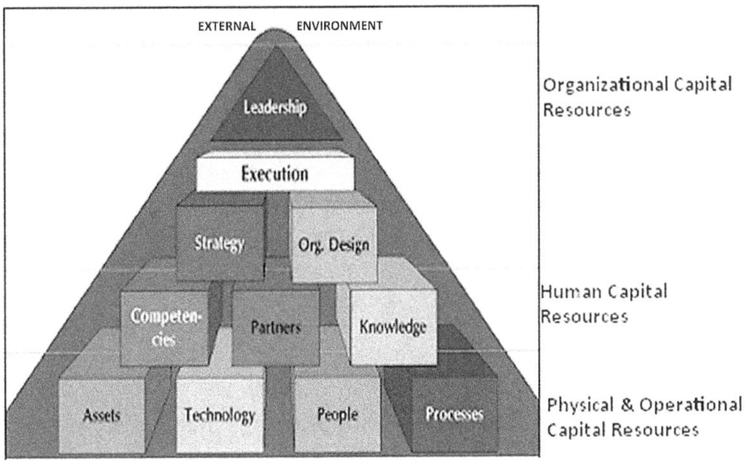

regard investment and time; it becomes easy on their kitty. Figure 5 gives the building blocks for SMEs completive advantage

FUTURE RESEARCH DIRECTIONS

Further studies which could enhance and deepen the understanding and also to spot the factors which create competitive advantages for SMEs include the effect of the networked economy, identifying the extent to which the firms use networks, methods, and approaches including framework industry wise to gain technology and spillover effects. Identifying pooled talent for enhanced retainer based utilization would also be an area for exploration. Focused studies on externalities as they are becoming increasingly important to remain competitive is required. A more general explanation is that substantial changes in the economic environment over the past 25 years involving internationalization, greater instability in product markets and more intense competition with a greater emphasis on quality/variety, is there. This at least for the first world, producers have increased the importance of flexibility, encouraging greater reliance on external than internal economies of scale (Gordona & Mccann, 2000). Fujita and Thisse (2002) suggest that these economies explain clustering. Therefore, research on how clustered approach proves and creates competitive advantages especially in emerging economies would be eye-opening and provide better strategies to make SMEs sustainable.

CONCLUSION

In the last decade, there have been numerous studies conducted on competitiveness and growth of economies. Porter (1990) first presented his conceptual framework of competitiveness and lot of water has flown under the bridge then until now. The ability of SMEs and any businesses to survive and compete in increasingly demanding market conditions, depends on a wide range of aspects such as the institutional efficiency, infrastructure, as well as the political and economic strength of their economy. Governments too have shown a growing interest to maintain the competitiveness of their economies with policies to stimulate SMEs and entrepreneurship development in both industrialized countries as well as emerging economies. This has resulted in enhancing the competitiveness of SMEs in some sectors. However, competitiveness is not an end in itself, but an indication of a way to go, a set of underlying forces to follow in pursuit of socio-economic success for any business and SME is no exception. To conclude, this study aims to clarify the factors, which create competitive advantages for SMEs and provides a building block approach, which we hope, will lead to enhanced understanding of factors that contribute most to the explanation of the global competitiveness of SMEs, irrespective of their stage of development.

REFERENCES

Abor, J., & Quartey, P. (2010). Issues in SME development in Ghana and South Africa, international research. *Journal of Financial Economics*, *39*, 218–228.

Andersen, T. L. (2006). Perspectives on Strategic Risk Management. Copenhagen Business School Press.

Ayanda, M. A., & Laraba, S. A. (2011). Small and medium scale enterprises as a survival strategy for employment generation in Nigeria. *Journal of Sustainable Development*, *4*(1), 200–206.

Banerjee, R. (2014). *SMEs financial constraints and growth*. BIS Working Papers, Bank for International Settlements.

Baporikar, N. (2014a). Strategic Management Overview and SME in Globalized World. In K. Todorov & D. Smallbone (Eds.), *Handbook of Research on Strategic Management in Small and Medium Enterprises* (pp. 22–39). Hershey, PA: Business Science Reference. doi:10.4018/978-1-4666-5962-9.ch002

Baporikar, N. (2014b). Innovation in the 21st Century Organization. In B. Christiansen, S. Yildiz, & E. Yildiz (Eds.), Transcultural Marketing for Incremental and Radical Innovation (pp. 339–365). Hershey, PA: IGI Global. doi:10.4018/978-1-4666-4749-7.ch016

Baporikar, N. (2015a). Role of Entrepreneurship in Networked Indian Economy. In P. Ordóñez de Pablos (Ed.), *Technological Solutions for Sustainable Business Practice in Asia* (pp. 36–59). Hershey, PA: Business Science Reference; doi:10.4018/978-1-4666-8462-1.ch003

Baporikar, N. (2015b). Distinctiveness of Techno-Entrepreneurship. *International Journal of Strategic Information Technology and Applications*, *6*(1), 15–25. doi:10.4018/IJSITA.2015010102

Baporikar, N. (2016). Understanding Knowledge Management Spectrum for SMEs in Global Scenario. *International Journal of Social and Organizational Dynamics in IT*, *5*(1), 1–15. doi:10.4018/IJSODIT.2016010101

Baporikar, N. (2017). Business Excellence Strategies for SME Sustainability in India. In P. Ordóñez de Pablos (Ed.), *Managerial Strategies and Solutions for Business Success in Asia* (pp. 61–78). Hershey, PA: IGI Global; doi:10.4018/978-1-5225-1886-0.ch004

Baporikar, N. (2018). Critical Success Factors for Executives in Global Economy. In A. Presenza & L. Sheehan (Eds.), *Geopolitics and Strategic Management in the Global Economy* (pp. 40–56). Hershey, PA: IGI Global; doi:10.4018/978-1-5225-2673-5.ch003

Baporikar, N., & Deshpande, M. (2017). SMEs and Branding Strategies. *International Journal of Applied Management Sciences and Engineering*, *4*(1), 43–55. doi:10.4018/IJAMSE.2017010104

Barney, J. (1991). Firm resources and sustained competitive advantage. *Journal of Management*, *17*(1), 99–120. doi:10.1177/014920639101700108

Barney, J. B., Ketchen, D. J. Jr, & Wright, M. (2011). The future of resource-based theory: Revitalization or decline? *Journal of Management*, *37*(5), 1299–1315. doi:10.1177/0149206310391805

Boulding, W., & Christensen, M. (2001). First Mover Disadvantage. *Harvard Business Review*, *79*(9), 20–21.

Clark, J., & Guy, K. (2010). Innovation and Competitiveness: A review. *Technology Analysis and Strategic Management*, *10*(3), 363–395. doi:10.1080/09537329808524322

Ferkolj, A. (2010). *Enterprise risk management analysis with suggestions for improvements for the selected company* (Master's thesis). University of Ljubljana Faculty of Economics, Ljubljana.

Fujita, M., & Thisse. (2002). *Economics of agglomeration Cities, industrial location, and regional growth.* Cambridge University Press.

Ghemawat. (1991). *Commitment, the Dynamics of Strategy*. Free Press.

Gordon, I. R., & McCann, P. (2000). Innovation, agglomeration and regional development. *Journal of Economic Geography*, *5*(5), 523–543. doi:10.1093/jeg/lbh072

Ha-Brookshire, J. E. (2009). Does the firm size matter on firm entrepreneurship: US apparel import intermediary case. *Journal of Small Business and Enterprise Development*, *16*(1), 131–145. doi:10.1108/14626000910932926

Hitt, M., Ireland, D., & Hoskisson. (1997). *Strategic management: Competitiveness and globalization*. West Publishing Company.

Leask, G., & Parnell, J. A. (2005). Integrating Strategic Groups and the Resource-Based Perspective: Understanding the Competitive Process. *European Management Journal*, *23*(4), 458–470. doi:10.1016/j.emj.2005.06.003

Makhija, M. (2003). Comparing the resource-based and market-based views of the firm: Empirical evidence from Czech privatization. *Strategic Management Journal*, *24*(5), 433–451. doi:10.1002mj.304

Marcotte, C. (2011). Country entrepreneurial profiles: Assessing the individual and Organizational levels of entrepreneurship across countries. *Journal of Enterprising Culture*, *19*(2), 169–200. doi:10.1142/S021849581100074X

Marcotte, C. (2012). Measuring entrepreneurship at the country level: A review and research agenda. *Entrepreneurship and Regional Development*, *25*(3/4), 174–194.

Marcotte, C., Sousse, S. A., Molz, R., Farashahi, M., & Hafsi, T. (2010). Strategy implementation in emerging countries: three theoretical approaches. In R. Molz & A. Taleb (Eds.), *The Multinational Enterprise in Developing Countries, Local versus Global Logic*. New York, NY: Routledge.

McGee, J., & Sammut-Bonnici, T. (2002). Network industries in the new economy. *European Business Journal, 14*(5), 116–132.

Olson, D. L., & Dash Wu, D. (2010a). A review of enterprise risk management in supply chain. *Kybernetes, 39*(5), 694–706. doi:10.1108/03684921011043198

Olson, D. L., & Dash Wu, D. (2010b). Enterprise risk management: A DEA VaR approach in vendor selection. *International Journal of Production Research, 48*(16), 4919–4932. doi:10.1080/00207540903051684

Omerzel, D. G., & Antoncic, B. (2008). Critical entrepreneur knowledge dimensions for the SME performance. *Industrial Management & Data Systems, 9*(108), 1182–1199. doi:10.1108/02635570810914883

Porter, M. E. (1980). *Competitive Strategy*. New York: Free Press.

Porter, M. E. (1985). *Competitive advantage: Creating and sustaining superior performance*. Free Press.

Porter, M. E. (1990). *Competitive Advantage of Nations*. New York: The Free Press. doi:10.1007/978-1-349-11336-1

Porter, M. E. (2001). *Strategy and the Internet*. Academic Press.

Porter, M. E., Schwab, K., & Sachs, J. (2004). *The global competitiveness report 2004-2005*. New York, NY: Palgrave Macmillan.

Powell, T. H., Thomas, H., & McGee, J. (2004). *Dynamic knowledge creation. Dynamics of Strategy*. University of Surrey.

Prahalad, C. K., & Hamel, G. (1990). Core competency concept. *Harvard Business Review, 64*, 56–64.

Rao, A. (2007). Evaluation of enterprise risk management (ERM) in Dubai – an emerging economy. *Risk Management, 9*(3), 167–187. doi:10.1057/palgrave.rm.8250031

Shortreed, J. (2010). Enterprise risk management and ISO 31000. *Journal of Policy Engagement, 2*(3), 8–10.

Soini, E., & Veseli, L. (2011). Factors influencing SMEs growth in Kosovo. *International Business Management, 75*, 8–64.

Stajano, A. (2010). *Research, Quality, Competitiveness. EU Technology Policy for the Knowledge-based Society*. Springer.

Subhan, Q. A., Mian Rahat Mehmood, M. R., & Sattar, A. (2013). Innovation in small and medium enterprises (SME's) and its impact on economic development in Pakistan. *Proceedings of 6th International Business and Social Sciences Research Conference.*

Taiwo, M. A., Awolaja, M. A., & Yusuf, A. B. (2012). Impact of small and medium enterprises on economic growth and development. *American Journal of Business and Management, 1*(1), 18–22. doi:10.11634/21679606170644

Teece, D. (2010). Business models, business strategy and innovation. *Long Range Planning, 43*(2-3), 172–194. doi:10.1016/j.lrp.2009.07.003

Wernerfelt, B. (1984). A resource-based view of the firm. *Strategic Management Journal, 5*(2), 171–180. doi:10.1002mj.4250050207

ADDITIONAL READING

Beal, R. M. (2000). Competing effectively: Environmental scanning, competitive strategy, and organizational performance in small manufacturing firms. *Journal of Small Business Management, 38*(1), 27.

Johnson, G. (2016). *Exploring strategy: text and cases*. Pearson Education.

Noe, R. A., Hollenbeck, J. R., Gerhart, B., & Wright, P. M. (2003). *Gaining a competitive advantage*. Irwin: McGraw-Hill.

Peteraf, M. A. (1993). The cornerstones of competitive advantage: A resource-based view. *Strategic Management Journal, 14*(3), 179–191. doi:10.1002mj.4250140303

Porter, M. E. (2008). The five competitive forces that shape strategy. *Harvard Business Review, 86*(1), 25–40.

Porter, M. E. (2008). *Competitive strategy: Techniques for analyzing industries and competitors*. Simon and Schuster.

Rivard, S., Raymond, L., & Verreault, D. (2006). Resource-based view and competitive strategy: An integrated model of the contribution of information technology to firm performance. *The Journal of Strategic Information Systems, 15*(1), 29–50. doi:10.1016/j.jsis.2005.06.003

Santos-Vijande, M. L., López-Sánchez, J. Á., & Trespalacios, J. A. (2012). How organizational learning affects a firm's flexibility, competitive strategy, and performance. *Journal of Business Research, 65*(8), 1079–1089. doi:10.1016/j.jbusres.2011.09.002

Smith, K. G., Grimm, C. M., & Gannon, M. J. (1992). *Dynamics of competitive strategy*. Sage Publications, Inc.

Weerawardena, J. (2003). Exploring the role of market learning capability in competitive strategy. *European Journal of Marketing, 37*(3/4), 407–429. doi:10.1108/03090560310459023

KEY TERMS AND DEFINITIONS

Business: Pertains broadly to commercial, financial, and industrial activities.

Competitive Advantage: An advantage that firms have over its competitors, allowing it to generate greater sales or margins and/or retain more customers than its competition. There can be many types of competitive advantages including the knowledge, skills, structure, product offerings, distribution network, and support.

Competitiveness: Act of competing for some honor, or advantage. A rivalry between two or more persons or groups for an object desired in common, usually resulting in a victor and a loser but not necessarily involving the destruction of the latter. The need for global competitiveness is much important for any industry to sustain in this competitive world.

Customer Service: An organization's ability to satisfy its customers' needs.

Decision-Making: A rational and logical process of choosing the best alternative or course of action among the available options.

Development: Means "steady progress" and stresses effective assisting in hastening a process or bringing about the desired end, a significant consequence or event, the act or process of growing, progressing, or developing.

Enterprises: The act or process of organizing; a structure through which individuals cooperate systematically to conduct business and/or the administrative personnel of such a structure.

Environment: It is important or essential about a plan of action; highly important to an intended objective.

Globalization: Globalization is the tendency of businesses, technologies, or philosophies to spread throughout the world, or the process of making this happen.

Government: The organization, machinery, or agency through which a political unit exercises authority and performs functions and which is usually classified according to the distribution of power within it and usually refers to a political system.

Innovation: Something new or different introduced, it is the act of innovating, which includes the introduction of new things or methods. Innovation is also the introduction of a new idea into the marketplace in the form of a new product or service, or an improvement in organization or process. The process of translating an idea or invention into a good or service to create value for which customers will pay.

Policy: Refers to guidelines as issued by the governance.

Small and Medium Enterprises (SMEs): Is a term for segmenting businesses and other organizations that are somewhere between the "small office-home office" size and the larger enterprise. Country to country this term may vary, but the basis usually is on the criteria of investment, number of employees, and turnover, etc.

Chapter 4
Micro Family Business and Socioeconomic Development:
Chilean Grocery Store

Alejandro Vega-Muñoz
https://orcid.org/0000-0002-9427-2044
Universidad Autónoma de Chile, Chile

Guido Salazar-Sepúlveda
https://orcid.org/0000-0002-4979-6869
Universidad Católica de la Santísima Concepción, Chile

ABSTRACT

This chapter studies family micro business in Chile and economic development generated around them, specifically in the commerce sector. Firstly, it introduces the micro, small, and medium enterprises context. Then, through a mixed methodology, narrative, and descriptive based on information from secondary sources such as legal bodies, reports, and databases generated by various Chilean State entities, it determines what is the micro family business in Chile and enterprises that are concentrated in the grocery stores. And finally, obtaining as main conclusions, the experience of these microentrepreneurs in opting to establish themselves as companies through an exceptional legal regime, based on the benefits gained from participating in the public technical cooperation program Grocery Stores of Chile is presented.

INTRODUCTION

The Chilean economy in recent decades is characterized as a commercially open market economy, but in which the economic role of the State remains as a regulatory entity, concentrating on strategic issues for the country. (Montero, 1997). According to Álvarez-Figueroa (2014), Chile, despite its low labor productivity and its scarce expenditure on research and development (R&D) occupies a prominent position in the Latin American region regarding international competitiveness. Although this competitiveness is of low sustainability in the long term, it founded its achievements mainly on comparative

DOI: 10.4018/978-1-5225-8939-6.ch004

advantages for the specialized export of low value-added non-renewable goods (mineral) and difficult renovation (forest resources). There is, above all macroeconomic benefits at the level of monetary policy (inflationary control and anti-subsidiarity of business activity), in addition to efficiency in government management. To which are added good level corporate directors, training policies for people with an organizational efficiency orientation, legal certainty as a result of a civil legal system and a reputation for serious business.

At the employment level, Barrero, Fuentes, and Mena (2018), account for a slowdown in the generation of employment in the Chilean economy between 2014 and 2017. And whose slowed growth from 2015 onwards is mainly explained by self-employed, as well as workers who perform a free exercise of the profession or operate their own company, but who do not have a job as a wage earner. This type of workers is those of lower university education (12%), mainly focused on the trade sector (33%) and whose income regarding hours worked is less than employees by one third (33%). The characteristics of this exploitation of an own company, give account for micro business. For the Internal Revenue Service (2018) of Chile, a micro business is an entity that regularly exerts an economic activity, whether handmade or other, individually or as a family or as a company, and whose annual sales are less than 2,400 Chilean development units, about 99,000 American dollars.

In the Chilean case, the draft on micro family business (MFB) was submitted to Parliament in June 1994, and its prosecution concluded seven years later, approved in July 2001 under Law 19,749 that establishes norms to facilitate the creation of family members of the micro business. Several factors converged so that for the first time to enact a law of this kind in Chile, which introduces an exceptional regime to encourage the establishment, formalization, and development of micro business operating in the family residence. Factors that are related to the growing concern to eliminate barriers to the development of micro and small business, whose relevance regarding potential in the creation of jobs and wealth began to be recognized strongly, since the nineties. (Valenzuela, Di Meglio, & Reinecke, 2006).

These ideas are related to those presented by Valencia and Darío (2012) regarding the promotion of these entrepreneurial initiatives, for the development of entrepreneurship as a means of generating employment and competitiveness. Those are implemented in Latin America from public promotion policies with the support of private initiatives to stimulate new companies (Echecopar et al., 2006). In Chile, the relative weight of multi-personal micro business (operating with partners, family members and/or dependent workers) was higher than the average for Latin America and accounts of half of the employees in the micro business segment. (Valenzuela, Di Meglio, & Reinecke, 2006).

According to Prahalad and Hart (2002), marginalized can alter the way of life and security of rich people, as poverty generates discontent. And while full income equality is a utopian dream, the use of business development to bring people out of poverty and give them the opportunity for a better life is fundamental to stability and health of global economy. In this way, improving the access of poor people to financial services allows these agents to build productive assets and improve their productivity and potential for sustainable livelihoods. Therefore, the final argument is the improvement of financial services supplying for poor people, can directly contribute to poverty reduction according to (Green, Kirkpatrick, & Murinde, 2006).

But this type of support mechanism often lacks a continuous evaluation and improvement process. Considering these problems, Nightingale and Coad (2014) re-evaluate the performance of entrepreneurial companies concerning innovation, job creation, economy, and growth. On the other hand, Velasco and Saiz (2007) point out that one of the most neglected areas of support programs for new entrepreneurs is the evaluation of business creation programs, that practically does not exist.

While Meier and Pilgrim (1994) affirm that the number of microbusinesses accessing these benefits is very low, we show that 70% of SMEs in developing countries ignore the existence of agencies created to support them. This fact is reaffirmed for Chile based on the results of the survey conducted by Ministry of Planning (MIDEPLAN) in 1997, where more than 85% of the micro business considered had not received any support in the 12 months preceding the application of this, which has an impact on the fact that they do not obtain support services. Such as Training courses, Advice / technical management, Credits. (Valenzuela, Di Meglio, & Reinecke, 2006). The situation is not very different from that expressed by the Technical Cooperation Service (2018: 20) in the case of Chile's Business Development Centers, which still demonstrate low levels of impact.

This latter aspect gains a greater importance degree since it recognizes that access to finance by micro, small and medium-sized enterprises (MSMEs) and vulnerable groups have critical importance for poverty reduction. Microfinance and credit programs for SMEs also believed to be well designed and targeted to be effective. These programs must be accompanied by other support services, such as training and capacity building, assistance in accessing markets and technologies, and the solution of other market failures (Zhuang et al., 2009).

On the other hand, contrary what might think by oneself, all micro businesses are directly or indirectly affected by the regulatory environment. This fact is true, even for those who operate without any type of record in state agencies. (Valenzuela, Di Meglio, & Reinecke, 2006, Moya, Guerrero, & Arregui, 2018).

DETERMINING THE CHILEAN MICRO FAMILY BUSINESS

From our research contribution, this chapter proposes to analyze from a mixed methodology, both qualitative of narrative type of topics (Salgado-Lévano, 2007, Blanco, 2011), and descriptive quantitative (Ramos, 2015), the case of Chilean micro business and their experience after having been established under an exceptional regulatory framework and how this has had impact both on their internal achievements and on the deployment of socio-economic support strategies, that have benefited them as micro family business.

The contribution of this research is to open the way to study this exceptional regime of smaller companies. Since research such as the one proposed here has scarcely been addressed in the scientific literature, which has focused more on justifying the reasons for public authorities' intervention on activity or, sometimes, to argue otherwise, as indicated Velasco and Saiz (2007). Mallard (2012), adds the resurgence of interest to study the "small urban production," between researchers and official institutions, in the domestic, community context, their identity, and personal development logic. Other authors such as Zhuang et al. (2009), point out that urgent research is needed how to sequence the development of the financial sector, how to balance the need for financial innovation and economic and financial stability, and how to make the programs of microfinance and credit programs for SMEs work. Best to reduce poverty.

Micro and small business is a key component of economic growth, job creation and poverty reduction in Chile. In other parts of the world, this role is maintained, As the case of Thai SMEs, which are becoming more and more the creator of new jobs and in the case of Vietnamese SMEs employ 64% of the industrial workforce. (Chittithaworn et al., 2011). Ideas that are related to those presented by Valencia and Darío (2012), regarding the promotion of these business initiatives, for the development of entrepreneurship to generate employment and competitiveness. Those are implemented in Latin America from public promotion policies with the support of private initiatives to stimulate new companies (Echecopar et al., 2006). In general terms, the ability to take advantage of market opportunities and create innovative value propositions that will generate wealth and employment requiring the presence of entrepreneurs (Quatraro, & Vivarelli, 2015). Vera-Oyarzún and Moreira-López (2009), already warned a decade ago for the case of Chile, that much economically relevant activity, especially in the job's creation, takes place in these micro businesses, on which there is scarce official information available.

But regarding promotion and support for entrepreneurship, sustainability of subsidized companies is often not analyzed. Focusing on this lack Santos, Neto and Serrano (2016) evaluate the mortality of subsidized entrepreneurial companies in Portugal, concluding that probability of persistence in the market increases with: investment, seniority of the firm and concentration of regional companies. Persisting doubts about the real economic effect of programmes to support product development in smaller companies' segments (Baker, 2000), also, urban-rural differences and minority ethnic component that present by Onphanhdala and Suruga (2010) in its study to 1700 micro and small companies in Laos. They would also be interesting to study for the case of Chile, given the high concentration of native ethnicities groups in some regions of the country.

According to Ministry of Economy, Development, and Tourism (2017), almost half of Chilean companies are family businesses (48%), understanding by family businesses those in which over fifty percent of their property as belonging to a family or family group. Figure that between micro and small and medium sized-enterprises reaches 49%, while in large companies it decreases to 40%. They are concentrating over 50% in economic sectors such as accommodation and food services where family businesses represent 58%, followed by the wholesale and retail trade sector with 55% and manufactures with 52%.

In the specific case of family micro business in Chile, the general definition of family property of the company is replaced by specific terms of Law Number 19,749 published in the Official Journal on August 25, 2001, has a main objective among others, facilitate and encourage the creation, location, development and operation of the so-called Micro Family Business (Ministry of Finance, 2001).

'Micro-family business' as indicated in the second subparagraph of article 26 of the Municipal Revenue Law Decree No. 3,063 of 1979 (Ministry of Interior, 2018), must be understood as the one whose activity is developed by gathering the following requirements: (a) the economic activity constituting its turn is exercised in the family home; (b) no more than five foreign workers in the family work; and (c) their productive assets, without considering the value of the property in which it works, do not exceed 1,000 Chilean development units (about 40,000 USD).

Also, according to Ministry of Finance of Chile (2002) in Article 2 of the Regulation of Law No. 19,749, the micro family business is a company that belongs to one or more natural persons residing in a dwelling. It can develop professional work, crafts, industry, or any other lawful activity, either to provide services or production of goods, excluding dangerous, polluting or annoying.

The main beneficiaries of this law are: (a) all those wishing to create a micro family business; (b) those who currently have a micro family business without being formalized, that is, they do not have a municipal license and/or have not started activities in the Service of Internal Taxes that covers its operation; and, (c) those micro family businesses that have not been able to formalize because they do not comply with the regulations on industrial or commercial zoning established by the respective territorial planning instruments.

According to the information published by the National Statistics Institute of Chile (2017), in its final report of the Fifth Micro-entrepreneurship Survey 2017, which considers as a micro-entrepreneur 'all those self-employed workers and employers with up to ten workers included, who carry out an economic activity of production of goods and services oriented to the market and that receives in return of that a

Figure 1. Regional distribution of formal Chilean micro business in 2015
Source: Internal Revenue Service (2018b)

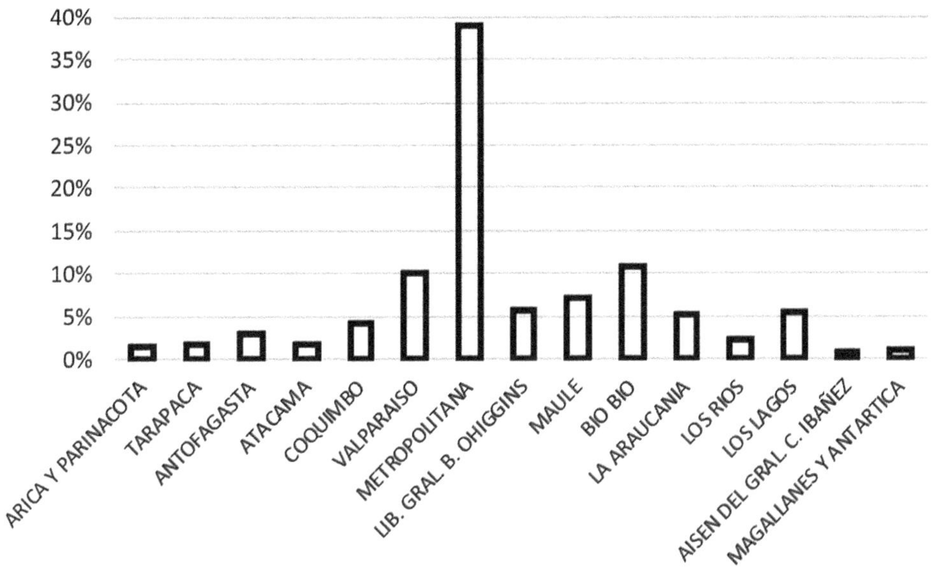

profit, species and/or monetary income." There are 1,992,578 Chilean micro-entrepreneurs, of which only 52% present formalization of their business activity before the Internal Revenue Service and about the origin of the business, it is mainly originated by necessity (58%) or to take advantage of latent business opportunities (30%). As for the smaller companies, these are strongly concentrated in the Metropolitan Region of Santiago, followed by regions with the largest population (Biobío and Valparaíso). Although they maintain a presence in the 15 regions of national territory, as shown in figure 1.

Of this total, only 83% correspond to self-employed workers (self-employment), and the remaining 17% are employers. Regarding gender, 61% are men, and 39% are women, a difference in gender that makes differences respect to the place where work activities are performed. Thus, only 29% of the activities of micro-entrepreneurs are developed within their homes, this figure amounts to 46% in the case of micro-entrepreneur women, but only 26% of micro-entrepreneurs in the country say they know about the system of micro business. A micro family business, being the total country level that has been constituted by this modality of only 8%. (National Statistics Institute, 2017). According to the National Statistics Institute (2017b), the working conditions of micro-entrepreneurs in the special family business scheme is 75% that of self-employed and only 25% of employer and in 49% of cases devoted to the commercial economic activity, with a geographic concentration of more than 30% in Metropolitan Region of Santiago.

Among the main features of the Chilean "micro family business" are characteristics presented in Table 1.

Regarding table 1, we find an age concentration among Chilean family micro-entrepreneurs, of over seventy percent in the range from 30 years to 54 years and whose average age is 45 years, who performed their work at home (65%) shared with other partners (69%). As far as gender distribution is concerned, there is a higher proportion of women over men, with 65% and 35% respectively, micro-entrepreneurs mostly married or living together (62%) and who commonly plays the role of head of household (57%)

Table 1. Main social characteristics of the Micro Family Business in Chile

Aspect	Indicator	Value
Shared House with partners	Yes	69%
Working facilities	Own (family, inheritance, succession)	65%
	Leased	26%
	Loaned	6%
Age	Mean (years)	45
	Minimum (years)	22
	Maximum (years)	77
	<30 years	10%
	≥ 30 years and <55 years	71%
	≥ 55 years	19%
Gender (sex, according to source)	Male	35%
	Female	65%
Marital Status	Or cohabiting	62%
	Single	20%
Nationality	Chilean	96%
Head of House	Yes	57%
Education level	Secondary education complete	51%
	Full professional	28%
	Complete primary education	14%
	Complete professional Technician	7%

Source: National Statistics Institute (2017b)

Regarding educational level, it is observed that 55% corresponds to family micro-entrepreneurs with full secondary education, followed by 28% with complete professional level, 14% with complete primary education and 7% with a technical level full professional. This result accounts for about a third of these micro-entrepreneurs with enough educational level to develop in professional work environments.

It can be observed in Table 2 that 100% of the micro family business consulted by the National Statistics Institute has developed business initiatives formally constituted and about eighty percent (83%) of those are faced as a natural person, with aid on average of 2 workers in addition it is observed that about one third of these companies does not exceed 2 years old of seniority.

In Table 3, we can see for those surveyed by the National Statistics Institute (2017), almost 90% of cases of their first venture. It is also important to note that a micro family business is far from being a family business because only 7% of them would have that reason to start their micro business as the main reasons would relate to obtaining higher income, family responsibilities, market opportunity, greater flexibility, temporary space and freedom in decision making. Reasons similar to those observed by Vega, Rojas, and Salazar (2018) in micro, small and medium-sized Chilean businesspeople, not necessarily attached to this exceptional business regime.

Table 2. Main economic characteristics of family micro-entrepreneurs

Aspect	Indicator	Value
Monthly incomes	income <390 USD	35%
	390 ≤ income <670 USD	27%
	670 USD ≤ income	38%
Registration with the Internal Tax Service	Yes	100%
	Natural Person	83%
	Legal Person	17%
Seniority	Same year	7%
	Of 1 to 2 years	28%
	From 3 to 4 years	17%
	From 5 to 6 years	12%
	From 7 to 8 years	6%
	From 9 to 10 years	10%
	More than 10 years	20%
Workers	Average	2
	1 worker	62%
	2 workers	22%
	≥ 3 workers	16%

Source: The National Statistics Institute of Chile (2017b)

Table 3. Main motivations for entrepreneurship of family micro-entrepreneurs

Aspect	Indicator	Value
Motivation	To obtain a higher income	25%
	Family responsibilities	15%
	Found an opportunity in the market	13%
	Has greater flexibility (schedule, place of work, etc.)	10%
	Make your decisions / be your boss	10%
	Family tradition /inheritance	7%
	He wanted to organize his own company	7%, He could
	Not find a job as a salaried employee	6%
	For health reasons	6%, He
	was fired from a salaried job	2%
Business undertook (including the current one)	Average	1
	1	89%
	2	10%
	3	1%

Source: The National Statistics Institute of Chile (2017b)

Given the characteristics, mentioned to this point, Chilean storekeepers micro-entrepreneurs, are a clear example of entrepreneurship originated at home with family work presence. Therefore, the analysis of micro family business will be focused on the support program of the Technical Cooperation Service, which provides coverage for this type of micro business.

MICRO FAMILY BUSINESS IN SMALL CHILEAN GROCERY STORES

It has been characterized the possible levels of 8% of Chilean companies that would be within those created by the exceptional regime of 'micro family business.' In its legal limits seem to be contained the 'neighborhood stores', since they comply with that: the economic activity that constitutes its turn is performed in the family home, in it no more than five workers work outside the family, and its productive assets, without considering that the value of property must not exceed 40,000 USD.

In Chile, as in other countries of the world, the productive structure is composed of micro, small and medium enterprises (MSMEs) that form the majority of the productive apparatus and generate most of the jobs, but, in contrast, their contribution to the national product is considerably smaller than large companies, because of its low productivity and difficulties in credit accessing. To change this situation, many countries have implemented policies to improve the productivity of MSMEs for decades, with discouraging results, on the one hand, because technical support activities have been dispersed and far from specific requirements of the MSMEs. Productive units and territorial conditions in which they operate; and, on the other, because the structural root of financial exclusion has not been attacked. (Moya, Guerrero, & Arregui, 2018).

Based on this, the state support program 'Grocery stores of Chile' is analyzed from a logic of the motivations of program beneficiaries, evaluation that these make with respect to processes and products of the program, delving into elements like the application experience to the program, the adequacy of amounts and the fulfillment of the deadlines. This program provides support to business micro-entrepreneurs, who are two-thirds women, concentrated in 28% between 50 and 60 years old, more than forty percent have complete secondary education (44%), and 57% are married.

Figure 2 shows the profile of clients that store micro-entrepreneurs have, where 61% of respondents say that their clients are mainly people living in the same neighborhood and 14% people who occasionally walk through the neighborhood. To a lesser extent, people who work and/or study in the neighborhood are mentioned, and 12% of storekeepers claim to have other types of clients, where tourists and people from other neighborhoods close to their stand out.

Regarding neighborhood stores as a source of employment, 44.3% have some worker. The result that accounts for 4 out of 10 small businesses of the trade have assistance to attend their businesses, and therefore they will not be devoted themselves to this task. Figure 3 shows the type of work they generate.

It could observe at figure 3, the detail of workers in the grocery stores, where 45% corresponds to paid workers who are not relatives and 27% to paid family members. It should be noted that 24% of these micro-entrepreneurs recognize the aid of family members who are not paid within the business, this could be due to the need of neighborhood storekeepers to have help, but do not have enough resources to formalize it.

Once characterized in a general way, this segment of micro businesses in the commerce sector will deepen on their experience and benefits obtained from the state support program to which they are hosted. In which the Technical Cooperation Service considers the delivery of up to 2,000,000 Chilean

Figure 2. Main customers of store micro-entrepreneurs
Source: Technical Cooperation Service (2016)

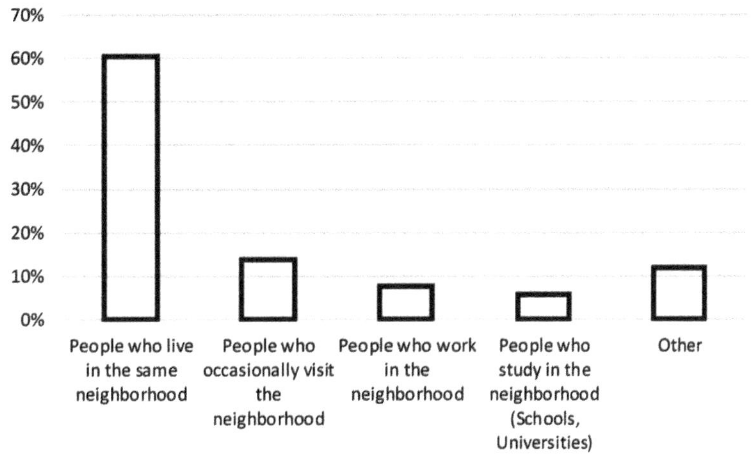

Figure 3. Main workers of micro-entrepreneurs
Source: Technical Cooperation Service (2016)

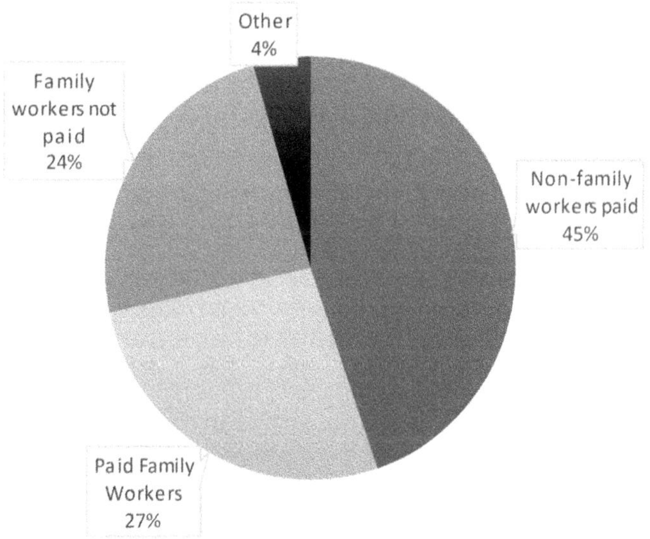

pesos (about 3,000 US dollars) to cover the financing of up to 80% of the activities detailed in their work plans, which should be used for both Business Management Actions as for Investments in assets, merchandise, among others. Also, the program considers a contribution of 20% of the same beneficiary (Technical Cooperation Service, 2018).

Thus, motivations of the micro-entrepreneurs of the trade beneficiaries from the 'Grocery stores of Chile' program, aimed mainly at improving their business regarding infrastructure, increase and improvement of products and/or services offered, among others (Technical Cooperation Service, 2018b).

As shown the following figure 4, improving the infrastructure or equipment of the grocery stores is a priority for beneficiaries, who consider that this aspect is fundamental for the improvement of their

Figure 4. Reasons why you decided to participate in the 'Grocery stores of Chile' Program
Source: Technical Cooperation Service (2016)

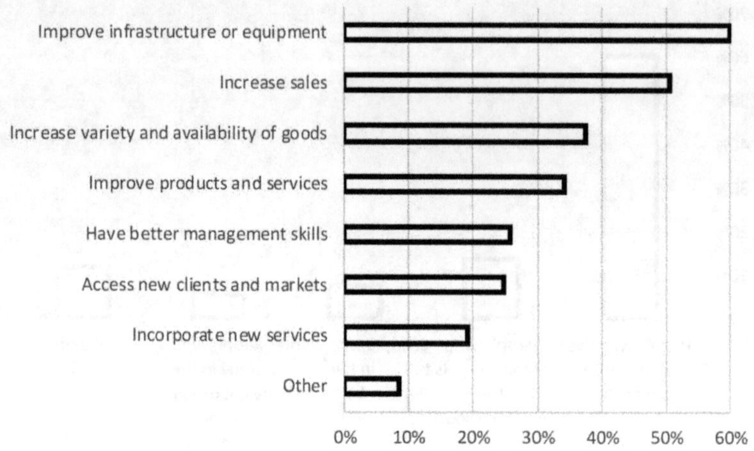

business. This fact could be related to seniority in businesses, since 55% who decided to participate for this reason are 11 years old or older, which would explain the interest of the beneficiaries to modernize their facilities. This fact is followed by the increase in sales with 51%, which is also essential for entrepreneurs. It is worth mentioning that among the less mentioned aspects is to access new markets and customers, with 25%, and only 19% had an interest in incorporating a new service to their business.

This fact is reflected in the testimony of the beneficiaries, who say that their main motivations to participate in the program have to do with the improvement of their business, both concerning infrastructure and improving the quality and variety of products offered. This fact is evident from some of the testimonies compiled by the Technical Cooperation Service (2016):

We had to make improvements; we had machines that were no longer working well, we had the part of the premises outside (...) we had bad curtains, I have been stolen several times so with all that it served me a lot.

... for me it was little, but maybe others covered them completely. All I did with that money was to buy a machine, fixed those curtains and the awning that you have out there ... it served me a lot, it was important, but it did not cover at least half of the needs I had

Well when they make an invitation, and obviously they tell him that he will apply to projects where the government is going to give him a money grant, I believe that, of course, no one can deny it, because it is logical that if you want to implement improvements in your business will do what is possible because it is so

I did not sell bread, did not sell mortadella and all those things ... And I had a manual weight hanging no more, now I have a digital table and to cut mortadella.

The evaluation of the amount granted by the Technical Cooperation Service to store micro-entrepreneurs is valued positively by 75% of store micro-entrepreneurs. On the other hand, it is observed that concerning the amount contributed by themselves, as co-financing, 70% considers t it is appropriate. in both cases there is a negative rate of the order 7%. Also, by consulting them what would have been the appropriate amount to deliver to meet the needs of their business, an average of one million and a half and a maximum of six million was recorded. Finally, 84% affirmed that deadlines for delivery of resources were fulfilled, while the figure in the opposite (16%) could be due by a delay in administrative processes or by difficulties in adjusting the expectations of the storekeepers.

Regarding the results and effects that the 'Grocery stores of Chile' program has had from the perspective of its beneficiaries, these range from increase in sales and improvement of infrastructure, to the improvement of store management, aspects that directly or indirectly, they respond to the objective pursued by the program enhancing the growth of this type of business, and its access to new market opportunities.

As can be seen in figure 5, the greatest contribution perceived by entrepreneurs is related to the improvement of business management, where 86% affirm that the program has contributed quiet or a lot in this regard. This fact could be a result of the first component of the program, related to the training that sought to deliver and update the storekeepers in the management of their businesses. In the same way, aspects such as the acquisition and renovation of machinery and the improvement of the stock of products offered are also mentioned.

On the contrary, the generation of jobs is the least mentioned effect. 52% claim that this has produced very little or nothing. This fact could be linked to the beneficiaries having difficulties in deriving functions and trusting other people for the operation of their business, or also that the profile of beneficiaries is linked to very small businesses to require the hiring of more staff. Above the average of two workers with which these types of businesses already count. It is worth mentioning that the generation of jobs is not part of the main focuses of the program, besides it is part of the motivation of entrepreneurs to participate in it. (Technical Cooperation Service, 2016)

Figure 5. The contribution of the program to family micro-entrepreneurs
Source: Technical Cooperation Service (2016)

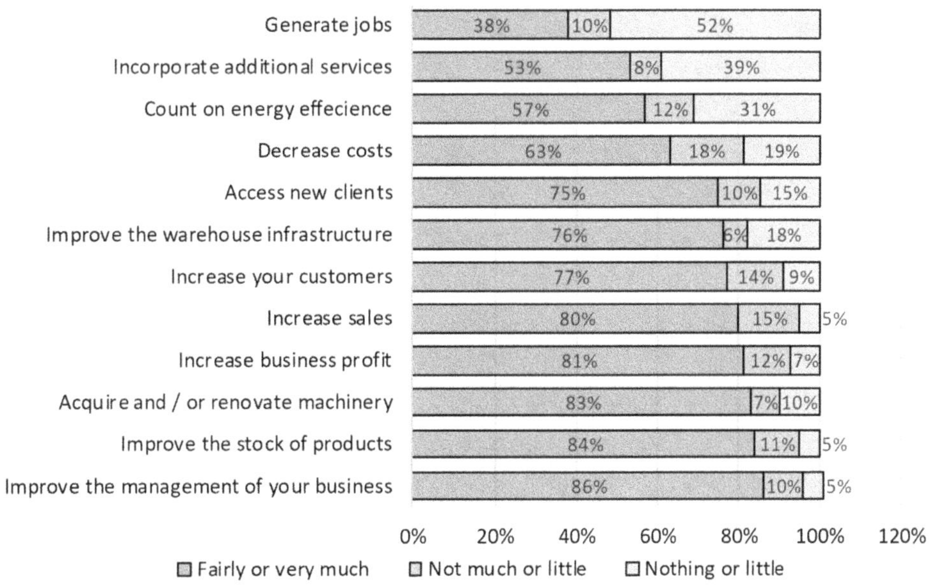

For entrepreneurs, improving the stock of products and acquiring and/or renewing machinery is a visible and immediate contribution, given that it allows them to make their businesses more competitive and attract more customers and, therefore, increase their sales income. On the other hand, a contribution of the program regarding business advertising is recognized. Making this type of investment for entrepreneurs means attracting a greater number of clients.

Figure 6 shows the distribution of the beneficiaries according to their perception of contribution with respect to the program, where 44% perceive a high contribution of the program regarding different aspects, such as the increase of sales, customers and the utility of the business, as well as to improve the management of their businesses, improve infrastructure, among other aspects. Likewise, 38% has a high average level, so it is possible to say that more than 80% of the beneficiaries have a positive view of the benefits obtained as family business micro-entrepreneurs, thanks to their participation in the program 'Grocery stores of Chile.'

As for the sales of store micro-entrepreneurs, it is observed from the Monthly Statement Form and Simultaneous Tax Payment (Form number 29), from April 2016 to May 2017, the average of sales, as shown in Table 4, reached 4.5 million Chilean pesos.

According to the perception of beneficiaries, after their participation in the program, sales increased, which in their opinion was expected due to the incorporation of new products and/or services.

Regarding the incorporation of new services, it is important to mention that at the beginning of the program only 24% of the beneficiaries expected to obtain this result from their participation. Bearing in mind the preceding, it should be noted that 35% claim that they have incorporated a service, while

Figure 6. Index of contribution received by the beneficiaries
Source: Technical Cooperation Service (2016)

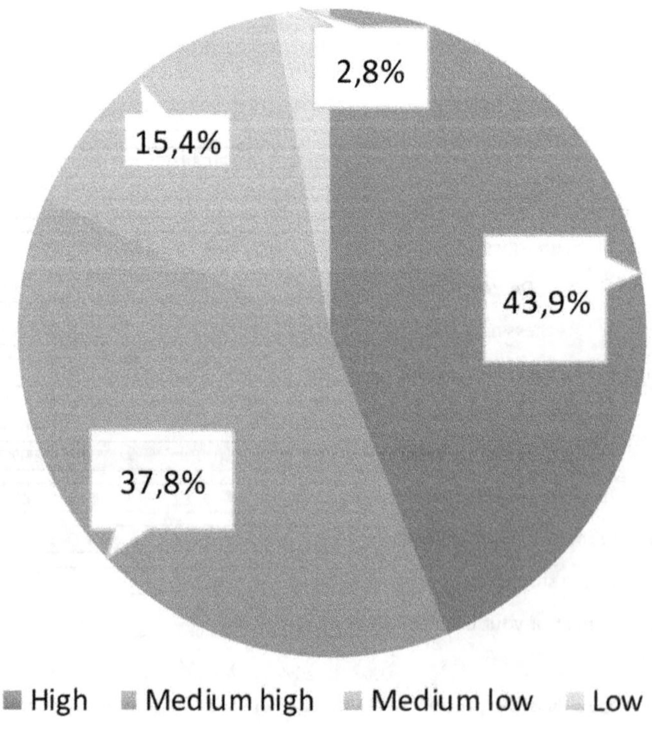

Table 4. The approximate annual sale of your store business micro-entrepreneurs during 2016

	Sales
Mean	$ 4,538,197
Median	$ 3,063,479
Mode	$ 1,393,206
Standard deviation	$ 4,470,838
Minimum	$ 133,880
Maximum	$ 23,861,191

Source: Technical Cooperation Service (2016)

more than half of the entrepreneurs affirm that, since their participation in the program, they have not incorporated any other service into their business (65%). This fact suggests that there is still a challenge in the incorporation of services that help the modernization of these stores, for which it is necessary to investigate the real needs and interests of the beneficiaries to incorporate these services.

In the case of those beneficiaries who claimed to have incorporated a service to their business based from the investment of the Technical Cooperation Service within the framework of the program, figure 7 shows that these are mainly library services, such as a photocopier (14.3%) and payment service through the Transbank payment network (12.0%). To a lesser extent, services such as 'Neighbor cash box' from Banco Estado (8.2%) and Bip! card charge (2.1%) were incorporated.

DISCUSSION AND RESULTS

There is a strong relationship between family micro-entrepreneurs who are in the business or storehouse sector and people who live in the neighborhood, where there is a theme of customer loyalty that has not

Figure 7. Percentage of the service that the entrepreneurs entered their business with the investment of SERCOTEC
Source: Technical Cooperation Service (2016)

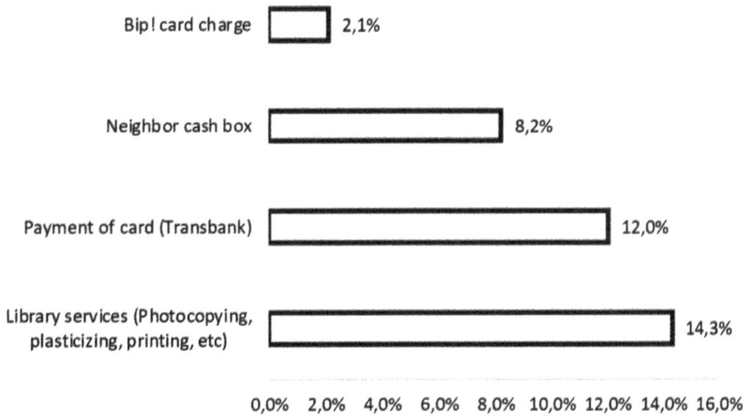

been incorporated as a key element of the business. This information would allow gathering from first source new needs that could be solved, and it would be interesting to survey.

Regarding the incorporation of more services for their businesses, more than half of the respondents said that they had not included any service. Whereas, while this is one of the main objectives of the work plans that are implemented in the 'Grocery stores of Chile' program, it is possible to conclude that there is a challenge regarding better managing of this element within the program. This element may be due to several factors, including the capture of new needs from customers, lack of knowledge or lack of motivation to carry out these new services and lack of human resources that could help to execute it.

On the incorporation of more human resources, even this does not obey to the objectives of the program, according to results entrepreneurs have family members who cooperate and work in the business in an unpaid way, which could benefit from a government plan such as Subsidy Youth Employment, Women's Work Bonus, among others. And in that way, regulate their work situation.

About the amounts delivered, they obtain moderate levels of satisfaction, which leads to thinking that the amounts may not be enough, concerning expectations of beneficiaries according to their shortfalls. This should necessarily be done together with other development instruments, allowing entrepreneurs to continue advancing in the improvement of their business and complementing investment made within the framework of this program, which can be insufficient to generate a greater impact on the business.

It is, undoubtedly, an essential aspect of maintaining technical assistance to family micro-entrepreneurs that is part of the people who work in this kind of programs.

CONCLUSION

Microbusiness in Chile, as in several parts of the world, generate an important source of employment, in Chile, there are around 2,000,000 companies of this size. To strengthen the formalization of microbusiness born in the home of micro-entrepreneurs, since 2001 an exceptional system of companies is created by law, which formally regulates what is understood in Chile as a 'micro family business.'

By facilitating a formalization path to that micro business that works irregularly, through this mechanism they can open new businesses, access working capital, improve their financing, contract services, expand their client portfolio and associate with other companies, among others.

Although the programs to finance micro business were not carried out from the beginning, they began to appear, as policymakers realized that one of the ways to reduce poverty is through the strengthening of micro business. However, this strengthening must go hand in hand with a robust and well-formed program, especially from technical advice and financing.

Within these programs there is one called 'Grocery stores of Chile', the main objective of which is to boost the growth of micro family business in commerce sector, and to provide them with access to new business opportunities, through the implementation of a work plan, which includes financing of investments and business management actions (training, technical assistance or other).

By identifying the profile of the beneficiaries of this program, we can highlight those main beneficiaries are in the Metropolitan Region. Regarding gender, 67% women participate and 33% men, with age between 50 and 60 years old, with a total education level of 44% on average, most of them are married (57%). All figures that are consistent with the general characteristics of micro-entrepreneurs in Chile.

Regarding the subsidy, it is used in 20% in management and 80% in fixed assets, for the first one it is disaggregated into 75% in Advertising and Promotion, followed by 15% in Technical Assistance Management. On the other hand, 61% goes to fixed assets and 15% to Technical Assistance and Management.

When evaluating the satisfaction of the beneficiaries on the perceived results achieved, in this program we find regarding the general satisfaction of the program users, that satisfaction is 90% while the dissatisfaction is only 3%. These results show a high level of user satisfaction, which is consistent with the satisfaction of each of the components of the program, both training and investment, which were evaluated with a higher satisfaction level than 80% in both cases. Finally, it is possible to say that the satisfaction of users is related to the fact that the program manages to boost the growth of its business.

ACKNOWLEDGMENT

The researchers of this study are grateful to Foundation School of International Affairs and the Chair of International Competitiveness and Territorial Development, for institutional sponsorship provided in the field of Entrepreneurial Studies.

REFERENCES

Álvarez-Figueroa, O. (2014). Competitiveness in International Economy Present Conditions. *Economia y Desarrollo*, *151*(1), 56–70.

Baker, J. (2000). *Evaluating the impact of development projects on poverty: a handbook for practitioners (Spanish)*. Washington, DC: World Bank. doi:10.1596/0-8213-4697-0

Barrero, A., Fuentes, M., & Mena, J. (2018). Formality and income gaps in the Chilean labor market. *Economía Chilena (Santiago)*, *21*(2), 108–127.

Blanco, M. (2011). Narrative research: A way of generating knowledge. *Argumentos (México, DF)*, *24*(67), 135–156.

Chittithaworn, C., Islam, M. A., Keawchana, T., & Yusuf, D. H. M. (2011). Factors Affecting Business Success of Small and Medium Enterprises (SMEs) in Thailand. *Asian Social Science*, *7*(5), 180–190. doi:10.5539/ass.v7n5p180

Echecopar, G., Angelelli, P., Galleguillos, G., & Schorr, M. (2006). *Seed capital for the financing of new companies Advances and lessons learned in Latin America*. Washington, DC: Inter-American Development Bank.

Green, C. J., Kirkpatrick, C. H., & Murinde, V. (2006). Finance for small enterprise growth and poverty reduction in developing countries. *Journal of International Development*, *18*(7), 1017–1030. doi:10.1002/jid.1334

Internal Revenue Service. (2018). *Taxpayers. Small Business*. Available in: http://www.sii.cl/contribuyentes/empresas_por_tamano/microempresas.pdf

Internal Revenue Service. (2018b). *Taxpayers: companies by size*. Available in: http://www.sii.cl/contribuyentes/contribuyentes.htm

Mallard, B. (2012). Micro enterprises and alternative socioeconomic dynamics in the BioBío region, (Chile). *Revista Márgenes Espacio Arte y Sociedad*, *9*(11), 169–184.

Meier, R., & Pilgrim, M. (1994). Policy-induced constraints on small Enterprise development in Asian developing countries. *Small Enterprise Development*, *5*(2), 32–38. doi:10.3362/0957-1329.1994.017

Ministry of Economy, Development, and Tourism. (2017). *Results report Companies in Chile, Fourth Longitudinal Survey of Companies*. Santiago de Chile: Division of Commercial and Industrial Policy of the Ministry of Economy, Development, and Tourism.

Ministry of Finance. (2001). *Law 19,749 Establishes Standards to Facilitate the Creation of Micro Family Business*. Available in: http://bcn.cl/1uxup

Ministry of Finance. (2002). *Decree 102. Regulates Law 19.749 That Establishes Standards to Facilitate the Creation of Family Micro Business*. Available in: http://bcn.cl/1v7mk

Ministry of Interior. (2018). *Decree 2385. Fixed and systematized text of Decree-Law number 3,063, of 1979, on Municipal Income*. Available in: http://bcn.cl/1v06x

Montero, C. (1997). State-business relations in a global economy. The case of Chile. *Nueva Sociedad*, *151*, 122–135.

Moya, X., Guerrero, R., & Arregui, R. (2018). Chile: Create and sustain employment through a combination of technical assistance and financial inclusion. *MktDESCUBRE*, *1*(9), 84–94.

National Statistics Institute. (2017a). *Final report Official Survey V Micro-Entrepreneurship Survey*. Chile: Author.

National Statistics Institute. (2017b). *Micro Entrepreneurship Survey. Full V database SPSS Micro Entrepreneurship Survey*. Chile: Author.

Nightingale, P., & Coad, A. (2014). Muppets and gazelles: Political and methodological biases in entrepreneurship research. *Industrial and Corporate Change*, *23*(1), 113–143. doi:10.1093/icc/dtt057

Onphanhdala, P., & Suruga, T. (2010). Entrepreneurial human capital and micro and small business in Lao PDR. *The Developing Economies*, *48*(2), 181–202. doi:10.1111/j.1746-1049.2010.00104.x

Prahalad, C.K., & Hart, S.L. (2002). The fortune at the bottom of the pyramid. *Strategy + Business*, *26*, 1–14.

Quatraro, F., & Vivarelli, M. (2015). Drivers of entrepreneurship and post-entry performance of newborn firms in developing countries. *The World Bank Research Observer*, *30*(2), 277–305. doi:10.1093/wbro/lku012

Ramos, C. A. (2015). The paradigms of scientific research. *Avances en Psicología: Revista de la Facultad de Psicología y Humanidades*, *23*(1), 9–17.

Salgado-Lévano, A. C. (2007). Qualitative research: Designs, evaluation of methodological rigor and challenges. *Liberabit, 13*(13), 71–78.

Santos, A., Neto, P., & Serrano, M. M. (2016). A long-term mortality analysis of subsidized firms in rural areas: An empirical study in the Portuguese Alentejo region. *Eurasian Economic Review, 6*(1), 125–151. doi:10.100740822-015-0035-4

Technical Cooperation Service. (2016). *Results evaluation of the Technical Cooperation Service programs*. Report No. 3 Final Results. Santiago of Chile: Technical Cooperation Service.

Technical Cooperation Service. (2018). *Small Business Development Center in Chile.* Technical Cooperation Service.

Technical Cooperation Service. (2018b). *Grocery stores of Chile. Fund.* Technical Cooperation Service.

Valencia, A., & Darío, G. (2012). Self-employment and entrepreneurship. A working hypothesis to explain one of the strategies adopted by governments to face the progress of the market. *Semestre Económico, 15*(32), 103–127.

Valenzuela, M., Di Meglio, R., & Reinecke, G. (Eds.). (2006). *From the house to the formality. Experiences of the Micro Family Business Law in Chile.* Chile: International Labor Organization.

Vega, A., Rojas, M.J., & Salazar, G. (2018). University Social Responsibility: Recent contributions to the Small Companies Development in Chile. *Revista Venezolana de Gerencia, 23*(1), 328-345.

Velasco, R., & Saiz, M. (2007). Business creation policies and their evaluation. *Working Papers, 118*, 1-70.

Vera-Oyarzún, M. B., & Moreira-López, V. H. (2009). Characterization of Small Agricultural Enterprises in Southern Chile. *Idesia, 27*(3), 89–99.

Zhuang, J., Gunatilake, H. M., Niimi, Y., Khan, M. E., Jiang, Y., Hasan, R., . . . Huang, B. (2009). *Financial Sector Development, Economic Growth, and Poverty Reduction: A Literature Review.* Asian Development Bank Economics Working Paper Series, No. 173, 1-46.

KEY TERMS AND DEFINITIONS

Bip! Card: A Chilean card that allows the payment in the transport in the Santiago Metropolitan Area (Chile).

Chilean Development Unit: The UF (for its acronym in Spanish *Unidad de Fomento*) is a unit of account used in Chile. The exchange rate between the 'UF' and the Chilean peso (CLP) is now adjusted continuously to the inflation rate so that the value of the Chilean development unit only remains on average constant daily during periods of low inflationary fluctuation.

Entrepreneur: Individuals who can identify business opportunities and then carry them out through some business plan.

Grocery Store: It is a store or shop which is serviced by a salaried worker or owner, in which products are sold mainly food, accompanied by a lot of other useful products varied.

Micro Family Business: Any productive activity or service that does not pollute is done at home, where most workers are familiar, and that has capital not exceeding 1,000 Chilean development units (equivalent to approximately 41,000 USD).

Microbusinesses: Companies whose annual revenues from sales, services and other activities of the line, do not exceed the 2,400 Chilean development units in the last calendar year, equivalent to about 98,000 USD.

Neighbor Cash Box: Service Banco Estado (Chile) to which people can access stores in your neighborhood, to perform some banking services.

Self-Employment: It is when the person creates his job to work directly and independently of an employer.

Storekeepers: Store owners in which their main products are food.

Technical Cooperation Service: Chilean Public Agency aimed to support entrepreneurs and micro and small businesses in the country.

Chapter 5
A Model for Social Entrepreneurship Education

Carlos Cuervo-Arango Martínez
Nebrija University, Spain

Carlos Torrejon-Martin
Nebrija University, Spain

ABSTRACT

This chapter reviews the factors that are relevant to promote an entrepreneurial attitude, identifying education as an element of vital importance that influences the disposition to start a venture and its results. This is particularly important in the case of social entrepreneurship projects, in which good intentions frequently overcome sound business realities. To deepen the understanding of the relationship between education and social entrepreneurship, the authors develop the model "pyramid of catalysts for entrepreneurship," which helps to understand the mechanism by which the educational process affects the quantity and quality of social entrepreneurship. This chapter also presents several elements of paramount importance in designing a program of social entrepreneurial education.

INTRODUCTION[1]

There is a broad consensus in identifying entrepreneurial activity as an element of vital importance for economic and social development of a country. This activity has become even more relevant in recent years, identified as an essential mechanism of generation of wealth, which in turn allows the improvement of the employment rate.

The same is true of social entrepreneurship. However, here the emphasis goes towards the social value generated by those entrepreneurs and their role in opening new pathways to solving large scale problems affecting social change, frequently for the benefit of the marginalized and disadvantaged.

The existing literature on entrepreneurship reviews various factors that help develop and enhance this activity: aspects such as the availability of financial resources, the provision of physical infrastructure, the economic, administrative, and regulatory environment and others. However, among the designated factors, one recurrently appears, as of particular importance; in fact, there is a consensus that the education received to play a decisive role in the predisposition to undertake.

DOI: 10.4018/978-1-5225-8939-6.ch005

It is possible that a large number of people, who are engaged in entrepreneurial activities, possess innate abilities that will enable them to face the complexities, institutional as well as relational, of the world. However, there is only a way to strengthen those capacities, both for those who already have them and also to cover the gaps and develop a predisposition to entrepreneurship in people who do not have such knowledge and skills. This mechanism is through education.

The role of education in fostering the capabilities of the social entrepreneur and the impact of the projects undertaken is as important, if not more still. The reason being that in addition to all the skills and abilities that foster the success of the usual entrepreneur, the social kind requires an added measure of leadership. The requirement comes from the need to be able to endure the hardships of moving people and institutions out of their regular paths and induce them to toddle new roads of action, setting up correspondingly new institutions. That rearranging of the existing reality is the usual outcome of the most successful social entrepreneurship projects, and this kind of transformation is difficult to achieve without an enhanced leadership capability.

There seems to be some correlation between the education level and the rate of entrepreneurship, and there are indications that higher education is more likely to lead to a higher level of entrepreneurship (GEM, 2012; GEM Special Report, 2008; High Impact Entrepreneurship Global Report, 2011). However, there seems to be a major gap in this field of study. A large majority of existing studies treat this relationship between education and entrepreneurship generically, without identifying and studying the precise way in which education can influence the predisposition of those that receive it to become entrepreneurs. Much less have been treated the special educational need of social entrepreneurs and their relationship to those of entrepreneurs at large.

Whether, for example, different training levels can impact on the quality of the entrepreneurship projects; if current educational systems, and its contents, are giving an adequate response to the needs of the potential entrepreneurs; or in-depth analysis of the mechanism by which education and training positively influence entrepreneurship. All these can help us to respond to such issues as the following:

- Are the entrepreneurs who demonstrate a higher level of education and qualification those that undertake projects more attractive and with more value generation?
- Are those entrepreneurs showing a higher level of training and qualification, the ones that have a greater likelihood of success in the ventures they start?
- Which is the most useful syllabus for the people who receive training aimed at the setting up and management of business projects?
- How do education and training impacts the entrepreneurial initiative?

As Moliterno and Playhart (2011, p. 3), have remarked, *Human capital theory predicts that individuals or groups who have higher levels of knowledge, skills, and other competencies will achieve greater performance results that those who possess lower levels.* This chapter delves into the relationship between education and entrepreneurship, both social and market-oriented, developing a model that allows a complete view of the inner workings of their interrelationship.

Since we think that education plays as large a role in the scope and success of social entrepreneurship as it does in the usual kind of entrepreneurship, all of the considerations on entrepreneurship and education apply as well to social entrepreneurship. Thus, we will not keep repeating the pertinence of the ideas discussed and the model developed for the education of the social entrepreneur but will include commentaries and extensions to that effect as we think fit. At the bottom, social entrepreneurs are *like other entrepreneurs; only they are in it for social improvement, not for money* (James, 2001, cited by Tracey & Phillips, 2007, p. 266).

The model developed, called the Pyramid of Catalysts for Entrepreneurship, will allow us to identify the mechanism by which the educational process has an impact on the quality and quantity of social entrepreneurship, and in stepping up its probability of success. We summarize this model in the following Figure 1.

EDUCATION AND ENTREPRENEURSHIP. WHAT IS AN ENTREPRENEUR?

If we want to deepen the relationship between education and entrepreneurship, one of the basic themes to be treated is the figure of the entrepreneur; what is an entrepreneur?

There are multiple definitions of the idea on "entrepreneur." Schumpeter (1965), for instance, defined entrepreneurs as *individuals who take advantage of the market opportunities through technical and/or organizational innovations.* Drucker (1970) talked about entrepreneurs as *people who take risks.* Bolton and Thompson (2000) defined entrepreneurs as *people that normally create or innovate to build something that adds value to the market.* Now, for entrepreneurs to set up and develop their projects, they need much more than dreams; they need other aspects beyond having a good idea and achieve funding to implement it; they need a set of knowledge, skills and specific capabilities that allow them to get the project underway and ensure that it bears fruit in due time.

Old fashioned as it may sound, we can go back to the year 1978, when Patrick Liles, then a Harvard Business School Professor, distinguished three types of companies: Companies with potential, attractive companies, and marginal companies. According to prof. Patrick Liles, 80% of existing businesses are marginal enterprises and do not represent for the entrepreneur anything else than self-employment.

Figure 1. The pyramid of catalysts for entrepreneurship
Source: Authors

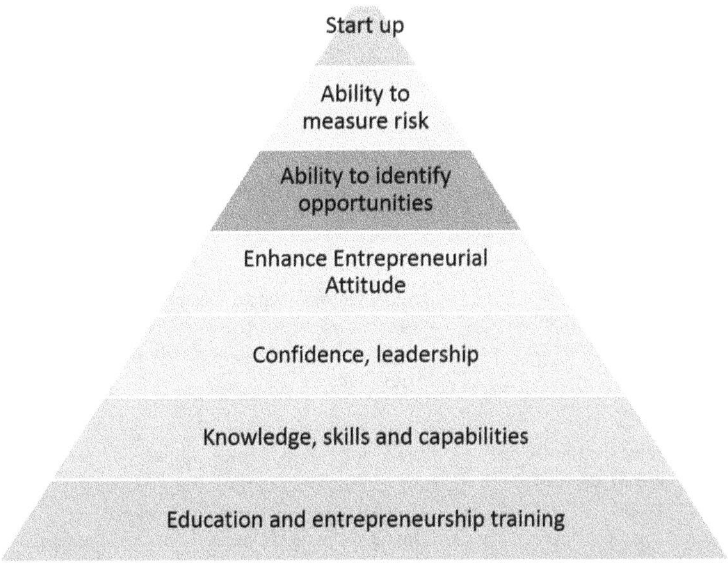

Prof. Liles emphasized that, when it comes to undertaking a project, it is very important to avoid marginalization. The goal would be projected with potential and attractions, and so he presented the three key elements to avoid project "marginality", also called mediocrity, as professionals (1) must have capabilities above the average; (2) should be offered something that people do want; there must be a genuine opportunity, and (3) must know how to convey to others what we offer them.

Almost 40 years after Professor Patrick Liles presented his ideas they are still valid, and the successive Global Entrepreneurship Monitor Reports have made them popular with the distinction between opportunity entrepreneurship and necessity entrepreneurship. If we relate the three objectives an entrepreneur should meet to be able to generate projects with high potential, with the possibilities offered by education to achieve them, we could summarize the situation in the following Figure 2.

It seems that education, both in knowledge and in specific skills for management and leadership, can have a critical impact in providing the entrepreneur with two key capabilities: Mastership of those professional skills that allow to properly identifying an opportunity and confidence enough to develop the project and, besides, to do it successfully.

Therefore, it seems worthwhile to study in deep the effects of education upon entrepreneurship, researching the process by which that impact obtains. In this connection, our basic hypothesis is as follows: Those social entrepreneurs who have education, both in skills and competencies, aimed at starting up a project, acquire greater security and confidence, showing a greater willingness to initiate projects of higher potential and with more chance of success than other entrepreneurs who have not enjoyed that kind of training.

However, since it is our special interest the application of these ideas to the educational process of social entrepreneurs, it is worthwhile to present a brief characterization of their aims and activities, to focus adequately in their unique features.

Figure 2. Patrick liles' theory
Source: Authors

THE SPECIAL EDUCATIONAL NEEDS OF SOCIAL ENTREPRENEURSHIP

The existence of serious difficulties to define with any degree of concreteness the term "social entrepreneurship" is a well-known reality in this field of study (Abu-Saifan, 2012; Martin & Osberg, 2007). However, no matter how short of a complete definition it may be considered, most interested people would agree that Wikipedia, of all sources, offers a good characterization of the role of social entrepreneurs when it says that they attempt to draw upon business techniques to find solutions to social problems.

The main advantage of the characterization proposed is that it places the business techniques that are typical of the entrepreneurship concept at the helm of our conception of social entrepreneurship. "In short, first a social entrepreneur is an entrepreneur" (Martin & Osberg, 2007, p. 2), only with a focus in a different range of problems, a differentiated set of tools and an aim in the creation of social value, rather than profits.

What the above amounts to, is to say that there is no success, measured by the social change obtained through the implementation of social entrepreneurship projects, if those projects are not adequately set-up and run. They have to be efficient enough to be able to live out of their stated sources of income, one of which frequently is, and rightly so, the income generated by the projects themselves. Only then will the social entrepreneur be able to fulfill its role as social transformer and change effecter.

Knowledge and skills for management are as useful to the social entrepreneur as to the rest of the entrepreneurs. To both, they allow the precise identification of opportunities, the fine valuation of their chances of success and the right mind for the implementation of whatever means could be required to attain the desired results.

Indeed, Wu, Kuo and Shen (2013) in a survey of 100 business schools, found that "there was no difference between social entrepreneurship education and entrepreneurship education " (p. 332). As the curricula and basic methods of teaching were common to both disciplines, perhaps with an emphasis on business ethics and the management of non-for profit ventures in the case of social entrepreneurship, they found differentiation in the activities developed in each case, with experiential learning and community service playing a larger role in the educational process of social entrepreneurs.

However, we could ask whether there are special skills needed by social entrepreneurs, required by the nature of their field of mission and the multidimensional nature of their call. In particular, by the challenge of having to manage a double bottom line, social and commercial (Tracey & Philips, 2007).

In this, we think there is a real difference. An entrepreneur of the usual sort has an objective simple and clearly stated, and the satisfaction of his shareholders depend crucially upon it. Not so the social entrepreneur; in his case, to the hardships of maintaining the project in operation, duly funded and efficient, it is added the task to express in realities of improvement the peculiar nature of his social call, always linked with some form of alleviation of a sorry lot of disfavored people.

Pongracz (2014) offers a clue to the special needs when she states that "because the manager in an environment of the social economy must deal with complex situations, it is necessary to reinforce all elements of his professionalism and develop his social, emotional and moral intelligence" (p. 420).

On the other hand, in their qualitative study on the required skills for social entrepreneurs, Muller, Chambers, and Neck (2014) identify three new skills that social entrepreneurs should develop, all of them linked to the "social" component of their bottom line. These are the ability to induce behavioral change; the ability to engage in co-creation with multiple stakeholders and the ability to develop solutions that aim to address the root cause of social problems.

Now, if we try to discover the basic trait of character, the key skill if you wish, that could allow the social entrepreneur to change the behavior of other people or to engage with them in planning and development steps of a broad social project, we will conclude that there is a need for a particular form of resilience.

Resilience is what allows the social entrepreneur, to face the natural resistance brought about by misperceptions and mistrust, and to overcome it with energy a vision. This is just what the idea of leadership is about, the skill to project one´s vision to engage others in the common pursuit, changing their behavior to the one adequate to the needs of the task. As Martin (2004) has remarked, "novel practices that unfreeze an unproductive status quo seldom establish themselves voluntarily," (p. 25). This is particularly true of the large-scale social problems, typical of the social entrepreneur endeavors, which require a level of commitment far above that of the common entrepreneur. Leadership reveals thus, as a key tool of the social entrepreneur.

Thus, looking for differentiation in the task of the social entrepreneurs, distinguishing them from the usual entrepreneur, we find it at several levels. Of course in the aims of their endeavors, profit in one case, social transformation in the other. Naturally, in the scope of their undertakings, narrow and focused in one case, broad and large scale in the other. Often in the drivers of their efforts, wealth in one case, a mission to deliver social value in the other. However, certainly not in the combination of skills needed to deliver their task and the nature of the education adequate to get them, except to the requirement of additional levels of leadership in the case of the social entrepreneur.

Hence, except for that characteristic skill, leadership, we shall maintain that the range and scope of the education required, does not depend crucially upon the adjective accompanying the entrepreneur, social or not, but in the requirements of entrepreneurship per se.

HELPING TO UNDERTAKE EDUCATION

As mentioned above, among all the elements that seem to encourage entrepreneurship, education and training of entrepreneurs obtain a clear pride of place (GEM 2013; GEM Special Report, 2008; Barba, 2012; High Impact Entrepreneurship Global Report, 2011, among others). Thus, we can consider that the entrepreneurial activity has one of its supporting pillars in the level of education that is available to the entrepreneur.

In 2008, the GEM Observatory carried out a special report on the issue, proceeding to a review of the existing literature to investigate the sources of entrepreneurial education as well as the effect of this training on the entrepreneurial initiative.

According to the study above, although there is considerable bibliography on entrepreneurship education, social and business, understood as the body of knowledge and skills necessary for the implementation of a business project, most of the studies focus on the evaluation or review of the educational programs themselves. They do not analyze nor try to respond to the questions we have previously formulated.

Little or nothing is known about what is taught in entrepreneurship training programs followed by those people that have provided information for this study, or about 'how' they are taught. Apart from a limited number of previous studies, (e.g., Sexton et al., (1997), one can´t know which part of the agenda of the training is the most valued by the entrepreneurs. (.....) Which lessons or experiences work better for those who receive training. Do they differ from the teachings that received those who developed or not developed into entrepreneurs? (Global Entrepreneurship Monitor Special Report, 2008, p. 51)

We start from the understanding that one of the primary objectives of the social entrepreneurial activity is to generate attractively, long-lasting projects that are able to generate value in social terms, that is, projects able to grow, create jobs, foster innovation and, at the bottom, transform the social reality upon which they act.

Now, from the existing literature on the subject (Alvord, Brown, & Letts, 2004; Fargion, Gevorgianiene, & Lievens, 2011; GEM, 2008; High Impact Entrepreneurship Global Report, 2011; Mottner & Wymer, 2011; Mueller, Chambers, & Neck, 2014; Schoenfeld, McDonald, & Youngblood, 1991; Tracey & Phillips, 2007), one can derive two relevant conclusions:

1. Despite its relevance, the issue of how education and training influence the quality of the entrepreneurship projects undertaken has not received adequate attention. Still less if the projects are social.
2. It has not been discussed in depth whether the orientation of training programs, especially in the higher educational levels, i.e., University and Business Schools, is adequate. That is if materials, content, and knowledge taught are what social entrepreneurs truly need to start their projects; or if there is a "gap" between the approach of education and the needs and expectations of the potential entrepreneurs.

WHAT MOTIVATES PEOPLE TO UNDERTAKE?

Perhaps one of the first aspects on which it is worthwhile to develop further research is the analysis of why a potential social entrepreneur decides to take the plunge and start a venture.

If we analyze the existing literature on the motivations of entrepreneurs, it seems that some aspects as relevant a priori as making money and being your boss are not by themselves sufficient reason to create and develop a business. This is obvious in the case of social entrepreneurs but also applies to business-oriented entrepreneurs (Barba-Sánchez, 2012).

The literature discusses the influence of multiple reasons weighting on entrepreneurs at the time of deciding to undertake. Among those reasons, they include the need for achievement, self-realization, independence, affiliation, competence, sense of power, all of which, together with interest in making money or developing a social project, can decide the implementation of a start-up.

To the above motivations, in the case of social entrepreneurs, we must add, a sense of mission, the willingness to innovate, and the desire to foster systemic change (Martin, 2004; Martin & Osberg, 2007).

Another key element is the availability of the financial resources that are necessary for the establishment of the business, the lack of start-up capital being one of the major obstacles identified by new social entrepreneurs (Dorado, 2006; Hoogendoorn, der Zwan, & Thurik, 2011; Zahra et al., 2009). However, in the majority of cases, the existence of financial support is insufficient by itself, if it is not accompanied by another set of incentives and resources for entrepreneurs, both material and motivational.

Among the resources or determining elements for entrepreneurship, Barba and Atienza (2012) present a key differentiator when it comes to deciding to take the plunge; the sense of confidence that entrepreneurs may have, to deal with the complexities of putting up a project, is revealed as a key component on the decision to undertake. It is noticeable that such confidence keeps building up, based on the knowledge and skills of the entrepreneur.

The High-Impact Entrepreneurship Global Report (2011) reaches the same conclusion, with the received education and training available appearing as key elements when it comes to providing that 'security' entrepreneurs seem to need. The studies carried out within the GEM project also reinforce this circumstance, since they show that individuals who receive entrepreneurship education and feel that they possess the necessary skills to start a new business tend to have higher rates of entrepreneurial activity.

Recent studies that are being conducted in the bosom of the GEM project, reveal that the formal teaching of entrepreneurship provides a gain in the field of entrepreneurial attitudes of the population that can subsequently result in a greater involvement of the same in the process of undertaking and also a benefit in the sense of promoting entrepreneurship of quality. Also, entrepreneurship learning can produce benefits in the pro-activity of employees within any entity or organization, so its implementation is advisable from any point of view" —possession of knowledge and skills to undertake (GEM, 2011, p. 71).

Also, Burke, Fitzroy, and Nolan (2002, p. 21), arrive at the same conclusion, stating, *in this context, education plays a great role in the development of entrepreneurship among individuals.*

Finally, Hemmen et al. (2015), using data from GEM for 34 countries, find that participative leadership and higher education represents the strongest factor in explaining the variance of the current rate of innovative entrepreneurship, this last concept being defined with traits very much implied in what we understand by social entrepreneurship

It seems safe, then, to state that the knowledge, capabilities, and skills that a formal training provide to potential social entrepreneurs may be relevant to their activity. Therefore, knowledge, capabilities, and skills form the first layer of need, the basis of a good social entrepreneurial education. We present this result in Figure 3 below.

CONFIDENCE AND LEADERSHIP OF THE ENTREPRENEUR

We know already that there is a clear relationship between the trust and confidence of the entrepreneur, and his motivation to undertake. Now, our question is the following: to what extent the education received help reinforce the confidence to launch an entrepreneurship project?

Figure 3. The first steps of education for entrepreneurship
Source: Authors

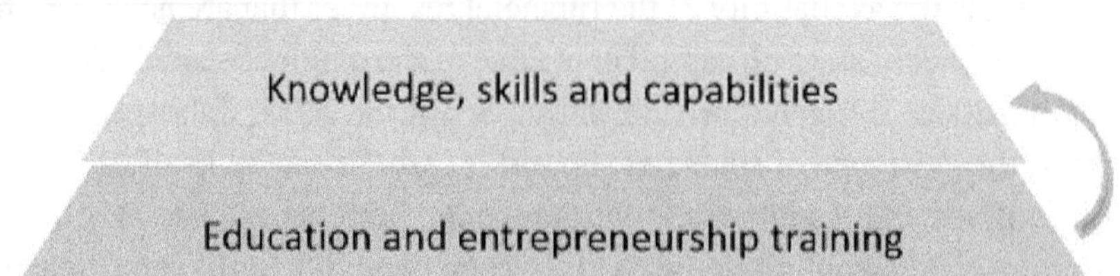

Popular myth saying that entrepreneurs are born, not made, has given way to a widespread consensus implying that the entrepreneurial spirit is a discipline and that just like any other discipline, it can be learned". (Drucker, 1985; Timmons, 2003, cited by ESADE, 2011, p. 19).

In the same line of thought, the "High-Impact Entrepreneurship Global Report" (2011) study, defines a particular group of entrepreneurs, those of "high and medium potential," which encompasses entrepreneurs that create the fastest growing companies, with the higher generation of jobs and value added. Now, this group is made up of those entrepreneurs that possess higher education and training levels, which corresponds to greater knowledge, competencies, skills, and abilities. As already mentioned above, those entrepreneurs acquire greater security and confidence, also lowering their perception of risk and their fear of failure, which predisposes them to take risks and to undertake (Barba & Atienza, 2012).

There are not many studies analyzing this possible correlation from a quantitative point of view, trying to find consistent evidence supporting that business education helps to promote and generate more and better entrepreneurs. De Clerc and Pia Arenius (2006) conducted a representative study, using GEM panel data for Belgium and Finland. They conclude that the probability of participating in entrepreneurship activities is positively correlated with the perception of having specific skills and knowledge to undertake and that this feeling reduces the fear of failure of those potential entrepreneurs and gives them a greater skill to detect opportunities.

Another relevant aspect highlighted by these authors is the positive influence of external experiences, i.e., meeting other entrepreneurs or having had previous experiences as an entrepreneur. In this sense, as analyzed later, it seems that the "knowledge," understood as the base of experiences necessary for the implementation of a project, acquired outside a formal program of education, reveals itself as a very important element for the social entrepreneurs and the success of their projects.

A particular case of the social capabilities so helpful to social entrepreneurs that have been revealed in the literature is their need of extensive networking skills, as required to cope with the complex relations and stakeholders' commitments that result from their management of a dual balance sheet (Sharir & Lerner, 2006; Haugh, 2007). Social entrepreneurs can seldom rely exclusively on external investors and should inspire, impel, mobilize the efforts of a variety of agents, from local governments to donors, volunteers, and partners. Thus the need for networking skills and, in the end, leadership capabilities.

McNally and Kay (2012) point out that in their review of the relevant literature, there are papers that seek to demonstrate a positive relationship between education, knowledge and the willingness to undertake, although there is a gap when the question is to explore the success of those ventures and the quality of their business results. However, after conducting the review of the quantitative literature in the context of the theory of human capital, they found that indeed there occurs a positive correlation between education, the development of human capital and entrepreneurship.

Finally, in the context of his study of the educational requirements in civil service development and public administration reform, a field not that far from social entrepreneurship, Ticlau (2014) finds a set of leadership challenges that impinge on the preparation of public leaders ready to tackle the new complex challenges of efficient and effective public services. He also explores the offerings of the top 5 MBA programs in the world and finds that three of them offer dual degree programs that combine business and public management education as a solution for the leadership challenges that lay ahead.

Now, as we have already noted, not only education but also the experiences are relevant. In this regard, Wennberg (2008) delves into the idea that knowledge and the experience of entrepreneurs are determinants for the survival and success of their business projects. In his model of creation and evolution of new businesses, the author introduces a new variable, speaking not simply of "education to undertake," but rather highlighting training and specific knowledge about the business and it works. These give the entrepreneurs a bonus at the time of launch, helping them significantly to identify possible business opportunities, have the confidence to start their projects and achieve a competitive advantage since this extensive training and experience will determine viability and profitability of the projects. It is thus shown that those firms whose founders have experience and good knowledge, tend to be better companies.

The same author introduces a concept very much relevant for the education of social entrepreneur. This is the concept of "founders with knowledge" whose importance is highlighted by the fact that companies whose founding team has experience and solid expertise, because of their having a previous job in a similar enterprise, have a greater chance of survival (Wennberg 2008, p. 24).

This idea of "founders with knowledge" calls for a deeper understanding of those elements of knowledge and skills acquired through experience and practical knowledge. These appear to be decisive when it comes to developing a prospective social entrepreneur´s ability to identify his field of action, and also feels the confidence of turning it into a viable project of social entrepreneurship with potential, attractive and with greater survival prospects that in other conditions it would have.

Thus, the next step in the building up of our "Pyramid of catalysts for entrepreneurship," must refer to the security and confidence of entrepreneurs, a trait very much linked to the leadership skill we found so important for the success of social entrepreneurship. These traits get strength from their knowledge, skills, and capabilities, and those, in turn, are themselves supported by the training and education received. With the understanding we are referring here not only to formal, normed education but also to education in the broadest sense, both formal and informal, steaming from experiences far away from those obtained in classrooms (figure 4).

THE ACTUAL SITUATION OF THE EDUCATION AND TRAINING FOR ENTREPRENEURSHIP

The generalization of the practice of social entrepreneurship has led to an increase in the numbers of social entrepreneurs that come to the business schools to acquire the competence and skills that they perceived as needed to build sustainable social projects (Tracey & Phillips, 2007).

Figure 4. Leadership, a key component
Source: Author

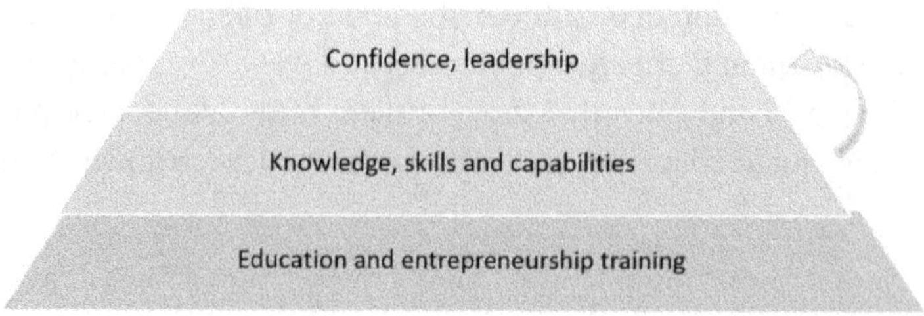

However, from the start, the question arises whether or not the proper location of those studies is within the business schools, as corresponds to their nearness with the entrepreneurial studies, or rather within other studies, more linked to humanities (Wu et al., 2013, p. 331).

From our viewpoint, it is clear that the proximity far exceeds the differences, so that it is best for the social entrepreneur to mingle and share with the kind of problems that they will encounter in developing a project, no matter the intention or the purpose of it.

This is not necessarily a consensus position, however, for there are authors that think that the social entrepreneurship education and the extracurricular activities it entails are not quite connected to the for-profit entrepreneurship being taught at most business schools (Dees, 2005; Austin et al., 2006). It is also true that many of the higher-level business training programs incorporate a traditional vision centered in theoretical knowledge of management, marketing, accounting, human resources, and finance. This generates a wealth of information and teaching material that often does not fit properly with the needs of the students, as future entrepreneurs, social or not, and is not sufficient to respond quickly to the pressing needs of setting up a project (Kohtamaki et al., 2010; Kollmann & Kuckertz, 2010; Siren et al., 2012).

However, we have seen that there is some consensus that it is not sufficient to educate just in knowledge, but that it is also essential to educate and train competences and skills. Among those skills, we can point up the following:

- Competences related to negotiation and networking help entrepreneurs to achieve their goals, and to convince stakeholders on their viability and credibility for success (Alvord et al., 2004; Gorman et al., 1977). Always taking into account that social entrepreneurs, because of the social nature of their endeavors, necessarily have at least one extra stakeholder concerned, namely, the recipients of the fruits of the project being undertaken (Doherty & Thompson, 2006).
- Competences for the management of people and their talent, leadership, given that human resources are limited, especially in a start-up and still more in the case of social projects (Aronsson, 2004; Martin, 2004).
- Creative thinking and the ability to translate that creativity in the continuous supply of new, innovative, processes and structures (Kuckertz et al., 2010).

As referred to in the GEM Special Report (2008, p. 52), *it is likely that education could increase entrepreneurial awareness, self-efficacy and the intention to undertake. However, it has less influence when it comes to increasing the ability to identify business opportunities and alleviate the fear of failure.*

Lastly, notice that the GEM above Special Report refers to the growing importance of informal training, as a means to compensate for the shortcomings of formal education.

The discovery that formal and informal training overlap implies that formal training may provide a basis, but that many people need specific knowledge and skills, perhaps when they begin to consider undertaking or have already started to do so. Profitable sources of training, as the self- study and programs based on Internet websites, constitute a way of responding to such needs. Entrepreneurs might consider access to these sources - or even to supply them with resources. GEM Special Report (2008, p. 53).

To develop this potential in the education for social entrepreneurship, we suggest some elements that educational institutions not always identify as "relevant", but which seem to be differential at the time of conveying and nurturing into the, potential social entrepreneurs, the original motivation that led them to start a path of social transformation and social value generation.

One of these elements we have shown to be the personal experiences; hence, the importance of having a faculty with a past of involvement in projects in social sectors and non-for profit ventures, so that they be able to pass those personal experiences to their students. It seems clear that such an interaction benefits the attitude and the interest of students about social entrepreneurship (Dees, 2005).

Perhaps more important in the case of social entrepreneurship is the "active" approach that relies on experiential learning methods, actual confrontation with real-world problems and hands-on involvement in the supply of public goods and community development projects (Martin, 2004; Gundlach & Zivnuska, 2010).

However short of a full commitment to an experiential learning method, the view that seeks to combine theoretical work with practical experiences is shared by the most relevant business schools involved in social entrepreneurship teaching, as they ensure that their faculty combines its research and teaching with consulting assignments. On the other hand, they also include among their part-time teaching faculty, social entrepreneurs and non-for profit institution managers.

We conclude that the security and confidence achieved by the entrepreneur, based on knowledge, skills, and capabilities, reinforces its potential entrepreneurial attitude, acting as an engine that gives an impulse to the starting of a project. Figure 5 shows this added building block of an effective social entrepreneurial education.

THE COMPREHENSIVE TRAINING

We have concluded that being a social entrepreneur encompasses much more than having an idea for developing a social project and get funding to start it up. It takes a series of knowledge, capabilities and specific skills. Some of them may be skills and abilities to take risks, innovate and manage people. Others consist of specific knowledge in administration, personnel management, marketing, and especially, economic knowledge, finances, and costs.

Figure 5. Building-up attitudes
Source: Authors

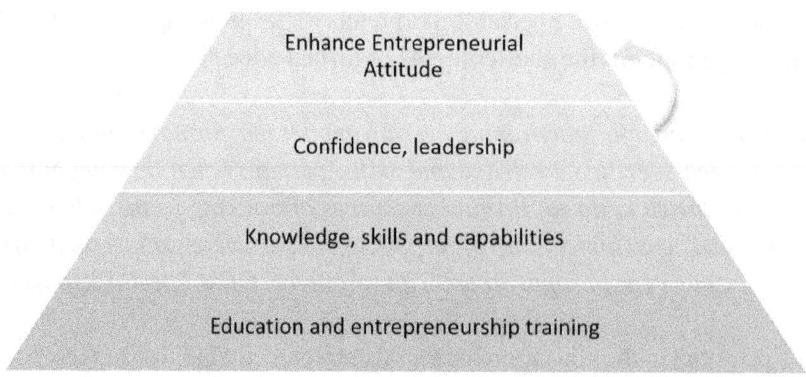

This follows a tradition coming back to Schumpeter, more than 50 years ago, that proposes that the future entrepreneurs and business managers need a holistic training, i.e., comprehensive and action-oriented training in all areas that will prove to be necessary to carry forward their projects. Entrepreneurs need to learn how to act in a complex and diverse environment, ever more changing nowadays. Figure 6 captures this intuition.

At this point, we can refer to Toca Torres (2010), that makes a distinction that seems relevant for understanding the type of education that social entrepreneurs seem to require. In her view, we can distinguish between two types of education, and one would be business education, meaning by "business," projects or activities relative to firms already underway or consolidated or, we may say, about social needs untended or social projects under review. On the other hand, education for entrepreneurship more oriented to the implementation of new social initiatives that seem to require another set of knowledge and abilities.

For Levenburg (2006), successfully starting a project requires mastering a combination of skills that are different from those needed to run a concern already established and operative. Different learning processes are needed, not only knowledge and tools, but also skills in communication, negotiation, opportunity recognition, leadership, networking, time management, and so on.

It certainly seems that both types of education should share some curricula, such as finance, accounting, marketing, business strategy, operations, management of people, and so on. However, in the particular case of social entrepreneurs, the combination of these elements seems to require a specific design, as well as a specific set of skills and capabilities, that may be not that important for success in already functioning, consolidated projects.

It is a fact that the vast majority of textbooks being used by students with the potential to be future social entrepreneurs, tends to incorporate the classic version of this knowledge and tools, but generally, do not consider many of the needs arising from the emerging business. More recently, Kozlinska (2011) insists in the same idea, proposing to jump over the traditional education systems to focus on the development of practical experiences by the students, centering their educational process in the so-called "Experiential Learning Theory," a methodology in which experience breads knowledge.

Figure 6. The comprehensive training
Source: Authors

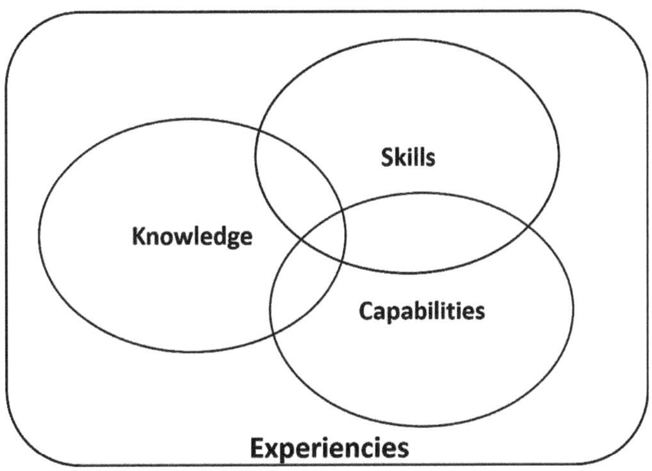

We can say, therefore, that for the design of an education geared specifically to social entrepreneurship, the appropriate combination of content will have a decisive impact on the strengthening of the entrepreneurial attitude of the educated people, improving their ability to identify real opportunities, decreasing the chances of failure and increasing the potential of the initiatives put in place. Always with the understanding, that the sum of knowledge + skills + abilities + experiences form the basis for such content. Figure 6, before, captures this broad view, that also informs our capping up of the Pyramid of Catalysts for Entrepreneurship model.

CONCLUSION

At the beginning of the paper, we referred to the professor Patrick Liles' theory. Back in the 1970s, he alerted about the prospects of marginal companies, which were created with the limited objective of providing average jobs, but that did not have the attributes necessary to make them attractive companies, with potential and long-lasting, due to the limitations of their inceptors.

Unfortunately, forty years later prof. Liles approach is still fully in force, since focusing in the field of social entrepreneurship, the vast majority of the new transformational projects tend to be marginal, frequently serving just the self-employment needs of their leaders and doomed to a limited horizon and a short life expectancy.

Through the model of the Pyramid of catalysts for entrepreneurship, we have been able to delve into the transmission mechanism through which an adequate, social entrepreneurship-oriented education, promotes the starting up of more and best social initiatives.

Figure 7. The pyramid of catalysts for entrepreneurship model
Source: Authors

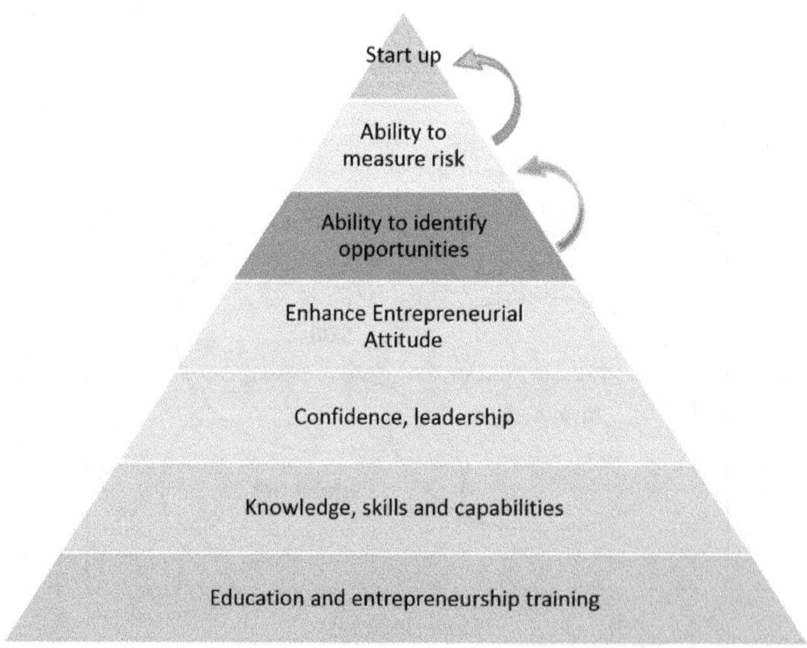

This educational process must contain a specific combination of knowledge, skills, and abilities, different from those present in most managerial curricula. These allow a fostering of social entrepreneurship by increasing the security and confidence of entrepreneurs. Through that mixture of skills and abilities´ building, with the right amounts of formal academic knowledge, social entrepreneurs develop a greater capacity to identify the soundest transformational projects, develop a hands-on approach to their involvement and lean to evaluate the risk and opportunities associated to any social entrepreneurship venture.

REFERENCES

Abu-Saifan, S. (2012). Social Entrepreneurship: Definition and Boundaries. *Technology Innovation Management Review*, *2*(2), 22–27. doi:10.22215/timreview/523

Alvord, S., Brown, D., & Letts, C. (2004). Social entrepreneurship and societal transformation. *The Journal of Applied Behavioral Science*, *40*(3), 260–282. doi:10.1177/0021886304266847

Barba, V., & Atienza, C. (2012). Entrepreneurial behavior: Impact of motivation factors on the decision to create a new venture. *Investigaciones Europeas de Dirección y Economía de la Empresa*, *18*(12), 132–138. doi:10.1016/S1135-2523(12)70003-5

Burke, A., Fitzroy, F., & Nolan, M. (2009). Is there a North-South divide in Self-employment in England? *Regional Studies*, *43*(4), 529–544. doi:10.1080/00343400701827360

Coduras, A., Levie, J., Kelley, D.J., & Sam. (2006). *Global Entrepreuneurship Monitor Special Report: Una perspectiva global sobre la educación y la formación emprendedora*. Madrid: Global Entrepreneurship Monitor.

De Clerc, D., & Arenius, P. (2006). The Role of Knowledge in Business Start-up Activity. *International Small Business Journal*, *24*(4), 339–358. doi:10.1177/0266242606065507

Dees, J. G. (2005). Social entrepreneurship and education. *Current Issues in Comparative Education*, *8*(1), 51–55.

Doherty, B., & Thompson, J. (2006). The diverse world of social enterprise. *International Journal of Social Economics*, *33*(5/6), 361–375. doi:10.1108/03068290610660643

Dorado, S. (2006). Social entrepreneurial ventures: Different values so different process of creation? *Journal of Developmental Entrepreneurship*, *11*(4), 319–343. doi:10.1142/S1084946706000453

Fargion, S., Gevorgianiene, V., & Lievens, P. (2011). Developing entrepreneurship in social work through international education. Reflections on a European intensive program. *The International Journal of Entrepreneurship Education*, *30*(8), 964–980.

Fossen, F. M., & Bütner, T. J. M. (2013). The returns to education for opportunity entrepreneurs, necessity entrepreneurs, and paid employees. *Economics of Education Review*, *37*(1), 68–84.

GEM. (2013). *Global Entrepreneurship Monitor España, 2012 y 2013*. Madrid, Spain: GEM.

Gundlach, M., & Zivnuska, S. (2010). An experiential learning approach to teaching social entrepreneurship, triple bottom line, and sustainability: Modifying and extending practical organizational behavior education. *American Journal of Business Education*, *3*(1), 19–29. doi:10.19030/ajbe.v3i1.364

Haugh, H. (2007). Community-led social venture creation. *Entrepreneurship Theory and Practice*, *31*(2), 161–182. doi:10.1111/j.1540-6520.2007.00168.x

Hemmen, S. (2015). Leadership styles and innovative entrepreneurship: An international study. *Cybernetics and Systems*, *46*(3-4), 271–286. doi:10.1080/01969722.2015.1012896

Hoogendoorn, B., der Zwan, P., & Thurik, R. (2011). *Social entrepreneurship and performance: The role of perceived barriers and risk. ERIM Report Series Research in Management. ERS-2011-016-ORG.* Rotterdam: Erasmus Research Institute of Management.

Irwin, R. (1978). New Business Ventures and the Entrepreneur. *American Journal of Small Business*, *37*(1), 160–168.

James, C. (2001). Social entrepreneurs. *Management.*, *10*, 58–67.

Kozlinska, I. (2011). Contemporary approaches to entrepreneurship education. *Journal of Business and Management*, *4*(1), 205–220.

Kuckertz, A. (2011). Entrepreneurship education. Status quo and prospective developments. *Journal of Entrepreneuship Education*, *16*(1), 59–71.

Kuckertz, A., Kollmann, T., & Krell, P. (2012). *Opportunity Recognition Propensity and Actual Opportunity Exploitation–Two Validated Scales.* Paper presented at the 16 Forum Gründungsforschung, Potsdam, Germany.

Lanero, A., Vázquez, J. L., Gutiérrez, P., & García, M. (2011). Evaluación de la conducta emprendedora en estudiantes universitarios. Implicaciones para el diseño de programas académicos. *Pecvnia. Universidad de León.*, *12*(1), 219–243.

Liles, P. R. (1977). New business ventures and the entrepreneur. *Harvard Business Review*, *5*(1), 184–193.

Liñán, F., Rodriguez-Cohard, J. C., & Rueda-Cantuche, J. M. (2011). Factors affecting entrepreneurial intention levels: A role for education. *The International Entrepreneurship and Management Journal*, *7*(2), 195–218. doi:10.100711365-010-0154-z

Lusardi, A., & Mitchell, O. (2007). Financial literacy and retirement preparedness: Evidence and implications for financial education. The problems are serious, and the remedies are not simple. *Business Economics (Cleveland, Ohio)*, *1*(1), 35–44. doi:10.2145/20070104

Martin, B., McNally, J., & Kay, M. (2013). Examining the formation of human capital in entrepreneurship: A meta-analysis of entrepreneurship education outcomes. *Journal of Business Venturing*, *28*(2), 211–224. doi:10.1016/j.jbusvent.2012.03.002

Martin, M. (2004). *Surveying Social Entrepreneurship: Toward an Empirical Analysis of the Performance Revolution in the Social Sector.* Available at SSRN: http://ssrn.com/abstract=1319499

Martin, R. L., & Osberg, S. (2007). Social Entrepreneurship: The Case for Definition. *Stanford Social Innovation Review*, *18*(1), 1–16.

Morris, R. (2011). *High Impact Entrepreneurship*. London, UK: Global Report Center for High Impact Entrepreneurship Endeavor and GEM.

Mottner, S., & Wymer, W. (2011). Non-profit education: Course offering and perceptions in accredited US business schools. *Journal of Nonprofit & Public Sector Marketing*, *23*(1), 1–19. doi:10.1080/10495142.2010.508207

Mueller, S., Chambers, L., & Neck, H. (2014). The Distinctive Skills of Social Entrepreneurs. *Journal of Enterprising Culture*, *21*(3), 301–334. doi:10.1142/S0218495813500131

Ployhart, R. E., & Moliterno, T. P. (2011). Emergence of the Human Capital Resource: A Multilevel Model. *Academy of Management Review*, *36*(1), 127–150. doi:10.5465/amr.2009.0318

Pongracz, E. (2014). Education as a key factor in the development of social entrepreneurship. In *13th. International Academic Conference, Antibes, Proceedings*. Prague: International Institute of Social and Economic Sciences.

Prats, J., & Agulles, R. (2009). Competencias que todo emprendedor debería desarrollar. Algo más que intuición para los negocios. *IESE Business Insight*, *2*, 50–57.

Sharir, M., & Lerner, M. (2006). Gauging the success of social ventures initiated by individual social entrepreneurs. *Journal of World Business*, *41*(1), 6–20. doi:10.1016/j.jwb.2005.09.004

Ticlau, T. C. (2014). Contemporary business education: A solution for global leadership challenges. *Anfiteatur Economic*, *16*(37), 885–901.

Toca, C. (2010). Consideraciones para la formación en emprendimiento: Explorando nuevos ámbitos y posibilidades. *Estudios Gerenciales*, *26*(4), 41–60.

Tracey, P., & Phillips, N. (2007). The distinctive challenge of educating social entrepreneurs: A postscript and rejoinder to the special issue on entrepreneurship education. *Computers in Human Behavior*, *16*(2), 264–271.

Van Praag, C. M., & Van der Sluis, J. (2004). Economic returns to education for entrepreneurs: The development of a neglected child in the family of the economics of education? *Swedish Economic Policy Review*, *11*(2), 183–225.

Velamuri, S. R., & Venkataraman, S. (2004). An empirical study of the transition from paid work to self-employment. *The Journal of Entrepreneurial Finance*, *10*(1), 1–16.

Vesper, K. (1979). Growing concerns. *Harvard Business Review*, *2*, 164–170.

Wennberg, K. (2009). Knowledge combinations and the survival of financial services ventures. *Journal of Evolutionary Economics*, *19*(2), 259–276. doi:10.100700191-008-0124-6

White Paper on Entrepreneurship in Spain. (2011). Barcelona, Spain: ESADE Business School.

Wu, Y. C., Kuo, T., & Shen, J. P. (2013). Exploring social entrepreneurship education from a web-based pedagogical perspective. *Computers in Human Behavior*, *29*(2), 329–334. doi:10.1016/j.chb.2012.08.012

Zahra, S. A., Rawhouser, H. N., Bhawe, N., Neubaumm, D. O., & Hayton, J. C. (2008). Globalization of social entrepreneurship opportunities. *Strategic Entrepreneurship Journal*, *2*(2), 117–131. doi:10.1002ej.43

KEY TERMS AND DEFINITIONS

Comprehensive Training: It is a type of training composed of a combination of knowledge, skills, and capabilities.

Entrepreneur: It is a person endowed of creation and the capacity of taking risks to add value to both the market and the firm.

Entrepreneurial Attitudes: It is a group of attitudes rooted in confidence, leadership, knowledge, skills, capabilities, education, and training.

Experiential Learning Theory: It is formed by the union of knowledge, skills, abilities, and experiences.

Genuine Opportunity: A sort of opportunities defined by being real, viable, and socially profitable.

Global Entrepreneurship Monitor: This is the most important international organization focused on entrepreneurship-related studies worldwide.

Social Entrepreneurship: It consists of a type of entrepreneurship focused on social change.

ENDNOTE

1. This chapter was also published in Saiz-Álvarez, J.M. (Ed.)(2016). *Handbook of Research on Social Entrepreneurship and Solidarity Economics*, Hershey, PA: IGI Global. DOI: 10.4018/978-1-5225-0097-1.ch010.

Chapter 6
Social Entrepreneurship and Its Competences: Implications for Higher Education

Sue Rossano
Münster University of Applied Sciences, Germany

Thomas Baaken
Münster University of Applied Sciences, Germany

Balzhan Orazbayeva
Münster University of Applied Sciences, Germany

Marieke C. Baaken
Georg-August-Universität Göttingen, Germany & RUG Rijksuniversiteit Groningen, The Netherlands

Bert Kiel
Münster University of Applied Sciences, Germany

Gideon Johannes Pieter Maas
Coventry University, UK

ABSTRACT

Entrepreneurship needs a vision and leadership skills to accomplish it and a motivation to build something new, which will develop and sustain it. And society needs social entrepreneurs, contributing to a new organization of the welfare system, while making a difference and helping each other. The central theme in the existing social entrepreneurship literature is the pursuit of a social mission or objective. Thus, social entrepreneurs play a role as reformers and revolutionaries, who are intending to solve social problems, and not being answered by governmental policies. Entrepreneurial thinking and acting as well as innovation driving managers is a need for society. However, it is not the organization but the people, united by a proactive and market-driven culture, that are innovative and which combine to populate and to equip the organization with the required competencies. The chapter proposes a methodology to analyze the competencies that should be fostered by higher education programs to provide graduates with the desired competencies for entrepreneurship and driving innovation.

DOI: 10.4018/978-1-5225-8939-6.ch006

INTRODUCTION[1]

Social entrepreneurship has gained popularity and support. Its popularity is reflected in the number of management and scholarly literature devoted to the topic (e.g., Chell, 2007; Chell et al., 2010; Dees and Anderson, 2006; Nicholls, 2010; Shaw and de Bruin, 2013, Sullivan Mort et al. 2003). In spite of the popularity of the field, there still remain questions with respect to the role of higher education in developing a solid set of skills among students as future social entrepreneurs and innovators. (Short et al., 2009)

Organizations such as the World Economic Forum (WEF) and the Organisation for Economic Co-operation and Development (OECD) have expressed concerns on the need for bridging the skills gap between what higher education systems nurture and what the society needs (Spear et al., 2013).

Social abilities such as coordinating with others and persuasion, as well as complex problem-solving skills, agility, and resiliency are essential in our society and the knowledge-based economy of the near future.

The question becomes whether a continued implementation of traditional approaches to learning is going to be helpful for students to be prepared for the economy and society in which they will have to operate. For today's entrepreneurs, the greater challenge is to reverse key negative trends that preceded current challenges, such as rising inequalities, lack of social responsibility among market actors, and reliance on public budgets to deal with the consequences (Waring, 2018). In this respect, the role of universities is perceived as going beyond preparing students to meet the demands of the labor market (Pavlin et al., 2014). Following Teichler (2013, p. 422) graduates additionally need to be trained to deal with the uncertainties created by the threat (and sometimes the actuality) of changing environmental conditions, such as economic, social and/or political crises. This fact situates universities as mediating structures for the creative process of social entrepreneurship in linking the means for entrepreneurship (e.g., entrepreneurial competences) with its end-goals (e.g., wealth creation, value creation) (Bowen, 2018).

A core contribution of the present article hereby lies on relating the competences for entrepreneurship at the individual level, with the environmental level, particularly with the environmental change in the light of social entrepreneurship. The underlying drive for social entrepreneurship is the creation of social value as opposed to personal or shareholder wealth (Noruzi, et al., 2010; Thake and Zadek, 1997) and the activity of such social value creation is characterized by pattern-breaking change or innovation (Munshi, 2010; Noruzi et al., 2010, p. 4), through the creation of new combinations (Defourny and Nyssens, 2010).

Hence, it is argued in the present chapter that social entrepreneurs need to possess a certain set of competences that have been proved to help organizations to thrive in times of uncertainty and rapid change, particularly in an era of constant innovation. These competences relate to agility, resilience, and leadership for collaboration that need to be developed through entrepreneurship education. The development of these competences forms the basis of a new paradigm in Higher Education concerning entrepreneurship education. (Bowen, 2018, Le Deist, 2009).

In the chapter, this set of competences is presented. Agility refers to the ability to respond and adapt to change quickly, is an increasingly crucial factor when facing innovation. Sambamurthy et al. (2003, p. 238) defined agility as "the ability to detect and seize market opportunities with speed and surprise." Resiliency is understood, in the context of this article as "the capacity for resisting, absorbing and responding, even reinventing if required, in response to fast change that cannot be avoided" (McCann et al., 2009, p. 45). Finally, leaders' pursuit of innovation in an environment of change is not done in isolation. This endeavor requires motivating and engaging highly qualified people that will thrive in times of uncertainty. Therefore, leadership for collaboration is the capacity of a leader to set a context for co-innovation and co-creation by providing venues for discussion, communication, and collaboration among employees and business partners. (Thorgren and Omorede, 2015)

Social Innovation and Social Entrepreneurship Skills

Entrepreneurship needs a vision, leadership skills to accomplish it and a motivation to build something new, which will develop and sustain; it also demands "talent, temperament and technique" (Thompson, 2000, p.331). Society needs social innovation and social entrepreneurs, who will contribute to the new organization of the welfare system, while making a difference, doing good, and helping each other (Lundström, 2014; Thompson et al., 2000). The central theme in the existing social entrepreneurship literature is the pursuit of a social mission or objective (Phillips et al. 2015). This need for modernization of the institutional systems requires having social innovators and Entrepreneurs. Social Entrepreneurs are Entrepreneurs, who immerse themselves in different activities with the motive to tackle an arising social problem; their actions are not perceived as doing a charity work, but as establishing a long-term vision for the enhancement of the social well-being (Dees, 2007; Sastre-Castillo et al., 2015, Bilán, et al., 2005). Thus, the social entrepreneurs play the role of reformers and revolutionaries who are, who would like to solve social problems, not being entirely solved by different governmental, philanthropic, or commercial organizations, via undertaking fundamental or systematic strategies to solve them (Shek and Lin, 2015).

There is no single definition for a social entrepreneur accepted in the literature, since it can be observed through divergent perspectives and applied in various areas (Dacin and Dacin, 2011, Harding, 2004, Mair and Martí, 2006, Weerawardena and Sullivan, 2006).

Social entrepreneurs are presented as "individuals or organizations engaged in entrepreneurial activities with a social goal" (Bosma and Amoros, 2013, Samer Abu-Saifan, 2012, p.25) presents an own definition, after examining the existing literature: "The social entrepreneur is a mission-driven individual who uses a set of entrepreneurial behaviors to deliver a social value to the less privileged, all through an entrepreneurially oriented entity that is financially independent, self-sufficient, or sustainable."

In his book "The rise of the social entrepreneur," Leadbeater (1997) examines the profile of the social entrepreneurs concerning their competences, motives, and drivers. The author depicts them as "the most important sources of innovation" (Leadbeater, 1997, p.2) since they are the people, who find a creative solution regarding how to use underutilized resources to tackle a social problem or social need. Leadbeater explains the term social entrepreneur, by addressing two aspects "social" and "entrepreneurial." First, social entrepreneurs are entrepreneurial; they know how to use resources to meet a market needs; they are motivated, charismatic, and innovative; Second social entrepreneurs are social and not solely directed by profit or shareholder value, rather they are following a mission. The social aspect is characterized by achieving innovations in the field of welfare, healthcare system, and the well-being of the society. They may use social capital (relationships, based on trust and cooperation) as assets; their innovations are part of the civil society. Nicholls et al. (2012) profile the social entrepreneurs, giving insights about which competences they need; the list is also complemented with other authors, research in this field:

- **Entrepreneurial**: Know where they can employ discarded resources to satisfy a social need. They also know how to find the resources needed (Thompson et al., 2000) and are ready to use different tools, as long as they work (Dees, 2007)

- **Innovative**: Find unconventional approaches concerning creating new products and services to solve a social problem
- **Transformatory:** They revolutionize the organizations that they lead through creativity and dynamics; additionally, they tolerate the usage of different operational and business models, as they adapt ideas and tools, used in them (Dees, 2007)
- **Leadership:** Social entrepreneurs possess all leadership skills; they know how to set their mission/purpose and how to activate and motivate the people around them for achieving even more than what was set as a goal on the first place. Thompson et al., 2000) complement that they are also ambitious and driven people.
- **Storytelling:** Social entrepreneurs, have to know how to communicate their mission to their followers and the rest of the world; they must be compelling and convincing while telling their stories
- **Managing and Working With People**: Social innovators work with people and opportunities, that is why they should know how to appreciate their most valuable resource – the people; they should be good at recruiting, managing, and communicating with people. Light (2009) mentions that even though social entrepreneurs can work individually, they gain more successful results when applying team-work.
- **Visionary**: Social entrepreneurs have a vision and communicate it with moral terms; they are opportunistic, but still realistic about the social innovation challenges that they face (also supported by Thompson et al., 2000)
- **Alliance Building**: They are good at networking and cooperating, since they realize that the own resources that they have at their disposal are not enough to tackle the chosen issues (Adomavičiūtė et al., 2012; Leadbeater, 1997); they are described as "ideological chameleons" by Leadbeater (1997, p. 56), since they are open-minded and flexible enough to work with partners from different political groups, institutional organizations, etc.; they know when they should be compassionate and when critical about a certain issue. Thompson et al. (2000) add that social entrepreneurs rely on trust and credibly when establishing their network.
- **Independence:** This competence could be seen both from a positive and a negative aspect; social entrepreneurs do not like the cumbersome bureaucracy and having constraints posed by any committees; at the same time this quality of theirs encourages their innovative thinking and makes them think out of the box
- **Understanding and Managing risk** (Thompson et al., 2000): Social entrepreneurs have to know how to estimate the risks that they take and how to possible decrease them and handle problematic issues, such as not enough financial resources
- **Technological Skills**: It is useful if social entrepreneurs do possess relevant technical skills, which can additionally contribute to their intention to do good for the society (Chavez et al., 2016; Thompson et al., 2000)

Are social entrepreneurs born or made? Talent, temperament, and technique are needed in all field of entrepreneurship (Thompson et al., 2000). The authors claim that some the entrepreneurs have a natural talent, but still appropriate training and development are necessary to help achieve the goal set. Moreover, other people have the potential for entrepreneurship, but their talent needs to be spotted and released, explain the authors. There are also leaders, who, however, are lacking the risk-taking abilities and do not have a vision for true entrepreneurship. Drucker also considers that most people have the potential to learn how to be entrepreneurs (Bornstein and Davis, 2010). Thus, Thompson et al. (2000)

share that entrepreneurs do need training in disciplines, such as finance, technologies, marketing. Smith and Woodworth (2012) also support the idea of training the skills needed for social entrepreneurship and proposes an identity approach via which the students at universities can become members in a social entrepreneurship community.

In addition to those findings, the following paragraphs will address entrepreneurial competences from a structured and new perspective, looking at agility, resiliency, and leadership as well as personal attitudes.

Entrepreneurial Competences for Today's Social Entrepreneurs

Agility

Doz and Kosonen (2010) provided a framework for strategic agility and corresponding leadership actions. They determined three main meta-capabilities that make an organization more agile: (1) strategic sensitivity, which is the awareness of and attention to strategic developments; (2) leadership unity, defined as the ability of the top decision-makers to make bold, fast decisions; and (3) resource fluidity, the capability to reconfigure capabilities and redeploy resources rapidly.

On his side, Mukerjee (2014) concluded that agility is "the ability to quickly respond and adapt to change," is an increasingly crucial factor when facing innovation. Sambamurthy et al. (2003, p. 238) defined agility as "the ability to detect and seize market opportunities with speed and surprise." Further, Mukerjee (2014) and Sambamurthy et al. (2003) stated that agility depends on three interrelated capabilities of customer agility, partnering agility, and operational agility. Operational agility means the ability of a firm to achieve speed, accuracy, and cost efficiency while addressing innovation opportunities quickly and competing effectively using the firm's business processes. Customer agility means the ability to relate to customers in such a way that their valuable input for product innovation is harnessed. Partnering agility is an organization's ability to make the best use of its partnerships with stakeholders (Sambamurthy et al., 2003, Caligiuri 2013).

To achieve organizational agility, Kotter (2012) proposed to set up a second operating system, which consists of an agile, network structure and an adapted set of business processes. Due to its characteristics, it should be able to assess the business continually and to respond with great agility. He added that many start-ups are organized as networks and offered more information on the second operating system by emphasizing that a level of individualism, creativity, and innovation could be achieved that not even the least bureaucratic hierarchy could provide. It requires the breakup of silo structures and hierarchical layers for information and knowledge to be shared with greater freedom and speed. To facilitate such an operating system, Kotter (2012) proposed eight accelerators: processes that enable the strategy network to work.

Resiliency

Gilbert et al. (2012) agreed that a two-track approach to transformation is best in a world characterized by innovation to achieve what they call 'organizational resiliency.' Their approach consists of reshaping/reinventing the core model and discovering a future business model. It is similar to Kotter's approach. Gilbert et al. (2012) stated that the objective of the 'reshape' form of transformation is to find the strongest competitive advantage your current model can sustain in the disrupted marketplace, while the objective of the 'discover' form of transformation is the discovery of a separate, new business model with its profit formula to develop innovations for future success.

McCann et al. explained that an adaptive capacity includes the important dimensions of agility and resiliency. "Organizations must build agility and resiliency to perform effectively." (McCann et al., 2009, p. 45). If a firm focuses on one dimension without investing in the other, it will result in an unstable business model, which will either be efficient or else be agile but delicate and costly. McCann et al. define agility as, "the capacity for moving quickly, flexibly and decisively in anticipating, initiating and taking advantage of opportunities and avoiding any negative consequences of change" (McCann et al., 2009, p. 45). Resiliency has been defined as, "the capacity for resisting, absorbing and responding, even reinventing if required, in response to fast change that cannot be avoided" (McCann et al., 2009, p. 45). Resiliency, as the robustness of the system, requires common values, purposes and shared beliefs. McCann et al. demonstrated with their results that both agility and resiliency have significant positive correlations with their performance measures.

In 2008, Raisch and Birkingshaw introduced the term 'organizational ambidexterity', meaning the ability of a firm to efficiently perform management of its business demands while at the same time adapting to changes. They emphasized the importance of senior executives in supporting ambidexterity. Building upon Raisch and Birkingshaw's concept, Prange and Schlegelmilch (2010) distinguished four coordination designs permitting organizations to engage in seemingly incompatible things simultaneously. They distinguished between structural ambidexterity: "Organizations may resolve the tension between exploration and exploitation by separating them into different parts of the firm" (Prange and Schlegelmilch, 2010, p. 48); contextual ambidexterity: "Ambidexterity also emerges when leaders, though not necessarily top managers, develop a supportive context" (Prange and Schlegelmilch, 2010, p. 48); punctuated ambidexterity: "Ambidexterity can also relate to business units, focusing on one type of innovation one day, and on a different set of innovations at another point in time" (Prange and Schlegelmilch, 2010, p. 48); and ambidexterity: "Another variant of ambidexterity is borrowed from genetics where the formation of a new species has often been tied to the idea of a founder who develops a new population" (Prange and Schlegelmilch, 2010, p. 48).

Leadership (In Collaboration)

In an economy where the creativity and talent of individuals are the main sources of innovation, all forms of recruiting, motivating and leading people do not work. Leaders must harness engaged communities of innovators; therefore skills for collaboration are crucial for the necessary leadership on an innovation-based economy.

Collaboration is a key element of innovation and entrepreneurship. Tapscott and Williams (2010, p. 63-64) highlight the role of the leader as responsible for setting a context for co-innovation and co-creation by providing venues for discussion and collaboration. Thus, leaders must develop a set of skills that can enable, employees and collaborators, to communicate and co-innovate. In addition Ernest et al. stated (2015) that [...] entrepreneurial competences are often psychological or social skills, not skills specific to a business or an academic sector, successful entrepreneurs are able to convince and inspire the required network members into reaching shared goals [...] (Ernest et al., 2015).

Within the literature on business innovation, "collaboration" is also one of the major success factors. Using a Delphi model, Lin and Hsia (2011) identified thirteen core capabilities for business innovation in three main areas; within the area of "collaboration," the core capabilities are:

1. Developing partnerships
2. Governing the value network
3. Enabling open innovation
4. Improving co-production and co-creating value

In this same line, cooperative business forms, including strategic value-added partnerships, networks and cross-company project orientated cooperation, need to foster a higher degree of "relational capacity" (Gassman and Enkel, 2004), where the leader requires highly-developed interpersonal, communication and management skills.

With the increased relevance of competences for an innovation-based economy, the relevant goals of teaching in higher educational institutes must include supporting students think and act in entrepreneurial and social ways (the entrepreneurial and social mindset) (Lawrence et al., 2012), and the mastery of competences endemic to this kind of thinking and acting (Morris and Kaplan, 2014; Wilson et al., 2007).

INDIVIDUAL COMPETENCES

An analysis of the Chartered Institute of Personnel and Development (CIPD) has shown that more than fifty percent of UK-based businesses use 'competency-based interviews' when recruiting managers (Robinson et al., 2007). "Job skills and experience combined have less impact on success than having the right set of competences" (Fleit, 2013). She remarked that half of the performance of successful marketing managers could be explained by their competences, followed by motivation and job experience. Tynan and Lee added that "Society at large is re-evaluating the types of skills and competences that graduates need to possess to be adequately prepared for work and life in the knowledge age" (Tynan and Lee, 2009, p 98.). Tynan et al. (2008) asked higher education institutions to react to these insights.

In addition Ernest et al. stated (2015) that "[…] entrepreneurial competences are often psychological or social skills, not skills specific to a business or an academic sector, successful entrepreneurs are able to convince and inspire the required network members into reaching shared goals […]" (Ernest et al., 2015).

Such insights are not new: Baaken (2002) stated that employers of graduates from higher education institutions require more than just professional expertise. While previously the level of professional expertise might have been the most decisive factor for the success of a job application, HR managers nowadays ask candidates to possess strategic competences, such as problem-solving ability, creativity, decisiveness, and interpersonal communication ability. (Mandyoli, 2016) Mansfield (2004) added that there is an increasing demand for 'multi-skilled workers,' who can adapt quickly to changing demands and changing work organizations.

Since business sectors are emphasizing the importance of competences in talent management, the education sector has agreed to align higher education programmes with the needs of the labor market (Mulder et al., 2009, Rausch et al., 2002). Teaching has evolved from a teacher-oriented lecture in which the participants are more or less passive learners, towards a more student-oriented activity in which participants are more active in the experience of learning (Kennedy et al., 2001). Norris (2013) remarked that the higher education sector is in a period of change. It has been developing from a factory model, which was characterized by a teacher focus, a focus on throughputs and outputs, seat time and little flexibility, towards an outcome-focused, learner-centric, just-in-time, personalized form of unbundled learning experiences. Christensen and Eyring (2011) recommended that higher education should use ICT technology as an enabler of innovation to transform their business models.

Morris and Kaplan (2014) declared that the relevant goals of teaching in higher educational institutes must include helping students think and act in entrepreneurial ways (the entrepreneurial mindset), and the mastery of competences endemic to this kind of thinking and acting. (also Miller et al., 2012)

With the European Qualification Framework (EQF), a competency framework for the European Union, "competence [itself] is described regarding responsibility and autonomy." Furthermore, it is defined as "the proven ability to use knowledge, skills and personal, social and/or methodological abilities, in work or study situations and professional and personal development (European Qualifications Framework, 2014).

However, Winterton (2009) remarked that in Europe there is no consensus for using a common competence definition or model. In contrast to the English National Qualification framework, which does apply a 'narrow' concept of competences based on work activities and task-based skills, French, Dutch and German national competence systems instead have conceived of competence in the sense of a more broadly defined occupational capacity (Brockmann et al., 2009).

KODE CHANGES IN THE PARAMETERS OF HIGHER EDUCATION AND THE ERPENBECK'S DIAGNOSTIC SYSTEM

The literature review highlighted the broad and still on-going scientific discussion about skills and competences for entrepreneurship and innovation. Some insights have been revealed. First of all, there is broad evidence that agility is an increasingly crucial factor in the field. Moreover, it has been underlined that about the concept of resiliency, two arguments apply. On the one hand, routines and ingrained habits may create 'competency traps,' on the other hand, there is a consensus that organizations require resiliency in addition to agility, sometimes also referred to as ambidexterity, to be successful. What, remains is to address these competences within a framework of Higher Education to develop them.

Over the last decades, the parameters of higher education have undergone several major changes – not only in Germany. The globalization of the economy, the shift from a manufacturing-based to an information-based society, as well as the development of new media and communication technologies have led to significant changes in the workplace and the conditions of work (Kennedy et al., 2001). Globalization has led to a continuous increase of the global-wide network density, and as a result of this, the speed and intensity of change as well as the complexity in the system 'earth' have risen. Such developments, combined with the emergence of the knowledge society, contribute to a new paradigm of knowledge production in higher education (Moravec, 2008). Universities have to respond to these developments (Tynan et al., 2008).

In the past, it was mainly the professional expertise that decided on the success of a job application, but today's personnel managers attach great importance to the strategic competences of the candidates such as problem-solving, creativity, presentation techniques, decisiveness and interpersonal communication ability (Baaken, 2002), entrepreneurial competences in a nutshell. Besides, there is a growing need for "multi-skilled workers" who can adapt quickly to changing skills demands and new methods of work organization (Mansfield, 2004). Given the importance attributed to competences in business, there is a wide agreement to align university curricula to the needs of society. (Mulder et al., 2009; Van der Sijde, 2012) But small businesses require skills and entrepreneurial competences that are very much different than from larger organizations (Tehseen and Ramayah, 2015).

Many authors discuss the concept of competence (Azemikhah, 2006; Mansfield, 2004) or even the competency era "that replaced the contents era" (Drexel, 2003; Van der Sijde, 2012). Within higher and vocational education the focus has changed from the content of the courses to the conveyance of competences and skills that allow adapting easily to new demands and tasks.

Barr and Tagg (1995) postulated in their highly discussed and recognized article "From Teaching to Learning – *A New Paradigm for Undergraduate Education"* that colleges no longer are institutions that exist to provide instruction, but institutions that exist to produce learning. They argue that higher education institutions should offer a creative environment that enables students to develop individual learning competences and strategies to acquire and construct new knowledge by themselves.

A concept looking at the issue from a different angle is the competence framework KODE of Erpenbeck and Heyse (which relates to the German understanding of competence). KODE is a multiple validated system for the diagnosis and development of competences. Its theoretical foundation is a theoretical model of self-organization derived from synergetic, management studies from Drucker, Malik and Probst, and Fromm's strengths-weaknesses paradox (Heyse, 2010).

Based on their empirical research, the four basic competence groups have been further subdivided into 64 strategic competences, thereby building a comprehensive competence map used for coding purposes.

Competences here are defined as abilities for self-organization of acting and thinking – in particular in changing situations and as the ability to conform in a comprehensive sense. Erpenbeck and Heyse structure the competences into four basic areas: (P) Personal Competence, (A) Activity and Action Competence, (M) Methods and Professional Competence and (S) Socio-Communicative Competence (Heyse and Erpenbeck, 2008).

Figure 1. Competences of an entrepreneurial thinking and innovation driving graduate
Source: Heyse & Erpenbeck 2009

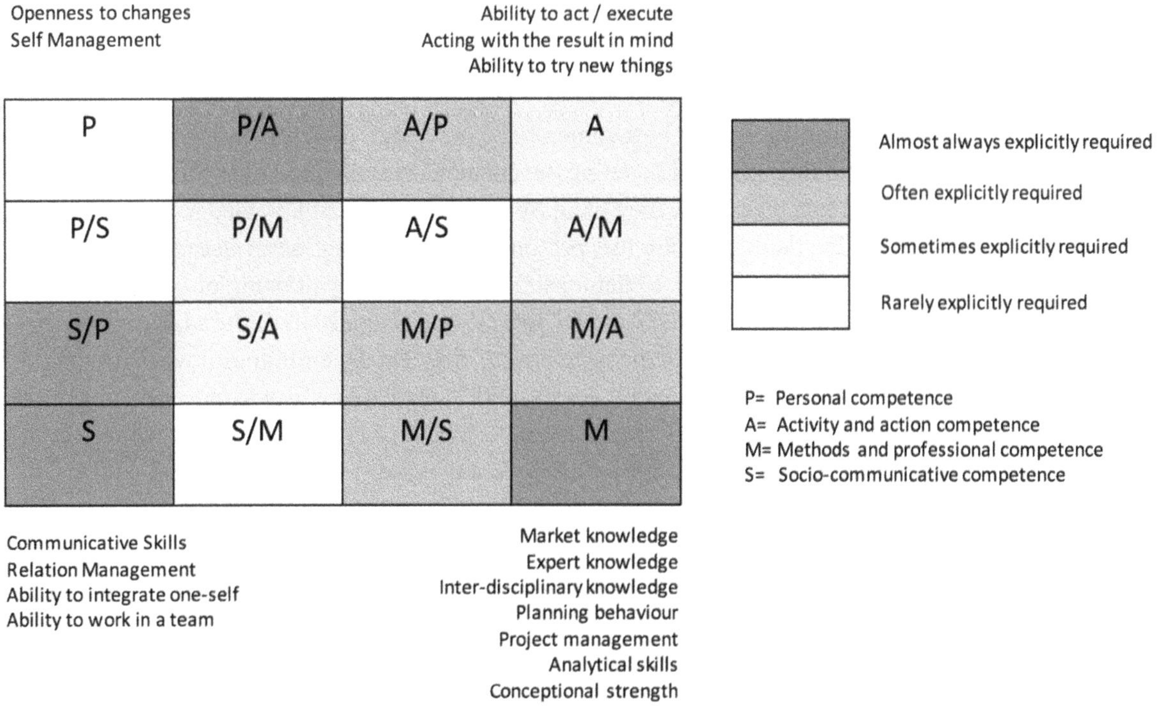

In higher education, competence profiles are generically composed for different levels of mastery (e.g., BSc, MSc level); in the higher education framework certain key competences have been emphasized (Heyse, 2014).

However, all those frameworks and studies have in common that they provide information on required competences across all industries and functional areas. As a result, a competence heat map for entrepreneurial and innovation-driving graduates has been generated as shown in Figure 1. Out of 64 strategic competences 16 have been identified as being of particular importance.

FRAMEWORK CONSOLIDATION

In each scientific article, the mentioned strategic competences have been identified. The importance of the competence groups P, A, M, and S has been determined for each article based on the frequency and emphasis with which strategic competences were mentioned. Similar to the method of the questionnaire from Erpenbeck and Heyse, and based on the assessed importance, for each article a rank order has been assigned to the four strategic competence groups, with the most prominently mentioned competence group receiving a score of 4, the second most important group receiving a score of 3, the third most important group receiving a score of 2, and the least important competence group receiving a score of 1.

The results show that the strategic competences that belong to competence groups P and A were mentioned particularly often in the articles. Such desirable strategic competences are, for example, creativity, openness to change, willingness to innovate, drive, decision-making ability, self-motivation, and personal responsibility. The strong emphasis on the personal competence group is attributed to the often mentioned desirable strong leadership skills and the need for charismatic leaders.

To achieve organizational agility, Kotter (2012) proposed setting up a second operating system, which consists of an agile, network-like structure. Graduates prospering in such a structure and fostering the success should have an appropriate strategic competence profile. It is further believed that such a strategic competence profile would be exceptional and that there is a development gap between the desired profile and the profile to be found in students. A highly developed personal competence (P) is desirable.

A different research project on how to best remember knowledge undertaken in 2001 by Baaken (2002) led to the following findings: By just listening, test persons remembered only 5% of the provided content. If they had to read a text on a topic, they increased the remembered knowledge base by another 5%. The amount of knowledge doubled when test persons had a combination of audio (listening) and visual (seeing) experience to 20%. The task to demonstrate knowledge by drawing or creating a model the level of memory raised by again some 10% to now 30%. If they had also to discuss the topic (+20%) or even apply it to a case, then the level of memory achieved 75%. The by far highest level was achieved by explaining knowledge to others (calls mates, guests): 90% of memory. It was not measured if the knowledge survived more than one month (Figure 2). Guests): 90% of memory. It was not guests): 90% of memory. It was not of memory. It was not of memory. It was not of memory.

Kennedy at al. (2006) reflected on a different system and list of domain-based competences. They came up with a hierarchy of cognitive domains. The following listing is naming the cognitive domains and – in brackets – the learning outcomes and competences which are achieved: Knowledge (Ability to remember facts without necessarily understanding, Collect, define, describe, find, identify, list, memorize, name, order, outline, recall, recognize, repeat, show, state); Comprehension (Ability to understand and interpret learned information, Clarify, contrast, convert, decode, defend, describe, differentiate, discuss,

Table 1. Rank order of competence groups as mentioned in the reviewed journal articles

Authors	P	A	M	S
Davey (2015)	4	3	3	3
Dobni (2008)	4	3	2	1
Doz and Kosonen (2010)	2	1	3	4
Ernest et al. (2015)	4	2	3	1
Gilbert (2012)	3	1	2	4
Herrmann and Nadkarni (2013)	4	1	2	3
Kagermann et al. (2013)	4	3	2	1
Kotter (2012)	3	2	1	4
McCann et al. (2009)	4	1	2	3
Morris and Kaplan (2014)	4	3	1	2
Mukerjee (2014)	3	4	2	1
Prange and Schlegelmilch (2010)	3	4	2	1
Scharmer and Käufer (2010)	2	4	3	1
Tehseen and Ramayah (2015)	4	1	3	2
Σ	**48**	**33**	**31**	**31**

Source: Adapted from Davey (2015); Dobni (2008); Doz and Kosonen (2010); Ernest et al. (2015); Gilbert (2012); Herrmann and Nadkarni (2014); Kagermann et al. (2013); Kotter (2012); McCann et al. (2009); Morris and Kaplan (2014); Mukerjee (2014); Prange and Schlegelmilch (2010); Scharmer and Käufer (2010); Tehseen and Ramayah (2015).

Figure 2. Potential to remember
Source: Baaken (2002); Baaken and Gosejohann (2009).red

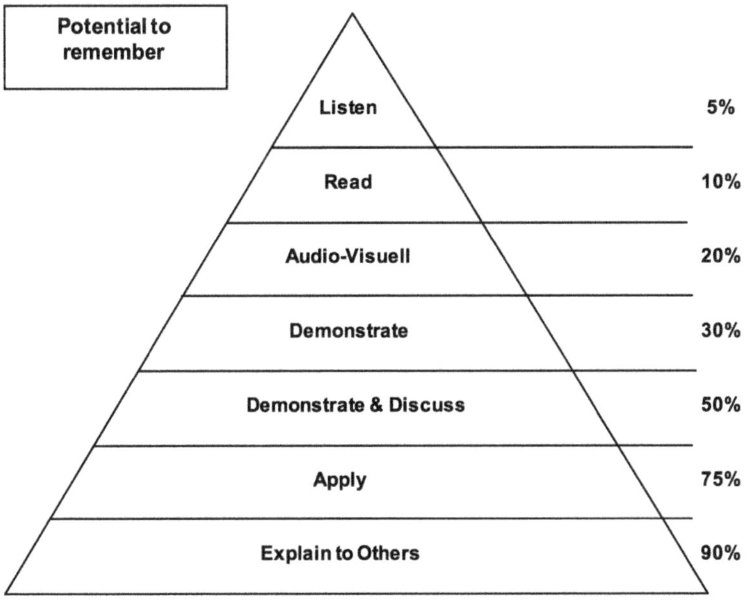

distinguish, explain, illustrate, predict); Application (Ability to use learned material in new situations, Apply, assess, calculate, complete, compute, demonstrate, develop, examine, interpret, produce, select, show, transfer); Analysis (Ability to break down information into its components, Analyse, appraise, break down, categorize, compare, connect, criticize, differentiate, divide, examine, investigate, examine); Synthesis (Ability to put parts together, Arrange, assemble, combine, compile, compose, construct, create, design, develop, generate, invent, make, plan, prepare); Evaluation (Ability to judge value of material for given purpose, Appraise, argue, conclude, convince, criticize, decide, evaluate, grade, interpret, judge, rate, recommend). (Kennedy et al., 2006)

If the two research projects will be combined with a new level of assessing competences creation is possible (Table 2).

There is a direct and significant correlation of how the learning is conducted and what level of knowledge of the hierarchy of cognitive domains can be achieved.

Figure 3. Cognitive domain based competences
Source: Kennedy, Hyland, and Ryan (2006)

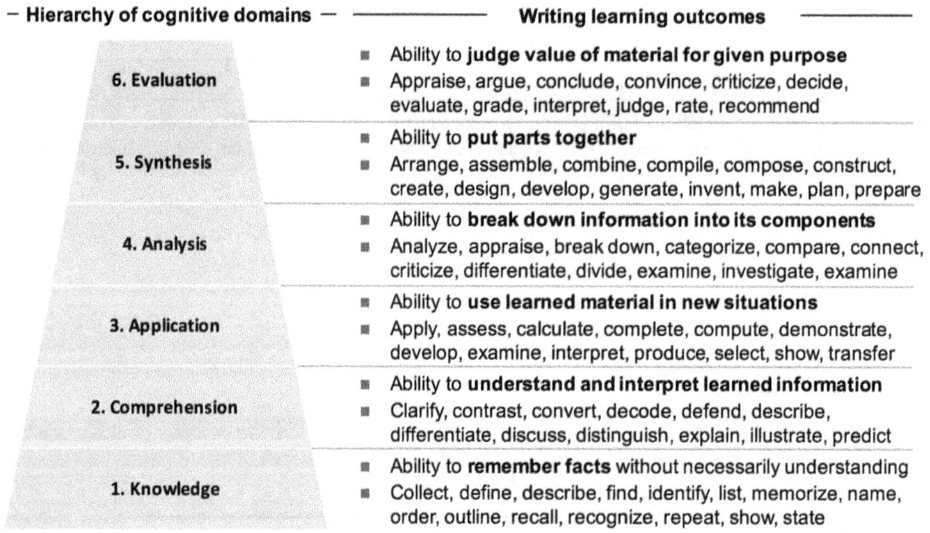

Table 2. Competence Creation by Learning Form

	Listen	Read	Audio-Visual	Demonstrate	Demonstrate & Discuss	Apply	Explain
Knowledge	●	●●	●●	●●●	●●●	●●●	●●●
Comprehension	●	●●	●●	●●	●●●	●●●	●●●
Application	●	●	●●	●●	●●	●●●	●●●
Analysis	-	●	●	●	●●	●●	●●●
Synthesis	-	-	-	●	●	●●	●●●
Evaluation	-	-	-	-	●	●●	●●●

Legend: ●●● = competence creation strong; ●● = competence creation; ● = competence creation weak;
- = no competence creation.
Source: Authors

Educational Implications

The following chapter is going to demonstrate how Higher Education Institution may act to follow those findings and improve their teaching and learning efficiency as well as achieving a far higher level of knowledge in entrepreneurship in the student base.

In all six involved authors' background units of the four universities (Science-to-Business Marketing Research Centre in Münster University of Applied Sciences in Germany, RUG Rijksuniversiteit Groningen & Georg-August-Universität Göttingen, and Centre for Transformational Entrepreneurship, Coventry University, UK), a project with external corporations is conducted. The following text is reflecting on the experiences by using the former findings of the paper.

The projects have in common to identify and formulate specific problems to investigate based on the task students are challenged by the industry partner. Second, the students have to decide on the appropriate information sources and data collection/analysis methods, and third, they have to develop a specific research proposal to meet not only the client's needs and cost constraints but also the time constraints of the class schedule (Moylan, 2008). Kennedy et al. (2001) argue that live business cases are powerful learning tools because they provide an "open-ended environment "that fosters the development of critical thinking and problem-solving skills" (Kennedy et al., 2001, p.147). Besides, most of the collaborative industry projects are conducted in student teams give students the opportunity to develop their team ability and their interpersonal skills. This fact is an important outcome given the changed requirements of employers towards the graduates of higher education mentioned before (Kennedy et al., 2001). Team projects offer in general many pedagogical benefits such as higher motivation of the students, multicultural experiences, positive peer modeling, cooperative learning, as well as the development of essential workplace skills including communication, group interaction and technical skills (Williams et al., 1991).

There are also problems attached to projects realized in student teams. One is the dilemma that team members might contribute unequally to accomplish the workload (Williams et al., 1991). There are several reasons why one or more students might not contribute fully to the project, from the simple desire to avoid effort and responsibility to more complex reasons such as lack of self-confidence and/or the bowing to very dominant personalities within the group. Either way, the consequences of inequitable contributions in group projects are negative as some students may learn less than what they would learn with individual assignments. Others might feel overstretched and might also reduce their effort because they fear that the grading system will not reward their contribution in a commensurate way. "In the worst instances, the group is unable to complete its task, and the instructor must deal with distraught students, anxious about how to proceed, fearful of grading consequences, angry about their teammates' failure to perform assigned tasks" (Williams et al., 1991, p. 49). They suggest different solutions to cope with the so-called 'free-rider-effect' in student groups. The most important key principle is the use of an appropriate award structure that also allows individual accountability for each student. For example, the instructor might sum up the individual scores of the students to get a group score which then builds the basis for the team grade. Other methods could be the use of peer evaluation forms, instructor observations, working papers, meeting reports, interaction logs or confidential reports to ensure individual accountability (Williams et al., 1991).

The objective of practice-oriented research projects in cooperation with industry is to offer the students real-life experiences and to make the theoretical know-how of the university lectures more tangible by using it in actual business case settings. Besides, the students are encouraged to organize and structure their learning process actively and to train – next to the study of marketing knowledge – also soft skills such as complex thinking, problem-solving capacity, presentation techniques, interpersonal communication competence, and team ability. Since to a large extent the students self-organize their projects a "learning by applying" and "learning by explaining it to their mates and later to the companies' delegates" a high level of understanding and cognitive-based competences are created (only "Apply" and "Explain" are listed due to findings in table 2).

Furthermore, Students occupy project leader, group leader, and task leader roles and are asked to teach applied methods and achieved results to the team and opposed to traditional student assessment techniques, the grades on project work, case studies or seminar papers. This system should be applied because self-determination of the students is regarded as a key factor.

According to statements of partners companies, they are most interested in running that kind of projects with universities as the projects provide very good 'value for money' (Baaken et al., 2014). For example, they receive new insights and solutions to their very specific problems and get to know graduates who might become employees of their company in the future.

The general setup of this kind of projects can be summarised as follows. At the semester start, the students are allocated to the projects. Depending on the amount of the expected workload and the interests of students, around 10 to 20 students are joining each project. In week two delegates of each partner company are handing out the briefing and task. This can be seen as a kick-off workshop. All kinds of questions are welcome. Week 3 is used for an internal discussion and development of a first project design to address the requirements and questions of the company. A re-briefing takes place (physically or via Skype) to make sure all stakeholders (students, lecturers, and company representatives) have the same understanding of the problem and get approval for the methodology which is part of the project design.

In the following weeks, the project is executed: questionnaires are developed, basic groups defined and organized, samples drawn, fieldwork was done, data analysis conducted, recommendations developed and a report created. This period lasts approximately ten weeks. Small groups of students work on parts of the project (work packages). Every week the entire group meets in a plenary session to present in between results of their sub-groups. Every plenary session minutes are written and the minutes (using a template provided by the lecturer) are sent to the partner company on the following day. By this procedure the project partner is constantly involved in the process, informed what happens in the project and has the opportunity to interfere in the project by providing additional background information, contributing

Table 3. Competence creation by learning form

	Student Projects for Industry Partners	
	Apply	**Explain**
Knowledge	●●●	●●●
Comprehension	●●●	●●●
Application	●●●	●●●
Analysis	●●	●●●
Synthesis	●●	●●●
Evaluation	●●	●●●

Legend: ●●● = competence creation strong; ●● = competence creation
Source: Authors.

to a discussion or adjusting a decision. After having finished the final report, the entire group will travel to the company's premises and present the results to delegates of the company.

Being onsite, some participants from the company can join in, and the students are put into a professional environment outside of the university, e.g., the board room of the company. Every student is delivering a part of the presentation and questions are answered by the group members, not only by the actual presenter. Students will get a qualified certificate, which is describing the projects in its key elements and assessing the groups' performance level. The certificate is printed on the company's letterhead and signed by responsible managers of the company so that the certificate helps graduates in their application process for a job. The company provides a budget for the project. The income is part of the university's third-party money stream and is partly spend on project research issues (database, fieldwork, etc.), and partly used for buying general equipment for the university (computers, publications, etc.). The project activities range from addressing potential clients, communicating with the client including transparent communication of the project's progress, developing and implementing an appropriate research strategy, and presenting the results to the client. For structuring the projects and developing appropriate solution concepts, methods and professional competence are required. For the daily execution of work within the projects' social-communicative competence' and 'activity and action-oriented competence' is required, and 'personal competence' is particularly demanded in leading roles. Overall, the project set-up of the teaching modules supports well the development of the previously identified competences.

A more detailed view on 'competence creation by the form of learning' is highlighted in the following table 4 (only "Apply" and "Explain" are listed due to findings in table 2).

Thus project student team members develop and train a whole set of different competences that are required in today's workplaces according to entrepreneurial thinking and acting. The students have to deal with the individualities of their teammates and therefore had the opportunity to train their communication, relationship and team ability. By developing a concept for the project, self-managing the project and developing knowledge about complex markets in a short time-frame the students fostered their 'methods and professional competence' as well as their 'personal competence.' Also, analytical skills were intensively trained in projects as the students were confronted with a research question of the industry partner and had to find suitable research methods and strategies to create answers to this question. The time pressure as well as the pressure of delivering a concise presentation of the results to the partner's attributed to a temporal emotional debilitation of the students, a necessity to permit training of such competences.

On top, the time pressure also created a frame for the development of project management and quality management skills. The lecturers provided coaching assistance and regular feedback to permit self-reflection. As most projects are conducted on an international level, the students also acquired know-how on global markets and international business relations. Generally, it can be concluded that student projects that are realized in cooperation with industry represent an effective 'learning by teaching' scheme that offers students a creative learning environment and the opportunity to develop individual learning strategies as well as comprehensive competences of a different kind.

Table 4. Competence creation by learning form

		Student Projects for Industry Partners	
		Apply	Explain
P	Openness to changes Self-Management	●●●	●●●
A	Ability to act/execute Acting with the result in mind Ability to try new things	●●●	●●●
M	Market knowledge Expert knowledge Inter-disciplinary knowledge Planning behavior Project management Analytical skills Conceptual strength	●●●	●●●
S	Communicative Skills Relation Management Ability to integrate one-self Ability to work in a team	●●●	●●●

Legend: ●●● = competencie creation strong
Source: Authors.

CONCLUSION

The discussion on entrepreneurship and innovation is ongoing. Nevertheless, entrepreneurship education has often focused on economic motivations and market-driven rationales. However, these perspectives do not entirely represent the field. The competences of agility and resiliency have been identified as being of great importance for successful management in the field.

Nevertheless, social entrepreneurs can also embrace these rationales, since social entrepreneurs seek by nature to tackle "problems" and "disparities" in society. It also requires a re-orientation of talent development to lead organizations and equip them well to face future challenges. This effort is the starting point to understand better the individual strategic competences required to manage in social entrepreneurship and social innovation successfully. The study offers initial insights that higher education programmes need to re-adjust to provide graduates with a desirable strategic competence profile.

New pedagogical theories have found their way into university didactic, e.g. the concept of 'learning by teaching' which is based on the idea that students are much more motivated to learn when they are given the opportunity to act as teachers themselves and to teach their fellow students the learning-matters of the course (Skinner, 1994; Grzega, 2003; Grzega & Schöner, 2008; Cortese, 2005; Eddy, 2006; Davey, 2015). 'Learning by Teaching also offers students the opportunity to practice and develop competences because it "encourages and demands creativity, independence, self-confidence and fundamental key qualifications (i.e. the ability to work in a team, complex thinking, the competence to seek and find information, explorative behaviour, presentation skills, project competence, internet competence, generating knowledge as well as disciplinary virtues like punctuality, reliability, patience)" (Grzega, 2005, p. 2). Innovative teaching methods that allow students to be more active in their learning process are also much more effective regarding the percentage of knowledge that is memorized (Baaken, 2002). Explaining the learning-matters to others was proven to be the most effective procedure of the innovative teaching method – corresponding to the above described 'Learning by Teaching.'

Another factor that exerts a strong influence on the academic education is the increasing competition between the different institutions of higher education. To attract the most talented students, universities are challenged to offer ambitious, diversified and innovative teaching methods (Lim & Svensson, 2007).

It is adopting a more proactive attitude in addressing the needs of its main stakeholders, such as the students and the society when designing courses is considered in this article an innovative way of carrying the mission of teaching from the university by integrating real-world industry projects into the teaching and learning setting (Baaken et al., 2009). Audretsch (2009) and Galloway et al. (2005) state that addressing the needs and concerns of the wider society is perhaps what makes the university one of the most resilient institutions in society.

REFERENCES

Abu-Saifan, S. (2012). Social Entrepreneurship: Definition and Boundaries. *Technology Innovation Management Review*, *2*(2), 22–29. doi:10.22215/timreview/523

Adomavičiūtė, E., Janiunaite, B., & Stuopyte, E. (2012). The Profile of Social Entrepreneurs Working for Non-governmental Organizations. *Social Sciences*, *77*(3), 17–29. doi:10.5755/j01.ss.77.3.2766

Audretsch, D. B. (2009). The entrepreneurial society. *The Journal of Technology Transfer*, *34*(3), 245–254. doi:10.100710961-008-9101-3

Azemikhah, H. (2006). The 21st Century, the Competency Era and Competency Theory, In Open Learning Institute of TAFE. In *AVETRA 9th Annual Conference*. University of Wollongong.

Baaken, T. (1989). *Bewertung technologieorientierter Unternehmensgründungen, Kriterien und Methoden zur Bewertung von Gründerpersönlichkeit, Technologie und Markt für Banken und Venture-Capital-Gesellschaften sowie für die staatliche Wirtschafts- und Technologieförderung*. Berlin, Germany: Erich Schmidt.

Baaken, T. (2002). Soft Skills und Schlüsselqualifikationen als integraler Ausbildungsbestandteil an Hochschulen. In F. Isenbart (Ed.), *Organisation und Management* (Vol. 25, pp. 4–18). Münster, Germany: Berichte aus der Hochschule.

Baaken, T., & Gosejohann, S. (2009). Higher Education in International Marketing by Integration of Industry Projects. *EDULEARN09 Proceedings, International Conference on Education and New Learning Technologies*, 5185-5195.

Baaken, T., Kiel, B., & Kliewe, T. (2015). Real World Projects with Companies Supporting Competence Development in Higher Education. *International Journal of Higher Education*, *4*(3), 129–139. doi:10.5430/ijhe.v4n3p129

Baaken, T., Kiel, B., Rossano, S., Baaken, M., & Maas, G. (2016). Competences in Entrepreneurship – Teaching Entrepreneurship in Higher Education from a new angle. In J. M. Saiz-Álvarez (Ed.), *Handbook of Research on Social Entrepreneurship and Solidarity Economics* (pp. 154–173). Hershey, PA: IGI. doi:10.4018/978-1-5225-0097-1.ch009

Barr, R. B., & Tagg, J. (1995). From Teaching to Learning – A new paradigm for undergraduate education. *Change*, *27*(6), 13–25. doi:10.1080/00091383.1995.10544672

Bilán, S. G., Kisenwether, E. C., Rzasa, S. E., & Wise, J. C. (2005). Developing and assessing students' entrepreneurial skills and mind-set. *Journal of Engineering Education*, *94*(2), 233–243. doi:10.1002/j.2168-9830.2005.tb00844.x

Bowen, H. (2018). *Investment in learning: The individual and social value of American higher education*. London, UK: Routledge. doi:10.4324/9781351309929

Brockmann, M., Clarke, L., & Winch, C. (2009). Competence and competency in the EQF and in European VET systems. *Journal of European Industrial Training*, *33*(8/9), 787–799. doi:10.1108/03090590910993634

Caligiuri, P. (2013). *Cultural Agility. Building a Pipeline of Successful Global Professionals*. San Francisco, USA: Wiley.

Chavez, V. A., Stinnett, R., Tierney, R., & Walsh, S. (2017). The importance of the technologically able social innovators and entrepreneurs: A US National Laboratory Perspective. *Technological Forecasting and Social Change*, *121*, 205–215. doi:10.1016/j.techfore.2016.09.002

Chell, E. (2007). Social enterprise and entrepreneurship: Towards a convergent theory of the entrepreneurial process. *International Small Business Journal*, *25*(1), 5–26. doi:10.1177/0266242607071779

Chell, E., Nicolopoulou, K., & Karatas-Özkan, M. (2010). Social entrepreneurship and enterprise: International and innovation perspectives. *Entrepreneurship and Regional Development*, *22*(6), 485–493. doi:10.1080/08985626.2010.488396

Christensen, C. M., & Eyring, H. J. (2011). The Innovative University. Changing the DNA of Higher Education from the Inside Out. San Francisco, CA: Jossey-Bass (The Jossey-Bass Higher and Adult Education Series).

Cortese, C. G. (2005). Learning through Teaching. *Management Learning*, *36*(1), 87–115. doi:10.1177/1350507605049905

Davey, T. A. (2015). Entrepreneurship at Universities - Exploring the factors influencing the development of entrepreneurship at universities. Amsterdam: Academic Press.

Dees, J. G. (2007). Taking social entrepreneurship seriously. *Society*, *44*(3), 24–31. doi:10.1007/BF02819936

Dees, J. G. (2017). The Meaning of Social Entrepreneurship. In *Case Studies in Social Entrepreneurship and Sustainability* (pp. 34–42). London, UK: Routledge.

Dees, J. G., & Anderson, B. B. (2006). Framing a theory of social entrepreneurship: Building on two schools of practice and thought. In R. Mosher-Williams (Ed.), *Research on social entrepreneurship: Understanding and contributing to an emerging field* (pp. 39-66). ARNOVA Occasional Paper Series.

Defourny, J., & Nyssens, M. (2010). Conceptions of social enterprise and social entrepreneurship in Europe and the United States: Convergences and divergences. *Journal of Social Entrepreneurship, 1*(1), 32–53. doi:10.1080/19420670903442053

Dobni, C. B. (2008). The DNA of innovation. *The Journal of Business Strategy, 29*(2), 43–50. doi:10.1108/02756660810858143

Doz, Y. L., & Kosonen, M. (2010). Embedding strategic agility. A leadership agenda for accelerating business model renewal. *Long Range Planning, 43*(2), 370–382. doi:10.1016/j.lrp.2009.07.006

Drexel, I. (2003). *Two Lectures. The Concept of Competence – an Instrument of Social and Political Change. Centrally Coordinated Decentralization – No Problem? Lessons from the Italian Case.* Stein Rokkan Centre for Social Studies, Working Paper 26. Bergen, Norway: Uni Research.

Eddy, J. (2006). Learning through teaching model results in improved student learning. *Teaching Matters, 10*(2), 1–31.

Ernest, K., Matthew, S. K., & Samuel, A. K. (2015). Towards Entrepreneurial Learning Competences. The Perspective of Built Environment Students. *Higher Education Studies, 5*(1), 20–30. doi:10.5539/hes.v5n1p20

European Commission. (2013). *Social economy and social entrepreneurship. In Social Europe guide* (Vol. 4). Brussels, Belgium: European Commission, Directorate-General for Employment.

European Qualifications Framework (EQF). (2014). Online at http.//ec.europa.eu/eqf/terms_en.htm

Fleit, C. (2013). *Direct marketing news. Core competences make the difference in marketing*. Online at http.//www.dmnews.com/marketing-leaders-must-get-results/article/275003

Galloway, L., Anderson, M., Brown, W., & Wilson, L. (2005). Enterprise skills for the economy. *Education + Training, 47*(1), 7–17. doi:10.1108/00400910510580593

Gilbert, C., Eyring, M., & Foster, R. N. (2012). Two Routes to Resiliency. Rebuild your core while you reinvent your business model. *Harvard Business Review, 90*(12), 66–73.

Grzega, J. (2003). *LdL in universitären Kursen. Ein hochschuldidaktischer Weg zur Vorbereitung auf die Wissensgesellschaft*. Retrieved from http://www. ldl. de/material/berichte/uni/ldl

Grzega, J. (2005). *Learning By Teaching. The Didactic Model LdL in University Classes*. Retrieved from http://www. ldl. de/material/berichte/uni/uni. htm

Grzega, J., & Schöner, M. (2008). The didactic model (Lernen durch Lehren) as a way of preparing students for communication in a knowledge society. *Journal of Education for Teaching, 34*(3), 167–175. doi:10.1080/02607470802212157

Herrmann, P., & Nadkarni, S. (2014). Managing strategic change. The duality of CEO personality. *Strategic Management Journal, 35*(9), 1318–1342. doi:10.1002mj.2156

Heyse, V. (Ed.). (2010). *Grundstrukturen menschlicher Kompetenzen. Praxiserprobte Konzepte und Instrumente*. Münster, Germany: Waxmann.

Heyse, V. (2014). *Aufbruch in die Zukunft, Erfolgreiche Entwicklung von Schlüsselkompetenzen in Schulen und Hochschulen*. Münster, Germany: Waxmann.

Heyse, V., & Erpenbeck, J. (2008). *Kompetenztraining. Informations- und Trainingsprogramme. 2., überarb. u. erg*. Stuttgart, Germany: Schäffer-Poeschel.

Kagermann, H., Wahlster, W., & Helbig, J. (2013). Umsetzungsempfehlungen für das Zukunftsprojekt Industrie 4.0. In H. Kagermann, W. Wahlster, & J. Helbig (Eds.), *Abschlussbericht des Arbeitskreises Industrie 4.0*. Frankfurt am Main, Germany: Forchungsunion and Acatech.

Kennedy, D., Hyland, A., & Ryan, N. (2006). Writing and using Learning Outcomes: A Practical Guide. In *Bologna Handbook: Implementing Bologna*. Berlin, Germany: European University Association.

Kennedy, E. J., Lawton, L., & Walker, E. (2001). The case for using live cases. Shifting the paradigm in marketing education. *Journal of Marketing Education, 23*(2), 145–151. doi:10.1177/0273475301232008

Kiel, B. (2014). Companies' Demand for Competences to Overcome Disruptive Changes. In T. Baaken & J. Teczke (Eds.), *Managing Disruption and Destabilisation* (pp. 91–108). Cracow, Poland: Cracow University of Economics.

Kotter, J. P. (2012). Accelerate! How the most innovative companies capitalize on today's rapid fire strategic challenges and still make their numbers. *Harvard Business Review, 90*(11), 44–58. PMID:23155997

Lawrence, T., Phillips, N., & Tracey, P. (2012). Educating Social Entrepreneurs and Social Innovators. *Academy of Management Learning & Education, 11*(3), 319–323. doi:10.5465/amle.2012.0224

Le Deist, F. (2009). Competence. Conceptual approach and practice in France. *Journal of European Industrial Training, 33*(8/9), 718–735. doi:10.1108/03090590910993599

Lim, M., & Svensson, P. (2007). The Embedded Critic: Marketing in the Future of the University. In *5th Critical Management Studies Conference*. Manchester Business School.

Lin, L. M., & Hsia, T. L. (2011). Core capabilities for practitioners in achieving e-business innovation. *Computers in Human Behavior, 27*(5), 1884–1891. doi:10.1016/j.chb.2011.04.012

Lundström, A., & Zhou, C. (2014). Rethinking social entrepreneurship and social enterprises: A three-dimensional perspective. In *Social Entrepreneurship* (pp. 71–89). Cham: Springer. doi:10.1007/978-3-319-01396-1_4

Mandyoli, B., Gervase Iwu, C., & Magoda, Z. (2016). Determining the Nexus between Social Entrepreneurship and the Employability of Graduates. *Socioeconomica, 5*(10), 279–298. doi:10.12803/SJSECO.51009

Mansfield, B. (2004). Competence in transition. *Journal of European Industrial Training, 28*(2/3/4), 296-309.

McCann, J., Selsky, J., & Lee, J. (2009). Building agility, resiliency, and performance in turbulent environments. *People & Strategy*, *32*(3), 44–52.

Miller, T. L., Wesley, C. L. II, & Williams, D. E. (2012). Educating the Minds of Caring Hearts: Comparing the Views of Practitioners and Educators on the Importance of Social Entrepreneurship Competences. *Academy of Management Learning & Education*, *11*(3), 349–370. doi:10.5465/amle.2011.0017

Moravec, J. W. (2008). A new paradigm of knowledge production in higher education. *On the Horizon*, *16*(3), 123–136. doi:10.1108/10748120810901422

Morris, M. H., & Kaplan, J. B. (2014). Entrepreneurial (versus managerial) competences as drivers of entrepreneurship education. Annals of Entrepreneurship Education and Pedagogy, 134-151.

Moylan, W. A. (2008). Learning by project: Developing essential 21st-century skills using student team projects. *International Journal of Learning*, *15*(9), 287–292. doi:10.18848/1447-9494/CGP/v15i09/45935

Mukerjee, S. (2014). Agility. A crucial capability for universities in times of disruptive change and innovation. *Australian Universities Review*, *56*(1), 56–60.

Mulder, M., Gulikers, J., Biemans, H., & Wesselink, R. (2009). The new competence concept in higher education. Error or enrichment? *Journal of European Industrial Training*, *33*(8/9), 755–770. doi:10.1108/03090590910993616

Munshi, N. V. (2010). Value creation, social innovation and entrepreneurship in global economies. *Journal of Asia-Pacific Business*, *11*(3), 160–165. doi:10.1080/10599231.2010.500569

Nicholls, A. (2010). The legitimacy of social entrepreneurship: Reflexive isomorphism in a pre-paradigmatic field. *Entrepreneurship Theory and Practice*, *34*(4), 611–633. doi:10.1111/j.1540-6520.2010.00397.x

Nicholls, A., & Murdock, A. (2012). The nature of social innovation. In *Social innovation* (pp. 1–30). London: Palgrave Macmillan. doi:10.1057/9780230367098_1

Norris, D., Brodnick, R., Lefrere, P., Gilmour, J., & Baer, L. (2013). Transforming in an age of disruptive change. Part 1. Back to the future, zooming to the present. *Planning for Higher Education*, *41*(2), 1–44.

Noruzi, M. R., Westover, J. R., & Rahimi, G. R. (2010). An exploration of social entrepreneurship in the entrepreneurship Era. *Asian Social Science*, *6*(6), 4–10. doi:10.5539/ass.v6n6p3

Pavlin, S., Kesting, T., & Baaken, T. (2016). An Integrative View on Higher Education and University-Business Cooperation in the Light of Academic Entrepreneurship. *European Journal of Education*, *51*(1), 3–9. doi:10.1111/ejed.12168

Phillips, W., Lee, H., Ghobadian, A., O'Regan, N., & James, P. (2015). Social Innovation and Social Entrepreneurship: A Systematic Review. *Group & Organization Management*, *40*(3), 428–461. doi:10.1177/1059601114560063

Prange, C., & Schlegelmilch, B. B. (2010). Heading for the next innovation archetype? *The Journal of Business Strategy*, *31*(1), 46–55. doi:10.1108/02756661011012778

Raisch, S., & Birkingshaw, J. (2008). Organizational ambidexterity. Antecedents, outcomes, and moderators. *Journal of Management*, *34*(3), 375–409. doi:10.1177/0149206308316058

Rausch, E., Sherman, H., & Washbush, J. B. (2002). Defining and assessing competences for competency-based, outcome-focused management development. *Journal of Management Development*, *21*(3), 184–200. doi:10.1108/02621710210420264

Robinson, M. A., Sparrow, P. R., Clegg, C., & Birdi, K. (2007). Forecasting future competency requirements. A three-phase methodology. *Personnel Review*, *36*(1), 65–90. doi:10.1108/00483480710716722

Sambamurthy, V., Bharadwaj, A., & Grover, V. (2003). Shaping agility through digital options. Reconceptualizing the role of information technology in contemporary firms. *Management Information Systems Quarterly*, *27*(2), 237–263. doi:10.2307/30036530

Sastre-Castillo, M. A., Peris-Ortiz, M., & Danvila-Del Valle, I. (2015). What Is Different about the Profile of the Social Entrepreneur? *Nonprofit Management & Leadership*, *25*(4), 349–369. doi:10.1002/nml.21138

Scharmer, C. O., & Käufer, K. (2010). In front of the blank canvas. Sensing emerging futures. *The Journal of Business Strategy*, *31*(4), 21–29. doi:10.1108/02756661011055159

Shaw, E., & de Bruin, A. (2013). Reconsidering capitalism: The promise of social innovation and social entrepreneurship? *International Small Business Journal*, *31*(7), 737–746. doi:10.1177/0266242613497494

Shek, D. T., & Lin, L. (2015). Nurturing university students to be social entrepreneurs: Relevance of service leadership education. *International Journal on Disability and Human Development: IJDHD*, *14*(3), 285–293.

Short, J. C., Moss, T. W., & Lumpkin, G. T. (2009). Research in social entrepreneurship: Past contributions and future opportunities. *Strategic Entrepreneurship Journal*, *3*(2), 161–194. doi:10.1002ej.69

Skinner, J.D. (1994). Learning by Teaching. *Zielsprache Englisch*, *2*(94), 38-39.

Smith, I. H., & Woodworth, W. P. (2012). Developing Social Entrepreneurs and Social Innovators: A Social Identity and Self-Efficacy Approach. *Academy of Management Learning & Education*, *11*(3), 390–407. doi:10.5465/amle.2011.0016

Spear, R., Aiken, M., Noya, A., & Clarence, E. (2013). *Boosting social entrepreneurship and social enterprise creation*. Paris, France: OECD.

Sullivan Mort, G., Weerawardena, J., & Carnegie, K. (2003). Social entrepreneurship: Towards conceptualization. *International Journal of Nonprofit and Voluntary Sector Marketing*, *8*(1), 76–88. doi:10.1002/nvsm.202

Tapscott, D., & Williams, A. (2010). Innovating the 21st-Century University: It's Time! *EDUCAUSE Review*, *45*(1), 16–29.

Tehseen, S., & Ramayah, T. (2015). Entrepreneurial Competences and SMEs Business Success. The Contingent Role of External Integration. *Mediterranean Journal of Social Sciences*, *6*(1), 50–61.

Teichler, U. (2003). Hochschule und Arbeitswelt: Konzeptionen, Diskussionen, Trends (Vol. 873). Frankfurt/M: Campus Verlag.

Thake, S., & Zadek, S. (1997). *Practical people, noble causes: How to support community social entrepreneurs*. London, UK: New Economics Foundation.

Thompson, J., Alvy, G., & Lees, A. (2000). Social entrepreneurship – a new look at the people and the potential. *Management Decision*, *38*(5), 328–338. doi:10.1108/00251740010340517

Thorgren, S., & Omorede, A. (2015). Passionate Leaders in Social Entrepreneurship. Exploring an African Context. *Business & Society*, *57*(3), 525–561.

Tynan, B., & Lee, M. J. W. (2009). Tales of adventure and change. Academic staff members' future visions of higher education and their professional development needs. *On the Horizon*, *17*(2), 98–108. doi:10.1108/10748120910965485

Tynan, B., Lee, M. J. W., & Barnes, C. (Eds.). (2008). Polar bears, black gold and light bulbs. Creating stable futures for tertiary education through instructor training and support in the use of ICTs. *Proceedings of World Conference on Educational Multimedia, Hypermedia and Telecommunications*.

Van der Sijde, P. (2012). Profiting from knowledge circulation. The gains from university-industry interaction. *Industry and Higher Education*, *26*(1), 15–19. doi:10.5367/ihe.2012.0082

Waring, M. (2018). *Social pressures and curriculum innovation: A study of the Nuffield Foundation Science Teaching Project*. London, UK: Routledge. doi:10.4324/9780429453922

Williams, D. L., Beard, J. D., & Rymer, J. (1991). Team Projects: Achieving their Full Potential. *Journal of Marketing Education*, *13*(2), 45–53. doi:10.1177/027347539101300208

Wilson, F., Kickul, J., & Marlino, D. (2007). Gender, Entrepreneurial Self-Efficacy, and Entrepreneurial Career Intentions: Implications for Entrepreneurship Education 1. *Entrepreneurship Theory and Practice*, *31*(3), 387–406. doi:10.1111/j.1540-6520.2007.00179.x

Winterton, J. (2009). Competence across Europe. Highest common factor or lowest common denominator? *Journal of European Industrial Training*, *33*(8/9), 681–700. doi:10.1108/03090590910993571

KEY TERMS AND DEFINITIONS

Cognitive Competences: A set of mental processes related to creative and critical thinking to develop new strategies for solving challenges and processes.

European Qualification Framework: It consists of a common reference guide used in the European Union to make qualifications more readable and understandable.

Free-Rider Problem: Market failure that occurs when people take advantage of being able to use a common resource, or collective good, without paying for it.

Organizational Ambidexterity: The ability of a firm to efficiently manage and, simultaneously, being adapted to changes.

Peripatric Ambidexterity: It is a sort of ambidexterity linked to genetics.

Resilience: The capacity of persistence without hesitation in face of a challenge or problem, until it is solved or reached.

Storytelling: Narrative technique used to convince others about the bondages of an idea or plan.

World Economic Forum: International non-profit organization aimed to reach a better world with the interaction of world leaders.

ENDNOTE

1 This chapter is an updated and rewritten version of Baaken, T.; Kiel, B.; Rossano, S.; Baaken, M.; Maas, G. (2016). Competencies in Entrepreneurship – Teaching Entrepreneurship in Higher Education from a new angle. In José Manuel Saiz-Álvarez (ed.): *Handbook of Research on Social Entrepreneurship and Solidarity Economics* (pp. 154-173), Hershey, PA: IGI Global.

Chapter 7
Proposal of a Business Model Based on the Triple Business Performance-E

Carlos Ricardo Rey-Campero
Universidad Externado de Colombia, Colombia

ABSTRACT

This chapter aims to analyze the relationship between business models and dynamic capabilities in firms of the systems development sector of Bogota (Colombia). Based on the theoretical framework of business models, the author applies an analysis based on principal categorical components and categorical regression. Results show a correlation between the elements of the business model (strategy and dynamic capabilities) and business performance. In conclusion, the author proposes a business model endowed with efficiency, effectiveness, and efficacy for newly created micro, small, and medium-sized family firms that highly correlates with business performance.

INTRODUCTION

This chapter emerges from the necessity to answer the following questions: how to maximize business results to compete better? And how to manage these dynamic environments? (Porter, 1991; Rumelt, Schendel & Teece, 1994; Becerra, 2009). Initially, this analysis was addressed to look over the position of the firm in the market and the external factors affecting it, where business behavior and its performance are both established in the market industry. Based on this fact, Porter (1980, 1985) develops a strategic model grounded on the sectorial analysis of the Porterian's five forces and the value chain. However, inefficient business performance invites stakeholders to analyze internal factors (Schmalensee, 1985; Rumelt, 1991), where business advantages are based on the resources and capabilities of the firm (Grant, 1991).

According to Barney (2007), the words "resources" and "capabilities" have been used as interchangeable words and sometimes are parallel. According to Grant (1991), "the resources and capabilities of a firm are the central considerations in formulating its strategy: they are the primary constants upon which a firm can establish its identity and frame its strategy, and they are the primary source of the

DOI: 10.4018/978-1-5225-8939-6.ch007

firm's profitability" (p. 133). As a result, the resources of the firm have an idiosyncratic meaning and are heterogeneous, and these resources are not sometimes available in the market, what is a problem in the strategic positioning model (Brunet, 2011; Dávila, 2009; Teece, 2009). Despite this fact, the competency model does not replace, but complements, the strategic positioning model (Barney, 1991; Mahoney & Padian, 1992; Peteraf & Barney, 2003).

The quality of the resources and the coordination coming from the firm leads to maintaining the firm's competitive advantage in the long term (Brunet, 2011). The approach to resources and capabilities is considered the most influential theoretical framework to understand the achievement of competitive advantages, and how these advantages can be timeless (Eisenhardt & Martin, 2000).

However, in most countries, their business context is now defined for having an ambiguous, unpredictable and non-linear fluctuations on their industrial structures, with blurred limits and changing business models and players (Eisenhardt & Martin, 2000) affecting to the loss of value of resources as a source of competitive advantage (Priem & Butler, 2001a,b). So, it is necessary to perform a constant change by using the dynamic capabilities of the firm by renewing knowledge for a more competitive one (Eisenhardt & Martin, 2000).

Dynamic capabilities arise in response to the difficulties that companies have in dynamic market environments (Eisenhardt & Martin, 2000), and consist of their ability to integrate, build and reconfigure their internal and external competencies to adapt to fast-track contexts change. Therefore, they reflect the organizational ability to achieve new and innovative forms of competitive advantage (Teece, Pisano, & Shuen, 1997; Teece, 2009). Moreover, it is important to have in mind that the management and performance of micro, small, and medium-sized enterprises (MSMEs) are influenced by the external environment where they operate (Zhara, 1996), and their ability to respond to these changes as part of their survival (Camisón, 1997).

Similarly, the analysis becomes relevant when talking about family business, since they are very important in the economy of practically all the countries of the world (Astrachan, Zahra, & Sharma, 2003). Between 80% and 98% of the firms in the planet are family businesses, and "around 85% of them fail within their first five years of operations" (Poza, 2005, p. 3), mainly because of financial problems and lack of education (Saiz-Álvarez, Muñiz, & Huezo, 2016).

The purpose of this chapter is to propose a business model based on performance and founded on the dynamic capabilities approach to allow newly-created[1] family MSMEs to be adapted to changing business environments. The article is divided into four sections: first, we theoretically develop the thematic areas of research where assumptions are present; second, we analyze the variables to propose and validate a proposed business model by using field research and different tools to proof the research hypotheses; third, the results are shown, and finally, we set some conclusions and recommendations.

THEORETICAL FRAMEWORK

The business model is at the heart of stories explaining how a firm works and answer questions like who is the consumer? How is the money obtained? How is the value distributed to the consumers? And how do firms appropriate this value? (Magretta, 2010). A business model is placed between the resources entry in a firm and the results of this at the market, which means "the business model is more than the financial market" (Teece, 2010, p. 179), and help to explain the creation and capture of the firm value, the performance, and the sustainable competitive advantage (Zott, Amit, & Massa, 2011). Having unclear conditions in whether a model is appropriate or not, makes it difficult to see the model interactions with the organizational variables, the existence of generic models, and how these methodologies are evaluated (Morris, Schindehutte, & Allen, 2005).

The business model, as a concept, has been confusing for many, because the term has lacked an agreed definition, and is used with different meanings in the daily business dialogue (Osterwalder, 2004). There is no unique definition of the business model. There is a large number of definitions that depend on the analysis point of view, which made it difficult to continue with the topic's development (Zott, Amit, & Massa, 2011).

Despite the emphasis on the practice of entrepreneurial initiative, the business model has received little attention from researchers; so much that there is no consensus regarding the definition, nature, structure, and evolution (Morris, Schindehutte, & Allen, 2005); furthermore, they lead to fragmented research (George & Bock, 2011).

Based on the different definitions found, the constitutive elements of the business model are summarized (Table 1). In which is observed that most of the elements are repeated, and can be grouped in the basic conception: create and capture value. The creation of value combines its elements such as the value proposition, the key resources and the processes that ultimately lead to the creation of value. Additionally, the financial model establishes the aspect of value capture within a cost-benefit analysis.

By recognizing the importance of the business model, and the difficulty of determining it, the first hypothesis of the investigation arises.

H1: Newly created firms that develop a business model using as basic elements: the value proposal, resources, processes, and financial model; they have a positive effect on performance.

However, it is important to highlight that this business model does not take into account a critical dimension of business performance: competition since this is the work of the strategy. Business models are not synonymous with a strategy (Teece, 2010). However, they facilitate the analysis, testing, and validation of strategic decisions of a company (Shafer, Smith, & Linder, 2005).

Teece's vision of the business model is quite practical "the company must select or create a particular business model that defines its marketing strategy and investment priorities" (Teece, 2009, p. 18), adding that it is presented considerable evidence that business success depends on the very good design of this.

From the above, the second hypothesis arises.

H2: The newly created companies that develop a business model using as basic elements: the value proposition, the resources, the processes, and the financial model; defined in a strategy of product and/or service differentiation, and cost efficiency, have a positive effect on performance.

In an environment of rapid changes and shortened product, future profit flows from existing operations are uncertain and companies have constantly look for new opportunities (Rauch, Wiklund, Lumpkin, & Frese, 2009). Today the business environment is increasingly dynamic due to the rapid and significant changes in technology, the life cycles of increasingly short products, increasing global competition, and rapid dissemination of knowledge and business practices increasingly aggressive (Teece, Pisano, & Shuen, 1997; Wang & Ahmed, 2007; Protogerou, Caloghirou, & Lioukas, 2008).

Dynamic environments are characterized by ambiguous industrial structures, blurred boundaries, fluid business models, ambiguous and changing players, and unpredictable and non-linear changes (Eisenhardt & Martin, 2000), while dynamic capabilities arise in response to the difficulties that companies have in having dynamic market environments (Eisenhardt & Martin, 2000). Dynamic capabilities that consist of their ability to integrate, build and reconfigure their internal and external competencies to adapt to fast-changing contexts.

Therefore, they reflect the organizational ability to achieve new and innovative forms of competitive advantage (Teece, Pisano, & Shuen, 1997; Teece, 2009) and specifically to detect, configure, take advantage of, empower and manage new opportunities. As a result, the third hypothesis is set.

Table 1. Different elements proposed for business models

No.	Authors	Elements
1	Chesbrough and Rosenbloom (2000)	1. Value Proposition 2. Market segment. 3. Structure of the value chain. 4. Cost structure and potential benefits to offer your product. 5. Describe the position of the company within the value system, relating suppliers and customers. 6. Formulate the competitive strategy through which the innovative company will be more competitive and will obtain a sustainable advantage.
2	Shafer, Smith, and Linder (2005)	1. Basic logic and strategy choice. 2. Creating value. 3. Value Capture. 4. A network of value.
3	Johnson Christensen and Kagermann (2010)	1. The proposition of consumer value. 2. The utility formula. 3. Key resources. 4. Operational, managerial, norms, rules and metrics processes.
4	Osterwalder and Pigneur (2010)	1. Market segment. 2. Proposed value. 3. Channels. 4. Relationship with the client. 5. Sources of income. 6. Key resources. 7. Key activities. 8. Key Partnerships. 9. Cost structure.
5	Morris, Schindehutte, and Allen (2005)	1. Factors related to the offer to the market. 2. Market factors. 3. Internal capabilities. 4. Competitive strategy. 5. Economic factors 6. Growth relative to investors
6	Teece (2010)	1. Selection of technology and features to be included in the product. 2. Determining the benefits to consumers from consumerism. 3. Identification of the target market segment. 4. Confirmation of the possibility of receiving income. 5. Design of mechanisms to capture value.
7	Venkatraman and Henderson (1998)	1. Interaction with customers. 2. Asset configuration. 3. Leveraging knowledge.
8	Amit and Zott (2001)	1. Content. 2. Structure. 3. Government.

Source: Author

H3: The newly created companies that develop a business model have a positive effect on performance when using as basic elements: (1) a strategy of product and/or service differentiation; (2) cost efficiency, and (3) the capacity to detect, configure, take advantage, empower, and manage new opportunities.

METHODOLOGY

To verify the hypothesis and the fulfillment of the objective of the chapter, further research is being developed to analyze the segment of newly created family-based MSMEs in the city of Bogota (Colombia). The industry chosen is the development of computer systems (planning, analysis, design, programming, testing) industry, computer consulting, and information services activities (codes 62 and 63), according to the International Standard Industrial Classification (ISIC) of all economic activities worldwide. Although there is no consensus on the definition of a family business (Astrachan, Klein, & Smyrnios, 2002), the most common way to define it (Kontinen & Ojala, 2010) is by combining ownership and management criteria (Gallo & Sveen, 1991; Saiz-Álvarez, 2011). In recent years the criterion of continuity has been added, in which family or generational succession is guaranteed. However, for the present investigation, this last criterion is not relevant.

In Colombia, MSMEs are defined for the number of employees and the value of the assets (Article 43 of Law 1450 of 2011, Article 2 of Law 590 of 2000, and Article 2 of Law 905 of 2004). There are 2,023 newly created MSMEs registered in the Chamber of Commerce of Bogota (Colombia), belonging to codes 62 and 63, between 2007 and 2011. Of them, 1,787 (88.33%) are dedicated to the development of information systems and 236 (11.67%) to information services activities.

Based on the above, a simple random sampling was carried out to identify the companies to be surveyed. In total, 320 telephone calls were made, of which 144 firms (7.12%) answered being family businesses, being micro (42 companies), small (78), and medium-sized (24). This percentage is acceptable since, and according to Cooper and Schindler (2008), the size of the sample is greater than 5% of the total population. The error of the sample was 7.87%.

Questionnaire

The information was collected through a questionnaire with forty-five questions about the three axes of the proposal: a) the basic elements of the business model, b) business strategies, and c) the dynamic capabilities of the firm. The first three questions were focused on specific data of the firm: a) Business creation date; b) the number of employees, and c) if they consider they are a family firm. The fourth question deals with the dynamic of the environment. Using SPSS 20.0, the questionnaire was measured using a 1-7 Likert scale (1 = totally disagree, 7 = totally agree) enriched with semantic differences developed by Miller and Friesen (1983), where it is asked about the frequency of market changes and the rate of obsolescence of products and services, the actions of the competitors, the demand and tastes of the consumers and technological changes.

Variables

The research is causal, which leads to use the statistical tools of multivariate analysis, and specifically the dependence and interdependence analysis. The dependency analysis consists of one or several dependent variables to be explained by several independent variables, while the analysis of interdependence consists of analyzing all the variables together, without considering any of them as dependent or independent, and trying to find some underlying structure (Hair, Anderson, Tatham, & Black, 2007). Besides, the investigation deals with ordinal or categorical variables, which measure the attributes of the different variables of the model. A characteristic of this type of variables is the difficulty of establishing a lower level in their measurement and the relationship between different measures since they are arbitraries (Domínguez, Blancas, Guerrero, & González, 2011), which imply "that the values of a variable represent ordered categories. Examples include attitude scales that represent the degree of satisfaction or confidence and preference rating scores" (Meulman & Heiser, 2012, p. 2).

Taking into account that the variables defined are categorical and used in an interdependence and dependence analysis, we proceeded by creating a main categorical components' analysis (CATPCA) complemented with a categorical regression (CATREG). As a result, the dependent variable of the model corresponds to the performance of the firm and is composed of profitability, growth in sales, assets, and the number of employees, as shown in Table 2.

Measurement of business performance is carried out using non-quantitative indicators, which has been used successfully by numerous researchers, given that one of the main advantages of this methodology lies on the high response rate (Covin & Slevin, 1989). As a result, the independent variables (Table 3) feed the model in three dimensions: a) basic elements of the business model, b) strategies used, and c) the dynamic capacities applied. In turn, each dimension analyzed has some components or attributes that support it.

The theoretical framework of the value proposition, the resources, the process, and the financial model are shown in table 4.

For the dimension of the strategy, three components are presented: the differentiation of the product and/or service, the cost efficiency and the combination of the two previous strategies (Table 4).

The dimension of the dynamic capacities (Teece, 2007 & 2009) is composed of: 1) The capabilities of detecting and configuring (CD1); 2) Take advantage and empower (CD2), and 3) Manage new business opportunities (CD3).

Table 2. Theoretical reference of the elements of the dependent variable

No.	Elements	Theoretical Reference
1	Profitability (DE1)	Financial measures include return on assets, the margin on sales and return on equity; being its objective results, simple, easy to understand and calculate (Chong, 2008).
2	Growth in sales (DE2)	The importance of growth in sales as a measure of performance lies in anticipating the achievement of sustainable competitive advantages and profitability (Markman & Gartner, 2002, Sexton, Pricer, & Nenide, 2002; Delmar, Davidsson, & Gartner, 2003).
3	Growth in assets (DE3)	The indicators of growth in assets and the number of employees have been considered as precursors to good performance. (Delmar, Davidsson, & Gartner, 2003).
4	Growth in the number of employees (DE4)	

Source: Author

Table 3. Dimensions of the proposed model

Dimensions	Components or Attributes
Basics elements of the business model	Value proposal
	Resources
	Processes
	Financial model
Strategies	Differentiation in projects
	Cost efficiency
Dynamic capabilities	Capabilities in detecting and configuring new business opportunities
	Capabilities to take advantage and empower new opportunities
	Capabilities to manage new opportunities

Source: Author

Analysis of Reliability and Validity

Reliability was determined with the Cronbach's alpha and was 0.897, so the result is good since they are above 0.80. On the other hand, the validity of the questionnaire was carried out with the help of three experts, who suggested eliminating three questions corresponding to the value proposal: PV6, PV7, and PV8; since they turned out to be quite "confusing" and "not very clear" at the time of being answered by eliminating the three components of the proposed value variable, the Cronbach's alpha increased to 0.907.

Categorical Principal Component Analysis

From the CATPCA, the elements of each variable that can be redundant are reviewed, this to suppress some of them and deliver a few without loss of information (Pérez, 2009).

For the first component of the basic elements of the business model corresponding to the value proposition, of seven factors, it has been reduced to three. According to the results, factor 1 explains 35.818% of the variance of the model and factor 2 explains 33.587%, which means that the two factors explain 69.405% of the variance (Table 7)

For the second component, the resources of eight elements are passed to only three factors. According to the CATPCA results, factor 1 explains 38.072% of the variance of the model and factor 2 explains 26.433%, which means that the two factors explain 64.505% of the variance (Table 8).

For the third attribute, the processes of the four elements are being reduced to two factors. According to the CATPCA results, factor 1 explains 71.394% of the variance of the model and factor 2 explains 21.201%, which means that the two factors explain 92.595% of the variance (Table 9).

For the fourth attribute, the financial model of three elements is passed to two factors. According to the CATPCA results, factor 1 explains 64.895% of the variance of the model and factor 2 explains 29.643%, which means that the two factors explain 94.538% of the variance (Table 10).

For the dimension of the strategy, of three elements, we turn to two factors.

According to the CATPCA results, factor 1 explains 64.273% of the variance of the model and factor 2 explains 24.263%, which means that the two factors explain 88.535% of the variance. The factor refers to offering strategies with customers' differentiation and lower costs in products and/or services.

Table 4. Components and theoretical reference of the value proposal, resources, process, and financial model

No.	Components	Theoretical Reference
1	Adding value to customers (PV1)	The value proposition generally refers to the reasons why a customer values what a company offers (Nagle & Holden, 2002; Kotler, 1999)
2	A positive assessment by customers (PV2)	The value proposition is the answer to the question of why customers should buy from your company (Kotler, 1999)
3	Segmentation (PV3)	Segmentation is the "division of the total market into smaller and relatively homogeneous groups" (Kurtz, 2012, p. 277). A good segmentation allows identifying groups of consumers with similar purchasing needs and behaviors (Lamb, Hair, & McDaniel, 2006).
4	Directed to deliver "more for more" (PV4), "more for the same" (PV5), "more for less" (PV6), "the same for less" (PV7) and "less for much less" (PV8)	Companies establish alternatives for value propositions in a broad manner, identified as strategies, which leads them to deliver differentiated products and/or services and/or with cost efficiency (Conner, 1991; Porter, 1985; Andrews, 1971). Resulting in products and/or services with specific benefits, with a clear reason to be purchased by the client. Thus, there are unique proposals around certain characteristics that lead to different value propositions (Kotler, 1999)
5	Communication in an appropriate manner (PV9)	The value proposal reaches the client through good communication. The set of communication tools that can carry a message to a target audience is known as promotion (Lamb, Hair, & McDaniel, 2006).
6	Easy access for the client, through a distribution channel (PV10)	Aspects such as coverage, experience, and performance must be taken into account when defining access channels for the client (Kotler & Keller, 2007)
7	Fixed assets (equipment, furniture, fixtures, etc.) (RE1)	They are easily identifiable and assessable. They are constantly revised in search of greater efficiencies in their operation, and in finding new possibilities for their use (Grant, 2010). A primary characteristic of tangible assets is the fact that they cannot be used simultaneously, that is, they are mutually exclusive.
8	Financial resources (RE2)	
9	Intangible resources such as copyright, patents, trademark registration, and developments (RE3)	They are invisible to financial statements. They are excluded and undervalued (Grant, 2010; Levy & Varela, 2003). Intangible assets are not exclusive; which leads them to have opportunity costs equal to zero, once the initial investment has been made. This leads them to have high initial investment costs, which are normally considered as sunken, and low operating costs, considered as incremental (Levy & Varela, 2003).
10	Knowledge of the entrepreneur given through experience and education in this type of business (RE4)	The knowledge of entrepreneurs obtained through experience and education have been studied by Stuart and Abetti (1990), Storey (1994), and Pfeffer (1994).
11	Knowledge of work activities by employees (RE5)	Companies need to have the knowledge, skills, and motivation of employees; These competences contain three types of knowledge: conceptual (knowing), procedural (know-how) and attitudinal (being) (Pinto, 1999) to form the 7-K (know-how, know-when, know-why, know-where, know-who, know-whom, and know-whose)(Saiz-Alvarez, 2018)
12	Skills on the part of employees for the development of different work activities. (RE6)	
13	Motivation on the part of employees for the development of different work activities. (RE7)	
14	With collective learning that results in conceptual, procedural and attitudinal skills of its employees, developed through routines. (RE8)	Collective learning results in the company having as a whole the set of conceptual, procedural and attitudinal competencies of its employees, elements necessary to achieve the objectives proposed by management. This learning is developed through routines, which as Winter (2003) says "are the behavior that is learned, very repetitive, repetitive or almost repetitive patterns, based in part on tacit knowledge - and the specificity of the objectives."
15	Strategic (PR1)	Orientation to the organization (Zaratiegui, 1999). They define how the business is organized (Beretta, 2002).
16	Operative (PR2)	Operative (PR2) Orientation expressly to the business (Zaratiegui, 1999). Adopting a process for the company implies taking into account the point of view of the client's needs, and implies placing a greater emphasis, rather than what is going to be delivered, in the process of how to deliver value to the consumer (Davenport, 1993).
17	Of support (PR3)	They complement other processes (Zaratiegui, 1999).
18	As a result of routines and/or activities that take place on a day-to-day basis. (PR4)	For Ray, Barney and Muhana (2004), processes are the result of routines and/or activities carried out by the firm in their day to day, which allow the company to achieve its goals.
19	Projection of future cash flows. (MF1)	The fundamental tool for the administration, control, and evaluation of the financial model corresponds to the cash flow (inflows and outflows of money over time)(Drucker, 1993).
20	Internal control of costs (MF2)	The financial model includes internal control issues, both accounting and administrative. "Internal control is a fundamental responsibility of top management" (Horngren & Foster, 1991, p. 1038).
21	It has real-time financial information. (MF3)	Companies, and specifically their employees and managers, must have sufficient and updated information to make better decisions and be proactive in the face of constant changes in the environment (Honeycutt, 2001).

Source: Author

Table 5. Components and theoretical reference of the strategy.

<table>
<tr><th>No.</th><th>Components</th><th>Theoretical References</th></tr>
<tr><td>1</td><td>Strategies with customers to differentiate the product and/or service (ES1)</td><td rowspan="3">The elements that allow reaching the creation and the capture of value are product and/or service differentiation, and cost efficiency; taking into account that both strategies are not mutually exclusive and can occur at the same time and used by the firm for years (Conner, 1991; Porter, 1985; Andrews, 1971).</td></tr>
<tr><td>2</td><td>Strategies with cost-efficient clients (ES2)</td></tr>
<tr><td>3</td><td>Strategies to differentiate clients and reduce costs in products and/or services (ES3)</td></tr>
</table>

Source: Author

Table 6. Theoretical reference of the control variables

No.	Variables	Theoretical Reference
1	Time from the creation of the firm	For purposes of the present research, a newly created firm has between three and seven years, on average five years of formally established; which have the potential to reach the size and has significant profitability (Bhide, 2000).
2	Number of employees	In Colombia, and until the National Government regulates Article 43 of Law 1450 of 2011, the definitions contained in Article 2 of Law 590 of 2000 and Article 2 of Law 905 of 2004, will continue in force. In other words, the number of employees and the value of the assets defines MSMEs.
3	Family business	There is no consensus on the definition of a family business (Astrachan, Klein, & Smyrnios, 2002). The most common way to define a family business (Kontinen & Ojala, 2010) is through a combination of ownership and management criteria (Gallo & Sveen, 1991). In recent years, the criterion of continuity has been added, in which the passage or generational succession of the family is guaranteed. However, for the present investigation, this last criterion is not relevant.
4	Dynamic environments	They are defined by unpredictable and rapid changes, increasing uncertainty for individuals and the companies that work within them (Duncan, 1972; Dess & Beard, 1984).

Source: Author

Table 7. Factors resulting from the value proposition

No.	Components	Factor 1	Factor 2	Factor 3
1	Adding value to customers, segmentation and addressing "more for more" and "more for the same."	FPV1		
2	Communication and access		FPV2	
3	Positive feedback from customers			FPV3

Source: Author

Table 8. The attributes of the resources variable

No.	Components	Factor 1	Factor 2	Factor 3
1	Entrepreneurial knowledge, motivation on the part of employees and collective learning.	FRE1		
2	Fixed assets, financial and intangible resources such as copyright, patents, trademark registration, and developments.		FRE2	
3	Knowledge and skills on the parts of employees.			FRE3

Source: Author

Table 9. Elements of the processes variable

No.	Components	Factor 1	Factor 2
1	Consolidation of strategic, operational and support processes in a formal manner.	FPR1	
2	As a result of routines and/or activities that take place on a day-to-day basis		FPR2

Source: Author

Table 10. Elements of the financial model variable

No.	Components	Factor 1	Factor 2
1	Projection of future cash flows and internal cost control	FMF1	
2	Real-time financial information is available		FMF2

Source: Author

For the analysis of the dynamic capacities, the first factor corresponds to the use of the capacities to take advantage of and empower the new business opportunities. The second factor corresponds to the use of capabilities to detect and configure new business opportunities, and the third factor corresponds to the use of the capabilities to manage new business opportunities, the latter contributes to the previous two capabilities. According to the CATPCA results, factor 1 explains 46.519% of the variance of the model and factor 2 explains 34.397%, which means that the two factors explain 80.916% of the variance.

Finally, performance (dependent variable) is composed of four variables: profitability, sales growth, assets growth, and employees growth. It has been averaged into a single variable, with the name of DETOT.

RESULTS

Regarding the first planted hypothesis, causality is corroborated using the CATREG analysis, resulting in an R squared of 0.643, where it can be stated that the performance in newly created family MSMEs is explained in 64.3%, that is, the model is adequate to describe the relationship that exists between these variables.

From the results of the analysis (Table 11), it can be observed that FMF1, corresponding to the use of projections of future cash flows and internal cost control, is a strong predictor of corporate performance since it has significance values lower than 0.05.

In the same way, it can be observed that the factors FPV3, corresponding to the positive valuation by the clients, and FRE3, corresponding to the knowledge and skills by the employees, have an inverse effect on the performance, however, are not significant factors in the analysis.

Finally, the utility test of the model is established in which it is verified if it provides significant information to the analysis (Table 12), contrasting and eliminating the null hypothesis (Ho) since the significance (0.000) is less than 0.05. The preceding indicates that at least one of the βj is different from zero, that is, there is a model.

Table 11. Coefficients of Categorical Regression indicating the significance of the variables of the business model in the performance of the company.

	Typified Coefficients		gl	F	Sig.
	Beta	Bootstrap (1000) Typical Error Estimate			
FPV1	0.164	0.127	3	1.672	0.177
FPV2	0.083	0.181	1	0.209	0.648
FPV3	-0.148	0.225	2	0.434	0.649
FRE1	0.168	0.111	3	2.279	0.083
FRE2	0.135	0.136	1	0.975	0.325
FRE3	-0.232	0.221	2	1.101	0.336
FPR1	0.129	0.201	2	0.410	0.664
FPR2	0.244	0.227	1	1.150	0.286
FMF1	0.660	0.203	2	10.598	0.000
FMF2	0.108	0.145	3	0.548	0.650

Dependent variable: DETOT
Source: Author

Table 12. Utility test of the model for the basic elements

	Sum of Squares	gl	Quadratic Mean	F	Sig.
Regression	92.559	20	4.628	11.066	0
Residual	51.441	123	0.418		
Total	144	143			

Dependent variable: DETOT
Predictors: FPV1 FPV2 FPV3 FRE1 FRE2 FRE3 FPR1 FPR2 FMF1 FMF2
Source: Author

Regarding the second hypothesis, the causality is corroborated using the CATREG analysis, with the result of the model an R-square of 0.661, where it can be affirmed that the performance in the newly created companies is explained by 66.1%, that is, the model is adequate to describe the relationship between these variables.

From the analysis (Table 13), it appears that the FMF1 factor, corresponding to the use of projections of future cash flows and internal cost control, is again a strong predictor of the performance of companies, since it presents values of significance less than 0.05.

Likewise, the factors FPV2, corresponding to communication and access by customers to products and services, and FRE3, corresponding to knowledge and skills on the part of employees, have an inverse effect on performance; however, they are factors not significant in the analysis.

Finally, the utility test of the model is established where it is verified if it provides significant information to the analysis (Table 14), contrasting and eliminating the null hypothesis (Ho) since the significance (0.000) is less than 0.05. The preceding indicates that at least one of the βj is different from zero, that is, there is a model.

Table 13. Coefficients of the categorical regression indicating the significance of the variables of the business model in the performance of the company

	Typified Coefficients		gl	F	Sig.
	Beta	Bootstrap (1000) Typical Error Estimate			
FPV1	0.036	0.163	2	0.049	0.952
FPV2	-0.122	0.202	2	0.361	0.698
FPV3	0.073	0.236	1	0.097	0.756
FRE1	0.152	0.120	2	1.601	0.206
FRE2	0.089	0.136	2	0.434	0.649
FRE3	-0.285	0.231	2	1.514	0.224
FPR1	0.080	0.253	1	0.099	0.753
FPR2	0.221	0.232	2	0.909	0.406
FMF1	0.603	0.203	2	8.800	0
FMF2	0.067	0.154	3	0.191	0.902
FES1	0.105	0.179	2	0.341	0.712
FES2	0.163	0.253	1	0.416	0.520

Dependent variable: DETOT
Source: Author

Table 14. Utility test of the model for the basic elements and the strategy

	Sum of Squares	gl	Quadratic Mean	F	Sig.
Regression	95.138	22	4.324	10.709	0
Residual	48.862	121	0.404		
Total	144	143			

Dependent variable: DETOT
Predictors: FPV1 FPV2 FPV3 FRE1 FRE2 FRE3 FPR1 FPR2 FMF1 FMF2 FES1 FES2
Source: Author

Regarding the third hypothesis, the causality is corroborated using the CATREG analysis, resulting in an R squared of 0.959, it can be stated that the performance in the newly created companies is explained in a 95.9%, that is, the model is adequate to describe the relationship that exists between these variables. It is observed that about the previous model when adding the factors of the dynamic capacities, the adjustment increases.

For this third hypothesis, it is established that FCD1, the use of capabilities to take advantage of and empower new business opportunities and FPV1, adding value to customers, segmentation and addressing "more for more" and "more so", and "same"; They are strong predictors of the performance of companies, since they have values of significance less than 0.05 (Table 15).

The following variables have an inverse effect on the results, although they are not significant factors (Table 15):

Table 15. Coefficients of the categorical regression indicating the significance of the variables of the business model, strategies and dynamic capabilities in the performance of the company

	Typified Coefficients		gl	F	Sig.
	Beta	Bootstrap (1000) Typical Error Estimate			
FPV1	0.323	0.170	2	3.602	0.030
FPV2	-0.056	0.073	2	0.595	0.553
FPV3	0.064	0.096	3	0.450	0.718
FRE1	-0.010	0.037	3	0.070	0.976
FRE2	-0.029	0.040	1	0.523	0.471
FRE3	0.008	0.076	1	0.011	0.917
FPR1	-0.094	0.089	2	1.117	0.331
FPR2	0.077	0.075	2	1.045	0.355
FMF1	0.103	0.136	1	0.575	0.450
FMF2	-0.028	0.064	1	0.186	0.667
FES1	0.038	0.048	4	0.636	0.638
FES2	0.036	0.063	1	0.321	0.572
FCD1	0.740	0.155	2	22.670	0
FCD2	0.069	0.062	2	1.256	0.289
FCD3	0.059	0.066	2	0.804	0.450

Dependent variable: DETOT
Source: Author

1. FPV2, communication, and access by customers to products and services;
2. FRE1, entrepreneurial knowledge, motivation by employees and collective learning;
3. FRE2, fixed assets, financial and intangible resources such as copyrights, patents, trademark registration, and developments;
4. FPR1, consolidation of strategic, operational and support processes in a formal manner; and
5. FMF2, corresponding to the fact of having real-time financial information,

Finally, the utility test of the model is established in which it is verified if it provides significant information to the analysis (Table 16), contrasting and eliminating the null hypothesis (Ho) since the significance (0.000) is less than 0.05. The preceding indicates that at least one of the βj is different from zero, that is, there is a model.

CONCLUSION AND RECOMMENDATIONS

The chapter presented a business model for newly created family MSMEs working in the system development sector of the city of Bogota (Colombia), using as basic elements: value proposition, resources, processes, and the financial model. This combination allows the firm to have a positive effect on their performance.

Table 16. Utility test of the model for the basic elements, strategy and dynamic capabilities

	Sum of Squares	gl	Quadratic Mean	F	Sig.
Regression	138.114	29	4.763	92.247	0
Residual	5.886	114	0.052		
Total	144	143			

Dependent variable: DETOT
Predictors: FPV1 FPV2 FPV3 FRE1 FRE2 FRE3 FPR1 FPR2 FMF1 FMF2 FES1 FES2 FCD1 FCD2 FCD3
Source: Author

The results of the categorical regression analysis give an R squared of 0.643, so the adjustment of the model is good and adequate to describe the relationship between these variables. Additionally, it is established that the FMF1 factor, corresponding to the use of projections of future cash flows and internal cost control, is a strong predictor of the performance of companies, since it has values with a significance less than 0.05.

Because of applying the analysis of main categorical components, the components of the basic elements were obtained. First, value proposition, which is defined by adding value addressed to deliver more for more, or more for the same, or more for less, and its positive assessment by customers with a clear segmentation. As a result, firms have adequate communication and easy access to distribution channels. Second, are resources, which are comprised of fixed assets, financial and intangible resources such as copyright, patent, trademark, registrations, and developments; additionally, the entrepreneur's knowledge and skills and motivations of the employees are available to increase different work activities, which allow collective learning and the growth of basic skills through routines. Third, the processes, which are oriented to the organization in strategic, operational and support issues. Finally, a financial model, with future cash flows, internal control of costs and real information.

So far, the business model is based on efficiency; however, this model is insufficient, since it does not ensure competitive advantage, and it becomes generic for companies, so it must be complemented and supported with a strategy of product and/or service differentiation and cost efficiency, which makes it a model that creates and captures value effectively.

For newly created family MSMEs developing business models, they use as basic elements: value proposition, resources, processes, and the financial model; and besides, they define a differentiation-based strategy for the product and/or service, and the efficiency in costs have a positive effect on performance.

The results of the categorical regression analysis give an R-square of 0.661, so the fit of the model is good and is adequate to describe the relationship between these variables. Again, it is established that the FMF1 factor, corresponding to future cash flows' projections and internal cost control, is a strong predictor of the business performance, as it has values of significance less than 0.05. Table 17 proposes a business model with efficiency and effectiveness for newly created family MSMEs that correlates with their business performance.

However, over time the business model is no longer effective, so it must adapt to dynamic environments, be sustainable over time and have sufficient business performance to create and capture value continuously, and therefore be effective. In short, for newly created companies that develop a business model using as basic elements: value proposition, resources, processes, there is a positive effect on performance due to the financial model, the product and/or service differentiation strategy, cost efficiency, and capabilities to detect, configure, take advantage, and manage new business opportunities. The results

Table 17. Proposed model with efficiency and effectiveness

Effectiveness	Differentiation and Efficiency Strategy	
Efficiency	Value proposition	Value creation
	Key resources	
	Processes	
	Financial model	Value capture

Source: Author

of the categorical regression analysis give an R squared of 0.959, so the adjustment of the model is good and adequate to describe the relationship that exists between these variables.

Besides, the FPV1 factors, adding value to customers with addressing "more for more" and "more for the same" and with an adequate segmentation; and FCD1, the use of the capacities to take advantage of and empower new business opportunities; They are strong predictors of the performance of companies, since they have values of significance less than 0.05. As a result, we propose a business model with efficiency, effectiveness, and efficacy for newly created family MSMEs that correlates with their business performance (figure 1). The model must have, not only an appropriate value proposal but also include key processes and resources to fit with a financial model by offering differentiated and cost-efficient strategies to customers in products and/or services. The business strategy appears where the dynamic capabilities allow taking advantage of empowering, detecting, configuring, and managing new business opportunities.

Figure 1. Proposed model for MSMEs with efficiency, effectiveness, and efficacy
Source: Author

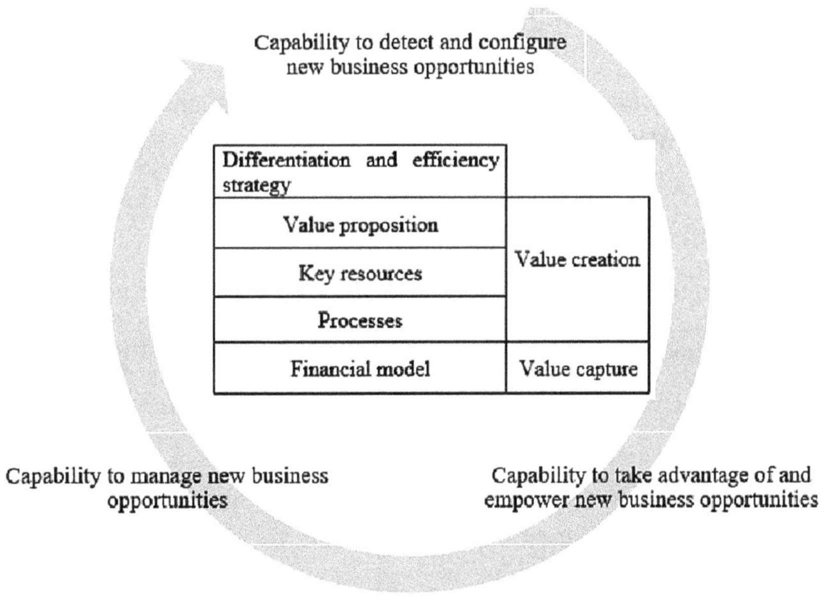

Finally, it is important to take into account the limitations of these results. First, they are limited to systems development's MSMEs and family firms of the city of Bogota (Colombia). Second, although the model presents a high correlation (for the third hypothesis is 0.959), they are not the only causes that explain the results. Third, the research is cross-sectional in a very specific view of the problem over time. As a result, new concerns arise that could give rise to new research: how applicable is the business model proposed to other sectors of the economy and other geographical areas? How different are the results of the application of the business model proposed between family MSMEs and those that are not? Moreover, how different are the results of the application of the business model proposed among family MSMEs in dynamic and non-dynamic environments? And finally, how different could the results be from replicating the research with longitudinal data, to get a more realistic view of the problem? These questions will be answered in future research.

REFERENCES

Amit, R., & Zott, C. (2001). Value creation in e-business. *Strategic Management Journal, 22*(6-7), 493–520. doi:10.1002mj.187

Andrews, K. (1971). *The Concept of Corporate Strategy*. Homewood, IL: Dow Jones-Irwin.

Astrachan, J. H., Klein, S., & Smyrnios, K. (2002). The F-PEC scale of family influence: A proposal for solving the family business definition problem. *Family Business Review, 15*(1), 45–57. doi:10.1111/j.1741-6248.2002.00045.x

Astrachan, J. H., Zahra, S. A., & Sharma, P. (2003). *Family-sponsored ventures*. Kansas City, MO: Kauffman Foundation.

Barney, J. B. (1991). Firm Resources and Sustained Competitive Advantage. *Journal of Management, 17*(1), 99–121. doi:10.1177/014920639101700108

Barney, J. B. (2007). *Gaining and Sustaining Competitive Advantage*. Upper Saddle River, NJ: Prentice Hall.

Becerra, M. (2009). *Theory of the Firm for Strategic Management*. Cambridge, UK: Cambridge University Press. doi:10.1017/CBO9780511626524

Beretta, S. (2002). Unleashing the integration potential of ERP systems. *Business Process Management Journal, 8*(3), 254–277. doi:10.1108/14637150210428961

Bhide, A. (2000). *The Origin and Evolution of New Businesses*. Oxford, UK: Oxford University Press.

Brunet, I. (2011). *Creación de Empresas. Emprendimiento e innovación*. Madrid, Spain: Ra-ma Editorial.

Camisón, C. (1997). *La competitividad de la PYME industrial española: estrategia y competencias distintivas*. Madrid: Civitas.

Chesbrough, H., & Rosenbaum, R. (2000). *The role of the business model in capturing value from innovation (working paper)*. Boston: Harvard Business School.

Chong, H. (2008). Measuring the performance of small and medium-sized enterprises: The grounded theory approach. *Journal of Business and Public Affairs*, *2*(1), 1–10.

Conner, K. R. (1991). A Historical Comparison of Resource-based Theory and Five Schools of Thought Within Industrial Organisation Economics: Do We Have a New Theory of the Firm? *Journal of Management*, *17*(1), 121–154. doi:10.1177/014920639101700109

Cooper, D., & Schindler, P. S. (2008). *Business Research Methods*. Boston: McGraw-Hill Irwin.

Covin, J. G., & Slevin, D. P. (1989). Strategic Management of Small Firms in Hostile and Benign Environments. *Strategic Management Journal*, *10*(1), 75–87. doi:10.1002mj.4250100107

Davenport, T. H. (1993). *The Process of Innovation*. Boston: Ernst & Young - Harvard Business School Press.

Dávila, J. C. (2009). *Capacidades dinámicas: un acercamiento a las teorías contemporáneas de la firma. Evidencias de dos organizaciones que operan en Colombia*. Bogotá, Colombia: Universidad de los *Andes*.

Delmar, F., Davidsson, P., & Gartner, W. (2003). Arriving at the high-growth firm. *Journal of Business Venturing*, *18*(2), 189–216. doi:10.1016/S0883-9026(02)00080-0

Dess, G., & Beard, D. (1984). Dimensions of organizational task environments. *Administrative Science Quarterly*, *29*(1), 52–73. doi:10.2307/2393080

Domínguez, M., Blancas, F. J., Guerrero, F. M., & González, M. (2011). Una revisión crítica para la construcción de indicadores sintéticos. *Revista de Métodos Cuantitativos para la Economía y la Empresa*, *11*, 41–70.

Drucker, P. F. (1993). *Gerencia para el Futuro*. Bogota, Colombia: Editorial Norma.

Duncan, R. (1972). Characteristics of organizational environments and perceived environmental uncertainty. *Administrative Science Quarterly*, *17*(3), 313–327. doi:10.2307/2392145

Eisenhardt, K., & Martin, J. (2000). Dynamic Capabilities. What are they? *Strategic Management Journal*, *21*(10/11), 1105–1121. doi:10.1002/1097-0266(200010/11)21:10/11<1105::AID-SMJ133>3.0.CO;2-E

Gallo, M. A., & Sveen, J. (1991). Internationalizing the Family Business: Facilitating and Restraining Factors. *Family Business Review*, *4*(2), 181–190. doi:10.1111/j.1741-6248.1991.00181.x

George, G., & Bock, A. J. (2011). The Business Model in Practice and its Implications for Entrepreneurship Research. *Entrepreneurship Theory and Practice*, *35*(1), 83–111. doi:10.1111/j.1540-6520.2010.00424.x

Grant, R. (1991). The Resource-Based Theory of Competitive Advantage: Implications for Strategy Formulation. *California Management Review*, *33*(3), 114–135. doi:10.2307/41166664

Grant, R. M. (2010). *Contemporary Strategy Analysis*. Chichester, UK: John Wiley & Sons.

Hair, J. F., Anderson, R. E., Tatham, R. L., & Black, W. C. (2007). *Análisis multivariante*. Madrid, Spain: Pearson-Prentice Hall.

Honeycutt, J. (2001). *Así es la Gestión del Conocimiento*. Madrid, Spain: McGraw-Hill Interamericana.

Horngren, C. T., & Foster, G. (1991). *Contabilidad de Costos. Un Enfoque Gerencial.* D.F., Mexico: Prentice Hall.

Johnson, M. W., Christensen, C. M., & Kagermann, H. (2010). Reinventing your Business Model. In *Harvard Business Review on Business Model Innovation* (pp. 47–70). Boston: Harvard University Press.

Kontinen, T., & Ojala, A. (2010). The internationalization of family businesses: A review of extant research. *Journal of Family Business Strategy, 1/2*(2), 97–107. doi:10.1016/j.jfbs.2010.04.001

Kotler, P. (1999). *El Marketing según Kotler*. Buenos Aires, Argentina: Editorial Paidos SAICF.

Kotler, P., & Keller, K. L. (2007). *A Framework of Marketing Management*. London, UK: Pearson Education.

Kurtz, D. L. (2012). *Marketing Contemporáneo*. D.F., Mexico: Cengage Learning Editores.

Lamb, C. W., Hair, J. F., & McDaniel, C. (2006). *Marketing*. D.F., Mexico: Thomson.

Levy, J. P., & Varela, J. (2003). *Análisis multivariable para las ciencias sociales*. Madrid, Spain: Pearson-Prentice Hall.

Magretta, J. (2010). Why Business Model Matter. In Harvard Business Review on Business Model Innovation (pp. 1-18). Boston: Academic Press.

Mahoney, J., & Padian, J. R. (1992). The Resource-Based View within the Conversation of Strategic Management. *Strategic Management Journal, 13*(5), 363–380. doi:10.1002mj.4250130505

Markman, G. D., & Gartner, W. (2002). Is Extraordinary Growth Profitable? A Study of Inc. 500 High-Growth Companies. *Entrepreneurship Theory and Practice, 23*(1), 65–75. doi:10.1111/1540-8520.t01-2-00004

Meulman, J., & Heiser, W. (2012). *SPSS Categories 20.0*. Chicago, IL: SPSS.

Morris, M., Schindehutte, M., & Allen, J. (2005). The entrepreneur's business model: Toward a unified perspective. *Journal of Business Research, 58*(6), 726–735. doi:10.1016/j.jbusres.2003.11.001

Nagle, T. T., & Holden, R. K. (2002). *Estrategia y Tácticas de Precios*. Madrid, Spain: Pearson-Prentice Hall.

Osterwalder, A. (2004). *The Business Model Ontology - A Proposition in a Design Science Approach.* Lausanne, Switzerland: University of Lausanne, Ecole des Hautes Etudes Commerciales.

Osterwalder, A., & Pigneur, Y. (2010). *Business Model Generation*. Hoboken, NJ: John Wiley & Sons.

Pérez, C. (2009). *Técnica de Análisis de Datos con SPSS 15*. Madrid, Spain: Pearson Educación.

Peteraf, M. A., & Barney, J. B. (2003). Unraveling the Resource-based Tangle. *Managerial and Decision Economics, 24*(4), 309–323. doi:10.1002/mde.1126

Pfeffer, J. (1994). *Competitive advantage through people*. Boston: Harvard Business School Press. doi:10.2307/41165742

Pinto, L. (1999). Currículo por competencia: Necesidad de una nueva escuela. *Tarea: Revista de Educación y Cultura*, *43*, 10–17.

Porter, M. E. (1980). *Competitive Strategy: Techniques for analyzing industries and competitors*. New York: Free Press.

Porter, M. E. (1985). *Competitive advantage*. New York: Free Press.

Porter, M. E. (1991). Towards a dynamic theory of strategy. *Strategic Management Journal*, *12*(S2), 95–117. doi:10.1002mj.4250121008

Poza, E. J. (2005). *Empresas de Familia*. D.F., Mexico: Thomson.

Priem, R., & Butler, J. (2001a). Is the resource-based "view" a useful perspective for strategic management research? *Academy of Management Review*, *26*(1), 22–40.

Priem, R., & Butler, J. (2001b). Tautology in the resource-based view and the implications of externally determined resource value: Further comments. *Academy of Management Review*, *26*(1), 57–66. doi:10.5465/amr.2001.4011946

Protogerou, A., Caloghirou, Y., & Lioukas, S. (2008). *Dynamic capabilities and their indirect impact on firm performance*. DRUID 25th Celebration Conference, Copenhagen, Denmark.

Rauch, A., Wiklund, J., Lumpkin, G., & Frese, M. (2009). Entrepreneurial Orientation and Business Performance: An Assessment of Past Research and Suggestions for the Future. *Entrepreneurship Theory and Practice*, *33*(3), 761–787. doi:10.1111/j.1540-6520.2009.00308.x

Ray, G., Barney, J. B., & Muhanna, W. A. (2004). Capabilities, business processes, and competitive advantage: Choosing the dependent variable in empirical tests of the resource-based view. *Strategic Management Journal*, *25*(1), 23–37. doi:10.1002mj.366

Rumelt, R. P. (1991). How much does Industry Matter? *Strategic Management Journal*, *12*(3), 167–185. doi:10.1002mj.4250120302

Rumelt, R. P., Schendel, D., & Teece, D. (1994). *Fundamental Issues in Strategy*. Cambridge, MA: Harvard Business School Press.

Saiz-Álvarez, J. M. (2011). Factores clave de éxito en la internacionalización de la empresa familiar: Una aplicación a la pyme. *Economía Industrial*, *380*, 57–62.

Saiz-Álvarez, J. M. (2018). Business Strategies and Advanced Techniques for Entrepreneurship 4.0. Hershey, PA: Information Science Reference (IGI Global).

Saiz-Álvarez, J. M., Muñiz, E., & Huezo, L. (2016). Informational Competencies, Entrepreneurship, and Integral Values in Higher Education. In Innovation and Shifting Perspectives in Management Education. Hershey, PA: Information Science Reference (IGI Global).

Schmalensee, R. (1985). Do markets differ much? *The American Economic Review*, *75*, 341–351.

Sexton, D., Pricer, R., & Nenide, B. (2002). Measuring performance in high growth firms. *Babson Entrepreneurship Research Conference*, Wellesley, MA.

Shafer, S., Smith, H., & Linder, J. (2005). The power of the business model. *Business Horizons*, *48*(3), 199–207. doi:10.1016/j.bushor.2004.10.014

Storey, D. (1994). *Understanding the Small Business Sector*. New York: Routledge.

Stuart, R. W., & Abetti, P. A. (1987). Start-up ventures towards the prediction of initial success. *Journal of Business Venturing*, *2*(3), 215–230. doi:10.1016/0883-9026(87)90010-3

Teece, D. J. (2007). Explicating Dynamic Capabilities: The Nature and Microfoundations of (Sustainable) Enterprise Performance. *Strategic Management Journal*, *28*(13), 1319–1350. doi:10.1002mj.640

Teece, D. J. (2009). *Dynamic Capabilities and Strategy Management*. New York: Oxford University Press Inc.

Teece, D. J. (2010). Business models, business strategy and innovation. *Long Range Planning*, *43*(2-3), 172–194. doi:10.1016/j.lrp.2009.07.003

Teece, D. J., Pisano, G., & Shuen, A. (1997). Dynamic Capabilities and Strategy Management. *Strategic Management Journal*, *18*(7), 509–533. doi:10.1002/(SICI)1097-0266(199708)18:7<509::AID-SMJ882>3.0.CO;2-Z

Venkatraman, N., & Henderson, J. C. (1998). Real strategies for virtual organizing. *Sloan Management Review*, *40*, 33–48.

Wang, C. L., & Ahmed, P. K. (2007). Dynamic capabilities: A review and research agenda. *International Journal of Management Reviews*, *9*(1), 31–51. doi:10.1111/j.1468-2370.2007.00201.x

Winter, S. G. (2003). Understanding dynamic capabilities. *Strategic Management Journal*, *24*(10), 991–995. doi:10.1002mj.318

Zahra, S. A. (1996). Technology strategy and financial performance: Examining the of the firm's competitive environment. *Journal of Business Venturing*, *11*(3), 189–219. doi:10.1016/0883-9026(96)00001-8

Zaratiegui, J. R. (1999). La Gestión por Procesos: Su papel e importancia en la empresa. *Economía Industrial*, *330*, 81–88.

Zott, C., Amit, R., & Massa, L. (2011). The business model: Recent developments and future research. *Journal of Management*, *37*(4), 1019–1042. doi:10.1177/0149206311406265

KEY TERMS AND DEFINITIONS

7-K: They are formed by combining the know-how, know-when, know-why, know-where, know-who, know-whom, and know-whose of the firm to determine business strategies and the settlement of goals.

Categorical Regression: A type of regression that quantifies categorical data by assigning numerical values to the categories, resulting in an optimal mathematical adjustment for the transformed variables.

Cronbach's Alpha: Originally used in the mid-1940s, it is a coefficient that measures the reliability of a scale of measurement.

Dynamic Capabilities: They are the type of capabilities formed by the combination of detecting and configuring new business opportunities and taking advantage, managing, and empowering new opportunities.

ISIC (International Standard Industrial Classification): It is the United Nations industry classification system used as an international reference classification of productive activities.

Newly Created Firm: It is a type of company between three and seven years of age, having on average five years of being formally established, which has the potential to achieve sustainable business growth.

Tacit Knowledge: Non-codified experiences, ideas, and skills that people have, so they are not easily expressed.

Value Proposition: It is composed by the value in products and services offered to the market to attract new clients for maximizing business profits.

ENDNOTE

1 For purposes of the present research, a newly created company has between three and seven years, on average five years of formally established; which have the potential to reach size and significant profitability (Bhide, 2000; Zott & Amit, 2007).

Chapter 8
Entrepreneurial Intention Among Academicians in Mexico:
A Descriptive Approach

Cynthia L. Franco-Rodriguez
Tecnologico de Monterrey, Mexico

Patricia Esther Alonso-Galicia
Tecnologico de Monterrey, Mexico

ABSTRACT

Scarce research was identified regarding the academic entrepreneur as a critical agent of change and its relation within the process of academic entrepreneurship, as well as the dynamics of different factors in the decision to become an entrepreneur. The study of academicians' entrepreneurial intention is of special relevance due to their roles as teachers and researchers, and because entrepreneurs are part of innovation ecosystems, entrepreneurial universities, entrepreneurship, and innovation itself. Accordingly, academic entrepreneurs have become the focus and strategic orientation of decision makers in the higher education system. Consequently, the purpose of this descriptive study is to contribute to the knowledge of the characteristics of academicians in Mexico and the way these characteristics influence the entrepreneurial intention. In this chapter, a sample of 209 scholars was obtained. The results show significant differences for entrepreneurial intention depending on previous work experience and formation.

INTRODUCTION

Given the growing need to strengthen the creation of new businesses, the entrepreneurial university is a crucial factor capable of playing an active role for economic and social development (Etzkowitz & Klofsten, 2005), and scientific growth (Etzkowitz, 2003). Therefore, one of the three missions of higher education institutions (HEIs) is to promote the culture of entrepreneurship in society. In the area of Academic Entrepreneurship, two main trends stand out: "creation of companies" and "entrepreneurial

DOI: 10.4018/978-1-5225-8939-6.ch008

universities" considered as possible catalysts for economic and social improvement in the regions and countries they operate. Empirical studies show the relationship between knowledge and economic growth, as the transmission of knowledge positively affects technological change and economic growth (Acs & Plummer, 2005; Acs & Varga, 2005; Audretsch & Keilbach, 2007; Varga & Schalk, 2004).

Although the most recent studies identify institutional and social determinants of entrepreneurial activity among scientists (Fini et al., 2009; Kenney & Goe, 2004; Nosella & Grimaldi, 2009), there is limited research on academic entrepreneurship in Mexico. HEIs have given importance in the monetary inputs (financing of basic and applied research) and outputs (patents and income generated by universities through licenses or spin-offs) only, with little attention on the role of the individual and their interaction among other individuals, organizations, environments, resources, and the processes involved in the commercialization of innovations.

Therefore, the goal of this chapter is to understand the topic of the entrepreneurial intention among academicians in Mexico, based on their general characteristics (gender, research area, age, the institution of origin, and academic experience). Results can be very useful for academicians and politicians responsible for the creation and implementation of the mechanisms and policies that can promote an entrepreneurial culture, as well as promoting the role that academicians have in knowledge transfer projects.

ACADEMIC ENTREPRENEURSHIP AND ENTREPRENEURIAL UNIVERSITY

The term "entrepreneurial university" has become valid since the third mission of the university in response to a series of demands from governments, industry, and society in general. In general, most HEIs overview with limitations regarding loans and public resources to meet their needs for going through a process of transformation, by acquiring capacities that allow them to be more flexible. This change or modification moves away from the traditional paradigm for being more innovative, proactive, and even "enterprising" (Clark, 2004). The entrepreneurial university continues to prioritize scientific research, but also increasingly produces technology, and even innovation (Etzkowitz & Viale, 2010). Therefore, an entrepreneurial university should promote various management techniques, strategic and competitive positions. Also, it has been suggested that they should be involved in associations, networks, and other types of relationships with public and private organizations to foster the interaction, collaboration, and cooperation with other HEIs (Annamária, 2004).

Entrepreneurial universities are more proactive, as they modify the classical model of teaching and research-oriented HEI by incorporating a new mission: the HEI as an engine of economic development and social context where it operates (Chrisman et al., 1995; Etzkowitz & Klofsten, 2005). As a result, Guerrero and Urbano (2014) define the entrepreneurial university as a survivor of competitive environments with a common strategy aimed at being the best in all of its activities (e.g., healthy finances, good students and teachers, high-quality research) trying to be more productive and creative when establishing links between education and research.

While the greater emphasis is given to the phenomenon of entrepreneurial universities in the world, the literature on this subject also expands rapidly, primarily in the United States and Europe. Research on the nature, background, and effects of entrepreneurial activities within universities has experienced rapid growth in the last two decades, due to the publication of special publications in various specialized journals, such as *Management Science*, *Journal of Technology Transfer*, *Research Policy* and

Journal of Business Venturing (Rothaermel et al., 2007), and more recently, *International Journal of E-Entrepreneurship and Innovation.*

Academic Entrepreneurship in Mexico

In general, entrepreneurial activities in Mexico are not characterized by having a high level social acceptance due, in part, to the negative image of entrepreneurship in Mexico, and the lack of entrepreneurial spirit among the population, who prefer the security of work for others to assume the risks inherent in the creation of a company. Despite this fact, and as also is happening in Europe, an increasing number of Mexican HEIs are becoming concerned about implementing business creation programs, so they are developing infrastructures to support them, such as the construction of science parks, business incubators and accelerators, and technology transfer offices (OTRIs).

It is well known that entrepreneurship is one of the driving forces behind the economic growth of a country. However, in Latin America, although there is a high incidence of entrepreneurs, these nations face generally weak macroeconomic growth. Moreover, Latin America is also a region with many small entrepreneurs, but lacks abundant innovation, and has low-valued exportations, due to its low level of innovation. This fact also includes large Latin American corporations (Lederman et al., 2014).

On the other hand, the quality of business education of HEIs is a national institutional characteristic that differs between nations (Hovne et al., 2014). So, increasingly in Mexico, business education is focused on the entrepreneurial spirit in HEIs and teaching and research. As a result, HEIs are increasingly inserted on triple helix (university-industry-government) linkages (Etzkowitz, 2015), so the combination of technology transfer (Link et al., 2013), spillovers (Acs et al., 2013), academic entrepreneurship (Shane, 2004), entrepreneurial universities (Guerrero et al., 2014a,b), national innovation systems (Nelson, 1993), and public entrepreneurship systems (Acs et al., 2014; Audretsch, 2007) is creating a society focused on business in Mexico.

Some academic institutions are adopting the role of investors to boost these startups, and some countries have developed and implemented innovation policies with a regional scope supported by external institutions dedicated to research (Ponds et al., 2010). One of the most important cases is found in Europe, where there is a significant volume of public investment to generate knowledge, carried out through public HEIs, based on policies to promote economic growth.

In Mexico, like other developing countries, most of the research in R&D (Research and Development) and innovation is mainly based on the resources granted by the federal government (Padilla-Pérez & Gaudin, 2014) through the National Council of Science and Technology (CONACYT). This public organization is mainly how the government grants funds to high-value projects to promote technological innovation in Mexico. The report *Global Entrepreneurship Monitor* (GEM) defines different levels of entrepreneurship in a country based on 12 pillars (Kelley et al., 2011). Consequently, nations can be classified as a factor-driven economy, efficiency-driven economy, and innovation-driven economy. Mexico is an efficiency-driven economy (Schwab, 2010).

On the other hand, the theory of endogenous growth, developed in late 1980s, identifies the knowledge capital as a factor associated with economic growth, establishing two fundamental propositions: first, the generation of knowledge and human capital takes place in response to market opportunities; and second, investment in the generation of knowledge is probably associated with other economic agents.

The accumulation of knowledge is highlighted as a factor that induces economic growth. At this respect, Audretsch and Keilbach (2004a) point out two conditions to have an increasing stock of knowledge from research, development, and education. First, knowledge must be transformed into economically useful knowledge; and, secondly, and the economy must be endowed with factors of production that can select, evaluate and transform knowledge for commercial use. Empirical evidence indicates that the presence of public research organizations, such as HEIs, has a significant influence on the degree of regional innovation (Goldstein & Drucker, 2006). Therefore, the growth of a knowledge society depends on the production of new knowledge, and the transmission, dissemination, communication and its use through new services-based and industrial-oriented procedures.

In this changing process, entrepreneurship plays a key role, as is defined as the process of discovery, evaluation, and exploitation of entrepreneurial opportunities; but also with the people who discover them, evaluate and exploit these new opportunities. People with an entrepreneurial spirit have the ability to innovate, they have the will to try new ventures or to manage them differently. As a result, entrepreneurs seek to develop capacities for change, they experiment with their ideas and react with greater openness and flexibility.

The university is the most important organization on which the new spin-off depends to receive specialized personnel, know-how, and business orientation (Smilor et al., 1990). Also, the entrepreneurial spirit presents a double facet. On the one hand, it develops new projects with independence, capable of tolerating risk, responsible, with intuition, and with possibilities of solving problems. Also, it can carry out the purposes of others with the same capacity for innovation, responsibility, and independence. To form an entrepreneurial spirit, students need to develop commitment, dedication, and responsibility. And at this respect, entrepreneurial education is related to knowledge, skills, discipline, motivation, and self-confidence.

Besides, entrepreneurship provides an extensive set of employment and innovation opportunities. The discussion on how to encourage it has gained relevance. The combination of skills, knowledge, and attitudes is necessary for the development of entrepreneurship and feeds the organization to grow in developed nations (Béchard & Toulouse, 1991; Kuratko, 2005; OECD, 2010), and in emerging economies (West, Bamford, & Marsden, 2008). For most of the countries included in the GEM special report on entrepreneurship education (Martinez, Levie, Kelley, Saemundsson, & Schott, 2010), more than a fifth of the population in their productive age has received some training on entrepreneurial spirit. Of this proportion, about 80% has been obtained it through formal education. However, in Mexico, only 10% of the population of productive age has received specific formal training at a higher or university level.

In recent years, many new companies have started operations within the ecosystems of entrepreneurship with characteristics and unique key elements. Davis (2013) described the eight key areas that were measured to classify the first 20 ecosystems that started in the world. These key areas are the number of companies formed (start-ups), financed, and performed to discover the startups' business mentality, trends, support infrastructure, talent, and ecosystems. At this respect, the USA has six (Silicon Valley, Los Angeles, Seattle, New York City, Boston, and Chicago) of the most important entrepreneurial ecosystems in the world that compete with other entrepreneurial ecosystems in Canada (Toronto, Vancouver, and Waterloo), Europe (London, Paris, Berlin, Madrid, and Moscow), South America (Sao Paulo and Chile), Australia (Sydney and Melbourne), Israel (Tel Aviv), Singapore, and India (Bangalore).

According to Davis (2013), some factors must be considered for the development of a business ecosystem. Some of them are traditional factors, such as financing and adopting the technology, while others may include unusual characteristics, such as entrepreneurial differentiation and government support. At this respect, Isenberg (2010) suggests the following principles of action to help governments towards the formation of a stronger entrepreneurial ecosystem by

1. Involving the private sector
2. Modifying cultural norms
3. Removing regulatory barriers
4. Encouraging and celebrating successes, emphasizing clusters and incubators, programs financing aimed at the rigors of the market and, above all,
5. Approaching the entire business ecosystem that will allow governments to create economic growth by encouraging the creation of self-sustaining companies.

However, the above principles of action must be adapted to the particular circumstances of the regions or countries, as for how to express interest in academic spin-offs is diverse in different social environments, as well as the role and the contribution they have in their performance (Gallurt Plá, 2010). For example, in Spain, the Organic Law of Universities (LOU) states that "The university will develop research of excellence with the objects of contributing to the advancement of knowledge, innovation and improvement of the quality of life of citizens and the competitiveness of companies" (LOU, article 41.1.) As a result, adopting policies based on financial support linked to the distribution of royalties is crucial for HEIs, while networks and the creation of economic structures and the freedom of the faculty are placed in the subsequent priorities respectively (Nadirkhanlou et al., 2013).

The main factors that prevent the creation of university spin-offs and, therefore, limit their participation in the development of the economy, are the lack of financial resources and entrepreneurial skills among entrepreneurs. The capacity to obtain capital is one of the most important points within the entrepreneurial activity, due to its impact on startups to self-finance their operations. Other elements that also concern for their survival are: the lack of work experience, the problems derived from management, and the lack of information about what happens in the market. This fact affects the relationship with stakeholders, as well as with external collaborators, which makes evident the absence of growth and the weak development of skills for management.

Although there are several studies that have analyzed the entrepreneur-opportunity relationship through various theories (e.g., human capital, social capital, financial capital, social network theory, etc.), little has been analyzed in developing countries where economic growth development matters (González, 2011), so there is a large area of opportunity in this discipline, for example, in the case of Mexico.

At this respect, Gonzalez (2011) studies the effect of human capital on the identification of opportunities, and the effect of social networks in the identification of opportunities, analyzing gender (González, 2008) and some descriptive studies of women entrepreneurs, aspects developed by Zabludovsky (2007), and Zabludovsky and Avelar (2001).

Moreover, Gutiérrez and Montemayor (2015) in a study focused on researchers belonging to the National System of Researchers (SNI in Spanish) in Mexico, show that the greater use and exposure to the entrepreneurship ecosystem created by institutions, as well as an adequate protection of intellectual property and a satisfactory entrepreneurial experience, give better access to the federal and state financial aid. These are some of the personal, organizational and economic factors that represent a strong and positive influence in the decision-making process to create new academic businesses by university researchers.

The amount of financial support received by researchers is not a determining factor in the decision to create or not create a new company (spin-offs). The commitment assumed by SNI researchers receiving financial support from the Mexican CONACYT (National Council of Science and Technology) implies reaching higher levels of scientific productivity shown by the number of publications in international journals, writing books or book chapters, as well as being invited speakers at important conferences and congresses. All this academic activity keeps them away from time-consuming activities, such as the creation of a new spin-off, while the origin of the SNI support negatively influences on the creation of new companies due to confidentiality and intellectual property imposed on researchers by private companies that finance their projects. This problem does not happen in projects financed with public funds.

Another important finding of this research is to confirm that diverse cultural and socioeconomic environments to which researchers are exposed in Mexico and abroad have a significant impact on the academic spin-offs they create. According to Monge et al. (2011, 2012), the main factors that contribute to the creation of university spin-offs are a) technical knowledge and b) identification of a business opportunity; Also, these authors observe that the financial support is the main problem of these newly-born companies. These results are relevant for academicians, authorities working in HEIs, and governmental agencies in considering promotion programs to benefit startups.

Universities are taking the role of investors to promote this type of business. In this sense, there are various expressions of interest that academic spin-offs are awakening in our society, for the role and contribution they make to their development (Gallurt Plá, 2010). In general, the entrepreneurial activities in Mexico are not very high in number, due in large part to the fear of failure and the social underestimation entrepreneurs have regarding their capacities to undertake (GEM, 2016). This aversion to risk and the lack of perception about the capacities to undertake is perceived to a greater degree among women.

Academic spin-offs are awakening in Latin America to reverse this situation, for the role and the contribution they make to their development (Gallurt-Plá, 2010). It is very important to know the configuration of the activities carried out by academicians and their perception of the creation of companies born from their research. This analysis will allow us to know more in detail the entrepreneurial phenomenon among the academicians through the following exploratory study. The variables we analyze are classified by HEIs and areas to which they belong, profession, previous work experience, age, gender, type of contract, belonging to the SNI, and attendance of business administration courses. The objective is to analyze these sociodemographic variables to find differences in the groups.

SAMPLE DESCRIPTION AND DATA COLLECTION

The quantitative study is formed by the selection of a group of professors from Tecnologico de Monterrey (Mexico) living in a relatively homogeneous geographic, cultural, normative, and political context to minimize the impact of variables that cannot be controlled in an empirical study (Hofstede, 1980). Data were obtained from full-time and part-time professors working in different areas of knowledge.

To apply the survey, the sample we obtained was formed by 500 Tecnologico de Monterrey's professors (of a total of 1,500) which represent 33.33% of the total population. We conducted a pilot test with 20 professors before the application of the questionnaire to verify it, who provided feedback regarding the questionnaire. Once the recommendations of the professors were incorporated, the survey was electronically and personally applied, with a request letter containing the instructions for completion, whose

Table 1. Research data

Sectors	Academicians of Tecnologico de Monterrey
Geographic Location	Mexico
Methodology	Structured questionnaire
Sampling Procedure	Consecutive non-probabilistic sampling
Size of the Study Population	1,500 professors located in 31campus
Sample Size (Response)	500 professors (209 valid)
Response Rate	41.8%
Period of Data Collection	January – May 2016

Source: Authors.

answers were received by e-mail. At the end of the data collection period, 209 questionnaires were valid and completed, which constitutes an outstanding response rate of 41.8% (Table 1).

The consecutive non-probabilistic sampling is a technique that attempts to include all the subjects that are available as part of the sample. The best non-probabilistic sample is recognized as one of the best, as it includes all available subjects and represents the study population to a greater degree (Sampieri et al., 1998). Because all measurements were obtained from the same collection instrument, the possibility of a common bias was tested with the one-factor Harman test (Konrad & Linnehan, 1995; Scott & Bruce, 1994). The classification of the different areas was considered regarding the organizational structure within the Tecnológico de Monterrey system, as shown in Table 2.

The highest proportion founded in the sample (209 professors (men 61.2%, women 38.8%), and 80.9% without experience in firms) is in the Business and Humanities Dept. (35.4%), followed by the School of Engineering, Architecture, and Health (32.1%), Entrepreneurship Dept. (24.9%) and, the Postgraduate School (7.7%).

Finally, 77% of the sample are SNI members, so they are granted economic incentives, and the amount varies according to the level achieved (Candidate, SNI-1, SNI-2, and SNI-3). This membership symbolizes the quality and prestige of scientific contributions in Mexico.

Entrepreneurial Intention

Of the sample of academicians analyzed, 31.58% have not taken any previous course in business administration, while 68.42% have taken it at some point in their life. A scale of Mueller (2011) was used

Table 2. Departments and areas of knowledge

Department	Code
Business and Humanities Dept.	ENH
School of Engineering, Architecture, and Health	EIAS
Postgraduate School	EP
Entrepreneurship Dept.	ENT

Source: Authors.

Table 3. Sample by age groups

	Frequency	Percentage	Accumulated Percentage
Up to 35 years	62	29.67	29.67
From 36 to 45 years	80	38.28	67.94
From 46 to 55 años	49	23.44	91.39
From 56 to 64 años	14	6.70	98.09
65 years and more	4	1.91	100
Total	209	100.0	

Source: Authors

Table 4. Type of professors in private universities.

Type of Contract	Description	Of the Sample
Full-time	Contract of indefinite labor regime whose main purpose is to carry out, teaching and research activities.	55.5%
Part-time	Contract of a definite time, full-time work regime, with the intention of carrying out teaching and research work.	30.1%
By hours	The exceptional contract in a definite time is working regime, for certain specific subjects that allow covering particular teaching needs that cannot be covered through full-time or full-time contracts.	14.4%

Source: Authors.

to assess the degree of academicians' willingness to venture. This construct measures the intention to start a business in the next five years ($\alpha = .94$) in the four items shown in Table 5. Responses were on a Likert scale from 1 (total agreement) to 7 (total disagreement).

To know the Academic Entrepreneurial Intention, we perform an ANOVA analysis. As a result, the entrepreneurial intention items responses were averaged and used as a factor to determine significant differences. Results are shown in Table 6.

The ANOVA analysis shows that the effect of professors' department, school or area on entrepreneurial intention is significant ($F(24, 184) = 1.57$, $p = 0.05$), and the effect on Business Administration courses taken by professors on entrepreneurial intention is also significant ($F(24, 184) = 1.95$, $p = 0.01$). Lastly, there is also a significant effect ($F(24, 184) = 1.78$, $p = 0.02$) between professors' previous work experience and the academic entrepreneurial intention.

Table 5. Entrepreneurial Intention items

1. I have planned to start my business in the following five years
2. I have begun starting my business (find information, discuss the idea with my friends, write a business plan, etc.)
3. I am convinced that I will start my business in the next five years
4. Being an entrepreneur is one of my professional goals

Source: Authors

Table 6. One-way analysis of variance of Entrepreneurial Intention by selected variables

Variable	Source	*SS*	*df*	*MS*	*F*	*p*
School or area	Between groups	48.92	24	2.04	1.57	0.05*
	Within groups	238.95	184	1.30		
	Total	287.88	208			
Profession	Between groups	9.45	24	0.39	0.89	0.61
	Within groups	81.11	184	0.44		
	Total	90.56	208			
Age	Between groups	25.26	24	1.05	1.23	0.22
experience	Within groups	157.63	184	0.86		
	Total	182.89	208			
Gender	Between groups	6.87	24	0.29	1.23	0.22
	Within groups	42.74	184	0.23		
	Total	49.61	208			
Business	Between groups	9.16	24	0.38	1.95	0.01**
administration	Within groups	36.00	184	0.20		
course	Total	45.16	208			
SNI	Between groups	5.69	24	0.24	1.39	0.11
membership	Within groups	31.28	184	0.17		
	Total	36.98	208			
Previous	Between groups	6.09	24	0.25	1.78	0.02*
work	Within groups	26.25	184	0.14		
experience	Total	32.34	208			

Note: SS = Squared sum; df = degrees of freedom; ms = mean squared
*$p < .05$; ** $p < .01$; *** $p < .001$(two-tailed).
Source: Authors

CONCLUSION

With this work, we wanted to advance in the understanding of the intention to undertake among professors using a descriptive approach. Therefore, the measurement instrument is based on the subjective perceptions of the sample and is subject to the biases of social desirability (Podsakoff & Organ, 1986). However, the anonymity of the information provided by the professors reduced this bias, even when their answers related to sensitive topics (Konrad & Linnehan, 1995). Regarding gender and entrepreneurial intention, our results agree with Díaz-García and Jiménez-Moro (2010), Goethner et al. (2009), and Shinnar et al. (2012).

As for our findings, age has an ambiguous effect still controlled by seniority. Some studies find a positive relationship (Boardman & Ponomariov, 2009; Haeussler & Colyvas, 2011; Link et al., 2007), while in others this relation is negative (Bekkers & Bodas-Freitas, 2008; Este & Patel, 2007; Este & Perkmann, 2011; Guiliani et al., 2010) or there is no relation whatsoever (Boardman & Ponomariov, 2009; Gulbrandsen & Smeby, 2005; Renault, 2006). Moreover, individuals who were trained when the commitment between HEIs and the industry was minor or even irrelevant, can be linked to the norms that are not compatible with the collaboration of private companies (Bercovitz & Feldman, 2008).

One of the great challenges in the economic-related field is to convert research results into commercial and industrial successes. As a consequence, there is a great interest in HEIs to strengthen the HEIs-industry collaboration, as well as the role of research, development, and innovation in the economic and social well-being of any region (Jaffe et al., 1993). The exploitation of results derived from research generated in HEIs has the potential to be a driver for economic growth (Agarwal & Shah, 2014; Audretsch & Keilbach, 2007, Etzkowitz & Viale, 2010). Understanding these issues offers opportunities to shape government interventions to help academic entrepreneurs who decide to start a new company or those who are already active in this regard (Fernández et al., 2014).

As limitations of this study are (1) variables are dynamic, so they can change over time, and as a result, the cognitive constructs of intention and action are conceptually different; and (2) the sample is limited to a specific geographical and institutional framework, so extreme caution must be exercised in generalizing the results to other countries or regions. Future research should further analyze the nature of the relationships between the analyzed variables and other cognitive and institutional factors that promote academic entrepreneurship.

REFERENCES

Acs, Z. J., & Plummer, L. A. (2005). Penetrating the 'knowledge filter' in regional economies. *The Annals of Regional Science*, *39*(3), 439–456. doi:10.100700168-005-0245-x

Acs, Z. J., & Varga, A. (2005). Entrepreneurship, agglomeration and technological change. *Small Business Economics*, *24*(3), 323–334. doi:10.100711187-005-1998-4

Annamária, I. (2004). The evolution of university-industry-government relationships during the transition. *Research Policy*, *33*(6–7), 975–995.

Audretsch, D. B., & Keilbach, M. (2004a). Does entrepreneurship capital matter? *Entrepreneurship Theory and Practice*, *28*(5), 419–429. doi:10.1111/j.1540-6520.2004.00055.x

Audretsch, D. B., & Keilbach, M. (2004b). Entrepreneurship and regional growth: An evolutionary interpretation. *Journal of Evolutionary Economics*, *14*(5), 605–616. doi:10.100700191-004-0228-6

Audretsch, D. B., & Keilbach, M. (2007). The theory of knowledge spillover entrepreneurship. *Journal of Management Studies*, *44*(7), 1242–1254. doi:10.1111/j.1467-6486.2007.00722.x

Audretsch, D. B., Lehmann, E. E., & Paleari, S. (2014). Academic policy and entrepreneurship: A European perspective. *The Journal of Technology Transfer*, *40*(3), 363–368. doi:10.100710961-014-9359-6

Béchard, J., & Toulouse, J. (1991). Entrepreneurship and education: A viewpoint from education. *Journal of Small Business and Entrepreneurship*, *9*(1), 3–13. doi:10.1080/08276331.1991.10600386

Bercovitz, J., & Feldman, M. (2008). Academic entrepreneurs: Organizational change at the individual level. *Organization Science*, *19*(1), 69–89. doi:10.1287/orsc.1070.0295

Chrisman, J. J., Hynes, T., & Fraser, S. (1995). Faculty entrepreneurship and economic development: The case of the University of Calgary. *Journal of Business Venturing*, *10*(4), 267–281. doi:10.1016/0883-9026(95)00015-Z

CONACYT. (2008). *Informe General del Estado de la Ciencia y Tecnología*. CONACYT.

CONACYT. (2010). *Informe General del Estado de la Ciencia y Tecnología*. CONACYT.

Davis, J. B. (2013). *The theory of the individual in economics: Identity and value*. Routledge.

Etzkowitz, H. (2003). Innovation in innovation: The triple helix of university-industry-government relations. *Social Sciences Information. Information Sur les Sciences Sociales*, *42*(3), 293–337. doi:10.1177/05390184030423002

Etzkowitz, H., & Klofsten, M. (2005). The innovating region: Toward a theory of knowledge-based regional development. *R & D Management*, *35*(3), 243–255. doi:10.1111/j.1467-9310.2005.00387.x

Etzkowitz, H., & Viale, R. (2010). Polyvalent knowledge and the entrepreneurial university: A third academic revolution? *Critical Sociology*, *36*(4), 595–609. doi:10.1177/0896920510365921

Fernández-Pérez, V., Alonso-Galicia, P. E., Del Mar Fuentes-Fuentes, M., & Rodriguez-Ariza, L. (2014). Business social networks and academics' entrepreneurial intentions. *Industrial Management & Data Systems*, *114*(2), 292–320. doi:10.1108/IMDS-02-2013-0076

Fini, R., Grimaldi, R., & Sobrero, M. (2009). Factors fostering academics to start up new ventures: An assessment of Italian founders' incentives. *The Journal of Technology Transfer*, *34*(4), 380–402. doi:10.100710961-008-9093-z

Gallurt Plá, P. (2010). *Creación de Spin-Offs en las Universidades Españolas: Un modelo de Intenciones (Doctoral Theses)*. Sevilla, Spain: Pablo de Olavide University.

GEM. (2016). *México. Reporte Regional Querétaro*. Querétaro, Mexico: Global Entrepreneurship Monitor.

Goldstein, H., & Drucker, J. (2006). The economic development impacts of universities on regions: Do size and distance matter? *Economic Development Quarterly*, *20*(1), 22–43. doi:10.1177/0891242405283387

Guerrero, M., & Urbano, D. (2014). Academics" start-up intentions and knowledge filters: An individual perspective of the knowledge spillover theory of entrepreneurship. *Small Business Economics*, *43*(1), 57–74. doi:10.100711187-013-9526-4

Guerrero, M., Urbano, D., & Gajón, E. (2014). The internal pathways that condition university entrepreneurship in Latin America: An institutional approach. In *Innovative Pathways for University Entrepreneurship in the 21st Century* (pp. 89–118). Emerald Group Publishing Limited. doi:10.1108/S1048-473620140000024004

Gutiérrez, H., & Montemayor, E. (2015). *Academic Entrepreneurship in Mexico An analysis of the most significant resources influencing university researchers to create academic spinoffs*. Panel Session 3: Entrepreneurial University and Triple Helix's development, 77.

Hovne, A. S., Hovne, B. S., & Schott, T. (2014). Entrepreneurs' innovation benefitting from their education and training and from national policy and culture: A global study. *International Journal of Entrepreneurship and Small Business*, *23*(1-2), 127–144. doi:10.1504/IJESB.2014.065312

Kenney, M., & Goe, W. R. (2004). The role of social embeddedness in professorial entrepreneurship: A comparison of electrical engineering and computer science at UC Berkeley and Stanford. *Research Policy*, *33*(5), 691–707. doi:10.1016/j.respol.2003.11.001

Kuratko, D. F. (2005). The emergence of entrepreneurship education: Development, trends, and challenges. *Entrepreneurship Theory and Practice*, *29*(5), 577–598. doi:10.1111/j.1540-6520.2005.00099.x

Lederman, D., Messina, J., Pienknagura, S., & Rigolini, J. (2014). *El emprendimiento en América Latina: muchas empresas y poca innovación*. World Bank Publications. doi:10.1596/978-1-4648-0284-3

Nadirkhanlou, S., Pourezzat, A. A., Gholipour, A., & Zehtabi, M. (2013). Requirements of Knowledge Commercialization in Universities and Academic Entrepreneurship. In *Innovation through Knowledge Transfer 2012* (pp. 179–194). Heidelberg, Germany: Springer. doi:10.1007/978-3-642-34219-6_20

Nosella, A., & Grimaldi, R. (2009). University-level mechanisms supporting the creation of new companies: An analysis of Italian academic spin-offs. *Technology Analysis and Strategic Management*, *21*(6), 679–698. doi:10.1080/09537320903052657

Ponds, R., Van Oort, F., & Frenken, K. (2010). Innovation, spillovers, and university-industry collaboration: An extended knowledge production function approach. *Journal of Economic Geography*, *10*(2), 231–255. doi:10.1093/jeg/lbp036

Ponomariov, B., & Boardman, P. C. (2008). The effect of informal industry contacts on the time university scientists allocates to collaborative research with industry. *The Journal of Technology Transfer*, *33*(3), 301–313. doi:10.100710961-007-9029-z

Rothaermel, F. T., Agung, S. D., & Jiang, L. (2007). University entrepreneurship: A taxonomy of the literature. *Industrial and Corporate Change*, *16*(4), 691–791. doi:10.1093/icc/dtm023

Schwab, K. (2010). *The global competitiveness report 2010-2011*. Geneva: World Economic Forum.

Shinnar, R. S., Giacomin, O., & Janssen, F. (2012). Entrepreneurial perceptions and intentions: The role of gender and culture. *Entrepreneurship Theory and Practice*, *36*(3), 465–493. doi:10.1111/j.1540-6520.2012.00509.x

Smilor, R. W., Gibson, D. V., & Dietrich, G. B. (1990). University spin-out companies: Technology start-ups from UT-Austin. *Journal of Business Venturing*, *5*(1), 63–76. doi:10.1016/0883-9026(90)90027-Q

Varga, A., & Schalk, H. (2004). Knowledge spillovers, agglomeration, and macroeconomic growth: An empirical approach. *Regional Studies*, *38*(8), 977–989. doi:10.1080/0034340042000280974

Zabludovsky, G. (2007). Las mujeres en México: Trabajo, educación superior y esferas de poder. *Política y Cultura*, *28*, 9–41.

Zabludovsky, G., & de Avelar, S. (2001). *Empresarias y ejecutivas en México y Brasil*. D.F., Mexico: UNAM.

KEY TERMS AND DEFINITIONS

Academician: A university professor who combines teaching and research among his or her professional tasks.

Entrepreneurial Intention: The cognitive concept for the degree of readiness that an individual has for business creation.

Entrepreneurial University: An institution that prioritizes scientific research produces technology and innovations. Also, it promotes various management techniques, strategic and competitive positions. It has been suggested that is involved in associations, networks and other types of relationships with public and private organizations that allow interaction, collaboration, and cooperation with other central elements in innovation systems.

Entrepreneurship: It is a dynamic process of creation and innovation, which is carried out by differentiated individuals (entrepreneurs) who can generate ideas, perceive market opportunities, manage uncertainty and risk, and combine, manage and take advantage of resources and institutions to create value in products and services.

GEM (Global Entrepreneurship Monitor): Founded by Babson College (USA) and London Business School (UK), this organization is the world's foremost study of entrepreneurship.

National System of Researchers (SNI): The public organization that economically encourages researchers working in public and private HEI in Mexico.

Triple Helix: It is formed by the creation of university-industry-government linkages to foster economic growth and social change to fight poverty and social exclusion.

Chapter 9
Affective and Emotional Determinants of Entrepreneurial Orientation Within Family Firms

Remedios Hernández-Linares
https://orcid.org/0000-0001-7836-4670
Universidad de Extremadura, Spain

María Concepción López-Fernández
Universidad de Cantabria, Spain

María José Naranjo-Sánchez
Universidad de Extremadura, Spain

Laura Victoria Fielden
https://orcid.org/0000-0002-6283-7610
Universidad de Extremadura, Spain

ABSTRACT

As a predominant form of business organization, family firms have attracted increasing attention by scholars, and especially by those researching entrepreneurial orientation with the aim of better understanding of entrepreneurial activities pursued by enterprises. However, the literature on the confluence of entrepreneurial orientation and family firms has paid scant attention to the influence of affective and emotional factors. To cover this research gap, the authors analyze the impact of affective commitment and concern for socioemotional wealth preservation on entrepreneurial orientation. To do so, they performed an empirical study using the data collected from 342 small and mid-sized family firms from Portugal, a country where family firms are under-researched even though they make up the backbone of the economy. Results show that both affective commitment and socioemotional wealth positively impact entrepreneurial orientation, pointing to the need to further research the relationships between such factors and strategic behaviors in the family business context.

DOI: 10.4018/978-1-5225-8939-6.ch009

INTRODUCTION

Entrepreneurial orientation ("EO") is defined as "a construct capturing the degree to which a firm's posture is entrepreneurial versus conservative, concerns how the firm's top managers support key entrepreneurial activities" (Morris et al. 2011, p. 956). EO has been the subject of more than 30 years of research (Wales et al. 2011) and is becoming a key construct within the management literature due to its ability to further our understanding of entrepreneurial activities pursued by organizations (Covin & Wales, 2012). As a result of these years of research, we know that organizational context impacts this strategic orientation (Covin & Slevin 1990; Wales et al., 2011).

Among the contexts influencing firm EO, the family business context deserves special attention, since family firms play a significant role in the worldwide economy as a predominant form of business organization (e.g., Astrachan & Shanker, 2003; Chittoor & Das, 2007; Litz, 1995; Sharma et al., 2012). Beyond its economic relevance, EO within family firms is attracting growing interest by literature (Hernández-Linares & Lópe-Fernández, 2018) and merits further research because in family businesses the presence of a family as the dominant coalition of the company (Chrisman et al. 2012) affects their strategic behavior (Carney et al., 2015; Pindado & Requejo, 2015). Specifically, the behavioral theory of the firm (Cyert & March, 1963) supports that stakeholders in a firm usually have many different goals instead of only one. This theory also points out that the dominant coalition in the company, in pursuing their goals, will influence the behavior and decision making of the firm (Argote & Greve, 2007). Family business researchers have used this theory to explore the effects of being a family, as the dominant coalition, in the firms' behavior (e.g., Chua et al., 1999; Ensley & Pearson 2005; Chrisman et al., 2012). However, the behavioral theory has scarcely been used in the exploration of EO in family firms (Revilla et al., 2016; Zahra, 2012).

Moreover, the heterogeneity of family firms is broadly accepted by scholars (Corbetta & Salvato, 2004; Dyer, 2006; Dyer & Dyer, 2009; Sciascia et al., 2014; Shanker & Astrachan, 1996; Sharma, 2004; Stanley et al., forthcoming; Westhead & Howorth, 2007). In this sense, previous research has shown that the ability to influence organizational behavior derived from the dominant position of the family does not warrant that the family will actually do so (Chrisman et al., 2012). The dominant family's willingness to influence family firm behavior has been called the essence of family influence and is at the root of family firms' heterogeneity (Chrisman et al., 2012). Among the indicators of family essence, we will address two in this work, the dominant family's affective commitment to the firm and the concern for socioemotional wealth (henceforth SEW) endowment preservation. Affective commitment to the firm reflects pride in belonging, as well as an emotional attachment, to the organization (Perry et al., 2016), and is still unresearched in relation to EO within family firms. This is so despite its inclusion as a control variable in a recent article (Hernández-Linares et al., 2018a). However, considering that affective commitment stems from the desire to support change (Chirico & Salvato, 2008), and is significantly related to EO (Hernández-Linares et al., 2018), it seems reasonable to call for further investigation into the influence of affective commitment on the EO of family firms. In a similar sense, SEW, which is rooted in the principles of behavioral agency theory (Wiseman & Gomez-Mejia, 1998), proposes that some firms are highly concerned with preserving their socioemotional endowment, while others attach less importance to such non-economic factors (e.g., Gómez-Mejía et al., 2007& 2011). Nevertheless, according to a recent review of the literature on the confluence of EO and family firms (Hernández-Linares & López-Fernández, 2018), only two empirical studies have included concern for SEW preservation among their variables (Kallmuenzer et al., 2017; Schepers et al., 2014). Therefore, further investigation is needed to shed light on the complexities derived from the existence of both a bright and a dark side to SEW (Kellermanns et al., 2012; Miller & Le Breton-Miller, 2014; Naldi et al., 2013). Finally, these consequences remain under-researched in some contexts, like in African countries or even in some European countries (Hernández-Linares & López-Fernández, 2018), such as in Portugal.

In short, increasing our knowledge about the singularities of EO in family firms is important for two main reasons. First, because virtually all economies today depend on promoting entrepreneurship for stability and growth, which as a consequence creates the need to stimulate the entrepreneurial behavior of family firms, especially in countries where family firms are at the forefront of socio-economic development. Secondly, the scant research on EO and family firm performance show inconsistent findings. This points to the need for further research on EO within family firms, paying special attention to their heterogeneity (Hernández-Linares & López-Fernández, 2018; Hernández-Linares et al., 2017; Sharma, 2004). For this reason, and given that such heterogeneity may be explained, for example, by the different levels of concern for SEW preservation, or by the different affective commitments to the firm, we believe that these aspects of family firms deserve further investigation (Berrone et al., 2012; Kellermanns et al., 2012 & 2014; Hernández Linares & López-Fernández, 2018).

To address these research gaps, our work aims to answer the two following questions, (1) is the affective commitment to the company associated with the EO within the family firm? And, (2) does the concern for SEW preservation affect the EO within the family firm? To answer these research questions, we performed an empirical study with a sample of 342 family small and medium enterprises (SMEs) from Portugal, a country where family firms make up the backbone of the economy.

This chapter is divided into seven parts. This introduction is followed by the literature review and hypotheses development section. The third part discusses the methodology used in the empirical study, by detailed describing study population and sample, as well as variables and measures used in the empirical part. The next section presents our results. The fifth section discusses such results in comparison with other studies' findings and suggests implications for family businesses literature and managerial implications, as well as research limitations and future research lines. The sixth section explains what the main contributions that this research does to literature are. The final section of our chapter presents our concluding remarks.

FRAMEWORK AND HYPOTHESES RATIONALE

Rooted in Mintzberg's (1973) strategic decision-making framework, EO originated with Miller (1983, p. 771), who did not use this name. He defined the concept of entrepreneurial organization as "one that engages in product-market innovation, undertakes somewhat risky ventures, and is first to come up with 'proactive' innovations, beating competitors to the punch." Both, this definition of the entrepreneurial firm, and the numerous definitions of EO appearing in literature imply that EO is not an individual action in time, but a strategic behavior (Covin & Slevin, 1991). This strategic business behavior may be determined by different organizational context (Lumpkin & Dess, 1996), and in this sense, the family business constitutes a unique setting for EO's research (Nordqvist & Melin, 2010). For this reason, in recent years, EO has generated increasing attention not only among scholars in the fields of entrepreneurship (Wales, 2016; Wales et al., 2013) but also among family business' researchers (Hernández-Linares & López-Fernández, 2018).

According to a recent literature review (Hernández-Linares & López-Fernández, 2018), empirical research exploring the antecedents of EO of family firms versus non-family firms have mostly explored the effect of family involvement in ownership, management or governance, yielding contradictory findings. For example, Kellermanns and Eddleston (2006) did not find a direct influence of family involvement on firm's EO, while other studies (Block, 2012; Miller & Le Breton-Miller, 2011) reported a negative relationship between these variables. Finally, other works find an inverted U-shaped relationship between family involvement and EO (Bauweraerts & Colot, 2017; Sciascia et al., 2013).

Thus, the origins of the family firm's EO remain unclear, and researchers should move toward the study of less explored areas to explain and predict EO (Rodrigo-Alarcón et al., 2018; Wales et al., 2013), which has also been pointed out in the literature review from Hernández-Linares and López-Fernández (2018). In this sense, the involvement of a family in the ownership, management and/or governance of a firm can only be considered as the necessary but not sufficient condition for the family exerting their influence on the behavior of the family firm (Chrisman et al., 2012). In a similar vein, the consideration of the dimensions of the essence of being a family business deserves much more investigation into family business research in general and the EO within family firms in particular (Hernández-Linares & López-Fernández, 2018). Family firms offer a unique phenomenon of study because they have not only economic endowments derived from business activities but also social and emotional endowments derived from family relationships (Basco & Pérez, 2011). This has consequences concerning the family's affective, emotional, and social needs (Gómez-Mejía et al., 2007). Indeed, research often assumes that family business pursues different goals and behave differently than their non-family counterparts due to emotional and socioemotional wealth that linked to family's involvement (Morgan & Gómez-Mejía, 2014), which affects decision making. However, this assumption has scarcely been tested (Aparicio et al., 2017). Our work aims to take a step in this direction, by empirically researching the relationships between affective commitment and family firms' EO, on the one hand, and between family firms' concern for SEW preservation and its EO, on the other. Each of these relationships is discussed in detail in the following sections.

Affective Commitment and Family Firm's EO

Affective commitment may be defined as an employee's "emotional attachment to, identification with, and involvement in the organization" (Meyer & Allen, 1991, p. 67), and is often associated with feelings, such as emotional attachment (Somers 2010), loyalty and belongingness (Allen & Meyer, 1990) or high identification (Morgan & Hunt, 1994). Affective commitment is the first type of organizational commitment (Mercurio, 2015) studied and measured (mainly through the Organizational Commitment Questionnaire first developed by Porter et al. (1974) and later validated by Mowday et al. (1979). Later some multidimensional models appeared, with the three-component model of organizational commitment (Meyer & Allen, 1991) being the most widely researched (Mercurio, 2015). This three-component model presents organizational commitment as a complementary relationship between "affective commitment (the desire to remain in the organization), continuance commitment (the need to remain in the organization), and normative commitment (the mindset of an obligation to remain in the organization)" (Mercurio, 2015, p. 396). However, empirical research and relevant meta-analyses indicate that affective commitment is the most relevant element of the multidimensional models (see Mercurio, 2015, for a review of those meta-analyses) and can, therefore, be considered the essence of organizational commitment (Mercurio, 2015). Despite organizational and affective commitment having been most researched in the area of human resources, they also exert their influence in many business behaviors and contexts (Ahlers et al., 2017).

Affective commitment is considered to be of special relevance to the family business context (Memili et al., 2013; Sieger et al., 2011), because family firms are distinguished from non-family businesses by the continued involvement of family members in the company's ownership and management (Chrisman et al., 2012). Hence, sustained affective commitment of family owners and managers are considered a key element for the survival of this type of organization. For this reason, affective commitment is attracting more and more attention from family firm scholars (e.g., Ahlers et al., 2017; Déniz-Déniz et al., 2018; Giménez et al., 2018; Hayek et al., 2018). However, the exploration of its effects on corporate entrepreneurship has been neglected, with only a few studies including the affective commitment as an independent (Salvato & Chirico, 2016) or control variable (Hernández-Linares et al., 2018a). Despite this lack of research, different arguments lead us to propose that it may be an antecedent for EO. First, literature argues that affective commitment translates into specific actions (Allen & Meyer, 1990; Gundlach et al., 1995), and shows that it favors knowledge integration in the organization (Randall et al., 1990). Besides, literature reports that affective commitment mediates the effect of human resources on innovation (Camelo-Ordaz et al., 2011), or that it boosts the firm's ability of successfully overcoming internal changes (Herscovitch & Meyer, 2002), all of these being strongly related to the EO of a company. In the case of family business, family members are expected to be highly committed to the company and its survival, given the desire of transgenerational transfer. Therefore, this affective commitment is expected to support change (Chirico & Salvato, 2008) and change constitutes the basis of any entrepreneurial behavior. Similarly, affective commitment is found to be an extremely significant (both directly and through knowledge internalization) variable in explaining new product development (Chirico & Salvato, 2016), which is a form of corporate entrepreneurship. Finally, the study including affective commitment as a control variable (Hernández-Linares et al., 2018a) found a significant and strong positive association between affective commitment and EO ($B = 0.224$, $p < 0.001$) in the context of Spanish family SMEs. Considering all the above arguments, our main objective is, therefore, to seek further confirmation of this last finding by testing the following research hypothesis,

Hypothesis 1: Affective commitment is positively associated with a firm's EO.

SEW and Family Firm's EO

Feelings and emotions mold information processing, comprising risk assessment and strategy formulation (Mittal & Ross, 1998), and in some cases, they can "outweigh rational considerations in decision making and other cognitive processes" (Baron 2008, p. 331). In addition, in her work on emotions and family firm creation, Stanley (2010) argues that emotions may push an individual toward one action versus another.

One of the concepts more closely linked to the emotional stock of the family firm is the concept of SEW, defined as "nonfinancial aspects of the firm that meet the family's affective needs, such as identity, the ability to exercise family influence, and the perpetuation of the family dynasty" (Gómez-Mejía et al., 2007, p. 106). Several scholars argue that this concern for SEW preservation may influence management practices and strategic decisions on firm performance (e.g., Cruz et al., 2014; Vardaman & Gondo, 2014). In line with them, and establishing a parallel with Stanley (2010)'s idea, it seems reasonable to investigate how the concern for SEW preservation may influence the firm's strategic behavior. In this sense, Hernández-Linares and López-Fernández (2018, p. 340) have recently argued that "it would be interesting to examine the direction and strength of the influence that the concern for SEW preservation has on EO," and we aim to address this suggestion for research.

Although the direct relationship between the concern for SEW preservation and family firm performance has not been previously researched, Kallmuenzer et al. (2018) proposed that prioritizing family-related goals would lead to inefficient use of all entrepreneurial capacities of the company. Also, such concern has been shown to lead family firms to maintain the status quo and be less innovative (Carney et al., 2015; Gómez-Mejía et al., 2007 & 2011). This is consequently the reason behind lower levels of EO in family firms versus non-family firms (Garcés-Galdeano et al., 2016). In line with the above arguments, we formally postulate our last research hypothesis,

Hypothesis 2: Concern for SEW preservation is negatively associated with a family firm's EO.

To test the two research hypotheses, we performed an empirical study, whose methodological characteristics are explained in the next section.

DESIGN/METHODOLOGY

Setting and Sample

Our work focuses on researching SMEs, defined as those non-listed private companies with 10 to 249 employees (e.g., Hernández-Linares et al., 2018a,b; Naldi et al., 2007), given they represent a significant share of the business landscape (Ayyagari et al., 2007). In particular, our study setting is composed of SMEs from Portugal, a country located in the southwest of Europe. We focused on this nation for different reasons. First, because SMEs have great relevance in the Portuguese social and economic fabric, being one of the main sources for jobs in the non-financial private sector in Portugal (Marques & Couto, 2017). Second, we focused on this area because a recent review of the literature on EO and the family business (Hernández-Linares & López-Fernández, 2018) has revealed that this is one of the lesser researched European countries, and as such, it generates more interest. Third, this area is of interest because family firms are the backbone of the Portuguese economy. The Associação das Empresas Familiares[1] (Family Businesses Association from Portugal) estimates that between 70% and 80% of all companies are family organizations and that they generate 60% of employment and 50% of the Gross Domestic Product (Figure 1).

In line with other studies of family business, entrepreneurship and SMEs (e.g., Altinay et al., 2016; Stenholm et al., 2016; Zellweger et al., 2012) fields, the data for this quantitative and empirical study, which is part of a wider research project, were collected using a survey instrument, in the year 2015. In particular, our questionnaire was first developed in English, then translated into Portuguese (with the help of Portuguese native speakers), and then back-translated into English to check for consistency. The Portuguese version was pre-tested. Once all received suggestions were collected, it was guaranteed that the questions raised were clearly perceived and that respondents would be able to respond them naturally and spontaneously. Then, the questionnaire was adjusted, and the survey conduction was begun. The first step in conducting the survey was distributing the questionnaire during the first half of 2015. To do this, we wrote a personalized e-mail to the CEOs of all the Portuguese SMEs included in the Iberian

Figure 1. The family business in the Portuguese economy
Source: Hernández-Linares (2017)

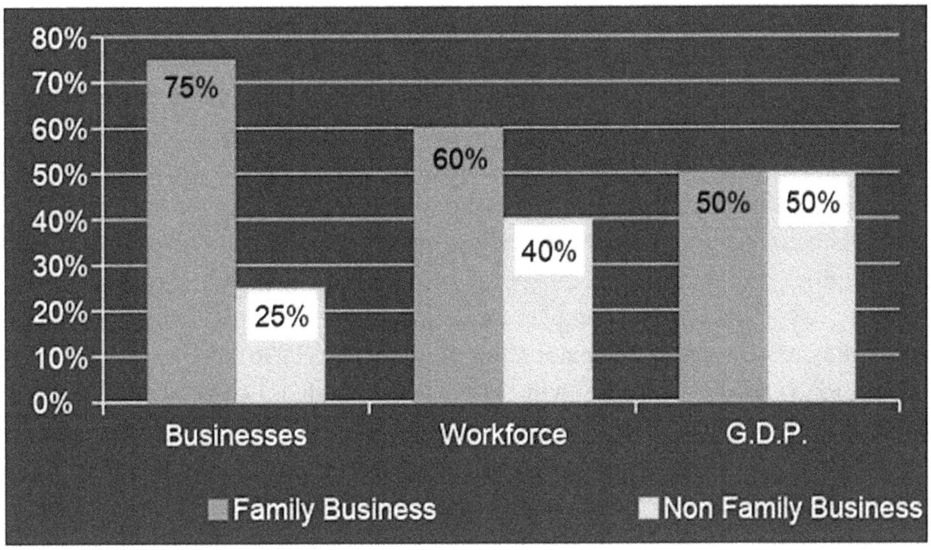

Balance Sheets Analysis System (SABI-Sistema de Análisis de Balances Ibéricos) database (March 2015), which has often been used in family business literature (e.g., Cruz et al., 2010; Diéguez-Soto & López-Delgado, 2018; Larrañeta et al., 2012; Rodrigo-Alarcón et al., 2018; Stanley et al., forthcoming). This e-mail was a personalized invitation to CEOs to complete an online survey, elaborated in limesurvey (www.limesurvey.org). The invitation included an offer to share summary reports as an incentive. From the surveys received, 557 were usable. However, only 342 of them were family firms, according to the perception of the key informant (Cooper et al., 2005; Hernández-Linares et al., 2018a). Among the myriad of the family business definitions appeared across fifty years of research (Hernández-Linares, Sarkar, & Cobo, 2018; Hernández-Linares et al., 2017), we used the self-perception as definitional criteria to capture the essence of being a family firm (Chua et al., 1999). Therefore, our final sample comprises 342 Portuguese family SMEs. The mean number of employees was 35.33, with a large majority of sample's firms (80.1 percent) having fewer than 49 employees.

Variables

All our constructs were adapted from previously validated scales, and all items used to measure constructs were five-point Likert-type scales unless otherwise noted. Key informants were asked to rate their perception on each item with "1" being "totally disagree" to "5" being "totally agree" for the variables, except socio-emotional wealth. In this case, the scale ranged from "not at all important" to "very important." All constructs, their items, and their Cronbach alpha are listed in Table 1.

Dependent Variables

Previous literature has proposed that EO is shaped by several dimensions, representing different characteristics of the firm's strategic orientation. Initially, Miller (1983) and Covin and Slevin (1989) proposed three aspects or dimensions to define EO, *innovativeness*, defined as the business's propensity to support new ideas, novelty, and creativity, and the process that results in new products, services, or technological processes (Lumpkin & Dess, 1996); *proactiveness,* which is understood as "a high level of opportunity-seeking, ideally ahead of competitors and combined with anticipation of future customer demands" (Engelen et al., 2014, p. 1354); and finally, *risk-taking*, which "captures the extent of riskiness reflected in various resource allocation decisions as well as choice of products and markets" (Venkatraman, 1989, p. 949). Two additional dimensions were added by Lumpkin and Dess (1996), *autonomy*, defined as "the independent action of an individual or a team in bringing forth an idea or a vision and carrying it through to completion", which generally means the ability and will to be self-directed in the pursuit of opportunities (Lumpkin & Dess, 1996, p. 140); and *competitive aggressiveness*, which refers to how firms relate to competitors and compete for demand, that is, to how firms respond to trends and demands that already exist in the marketplace (Lumpkin & Dess, 1996).

While Miller (1983) and Covin and Slevin (1989) conceptualize EO as the simultaneous presence of the three dimensions of innovativeness, proactiveness, and risk-taking; Lumpkin and Dess' (1996) approach recognizes that each dimension can vary independently and might not necessarily be beneficial or desirable at different contexts or points in time. Recent reflections suggest that neither approach is intrinsically superior (Covin & Wales, 2012). Indeed, recent studies (Hernández-Linares et al., 2018a) have adopted an intermediate view, considering both the three dimensions of EO initially proposed by Miller and Covin and Slevin (innovativeness, proactiveness, and risk-taking) and the additional dimensions from Lumpkin and Dess (autonomy and competitive aggressiveness) under an aggregated approach. Thus, and in line with these recent studies, we have considered it more adequate for our research purposes to operationalize EO as a second-order construct consisting of five dimensions (autonomy, competitive aggressiveness, innovativeness, proactiveness, and risk-taking). Specifically, it was measured using Hughes and Morgan's (2007) 18-item scale, which has been validated by numerous studies (e.g., Hernández-Linares et al., 2018a; Shan et al., 2016; Stanley et al., forthcoming). The average of the items was used to represent the dimensions, autonomy (6 items), competitive aggressiveness (3 items), innovativeness (3 items), proactiveness (3 items), and risk-taking (3 items). The average of the five dimensions was used to calculate the EO's measure.

Independent Variables

Concerning family business, we first note that empirical literature has used a wide assortment of proxies to define family firms (e.g., Schepers et al., 2014). In this study, we use the self-definition criterion to establish an operational definition of family firms. We have chosen this criterion due, on the one hand, to the increasing relevance of this criterion within the definitional debate on family firms (Hernández-Linares et al., 2018), and on the other hand, to the fact that it allows us to capture the "essence" of being a family business (Chua et al., 2009). This is a reason that scholars foresee the "self-definition" will gain importance in future family business definitions (Hernández-Linares et al., 2018). Thus, we asked the CEOs or top managers whether or not they perceived their firm as a family business (e.g., Cooper et al., 2005), and coded their answers as a binary dummy taking the value of one if the firm was family-classified, and the value of zero otherwise.

SEW was measured by using the Schepers et al.'s scale (2014), which was the only instrument empirically tested at the time the study was performed. This measurement, which has been also used by others (Goel et al., 2013; Vandekerkhof et al., 2015), is based on selection criteria taken from the Strategic

Orientations of Small and Medium-Sized Enterprises (STRATOS) questionnaire (Bamberger 1994, p. 399; Bamberger & Weir, 1990) that addressed the main dimensions of SEW. In this case, the respondents were asked to indicate the importance they attach to each item, from "totally unimportant" (1) to "very important" (5). The average of the items was used to represent the SEW variable.

Affective commitment was measured by using a three-item scale taken from Eddleston et al. (2013), which, in turn, was derived from an organizational commitment scale developed by Porter et al. (1974). This scale has recently been used in the family business literature (Hernández-Linares et al., 2018a).

Control Variables

To improve the robustness of our models, we included several control variables. First, we controlled for business size, which is common in family firm research (e.g., Barros et al., 2017). Business size was measured as the logarithm of the number of employees (Cruz & Nordqvist, 2012; Engelen et al., 2014; Kraiczy et al., 2014), because EO seems to be a resource-consuming strategic posture (Boling et al., 2016) and larger firms might have more slack resources to engage in corporate entrepreneurship (Zahra et al., 2004). However, literature also points out that smaller firms are more agile and faster regarding pursuing entrepreneurial initiatives (Rauch et al., 2009). Literature also notes that larger firms tend to have more mechanical structures and be more technocratic in decision-making (Green et al., 2008), which may hinder their EO (Rodrigo-Alarcón et al., 2018). Second, and given that different industries may exhibit different organizational and environmental characteristics (Wiklund & Shepherd, 2005), we controlled for industry effects in line with recent studies (Stanley et al., forthcoming). Thus, following NACE coding (statistical classification of economic activities in the European Community) we used three dummy variables, manufacturing, construction, and services sector; the agricultural sector being used as default. Thus, manufacturing, construction, and services were included as the second to fourth control variables. Fifth, and in line with other studies (Eddleston et al., 2008) we controlled for the existence of a strategic plan that includes the business goals, as well as the resources and capabilities required to achieve them. This variable was coded with a dichotomous response format. Then, consistent with recent studies (Boling et al., 2016; Hakala et al., 2016), we included as the sixth control variable, environmental dynamism, understood as the frequency of changes, the differences involved in each change, and the irregularity in the overall pattern of change characterizing organizational environment (Child, 1972). To do so, we used a three-item scale, taken from Jansen et al. (2005), and commonly used by family business scholars (e.g., Chirico et al., 2011; Hernández-Linares et al., 2018a). Seventh, we controlled for the existence of a board of directors by including a dichotomous variable, where the number 1 was assigned in this case. The existence of a board was controlled because it is considered a key corporate control mechanism of the company (Bauweraerts & Colot, 2017), that may impact its strategic behavior. Finally, we controlled for the existence of financial stakeholders who were not workers by asking key informants if there were financial stakeholders that did not work in the company similar to Hernández-Linares, López-Fernández, and Fielden (forthcoming) because the presence of stakeholders not working in the company can limit the ability of those involved in management to pursue their own goals (Wong et al., 2010).

To test for reliability, Cronbach alpha coefficients were calculated for each scale. The Cronbach alphas of EO, socioemotional wealth and environmental dynamism successfully satisfied Nunnally's (1978) threshold level of reliability of 0.7, with coefficients of 0.79 or greater in each case (Table 1). In the case of the affective commitment construct, its Cronbach alpha did not surpass this threshold point. However, in line with recent works (Covin & Wales, 2012), a Cronbach's alpha greater than 0.6

was considered adequate since a high coefficient alpha does not always mean a high degree of internal consistency, and such a coefficient may also be affected by the length of the test or the number of items per construct (Merschmann & Thonemann, 2011; Tavakol & Dennick, 2011). Hence, we considered this limit of 0.6 to be reasonable (Nunnally & Bernstein, 1994), as this is a broadly accepted construct in the literature (e.g., Covin & Wales, 2012).

RESULTS

Analysis of Common Method Variance

This cross-sectional study uses self-reported data from single informants, which introduces the potential for hindering interpretation of the relationships between measures (common method variance bias). To alleviate concerns about common method bias, similarly to other studies (e.g., Deb & Wiklund, 2017; Hernández-Linares et al., 2018; Lonial & Carter, 2015; Zahra et al., 2004), we conducted the Harman's single-factor test (Harman, 1967), following the procedure suggested by Podsakoff and Organ (1986) in line with recent studies. We entered all variables into an exploratory factor analysis with a Varimax rotation using the eigenvalue greater than one criterion. More than one factor emerged from this analysis, and no factor accounted for the majority of variance in these variables. The first factor captured only 26.28 percent of the variance in the data.

Additionally, we obtained four of the control variables from a secondary database (SABI), firm size, the manufacturing sector, construction sector, and the services sector. As a result, we concluded that the variance in this study could be attributed to the constructs of interest rather than the measurement method. Hence, common method variance bias is not a serious concern in this study.

Descriptive Analysis

Table 2 presents the descriptive statistics (means and standard deviations), and intercorrelations for the study's variables used in the econometric analysis.

Testing the Hypotheses

The research hypotheses were tested using ordinary least squares (OLS) estimation with robust standard errors (see Table 3). To test hypothesis 1 and 2, we first run the base model containing only the control variables (see Model 1, Table 3). Control variables explained more than 26% of the variance (R-square = 0.267; $p < 0.001$). Manufacturing sector ($b = -0.288$; $p < 0.05$) is significantly and negatively associated with EO in the context of family firms from Portugal, and services sector ($b = -0.220$; $p < 0.1$) is also negatively related to Portuguese family firms' EO, although in this case, the association is only partially significant. Strategic planning ($b = 0.361$; $p < 0.001$) and the existence of a board (0.151; $p < 0.01$) are significantly and positively related to family business' EO, while the existence of shareholders not working in the company ($b = -0.136$; $p < 0.01$) is significantly and negatively related to its EO. Finally, Model 1 also shows a significant and positive association between environmental dynamism ($b = 0.188$; $p < 0.05$) and EO in the Portuguese family businesses context. In a second step, we added

Table 1. Scale items and reliabilities

Dependent Variable
Entrepreneurial Orientation ($\alpha = 0.877$)
The term 'risk taker' is considered a positive attribute for people in our business. (RT)
People in our business are encouraged to take calculated risks with new ideas. (RT)
Our business emphasizes both exploration and experimentation for opportunities. (RT)
We actively introduce improvements and innovations in our business. (INNOV)
Our business is creative in its methods of operation. (INNOV)
Our business seeks out new ways to do things. (INNOV)
We always try to take the initiative in every situation (e.g., against competitors, in projects and when working with others). (PROACT)
We excel at identifying opportunities. (PROACT)
We initiate actions to which other organizations respond. (PROACT)
Our business is intensely competitive. (COMPAGGR)
In general, our business takes a bold or aggressive approach when competing. (COMPAGGR)
We try to undo and out-maneuver the competition as best as we can. (COMPAGGR)
Employees are permitted to act and think without interference. (AUT)
Employees perform jobs that allow them to make and instigate changes in the way they perform their work tasks. (AUT)
Employees are given freedom and independence to decide on their own how to go about doing their work. (AUT)
Employees are given the freedom to communicate without interference. (AUT)
Employees are given authority and responsibility to act alone if they think it to be in the best interests of the business. (AUT)
Employees have access to all vital information. (AUT)
Independent Variables
Affective Commitment ($\alpha = 0.681$)
I am proud to tell others that I am part of this organization.
I really care about the fate of this organization.
For me, this is the best of all possible organizations for which to work.
Socioemotional Wealth ($\alpha = 0.796$)
Maintaining family traditions/family character of the business. [a]
Creating/saving jobs for the family (both may be considered as proxies for the perpetuation of the family dynasty). [a]
Independence in ownership. [b]
Independence in management (both may be considered as proxies for the ability to exercise family influence and maintaining family control). [b]
Control Variables
Environmental Dynamism ($\alpha = 0.809$)
Environmental changes in our local market are intense.
Customers regularly ask for completely new products and services.
In our market, changes are taking place continuously.
[a]both may be considered as proxies for the perpetuation of the family dynasty. [b]both may be considered as proxies for the ability to exercise family influence and maintaining family control.

Table 2. Descriptive statistics and pairwise correlations¥

	Mean	SD	1	2	3	4	5	6	7	8	9	10
1. EO	3.831	0.489										
2. Size	3.192	0.784	.056									
3. Manufacturing sector	0.342	0.475	- 0.059	0.157**								
4 Construction sector	0.085	0.279	- 0.016	0.029	- 0.219							
5. Services sector	0.541	0.499	0.045	- 0.155**	- 0.783***	- 0.330***						
6. Strategic planning	0.740	0.438	0.355***	0.066	0.044	- 0.061	- 0.019					
7. Board	0.290	0.456	0.142**	0.343***	0.133**	- 0.057	- 0.053	0.084				
8. Shareholders not workers	0.480	0.500	- 0.104*	0.205***	0.048	- 0.082	0.003	0.070	0.271***			
9. Environmental dynamism	3.668	0.856	0.354***	0.029	- 0.046	0.000	0.074	0.092*	0.074	- 0.088		
10. Affective Commitment	4.343	0.563	0.515***	0.032	- 0.093*	- 0.011	0.092*	0.244***	0.061	- 0.117*	0.298***	
11. SEW	3.773	0.882	- 0.067	- 0.090	0.002	- 0.014	- 0.033	0.080	- 0.057	- 0.003	0.025	0.088

* $p < .05$; ** $p < .01$; *** $p < .001$; ¥Standardized regression weights; [1] number of employees logarithmized

"affective commitment" and "SEW" variables to the control variables. The results of this new analysis are shown in Model 2 of Table 3.

A significant change in R-square was observed (ΔR-square = 0.133; $p < 0.001$). Affective commitment (0.334; $p < 0.001$) shows a significant and positive association with the family firms' EO, supporting hypothesis 1. Hypothesis 2, which proposed that concern of family firms for SEW preservation would be negatively associated with their EO, was also supported. All these results are discussed with detail in the next section.

DISCUSSIONS

The findings of this study offer new evidence about the heterogeneity of the family firms regarding two relevant indicators of the family firm's essence, affective commitment and the concern for SEW preservation. Our results offer further evidence about how these two variables affect EO in family firms, which in turn reveal interesting insights into the management of family SMEs.

To begin with, our research shows that affective commitment is positively and significantly associated with EO in the Portuguese family firms' context. This means that affective commitment constitutes an important antecedent for EO. This result is especially relevant because, despite the importance of affective factors in strategic decision making (e.g., Daniels 1998; Delgado-García & De la Fuente-Sabaté, 2010), to the best of our knowledge, this is the first time that the positive effect of affective commitment in EO has been empirically tested, both in general and in the family firm literature. This result confirms that affective commitment in family business helps this type of firms to adopt an EO. This result confirms as well the relevance of affective commitment for corporate entrepreneurship as found in previous research (Chirico & Salvato, 2016). What is more, our results show that the concern for SEW preservation negatively and significantly affects EO within family firms, which allow us to empirically corroborate the negative effect of SEW pointed out by other scholars (Garcés-Galdeano et al., 2016).

Table 3. Results of linear regression analysis, four models¥

Variables	Model 1	Model 2
	B (S.E.)	B (S.E.)
Firm size	0.012 (0.032)	- 0.003 (0.029)
Manufacturing sector	- 0.288* (0.135)	- 0.267* (0.124)
Construction sector	- 0.237 (0.151)	- 0.242† (0.138)
Services sector	- 0.220† (0.133)	- 0.244* (0.121)
Strategic planning	0.361*** (0.053)	0.276*** (0.050)
Board	0.151** (0.056)	0.122* (0.051)
Stakeholders not workers	- 0.136** (0.049)	- 0.084† (0.045)
Environmental dynamism	0.174*** (0.027)	0.121*** (0.026)
Family business		
Affective commitment		0.334*** (0.041)
SEW		- 0.072** (0.024)
ΔR^2	.267***	.133***
R^2	.267	.400
Adjusted R^2	.249	.382
F	15.140***	22.069***

Globally considered, our findings help to explain why some family firms are more entrepreneurially oriented than others. At the same time, these results then corroborate the diversity of family firms (Chua et al., 2012). They also allow us to compare the relevance of both effects and to say that the effect of affective commitment is more significant and stronger than the effect of SEW.

Practical Implications

The chapter's findings offer practical implications for family firms management. Even though EO is important to sustain a firm's performance (Rauch et al., 2009) the chapter's results suggest that family firms' managers should be aware that the affective and emotional factors that characterize the family relationships may both boost and reduce the organization's EO. For example, they may establish control mechanisms to avoid the negative influence of the concern for SEW preservation on EO, such as the inclusion of external members on the board. Similarly, considering its role as the antecedent of a family firm's EO, managers of this type of firm may boost affective commitment by promoting personal relationships between family and non-family employees.

Limitations and Future Research

As with all research, there are also some limitations to the current study. First, due to the cross-sectional nature of the data, the analyses examined the association between affective commitment and family firm performance and between concerns for SEW preservation and family performance, rather than how such concern and affective commitment might affect organizational performance in the family business context. That is, the static nature of this type of study, although common in family business literature (Rodrigo-Alarcón et al., 2018) does not allow for the establishment of causal relationships. This makes it impossible to capture the dynamic essence and the effects of SEW (Barros et al., 2017). Thus, a future line of research emerges, carrying out a longitudinal study that considers the time evolution in the characterization of both the affective commitment and the concern for preserving SEW, as well as family firm performance, because it would allow a better explanation of the causal effects within the variables considered.

Second, we have analyzed EO as a higher order construct, contrary to works suggesting the need for analysis of each dimension of these constructs and their individual effects (Casillas & Moreno, 2010; Casillas et al., 2010; Hughes & Morgan, 2007). Consequently, a new line of research unfolds, the analysis of the potential heterogeneity in the effects of affective commitment and the concern for SEW preservation on each dimension of a business' EO (autonomy, competitive aggressiveness, innovativeness, proactiveness, and risk-taking).

Third, we selected family firms based on a subjective criterion (self-perception). Although this is common in family firm literature (e.g., Cooper et al., 2005), we encourage scholars to reply to our analysis by employing other criteria for classifying firms as family or non-family.

Fourth, we operationalized the SEW construct in line with Schepers et al. (2014). However, to disentangle the complexity of the influence of SEW on EO within family firms, the multidimensional nature of SEW should be explored (Hernández-Linares & López-Fernández, 2018), by employing, for example, the FIBER scale proposed by Berrone et al. (2012).

A fifth limitation of our research is that the study variables were measured at the same time from the same source. Hence, common method variance cannot be ruled out (Podsakoff & Organ, 1986). Spector (2006) suggested that the presence of a common method for collecting data does not necessarily mean that results are biased. However, we conducted Harman's single-factor test for common method bias, and its results report that common method bias is not a concern in this study (Harman, 1967; Podsakoff & Organ, 1986). Although this method may also have its limitations, as the test suggests, this concern is diminished (Podsakoff et al., 2003). Despite this, we recommend taking care of generalizing the results.

Finally, we have analyzed the influence of affective commitment and emotional factors on the family firm's EO. However, we believe it would be expedient to analyze the effects of such factors on other variables, such as the family firm's market orientation or its corporate social responsibility.

RESEARCH CONTRIBUTIONS

The chapter contributes to the discussion about the link between entrepreneurship and family firm in at least three ways. First, this research adds to the increasing research on the confluence of EO and family firms (Hernández-Linares & López-Fernández, 2018) by empirically exploring the relationship between family business heterogeneity and firm EO. This is confirmed in the context of SMEs from Portugal, a country generally neglected by the literature on EO within family firms. Second, our work addresses the recent claim for further investigation on the origins of EO by moving toward the study of less explored areas (Rodrigo-Alarcón et al., 2018), in our case affective and emotional factors. We explore how concern for SEW preservation contributes to an organization's EO, and report that such concern reduces the EO of the firm. In this way, we address the third suggestion for future research offered by Hernández-Linares and López-Fernández (2018). Besides, we are pioneering research on the effect of affective commitment on the EO within family firms, by highlighting that such commitment boosts EO within family firms. These results open the door to explore how affective and emotional factors affect EO within family firms.

CONCLUSION

This is the first research effort to study the role of affective and emotional factors as antecedents of the family firm's EO. Due to the confluence of family and firm, in the family firm, there is a unique affective and emotional stock that has been traditionally neglected by the research on EO. However, we find evidence of such factors, mainly affective commitment and SEW, are strongly associated with the entrepreneurial behavior of the company. This finding contributes to the family business literature and suggests new opportunities for future research. Therefore, we hope this chapter is the first step of a fruitful line on how emotions and affective traits influence the strategic and entrepreneurial behaviors of family firms.

REFERENCES

Ahlers, O., Hack, A., Madison, K., Wright, M., & Kellermanns, F. W. (2017). Is it all about money? Affective commitment and the difference between family and non-family sellers in buyouts. *British Journal of Management*, *28*(2), 159–179. doi:10.1111/1467-8551.12178

Allen, N. J., & Meyer, J. P. (1990). The measurement and antecedents of affective, continuance and normative commitment to the organization. *Journal of Occupational Psychology*, *63*(1), 1–18. doi:10.1111/j.2044-8325.1990.tb00506.x

Altinay, L., Madanoglu, M., De Vita, G., Arasli, H., & Ekinci, Y. (2016). The interface between organizational learning capability, entrepreneurial orientation, and SME growth. *Journal of Small Business Management*, *54*(3), 871–891. doi:10.1111/jsbm.12219

Aparicio, G., Basco, R., Iturralde, T., & Maseda, A. (2017). An exploratory study of firm goals in the context of family firms, An institutional logics perspective. *Journal of Family Business Strategy*, *8*(3), 157–169. doi:10.1016/j.jfbs.2017.08.002

Argote, L., & Greve, H. R. (2007). A behavioral theory of the firm—40 years and counting, Introduction and impact. *Organization Science*, *18*(3), 337–349. doi:10.1287/orsc.1070.0280

Astrachan, J. H., & Shanker, M. C. (2003). Family businesses' contribution to the US economy, A closer look. *Family Business Review*, *16*(3), 211–219. doi:10.1177/08944865030160030601

Ayyagari, M., Beck, T., & Demirguc-Kunt, A. (2007). Small and medium enterprises across the globe. *Small Business Economics*, *29*(4), 415–434. doi:10.100711187-006-9002-5

Bamberger, I. (1994) *Product/Market Strategies of Small and Medium-Sized Enterprises*. Aldershot, UK: Ashgate Publishing Group.

Bamberger, I., & Weir, A. (1990). Strategic orientations of small European businesses, The STRATOS group. Aldershot, UK: Gower Publishing Company.

Baron, R. A. (2008). The role of affect in the entrepreneurial process. *Academy of Management Review*, *33*(2), 328–340. doi:10.5465/amr.2008.31193166

Barros, I., Hernández-Gómez, J., & Martín-Cruz, N. (2017). Familiness and socioemotional wealth in Spanish family firms, An empirical examination. *European Journal of Family Business*, *7*(1-2), 14–24. doi:10.1016/j.ejfb.2017.06.004

Basco, R., & Pérez, M. J. (2011). Ideal types of family business management, Horizontal fit between family and business decisions and the relationship with family business performance. *Journal of Family Business Strategy*, *2*(3), 151–165. doi:10.1016/j.jfbs.2011.07.004

Bauweraerts, J., & Colot, O. (2017). Exploring nonlinear effects of family involvement in the board on entrepreneurial orientation. *Journal of Business Research*, *70*(1), 185–192. doi:10.1016/j.jbusres.2016.08.020

Berrone, P., Cruz, C., & Gómez-Mejía, L. R. (2012). Socioemotional wealth in family firms, Theoretical dimensions, assessment approaches, and agenda for future research. *Family Business Review*, *25*(3), 258–279. doi:10.1177/0894486511435355

Block, J. H. (2012). R&D investments in family and founder firms, An agency perspective. *Journal of Business Venturing*, *27*(2), 248–265. doi:10.1016/j.jbusvent.2010.09.003

Camelo-Ordaz, C., García-Cruz, J., Sousa-Ginel, E., & Valle-Cabrera, R. (2011). The influence of human resource management on knowledge sharing and innovation in Spain, The mediating role of affective commitment International. *Journal of Human Resource Management*, *22*(7), 1442–1463.

Carney, M., van Essen, M., Gedajlovic, E. R., & Heugens, P. P. (2015). What do we know about private family firms? A meta-analytical review. *Entrepreneurship Theory and Practice*, *39*(3), 513–544. doi:10.1111/etap.12054

Casillas, J. C., Moreno, A. M., & Barbero, J. L. (2010). A configurational approach of the relationship between entrepreneurial orientation and growth of family firms. *Family Business Review*, *23*(1), 27–44. doi:10.1177/0894486509345159

Casillas, J. C., & Moreno, M. (2010). The relationship between entrepreneurial orientation and growth, The moderating role of family involvement. *Entrepreneurship Theory and Practice*, *22*(3-4), 265–291.

Child, J. (1972). Organizational structure, environment and performance, The role of strategic choice. *Sociology*, *6*(1), 1–22. doi:10.1177/003803857200600101

Chirico, F., & Salvato, C. (2008). Knowledge integration and dynamic organizational adaptation in family firms. *Family Business Review*, *21*(2), 169–181. doi:10.1111/j.1741-6248.2008.00117.x

Chirico, F., & Salvato, C. (2016). Knowledge internalization and product development in family firms. When relational and affective factors matter. *Journal of Business Venturing*, *40*(1), 201–229.

Chirico, F., Sirmon, D. G., Sciascia, S., & Mazzola, P. (2011). Resource orchestration in family firms. Investigating how entrepreneurial orientation, generational involvement, and participative strategy affect performance. *Strategic Entrepreneurship Journal*, *5*(4), 307–326. doi:10.1002ej.121

Chittoor, R., & Das, R. (2007). Professionalization of management and succession performance - A vital linkage. *Family Business Review*, *20*(1), 65–79. doi:10.1111/j.1741-6248.2007.00084.x

Chrisman, J. J., Chua, J. H., Pearson, A. W., & Barnett, T. (2012). Family involvement, family influence, and family-centered non-economic goals in small firms. *Entrepreneurship Theory and Practice*, *36*(2), 267–293. doi:10.1111/j.1540-6520.2010.00407.x

Chua, J. H., Chrisman, J. J., & Sharma, P. (1999). Defining the family business by behavior. *Entrepreneurship Theory and Practice*, *23*(4), 19–39. doi:10.1177/104225879902300402

Cooper, M. J., Upton, N., & Seaman, S. (2005). Customer relationship management, A comparative analysis of family and nonfamily business practices. *Journal of Small Business Management*, *43*(3), 242–256. doi:10.1111/j.1540-627X.2005.00136.x

Corbetta, G., & Salvato, C. A. (2004). The board of directors in family firms, one size fits all? *Family Business Review*, *17*(2), 119–134. doi:10.1111/j.1741-6248.2004.00008.x

Covin, J. G., & Slevin, D. P. (1990). New venture strategic posture, structure, and performance, An industry life cycle analysis. *Journal of Business Venturing*, *5*(2), 123–135. doi:10.1016/0883-9026(90)90004-D

Covin, J. G., & Slevin, D. P. (1991). A conceptual model of entrepreneurship as firm behavior. *Entrepreneurship Theory and Practice*, *16*(1), 7–25. doi:10.1177/104225879101600102

Covin, J. G., & Wales, W. J. (2012). The measurement of entrepreneurial orientation. *Entrepreneurship Theory and Practice*, *36*(4), 677–702. doi:10.1111/j.1540-6520.2010.00432.x

Cruz, C., Larraza-Kintana, M., Garcés-Galdeano, L., & Berrone, P. (2014). Are family firms really more socially responsible? *Entrepreneurship Theory and Practice*, *38*(6), 1295–1316.

Cruz, C., & Nordqvist, M. (2012). Entrepreneurial orientation in family firms, a generational perspective. *Small Business Economics*, *38*(1), 33–49. doi:10.100711187-010-9265-8

Cruz, C. C., Gómez-Mejía, L. R., & Becerra, M. (2010). Perceptions of benevolence and the design of agency contracts, CEO-TMT relationships in family firms. *Academy of Management Journal*, *53*(1), 69–89. doi:10.5465/amj.2010.48036975

Cyert, R. M., & March, J. G. (1963). *A behavioral theory of the firm*. Englewood Cliffs, NJ: Prentice-Hall.

Daniels, K. (1998). Towards integrating emotions into strategic management research, trait affect and perceptions of the strategic environment. *British Journal of Management*, *9*(3), 163–168. doi:10.1111/1467-8551.00081

De Clercq, D., Dimov, D., & Thongpapanl, N. T. (2013). Organizational social capital, formalization, and internal knowledge sharing in entrepreneurial orientation formation. *Entrepreneurship Theory and Practice*, *37*(3), 505–537. doi:10.1111/etap.12021

Deb, P., & Wiklund, J. (2017). The effects of CEO founder status and stock ownership on entrepreneurial orientation in small firms. *Journal of Small Business Management*, *55*(1), 32–55. doi:10.1111/jsbm.12231

Delgado-García, J. B., & de La Fuente-Sabaté, J. M. (2010). How do CEO emotions matter? Impact of CEO affective traits on strategic and performance conformity in the Spanish banking industry. *Strategic Management Journal*, *31*(5), 562–574.

Déniz-Déniz, M. C., Cabrera-Suárez, M. K., & Martín-Santana, J. D. (2018). Family firms and the interests of non-family stakeholders, The influence of family managers' affective commitment and family salience in terms of power. *Business Ethics European Review*, *27*(1), 15–28. doi:10.1111/beer.12155

Diéguez-Soto, J., & López-Delgado, P. (2018) Does family and lone founder involvement lead to similar indebtedness? *Journal of Small Business Management*. doi:10.1111/jsbm.12422

Dyer, W. G. (2006). Examining the "family effect" on firm performance. *Family Business Review*, *19*(4), 253–273. doi:10.1111/j.1741-6248.2006.00074.x

Dyer, W. G. Jr, & Dyer, W. J. (2009). Putting the family into family business research. *Family Business Review*, *22*(3), 216–219. doi:10.1177/0894486509333042

Eddleston, K. A., Kellermanns, F. W., Floyd, S. W., Crittenden, V. L., & Crittenden, W. F. (2013). Planning for growth, Life stage differences in family firms. *Entrepreneurship Theory and Practice*, *37*(5), 1177–1202. doi:10.1111/etap.12002

Eddleston, K. A., Kellermanns, F. W., & Sarathy, R. (2008). Resource configuration in family firms, Linking resources, strategic planning and technological opportunities to performance. *Journal of Management Studies*, *45*(1), 26–50.

Engelen, A., Kube, H., Schmidt, S., & Flatten, T. C. (2014). Entrepreneurial orientation in turbulent environments, The moderating role of absorptive capacity. *Research Policy*, *43*(8), 1353–1369. doi:10.1016/j.respol.2014.03.002

Ensley, M. D., & Pearson, A. W. (2005). An exploratory comparison of the behavioral dynamics of top management teams in family and non-family new ventures, Cohesion, conflict, potency, and consensus. *Entrepreneurship Theory and Practice*, *29*(3), 267–284. doi:10.1111/j.1540-6520.2005.00082.x

Garcés-Galdeano, L., Larraza-Kintana, M., García-Olaverri, C., & Makri, M. (2016). Entrepreneurial orientation in family firms, The moderating role of technological intensity and performance. *The International Entrepreneurship and Management Journal*, *12*(1), 27–45. doi:10.100711365-014-0335-2

Giménez, D. A., Calabrò, A., Edelman, L. F., Minola, T., & Cassia, L. (2018) The impact of affective commitment and in-group-collectivism on daughters' succession intentions. *Academy of Management Proceedings, 18*(1). Available in https://journals.aom.org/doi/abs/10.5465/AMBPP.2018.223

Goel, S., Voordeckers, W., Van Gils, A., & van den Heuvel, J. (2013). CEO's empathy and salience of socioemotional wealth in family SMEs–The moderating role of external directors. *Entrepreneurship and Regional Development, 25*(3-4), 111–134. doi:10.1080/08985626.2012.710262

Gómez-Mejía, L. R., Cruz, C., Berrone, P., & De Castro, J. (2011). The bind that ties, Socioemotional wealth preservation in family firms. *The Academy of Management Annals, 5*(1), 653–707. doi:10.5465/19416520.2011.593320

Gómez-Mejía, L. R., Haynes, K. T., Núñez-Nickel, M., Jacobson, K. J., & Moyano-Fuentes, J. (2007). Socioemotional wealth and business risks in family-controlled firms, Evidence from Spanish olive oil mills. *Administrative Science Quarterly, 52*(1), 106–137. doi:10.2189/asqu.52.1.106

Green, K. M., Covin, J. G., & Slevin, D. P. (2008). Exploring the relationship between strategic reactiveness and entrepreneurial orientation. The role of structure style fit. *Journal of Business Venturing, 23*(3), 356–383. doi:10.1016/j.jbusvent.2007.01.002

Gundlach, G. T., Achrol, R. S., & Mentzer, J. T. (1995). The structure of commitment in exchange. *Journal of Marketing, 59*(1), 78–92. doi:10.1177/002224299505900107

Harman, H. H. (1967). *Modern factor analysis.* Chicago: University of Chicago Press.

Hayek, M., Randolph-Seng, B., Atinc, G., & Montalvo, D. (2018). The influence of political skill on career success in an Ecuadorian family firm, The mediating role of affective commitment. *International Journal of Cross Cultural Management, 18*(2), 175–190. doi:10.1177/1470595818768347

Hernández-Linares, R. (2017). *Análisis de la relación entre orientación emprendedora, orientación al mercado, orientación al aprendizaje y rendimiento de la organización. La influencia del contexto organizacional, empresa familiar versus empresa no familiar* (Unpublished doctoral dissertation). University of Cantabria, Spain.

Hernández-Linares, R., Kellermanns, F. W., & López-Fernández, M. C. (2018a). A note on the relationship between learning, market, and entrepreneurial orientations in family and nonfamily firms. *Journal of Family Business Strategy, 9*(3), 192–204. doi:10.1016/j.jfbs.2018.08.001

Hernández-Linares, R., Kellermanns, F. W., & López-Fernández, M. C. (2018b). Dynamic capabilities and SME performance, The moderating effect of market orientation. *Journal of Small Business Management.* doi:10.1111/jsbm.12474

Hernández-Linares, R., & López-Fernández, M. C. (2018). Entrepreneurial orientation and the family firm, Mapping the field and tracing a path for future research. *Family Business Review*, *31*(3), 318–351. doi:10.1177/0894486518781940

Hernández-Linares, R, López-Fernández, MC, & Fielden, L.V. (forthcoming). The moderating effect of the family firm status on the relationship between entrepreneurial orientation and SMEs performance. An empirical study in Portugal.

Hernández-Linares, R., Sarkar, S., & Cobo, M. J. (2018b). Inspecting the Achilles heel, a quantitative analysis of 50 years of family business definitions. *Scientometrics*, *115*(2), 929–951. doi:10.100711192-018-2702-1

Hernández-Linares, R., Sarkar, S., & López-Fernández, M. C. (2017). How has the family firm literature addressed its heterogeneity through classification systems? An integrated analysis. *European Journal of Family Business*, *7*(1-2), 1–13. doi:10.1016/j.ejfb.2017.06.003

Herscovitch, L., & Meyer, J. P. (2002). Commitment to organizational change, Extension of a three-component model. *The Journal of Applied Psychology*, *87*(3), 474–487. doi:10.1037/0021-9010.87.3.474 PMID:12090605

Hughes, M., & Morgan, R. E. (2007). Deconstructing the relationship between entrepreneurial orientation and business performance at the embryonic stage of firm growth. *Industrial Marketing Management*, *36*(5), 651–661. doi:10.1016/j.indmarman.2006.04.003

Jansen, J. J., Van Den Bosch, F. A., & Volberda, H. W. (2005). Managing potential and realized absorptive capacity. How do organizational antecedents matter? *Academy of Management Journal*, *48*(6), 999–1015. doi:10.5465/amj.2005.19573106

Kallmuenzer, A., Strobl, A., & Peters, M. (2017). Tweaking the entrepreneurial orientation-performance relationship in family firms, The effect of control mechanisms and family-related goals. *Review of Managerial Science*, *12*(4), 855–883. doi:10.100711846-017-0231-6

Kellermanns, F. W., Dibrell, C., & Cruz, C. (2014). The role and impact of emotions in family business strategy. New approaches and paradigms. *Journal of Family Business Strategy*, *5*(3), 277–279. doi:10.1016/j.jfbs.2014.08.002

Kellermanns, F. W., & Eddleston, K. A. (2006). Corporate entrepreneurship in family firms, A family perspective. *Entrepreneurship Theory and Practice*, *30*(6), 809–830. doi:10.1111/j.1540-6520.2006.00153.x

Kellermanns, F. W., Eddleston, K. A., & Zellweger, T. M. (2012). Extending the socioemotional wealth perspective, A look at the dark side. *Entrepreneurship Theory and Practice*, *36*(6), 1175–1182. doi:10.1111/j.1540-6520.2012.00544.x

Kraiczy, N. D., Hack, A., & Kellermanns, F. W. (2014). New product portfolio performance in family firms. *Journal of Business Research*, *67*(6), 1065–1073. doi:10.1016/j.jbusres.2013.06.005

Larrañeta, B., Zahra, S. A., & González, J. L. G. (2012). Enriching strategic variety in new ventures through external knowledge. *Journal of Business Venturing*, *27*(4), 401–413. doi:10.1016/j.jbusvent.2011.11.004

Litz, R. A. (1995). The family business, Toward definitional clarity. *Family Business Review*, *8*(2), 71–81. doi:10.1111/j.1741-6248.1995.00071.x

Lonial, S. C., & Carter, R. E. (2015). The impact of organizational orientations on medium and small firm performance, A resource-based perspective. *Journal of Small Business Management*, *53*(1), 94–113. doi:10.1111/jsbm.12054

Marques, A. P., & Couto, A. I. (2017). SMEs and family SMEs, Specificities from the Portuguese socio-business context. *European Journal of Economic Business Studies*, *3*(2), 190–199. doi:10.26417/ejes.v8i1.p190-199

Memili, E., Zellweger, T. M., & Fang, H. (2013). The determinants of family owners-managers' affective organizational commitment. *Family Relations*, *62*(3), 443–456. doi:10.1111/fare.12015

Mercurio, Z. A. (2015). Affective commitment as a core essence of organizational commitment. An integrative literature review. *Human Resource Development Review*, *14*(4), 389–414. doi:10.1177/1534484315603612

Merschmann, U., & Thonemann, U. W. (2011). Supply chain flexibility, uncertainty and firm performance, An empirical analysis of German manufacturing firms. *International Journal of Production Economics*, *130*(1), 43–53. doi:10.1016/j.ijpe.2010.10.013

Meyer, J. P., & Allen, N. J. (1991). A three-component conceptualization of organizational commitment. *Human Resource Management Review*, *1*(1), 61–89. doi:10.1016/1053-4822(91)90011-Z

Miller, D. (1983). The correlates of entrepreneurship in three types of firms. *Management Science*, *29*(7), 770–791. doi:10.1287/mnsc.29.7.770

Miller, D., & Le Breton-Miller, I. (2011). Governance, social identity, and entrepreneurial orientation in closely held public companies. *Entrepreneurship Theory and Practice*, *35*(5), 1051–1076. doi:10.1111/j.1540-6520.2011.00447.x

Miller, D., & Le Breton-Miller, I. (2014). Deconstructing socioemotional wealth. *Entrepreneurship Theory and Practice*, *38*(4), 713–720. doi:10.1111/etap.12111

Mintzberg, H. (1973). Strategy-making in three modes. *California Management Review*, *16*(2), 44–53. doi:10.2307/41164491

Mittal, V., & Ross, W. T. Jr. (1998). The impact of positive and negative affect and issue framing on issue interpretation and risk-taking. *Organizational Behavior and Human Decision Processes*, *76*(3), 298–324. doi:10.1006/obhd.1998.2808 PMID:9878512

Morgan, R. M., & Hunt, S. D. (1994). The commitment-trust theory of relationship marketing. *Journal of Marketing*, *58*(3), 20–38. doi:10.1177/002224299405800302

Morgan, T. J., & Gómez-Mejía, L. R. (2014). Hooked on a feeling, The affective component of socio-emotional wealth in family firms. *Journal of Family Business Strategy*, *5*(3), 280–288. doi:10.1016/j.jfbs.2014.07.001

Morris, M. H., Webb, J. W., & Franklin, R. (2011). Understanding the manifestation of entrepreneurial orientation in the nonprofit context. *Entrepreneurship Theory and Practice*, *35*(5), 947–971. doi:10.1111/j.1540-6520.2011.00453.x

Mowday, R. T., Steers, R. M., & Porter, L. W. (1979). The measurement of organizational commitment. *Journal of Vocational Behavior*, *14*(2), 224–247. doi:10.1016/0001-8791(79)90072-1

Naldi, L., Cennamo, C., Corbetta, G., & Gómez-Mejía, L. (2013). Preserving socioemotional wealth in family firms, Asset or liability? The moderating role of business context. *Entrepreneurship Theory and Practice*, *37*(6), 1341–1360. doi:10.1111/etap.12069

Naldi, L., Nordqvist, M., Sjöberg, K., & Wiklund, J. (2007). Entrepreneurial orientation, risk-taking, and performance in family firms. *Family Business Review*, *20*(1), 33–47. doi:10.1111/j.1741-6248.2007.00082.x

Nordqvist, M., & Melin, L. (2010). Entrepreneurial families and family firms. *Entrepreneurship and Regional Development*, *22*(3-4), 211–239. doi:10.1080/08985621003726119

Perry, S. J., Hunter, E. M., & Currall, S. C. (2016). Managing the innovators, Organizational and professional commitment among scientists and engineers. *Research Policy*, *45*(6), 1247–1262. doi:10.1016/j.respol.2016.03.009

Pimentel, D., Couto, J. P., & Scholten, M. (2017). Entrepreneurial orientation in family firms, Looking at an outermost European region. *Journal of Enterprising Culture*, *25*(4), 441–460. doi:10.1142/S0218495817500169

Pindado, J., & Requejo, I. (2015). Family business performance from a governance perspective, a review of empirical research. *International Journal of Management Reviews*, *17*(3), 279–311. doi:10.1111/ijmr.12040

Podsakoff, P. M., MacKenzie, S. B., Lee, J. Y., & Podsakoff, N. P. (2003). Common method biases in behavioral research. A critical review of the literature and recommended remedies. *Applied Psychology*, *88*(5), 879–903. doi:10.1037/0021-9010.88.5.879 PMID:14516251

Podsakoff, P. M., & Organ, D. W. (1986). Self-reports in organizational research, Problems and prospects. *Journal of Management*, *12*(4), 531–544. doi:10.1177/014920638601200408

Porter, L. W., Steers, R. M., Mowday, R. T., & Boulian, P. V. (1974). Organizational commitment, job satisfaction, and turnover among psychiatric technicians. *The Journal of Applied Psychology*, *59*(5), 603–609. doi:10.1037/h0037335

Randall, D. M., Fedor, D. B., & Longenecker, C. O. (1990). The behavioral expression of organizational commitment. *Journal of Vocational Behavior*, *36*(2), 210–224. doi:10.1016/0001-8791(90)90028-Z

Revilla, A. J., Pérez-Luño, A., & Nieto, M. J. (2016). Does family involvement in management reduce the risk of business failure? The moderating role of entrepreneurial orientation. *Family Business Review*, *29*(4), 365–379. doi:10.1177/0894486516671075

Rodrigo-Alarcón, J., García-Villaverde, P. M., Ruiz-Ortega, M. J., & Parra-Requena, G. (2018). From social capital to entrepreneurial orientation, The mediating role of dynamic capabilities. *European Management Journal, 36*(2), 195–209. doi:10.1016/j.emj.2017.02.006

Schepers, J., Voordeckers, W., Steijvers, T., & Laveren, E. (2014). The entrepreneurial orientation-performance relationship in private family firms, the moderating role of socioemotional wealth. *Small Business Economics, 43*(1), 39–55. doi:10.100711187-013-9533-5

Sciascia, S., Mazzola, P., & Chirico, F. (2013). Generational involvement in the top management team of family firms, Exploring nonlinear effects on entrepreneurial orientation. *Entrepreneurship Theory and Practice, 37*(1), 69–85. doi:10.1111/j.1540-6520.2012.00528.x

Sciascia, S., Mazzola, P., & Kellermanns, F. W. (2014). Family management and profitability in private family-owned firms, Introducing generational stage and the socioemotional wealth perspective. *Journal of Family Business Strategy, 5*(2), 131–137. doi:10.1016/j.jfbs.2014.03.001

Shan, P., Song, M., & Ju, X. (2016). Entrepreneurial orientation and performance. Is innovation speed a missing link? *Journal of Business Research, 69*(2), 683–690. doi:10.1016/j.jbusres.2015.08.032

Shanker, M. C., & Astrachan, J. H. (1996). Myths, and realities, Family businesses' contribution to the US Economy. A framework for assessing family business statistics. *Family Business Review, 9*(2), 107–123. doi:10.1111/j.1741-6248.1996.00107.x

Sharma, P. (2004). On overview of the field of family business studies, Current status and directions for the future. *Family Business Review, 17*(1), 1–36. doi:10.1111/j.1741-6248.2004.00001.x

Sharma, P., Chrisman, J. J., & Gersick, K. E. (2012). 25 years of family business review, Reflections on the past and perspectives for the future. *Family Business Review, 25*(1), 5–15. doi:10.1177/0894486512437626

Sieger, P., Bernhard, F., & Frey, U. (2011). Affective commitment and job satisfaction among non-family employees, Investigating the roles of justice perceptions and psychological ownership. *Journal of Family Business Strategy, 2*(2), 78–89. doi:10.1016/j.jfbs.2011.03.003

Somers, M. J. (2010). Patterns of attachment to organizations, commitment profiles and work outcomes. *Journal of Occupational and Organizational Psychology, 83*(2), 443–453. doi:10.1348/096317909X424060

Spector, P. E. (2006). Method variance in organizational research, Truth or urban legend? *Organizational Research Methods, 9*(2), 221–232. doi:10.1177/1094428105284955

Stanley, L. (2010) Emotions and family business creation, an extension and implications. *Entrep Theor Pract, 34*(6), 1085–1092.

Stanley, L., Hernández-Linares, R., López-Fernández, M. C., & Kellermanns, F. (2019). (forthcoming). A typology of family firms, An investigation of entrepreneurial orientation and performance. *Family Business Review.*

Stenholm, P., Pukkinen, T., & Heinonen, J. (2016). Firm growth in family businesses, The role of entrepreneurial orientation and the entrepreneurial activity. *Journal of Small Business Management*, *54*(3), 691–713.

Tavakol, M., & Dennick, R. (2011). Making sense of Cronbach's Alpha. *International Journal of Medical Education*, *2*, 53–55. doi:10.5116/ijme.4dfb.8dfd PMID:28029643

Vandekerkhof, P., Steijvers, T., Hendriks, W., & Voordeckers, W. (2018). Socioemotional wealth separation and decision-making quality in family firm TMTs, The moderating role of psychological safety. *Journal of Management Studies*, *55*(4), 648–676. doi:10.1111/joms.12277

Vardaman, J. M., & Gondo, M. B. (2014). Socioemotional wealth conflict in family firms. *Entrepreneurship Theory and Practice*, *38*(6), 1317–1322.

Venkatraman, N. (1989). Strategic orientation of business enterprises, The construct, dimensionality, and measurement. *Management Science*, *35*(8), 942–962. doi:10.1287/mnsc.35.8.942

Wales, W., Monsen, E., & McKelvie, A. (2011). The organizational pervasiveness of entrepreneurial orientation. *Entrepreneurship Theory and Practice*, *35*(5), 895–923. doi:10.1111/j.1540-6520.2011.00451.x

Wales, W. J., Gupta, V. K., & Mousa, F. T. (2013). Empirical research on entrepreneurial orientation, An assessment and suggestions for future research. *International Small Business Journal*, *31*(4), 357–383. doi:10.1177/0266242611418261

Westhead, P., & Howorth, C. (2007). 'Types' of private family firms. An exploratory conceptual and empirical analysis. *Entrepreneurship and Regional Development*, *19*(5), 405–431. doi:10.1080/08985620701552405

Wiklund, J., & Shepherd, D. (2005). Entrepreneurial orientation and small business performance, A configurational approach. *Journal of Business Venturing*, *20*(1), 71–91. doi:10.1016/j.jbusvent.2004.01.001

Wiseman, R. M., & Gómez-Mejía, L. R. (1998). A behavioural agency model of managerial risk taking. *Academy of Management Review*, *23*(1), 133–153. doi:10.5465/amr.1998.192967

Wong, Y.-J., Chang, S.-C., & Chen, L.-Y. (2010). Does a family-controlled firm perform better in corporate venturing? *Corporate Governance*, *18*(3), 175–192. doi:10.1111/j.1467-8683.2010.00792.x

Zahra, S. A. (2012). Organizational learning and entrepreneurship in family firms, Exploring the moderating effect of ownership and cohesion. *Small Business Economics*, *38*(1), 51–65. doi:10.100711187-010-9266-7

Zahra, S. A., Hayton, J. C., & Salvato, C. (2004). Entrepreneurship in family vs. non-family firms, A resource-based analysis of the effect of organizational culture. *Entrepreneurship Theory and Practice*, *28*(4), 363–381. doi:10.1111/j.1540-6520.2004.00051.x

Zahra, S. A., & Nielsen, A. P. (2002). Sources of capabilities, integration and technology commercialization. *Strategic Management Journal*, *23*(5), 377–398. doi:10.1002mj.229

Zellweger, T. M., Nason, R. S., Nordqvist, M., & Brush, C. G. (2013). Why do family firms strive for nonfinancial goals? An organizational identity perspective. *Entrepreneurship Theory and Practice*, *37*(2), 229–248. doi:10.1111/j.1540-6520.2011.00466.x

KEY TERMS AND DEFINITIONS

Affective Commitment: It is the desire to remain in the organization.

Continuance Commitment: It is generated by the need to remain in the organization.

Entrepreneurial Orientation: It is how the CEO and the Board of Directors design business strategies support key entrepreneurial activities.

Normative Commitment: It is the mindset of an obligation to remain in the organization.

Proactiveness: It consists of the high level of opportunity-seeking, ideally ahead of competitors and combined with anticipation of future customer demands.

Socioemotional Wealth: It consists of the dominant family's affective commitment to the firm.

ENDNOTE

1 http, //www.empresasfamiliares.pt/quem-somos

Chapter 10
Orange Economy and Digital Entrepreneurship in Latin America:
Creative Sparkles Among Raw Materials

Alejandro Vega-Muñoz
https://orcid.org/0000-0002-9427-2044
Universidad Autónoma de Chile, Chile

Guillermo Bustamante-Pavez
Universidad Finis Terrae, Chile

Guido Salazar-Sepúlveda
https://orcid.org/0000-0002-4979-6869
Universidad Católica de la Santísima Concepción, Chile

ABSTRACT

This chapter gives an account of how the orange economy begins to penetrate the traditional economy of Latin American countries, which are oriented towards the export of generic products and low commercial value. For this, the authors have analyzed the experiences of 18 Latin American creative companies identified by the Inter-American Development Bank. Cases selected concentrates in the media and software platforms sectors of the orange economy, with a qualitative approach and a narrative design through the analysis of the information of these 18 extreme cases of business success describes the possibilities that in the Latin American reality can be visualized. As a result, this chapter allows us to understand the opportunities of entrepreneurship, through the orange economy in Latin America, and to distinguish how this economic, social, and cultural phenomenon is observed, starting from the Latin American academic discourse, contributing to the construction of a definition that tries to achieve a greater conceptual precision concerning Orange economy.

DOI: 10.4018/978-1-5225-8939-6.ch010

INTRODUCTION

This chapter gives an account of how orange economy begins to permeate the traditional economy of Latin American countries, which are commonly oriented to export generic products and a low commercial value (Vega & Rodriguez, 2015). Although for some authors the concept of orange economy lacks conceptual precision (Durand-Grahammer & Durand-Grahammer, 2017; Morales-Astola, 2016; Reyes Godínez, 2016), it will be understood by orange economy, a sort of economy that implies an economic, social and cultural development, by means of transformation of ideas into goods and services generated by the creative industries, and driven by digital technologies, strongly linked with the economy of information and knowledge, and intangible capital (knowledge, know-how, intellectual property, relational capital, positioning and human talent), which arise from the links between artistic creation and cultural demand, socioeconomic and cultural dynamics, and business political demand and cultural supply (Blanco-Valbuena et al., 2018; Castañeda-Rivera & Garduño-Bello, 2017; Jiménez, Millán & Suárez, 2017). In this sense, Bayardo (2016) adds that this form of the economy should be stimulated through public policies.

For this reason, experiences of eighteen Latin American creative ventures, identified by the Inter-American Development Bank (Luzardo, De Jesus, & Pérez, 2017), are analyzed. The cases chosen for this chapter are concentrated in sectors of Media and Software / Digital Platforms of the orange economy, with geographical origins in Argentina, Brazil, Chile, Colombia, Jamaica, Mexico, and Peru. Countries whose economic sectoral composition in typical triadic terms (agriculture, industry, services) is concentrated between 56% and 73% on services, and whose global position per GDP - per capita ranges from 83 to 145 out the total of 229 countries (Central Intelligence Agency, 2018).

ORANGE ECONOMY AND DIGITAL ENTREPRENEURSHIP

Overcome of shortage by appropriation of creative transformations of added value, is the component of the economy that in contemporary terms has been called the orange economy. This is focused on creative or cultural industries, space that among others is home to digital entrepreneurship, which allows the generation of new business models based on means and technologies usage, by this ubiquity can have a wide global impact.

An Orange Component in the Economy

The orange economy is operationally defined, that is, based on activities to this gives coverage, being its essence to give way for ideas which are transformed into creative goods and services, whose added values is produced according to its intellectual property (Jiménez, Millán, & Suárez, 2018). In broad terms, these activities are associated to 'cultural sector' as economic activity and, at the same time, as an empowering activity of local cultures, giving space to recovering of local cultures in a context as alienating as globalization (Szpilbarg & Saferstein, 2014). This local development is not strictly restricted to a local market and is an evident issue in the tourism industry (Otero-Gómez & Giraldo-Pérez, 2018).

Respect to creative territories development, these rather depend on personal creativity and ability to 'attract, retain and generate creatives individuals' (Sánchez-Serra, 2016: 29). And it does not strictly depend on the size and condition of rurality of urbanity of such places (Escalona-Orcao & Escolano-

Utrilla, 2016). In Europe, increasing interest on linked activities to the creative economy is due to the need to deal with economic crisis, and the need to identify and develop strategic activities to allow cities a better adaption to changing environments before many urban centers start to promote those type of goods and services to the challenges faced by individuals, societies or territories (Méndez, Michelini, Prada, & Tébar, 2012).

During last years, globalization and sustained development in the rise of new information and communication technologies (ICTs) have given a considerable advantage to proliferation and exportation of ideas, projects, and business born under the waves of creative economy (Morales, 2018). A previous example is Uber and Airbnb that is used practically around the world, like a new collective transportation system and hotel rental, respectively.

Despite of the benefits that can bring with it the creative economy, to develop a geographical space by means of ideas transmission, poses as challenges the human capital development and economic and social value that this kind of services make to the gross domestic product of each country (Sánchez-Trujillo, Molina-Ruiz & García-Vargas, 2018) in conjunction with legal aspects that involve the startup of this type of creative solutions in legal statements not entirely adapted to this type of process (Muñoz, 2016) According to Oliva and Lázaro (2018), in Latin America, the creative economy has gained great importance, not only in regional cultures policies, but also in strategies of social and economic areas. Nevertheless, data are still necessary that guarantee where to invest and the necessary criteria to do it.

However, creative economy actions' spheres had demonstrated that in Latin America exist a high strength to contribute to the generation of 'happier lives, richer and worthier for everyone (...) so economy and cultural creative contribute to creating societies in which worth to live, vibrating, expressive and cheerful (Finlev, Maguire, Oppenheim, & Skvirsky, 2017, p. 18), but for those it is required that both businesspeople and governments take new procedures to the development of this industry away from the traditional ones that are rather tied to product/service sensibility.

For Latin America, the development and strengthening of the orange economy should be directly related to the economic development of the region, even more considering with data of International Labor Organization in 2015, companies belonging to this industry contribute with 1.9 million jobs in all region, some jobs that generate in economies like Uruguay and Costa Rica (Luzardo, De Jesus, & Pérez, 2017). One of the bigger engines of the orange economy is entrepreneurship and with it, the resurgence of companies that stir up the global market and the way how to be understanding. With an important technological base and a solid certainty to solve people real problems of this kind of companies it is attracting more and more customers and, with it, new stockholders and talents that add to them. The previous make possible even more the economic increasing of the region.

In this digital economy described, arise ideas by Pereira de Castro Pacheco, Benini and Pasquotto-Mariani (2017) which point out that Creative Economy emerge in the middle of the economic singularity discover by an industrial conglomerate with plentiful symbolic assets, knowledge, and ideas (Hesmondhalgh, 2002). John Hartley defined the concept since the incorporation of information technologies, in an intersection between culture and technologies. '[...] The idea of Creative Industry seeks to describe the conceptual and practical convergence of creative arts (individual talent) with cultural industries (mass scale), into the context of mass new technologies (ICTs) in a new knowledge economy to the interactive usage of new consumer citizens' (Hartley, cited by Fonseca-Reis, 2008: 21).

Digital Entrepreneurship and Its Effects on the Economy

To introduce in the contextual framework of digital entrepreneurial, it has to start to recognize that currently economy and its development are strongly build in an digital environment promoted by the Fourth Industrial Revolution, making up in a digital economy that, although it is not by universal access, it creates spaces to individuals whose ability is to use mass media and digital technologies, so that can solve world challenges through this or create new business opportunities (Pombo, Gupta, & Stankovic, 2018). According to Luzardo, De Jesus and Pérez (2017), the combination of software and new information technologies are the key clues to lead transformation and promote digital entrepreneurial, but creativity must be the starting point. Without it, digital entrepreneurship is not possible to understand in the orange economy.

The contribution of digital entrepreneurial is the consequence of Sustainable Development Objectives (SDO) in Latin America is a recent phenomenon. So far, there is some clarity respect how digital entrepreneurs -assuming a role from social innovation- can contribute to a greater extent to his achievement. (Buckland, Garmilla, Murillo, Leticia, & Flores, 2018). That is not all, but together with digital entrepreneurship, also it has valued the development of services as one of the ways of how the Latin American economy is competing into the global market. Since this point, the increasing of companies based on knowledge-intensive services has started to highlight. This type of services is strongly linked to the high specialization of human capital employment and their basis in the usage of available technologies or their creation to serve based on their clients' information and knowledge (López, Niembro & Ramos, 2014)

To understand digital entrepreneurship, it is necessary to go back to different conceptions of entrepreneurship that had been developed throughout history, so they are the necessary basis to understand the current changes that creative economy generates. Because of this fact, the evolution of an entrepreneur has changed. In the beginning, they were considered like who started the construction of greater acts by order (Verin, 1982; Rodríguez-Ramírez, 2009), but now they are capable people to transform human wishes in a combined act of thinking and action (Aktouf, 2001 cited by Rodríguez-Ramírez 2009).

Besides, according to Rodríguez-Ramírez (2009), entrepreneurship can be understood from the following perspectives,

1. **Behavioral Perspective:** This viewpoint studies entrepreneur from an entrepreneur glance and the role it plays in business creation.
2. **Psychological or Cognitive Perspective:** In this line, it studies risks and, therefore, failures that entrepreneurs assume at the moment to carry out their projects.
3. **Economic Perspective:** From this glance, entrepreneur and entrepreneurship are comprehending as the revitalizing of economic development, because the company's results have a direct impact into the society.
4. **Processing Perspective:** From this vision, it focuses on the development and the creation of economic value. For this fact, they study how relationships between entrepreneurs affect social development resulted from established challenges into the entrepreneurial phenomena.

Following this line of thinking, it is possible to point out that digital entrepreneurship can be understood under a double economic and processing perspective, to consider both spaces as necessaries to strengthen an orange economy. It is necessary to have some elements to make easier its incorporation to societies by accelerating some processes and making things happen to make digital entrepreneurship survive. This element set up dynamic entrepreneurial ecosystems that contemplate the participation of, at least, four key actors for this process: public and private sectors, civic and academia.

For Duque-Escobar (2015), in line with the 'Urban and Economical development of Manizales', says that a form to develop the third sector, is strengthened ICTs, biotechnology and the orange economy, where the main barriers are in the primary educational sector, given the currently educative model is still thought for the industrial society of yesterday, and a low educational level of population of the Department of Caldas in Colombia only reaches to overcome 4 years in rural zone and ten years in the urban zone. According to Landsdale, Abad, and Vera (2012), dynamic ecosystems of entrepreneurship are limited for the political, institutional and social contexts, government's policies, financial support, education, training, capacity to undertake, social and cultural rules, and markets opening. The same author points out that the private sector can be responsible for entrepreneurship execution through market opening; the public sector is in charge of supply mechanisms and regulations that promote entrepreneurship; the civil society, made by non-governmental organizations, must promote entrepreneurship with technical assistance and training, while academia must encourage the necessary creative space to develop entrepreneurially. The participation of these actors is more than relevant because of the main concerns for dynamic ecosystems of entrepreneurship are, besides, that new companies will be born, they will survive, and they will grow in a significant way to be consolidated in local and international markets.

In this way, and according to Auletta and Rivera (2011), it is possible to point out a dynamic ecosystem of entrepreneurship as a business community where a set of individuals and organizations produce and combine business ideas, skills, finance and non-finance resources that become in dynamic enterprises. As a result, dynamic entrepreneurship is composed of those companies born with a competitive advantage and, therefore, are capable of generating a higher number of jobs and grow with a very higher average rate compared to their competitors. Consequently, for Du, Pan, Zhou, and Ouyang (2018) 'digital entrepreneurial spirit are found in digital technologies and entrepreneurial spirit intersection.' In this sense, in a digital technology following an entrepreneurship perspective (Nambisan, 2017), Davidson and Vaast (2010) argue that the essence of the digital entrepreneurial spirit is the search for business opportunities presented by digital technologies. This opportunity grows fastly, thanks to technological advances, such as mobile Internet, artificial intelligence, and cloud computing (Manyika et al., 2013). For Shen and Lindsay (2018) the digital entrepreneurial spirit includes companies and the existing business transformation by the creation of original technologies and/or original use of such technologies. Many countries consider digital entrepreneurship as a critical pillar for digital economic development. So, it is imperative to develop a detailed comprehension of digital entrepreneurial spirit.

For this fact, an alternative is the measuring of a digital ecosystem of each region as a scalable space, self-organized, sustainable, open, decentralized, and dynamic in which it is promoted information flow, collaboration and innovation (Li et al., 2012; Sussan et al., 2016; Fernandez y Hernandez, 2018). This system is composed by agents (entrepreneurs) and users (consumers) that hold multilateral relations, interacting collaboratively to feed digital space content (Boley & Chang, 2007; Evans & Schmalensee, 2016; Sussan et al., 2016). The digital system spine is, on the one hand, ICTs which interact with agent networks (Li et al., 2012), and on the other, the digital citizenship that takes part in the digital space (de Moraes & de Andrade, 2015; Sussan et al., 2016). Under this dynamic it is possible to understand, in a first approach, the digital citizen participation as the capacity of people to act within digital media (de Moraes & de Andrade, 2015) A second approach is the United Nations' definition as an *electronic participation consisting of encouraging civic agreement and opening a participatory government through ICTs. The growing evidence points to electronic participation fast expansion as a tool for the commit end and strengthening of cooperation between government and citizens. Its objective is improving access to information and public services, as well to promote participation in policy formulation, as much for individual citizen empowerment and benefit of society at large.*

Together with the widespread Internet growth, it has happened changes in both channels and the participation process with the use of several electronic media to interact and communicate. In this line, a study of Yusuf, Adams, and Dingley (2016) point that citizen participation is important to make successful activity in various government fields, one of them is political participation where the policy formulation has a significant impact, and the other is economic activities. It is important to point out that social interactions consider, on the one hand, the combination of digital activism, content creation, and the dissemination of public and personal information (e.g., Facebook and Twitter) (Sussan et al., 2016). On the other hand, it is related to digital market quality which explains the ability to keep commercial relations between agents and users and vice versa. Under a market point of view, digital interaction is the space where users and agents cooperate to value creation (Sussan et al., 2016) and in the consumer decisions, making digital market in line with Kumar et al. (2018) who affirm that the more deciding factor is being 'innovative and modern' followed by 'brand and quality' and 'compliance and time and energy.'

Respect to the digital market, it can be composed of private goods as users use tools for good sales, as well as the creation of public goods with a collaborative content generation (e.g., Wikipedia). On the other hand, digital infrastructure measures the physical and regulatory capacity of an entrepreneurship system to hold digital activities (Sussan et al., 2016). Within this measure, there are competition metrics to quantify digital standards and decentralize the level of Internet connection services suppliers.

According to Cominetti (2002), the origin of a new model in the telecommunication industry, as a result of signals and development of the Internet digitalization, offers conditions to an extreme transformation in the way of how the economic and social relations can carry out, promoting a more efficient and democratic form, contributing to higher competition, participation, and equality. Particularly, the substitution of traditional mechanisms to perform transactions and procedures for communication, in general, by methods doing an intensive use of ICTs, are originated a 'new digital economy,' whose benefits regarding productivity make it necessary to be incorporated quickly and massively to the networks' economic agents.

The concept of technological innovation is employed to describe the process through which it is producing technological advances — reflecting variations that available technologies experiment in a period (Antolin, 2003). Innovation process includes, thus, a set of activities that contribute to increase the ability to produce goods and services (innovations in the product) and, start up new production's forms (innovations in the process). Therefore, the concept of technological innovation is related to a flow - generation, implementation, and dissemination- of technological ideas. As a result, innovation is an integration of generalized metric of new productive processes and creation of new products in the market (Audretsch & Belitski, 2017). In other words, it is an innovative activity to measure and create new technologies into the system. Also, it includes the adoption of new technologies, so it concentrates on the technological adoption by producers. The previous issue generates that systems include patterns of technological adoption, and have a greater technical knowledge transmission among firms to impact positively in new process and products' creation.

In consonance with Di-Noia et al. (2004), more available resources into Web incentives a growing need of infrastructures to satisfy demand with supply in an electronic market. Several matchmakers' creators trust in simply concordance of keywords, but significant concordance results only can be obtained by exploding inherent semantic in structured descriptions. Digital Matchmakers is a metric that captures the system capacity to promote and hold tools that they promote streamlining of disused resources. Besides, it captures the dynamic of users and agents pairing through digital platforms for value creation (Evans & Schmalensee, 2016). This is an important component of digital entrepreneurship system and is a key to encourage a multi-directional relationship between users and agents.

Finally, access to finance is related to system ability to supply financing resources to digital entrepreneurship. This fact can refer to formal financing through banking or other financial institutions, as well as more informal mechanisms, like personal loans and business angel. Besides, the ability of collaborative investments platforms allows matching entrepreneurs in search of finance with individuals and institutions that search for financing specific projects.

ORANGE ENTREPRENEURSHIP IN LATIN AMERICA

Through a study based on a qualitative approach and a narrative design, information is analyzed of eighteen extreme cases, Hernández, Fernández, and Baptista (2014) and Salgado (2007) investigate how in the Latin American reality they begin to visualize 'cases of entrepreneurial success', and how this success is managed to insert a Latin American vision of the orange economy (Hira, 2016) generated by researchers from Argentina (Bayardo, 2016; Vera 2017), Brazil (Pereira de Castro Pacheco, Benini & Pasquotto Mariani, 2017), Chile (Tironi-Rodó, 2010), Colombia (Blanco-Valbuena, Bernal-Torres, Camacho, & Díaz-Olaya, 2018; Jiménez, Millán, & Suárez, 2018), Jamaica, Mexico (Castañeda-Rivera & Garduño-Bello, 2017; Reyes-Godínez, 2016) and Peru (Durand-Grahammer & Durand-Grahammer, 2017), among others.

According to what is described by Pereira de Castro Pacheco, Benini, and Pasquotto Mariani (2017), and pointed out by Fonseca-Reis (2008: 24-27), they present a conceptual framework summary of the creative economy around the world, and they show that it can be understood through four approaches:

1. **Creative Industries:** Characterized by specific economic sectors of each country, considering the riches generation.
2. **Creative Economy:** It covers not only creative industries but also impacts of the goods and services' interaction with other economic processes.
3. **Creative Cities and Spaces:** They are seen under the perspective of the struggle against inequalities, in the promotion of worldwide creative poles in articulation with tourism policies and restructuration of urban socioeconomic-related issues.
4. **The Creative Economy as Development Strategy:** It is formed by complementary approaches recognition of creativity as human capital, integrated to social, cultural and economic objectives that follow a new development paradigm.

In Brazil, efforts to include this concept in a governmental agenda were initiated through the implementation of Creative Economy Secretary, in the area of Ministry of Culture together with the Creative Economy National Plan. This plan defines the Brazilian creative economy from '[...]of cultural, social and economic dynamics built from creation, production, distribution/ circulation/ dissemination cycle, and consume/enjoyment of goods and services it born from creative sectors, characterized by the prevalence of symbolic dimension' (Brazil, 2012: 23).

According to Blanco-Valbuena et al. (2018), the contribution to the Colombian economy to creative and cultural economies is about 3.3%, and employment is about 3.3% (Buitrago & Duque, 2013). In this way, Colombia occupies the third place in Latin America in employment in this sector, after Mexico and Brazil.

Entrepreneurs are in each one of these cases to make us know the essential ideas behind their entrepreneurship:

Our dream is to unite all the actors of society behind just and humanitarian causes. cmed01.

ArchDaily is a bridge of communication between architects of the world and seeks to be the source of inspiration, knowledge, and tools for them to face the challenges presented by cities. cmed02.

Table 1. Sectoral economy from Latin American countries where are located the chosen cases by inter-American development bank

Country	% Agriculture	% Industry	% Services	Rank GDP - per Capita (PPP) of 229 Countries
Argentina	11	28	61	89 of 229
Brazil	6	21	73	110 of 229
Chile	4	32	64	83 of 229
Colombia	8	31	61	117 of 229
Jamaica	8	23	69	145 of 229
Mexico	4	32	64	91 of 229
Peru	8	36	56	120 of 229

Source: Central Intelligence Agency (2018).

Table 2. Orange Economy cases selected by the Inter-American Development Bank in the category of media

	Country	Since	Entrepreneurial Case	Entrepreneurs
cmed01	Argentina	2012	Posibl	Martín Parlato
cmed02	Chile	2008	Arch Daily	David Basulto, and David Assael
cmed03	Colombia	2006	Dynamo	Andrés Calderón, Diego Ramírez Schremp, Rodrigo Guerrero Rojas, and Cristian Conti.
cmed04	Colombia	2011	Zambo Dendé	Nicolás Rodríguez
cmed05	México	2002	Ánima Estudios	Fernando de Fuentes, and José C. García de Letona

Source: Luzardo, De Jesús, and Pérez (2017).

We saw an opportunity to boost the film industry in Colombia and give it international status. cmed03.

It is time for the entertainment industry to be prepared because Colombia and Latin America are the new creative hub of the planet. cmed04.

Every time there is more appetite for Mexican animated films ... we can tell universal stories with a taste of Mexico. cmed05.

Approaching an operational definition of Latin American, in the orange economy in the media category can be distinguished as common and central ideas:

- A dedication to the production of multimedia contents, under different formats:

... the multimedia company that produces and distribute content .... cmed01.

... the trajectory in production ... of self-content and formats for cinema, television and digital platforms ... cmed03.

... a transmedia project that includes a video game, animated series, television series, animated short film, feature film, comic, interactive apps and toys line ... all sceneries and environments are created through digital animation .... cmed04.

architecture web page...the more completed projects database... A platform has achieved to digitized content that previously it was only in printed magazines ... cmed02.

... it has produced several box offices draw and awarded feature films ... production of successful series for television ... cmed05.

- The trend towards the internationalization of global coverage:

... With the presence of 5 continents and activity in 161 countries ... cmed01.

... one of the producers of higher increase and recognition in Latin America, ... There are Colombian movies of greater international recognition... developed and distributed the Latin American content around the world .... cmed03.

... the success of their productions have made them a benchmark for the industry in worldwide level ... cmed04.

.. it is the Architecture-related web page more visited in the world, it gathers... data... about architectonic projects and products ... around the world ...cmed02.

- A business model that incorporates the distribution of greater content from producers and/or distributors:

... Among their success for television, appear the Narcos' series for Netflix ... cmed03.

... The project has with the support of Disney and Fox Colombia ... cmed04.

... It is the first study in Latin America that produce an original series for Netflix. ... cmed05.

Thus, the orange economy in the Latin American media industry produces multimedia content as a tendency to internalization of worldwide coverage. A strategy based on a business model that incorporates big production companies and content distributors. Emphasized as the main motivation to create an orange business, from the five cases of media industry selected by Inter-American Development Bank, we select the following force ideas:

1. To participate in the orange economy, with the goal of sustainable development, is by achieving an economical, social and environmental balance (Salas-Muñoz, 2018):

.... capable of creating empathy, to promote solidarity and to achieve a positive social impact. Connection with people with humanitarian causes is essential to produce a change in the world. cmed01.

... environmental and social challenges of our cities... opening way to its recognition in different markets. The global platform answers to ... opportunities to achieve a fairer society ... cmed02.

2. To strengthen the Latin American creative industry by increasing its presence in international markets

... to support the development of new talents, stimulating a higher growth in audiovisual productions and filling the demand for national cinema to exports ... promote the development of the film industry in Colombia and Latin America, betting on its growth and financing ... the initial stages of each project. cmed03

... to show that in Latin America can achieve projects of Hollywood quality, creating new market opportunities and spreading out its creative offer. cmed04.

Through internalizations of products...contribute...to the global entertainment industry, opening spaces to tell the Mexican and Latin American...and thus to conquer new audiences cmed05.

Regarding software category and digital platforms, the Inter-American Development Bank has selected the detailed cases in table 3.

As with media category, orange entrepreneurs of software and digital platforms creative industry from these cases, make known the essential ideas that are behind of their entrepreneurship:

FazGame is changing the way we learn so that all young people can have a quality education and thus provide equitable access to opportunities. csdp01.

Table 3. Orange economy cases selected by Inter-American Development Bank in the software category and digital platforms

	Country	Since	Entrepreneurial Case	Entrepreneurs
csdp01	Brazil	2013	FazGame	Carla Zeltzer
csdp02	Brazil	2015	Frei.re Lab	Américo Amorim
csdp03	Chile	2013	allGreenup	Andrés and Sebastián Luongo
csdp04	Colombia	2014	Lorapp	Camilo Lucero
csdp05	Colombia	2012	Nativo Digital	Ilana Milkes
csdp06	Colombia	2002	PayU	José Vélez
csdp07	Colombia	2012	Torre	Alex Torrenegra and Tania Zapata
csdp08	Jamaica	2013	BookFusion	Dwayne Campbell
csdp09	Mexico	2012	Carrot	Jimena Pardo and Diego Solórzano
csdp10	Mexico	2011	Fondeadora	René Serrano and Norman Müller
csdp11	Mexico	2014	Kernaia	Carlos Mondragón Álvarez
csdp12	Mexico	2012	Mi Cartelera MX	Guillermo Fernández Merchant
csdp13	Peru	2012	Arte Manifiesto	Luis E. Uyejara and Gianmarco A. Delgado

Source: Luzardo, De Jesús and Pérez (2017).

In Latin America, half of our students do not understand what they read and may never meet their potential. csdp02.

82% of consumers have good intentions, but only 16% are willing to comply, so it is necessary to encourage them. csdp03.

Innovation is born by asking the why of things, thinking that every problem has more than one solution. csdp04.

In emerging markets, only one in ten children is considered a digital native versus eight out of ten children in developed economies. csdp05.

Any business with an online or new presence in e-commerce and also any natural person who wants to enter the sector can open a PayU account and start exploring the solutions. csdp06.

At Torre, our mission is to make work rewarding for everyone. We dream of the day when the seven billion human beings, regardless of their gender, nationality, location and socio-economic origin, can participate in a fair way in the global market. csdp07.

The editors and authors of emerging markets have not yet made the transition to the digital world. The problem is that they do not trust the available solutions from existing platforms and there is little penetration of credit cards, which in turn limits readers 'access to e-books'. csdp08.

Carrot is part of a solution that allows the abandonment of the irrational use of the car. We seek to change the way we move to have a better quality of life. csdp09.

Mexico is in a special position for the creative industries ... When a leader emerges in an industry branch, it accelerates. csdp10.

In large cities, many people speak an indigenous language and do not have access to content. What we do is to train natives in the languages to produce that content, distribute it digitally and find the audience that wants to consume it. csdp11.

My Billboard MX is a communication bridge between creators and their audiences. We seek to revolutionize the diffusion market of performing arts in Mexico and Latin America. csdp12.

Because we believe that Latin America is a continent of artists, craftsmen, and creators, Manifest Art makes them visible and makes the creators dedicate themselves to creating full time. Manifest Art, Latin creators for the world. csdp13.

They are extracting from these thirteen testimonies, central elements in their entrepreneurship, such as contribution to education in different areas, valuation of environmental problems and support to entrepreneurs, especially to others orange entrepreneurs.

These thirteen relevant cases, chosen by Inter-American Development Bank, allow getting in touch with the meaning of 'startup in orange' in software and digital platforms area in Latin America, distinguishing next categories within testimony the expressed:

- Presence of commercialization alternative forms in traditional markets:

... break with intermediaries... it helps to expand its work to other audiences and generate new markets ... csdp13.

... to rent academy book chapters at a similar price to the photocopies digitally... Pay to the authors and editorials for each rented reading, generating a simple, legal and economical alternative...editorials get their money back they did not receive because of piracy ... csdp04.

... first car-sharing service, pioneers of the shared economy in Mexico ... csdp09.

... crowdfunding platform pioneer in the Mexican market... to finance their projects by means community donations ... csdp10.

... Activities give 'green points' to the user, who, later, can change for benefits in associate commerce... certification as B business, authenticating its social and environmental benefits. csdp03

... First app dedicated to theatre and show world in Mexico City ... csdp12. ...

... it finds to redefine reading experience, integrating audiovisual elements and multimedia tools for venture ...csdp08.

... digital bank of professional voices to producers and content creators...The crowdsourcing platform online has a database of 135.000 dubbing and storytelling actors ... its product offer includes translating services, redaction, and research under a creative model on demand csdp07.

- The vocation to support education and environment:

... undergraduates can digitally rent academic book chapters ...casdp04.

... software where undergraduates can create interactive games without the need for knowledge on design and programming ... it allows developing logical reasoning, problem-solving, creative thinking and collaborative work ... csdp01.

... it makes easier school innovation through interactive games ... makes possible that parents without much education participate in school teaching of their children ... gives the option to the teachers to adapt classes according to the student needs.

The platform is visited by students and teachers of 49 countries. csdp02.

... to contribute to preservation, dissemination and strengthen of natives' language....it finds the integration of vulnerable communities to the digital world. csdp11.

... it reduces the environmental impact of traffic overdoes in megacities...Mexico City, Monterrey, and Puebla ... hybrid and electric vehicles fleet ...csdp09.

... it teaches, measures and encourages friendly activities for natures and in this way it promotes a more sustainable lifestyle ...csdp03.

... it allows to students the access to a better reading form that facilitates interactive learning to retain information ... csdp08.

... it takes the skills of programming and codes....to hundreds of millions of children in emerging markets. csdp05.

- The dynamic role in the market in general and in self orange economy

... a digital platform that allows the access to car demand " csdp09.

A virtual art gallery ... to show artists and to connect with potential buyers ...csdp13.

... software development to the sales handles without the need to have a web platform, even to receive credit card payment and bank transfer ... csdp06.

... crowdfunding platform pioneer in the Mexican market and it focuses on creative sector...user stops being a new spectator to participate and decide that he believe. csdp10.

... FazGame is software where students can create interactive games without the need to design and programming knowledge. ... csdp01.

... it makes easier electronic tickets buying and adapts to wishes and preferences of its users... csdp12.

... marketplace to voices talents that identify the best talent for each project among thousands of voices in the database " csdp07.

- Use of different resources of software and digitals platforms:

... It used the Internet, e-commerce and augmented reality ...csdp13.

... theme library, sceneries, characters and objects, students research a topic to develop their games ... csdp01.

... through a web page and a mobile app ...csdp09.

... e-learning software... it allows, ...to produce interactive learning content... through their mobile app in their cell phones ... csdp02.

... digital platform to the creation, dissemination, and commercialization of contents ... csdp11.

... platform to the creation and, dissemination of e-books ... integrating audiovisual elements and multimedia tools ... csdp08.

... first multi-platform app...it combines adaptive and emotional technologies ... and data processing. csdp05.

... application programming interface (API) company...owner algorithm ... csdp07.

- An associated presence that strengthens business model:

... inspired in Kickstarter, from the United States and after five years....it achieves an official alliance with this leader company ... csdp10.

... part of PayU Group after a strategic alliance...with Naspers, South African company that gives the same service in emerging countries. csdp06.

... it has been supported by ImagineLab, by Microsoft ... csdp03.

... Among their clients appears recognized producers such as Apple, Disney, Amazon, Spotify, and Pixar .. csdp07.

- The interaction with the local economy:

... a new of business for local art ... csdp13.

... to offer services that it is adapted to the needs of the region ... csdp06.

... to contribute to preservation, dissemination and strengthen of natives language ...csdp11.

... in the Mexico City connects, with a cultural offer with the interested public to assist ...csdp12.

Thus, the orange economy in the Latin American software and digital platforms industry is characterized to get alternative ways of commercialization in traditional markets to support education and environment in dynamic markets and creatives industries. Industries based on different sources of information and technologies, and supporting associated networks that strengthen the business model in connexion with the local economy.

Regarding motivations to start in the orange economy context, theses selected thirteen cases important in the software and digital platforms category by Inter-American Development Bank, stand out:

- To take advantage of e-commerce to interact with their clients:

... The Internet offers an opportunity in the unlimited reinvention of space, time or geographical. Actually, Manifesto Art welcomes over five thousand artist portfolios, with more than twenty thousand artworks and creation. csdp13.

... PayU since 2002, when it does not exist any payment service and electronic taking money. Today it offers solutions to more than 20.000 commerce in the region, with around 75 payment options and it generates 300 directs jobs. csdp06.

... An electronic ticket purchase service easy, efficient and low cost provides to the increasing of scenic arts in Mexico. csdp12.

... BookFusion facilities to their authors and editors the technology to distribute their creative and cultural content, with greater control about rights and discounts for its commercialization. csdp08.

It is more relevant than ever to revitalize sectors with obsoletes practices through digitalization, programming, and Internet ... Now thanks to this innovation, a voice professional can find projects directly, record it in 30 minutes, to an accessible cost to the producer. csdp07.

- To incorporate friendly solutions with the environment:

In Latin America, there are 20 million undergraduates, and 99% of them use photocopies to study, incur annual costs of more than 1,100 million dollars in illegal photocopies. Besides ecological impact, it is reduced the piracy problem, to offer a legal alternative to photocopies. csdp04.

A company as Carrot propose a sustainable solution that it not only increase mobility in the city for the public in general, but it reduces environmental impact.csdp09.

... AllGreenup allows to insert the issue in daily life using mobile and bring the sustainability subject to the users simply and funnily and where everybody gets a benefit. csdp03.

- To put technology into education service:

There are 11 million children in Brazil and 7 million in Latin America who can benefit from learning to read and write in fun and interactive way through games and new technologies. This, in turn, reduces the statistics of dropout. csdp02.

Games and digital innovation are tools that help to reduce dropouts. With educational applications, it can prepare for young people with the skills needed to be successful in the 21st century. csdp01.

... The purpose is to preserve cultural heritage, tell stories and facilitate access to alternative contents, generating a meeting point among creators, languages, and audiences.. csdp11.

... The Digital native's mission is to get each student to receive a technology education, designing and developing innovative and attractive solutions for emerging and unattended markets. csdp05.

For these entrepreneurs, there is a clear motivation to open up to the use of information technology to expand their markets, as well as to provide support with this kind of tools to care for the environment and education in Latin America.

RECOMMENDATIONS

Latin American's orange entrepreneurship, in the case of the creative industries, analyzed: media, and software and digital platforms show a great interest for reaching the international market to increase potential customers and the profits of each entrepreneurship. In this regard, the eighteen cases selected by the Inter-American Development Bank and analyzed in this chapter, show being the main allies of large consolidated companies worldwide or are parts of initiatives that this type of companies promote and finance. This fact generates two types of reflections:

First, in these cases both the State and HEI (higher-education institutions) are absent. Therefore, the quadruple helix model (formed by business, non-governmental organizations, HEIs, and firms) (Saiz-Álvarez, 2019) is not created, so a joint development of a socially integral business strategy is not possible to achieve. Therefore, it is advisable to have a greater interaction of HEIs to investigate the orange economy and of Latin American governments to increase their efforts to encourage and co-finance the orange entrepreneurship as, according to the cases analyzed, their scaling would be contingent on achieving alliances with large international companies.

Second, there is an incipient interest to develop local firms based on ICTs to answer market needs better rather than foreign firms. And at least in the studied industries, especially in the software industry and digital platforms, to provide intermediation and cultural industry's dynamics by providing technical support to the development of the cultural industry. That fact should emphasize, on incentive training and financing of initiatives aiming greater interdisciplinary between ICTs and local cultural development.

CONCLUSION

Based on cases selected by the Inter-American Development Bank, this chapter analyzes the emergence of a Latin American orange economy rooted in the digital creative industry (media and software and digital platforms), but not from any entrepreneurship. Therefore, it is possible to observe a business frontier condition that establishes the necessary recommendations to achieve orange entrepreneurship in the country. Thus, it has been possible to specify the orange entrepreneurship operationally from a multiple economic, social and cultural vision, by following a Latin American entrepreneurial discourse. The orange economy in a digital creative industry is an economy oriented to sustainability (economic, social and environmental), but having in mind that, on the one hand, the Latin American media industry deals with the production of multimedia content strongly orientated towards the leveraged internationalization of large companies in producing and distributing content and, therefore, mainly responding to tastes and preferences of global consumers with a local perspective.

On the other hand, in the aspect of the use of software and digital platforms in the Latin American creative industry, ICTs dynamize and expand the market in general through new forms of commercialization of traditional cultural businesses, and especially those strongly oriented to support education and environment. Also relevant in this area are the networks of partners established with large international firms. These firms achieve their results independently, and although to a lesser extent, they would exist by operating in the local economy only. Consequently, the success of orange entrepreneurship in Latin American requires combining creativity, work experience, public and private financing, and international-based contact networks for accelerating and maximizing business results.

ACKNOWLEDGMENT

We are grateful to Universidad de Los Andes (Chile) for the access provided to its electronic references for research, and Fundación Escuela de Asuntos Internacionales for its institutional sponsorship provided in the field of Entrepreneurship Studies.

REFERENCES

Audretsch, D. B., & Belitski, M. (2017). Entrepreneurial ecosystems in cities: Establishing the framework conditions. *The Journal of Technology Transfer*, *42*(5), 1030–1051. doi:10.100710961-016-9473-8

Auletta, N., & Rivera, C. (2011). An ecosystem for entrepreneurship. *Debates IESA*, *16*(4), 12–17.

Bayardo, R. (2016). From culture to creativity. Some reflections from Argentina. *Revista Uruguaya de Antropología y Etnografía*, *1*(1), 39–46.

Blanco-Valbuena, C. E., Bernal-Torres, C. A., Camacho, F., & Díaz-Olaya, M. (2018). Creative and Cultural Industries: Study from the Knowledge Management Approach. *Información Tecnológica*, *29*(3), 15–28. doi:10.4067/S0718-07642018000300015

Boley, H., & Chang, E. (2007). *Digital ecosystems: Principles and semantics. In Inaugural IEEE-IES Digital EcoSystems and Technologies Conference*. Cairns, Australia: IEEE.

Buckland, H., Garmilla, A., Murillo, D., Leticia, M., & Flores, S. (2018). *The digital revolution is facing the great challenges of the world*. Barcelona, Spain: Social Innovation Institute of ESADE.

Buitrago, F., & Duque, I. (2013). *The Orange Economy: An infinite opportunity*. Washington, DC: Inter-American Development Bank.

Castañeda-Rivera, E., & Garduño-Bello, B. (2017). Map of the creative industries in Mexico. A projection for CENTRO. *Economía Creativa*, *7*, 118–166.

Central Intelligence Agency. (2018). *The World Factbook*. Washington, DC: CIA.

Davidson, E., & Vaast, E. (2010). Digital entrepreneurship and its socio-material enactment. *Proceedings of the 43rd Annual Hawaii International Conference on System Sciences*, 1–10.

De Moraes, J., & Benvenutti De Andrade, E. (2015). Who are the citizens of the digital citizenship? *International Review of Information Ethics*, *23*, 4–19.

Di-Noia, T., Di Sciascio, E., Donini, F. M., & Mongiello, M. (2004). A System for Principled Matchmaking in an Electronic Marketplace. *International Journal of Electronic Commerce*, *8*(4), 9–37. doi:10.1080/10864415.2004.11044308

Du, W., Pan, S. L., Zhou, N., & Ouyang, T. (2018). From an electronics marketplace to a digital entrepreneurial ecosystem (DEE): The emergence of a meta-organization in Zhongguancun, China. *Information Systems Journal*, *28*(6), 1158–1175. doi:10.1111/isj.12176

Duque-Escobar, G. (2015). The urban and economic development of Manizales. *The POT of Manizales: 'Collective Let's Get on the Bus of the POT' SMP of Manizales Conference*.

Escalona-Orcao, A. I., & Escolano-Utrilla, S. (2016). The potential for the intelligent development of rural areas: The spatial clusters of creative activities in Spain. *Revista de Geografía Norte Grande*, *65*, 91–107. doi:10.4067/S0718-34022016000300005

Evans, D. S., & Schmalensee, R. (2016). *Matchmakers: the new economics of multi-sided platforms*. Boston: Harvard Business Review Press.

Fernández, J., & Hernández, F. (2018). *Measurement and Diagnosis of Digital Entrepreneurship Ecosystems (MIDE-Digital) – Metropolitana*. Santiago, Chile: Universidad del Desarrollo.

Finlev, T., Maguire, R., Oppenheim, B., & Skvirsky, S. (2017). *Future Landscapes of the Orange Economy: Creative Pathways for Improving Lives in Latin America and the Caribbean*. Washington, DC: Inter-American Development Bank.

Fonseca-Reis, A. C. (2008). *Creative economy: as a development strategy: a view of developing countries*. São Paulo, Brazil: Itaú Cultural.

Grahammer, J. C. D., & Grahammer, C. D. (2013). Lost in Theorization: On the Effectiveness of Policies to Promote Creative Industries in Peru. *Derecho & Sociedad*, *49*, 39–54.

Hernández, R., Fernández, C., & Baptista, P. (2014). Research Metodology (6th ed.). Mexico D.F., Mexico: McGraw-Hill.

Hesmondhalgh, D. (2002). *The cultural industries*. London, UK: Sage Publications.

Hira, S. (2016). The long journey of decolonizing the mind in Latin America. *Tabula Rasa*, *25*, 175–194. doi:10.25058/20112742.80

Jiménez, I. F., Millán, M. F., & Suárez, D. F. (2018). Effect of the added value of cultural consumption: An approach to the orange economy in Colombia. *Ploutos*, *7*(2), 4–11.

Kantis, H., Federico, J., & Menéndez, C. (2012). *Policies to promote dynamic entrepreneurship in Latin America: trends and challenges. CAF Documento de Trabajo, 9*. Caracas, Venezuela: CAF.

Kumar, A., Mangla, S. K., Luthra, S., Rana, N. P., & Dwivedi, Y. K. (2018). Predicting changing pattern: Building model for consumer decision making in the digital market. *Journal of Enterprise Information Management*, *31*(5), 674–703. doi:10.1108/JEIM-01-2018-0003

Landsdale, D., Abad, C., & Vera, D. (2012). Key drivers to establish the dynamic ecosystem of entrepreneurship in Ecuador. *Polémika*, *9*(1), 18–25.

Li, W., Badr, Y., & Biennier, F. (2012). Digital ecosystems: challenges and prospects. In *Proceedings of the international conference on management of Emergent Digital EcoSystems* (pp. 117-122). Addis Ababa, Ethiopia: ACM.

López, A., Niembro, A., & Ramos, D. (2014). The competitiveness of Latin America in the trade of services based on knowledge. *Revista de la CEPAL*, *113*, 23–41.

Luzardo, A., De Jesús, D., & Pérez, M. (2017). *Orange Economy: Innovations you may not know were from Latin America and the Caribbean*. Washington, DC: Inter-American Development Bank.

Manyika, J., Chui, M., Bughin, J., Dobbs, R., Bisson, P., & Marrs, A. (2013). *Disruptive technologies: Advances that will transform life, business, and the global economy*. New York: McKinsey Global Institute.

Méndez, R., Michelini, J. J., Prada, J., & Tébar, J. (2012). Creative economy and urban development in Spain: An approach to its spatial logics. *EURE (Santiago)*, *38*(113), 5–32.

Ministry of Culture. (2012). *Plan of the Creative Economy Secretary: Policies, Guidelines, and Actions 2011 to 2014*. Brazil, Ministry of Culture.

Morales-Astola, R. (2016). Border cultural management and the challenge of Latin America. In U. Bustamante-Lozano, J. L. Mariscal-Orozco, & C. Yáñez-Canal (Eds.), *Forms and configurations of cultural management in Latin America*. Universidad Nacional de Colombia.

Muñoz, P. J. (2016). Italy launches to regulate the collaborative economy: About the Bill Discipline of digital platforms for sharing goods and services and provisions for promoting the sharing economy. *Revista Democracia Digital e Governo Eletrônico, 1*(14), 83–95.

Nambisan, S. (2017). Digital Entrepreneurship: Toward a Digital Technology Perspective of Entrepreneurship. *Entrepreneurship Theory and Practice, 41*(6), 1029–1055. doi:10.1111/etap.12254

Nieto-Antolín, M. (2003). Dynamic characteristics of the process of technological innovation in the company. *Investigaciones Europeas de Dirección y Economía de la Empresa, 9*(3), 111–128.

Oliva, R., & Lázaro, I. (2018). *Creative economy in Latin America and the Caribbean: Measurements and challenges (No. IDB-TN-01488)*. Washington, DC: Inter-American Development Bank.

Otero-Gómez, M. C., & Giraldo-Pérez, W. (2018). Cultural Consumption as a means for International Tourist development. An analysis applied to Villavicencio–Colombia. *Encuentros, 16*(1), 64–77.

Pereira de Castro-Pacheco, A., Benini, E. G., & Pasquotto-Mariani, M. A. (2017). The creative economy in Brazil: The development of local tourism in the southern marsh of Mato Grosso. *Estudios y Perspectivas en Turismo, 26*(3), 678–697.

Pombo, C., Gupta, R., & Stankovic, M. (2018). *Social Services for Digital Citizens: Opportunities for Latin America and the Caribbean*. Washington, DC: Inter-American Development Bank.

Reyes-Godínez, M. (2016). Economy and culture in Mexico. Notes of an agenda under construction. Periférica Internacional. *Revista para el análisis de la cultura y el territorio, 17*, 209-229.

Rodríguez-Ramírez, A. (2009). New perspectives to understand business entrepreneurship. *Pensamiento & Gestión, 26*, 94–119.

Saiz-Álvarez, J. M. (2019). Managing Social Innovation Through CSR 2.0 and the Quadruple Helix: A Socially Inclusive Business Strategy for the Industry 4.0. In A. Guerra Guerra (Ed.), Organizational Transformation and Managing Innovation in the Fourth Industrial Revolution (pp. 228-244). Hershey, PA: IGI Global.

Salas-Muñoz, R. (n.d.). A critical analysis of the conceptual framework of sustainable development and their measurement tools. *Revista En-Contexto, 6*(8), 171-184.

Sánchez-Serra, D. (2016). Location determinants of creative industries' firms in Spain. *Journal of Regional Research, 34*, 23–48.

Sánchez-Trujillo, M. G., Molina-Ruiz, H. D., & García-Vargas, M. L. (2018). The economic dimension of the creative economy. *TEPEXI Boletín Científico de la Escuela Superior Tepeji del Río, 5*(9). doi:10.29057/estr.v5i9.2971

Shen, K. N., Lindsay, V., & Xu, Y. (2018). Digital entrepreneurship. *Information Systems Journal, 28*(6), 1125–1128. doi:10.1111/isj.12219

Sussan, F., Autio, E., & Kosturik, J. (2016). *Leveraging ICTs for Better Lives: The Introduction of an Index on Digital Life. CPRLATAM Conference*, Mexico.

Szpilbarg, D., & Saferstein, E. (2014). From 'culture industry' to creative industries: An analysis of the mutation of the concept and its contemporary uses. *Estudios de Filosofía Práctica e Historia de las Ideas, 16*(2), 99–112.

Tironi-Rodó, M. (2010). What is a cluster? Geographies and practices of the experimental music scene in Santiago, Chile. *EURE. Revista Latinoamericana de Estudios Urbano Regionales, 36*(109), 161–187.

Valdivia-López, M., & Cuadrado-Roura, J. M. (Eds.). (2017). The economics of creative activities: a perspective from Spain and Mexico. Ciudad de Mexico, Mexico: Regional Center for Multidisciplinary Research, Universidad Nacional Autónoma de México.

Vega, A., & Rodríguez, P. (2015). Regionalisms in South America and their effects on intraregional development from an economic, scientific and technological perspective. *Espaciotiempo. Revista Latinoamericana de Ciencias Sociales y Humanidades, 8*(9), 7–16.

Vera, P. (2017). Processes of urban requalification and innovation imaginaries. The Rosario case, Argentina. *EURE. Revista Latinoamericana de Estudios Urbano Regionales, 43*(129), 209–234. doi:10.4067/S0250-71612017000200010

Yusuf, M., Adams, C., & Dingley, K. (2016). Digital citizen participation within schools in the United Kingdom and Indonesia: An Actor-Network Theory (ANT) perspective. *Information, 7*(4), 69–81. doi:10.3390/info7040069

ADDITIONAL READING

Ayhan, B. (2017). *Digitalization and Society*. Bern, Switzerland: Peter Lang International Academic Publishers. doi:10.3726/978-3-653-07022-4

Boccia, F., & Leonardi, R. (Eds.). (2016). *The Challenge of the Digital Economy: Markets, Taxation, and Appropriate Economic Models*. Palgrave Macmillan-Springer. doi:10.1007/978-3-319-43690-6

Chandra, A., & Khanijo, M. K. (Eds.). (2009). *Knowledge Economy: The Indian Challenge*. New Delhi, India: SAGE Publications India. doi:10.4135/9788132101222

Cominetti, R. (2002). La infraestructura de soporte para la economía digital en Chile. *Revista de la CEPAL, 77*, 163–177.

García, A. M., & Marín, S. R. (2018). *Aspectos legales de la economía colaborativa y bajo demanda en plataformas digitales*. Barcelona, Spain: Editorial Bosch.

Malecki, E. J., & Moriset, B. (2007). *The digital economy: Business organization, production processes and regional developments*. London, UK: Routledge. doi:10.4324/9780203933633

Mark, R. V. D. (2018). Virtual Competition: The Promise and Perils of the Algorithm-Driven Economy, by Ariel Ezrachi & Maurice E. Stucke. *Osgoode Hall Law Journal*, *55*(2), 614–619.

Mossberger, K., Tolbert, C. J., & Franko, W. W. (2012). *Digital Cities: The Internet and the Geography of Opportunity*. New York, USA: Oxford University Press. doi:10.1093/acprof:oso/9780199812936.001.0001

Ng, I. C. L. (2014). *Creating new markets in the digital economy: Value and Worth*. Cambridge, UK: Cambridge University Press.

Oncioiu, I. (2013). *Business Innovation, Development, and Advancement in the Digital Economy* (pp. 1–354). Hershey, PA: IGI Global. doi:10.4018/978-1-4666-2934-9

Shaw, M. J. (Ed.). (2006). *E-Commerce and the Digital Economy. Advances in Management Information Systems* (Vol. 4). Armonk, NY, USA: M.E. Sharpe.

Torres-Coronas, T. (2012). *Social E-Enterprise: Value Creation through ICT: Value Creation through ICT*. Information Science Reference.

KEY TERMS AND DEFINITIONS

Crowdfunding: A way of seeking financing for an idea, business or entrepreneurship by who those are seeking funding make public the idea on a public platform on the Internet through different users bring small sums of money to achieve the target.

Crowdsourcing: It is execution and development of products modality collaboratively, in which responsibility and workloads of projects are distributed in public and open platforms in where different users contribute to the online project development and receiving a payment for the contribution.

Dynamic Entrepreneurship Ecosystem: Community where it develops and lives with different public actors, privates, and academics that interact in an economy to promote entrepreneurship.

Intellectual Property: Is called to the regulation that protects the intellectual creation in any of its areas. This legal body is characteristic of each country that protects differently, in form but similar in substance, to the creators.

Know-How: It is understood as a way to do an activity correctly. It is how to do it well; it can be understood as the differential of an entrepreneur if you know how to do an activity better than the rest, has an important part of your business done.

Knowledge: It is the basis of current society, where thanks to its companies, businesses, and countries manage to position themselves and contribute value in different areas.

Relational Capital: It is the product of shared knowledge when it is effectively incorporated into an organization.

Shared Economy: It is an interchange model of goods and/or services among privates. This type of economy has become the basis of new platforms such as Uber, Cornershop, Airbnb in which the exchange is done directly among individuals through an online platform.

Talent: It is the foundation of creativity and therefore of entrepreneurship. Talent is a condition of humans and relates to the ability to learn and the ability to effectively develop an action.

Chapter 11
The Electronic Obsolescence as an Opportunity for Social Entrepreneurship:
The Case of EEE in Manizales, Colombia

Diego Lopez Cardona
University of Manizales, Colombia

Rocio del S. Tabares Hoyos
https://orcid.org/0000-0002-3613-1366
Universidad de Manizales, Colombia

ABSTRACT

The chapter contains the concepts of social entrepreneurship, planned and perceived obsolescence, corporate social responsibility, the legal framework for electrical and electronic equipment (EEE) waste, and reverse logistics, as theoretical support from different authors. Applied to Manizales, Colombia, the study was conducted with a quantitative and qualitative approach. The information was collected through surveys and interviews with 26 entrepreneurs and 331 households' consumers to know the type of appliances, how they buy, change, and use them, and the chain of intermediaries. With planned and perceived obsolescence, products lose their life in a short time, are dumped as waste of electrical and electronic equipment (WEEE), and collected by people of a low educational and economic level that survive in precarious conditions. Due to these results and conclusions, the authors offer in the chapter the opportunity to generate proposals for their inclusion and social development.

DOI: 10.4018/978-1-5225-8939-6.ch011

INTRODUCTION[1]

In Colombia, due to the few public policies related to environmental management, and specifically the control of manufacturing, distribution, and sales of electrical and electronic equipment (EEE), some market strategies concerning to Planned and Perceived Obsolescence[2] (Valquíria & Bonifacio, 2013) have been implemented to reduce the time of use of products by consumers. Having completed its life cycle, the Waste of Electrical and Electronic Equipment (WEEE) is thrown in the trash mixed with other organic, building, and metalworking wastes. As a result, pollution increases and a huge problem arises as a great challenge for the society and the authorities that manage and regulate the country or region, given the large volume of EEE waste, which mostly gets tossed.

This chapter is intended to address how social entrepreneurship can be an opportunity for social inclusion of those who collect, recycle and reuse waste products. The problem lies in the few opportunities offered by the agents involved in the collection process, and belonging to a parasitic intermediation chain, using people with low educational level, with few job opportunities and many social problems, being most individuals who are not associated or included in a program of social inclusion. Similarly, the concepts of planned and perceived obsolescence as trading strategies result in businesses and industries engaged in selling products in different versions to force change, so that the user feels an unconsciously need to have analyzed this increasingly older product and compare it to the new products launched on the market.

Selective harvesting strategies and environmental management of waste computers and-or peripherals, as well as EEE, is now just beginning to be regulated, to prevent and control environmental degradation. Collecting programs are now producing small results, as they are based on routes established by the firm that has the monopoly of waste management. Vehicles generally guided by employees endowed with a low educational level that select different types of waste, such as plastics, cardboard, heavy metals, and some high-volume WEEE to classify them afterward. These informal workers carry this waste to a collection center, according to their specialty. Some intermediaries buy according to the law of supply and demand. This intermediary is responsible for selling the volume of raw material to companies.

Therefore, based on the potential of social entrepreneurship as an opportunity to form working groups with people who collect WEEE and training them in the extraction of precious metals which are manufactured, we can establish a project of social innovation grouping this community with low level of education, low income, health conditions, and deplorable housing, and we can step in improving their quality of life. WEEE recycling becomes an opportunity for social entrepreneurship.

The case study presented a response to an inventory of consumption of electrical and electronic equipment (EEE) in the city of Manizales. It was made from conducting surveys to recycling companies (26) and consumers (331), which allowed knowing the type of EEE used in homes, the life, the way of acquisition, the frequency with which they change the reasons for that change and the final repository once it has completed its life cycle.

With the results, we hope to contribute to alternative solutions to the problem of the current economic system of production that does not conform at all to harmony and balance that nature requires. Therefore, to counter planned obsolescence, the key will be the commitment and responsibility with which the laws of manufacture of each product are met, of course, without neglecting corporate growth by implementing new business models to rectify this phenomenon.

CONCEPTS OF SOCIAL ENTREPRENEURSHIP

One of the major purposes of social entrepreneurship is the social inclusion of vulnerable groups into the economic dynamics that through the creation of value can generate opportunities for social change. It draws attention to the importance of social entrepreneurship as a solution to many global crises that occur daily. For Yunus (2010), Nobel Peace Prize in 2006, "*the financial crisis is just one of the many crises that threaten humanity. We also have a global food crisis, energy crisis, environmental crisis, health care and the continued economic and social crisis of massive poverty* ". According to Yunus (2010), social business is an initiative that contributes to the development not only of opportunities for citizen participation but also processes of social, economic inclusion, employment and contributes to overcoming welfare and poverty.

Social entrepreneurship is the construction, evaluation, and pursuit of opportunities for transformative social change conducted by visionary individuals, passionately dedicated (Roberts & Woods, 2005). Emphasize that social entrepreneurship is key aspects such as social opportunities that are not discovered, but constructed due to the generation of ideas. Taking into account the characteristics of entrepreneurs, Austin, Stevenson, and Wei-Skillern (2006) define social entrepreneurship as an innovative activity, creating social value, which occurs within and across sectors, non-profit, business and government, which implies that social entrepreneurship and business entrepreneurship coexist, go hand in hand.

All entrepreneurial process involves a balance of social behavior and economic behavior, which in turn, allows the generation of social and economic value (Chell, 2007; Guzman & Trujillo, 2008). In an environment characterized by the values of individuals inserted into a "*paradigm of competition*" with the capacity of having initiative, creativity, and proactivity to overcome the usual risky projects involving all business needs. Thus, to meet the challenges and the economic model of globalization requires high entrepreneurial capacity (Guzman & Santos 2008; Santos, 2004; Santos, Barroso, & Guzman, 2013).

Yunus (2006) classifies social entrepreneurs into (a) social entrepreneurs based on the market, and (b) social entrepreneurs not based on the market. The difference lies in their pursuit of profit, i.e., that social firms not based on the market pursue social purposes (associations, foundations), and social firms based on the market follow social purposes and business profits (cooperatives, labor companies). The Red Senk[3] defines social entrepreneurship as actions performed with the explicit purpose of creating social value. Performing actions from purely philanthropic to business projects aimed at improving the quality of life of the people, and at the same time, to improve the economic performance of companies. These actions can be carried out by an organized community or by a company, i.e., the need to create value ignores the subject to do so. In other words, the need for economic performance goes hand in hand with the aim of improving the quality of life of its members, two elements which must stay together in theory and practice (De Pablo, 2005).

Social enterprises are also defined as those whose purpose is to ease community development, as they are not-for-profit and are guided by a social mission only to explore and recognize opportunities to create social value. As a result, the primary objective of their economic value is to guarantee sustainability (Seelosa, 2005). Different authors agree on three fundamental characteristics: (a) the development of community service; (b) focus on the solution to a problem, and (c) a change generator to define cooperative entrepreneurship where converges most of the attributes of the entrepreneur (Mozas, 2013).

Another feature is the development of goods and services. This feature allows social firms to become a service-oriented firm to the community seeking to solve territorial problems and allowing the generation of change in the company to impact the territory, taking into account sustainability, which will allow an impact for a longer period. Social enterprises are effective as are a fundamental pillar of leadership if they have an adequate strategy for the fair distribution of resources. The market of social entrepreneurship is the world population with their various challenges and needs, taking into account education, gender equality, reducing child mortality by combating diseases, environmental sustainability, and improving the quality of life, among others (Alemán & Coronado, 2014, p. 6).

Leadership in Social Entrepreneurship is defined as "the ability to make changes and achieve outstanding results." (Céspedes, 2009, p. 6). It is necessary to establish mechanisms for quality control in the production, as well as pride on the product, and the values of creativity and honesty with the user seeking fair terms of trade and the value of cooperation. They need to develop information-based systems that allow making proper decisions on economic activity, as well as the inclusion of entrepreneurship in the community.

The evolution of the world economy and the existence of overwhelming inequality and poverty leave important lessons regarding wealth generation and the challenge of generating greater social mobility within societies. And it is here where the project becomes a powerful tool for this purpose (Pumarino, 2011; Wompner, 2012). Social firms can be transformed into a platform for social mobility. Therefore, entrepreneurial activity is the best tool for economic and social development, and entrepreneurial education and business management are key actors for social mobility and fight against poverty.

Training in Social Entrepreneurship

Training in social entrepreneurship by implementing values, social models and techniques enable the creation of wealth; avoid and ignores political opportunism. Among the results expected with education on social entrepreneurship is the increase in jobs that allow developing a local economy, and even regional, producing a virtuous circle between an educational system based on social entrepreneurship and students with vocational entrepreneurship. These virtuous circles create human capacities to produce and use knowledge in a changing, challenging and competitive environment, to meet the economic, industrial, organizational, and social needs of people, and also encouraging future generations (Silakalne-Araja & Arajs, 2012).

Social entrepreneurship based on education and taking practical experienced and theoretical models, improve the culture of innovation (Zain et al., 2013), the responsibility of persons involved, and the development of skills and knowledge (Dejaeghere, 2013); including the creation and use of courses and seminars for business performance (Daghbashyan & Harsman, 2014), by ensuring a good coverage of jobs, sustainability and the development of the local and regional economy (Li & Zuo, 2013), and by improving academic performance (Johansen, 2014), and self-employment self-esteem (Yin & Li, 2013). Entrepreneurship creates a virtuous cycle of creativity and innovation (Sudharson, Ali, & Sermakani, 2012), incentives economic growth and productivity (Egbe-Okpenge & Igbo, 2012), and creates tacit and explicit knowledge (Ndou & Del Vecchio, 2013), and technology transfer (Spulber, 2012)

In summary, and according to several authors, it is necessary and important to encourage and promote the implementation of social entrepreneurship, as it is a viable solution for social wealth and sustainable economic growth. If companies want to succeed, they must be adapted to difficult cultural environments (Alam et al., 2010), manage a good public-private partnership based on solidarity, social networks, joint ventures, innovation, and marketing (Racic & Viduka, 2013) to accelerate economic growth (Grundey et al., 2008; Kayasan, 2011) and increase competitiveness with the participation of other innovative companies (Grundey et al., 2008). All these activities are more profitable when companies that encourage social entrepreneurship pursuing a social purpose use business models defined by being inclusive. A reasonable return on investments also benefit stakeholders endowed with social and environmental responsibility, transparency, and protection of assets.

CONCEPTS OF PERCEIVED AND PROGRAMMED OBSOLESCENCE

The problem of a consumer society based on Corporate Social Responsibility (CSR) under the principle of profitability is that technology cannot maintain a viable rate of profit for the owners of the means of production (Mahecha & Zambrano, 2013), which results into an unethical business practices defined by selling products with programmed obsolescence. Since the early twentieth century, products have a limited life; for example, manufactured bulbs have a limited lifetime (Guerrero, 2012). This model has been applied after the Second World War for all industries, regardless of the ecological and environmental damages, only to dominate the consumer market, driving customers to throw their products away.

While these processes are maintained to sustain an economy of inequitable consumption, it will continue to produce unlimited amounts of low-quality products to be damaged in time, which will end up being sold in developing countries by multinationals, which causes a considerable social and ecological impact, no matter how green we are when we recycle.

Using three basic instruments such as advertising, planned obsolescence, and credit, companies come to the perceived obsolescence where new followers of fashion products, become obsolete to those who have not used, almost forcing them to dump products still they serve for the sake of change model, or use products that others have. Most times these goods become social consumption, since they depend on the acceptance of the person in human groups, affecting social inclusion in the study, work and institutions.

These two types of obsolescence create a consumer society, social problems connecting to environmental consumption, emphasizing the need for a more sustainable and just world. These trends affirm what Victor Lebow, ideologist of this way of life, in 1955 said: "Our enormously productive economy ... ask that we make consumption our way of life, that we convert the buying and use of goods in a ritual to seek our spiritual satisfaction, our ego satisfaction, in consumption (...) We need things consumed, burned up, replaced and discarded at an accelerated pace." The acceleration of this consumption depletes natural resources, wastes energy, and produces large volumes of waste.

The current economic model is more ideological than technical, as buying, selling and credit are facilitators that make obsolescence operate without major problems encouraging mass production and the consumer society. Great efforts are made by environmental organizations to process or reuse the waste generated by excessive consumption. These organizations seek to reuse "electronic waste" materials by seeking a social responsibility extended to the producer, trying to create an infrastructure prepared for the disposal, storage, transportation, and recycling of WEEE.

Social entrepreneurship arises as an opportunity to implement new business models where obsolescence should be seen as an opportunity to extend the life of products by creating new ventures. In the city of Manizales, located in the center of Colombia, it was conducted the study entitled "Planned and Perceived Obsolescence in Manizales in the Appliances Sector" (Lopez & Tabares, 2013) with the purpose of conducting a technological inventory as, for appliances, their use and frequency of change generate industrial waste.

Technical obsolescence can diminish by rethinking the engineering and production process focused on sustainable industries by using organic raw materials, so when are discarded they become an energy source for other processes (Thackara, 2006, p. 89) from cradle to cradle (McDonough & Braungart, 2005). Also, the Theory of Decline breaks with the paradigm of the infinite. A growth that does not fit in a world with exhaustible sources of raw materials, so changing the logic of excess by reducing the footprint of waste, overproduction and overconsumption is needed to produce other inexhaustible sources, such as friendship or knowledge (Kumar & Putnam, 2008; Krikke, Van Harten, & Schuur, 1999).

If happiness depends on the level of consumption, given the higher esteem that generates, today people should be supremely happy as they consume 26 times more than 70 years. Sharing the vision of Gandhi: "the world is big enough to meet everyone's needs, but will always be too small for the greed of some" (Latouche & Harpages, 2010, p. 78). The effort to achieve sustainability is wasted because firms do not reduce production to protect the environment (Genchev, 2009).

The combination of increasingly products' life-shortening (planned obsolescence) and effective marketing campaigns is generating serious consequences. Two types of obsolescence can be considered: (a) *Quality perceived obsolescence* carried out by introducing recurrent small technical changes in the product, as users think new products are better (Slade, 2006), and (b) *Psychological perceived obsolescence* (e.g., fashion in the clothing industry), when the design and appearance of things become very important for social status and make him/her comfortable with their use (Valquíria & Bonifacio, 2013).

Some decades ago products were produced to be used for a long time, and it was normal to repair or maintain any item purchased for keeping the same operability. Today, things have changed; the useful life of each product purchased has become shorter. Society is wrapped by consumerism, a phenomenon that increasingly appropriates most of the present generation, which is stimulated by new inventions, innovations, modernization, and different changes in production, which has led to generate a large collection of waste and garbage that destroy, in most cases, the natural resources that are essential for sustainability and human development (Contreras, Fraile, & Silva, 2013).

It seems contradictory to speak of the environment and CSR to a consumer society which has as the main paradigm to satisfy all material needs and create new ones using various means to achieve this goal, such as advertising, credit facilities and of course, planned obsolescence. The planet has become a world full of products that everyday consumers are encouraged to be obtained through advertising, innovation and new and striking features in each device, so each is tempted to consume no matter the amount of damage to the environment and the community. TV and Internet commercials are the best tool for companies to sell their products and services (sometimes by using false information) with the irrational desire of people for the purchase. This fact results in people that every day are buying only to improve their self-esteem or simply for the attention of other individuals. The lack of awareness and responsibility make those purchased products and services without considering the future consequences caused because they are involved in a consumer world where unneeded items are bought.

CONCEPTS OF CORPORATE SOCIAL RESPONSIBILITY

Following the devastating rise of consumerism, every day becomes more important the concept of CSR, and this importance is greater in Latin America where the environmental damage, mainly caused by foreign multinationals with the approval of corrupted governments, is very high. There are many definitions of CSR, but in the context of the WEEE generation, it is important to know some aspects related to their manufacture, such as (a) pieces that can be reused; (b) parts that can be reassembled; (c) which parts are biodegradable, (d) how this wasted devices will be collected and are environmentally and socially dangerous, among others.

Culturally, CSR-related policies change in each country, as they are particularly dependent on public policy and the institutional development promoted by the interests of the nation (Vives & Peinado, 2011). Thus, CSR practices must be adapted to the social, political, and economic environment. In developed countries, there are strict practices for certain activities which require the companies transfer to other countries to grow. As a result, the philosophy of CSR (sustainable and responsible practices contribute to the country's development) is ignored by these firms.

Approaches to the Concept of CSR

To clarify the concept of CSR, we must take into account the processes leading to sustainable development. Initially, economic development was made in stages with the idea of being easily assimilated by other countries. To make such development, it is required that the country uses capital goods (machinery and equipment) to produce goods and services not only for subsistence but also for people to have entertainment and education, i.e., to improve their quality of life. This fact forces the country to attract foreign investment when necessary, to stimulate the production of consumer goods. As a result, a mandatory planning policy development is set where tax incentives, tariffs, and credits with specific conditions are approved.

This purely economic perspectives changes when health, education, and culture are being added. The vision of sustainable development appears where the system must be preserved for future generations. As a result, the intergenerational equity is included, as well as the concept of sustainability as a joint process of a threefold environmental, economic and social dimension. In short, governments, businesses, and institutions working for sustainable development are being used as a reference to create the triple bottom line (economic, social, and environmental) for the social wellbeing.

Different Concepts of CSR

The concept of CSR is formed by the association of an economic concept (Return On Investment, ROI), a legal term (required obligations), ethics (what society expects as there is no legal requirement), and philanthropy (donations) (Carroll, 2006). Given this fact, CSR is multidimensional, so corporate citizenship can also be included (Crane & Matten, 2006). According to these conceptions, different definitions have emerged:

- **Global:** The CSR is a guide for companies to assume their responsibilities (Caravalo, 2011) related to sustainability. As a result, the World Business Council for Sustainable Development (WBCSD) commit firms to sustained economic development by working with employees and their families, the local community and the society at large to improve their quality of life. This concept is similar to the notion of freedom and equality, and it will always be redefined according to changing needs and circumstances. The UN's Global Compact or Global Pact defines principles under increasing globalization due to the generally disastrous environmental impact of the transnational corporations in the 1990s, involving them in social and environmental challenges.

- **In the United States of America:** Companies have played an important social role in this country defined by free market and single entrepreneurship. CSR is inserted in the philanthropic culture of companies and citizens, not only in charity programs, but also in the promotion of art, scientific research, and education, leading to a more comprehensive understanding which makes possible the redefinition of traditional philanthropy. This redefinition has allowed some facts that information are assimilated to the concept of social responsibility as:
    - Employees work best when they understand the meaning of their tasks in the company, in favorable working environments with reasonable wages. They enjoy healthy stability between work and family life.
    - Employers constantly encourage their human resources to work constantly looking for personal and professional growth.
    - Firms set aside autocratic, authoritarian and abusive methods in the workplace guided by tyranny and intimidation.
    - In the long term, companies work best when they are located in healthy working communities.
    - Firms dealing concerning the natural environment usually reduce their waste, while obtaining efficient products and services defined by higher quality to maximize their resources, including capital investments.
    - Companies have a long-term vision to benefit the affected communities.
    - With CSR, business reputation, social recognition, and credibility are enhanced.
- **In the European Union:** Public intervention has a greater role in social and economic affairs. European societies have been more attentive to environmental issues and are very sensitive to these problems. From the perspective of CSR, companies have changed their way of doing business, by incorporating the concept of sustainable development and achieving savings opportunities where previously only perceived costs and difficulties. They have achieved cleaner technologies, extending the vision of CSR to all parts of the company transforming the concept of reliability by openness and transparency.

For the European Commission, CSR is the voluntary integration by firms of social and environmental considerations into their commercial activities and their relations with stakeholders' concerns (Renaut, 2005). Efforts have been made to promote the voluntary nature of CSR; however, different trade unions have pointed out that one should not confuse CSR as an alternative to the responsibilities of governments, assuming that the starting point should be a voluntary focus, not excluding the regulatory approach supervision.

- **In Latin America:** Relationships and links between different social classes defined by paternalism are one of the most influential factors in the formation of governments, business communities, and societies, which has contributed into the marked inequality in both income distribution and the unequal concentration of political, economic and social power. As a result, poverty persists in these nations. Poverty level partially reduced due to religion, traditional families, and philanthropy from SMEs (small and medium enterprises) and large firms. Some business and social leaders have been given the task of dismantling this paternal culture-dependent society to build another philanthropic and CSR-based economy.

The problem in Latin America surges because transnational corporations, coming from countries where CSR is voluntary, and technology is accessible to apply socially responsible processes imposed by the global market, do not adapt their CSR policies to the social environment. They try to complement local initiatives to act responsibly, but this task of cultural and social transformation is of great difficulty. For this reason, the practice of CSR remains charitable, and this modification is very difficult to achieve. CSR policies should be conceived as the commitment leading to economic development focused on social welfare to improve the quality of life for employees, families and the community at large (Martínez, 2005). And in this sense, stronger collaboration with the public administration is needed, especially when dealing with WEEE.

THE COLOMBIAN LEGAL FRAMEWORK OF WEEE

The Ministry of Environment, Housing, and Territorial Development, by Resolution No. 1512 of August 5, 2010, established separate collection systems and environmental management of waste computers and/or peripherals. Colombia also signed the Basel Convention on the Control of Transboundary Movements of Hazardous Wastes and their Disposal[4], to prohibit the passage of these wastes between OECD and non-OECD. This agreement was signed by Law 253 of 1996, which became effective on March 31, 1997, acquiring a series of obligations to trade, processing, reduction and elimination of all types of hazardous waste.

The Ministry of Environment and Sustainable Development of Colombia, by law No. 1672 of July 19, 2013establishes the guidelines for the adoption of a policy of integrated management of electrical and electronic equipment waste, which defines the concepts established to know clearly who are producers and marketers to define the product life cycle to control WEEE. It also defines the responsibilities and obligations of producers, traders, users or consumers, and managers. Post-consumer programs have established some WEEE collection programs through chain stores, foundations, educational institutions, and agencies. These processes are just getting approved as programs to provide waste not only to industry, but also to other WEEE products, such as paper, plastics, and glass, among others.

Electrical and Electronic Equipment

The term WEEE (or e-Waste) refers to damaged, discarded or obsolete devices that consume electricity, so it includes extensive reference devices like appliances, computers, cell phones, and electronic devices. The WEEE symbol is used as a general term for all types of waste containing electricity consumption products that are dangerous, rare, and valuable or have interesting materials. Products containing lead, mercury, cadmium, hexavalent chromium, polybrominated biphenyls or polybrominated diphenyl ethers are included. The categories were defined by the decree adopted by WEEE Colombia (Table 1). According to this classification, categories 1, 2, 3 and 4 cover more than 50% of waste in Colombia (RAEE Colombia, 2014).

The government sanctions people and firms involved in throwing garbage in inappropriate places, and Colombians linked to a waste program, affirm that 32% return their devices to stores and warehouses, 29% phone local authorities to collect them, 21% take them to the collector garbage truck, and 18% leave them in municipal collection sites.

Table 1. EEE (electrical and electronic equipment) classification

No.	Category	Items
1	Major appliances	Refrigerators, freezers, washers, dryers, dishwashers, stoves, electric stoves, microwave ovens, heaters, fans, air conditioners
2	Small appliances	Vacuum cleaners, sewing machines, knitting, irons, toasters, deep fryers, coffee makers, grinders, electric knives, devices for cutting and drying hair, shaving, massage, clocks, scales
3	IT and telecommunications equipment	Computers, laptops, printers, copiers, electric typewriters, calculators, fax, telephones, answering machines
4	Consumer electronics appliances	Radios, televisions, camcorders, sound amplifiers, musical instruments
5	Lighting appliances	Lighting equipment used to spread or to control light except for filament bulbs.
6	Electrical and electronic tools	Sewing machines, drills, saws, lawn mowers, among others
7	Toys or sports and leisure equipment	Electric trains, video games, slot machines
8	Medical devices	Radiotherapy, cardiology, dialysis appliances, nuclear medicine, analyzers
9	Monitoring and control instruments	Smoke detectors, heating regulators, thermostats, surveillance cameras, sensors
10	Vending machines	Hot drinks, hot or cold bottles or cans of solid products, money

Source: RAEE Colombia (2014)

Estimate of WEEE to Colombia

According to the information provided by the associations that manage the production, distribution, marketing and final inspection of the EEE in Colombia, for the year 2008, there was an installed base of over 133,000 tons of production of appliances, where 40,500 tons is waste equipment. For 2008 it was estimated that the amount of WEEE in Switzerland was 14 kilos per inhabitant, while in Colombia was 0.7 kg. This quantity will increase if it grows the quality of life of the Colombian citizen.

REVERSE LOGISTICS

To create a more sustainable environment and due to the shortage of some raw materials and rapidly increasing waste, some time ago, within the framework of integrated logistics, it has been heard the concept of Reverse Logistics, It aimed at ensuring, through recovery techniques, reuse of all waste materials and any product in the final stage of use, so that they come back to their original producer giving a total or partial reuse of these wastes, adding renovation and reprocessing methodologies to finally turn them into raw material for the industry itself or other organizations that can benefit by reducing the environmental impact it generates.

This process involves moving products from their final destination uphill in the supply chain to achieve added value or ensure their proper disposal. As more clearly indicated Blumberg (2004): "*A supply chain that is redesigned to manage the flow of products for reprocessing, reuse, recycling or destruction, correctly using all its resources efficiently.*"

According to Martí Frias (2014), the relationship between conventional logistics and reverse logistics is broadly given that the primary action of conventional logistics is to get the raw materials from reaching the organization at the right time to have the products in consumers' hands in the planned time and at less cost. For reverse logistics, the environment and CSR are crucial.

Reverse Logistics Management

Reverse logistics plan, manage and control the flow of products and materials that have been deemed defective, excess inventory, customer returns, inventory or seasonal products obsolete, to be taken from the place of consumption to the point of origin of the manufacturer or supplier including information associated to assess the causes of the return (Atún, 2004). In reverse logistics, strategic cost, quality, customer service, environmental concerns, and legal concerns are keys for success (Dowlatshahi, 2000), as well as operational factors such as cost-benefit analysis, transport, storage, supply management, remanufacturing, recycling, and packaging. These factors together make the knowledge of state of the art on the keys to successful design and management of reverse logistics systems.

Processes Involved in Reverse Logistics

Reverse logistics processes focus on five key objectives (Mora, 2008):

1. **Procurement and Shopping:** It involves the production, supplier development, and procurement of raw materials, components, packaging materials, packaging, packing and handling units that are "environmentally friendly."
2. **Reduction of Virgin Inputs:** It is composed by activities of product engineering and re-training of human resources to evaluate the surplus materials reuse and the preference for recycling materials to choose containers, packaging, and handling reusable and recyclable units to promote the culture of return.
3. **Recycling:** The development of recycling policies respecting performance or product standards by using recycled source materials, technological innovations, and virgin raw materials.
4. **Replacing:** The increase in the rate of innovation in recycling processes should promote the substitution of materials, i.e. heavier particles by lighter ones with equal or superior performance, as is the case in the automotive industry where plastic parts are replacing massively metal and glass in automobiles, as well as aluminum or composite materials in new truck chassis to decrease the tare and increase the charging unit for equal axle weight.
5. **Waste Management:** The material procurement policies should evaluate the rate of utilization of waste materials and the acceptance of samples. Reverse logistics is a philosophy that any company should use to preserve the environment.

In Colombia, although no law specifies the terms of reverse or inverse logistics, some decrees protect the environment to regulate the handling of certain waste. The Ministry of Environment puts special emphasis on the definition of waste to set the obligations and responsibilities of producers and consumer, but there is no mention of the possibilities for reusing waste. This fact has been made at the regional and local level, as in the case of the city of Manizales (Colombia).

CASE STUDY

The sample surveyed is composed of 3-4 members' families whose members (79%) are aged between 18 and 33 years old, and mostly belong to 3 (low-medium social class), 4 (medium social class), 5 (high-medium social class), and 6 (high social class) strata in the city of Manizales (Colombia). The asked to a questionnaire about the appliances they use and belonging to the white line, brown line, food preparation appliances, devices for home care, and personal grooming appliances. They were consulted about the equipment used, the number of them, how they purchased them, how many times and why they changed.

Results show that the most owned appliances are TV, computer, phone, video player, audio player, keeping it from two to four devices per household, which implies that they are items of high consumption and fashion by different members of the households, services, and benefits for entertainment, work, and communication, and accounting; other high consumption devices are the refrigerator, stove, blender, washing machine, rice cooker, justified by the roles of conservation and food preparation, hygiene and beauty.

Products going out of style are televisions and mobile phone, as respondents see the need for change to keep up with new technology. The perceived obsolescence is subjective in respondents, as these items are assimilated as old and obsolete, but they are in good condition. A large percentage of respondents consider the useful life of products because they are concerned about not losing the invested money, quality, and utility of the product, or the need for what they bought them. Popular products owned at home by the majority of the population are a fridge, stove, washer, blender, rice cooker, cellular, blender, iron, hair dryer, hair iron, because they are everyday devices for storing food, heat, work, communicate, or entertain. They are essential for having a good quality of life.

Reasons for Buying Appliances Knowing Their Limited Useful Lifetime

The responses are classified into

1. **Necessity:** Consumers prefer products of better quality, better performance and/or innovative features, and people make them wishes and needs no matter how long they would last, what matters is the satisfaction generated.
2. **Quality:** People are willing to buy an expensive product when their brands are good because they provide good service and are characterized by being considered more durable, thin, have good quality, and better performance. For most people, the life of a product has to do not only with the durability and price but also with the quality of the materials used. Quality becomes a decisive condition for the consumption of certain products. It is definitive to develop superior products with better performance because, over time, buyers will value and appreciate a product specifically for its quality.
3. **Functionality:** When buying any device, people expect to fulfill some functions during the time of usage, to take full advantage of the investment made, and enjoy it 100% during its lifetime, because if an appliance fails, it should be counted as an expense. Buyers seek comfort and take into account the value and service provided.

Reasons for Not Buying the Appliance

1. **Economic:** Many consumers say they would not buy an expensive product if that lasts only for a short time, as it would be a waste of money. So, they tend to search for something cheaper or at the same price, but better quality.
2. **Environmental:** People would not buy the appliances because it does not justify investing money in a product or brand that soon is damaged, because it generates more expense, greater pollution, and environmental damage. This fact suggests that although environmental awareness is lacking to some extent, it is manifesting a certain environmental responsibility, even though, people seldom realize the consequences that will bring the discard of these appliances. Respondents have certain environmental awareness and responsibility for the accumulation of waste.

Recycling Programs

81% of respondents said they did not know recycling programs, which allows us to infer that there is ignorance and/or there are not many recycling programs founded in the city. 19% of the sample did know them. As a result, we can deduce that the level of ignorance about recycling is high in the city, perhaps because of a lack of an efficient publicity campaign made by the town hall and private companies, so it is necessary to work and make collective efforts to achieve a recycling awareness of all kinds of appliances to be reused.

The most disposed appliances in the city of Manizales are washing machines, refrigerators, and microwaves, mostly discarded in very bad conditions, very few in perfect conditions. These discarded appliances are purchased as follows: 72% buy them, 16% give them away, and 12% acquire them by collecting or requesting. Of waste collected, 60% disarm pieces, 20% sell them for parts, 16% resell entirely, and 4% repair them. As for the benefits of these wastes, 48% are a cheap buy, 24% serve as raw material, 24% is a business opportunity, and 4% have another type of benefit. When items do not work, 54% are thrown away, 33% are lead to the public authorities, 8% reuse them, and 4% give them as a gift. Regarding the environmental impact of this waste, 60% believe they cause damage to the environment, while 40% do not think so.

CONCLUSION

There is a growing number of new products in the household appliances sector which are continuously put on the market. As the supply of goods is greater than the demand, programmed obsolescence becomes a sales strategy to encourages the purchase. Today's consumer is increasingly informed and demanding person seeking higher quality and not only wanting to buy essential goods for their daily activities. They buy products that give value to life.

According to the findings, when people change appliances for consumption, they have little awareness of how to dispose of the product, given that most times these are thrown or given away, not recycled properly. When people buy EEE, they are seeking innovation requirements and conditions, warranty, safety, welfare, and care of these devices to allow a more convenient and comfortable life. In this sense, social innovation, social entrepreneurship, and reverse logistics are related as they are strategies focused on promoting processes to generate a return and contribute to preserving the environment, given the environmental damage resulted from production and consumption processes.

Companies must develop an effective policy to manage recycled and recovered items, using the theories of reverse logistics, the cradle to the cradle, and the theory of decline, trying not to affect the structure of costs having in mind that most of the parts of the product, once discarded, become raw material for upgrade, or other products.

The role of science, marketing, advertising and universities in the world, and especially engineering, is crucial to reduce waste and to increase recycling from the design and development of products. Some laws protect consumers' rights against possible abuses from market makers. Consumers have the final decision to reject or choose devices defined by planned obsolescence, so it is crucial to educate them to have a responsible consumption. To overcome the problem of perceived obsolescence, the education for a more responsible consumption is basic, as well as the support social entrepreneurship and alternative ideas to reduce the effects of the large amount of WEEE. In this process, it is important to reduce the chain of both intermediaries, only interested in participating in the market supply, and gatherers, with no social security and excluded from conversion programs. In the city of Manizales, there are few recycling programs and are only aimed at garbage collection. Therefore, public-based WEEE collection programs are an opportunity for the social inclusion of gatherers through the use of social entrepreneurship.

REFERENCES

Alam, M. S. (2010). Transición Cultural y Emprendimiento Innovador. *5th International Conference on Product Innovation Management*, 1-2, 757-761.

Alemán, F., & Coronado, C. I. (2014). Emprendimiento social innovador: el caso de Biored Colombia SAS. *Global Conference on Business & Finance Proceedings*, *9*(2), 508-516.

Atún, J.P. (2004). Logística Verde: Estrategias para implantarla y casos exitosos en Latinoamérica. *Revista Zona Logística, 1*, 12–19.

Austin, Stevenson, H., & Wei-Skillern, J. (2006). Social and Commercial Entrepreneurship: Same, different or both? *Entrepreneurship Theory and Practice*, *30*(1), 1–22. doi:10.1111/j.1540-6520.2006.00107.x

Blumberg, D.F. (2004). *Introduction to Management of Reverse Logistics and Closed Loop Supply Chain Processes*. CRC Press.

Caravalo, B. (2011). *Desarrollo sostenible, ética, filantropía y responsabilidad social*. Bogota, Colombia: Ediciones Econ.

Carroll, A., & Buschholtz, A. (2006). *Business & Society: Ethics & Stakeholder Management* (6th ed.). Thompson.

Céspedes, A. H. (2009). *Emprendimiento Social y su Sustentabilidad*. Bogota, Colombia: HCGlobal Group.

Chell, E. (2007). Social Enterprise and Entrepreneurship: Towards a Convergent Theory of the Entrepreneurial Process. *International Small Business Journal*, *25*(5), 12–21.

Conteras, E. D., Fraile, A. M., & Silva, J. D. (2013). Diseño de un sistema de logística inversa para la recolección de envases y empaques vacíos de plaguicidas. *Revista Ingeniería Industrial, 2*, 29–42.

Contreras, E., Tordecilla, R., & Silva, J. (2013). Revisión de estudios de caso de carácter cualitativo y exploratorio en logística inversa. *Revista EIA, 10*, 153–164.

Crane, A., & Matten, M. (2006). *Business Ethics*. London, UK: Oxford University Press.

Daghbashyan, Z., & Harsman, B. (2014). Universidad Elección y Emprendimiento. *Pequeña Economía de la Empresa, 42*(4), 729–746.

De Pablo López, I. (2005). *El emprendizaje social: motor de desarrollo y cohesión social. V Seminario de creación de empresas. Cantoblanco*. Madrid, Spain: Autonomous University of Madrid.

Dees, G. E. (2001). *Strategic tools for social entrepreneurs*. John Wiley & Sons.

Dejaeghere, J. (2013). La educación, las habilidades y la ciudadanía: Un modelo emergente de la iniciativa empresarial en Tanzania. *Education and Computing, 49*(4), 503–519.

Dowlatshahi, S. (2000). Developing a Theory of Reverse Logistics. *Interfaces, 30*(3), 143–155. doi:10.1287/inte.30.3.143.11670

Egbe-Okpenge, E. G., & Igbo, H. I. (2012). Relación entre la Consejería y Emprendimiento Desarrollo de Habilidades de Nigerianos Fin de Carrera de Pregrado. *III World Conference on Psychology, Counseling, and Orientation (WCPCG 2012), 84*, 120-127.

Fernández, A. D., Adenso, D. F., Gil, M. J. A., José, Á. G. M., Torre, P. G., & Pilar, G. T. (2004). *Logística inversa y medio ambiente: aspectos estratégicos y operativos*. Madrid, Spain: McGraw-Hill Interamericana de España S.L.

Genchev, S. E. (2009). Reverse logistics program design: A company study. *Business Horizons, 52*(2), 139–148. doi:10.1016/j.bushor.2008.09.005

Grundey, D., & ... . (2008). El Papel de la Política Institucional de Desarrollo de Emprendimiento Innovador en Lituania. *Transformaciones en Negocios y Economía, 7*(2), 86–101.

Guerrero, L. (2012, Sep 28). Obsolescencia programada y e-waste. *Revista Fortuna*.

Guzmán-Vásquez, A., & Trujillo-Dávila, M. A. (2008). Emprendimiento social-revisión de literatura. *Estudios Gerenciales, 24*(109), 105–125. doi:10.1016/S0123-5923(08)70055-X

Johansen, V. (2014). Educación Emprendimiento y Rendimiento Académico. *Scandinavian Journal of Educational Research, 58*(3), 300–314. doi:10.1080/00313831.2012.726642

Kayasan, O. (2011). Papel del Estado en la innovación para estimular el espíritu empresarial: Países Emergentes Perspectivas. Actas de la VI Conferencia Europea sobre Innovación y Emprendimiento (ECIE), 1-2, 511-518.

Krikke, H. R., van Harten, A., & Schuur, P. C. (1999). Business case Océ: Reverse logistic network redesign for copiers. *OR-Spektrum, 21*(3), 381–409. doi:10.1007002910050095

Kumar, S., & Putnam, V. (2008). Cradle to cradle: Reverse logistics strategies and opportunities across three industry sectors. *International Journal of Production Economics*, *115*(2), 305–315. doi:10.1016/j.ijpe.2007.11.015

Latouche, S., & Harpages, D. (2010). *L'heure du décroissance*. Paris, France: Editions Thierry Magnier.

Li, H., y Zuo, X. (2013). Investigación de Empleo del Colegio de Graduados y Emprendimiento - Tomando Estudiantes Formación Superior en especialidades como productor del sector servicios para un ejemplo. *Actas de la Conferencia Internacional sobre Educación de Tecnología y Sistema de Información (ICETIS 2013)*, 126-133.

López-Cardona, D., & Tabares-Hoyos, R. (2013). La obsolescencia programada y percibida en el sector de electrodomésticos de Manizales. Simposio ASPROMER.

Mahecha, E., & Zambrano, C. (2013). La inviabilidad del capitalismo en el siglo XXI. *Educación y Desarrollo Social*, *8*(1), 10–47.

Martí Frías, B. (2014). *La logística inversa: Gestión de RAEEs*. Valencia, Spain: Polytechnic University of Valencia.

Martínez, H. (2005). *El marco ético de la Responsabilidad Social Empresarial*. Bogota, Colombia: Pontificia Universidad Javeriana.

Mcdonough, W., & Braungart, M. (2005). *Cradle to Cradle: De la Cuna a la Cuna: Rediseñando la forma en que hacemos las cosas*. Madrid, Spain: McGraw-Hill Interamericana de España.

Mora, G. L. A. (2008). *Gestión logística integral*. Bogota, Colombia: Ecoe Ediciones.

Mozas-Moral, A. (2013). Emprendimiento y Economía Social. *C.I.R.I.E.C. España*, *78*, 7–9.

Ndou, V., & Del Vecchio, P. (2013). Fomento del espíritu empresarial innovador de desarrollo de activos de conocimiento: una evaluación de la situación en los países de los Balcanes Occidentales. In Quinta Conferencia Anual de la Asociación Euromediterránea de la Academia EUROMED de Negocios (pp. 1187–1197). Montreux, Switzerland: Academic Press.

Prahalad, C. (2010). *The Fortune at the Bottom of the Pyramid: Eradicating Poverty Through Profits*. Upper Saddle River, NJ: Prentice Hall. doi:10.19177/reen.v1e220081-23

Racic, D., & Viduka, Z. (2013). Desarrollo de Emprendimiento Innovador en Croacia: Análisis y Recomendaciones de Política. In Actas de la Conferencia Internacional de Innovación Valle-Beijing 2013 Suzhou-Silicio (SIIC): Innovación Tecnológica y Diásporas en una Era Global (pp. 56–60). Suzhou, China: Academic Press. doi:10.1109/SIIC.2013.6624166

RAEE Colombia, . (2014). *Cifras y estimativos para Colombia*. Electrodomésticos.

Red Senk. (2011). *Escala e Impacto en Negocios sociales en Iberoamérica*. Retrieved from http://www.sekn.org/cms/index.php/proyectos.html

Renaut, A. (2005). *La Responsabilidad Social de las empresas en Europa: ¿tiene el diálogo social alguna oportunidad?* International Labor Organization.

Roberts, D., & Woods, C. (2005). Changing the world on a shoestring: The concept of social entrepreneurship. *University of Auckland Business Review*, *23*, 45–51.

Santos, F. J. (2004). Crecimiento, desarrollo y empresarialidad en el proceso de globalizacion economica. *Revista de Economía Mundial*, *10/11*, 171–202.

Santos, F. J., Barroso, M., & Guzmán, C. (2013). La economía global y los emprendimientos sociales. *Revista de Economía Mundial*, *35*, 21–45.

Seelosa, C., & Mair, J. (2005). Social entrepreneurship: Creating new business models to serve the poor. *Business Horizons*, *48*(3), 241–246. doi:10.1016/j.bushor.2004.11.006

Silakalne-Araja, D., & Arajs, R. (2012). Promoción de la Educación de Adultos en el negocio innovador. *Scientific International Conference on Society, Integration, and Education 2012*, 429-440.

Slade, G. (2006). *Made to break: technology and obsolescence in America*. Boston: Harvard University Press.

Spulber, D. F. (2012). El conocimiento tácito con el emprendimiento innovador. *Revista Internacional de Organización Industrial*, *30*(6), 641–653.

Sudharson, K., Ali, A. M., & Sermakani, A. M. (2012). Una perspectiva organizativa de Comunicación del Conocimiento en Desarrollo de Emprendimiento Educación para Estudiantes de Ingeniería. In *Actas de la Segunda Conferencia Internacional de Información Integrado* (Vol. 73, pp. 590–597). Budapest, Hungary: IC-ININFO.

Thackara, J. (2006). *In the bubble. Designing in a complex world*. Boston: MIT Press.

Valquíria, B., & Renata, C.A. (2013). *Historia secreta de la obsolescencia programada*. Academic Press.

Vives, A., & Peinado-Vara, E. (2011). *La Responsabilidad Social de la Empresa en América Latina. Manual de gestión*. Montevideo, Uruguay: Inter-American Development Bank.

Wompner, F. H. (2012). El emprendimiento como factor de movilización social. *Nómadas*, *36*, 58–69.

Yin, L., & Li, J. (2013). Estudio sobre la situación actual de la educación empresarial. III Conferencia Internacional de Educación y Gestión de la Educación (EEM), 188-191.

Yunus, M. (2006). *El banquero de los pobres: los microcréditos y la batalla contra la pobreza en el mundo*. Barcelona, Spain: Paidós.

Yunus, M., Moingeon, B., & Lehmann, L. (2010). Building Social Business Models: Lessons from the Grameen Experience. *Long Range Planning*, *43*(2-3), 308–325. doi:10.1016/j.lrp.2009.12.005

Zain, S. M. (2013). Educación Sostenible y Emprendimiento disparadores Innovación Cultura en 3R. VI Foro Internacional sobre la Enseñanza de la Ingeniería (IFEE), 128-133.

KEY TERMS AND DEFINITIONS

Chain of Intermediaries: Parasitic agents are not adding value, just higher costs.

Corporate Social Responsibility: The commitment of a company to help economic development, welfare, and improve employees' life quality, including families and society.

Manizales: Capital of the Department of Caldas, Republic of Colombia, located in the center of the country, coffee region, with over 400,000 inhabitants.

Planned Obsolescence: To reduce product quality life programming to make people throw away products.

Perceived Obsolescence: Due to technological progress this is the effect of changing products because of advertising and fashion.

Reverse Logistics: Reuse of all waste materials and any product in the final stage of use to benefit the environment.

Social Enterprise: Firm aiming social impact rather than making economic profits.

Social Entrepreneurship: Actions to create social value from philanthropy to improve the quality of life in the society, and simultaneously, the economic performance of firms.

WEEE (Waste Electrical and Electronic Equipment): A set of materials, components, consumables, and subassemblies that comprise, from households or firms, from the time they became waste.

ENDNOTES

1 A previous version of this chapter has been publish in the *Handbook of Research on Social Entrepreneurship and Solidarity Economics*, IGI Global (doi: 10.4018/978-1-5225-0097-1.ch023).

2 To program in the design phase the end of the useful life of a product. As a result, it becomes obsolete, useless or unusable.

3 It is a collaboration network among ten of the most renowned business schools in Latin America.

4 This convention was adopted by the Diplomatic Conference in Basel (Switzerland) in 1989 and entered into force in May 1992. Since November 1997, a total of 114 states and the European Union are part of the agreement, adopting an instrument governing the transboundary movement of hazardous wastes.

Chapter 12
Joint Liability Lending, Entrepreneurial Development, and Poverty Reduction

Christopher Boachie
Central University, Ghana

ABSTRACT

The purpose of this chapter is to examine the effect of joint liability lending on micro businesses in Madina municipality. Joint liability lending has become a popular and fashionable word in financial and development circles. It is a cross-sectional survey study and used both primary and secondary data on joint liability lending. The study reveals that joint liability lending improves entrepreneurship and reduces poverty. There exists a significant relationship between joint liability lending and a high repayment rate. The implications are that individual within the group are encouraged to continue saving and microfinance institutions should continue investing in educating and training clients to improve upon their micro businesses.

INTRODUCTION

Microfinance institutions have played a fundamental role in delivering broader access to financial services such as credit, savings, and insurance to the poor; however, it is still unclear what policies allow microfinance institutions to offer these services successfully and whether or not the success of such policies depends on the socioeconomic environment in which the institution operates. Group liability claims to improve repayment rates and lower transaction costs when lending to the poor by providing incentives for peers to screen, monitor and enforce each other's loans. However, some argue that group liability creates excessive pressure and discourages good clients from borrowing, jeopardizing both growth and sustainability. Therefore, it remains unclear whether group liability improves the borrower's overall economic situation and the poor's access to financial markets. The purpose of this chapter, therefore, is to investigate whether joint liability lending can lead to entrepreneurial development and thereby reduce poverty.

DOI: 10.4018/978-1-5225-8939-6.ch012

The vast majority of studies in the microfinance literature have focused on the mechanisms behind the success of the group lending model that is used by the Grameen Bank in Bangladesh and by many other microfinance institutions around the world. On the theoretical side, researchers have studied how joint liability contracts help to overcome the problems of adverse selection (Armendariz de Aghion & Gollier 2000), moral hazard (Stiglitz, 1990; Varian, 1990), and enforcement (Besley & Coate, 1995). Some theories view the existing level of social capital as critical to the performance of group lending, and state that joint liability contracts can improve repayment because borrowers have better information about each other's type; can more easily monitor each other's investment, and can make use of social sanctions to force people to pay back a loan. Other theories contend that joint liability lending may succeed whether or not the contract is implemented among borrowers with high levels of social capital. Empirical studies show mixed results. Some of them provide evidence that social pressure or social cohesion are positively associated with group performance (Wenner, 1995; Abbink *et al.,* 2006; Karlan, 2001); while others show that strong social ties within borrowing groups make it more difficult to pressure members to repay loans (Wydick, 1999; Ahlin & Townsend, 2007). The effectiveness of microcredit as a tool to combat poverty is much debated now that, after years of rapid growth, microfinance institutions (MFIs) in various countries are struggling with client over-indebtedness and repayment problems. This chapter seeks to review and assess the role of joint liability lending in improving social entrepreneurship by focusing on the level of income, loan repayment and savings habits of beneficiaries of Joint Liability Lending.

Under joint liability lending, small groups of borrowers are responsible for the repayment of each other's loans. All group members are treated as being in default when at least one of them does not repay, and all members are denied subsequent loans. Because co-borrowers act as guarantors they screen and monitor each other and in so doing reduce agency problems between the MFI and its borrowers. A potential downside to joint-liability lending is that it often involves frequent and time-consuming repayment meetings and exerts strong social pressure, making it potentially onerous for borrowers. This fact is one of the main reasons why MFIs have started to move from joint to individual lending. The remainder of the chapter is organized as follows: Section 2 reviews the literature on joint liability lending and a description of joint liability loans. Section 3 presents the relationship between joint liability lending and poverty reduction with empirical evidence. Then, section 4 presents the strengths and weaknesses of joint liability lending and finally concludes.

BACKGROUND

Over the last forty years, microfinance has evolved from the provision of small, agricultural loans disseminated to impoverished farmers in rural areas to include services in urban centers administered to a wide range of households. These institutions now offer services beyond microcredit and operate within diverse organizational structures and institutional environments. Scholars debate the impact of this organizational metamorphosis regarding the outcomes of the institution and the sustainability of this form of development aid. It seems that microfinance institutions intend to fulfill mission-directed outcomes but are coming under pressure to become sustainable financial institutions. The mission of the organization, in theory, determines the target market served and guided the provision of services, concerning outputs, to specific types of clients. In this piece, this distinction will be framed regarding a welfarist *versus* institutionalist philosophy of lending, each with a focus on a particular clientele, desired outcome, and attained by particular administration of services.

Sharma (2006) writes that the spectacular growth of microfinance industry has been fuelled not by market forces but by conscious actions of national governments, non-governmental organizations (NGOs), and donors who view microfinance as an effective tool for alleviating poverty. Even with Sharma (2006) explanation, there remains a very intriguing question: How has it been possible that microfinance institutions have achieved such tremendous growth within the last three decades? How is it that microfinance institutions have succeeded in serving the poor with financial services while the formal financial institutions have constantly failed? Kiiru and Kenia (2007) argued that poverty and desperation of households make them a prime market for microfinance services. The writers argued that the poor are a prime market for credit services because of their liquidity needs for either consumption smoothing or micro-entrepreneurship purposes. Little wonder that Asia, where high population density coupled with a high level of poverty and lack of alternative finance, is a prime market for microfinance.

To reach economically disadvantaged clients with financial services requires innovative strategies. Joint liability lending institutions use "unconventional" methods to lend successfully to the poor. There is evidence that in many circumstances an unconventional lender such as the Grameen Bank can lend to poor people that no ordinary commercial bank would want for a customer. The unconventional lender can do so with a reasonable degree of financial self-sufficiency and achieve repayment rates that are significantly higher than for comparable loans by conventional lending institutions (Schreiner, 2003). This chapter identifies four distinct but complementary reasons for this success. First, many (but not all) of these lending programs ask borrowers to form a group in which all borrowers are jointly liable for each other's loans. Second, individual group members engage in intensive monitoring to each other. Third, microfinance institutions rely heavily on the promise of repeat loans (dynamic incentives) for borrowers who perform well. Finally, microfinance institutions impose forced savings by individual group members to lower the risks of moral hazards.

In analyzing joint liability lending institutions, economists have focused on either the effects of joint liability on the pool and behavior of borrowers or on the fact that lending to groups, as opposed to individuals, is a way to reduce transactions costs for the microfinance institutions. If the socioeconomic characteristics of the borrowers are comparable to a large extent, it would be possible to put them together in a group to save on processing, screening and loan collection costs. This way the group enables the microfinance institution to avoid the cost of performing a costly audit every time an individual borrower declares an inability to pay due to low output. This fact is because the microfinance institution will induce the rest of the group to undertake liability for the defaulting member. The microfinance institution will only audit when the whole group declares an inability to repay. That group lending enables a reduction in transactions costs per loan for the microfinance institution. The most hailed advantage of group lending is that it makes it possible for the poor in the informal sector who have no collateral to access credit as long as they can be able to join a group. Some writers have even described it as "the apparent miracle of giving solvency to a community composed almost entirely of insolvent individuals."

Poverty reduction researchers have a distinct question of whether joint-liability lending helps the poor. As a logical matter, a microfinance institution could function very well regarding repayment rates but have little impact on poverty — this question, which is also the focus of this chapter, has also been asked before. Pitt and Khandker (1998) find, using data from three programs in rural Bangladesh, that borrowing from group-lending schemes increased consumption of poor households. However, Morduch (2008) has argued that Pitt and Khandker's result reflects program selection effects rather than the impact of borrowing per se. This chapter, therefore, seeks to focus on the effects of joint liability on the individual in the pool and behavior of borrowers rather than analyze joint liability as a cost mitigation measures by the microfinance institution.

Theoretical Framework

Existing theories on joint liability lending motivate the analysis in this paper. Following Ahlin and Townsend (2007), I focus on four of the best-known and most representative papers in the literature to motivate my conceptual and empirical work. These papers are Stiglitz (1990), Banerjee *et al.* (1994), Besley and Coate (1995), and Ghatak (1999). In this section, the repayment implications of these four joint liability lending models are briefly described using the corresponding extended version of the models developed.

In general, the theories that are analyzed below assume that groups consist of two borrowers and that both of them face the same contract terms.

Moral Hazard Model of Stiglitz (1990)

The theoretical model by Stiglitz (1990) shows how peer monitoring under joint liability lending can help to mitigate ex-ante moral hazard. In this model, all individuals receive a loan L and choose to undertake a risky or safe project. If successful, the risky project will yield a return of $Y_R(L)$ with probability P_R, while the safe project will yield a return of $Y_S(L)$ with probability $P_S > P_R$. If a project fails, returns are zero. The model assumes that the safe project yields a higher expected return than the risky project, but it yields a lower return when successful. Individuals maximize their expected utility, where utility is a standard utility function that depends on the net return of the project.

Limited liability implies that the lender will get rL from a borrower who succeeds, and zero from a borrower who fails. Thus, limited liability increases the incentives to choose the risky project. To mitigate this problem, the lender offers a joint liability contract in which he gets nothing from a borrower who fails; rL from a borrower who succeeds; and an additional payment qL from a borrower who succeeds and whose partner fails. Also, the author imposes symmetry in the choice of a project and assumes borrowers behave cooperatively; that is, borrowers, decide together whether to undertake the safe or the risky project.

Stiglitz (1990) shows the repayment rate decreases with the interest rate and the size of the loan. In both cases, success becomes a less attractive outcome compared to the case in which the project fails; therefore, an increase in the interest rate or the size of the loan causes the risky project to dominate the safe project. Also, Ahlin and Townsend (2007) show that the repayment rate is lower for groups with a higher degree of joint liability and higher for groups acting cooperatively. First, higher joint liability reduces the payoff of risky and safe projects; however, the reduction in the payoff of safe projects is larger than the reduction in the payoff of risky projects choosing the safe project implies paying for delinquent borrowers more often and during times in which the returns are lower. Therefore, an increase in the degree of joint liability encourages the choice of risky projects. Similarly, if borrowers do not act cooperatively regarding the choice of the type of the project, then both of them have incentives to deviate to risky projects and free-ride on their partner's safe behavior. Hence, when groups do not act cooperatively they choose risky projects more often; this, in turn, reduces the repayment rate.

Moral Hazard Model of Banerjee et al. (1994)

Banerjee *et al.* (1994) also study how joint liability lending can help to overcome the problem of *ex-ante* moral hazard. The authors introduce monitoring and demonstrate how local information facilitates the role of borrowers as monitors since they can impose higher penalties on their peers in case of default. Groups consist of one borrower and one cosigner, who assumes the role of monitor.

The borrower receives one unit of capital and chooses a project with a probability of success *p*. The return of the project is a function of the probability of success and is equal to zero if the project fails. If the project succeeds, the borrower pays the interest to the lender; if the project fails, the cosigner has to respond for the borrower.

As in Stiglitz (1990), limited liability increases the incentives to choose riskier projects. The model assumes the co-signer acts as a monitor and can penalize the borrower in case she opts for a risky project. The more the co-signer monitors, the less likely she will end up paying back the borrower's loan; however, monitoring is costly. The monitor chooses the optimal project riskiness to maximize his payoff. In this context, a higher degree of joint liability increases the benefit from monitoring; and, as a result, repayment rates are higher. This result contradicts the prediction of the Stiglitz model. Also, Ahlin and Townsend (2007) show repayment rates are lower for groups with larger loans or higher interest rates. Both cases make it more attractive to repay the loan less often; so the borrower has incentives to choose riskier projects. Similarly, the authors introduce cooperation in the model and find that repayment rates are higher for groups that cooperate and enforce a joint agreement as long as the marginal cost of penalizing is greater than one; otherwise, the non-cooperative case results in higher repayment rates as it is cheaper for the monitor to enforce a higher probability of repayment.

Strategic Default Model of Besley and Coate (1995)

Besley and Coate (1995) analyze the borrowers' decision regarding whether to repay the loan or not after the project returns are realized. This decision depends on the cost of repayment (*i.e.,* the gross interest rate, *r*) and the severity of the penalties imposed by the lender and the group or community.

In this model, each borrower undertakes a project that requires one unit of capital and yields *Y* units of income. The model assumes that returns are drawn independently on *[0, Y]*from distribution *F(Y)*; thus, repayment decisions are made non-cooperatively. Under the joint liability contract, if the lender does not receive the full repayment amount from the group, he imposes a penalty on each borrower. This feature of the contract introduces interdependence between the borrowers' decisions. It is assumed that the penalty is increasing on the projected return; consequently, borrowers who realize high returns will choose to repay, and borrowers who realize low returns will choose to default. The authors identify situations in which there is disagreement in the borrower's decision to repay or not the loan and in which neither borrower is willing to bail out the group; as a result, the group default. They show how unofficial penalties can increase the willingness to repay the low return borrower in these situations of disagreement. The severity of these penalties will depend on the partner's desire to repay which is assumed to be proportional to his gain from repayment relative to default.

Besley and Coate's model predicts that repayment rates increase with the severity of official and unofficial penalties, as these penalties raise the cost of default and do not affect the cost of repayment; and that repayment rates decrease with the gross interest rate as this implies an increase in the cost of repayment. The extended model by Ahlin and Townsend (2007) includes cooperation; their analysis shows that repayment rate is lower for groups acting cooperatively if unofficial penalties are greater than the loss of the non-defaulting borrower from default, and vice versa.

Adverse Selection Model of Ghatak (1999)

As in Stiglitz (1990) and Banerjee *et al.* (1994), limited liability makes borrowing more attractive to risky than to safe borrowers; and thus less profitable to lenders as risky borrowers default more often. Ghatak (1999) analyzes how joint liability lending programs take advantage of local information that borrowers have about each other's projects through self-selection of group members. In this model, a borrower is characterized by the probability of success of her project $p \in [p, 1]$; the type of project is fixed and is observable among borrower, but not to the lender; and the return of a type p project is a random variable which takes two values, Y(p)˃ 0 if successful and 0 otherwise. Also, it is assumed the contract stipules an individual liability component r, and a joint liability component q. Thus, given the limited liability restriction, if the project fails the borrower pays nothing to the lender; however, if the project is successful, then the borrower has to pay her debt plus an additional joint liability payment per member of the group whose project has failed.

Under this economic environment, a borrower has two decisions to make. First, she has to decide with whom to borrow. Ghatak shows that the self-selection process results in homogenous groups, which make the market more attractive for safer borrowers who would otherwise have been excluded from the market. Second, a borrower has to decide whether or not to borrow. The model assumes all borrowers get the same expected return; however, safer borrowers exhibit higher expected repayment as they succeed more often. Hence, borrowers will choose to borrow if their expected net return is higher or equal to their non-borrowing outside option. This fact implies that only borrowers riskier than some cutoff risky-type will borrow, and safer borrowers will opt for the outside option.

Note that any change that makes borrowing more attractive draws in safer borrowers, which increases repayment rates. Ghatak's model predicts that repayment rates decrease with the degree of joint liability, as higher joint liability makes borrowing a less attractive option for safer borrowers. Also, their payment predictions of the extended version of the model developed by Ahlin and Townsend (2007) are as follows: first, if borrowers cannot screen other borrowers, the matching process in groups is random; this makes borrowing less attractive to safer borrowers since their projects succeed more often. Second, a higher loan size makes borrowing more attractive relative to the outside option; this attracts a greater number of safer borrowers and, in turn, increases repayment rates. However, the authors note that a higher loan size decreases repayment rates. This fact is explained by the fact that, under diminishing returns to capital, the borrower's marginal product is low; and observing a large loan implies that the borrower's cost of capital is even lower than her marginal product. Since the cost of capital declines with risk, as the loan size increases the pool of borrowers becomes riskier which, in turn, reduces repayment rates. And third, a higher correlation of project returns results in higher group repayment rates. In particular, higher correlation means that if a borrower is successful, her partners are more likely to be successful; this makes borrowing more attractive compared to the outside option, and safer borrowers are drawn into the market.

JOINT LIABILITY LOANS

Group lending arrangements delegate the task of monitoring to the borrowers themselves rather than to an outside monitor. One obvious potential advantage of this approach that has been frequently mentioned in the literature is that borrowers may be more effective monitors because they belong to the same social networks and may already interact in other economic exchange relationships. But joint liability loans may offer advantages that go beyond this effect.

In a peer-monitored loan, each member of the group must be given incentives to act both as a borrower and as a delegated monitor choosing the optimum intensity c at which to monitor and/or otherwise attempt to control the actions of other members in the group. Since neither activity is observable to an outside lender, the structure of the problem is that of a multi-task principal-multi-agent problem.

Just as the outside intermediary monitor could not, group members cannot observe each other's diligence level in production directly. Nor need we assume that monitoring intensities are directly observed. Borrowers only infer what the other borrower's production and monitoring actions are likely to be from the known terms of the contract, and they choose their actions accordingly.

One might well imagine, especially in the context of small, tight-knit communities that peer-monitoring operates through somewhat different channels than monitoring by an outsider. For example, a borrower might be less likely to divert funds to private purposes because he would feel guiltier or be more likely to face costly social retaliation for cheating on a friend or community member that he would for cheating on a bank clerk or hired intermediary to whom he owes no particular allegiance. This fact would especially be the case when that friend or community member has demonstrated a willingness to bear liability for the borrower's failures and has spent time and energy on the group project. On the other hand, collusion also seems more likely to occur amongst borrowers.

The capacity of the poor to borrow and save may not be so obvious, yet one thing that can be least disputed is that their need to borrow and save may be greater than for better off people. This fact is because their incomes are tight and even volatile. Given the volatility of incomes, it would be very useful to have financial institutions that can help the poor manage their finances in a way that they can save when for example they receive remittances or have sold some farm product or whenever they receive any extra money.

On the other hand, they would also borrow when there has been a shock in the household or just for consumption smoothing. Such a financial institution would be a matter of survival for poor households. Although they seem opposites, saving and borrowing could help the poor cope with the volatility in their incomes and maintain more stable consumption habits (Roodman & Qureshi, 2006). This fact implies that there is already the opportunity to serve the poor with financial services since in principle they need the service; yet availing these services to the poor has been quite a challenge for formal financial institutions. Roodman and Qureshi (2006) observe that the genius of microfinance is the ability to find a suite of techniques that solve the complex business problems of building loan volumes, maintaining high repayment, retaining customers and minimizing the scope for fraud while dealing with very poor borrowers.

Policies on Compulsory Savings and Training

In this section, the effect on repayment of two practices that can be used with joint liability lending to ensure timely repayment is analyzed. In particular, in light of the joint liability models presented above, I examine the effect of using compulsory savings to secure loans; and the effect of providing training to borrowers to enhance the project's probability of success are examined.

Compulsory Savings Component

Assume the lender requires borrowers to accumulate savings before borrowing or during borrowing, and that savings are used to secure loans. In the Stiglitz model, introducing a compulsory savings component decreases the payoff of safe and risky projects, but the reduction in the payoff of risky projects is larger than the reduction in the payoff of safe projects. This fact is explained by the fact that choosing the risky project implies defaulting on the loan more often; and, therefore, losing the accumulated savings that are used to secure the loan. Consequently, using a compulsory savings scheme promotes the choice of safe projects; which in turn results in higher repayment rates.

Similarly, Banerjee et al. (1994) posited that a compulsory savings scheme increases the incentives to choose safer projects. In this model, the minimum penalty needed to enforce a project with a probability of success decreases by requiring the borrower to accumulate savings. This fact is because if the project fails, the borrower loses her accumulated savings. A decrease in the size of the additional penalty needed to lower cost reduces the cost of monitoring without affecting the benefit. Hence, using a compulsory savings component increase the incentives of the borrower for performing well which results in choosing more often safer projects.

In the strategic default model of Besley and Coate (1995), requiring borrowers to accumulate savings is similar to increasing official and unofficial penalties. First, official penalties increase as the borrower consequentially loses her savings in case of default. Likewise, unofficial penalties increase as the desire to repay the borrower's partner increases for the same reason. In both cases, the cost of default increases, while the cost of repayment remains constant. Hence, repayment rates increase when the lender uses a compulsory savings component.

Training Component

Next, assume the lender requires borrowers to undergo training on basic financial concepts that may be useful to cope with the managerial aspects of their projects. This educational component may help borrowers to increase their loan productivity. In this way, the effect on repayment of including a training component into the models of joint liability is similar to the effect of borrower productivity analyzed by Ahlin and Townsend (2002). The authors show that the four models predict that repayment rates increase with borrower productivity; thus, including a training component may increase repayment rates. In particular, in Stiglitz (1990) and Banerjee et al. (1994), the result is explained by the fact that higher borrower productivity increases the payoff of safe projects relative to risky projects. Thus, training may encourage the choice of safer projects. In the model by Besley and Coate (1995), the effect of training on repayment can be explained by the fact that both official and unofficial penalties are increasing on the projected return; hence, a training component increases the cost of default and does not affect the cost of repayment.

This fact, in turn, results in higher repayment rates. Finally, in the Ghatak model, higher productivity makes the borrowing option more attractive compared to the outside option; this draws safer borrowers into the market and, consequently, results in higher repayment rates.

RELATIONSHIP BETWEEN JOINT LIABILITY LENDING AND POVERTY REDUCTION

Most studies that have examined the impacts of group lending on poverty have employed loan repayment as a proxy for poverty reduction, and they show mixed results. For instance, Gomez and Santor (2003), using data from two Canadian microfinance institutions found evidence that group lending lowered borrower default compared to individual lending and that group lending effects operated through self-selection into lending groups and once inside the group, greater group borrower effort. Karlan (2003) used data from FINCA-Peru and discovered that group lending engendered higher loan repayment and higher savings. Data collected from another group credit program, FINCA- Costa Rica, showed that groups that screened their members and relied on local information had higher repayments rates than those who did not (Wenner, 1995). Mckernan (2002) also found that being a member of Grameen increased self-employment profits by about 126% after controlling for the direct benefits of access to loans. This increment was attributed to the increased social and human capital derived from group meetings. Finally, it is envisaged that group lending increases the efficiency of delivery of financial services to the poor and reduce transaction costs of microfinance institutions which, hopefully, might translate into lower cost of borrowing for service users.

Other studies such as Ahlin and Townsend (2007) and Wydick (1999) have examined how social ties affect group lending and the effect of group lending on repayment rates. Ahlin and Townsend (2007), employed survey data from joint liability groups of the Bank for Agriculture and Agricultural Cooperatives (BAAC) in Thailand and found the issue of screening during group formation as the most important and had a positive impact on repayments among the wealthier clients. Stronger social ties among the poorer clients reduced repayments. However, in a limited contract enforcement environment, such as in a village, sanctions tended to increase repayment. Wydick's (1999) study in Guatemala indicated no significant effect of social ties on group behavior. Group members tended to function best as peer monitors. The author stated that social ties were likely to create a conflict of interest for groups, making threats of ejection from the group more difficult.

Interestingly, the rural/urban divide appeared to enforce in groups through different means: urban groups mainly through intensive peer monitoring and for groups in rural communities social pressure, that is, threats of expulsion from the group. The next section is empirical evidence of the impact of Joint Liability Lending on poverty reduction by using repayment, savings and level of income as a proxy for entrepreneurial development and poverty reduction. The table below shows the amount borrowed, repayment period and the percentage of repayment.

From the statistics in the cross tabulation, it was realized that the repayment period of the group loans between GHS 1,000.00 and GHS 6,000.00 are generally spread between 6 to 18 months. This fact depends on the characteristics of the group accessing such loans. Where the primary collateral which is the savings of the customer of the group is the only guarantee it was demanded that the loan facility is paid within six months; such was the case for all loans in the value of GHS 3,000.00. Loans that attract repayment beyond one year are mostly those that exceed GHS 10,000 to as much as GHS 25,000.000.

Table 1. Loan amount and repayment

The Amount Borrowed per Group (GHS)	Loan Repayment Period			Total	% Repayment
	6 Months	1 Year	18 Months		
3000	4	0	0	4	85
4000	12	24	1	37	100
6000	5	13	11	29	100
10000	0	1	19	20	100
15000	0	0	16	16	98
20000	0	0	17	17	100
25000 +	0	0	18	18	100
Total	21	38	82	141	

Source: Author

However, the majority of the customers are those who took loans not exceeding GHS6, 000.00. This fact may be due to the size of their business, lack of appropriate or commensurate collateral to enable them to access larger amounts. The small size of this loans again attests to the fact that microfinance concept was meant for the poor who according to Harper (2005) are helped to access cheap credit loans with the savings of the member. The amount of loan and the repayment period therefore strongly correlated and confirm literature that microfinance provides short term funds to the poor to gradually help to empower them economically to improve their livelihood. The percentage of repayment indicates the greater benefit of joint liability lending. Almost all groups paid over 95% of the gross amount borrowed was paid within the stipulated period except the group who borrowed GHS3,000.00

Savings Habit of Clients Before and After Microfinance

The figure below shows the savings habit of clients before and after sourcing funds from a microfinance institution. These individuals are members of the joint liability groups and were interviewed separately. According to the figure, 60 percent of the respondents explained that they had managed to earn a small amount of money and open saving account in the MB microfinance, after joining while 20.4 percent of them saved in the bank. The rest 19.6 percent did not have a savings account at all. However, before joining MB, only 18 percent of them had a saving account with a bank, and the rest did not have their own savings account.

This fact indicates that the number of clients that have been able to save has increased after joining MB microfinance.

As per the MB member of joint liability, a majority of the respondents indicated they had savings account in the MB but were not aware of the amounts they had and the applicable interest rates. In some cases, the clients withdrew all or some amount of their savings, and then they would start all over again to save. The respondents explained that they had a very small amount of money on hand before joining MB which they were ashamed to lodge at the bank. This fact according to the group members did not have the time to go to the bank before becoming members of the MB. They reiterated that it became possible for them to save because the MB had agents who came round to collect their daily/weekly savings.

Figure 1.

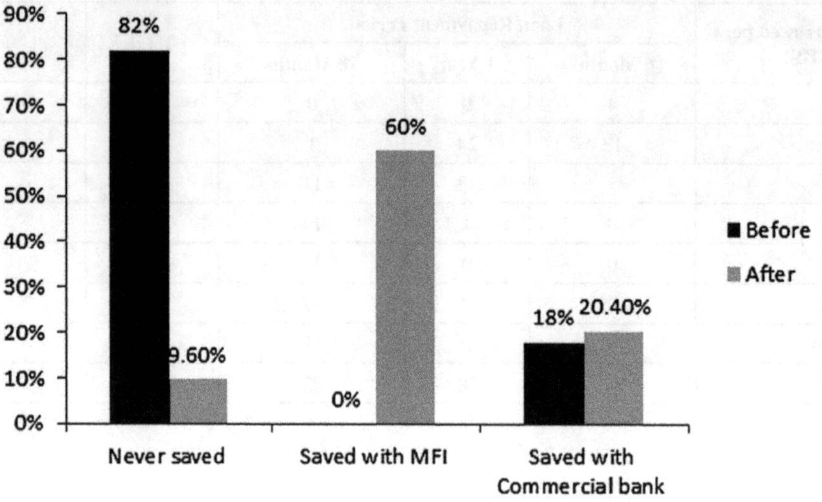

Income Levels Before and After Microfinance

The Table below shows that after joining MB, 20 percent of the respondents have acquired income up to GHS 100, while 26 percent have earned between GHS 101-150. The percentage of respondents that earned between GHS 151 and 200 was 27.6 percent. Those who earned between GHS 201 and 300 were 13.2 percent, leaving the remaining 7.6 percent to those earning GHS 300 and above per month. There were others, however, who did not see any increase in their levels of income.

Comparing the two levels of income indicate that some of the clients had managed to increase their incomes after they joined the MB although the levels of change were not so significant. Given the average levels of income in the Ghanaian household as GH 1,217.00 based on the fifth round of the Ghana Living Standard Survey in 2008, it can be concluded that the MB was able to raise the income of about 35 percent of the borrowers to the average, and push about 20 percent above the national average.

Table 2. Income levels before and after microfinance

Level of Income (GHS)	Before		After	
	Frequency	Percent	Frequency	Percent
300 - 500	98	39.2	19	7.6
550 - 1000	72	28.8	50	20
1001 -1500	40	16	65	26
1051 - 2000	26	10.4	69	27.6
2001 - 3000	9	3.6	28	11.2
3000 +	5	2	19	7.6
Total	**250**	**100**	**250**	**100**

Source: Author

Peer Support in Joint Liability Lending

When peer pressure and sanctions have been applied and have failed to result in repayment, other members in the group have to make good the default. This fact should logically have been the last or fourth stage of the model. Simtowe and Zeller (2006) call this the problem of limited liability. It can, however, be argued that joint liability is not just a stage in the group lending scheme, but underlies the entire process of group lending (Ghatak and Guinanne, 1999). Service users have joint liability in mind when they organize themselves into groups. It is the idea that all members of a group are jointly liable for any loan default that compels peers to monitor and apply pressure and sanctions to ensure repayment.

Although joint liability is perceived as the basis of group lending, it is not enforced in some microfinance interventions. Jain (1996) observed in the Grameen Bank that even though there were much discussion and emphasis on the concept of joint liability, it was the individual defaulter who was pursued. Other members of the group did not have to suffer jointly for the non-payment of the loan by the individual. The Grameen Bank as a whole has evolved: Grameen Classic System has evolved into the Grameen Generalized Scheme or Grameen Bank II, which has essentially abolished joint liability (Reggiani, 2005). Even though the new Grameen claims to have abolished the joint liability scheme, it has instituted the system of rewards for branches that achieve 100% repayment rates among others. This reward scheme is likely to compel Grameen staff and/or groups to surreptitiously force recalcitrant service users to pay up or help them to repay.

Joint liability is not without risk to service users. For example, when microfinance institutions decide to form groups without recourse to self-selection and also insist on a joint liability, it is likely to create a problem for service users. For instance, what will happen to the issue of joint liability when the level of heterogeneity about risk and socio-economic status is high? Few studies have been found that have comprehensively examined the effects of group formation and joint liability on service users.

POSITIVE AND NEGATIVE CONTRIBUTIONS

Joint Liability Lending: Positive Contributions

Joint liability lending contracts effectively make a borrower's neighbors' co-signers to loans, mitigating problems created by informational asymmetries such as adverse selection, moral hazard, and enforcement. Thus, in group-lending programs, the functions of screening, monitoring and enforcing repayments are to a large extent transferred from the bank agent to group members.

1. **Mitigation of Adverse Selection Problems:** One of the advantages of joint liability lending is the mitigation of adverse selection problem, which in turn reduces the problem of credit rationing and brings the safe borrowers back to the credit market. The process of group formation group members is expected to screen each other. Theoretical and empirical studies show that people try to investigate each other's behavioral integrity and creditworthiness with the help of existing social networks before they allow others to join their group. Through peer screening, they try to prevent irresponsible and credit risk individuals from joining their group.
2. **Mitigation of Moral Hazard Problems:** Another advantage of group-based lending is the mitigation of the moral hazard problem. This fact is an incentive rather than a selection problem. After

members have received a loan, they have to monitor each other to make sure that every member has invested the loan in a safe project, which will guarantee repayment. Members make use of their social ties to acquire the necessary information and create social sanctions and pressure on non-performing members.

This is a costly activity for the members, as they have to spend time and energy monitoring each other. However, the creditor can now afford to lower the interest rate, which will offset to some extent the burden of these costs for the borrowers. Also, the microfinance institute can lower the interest rate as its monitoring costs have been shifted to members, and the probability of repayment of its loans has increased.

3. **Mitigation of Costly State Verification:** The joint liability lending contract also provides appropriate incentives to avoid the problem of costly state verification. This is sometimes called ex-post moral hazard. It occurs once actions or efforts have been undertaken and returns of the product activity have been realized. Yet, the lender cannot observe the yield from the project. The borrower might find it optimal to divert funds for repayment of the loan to other purposes and default. In group-based lending, schemes group members live close to each other, and they are well informed of each other's economic activities. Therefore, they face a lower cost of verifying each other's output as compared to a distant lender. Moreover, each member has the incentive to audit his partner.
4. **Peer Pressure:** Peer pressure is a mechanism group member used in the process of mitigating moral hazard and enforcing punctual repayment. To secure future access, members are obliged to monitor each other. Once the output is realized, and a member proves unwilling to repay, other members can use peer pressure and social sanctions to make him repay.

In most cases, groups are formed from communities with many social connections and a lot of interdependence. Individual community members follow and respect shared social values and norms such as mutual assistance, managing communal properties, etc., and this social system constitutes a powerful device to reinforce repayment among group members. In such communities, if a borrower fails or refuses to repay his share, other community members may turn to social penalties such as warning and hassling, telling the rest of the community that he refuses to repay or complaining to community chieftains (i.e., traditional legal action). This fact could damage the bad borrower's reputation, and it might isolate him socially. Thus, the ability of groups to harness social sanctions and make use of such sanctions in inducing members to repay their shares can be an important mechanism to sustain groups and improve repayment performance of programs.

5. **Minimum Transaction Costs:** Providing loans to small individual borrowers who live in geographically dispersed areas and work in relatively risky economic environments leads to high loan transaction costs for the lender. Distributing loans through groups of borrowers is assumed to result in lower transaction costs for both the lender and the individual borrowers. The lender's costs are minimized, as he is dealing with the group as a whole, rather than with individuals within a group. At the same time, since the group is responsible for distributing loans and collecting repayments the costs to individual borrowers are also reduced. There is an inverse correlation between the size of the group and groups transaction costs. On the one hand, the transaction costs are fixed costs and the larger the group, the lower the cost to individual members.

On the other hand, group size cannot be increased beyond a certain level without negatively influencing group efficiency in monitoring, screening and enforcing. When the group is small, the time and effort spent by each member of the group on monitoring are manageable, but with the increase in size the monitoring effort may end up being demanding, and the situation may lead to free riding by some members. Hence, there is a tradeoff between the reduction of group transaction cost and effectiveness of peer monitoring, which has to be taken into account

Joint Liability Lending: Limitations

This section will discuss group-based lending limitations and shortcomings.

Domino effect. In group-based lending programs, the possibility of collision of all members not to repay cannot be ruled out. The very assumption of joint liability might make the decision for or against loan repayment a strategic one that is taken by all borrowers. Apparently, a group member will not be prepared to repay his loan if he expects other members to default because if this happens, he will be denied access to additional credit or his share in making payments for others increases. This fact is also called the domino effect, which may take place when defaulting borrowers inflict negative externalities on good borrowers, inducing others not to repay whereas they might have repaid in case of individual lending.

Recording the experience of borrowers from Zimbabwe, Bratton (1986) stated that during a good agricultural season farmers show higher repayment performance. However, when farmers are unable to meet their expected production, potentially creditworthy borrowers might expect some members of their group to default. This fact may lead them to decide to default, which leads to a dramatic rise in the default rate. Paxton, Graham, and Thraen (2000) found that the domino effect was a strong and significant determinant of group loan-repayment in her study of Burkina Faso's group-based lending program.

Joint liability is not optimal. In group-based lending, the joint liability contract is seen as the main driving force for members to actively monitor and reinforce repayment. Denying future loans as a punishment is a deadweight loss to a borrower when this borrower has enough output to pay for himself but not for his defaulting members. Rai and Sjöström (2004) therefore argue that the joint liability mechanism is not optimal and has to be augmented by cross-reporting. Through cross-reporting, the successful borrower may be induced to help to repay the loans of unsuccessful borrowers when he can minimize this loss. Rai and Sjöström (2004) observed that in the weekly borrowers' meetings of the Grameen Bank borrowers implicitly used cross-reporting in enforcing successful members to pay for the unsuccessful ones. Based on their observations they argue that the conditions under which joint liability is optimal are narrow and unlikely to hold in practice and they claim that joint liability will not be enough to induce borrowers to help each other efficiently.

Limitations of social collateral. As is mentioned before, one of the key problems that led to group-based lending is the poor or lack of any sizeable physical assets that can be used as collateral in enforcing repayment.

Therefore, joint liability lending programs rely on credit denial and social sanctions in enforcing repayment and these alternatives are often grouped and termed social collateral. But it is difficult for the bank to lend effectively on social collateral, as the lender does not have a very good idea of what the value of social collateral is to the borrower. For instance, access to future credit is not a traded good, so it does not have a market value. The lender must try and appraise the value the borrower attaches to access to future credit. This value may be significant, but it may also be zero if the borrower knows he can raise funds from other sources if extra credit is not expected in the future.

Group size and free riding. The extent to which group-based lending can minimize the asymmetry of information problem depends among other things on the optimal group size. Certain programs using VB models in Latin American and West African countries use larger group sizes to the detriment of their efficiency (Kapkiyai et al., 2015). In certain Burkina Faso programs, MkNelly and Kevane (2002) observed that large-sized groups usually face free-riding problems, where some group members hide behind the large group to dodge monitoring and other responsibilities. Therefore, the existence of large groups can lead to imperfect information and moral hazard, and it can make group solidarity an impractical mechanism.

Matching problems between demand and supply. Another negative influence on repayment occurs when the credit terms and conditions are no longer appropriate for each member, creating an inherent "matching problem" as group-based lending is repeated over time (Paxton et al., 2000). At the beginning of a lending program, borrowers may be able to find group members with the same demand for loans and a similar supply, but the probability of the same group desiring consecutive loans with similar loan amounts diminishes over time. Thus, harmonizing supply and demand for credit among group members becomes more and more challenging over time and may result in defaulting if one or more members are no longer satisfied. This matching problem may occur when different members have received different amounts of loans, and those who wished to get a smaller amount of loans may lose the incentive to cover for their defaulting co-members, especially when the defaulting members have obtained larger amounts of money. Therefore, in some lending programs, the loan terms are restricted by what the group feels it can guarantee jointly, so clients with growing businesses as compared to their peers may find that the group contract impedes their activities.

FUTURE RESEARCH

The empirical and conceptual discussion has focused on the effect of joint liability lending on poverty reduction. Given the underdeveloped state of the empirical literature, I do not claim that joint-liability lending is the most important feature of successful micro-lenders such as the Grameen Bank. There is clear evidence that joint-liability improves repayment, but these institutions use other instruments as well, and no study yet tries to apportion the reasons for success. Whether the Grameen Bank and similar joint-liability programs will ever be completely self-sustaining is not clear, as Morduch argues in this issue. In cases of the impact of joint liability, a regional analysis could be employed instead of just a microfinance institution.

CONCLUSION

This chapter provides a review of the literature on joint liability lending and empirical analysis of the effect of the loan facility. The central issue in such credit markets is twofold: the lender does not know much about the borrower asymmetric information, and effective, commonly used contractual arrangements for contending with asymmetric information do not work because the borrowers are too poor for the lender to use financial sanctions to achieve repayment of loans. It was shown that joint liability could achieve better screening to contend with adverse selection, encourages peer monitoring to reduce moral hazard, gives group members incentives to enforce the repayment of loans, and reduces the lender's audit costs for cases where some group members claim not to be able to repay. The empirical analysis suggests that the joint liability payment of the group leader lowers the days of late repayment while the joint liability payment of the rest of the group members has no predictive power on repayment.

This chapter may have important policy implications for product design in microfinance. In particular, when implementing microcredit programs in certain social environments and/or contexts, MFIs need to consider the social collateral that their clients can pledge. One policy message based on the analysis may be that using joint liability group lending may work better in rural areas than in urban ones. More generally, it may be important for loan officers in a microfinance program to be informed about the social embeddedness of group borrowers in the community in which they reside. The loan policy of the bank must be customer oriented. It must take into consideration the needs and the aspiration of the customers to come out with a loan product that will be beneficial to the customer to enhance repayment. Policymakers' need to implement a comprehensive legal framework to govern and regulate the activities of both MFIs and borrowers

All of the above suggestions may be taken into account and can be incorporated into future elaborations of our model. This fact will enable us to explore further the role social capital plays in determining the screening, monitoring and enforcement behavior of group members and to what extent it has an impact on the repayment performance of borrowing groups. Another important and potentially fruitful future research avenue would be to test the outcomes of our model empirically. This involves collecting detailed information about the nature of social ties borrowers have with group members as well as with other members of the community in which they live.

REFERENCES

Abbink, K., Irlenbusch, B., & Renner, E. (2006). Group Size and Social Ties in Microfinance Institutions. *Economic Inquiry*, *44*(4), 614–628. doi:10.1093/ei/cbl001

Ahlin, C. R., & Townsend, R. M. (2002). *Using repayment data to test across models of joint liability lending*. Working Paper No. 02-W27, Department of Economics, Vanderbilt University.

Ahlin, C. R., & Townsend, R. M. (2007). Using Repayment Data to Test across Models of Joint Liability Lending. *Economic Journal (London)*, *117*(517), F11–F51. doi:10.1111/j.1468-0297.2007.02014.x

Armendariz de Aghion, B., & Gollier, C. (2000). Peer Group Formation in an Adverse Selection Model. *Economic Journal (London)*, *110*(465), 632–643. doi:10.1111/1468-0297.00557

Banerjee, A. V., Timothy, B., & Timothy, W. G. (1994). The neighbor's keeper: Design of a credit cooperative with theory and a test. *The Quarterly Journal of Economics*, *102*(9), 491–515. doi:10.2307/2118471

Besley, T., & Coate, S. (1995). Group lending, repayment incentives, and social collateral. *Journal of Development Economics*, *46*(1), 1–18. doi:10.1016/0304-3878(94)00045-E

Ghatak, M. (1999). Group Lending, Local Information, and Peer Selection. *Journal of Development Economics*, *60*(1), 27–50. doi:10.1016/S0304-3878(99)00035-8

Ghatak, M., & Guinnane, T. W. (1999). The economics of lending with joint liability: Theory and practice. *Journal of Development Economics*, *60*(1), 195–228. doi:10.1016/S0304-3878(99)00041-3

Gomez, R., & Santor, R. (2003). *Do peer group members outperform individual borrowers? A test of peer group lending using Canadian micro-credit data.* Bank of Canada Working Paper, No. 33.

Harper, M., & Vogel, R. (2005). The Role of Savings as a form of MFI Funding: Debate. *MicroBanking Bulletin, 11*, 5–9.

Jain, P. S. I. (1996). Managing Credit for the Rural Poor: Lessons from the Grameen Bank. *World Development, 24*(1), 79–89. doi:10.1016/0305-750X(95)00116-T

Kapkiyai, C., Kimitei, E., Mutwol, P., & Kimaiyo, I. K. (2015). Effects of Group Lending on Accessibility of Micro Credit Facilities among Low-Income Households in Keiyo South District. *European Journal of Business and Management, 7*(3), 39–46.

Karlan, D. S. (2001). *Social Capital and Group Banking.* Boston: Boston University, Department of Economics.

Karlan, D. S. (2003). *Social Capital and Group Banking. Mimeo.* Princeton, NJ: Princeton University.

Kiiru, M. J., & Kenia, M. (2007). *The Impact of Microfinance on Rural Poor Households' Income and Vulnerability to Poverty: Case Study of Makueni District, Kenya.* Bonn, Germany: University of Bonn.

McKernan, S. (2002). The Impact of Microcredit Programs on Self-Employment Profits: Do Noncredit Program Aspects Matter? *The Review of Economics and Statistics, 84*(1), 93–115. doi:10.1162/003465302317331946

McNelly, B., & Kevane, M. (2002). Improving Design and Performance of Group Lending: Suggestions from Burkina Faso. *World Development, 30*(11), 2017–2032. doi:10.1016/S0305-750X(02)00119-5

Morduch, J. (2008). *How can the poor afford microfinance? Financial Access Initiative. Wagner Graduate School*, New York University.

Paxton, J., Graham, D., & Thraen, C. (2000). Modeling group loan repayment behavior: New insights from Burkina Faso. *Economic Development and Cultural Change, 48*(3), 639–655. doi:10.1086/452613

Pitt, M. M., & Khandker, S. R. (1998). The Impact of Group-Based Credit on Poor Households in Bangladesh: Does the Gender of Participants Matter? *Journal of Political Economy, 106*(5), 958–996. doi:10.1086/250037

Rai, A. S., & Sjöström, T. (2004). Is Grameen lending efficient? Repayment incentives and insurance in village economies. *The Review of Economic Studies, 71*(1), 217–234. doi:10.1111/0034-6527.00282

Reggiani, T. (2005). *Grameen Bank II: a possible analysis with a relational perspective. MPRA (Munich Personal RePec Archive) Paper, 1526.* Munich, Germany: University Library of Munich.

Roodman, D., & Qureshi, U. (2006). *Microfinance as Business.* Washington, DC: Center for Global Development.

Schreiner, M. (2003). A cost-effectiveness analysis of the Grameen Bank of Bangladesh. *Development Policy Review, 21*(3), 357–382. doi:10.1111/1467-7679.00215

Sharma, S. (2006, August). Are micro-finance institutions exploiting the poor? *InfoChange News & Features*.

Simtowe, F., & Zeller, M. (2006). *Determinants of Moral Hazards in Microfinance: Empirical Evidence from Joint Liability Lending Programs in Malawi. MPRA (Munich Personal RePec Archive) Paper, 461*. Munich, Germany: University Library of Munich.

Stiglitz, J. E. (1990). Peer Monitoring and Credit Markets. *The World Bank Economic Review*, *4*(3), 197–203. doi:10.1093/wber/4.3.351

Varian, H. (1990). Monitoring agents with other agents. *Journal of Institutional and Theoretical Economics*, *146*, 155–174.

Wenner, M. D. (1995). Group Credit: A Means to Improve Transfer and Loan Repayment Performance. *The Journal of Development Studies*, *32*(2), 263–281. doi:10.1080/00220389508422414

Wydick, B. (1999). Can Social Cohesion Be Harnessed to Repair Market Failures? Evidence from Group Lending in Guatemala. *Economic Journal (London)*, *109*(457), 463–475. doi:10.1111/1468-0297.00457

KEY TERMS AND DEFINITIONS

Adverse Selection: It is a risk exposure that exists before the money is lent to group members. It occurs when bad credit risks become more probable to acquire loans than good credit risks. Because of information asymmetry, lenders tend to have a hard time differentiating between good credit risks and bad credit risks. As a result, lenders end up with a loan portfolio comprising almost entirely of bad credit risks.

Informal Economies: It is the part of an economy that is neither taxed nor monitored by any form of government. The informal economy is the diversified set of economic activities, enterprises, jobs, and workers that are not regulated or protected by the state. The concept originally applied to self-employment in small unregistered enterprises. It has been expanded to include wage employment in unprotected jobs.

Joint Liability: It is microfinance lending methodology where a group of individuals is all responsible for each other's loans if one member defaults. Group liability may improve repayment rates, but it also raises the possibility that bad clients will take advantage of good clients in their liability group.

Microenterprise: It is a business operating on a very small scale, especially one in the developing world that is supported by microcredit.

Microfinance: It is a source of financial services for entrepreneurs and small businesses lacking access to banking and related services. The two main mechanisms for the delivery of financial services to such clients are (1) relationship-based banking for individual entrepreneurs and small businesses; and (2) group-based models, where several entrepreneurs come together to apply for loans and other services as a group. In some regions, for example, Africa, microfinance is used to describing the supply of financial services to low-income employees, which is closer to the retail finance model prevalent in mainstream banking.

Moral Hazard: Moral hazard occurs after the money has been disbursed to the borrower and it arises out of the fact that the borrower may have an incentive to breach the loan covenants by investing in "immoral projects" which are unacceptable in the eyes of the borrower because inasmuch as they have a high possibility of gain to the borrower, they also have a high possibility of failure which will have the most detrimental effect on the lender. Information asymmetry causes moral hazard because of the lender's lack of knowledge about the borrower's activities.

Transaction Cost: It is a cost incurred in making an economic exchange. The economic exchange here represents the given out of loan facility to the group members and the group members paying back the facility.

Chapter 13
Going Beyond GDP:
The Role of Social Innovation in Building a Welfare State

Seyithan Ahmet Ates
Ankara University of Social Sciences, Turkey

Muradiye Ateş
Konya Necmettin Erbakan University, Turkey

Murat Ali Yülek
Istanbul Commerce University, Turkey

ABSTRACT

A redirection towards wellbeing with a view to produce lasting social and economic vitality for the global civilization necessitates moving from conventional economic methods towards innovative solutions, which are necessary to face challenges of today and the future to foster sustainable growth. Social innovation and its agents can be considered as a toolbox which may facilitate a transition by positively influencing wellbeing, developing ways of integrating it into policy, and promoting it as an alternative measure of progress. Social innovation may increase the role of civil society in solving social problems, while sustaining and improving people's wellbeing beyond increasing their welfare in monetary term. By providing up-to-date solutions to challenges ranging from global warming to fair income distribution, and from social innovative entrepreneurs to grass-rooted innovation, social innovation seems to be capable of transforming the society in a way to tackle with a new kind of societal problems, and of exploring new ways to create added value for the economy.

DOI: 10.4018/978-1-5225-8939-6.ch013

INTRODUCTION[1]

A growing number of economists are realizing that simple economic activity measured by the GDP is, alone, not enough to represent the well-being of citizens. In recent years, some scholars and some politicians have embarked on efforts to conceptualize and theorize new economic paradigms. Former president of the European Commission, Manuel Barroso, once featured that "*Despite being an invaluable tool for economic policy, Gross Domestic Product (GDP) is unfit to reflect many of today's challenges, such as climate change, public health, and the environment. We cannot face the challenges of the future with the tools of the past*" (European Parliament, 2009, p.24)). Innovative solutions are necessary to face the challenges of the future and foster sustainable growth. Measuring a prosperous society as a whole is more complex and necessitates considering several other elements besides robust GDP growth, such as peace and happiness, economic and financial well-being, and individual freedoms and liberties (Urama & Acheampong, 2013). A redirection towards sustainability and well-being, which produces lasting social and economic vitality for global civilization as a whole may be the most viable option for further development (Rogers et al., 2012)(Fullerton, 2015).

There are numerous economic, social and technical developments which led governments and societies to seek new approaches to overcome related contemporary challenges and provide sustainable well-being. Shifting focus of economies to a greener form of production, engagement of cities throughout the world in the promotion and pursuit of mitigating climate activities, growing attention on ecological developments are some of the illustrative cases of big shifts.

We argue that social innovation is capable of providing new means to overcome today's challenging problems, ranging from zero-carbon housing to fair economic system by providing social capital needed for the improvement of the human well-being and social progress. In this process, social innovation is expected to change beliefs, basic practices, resources and social power structures profoundly by providing a unique opportunity to step back from a narrow way of thinking about social enterprises, business engagement, and philanthropy and to recognize instead the interconnectedness of various factors and stakeholders (Urama & Acheampong, 2013).

The main objective of this chapter is to highlight the shifting dynamics by elaborating the drivers of the change and shedding light on the potential role of social innovations praxis in improving the welfare of the people. After the introduction, the second section of the chapter addresses the beyond GDP approach from various aspects with a particular focus on the "new economy" discussion. In the third section, by following conceptual heuristic, foundational drivers of new economic paradigms, namely exogenous developments, socio-technical transformation, socio-ecological transformation, economic crisis and the shifting the role of government and society are elaborated as the drivers of the "new economy." In the fourth section, we analyze the role of social innovation from various aspects as a facilitator in building the welfare state. Possible contributions of social innovations have been highlighted in four illustrative cases. In this context, the role of social innovation is investigated in four categories including creating a fair economic system, facilitating the social transition, providing sustainable added value, empowering the community to adapt itself to socio-ecological transition and building a "competitive advantage" in the applied country.

BEYOND GDP: THE NEED FOR A NEW ECONOMIC PARADIGM

In the face of massive advancement in technological and scientific areas, we are witnessing today rapid paradigm change, extensive structural transformation and a dimensional shift in many fields including human being-technology, human being-environment, and human being-material prosperity relationships. As a result of various symptoms relating to this shift, a growing number of scholars and politicians started recently envisaging contemporary approaches to the so-called "state-of-the-art challenges" including resource shortages, demographic realities, and planetary boundaries. In this respect, content, and motivation for economic development has been one of the subjects of intensive discussions. The Beyond GDP measurement agenda will continue to play a critical role in helping us to overcome these challenges (Stiglitz, 2018)

The most distinctive feature of modern economic growth has been the combination of a high rate of aggregate growth with disrupting effects and new problems (Kuznets, 1973). Conventional economic growth theories focus on the development of per capita income, output or productivity levels over time (Hobijn & Franses, 2001). As a result of this common development approach, the drive for material economic wealth has resulted in resource capture by some groups to the exclusion of others, leading to inequalities in not only monetary wealth but also in health, education and basic freedoms (Rogers et al., 2012). Many leading economists, among others (Stiglitz, Sen, & Fitoussi, 2010; Costanza et al., 2004; Distaso, 2007; Dasgupta, 2008) echoed the view that the GDP is an indicator of economic market activity, and it was not intended to be an accurate measure of well-being.

Since the indicators we choose to define success become the things we strive for, it follows that if we measure the wrong inputs, we get the wrong outcomes (Hall, 2010). As a result of that, GDP growth became the dominant goal of policymakers. In line with this, Simon Kuznets' main objective was "to provide policymakers a theoretically robust empirical framework for measuring the economy in terms of production and income potential; to give the total economic value of all final goods and services produced in an economy in a stipulated time using market prices", as he introduced the GDP approach (S. S. Kuznets & Murphy, 1966).

Current calculation methodology and the perception of GDP are criticized mainly from three aspects (Fox, 2012):

- GDP is, even on its own terms, a faulty measure;
- It takes no account of sustainability or durability; and
- Progress and development can be better gauged with other metrics.

In the light of these reservations on GDP, a new economic development paradigm is expected to be more oriented towards social progress and the well-being of the people while considering the GDP growth as well. Useful measures of social progress and human well-being is expected to measure the degree to which society's goals (i.e., to sustainably provide basic human needs for food, shelter, freedom, participation, etc.) are met, rather than measures of the mere volume of marketed economic activity, which is only one means to that end (Costanza et al., 2009), as shown in Table 1.

A new development agenda, according to Nobel Prize-winning economist Joseph Stiglitz, must center around (Stiglitz, 2011);

Table 1. Milestones in the beyond-GDP discussions

Year	Actor	Event
1937	Simon Kuznets	GDP is born - original formulation of Gross Domestic Product in his report to the U.S. Congress, "National Income, 1929-35."
1944	Bretton Woods Conference	GDP becomes the standard tool for sizing up a country's economy
1959	Moses Abramovitz	One of the first to question whether GDP accurately measures a society's overall well-being
1972	Jigme Singye Wangchuck	King of Bhutan, Jigme Singye Wangchuck declares his aim is not to increase GDP, but GNH "Gross National Happiness."
1978	Irving B. Kravisand Robert Summers	Compile the first estimates of GDP per capita worldwide, with figures for more than 100 countries.
1990	United Nations	The United Nations launches the Human Development Index, which measures such factors as education, gender equality, and health. U.N. economist Mahbubul Haq convinces future Nobel laureate Amartya Sen to create "an index as vulgar as GDP, but more relevant to our own lives," as Sen remembers it.
1999	U.S. Commerce Department	Declares GDP "one of the great inventions of the 20th century."
2001	United States	The bursting of the tech bubble and the 9/11 attacks send the U.S. economy into a temporary tailspin. During the subsequent recovery, something unexpected happens: Although GDP rises between 2002 and 2006, personal incomes fall.
2006	China	China creates a new index for "green GDP" — a measure of national economic output that considers environmental factors.
2008	United States	The U.S. government begins funding the State of the USA project, designed to create a "key national indicator system" with hundreds of new data points to add nuance to standard GDP stats.
2009	France	The French government releases a report, co-authored by Nobel Prize-winning economist Joseph Stiglitz, calling for an end to "GDP fetishism."
2010	United Kingdom	British Prime Minister David Cameron's government announces that it will, for the first time, survey happiness in addition to other economic measures.
2014	European Union	Beyond GDP Conference
2015	Shanghai/China	Shanghai is the first major city or province in China, which discarded its official economic growth target for 2015. Instead of setting numerical targets for local GDP, in his annual work report mayor, Yang Xiong defines the maintenance of steady growth and structural optimization as economic goals
2016	Germany	A national dialogue group was set up with an aim to identify the issues that are most important for quality of life in the country. The chancellor, members of government and the ministers participated in 50 meetings.
2017	French	The French Government and the National Institute of Statistics and Economic Studies (INSEE) published the report on the new wealth indicators (Nouveaux Indicateurs de richesse). The indicators are also included in the progress report on the French economy.
2017	Africa	The African Union Commission (AUC), the United Nations Economic Commission for Africa (ECA), the African Development Bank (AfDB), and the United Nations Development Programme (UNDP), have jointly published the African Sustainability Report. The report covers all 54 African countries with variable data coverage, utilizing 241 indicators.
2018	Global movement	A small group of countries, initiated by Scotland, has formed the Wellbeing Economy Alliance -
2018	Australia	Australia has started to provide an annual overview of Australia's implementation of the Sustainable Development Goals (SDGs).
2018	Netherland	Statistics Netherlands (CBS), the Dutch government's statistical body, has published the first "Monitor of Well-being" report comprising 21 indicators of broad well-being (Brede Welvaart) trends (or BWTs).
2018	Belgium	The Belgian Federal Planning Bureau (BFP) has published the 2018 Report on Complementary Indicators to GDP, an annual publication showing the evolution of complementary indicators to GDP during 1990-2016.

Source: Compiled from Gertner (2010), Lelyveld (2015), Dickinson (2011) and various online resources.

- Identifying and explaining key characteristics of developing countries, and especially those that differentiate them from the more developed ones; and exploring the macro-economic implications, e.g., for growth and stability; and
- Describing the process of change, how institutions, including social and political institutions, and economic structures are altered in the process of development.

On the other hand, the term 'development,' in the ideal case, should involve economic as well as social and environmental progress. The well-being of the people should also be the main dimension of economic development. Well-being, in fact, is a multidimensional and context-specific term. However, it must be approached in a way that preserves cultural diversity and societal autonomy while meeting universal human needs (Rogers et al., 2012). Given that, 'development' is expected to address the complex relationships among various aspects of development, including population growth, economic growth, improvements in education and health, urbanization, and globalization (Soubbotina, 2004)(Soubbotina & Sheram, 2000)

In assessing development programs, one should consider the program's impacts on GDP, along with the impact on the environment, poverty, and democracy considering sustainability aspects (Stiglitz, 2011). For all these reasons, we need a smarter approach to development and well-being: one that addresses the underlying issues and root causes of inadequate human well-being, and solves these problems within the context of environmental limits which will obviously require a new focus and fundamental societal transition (Rogers et al., 2012). The question arises at this point is, whether there are appropriate tools to address those challenges and achieve a smooth transition. Social innovation and associated tools are capable of doing that by positively influencing wellbeing, developing ways of integrating it into policy, and promoting it as an alternative measure of progress (NEF, 2015). In the next paragraphs, we will elaborate the social innovation tools used to address the above mentioned contemporary challenges by giving relevant case examples from various countries.

DRIVERS FOR CHANGE

There are numerous developments, such as economic, social and technical ones, which led to governments and societies seeking new approaches to overcome related contemporary challenges and provide sustainable well-being. Shifting focus of economies to a greener form of production, engagement of cities throughout the world in the promotion and pursuit of mitigating climate activities, growing attention on ecological developments are some of the illustrative cases of big shifts. The core process for transitions is a shift in belief systems, ideologies and public opinion which not only influence consumer preferences and values, but also create credibility pressure on them, and add legitimacy for policymakers and civic societies to introduce new perspectives and alternatives (Geels, 2010). In this regard, Braudel & Mayne (1995) distinguish three phases in the transition to the conventional Welfare States:

1. The ideological phase (1815–1870), where social reformers drew attention to poverty-related problems and developed new ideas and vocabularies with words like industrialist, capitalist, exploitation, proletariat, the masses, and Socialism;
2. The phase of mobilization (1870–1914), where militant labor (trade unions, and new political parties) engaged in power struggles to further their interests,

3. The political/governmental phase (after World War I), where the State increasingly implemented new laws, programs and social measures.

However, it seems that the Welfare State Approach, as a result of so-called contemporary challenges and developments, has also entered a new era. After some shortcomings of political/governmental led by the Welfare State Approach, and the crisis of mixed economy systems in the final quarter of the 20th century, some European countries saw a reawakening of interest in social economy as new business alternatives to the models of the capitalist and public sectors, such as cooperatives and mutual societies, or non-market organizations – mostly associations and foundations (Monzón & Chaves, 2012).

It is argued by some European scholars that the "Welfare State" Approach should be re-examined and adjusted by addressing to the core question: which kind of welfare architecture will further Europe's stated goal of maximum social inclusion and justice, since the current era requires new approaches towards the aged society, profound changes in working life; the new risks and needs that arise in households and, especially, in child families; the challenges of creating gender equality and the sustaining the daily life quality while considering the planetary boundaries (Esping-Andersen, 2002). In line with that, an open letter to the European Commission underscored the importance of social enterprises in providing effective solution to sustain the wellbeing of the EU citizens by stating the need for rediscovering the core social elements of the European economic model, and argued that the EU needs to move beyond the conventional paradigm that sees private for-profit firms and public institutions as the only relevant actors and move towards a pluralist view that recognizes the varied roles that different forms of enterprise can play with respect to our collective social and economic goals in order to create a healthier competitive environment with firms that have different goals, strategies and behaviors, resulting in diversity of forms and functions, thus enhancing the capacity of the European society to evolve effective solutions to its challenges (Scholars, 2010).

There are various factors which are illustrative of the need for remodeling the Welfare State Approach and developing new tools to accomplish the wellbeing. One of the main drivers of this quest is the socio-ecological transition. New environmental problems, such as climate change, biodiversity, and resource depletion, are needed to be addressed fairly well with incremental clean technologies and require more substantive 'transitions' in the coming decades, i.e., major changes in energy, transport, and agri-food systems (Geels, 2010). According to Geels (2010), sustainability transitions may require a shift towards new approaches covering the catchwords as 'green', 'sustainable development', 'ecological footprint', 'carbon trading', 'environmental impact assessment', 'lifecycle analysis', and such a shift would require a greater sense of urgency about the new environmental problems and widespread beliefs that radical 'green' innovations are feasible and desirable. However, the main challenge arises at this point is the necessary means to accomplish this so-called "sustainability transition."

Recent developments in market economies also require new approaches and innovative solutions the problems as massive long-term unemployment, social exclusion, welfare in the rural world, and run-down urban areas, health, education, the quality of life of pensioners, sustainable growth and other issues (Monzón & Chaves, 2012). In line with that, the global financial crisis has cast doubt over the neoclassical paradigm in advanced industrial countries, and much of development economics had been viewed as asking how developing countries could successfully transition toward the kinds of market-oriented policy frameworks (Stiglitz, 2011).

Social innovation and its agents could play an important role in future, bearing in mind the limitations that the State encounters in providing social welfare related to goods and services, and the limitations and imbalances of private sector provision (Brazda, Dellinger, & Rößl, 2012).

As seen, various forms of contemporary developments have resulted in questing the state-of-the-art solutions to overcome these challenges in the face of shifting the role of governments, companies and social economy actors. We argue that social innovation and associated means may play a vital role in providing state-of-the-art solutions to the challenges arise as a result of abovementioned driving forces. In the coming section, we will further elaborate on the facilitating role of social innovation in providing and sustaining the well-being of the people.

SOCIAL INNOVATION: A FACILITATOR IN BUILDING THE WELFARE STATE

The concept and power of social innovation have been gradually explored. The experiencing of the boundaries of conventional economics in providing well-being to the society is leading to a search for social innovation and associated tools as a state-of-the-art alternative providing solutions to various challenges ranging from global warming to equal distribution of wealth, from innovative social entrepreneurs to grassroots innovation to proliferate the utilization of renewable energy systems. Social innovation has become particularly attractive to policy-makers because of the difficulties traditional welfare systems face in meeting the growing and diverse needs of society (Borzaga vd., 2014). On the one hand, social innovation seems to have a potential in transforming society to tackle new kinds of societal problems. On the other hand, it enables exploration of new ways to create added value for the economy and the society.

There are various possible roles for social innovation in improving social wellbeing. For instance, Reinstaller (2013) sheds light on the three dimensions of social innovation in the context of people's wellbeing;

- Social innovation affects the achievements and opportunities of individuals and as a consequence their well-being; it changes the freedom of human beings to live alternative lifestyles. The extent to which this is possible depends on the institutional framework conditions.
- Social freedom depends on some contingent circumstances such as personal heterogeneities or environmental diversities. This fact explains the many different manifestations of social innovation;
- To assess the impact of social innovation a generally valid normative conception of what makes a good life is needed. The capabilities approach is a potentially interesting starting point for the assessment of the welfare impact of social innovation, even though this approach has some important shortcomings.

Social innovation refers to innovative activities and services that are motivated by the goal of meeting social needs predominantly diffused through organizations whose primary purposes are social as opposed to business innovation which is generally motivated by profit maximization, and is diffused through organizations are primarily motivated by profit maximization (Mulgan, 2006). Social innovations were conceptualized as new services, practices or ideas at the micro-level of niches (Avelino et al., 2014). Across the globe, social innovation, social entrepreneurship or social enterprise have turned into mainstream concepts in politics that comprehend a heterogeneous set of policies and measures to support the provision of public goods, or more generally strengthen the innovative capabilities of countries by other means than the public sector (Reinstaller, 2013). For European Union, U.S.A., Great Britain, and Japan, social innovation is a key concept in realizing sustainable and inclusive growth (Eriksson, Einarsson, & Wijkström, 2014)(Fujisawa, Ishida, Nagatomi, & Iwasaki, 2015)(Lake, 2015).

In the last decade, we have witnessed growing attention and expectation in civic societies, governmental bodies, and non-profit organizations towards social innovation. The quest towards understanding how to increase the role of civil society in solving social problems, sustaining and improving the wellbeing of the people beyond increasing the monetary term welfare has triggered the interest in social innovation.

In the remaining part of this section, we aim at highlighting the functions and contributions of social innovation in a society with relevant examples.

The Role of Social Innovation in Creating the "New Economy"

Both Neoliberal and Keynesian economics use GDP – a measure of the value of goods and services produced nationally – as the primary measure of economic performance, while considering robust and stable GDP growth as the sole objective of economic policy complemented by macroeconomic variables, such as inflation rate and budget balance.

In contrast, a range of "New Economy" efforts, as shown in Table 2, now call for alternatives to GDP measuring outcomes of progress and prosperity (Fullerton, 2015). The idea that we need a "new economy" with radical new economic structure and preferences is highlighted by numerous scholars including Schumacher (1973), Meadows, Meadows, Randers, & Behrens (1972), Latouche (2007), Pikkety (2014), and Jacobs (1961).

The 'new economy' is long-term and social benefit oriented. Sustainability and better distribution of income and opportunities across the society are its key drivers. Intangible factors and outputs of economic and social activity have a significantly higher weight in the new economy compared to the conventional economy. The range of innovation activities is much broader in the new economy encompassing innovation in social areas in addition to economic ones. That is likely to enhance the efficiency and effectiveness the innovation activity by triggering positive economic spillovers from social innovations.

As pointed out in the previous section, the sustainability of the existing financial and economic system has become a subject of hot discussion, particularly after the global financial crisis. Deepening appreciation, over the past few decades, of the profound ecological challenges facing the planet and growing despair at the inability of traditional economics and politics to address economic failures have fueled a growing amount of experimentation by activists, economists and socially-minded business leaders (Alperovitz, 2011). In addition to ecological challenges, unequal distribution of wealth and opportunities have resulted in a quest for new economic narratives beyond GDP and growth based ones.

In line with this pursuit, a North American think tank, Capital Institute, concluded that "*to avoid social, environmental and economic collapse, the world needs to move beyond the standard choices of capitalism or socialism*" (Fullerton, 2015, p. 80). The main argument of the report is that conventional economic systems based on socialistic or capitalistic are unsustainable, thus requiring a new and holistic approach to incorporate environmental and human aspects along into economic activities.

Instead of trying to find globalized one-size-fits-all approaches to change, it is vital to recognize that each community consists of a "mosaic of peoples, traditions, beliefs, and institutions uniquely shaped by long term pressures of geology, human history, culture, local environment, and changing human needs"(Confino, 2015, p. 1). Thus, the key agents of change can be social innovators and entrepreneurs in each community. Social innovators and entrepreneurs around the world have already started to cre-

Table 2. Comparison of "new" and "conventional" economy perspectives

New Economy	Conventional Economy
Focuses on 'how' the system grows as the key to long-run prosperity, not only the growth of the system *per se*.	Focuses on the growth of the system measured by GDP as the primary path to prosperity.
Acts in ways that support the long-term health of the whole society and the planet, with feedback loops designed into the system to ensure systemic health rather than treating the symptoms of ill health.	Acts in ways that tend to benefit the wealthy and powerful, often at the expense of harm done to other parts of the system, subject only to after-the-fact mitigation by government policy.
Maximizes long-term economic health by ensuring equitable benefits to all stakeholders.	Maximizes profits to owners by minimizing benefits to other stakeholders.
Favors intangible things like ideas, information, and relationships.	Favors mostly tangible things like GDP, trade deficit, central bank reserves.
Values the long-term vitality of human beings and the essential ecosystem function.	Values money and short-term profit ahead of human beings and the environment.
Circulates money/wealth/information robustly.	Concentrates money/wealth/information increasingly, subject only to regulation/redistribution debates.
Balances the freedom upon which innovation thrives, and the constraints necessary for a collaborative community by building self-regulating mechanisms into the design of systems aligned with principles of systemic health.	Polarizes the debate over the value of individual freedom (*laissez-faire*) *versus* the need for government regulation in response to market deficiencies.
Centers on reciprocity, mutual benefit, and common cause.	Stresses selfishness and effective exploitation of land and labor for the benefit of capital.
Invests long term in people and common-cause infrastructures.	Impulses long-term investment displaced by short-term Reinforces speculation and manipulation of the system benefitting a small elite.
Argues that addressing social, economic and environmental crises provides an excellent way to increase both profits and economic health.	Ignores looming social, economic, and environmental crises, arguing that profits and growth must come first because they are the key to economic strength.

Source: Compiled from Fullerton (2015), and Kelly (1999)

ate many enterprises and led many movements of sustainability initiatives, shared economy activities, grass-roots innovations, impact investing and initiatives were addressing local challenges.

For instance, hundreds of 'social enterprises' that use profits for environmental, social or community-serving goals are also expanding rapidly and in many communities urban agricultural efforts have made common cause with groups concerned about healthy non-processed food (Alperovitz, 2011). For example, Mexico's Grupo Ecológico_has worked to fund impoverished small farmers and ranchers, giving them the economic freedom to preserve and regenerate their own land (Confino, t.y.). Similarly, Australia's Bendigo Community Bank splits its net income with local community enterprises. It directs a portion of community branch earnings toward grantmaking, giving local leaders the opportunity to become active players in their communities.

Even some conventional forms of social innovation, like cooperatives, with their updated structures, are becoming increasingly important in the new-economy efforts. The Evergreen Cooperatives in Maryland/U.S.A., for instance, are linked through a nonprofit corporation, a revolving loan fund and the common goal of rebuilding the economically devastated Greater University Circle neighborhood. A thoroughly green industrial-scale laundry, a solar installation company and a large-scale commercial greenhouse (capable of producing about 5 million heads of lettuce a year) make up the first of a group of linked cooperation initiatives projected to expand in the years to come. The effort is unique in that

Evergreen is building on the purchasing power of the area's large hospital, university and other anchor institutions, which buy some $3 billion of goods and services a year—virtually none of which, until recently, had come from local business (Alperovitz, 2011).

Role of Social Innovation in Facilitating the Social Transition

In the face of profound challenges relating environment, society, and economy, there is an urgent need for new governance and management systems along with the transformation will and capacity of the society.

According to Howaldt & Kopp (2012), social innovations are gaining importance over technical innovations when it comes to dealing with societal challenges, and that social innovations "*can contribute proactively with regard to anticipated developments, such as demographic developments or the effects of climate change "to modify, or even transform, existing ways of life should it become necessary to do so*" (p. 44).

For instance, when it comes to planetary boundaries of Rockström et al. (2009), comprehensive transformations are necessary for terms of human-environment interactions to sustain the current level of well-being. According to Olsson & Galaz (2011), "*social innovation, including new technology, strategies, concepts, ideas, institutions, and organizations that enhance the capacity of ecosystems to generate services and help steer away from multiple earth-system thresholds*" (p. 225). Regarding economic challenges, social innovation also has substantial potential to cultivate new kind of cross-sectoral economic activities in a sense to transform the economy along with society. In line with that, the Bureau of European Policy Advisors (BEPA) argues that social innovations provide an effective way to "empower people" and "drive societal change", "*at a time of major budgetary constraints, social innovation is an effective way of responding to social challenges, by mobilizing people's creativity to develop solutions and make better use of scarce resources*" (Defourny, Hulgård, & Pestoff, 2014, p. 68)(Avelino et al., 2014).

This part of the chapter aims at highlighting the role of social innovation in facilitation these transformations by dealing with relevant social innovation applications.

There are mainly three developments which necessitate profound transformations in respective dynamics and systems: economic crisis, climate change, IT revolution. Such societal transformation requires a simultaneous change in multiple dimensions of social systems, with these changes occurring widely across society(Avelino et al., 2014). Those three main transformative discourses and respective social innovation fields are illustrated in table 3 below.

Table 3. Transformative social innovation

Transformative Discourses	Social Innovations
Financial Crisis	Innovations in ownership, business models, methods of exchange *Policy areas: Health, welfare, employment, finance.*
Climate Change	Innovations in life-styles, daily practices, consumer habits. *Policy areas: Energy, mobility, food, agriculture, water.*
ICT Revolution	Innovations in research, production, sharing of information *Policy areas: R&D, education, participation, employment.*

Source: Jorgensen, Dorland, Pel, & Wittmayer (2015)

As the transitions in various fields are required by financial crisis, climate change and ICT revolution, Grin, Rotmans, & Schot (2010) claim that system innovations should be the first step since system innovations are "profound transformations in social systems", which involve "changes in established patterns of action as well as in structure, which includes dominant cultural assumptions and discourses, legislation, physical infrastructure, the rules prevailing in economic chains, knowledge infrastructure, and so on" (Grin et al. 2010, p 140). For instance, challenges of climate change require innovations in life-styles, daily practices, consumer habits, thus in the areas including energy, mobility, food, agriculture, and water. However, the change in consumer habits or lifestyles requires a system innovation, beyond product innovations towards clean technologies. System innovations in ownership, business models, or in lifestyle and daily practices are enabled by innovative social practices along with technical innovations. In line with that, founder of the Ashoka once said that "*Social entrepreneurs are not content just to give a fish or teach how to fish. They will not rest until they have revolutionized the fishing industry*" (Drayton, 2015, p. XIV). Time Banks, for instance, are seen as an innovation in lifestyle and methods of change, thus a tool in overcoming the challenges of climate change and economic crisis. In Time Banks, participants give and receive services in exchange for time credits. Everyone's time is valued equally, and taken-for-granted (but sometimes scarce) skills and abilities, such as time for listening sympathetically, companionship, doing someone's shopping, walking a dog, light gardening or home repairs, are recognized, valued and rewarded, thus participants enjoy the social networking, sense of being useful, an opportunity to help others, they are also imbued with alternative values relating to the nature of work, how people are valued as assets; they respond to incentives to perform the types of neighborhoods work needed to build healthy communities (Seyfang & Smith, 2007). The values expressed through this time-based system of exchange value all productive labor equally contrast with the conventional economy (O'Boyle, 2005).

When it comes to the economic crisis or for those with little income, innovative social applications may also be utilized to provide economic and social solutions. Transition Towns Movement, for example, has the vision of empowering citizens to build community resilience by (re)discovery of (new combinations of) old and new skills and services to increase socioeconomic independence (e.g., permaculture design principles for urban farming and local food production)(Avelino et al., 2014). These examples are illustrative of transformative role of social innovation and its capacity in empowering and preparing communities in tackling with challenges of economic crisis, climate change or ICT (Information & Communication Technologies) revolution.

Role of Social Innovation in Providing Sustainable Added Value

Creating sustainable value added is vital for any country aiming at providing well-being to its citizens. Conventional welfare approaches mainly focus on the economic value added without considering the social value added aspect. New business concepts of social innovation perspective argue that instead of "either profit or social value" thinking, we need to implement an "economic and social value added" perspective, and indeed there are numerous proven examples of this method today (Osburg & Schmidpeter, 2013). It is obvious that this new approach illustrated in figure 1 is likely to assure a more sustainable future for society by encouraging the business to implement social innovation aspects into their business.

Figure 1. Social innovation: Added values for business and society
Fuente: Osburg & Schmidpeter (2013)

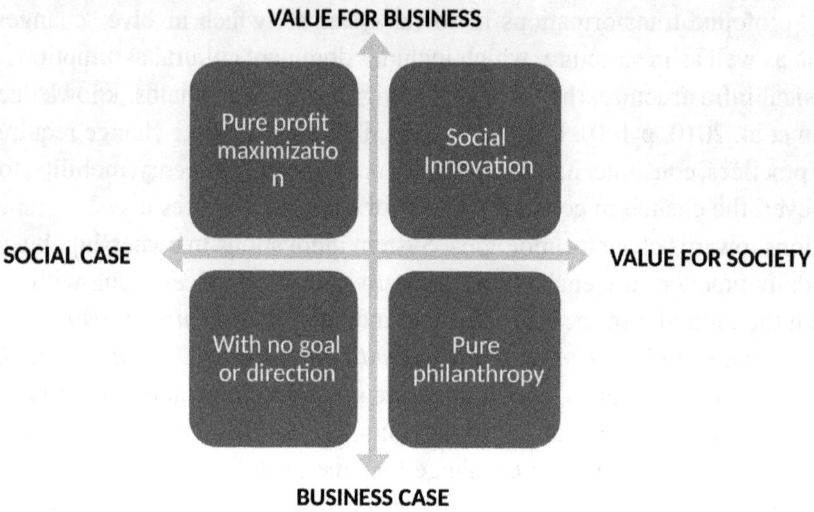

Social entrepreneurs are the fundamental components of social innovations in providing social value. There are numerous examples of social entrepreneurs around the world which address a social problem and create social value added simultaneously. Regarding social entrepreneurship, the charitable activity must still reflect economic realities, while economic activity must still generate social value (Austin, Stevenson, & Wei-Skillern, 2006). Although the economic value is assessed only in monetary terms, social values provided by social innovations may comprise various forms, including increasing creativity, emancipation, social inclusiveness, responsibility, transformation capacity, self-actualization, and social awareness.

For instance, Ecosia (www.ecosia.org) has developed a creative and sustainable business form that helps plant trees and conserved rainforests. Ecosia is a web-based search engine working over google and generate money by searching and shopping on the web. 80% of the generated revenue is used for planting trees. As of May 2015, Ecosia has planted over 2 million trees around the world.

KaBOOM!, on the hand, is a U.S. based national non-profit organization which is "*dedicated to bringing balanced and active play into the daily lives of all kids, particularly those growing up in poverty in America*" (Kaboom, 2015)(Dees, Anderson, & Wei-Skillern, 2004, p. 28). By creating appropriate places for children to play, KaBOOM! inspires communities to promote and support play, and work to drive the national discussion about the importance of play in fostering healthy lives and communities.

In the education sector, a growing number of initiatives pop up to address state-of-art challenges faced by the education sector. GACEMER is one of those socially innovative initiative dedicated to making learning and exploring more exciting. As an innovative app combining creativity and technology with a higher level of questioning and To Do challenges, GACEMER encourages active learning and promotes student engagement in a fun, exciting ways involving interesting tasks like visiting assigned sites, answering multiple choice questions, photo shooting, video recording, solving puzzles, watching videos.

Role of Social Innovation in Providing "Competitive Advantage"

Innovation, including technological, organizational or social innovation, heavily affects competitiveness and vice versa. In fact, many are in the opinion that "social innovation" and "competitiveness" cannot be aligned with each other since it is assumed that competition is something reserved for the for-profit world (West & Posner, 2013). However, in order to improve the service quality of social innovative businesses and NGOs, or increase the market share of their "products", on the one hand, and provide resilience to the community and explore the way community can create state-of-the-art solutions on the contemporary challenges ranging from energy saving to advanced education methods, on the other hand, one should also address the competitiveness aspect of social innovation.

Competitive Strategy guru Michael Porter asserted in 2008 that "*a nation's competitiveness depends on the capacity of its industry to innovate and upgrade*"(Porter, 2008, p. 171). Michael Porter's point of view is illustrative of an incomplete and outdated concept of competitiveness. As a result of global challenges and shifting dynamics in many areas in the meantime, we are in the opinion that a nation's competitiveness depends not only on the capacity of its industry but also on its community to innovate, upgrade and to become resilient against global warming, economic and social shocks, and disasters to manage their well-being in a sustainable way.

Although there are numerous researches about the influence of the different form of innovations on the competitiveness of a company, country or non-profit enterprises, the role of social innovation in this respect is rarely investigated. However, with its capacity and available tools, social innovation can play a vital role in providing competitiveness in various forms.

As stated recently by the founder of World Economic Forum, Claus Schwab, "*In the new world, it is not the big fish which eats the small fish, it's the fast fish which eats the slow fish*" (Schwab, 2015). Having said that, one should recognize countries, NGOs, for-profit or non-profit enterprises cannot be considered in isolation from the wider economic or political context. Additionally, given the fact that existing challenges require immediate actions, social innovations can support communities or countries in exploring community/culture/region specific strengths in tackling those challenges efficiently and effectively. For instance, regarding climate change, the way countries or communities fight climate change is highly dependent on the conditions, strength and available means of the respected community or region. At this stage, innovative social enterprises can explore the strength of the respected region and configure their work accordingly.

In combating climate change, for instance, experienced locals of Tanzania might be more capable of launching innovative community-led deforestation campaign than other parts of the world, and small-scale local associations have a potential to facilitate collective experimentation and risk management, contributing to the resilience and sustainability of the social-ecological system (Rodima-Taylor, 2012). In the United Kingdom and Germany, on the other hand, as a result of technical knowledge, accessibility to economic or technical means and regulatory conditions, growing number of grassroots social innovations are launched with an aim to proliferate the utilization of renewable energy, such as Pauls (2013), Breitenbach (2015), and Seyfang, Hielscher, Hargreaves, Martiskainen, & Smith (2014).

These social enterprises do not only support the community, but it improves the respected enterprises' competitive advantage within a key market segment. By creating sustainable, need-driven and community/region based solutions, innovative social enterprises contribute to the development of competitive advantages of the respective region.

CONCLUSION

In the face of tremendous developments in economic, social and technical areas, it is inevitable for governments and societies to seek new approaches to overcome related contemporary challenges and provide sustainable well-being.

Given the complex nature and interdependencies of today's challenges, achieving social and human progress entails a new mindset, new approaches, collaborative actions, and a profound transformation.

As a result of this need, content, and motivation of economic development has been one of the subjects of intensive discussions recently. The focus of the countries is gradually shifting from GDP-led growth to sustainability, and social progress focused development. It is obvious that there are various driving forces which resulted in a pressing the need for a comprehensive transition. Shifting focus of economies to a greener form of production, engagement of cities throughout the world in the promotion and pursuit of mitigating climate activities, growing attention on ecological developments are some of the illustrative cases of big shifts. A redirection towards sustainability and well-being, which produces lasting social and economic vitality for global civilization as a whole may be the most viable option for further development (Rogers et al., 2012)(Fullerton, 2015). However, the challenge is, how to realize this "redirection" towards sustainability and well-being with conventional methods whereas those "conventional" methods are falling short to propose up-to-date solutions and to a great extent responsible for the current outcomes. Innovative solutions are necessary to face the challenges of the future and foster sustainable growth.

The quest towards understanding how to increase the role of civil society in solving social problems, sustaining and improving the wellbeing of the people beyond increasing the monetary term welfare has triggered the interest in social innovation.

Social innovation and its agents can be considered as a toolbox which may facilitate the transition by positively influencing wellbeing while developing ways of integrating it into policy and promoting it as an alternative measure of progress.

By providing up-to-date solutions to various challenges ranging from global warming to equal distribution of wealth, from social innovative entrepreneurs to grassroots innovation to proliferate the utilization of renewable energy systems, social innovation seems to be capable of transforming the society in a way to tackle with the new kind of societal problems, and exploring new ways to create added value for the economy.

REFERENCES

Alperovitz, G. (2011). The New-Economy Movement. *The Nation*. Retrieved from http://www.thenation.com/article/160949/new-economy-movement

Austin, J., Stevenson, H., & Wei-Skillern, J. (2006). Social and Commercial Entrepreneurship: Same, Different, or Both? *Entrepreneurship Theory and Practice*, *30*(1), 1–22. doi:10.1111/j.1540-6520.2006.00107.x

Avelino, F., Wittmayer, J., Haxeltine, A., Kemp, R., O'Riordan, T., Weaver, P., … Rotmans, J. (2014). *Game Changers and Transformative Social Innovation. The Case of the Economic Crisis and the New Economy*. TRANSIT Working Paper.

Borzaga, C., Bodini, R., Carini, C., Depedri, S., Galera, G., & Salvatori, G. (2014). *Europe in transition: The role of social cooperatives and social enterprises*. Academic Press.

Brazda, J., Dellinger, M., & Rößl, D. (2012). *Genossenschaften im Fokus einer neuen Wirtschaftspolitik. Bericht der XVII. Internationalen Genossenschaftswissenschaftlichen Tagung*. IGT.

Chaves Avila, R., & Monzon, J. L. (2012). *The social economy in the European Union*. Retrieved from http://roderic.uv.es/handle/10550/39363

Confino, J. (2015). *Beyond capitalism and socialism: could a new economic approach save the planet?* Retrieved from http://www.theguardian.com/sustainable-business/2015/apr/21/regenerative-economy-holism-economy-climate-change-inequality

Costanza, R., Erickson, J., Fligger, K., Adams, A., Adams, C., Altschuler, B., ... Kelly, J. (2004). Estimates of the genuine progress indicator (GPI) for Vermont, Chittenden County, and Burlington, from 1950 to 2000. *Ecological Economics, 51*(1), 139–155. doi:10.1016/j.ecolecon.2004.04.009

Dasgupta, P. (2008). Nature in economics. *Environmental and Resource Economics, 39*(1), 1–7. doi:10.100710640-007-9178-4

Dees, J. G., Anderson, B. B., & Wei-Skillern, J. (2004). Scaling social impact. *Stanford Social Innovation Review, 1*(4), 24–33.

Defourny, J., Hulgård, L., & Pestoff, V. (2014). *Social Enterprise and the Third Sector: Changing European Landscapes in a Comparative Perspective*. Routledge. doi:10.4324/9780203487747

Distaso, A. (2007). Well-being and/or quality of life in EU countries through a multidimensional index of sustainability. *Ecological Economics, 64*(1), 163–180. doi:10.1016/j.ecolecon.2007.02.025

Drayton, B. (2015). *Social entrepreneurs are not content just to give a fish or teach how to fish Ashoka - USA*. Retrieved from http://usa.ashoka.org/social-entrepreneurs-are-not-content-just-give-fish-or-teach-how-fish

Eriksson, M., Einarsson, T., & Wijkström, F. (2014). Report on the European social innovation policy framework in light of the third sector and civil society actors. A deliverable of the project: 'Impact of the Third Sector as Social Innovation' (ITSSOIN), European Commission–7th Framework Programme, Brussels, Belgium.

Esping-Andersen, G. (2002). *Why we need a new welfare state*. Oxford University Press. doi:10.1093/0199256438.001.0001

Fox, J. (2012). *The Economics of Well-Being*. Retrieved from https://hbr.org/2012/01/the-economics-of-well-being

Fujisawa, Y., Ishida, Y., Nagatomi, S., & Iwasaki, K. (2015). A Study of Social Innovation Concepts: A Japanese Perspective. *Japan Social Innovation Journal, 5*(1), 1–13. doi:10.12668/jsij.5.1

Fullerton, J. (2015). *Regenerative Capitalism - How Universal Principles And Patterns Will Shape Our New Economy*. Greenwich, CT: Capital Institute. Retrieved from http://capitalinstitute.org/wp-content/uploads/2015/04/2015-Regenerative-Capitalism-4-20-15-final.pdf

Geels, F. W. (2010). Ontologies, socio-technical transitions (to sustainability), and the multi-level perspective. *Research Policy*, *39*(4), 495–510. doi:10.1016/j.respol.2010.01.022

Hall, J. (2010). Measuring what Matters to Make a Difference. *Journal of Futures Studies*, *15*(2), 151–154.

Hobijn, B., & Franses, P. H. (2001). Are living standards converging? *Structural Change and Economic Dynamics*, *12*(2), 171–200. doi:10.1016/S0954-349X(00)00034-5

Jacobs, J. (1961). *The death and life of great American cities*. Vintage.

Kaboom. (2015). *Play Matters*. Retrieved from http://kaboom.org/

Kelly, K. (1999). *New rules for the new economy*. Penguin.

Kuznets, S. (1973). Modern economic growth: Findings and reflections. *The American Economic Review*, 247–258.

Kuznets, S. S., & Murphy, J. T. (1966). *Modern economic growth: Rate, structure, and spread (C. 2)*. Yale University Press.

Lake, R. W. (2015). The Financialization of Urban Policy in the Age of Obama. *Journal of Urban Affairs*, *37*(1), 75–78. doi:10.1111/juaf.12167

Latouche, S. (2007). De-growth: An electoral stake? *The International Journal of Inclusive Democracy*, *3*(1), 14–18.

Meadows, D. H., Meadows, D. L., Randers, J., & Behrens, W. W. (1972). *The limits to growth*. Retrieved from https://www.google.com/books?hl=tr&lr=&id=vb8_BAAAQBAJ&oi=fnd&pg=PA25&dq=%22limits+to+growth%22&ots=7pmu7LshCf&sig=ktZdt_jikOFMt7NCcgRJMSbVa0s

Mulgan, G. (2006). The process of social innovation. *Innovations*, *1*(2), 145–162. doi:10.1162/itgg.2006.1.2.145

NEF. (2015). *Wellbeing*. Retrieved from http://www.neweconomics.org/issues/entry/well-being

O'Boyle, E. J. (2005). Homo Socio-Economicus: Foundational to social economics and the social economy*. *Review of Social Economy*, *63*(3), 483–507. doi:10.1080/00346760500255635

Osburg, T., & Schmidpeter, R. (2013). *Social Innovation: Solutions for a Sustainable Future*. Springer Science & Business Media. doi:10.1007/978-3-642-36540-9

Pikkety, T. (2014). *Capital in the 21st century*. Harvard University Press.

Porter, M. E. (2008). *On competition*. Harvard Business Press.

Reinstaller, A. (2013). *An evolutionary view on social innovation and the process of economic change*. WWW for Europe.

Rodima-Taylor, D. (2012). Social innovation and climate adaptation: Local collective action in diversifying Tanzania. *Applied Geography (Sevenoaks, England)*, *33*, 128–134. doi:10.1016/j.apgeog.2011.10.005

Rogers, D. S., Duraiappah, A. K., Antons, D. C., Munoz, P., Bai, X., Fragkias, M., & Gutscher, H. (2012). A vision for human well-being: Transition to social sustainability. *Current Opinion in Environmental Sustainability*, *4*(1), 61–73. doi:10.1016/j.cosust.2012.01.013

Scholars, E. (2010). *From words to action: supporting cooperative and social enterprises to achieve a more inclusive, sustainable and prosperous Europe | Euricse*. Retrieved from http://www.euricse.eu/publications/from-words-to-action-supporting-cooperative-and-social-enterprises-to-achieve-a-more-inclusive-sustainable-and-prosperous-europe/

Schumacher, E. F. (1973). *Small is beautiful: Economics as if people really mattered*. London: Abacus.

Schwab, C. (2015). *Are you ready for the technological revolution?* Retrieved from https://agenda.weforum.org/2015/02/are-you-ready-for-the-technological-revolution/

Seyfang, G., Hielscher, S., Hargreaves, T., Martiskainen, M., & Smith, A. (2014). A grassroots sustainable energy niche? Reflections on community energy in the UK. *Environmental Innovation and Societal Transitions*, *13*, 21–44. doi:10.1016/j.eist.2014.04.004

Seyfang, G., & Smith, A. (2007). Grassroots innovations for sustainable development: Towards a new research and policy agenda. *Environmental Politics*, *16*(4), 584–603. doi:10.1080/09644010701419121

Soubbotina, T. P. (2004). *Beyond economic growth: An introduction to sustainable development*. World Bank Publications. doi:10.1596/0-8213-5933-9

Soubbotina, T. P., & Sheram, K. (2000). *Beyond economic growth: Meeting the challenges of global development*. World Bank Publications.

Stiglitz, J. E. (2011). Rethinking Development Economics. *The World Bank Research Observer*, *26*(2), 230–236. doi:10.1093/wbro/lkr011

StiglitzJ. E. (2018). *Beyond GDP*. Retrieved from https://www.project-syndicate.org/commentary/new-metrics-of-wellbeing-not-just-gdp-by-joseph-e-stiglitz-2018-12

Stiglitz, J. E., Sen, A., & Fitoussi, J.-P. (2010). *Report by the commission on the measurement of economic performance and social progress*. Paris: Commission on the Measurement of Economic Performance and Social Progress.

Urama, Ke., & Acheampong, E. (2013). Social Innovation Creates Prosperous Societies. *Stanford Social Innovation Review*. Retrieved from http://www.ssireview.org/articles/entry/social_innovation_creates_prosperous_societies

West, M., & Posner, A. (2013). Defining Your Competitive Advantage. *Stanford Social Innovation Review*. Available from: http://www.ssireview.org/blog/entry/defining_your_competitive_advantage

KEY TERMS AND DEFINITIONS

GACEMER: A socially innovative app to incentive active learning by combining creativity and technology with a higher level of questioning and To Do challenges based on multiple choice questions, photo shooting, video recording, solving puzzles, and watching videos.

KaBOOM!: A U.S.-based national non-profit organization focused on bringing balanced and active play to poor U.S. kids.

New Economy: Defined by the Industry 4.0, it appears in the transition from a manufacturing-based economy to a service-based economy.

Social Innovation: Social practices focused on ameliorating the lives of the poor and the most disadvantaged.

State-of-the-Art Challenges: They are composed of the study of resource shortages, demographic realities, and planetary boundaries to maximize sustainable economic development.

Think Tank: Non-profit organizations, in general, devoted to analyze topics of common interest to impact on governments and societies.

World Economic Forum: Founded in 1971, it has the commitment to improving the state of the world by engaging business, political, academic, and other leaders of society to shape global, national, regional, local, and industry agendas.

Zero-Carbon Housing: Also known as Energy Housing, it is used to define single family dwellings with a very high energy efficiency rating measured by zero-emissions.

ENDNOTE

1 Earlier version of the chapter was published in the *Handbook of Research on Social Entrepreneurship and Solidarity Economics*, IGI Global - 2016, Edited by Jose Manuel Saiz-Alvarez.

Section 2
Digital Marketing

Chapter 14
Digital Moms:
Devices, Social Networking Sites, and Perceptions Towards Digital Marketing Strategies

Teresa Treviño
Universidad de Monterrey, Mexico

ABSTRACT

Given the rise of new technologies and the resultant changes in consumer behavior, marketing practices need to evolve, which requires organizations to rethink their strategies. Having a digital marketing strategy can establish a direct dialog with customers, thereby increasing knowledge about customers, suppliers, and partners, as well as building, consolidating, and maintaining brand awareness. However, little is known about the attitudes and perceptions of consumers toward popular digital marketing tools that can strategically be used in an integrated digital marketing strategy. Therefore, the objective of this research is to understand the perceptions of digital moms toward technology and digital marketing strategies. Following a qualitative and interpretative approach, the results contribute to the literature by (1) addressing the symbolic meanings that technological tools have in the lives of this group of consumers and (2) providing insights on how different digital marketing strategies commonly implemented by brands are perceived by digital moms.

INTRODUCTION

Presently, our social world is going digital. New technologies and tools are changing the way we communicate, interact, and have relationships with others. Consumers around the world are becoming more connected by owning several devices that allow continuous Internet access, enabling them to communicate, find information, make purchases, and interact with brands. This phenomenon, called the "mobile lifestyle," has changed many aspects around companies and brands; therefore, many interesting opportunities arise from these changes.

DOI: 10.4018/978-1-5225-8939-6.ch014

As a first step, managers must understand these changes, and it becomes relevant to analyze the meaning that new technological tools have in consumers' lives. It is well known that people assign meanings to the objects they own; therefore, we can expect something almost similar to occur for digital tools and technology itself. In the past, research has questioned whether new technological tools carry symbolic meanings (Trevino, Lengel, & Daft, 1987). Understanding such meanings and roles in today's context can contribute to a better comprehension of the audiences of brands in the online environment as a prerequisite for successful brand performance (Singh & Sonnenburg, 2012).

From a marketing perspective, it is interesting to understand different online audiences to implement better digital marketing strategies that appeal to a specific target. In Mexico, previous literature has suggested that several groups of Internet users can be classified based on demographics and psychographic characteristics such as teens, executives, silver surfers, and digital moms (IAB México & Millward Brown, 2014). In this chapter, the digital moms' segment will be analyzed, considering that research has recognized this segment to have important implications for online marketing strategies (Treviño, 2017).

Furthermore, with the rise of information and communication technologies (ICTs), marketing practices have also been evolving in response to changes in consumer behavior, and this change requires organizations to rethink their strategies. It is well known that companies are seeking to establish long-term relationships with their customers now require a digital marketing strategy. Previous literature has found that companies report several benefits of having a digital marketing strategy. For example, it helps establish a direct dialog with the customer and increases knowledge about customers, suppliers, and partners. It further assists in building, consolidating, maintaining brand awareness, as well as improving the overall communication process (Tiago & Veríssimo, 2014). Considering the importance of this topic, literature addressing the impact of such marketing efforts is insufficient. Specifically, there is an opportunity to understand how consumers perceive the different digital marketing strategies such as social networking sites, email marketing, search engine optimization (SEO), search engine marketing (SEM), and website design. Research on such topics can help managers develop suitable digital marketing strategies.

Therefore, the objective of this research is to understand the perceptions of digital moms toward technology and digital marketing strategies. Particularly, the results contribute to the literature by (a) addressing the symbolic meanings that technological tools have in the lives of this group of consumers, and (b) providing insights on how digital moms perceive different digital marketing strategies commonly implemented by brands.

The following chapter is structured as follows. First, a description of the digital mom segment as Internet users is provided to understand the context of this study. Next, the literature on the symbolic meanings of technology is addressed. Then, common digital marketing strategies are presented and described as a basis for this research. The methodology employed and results obtained is described. Finally, the chapter concludes with discussing some implications for theory and practice as well as analyzing limitations and possible future research on the topic.

Digital Moms as Internet Users in Mexico

There are 71.5 million Internet users in Mexico, and 44% are between the age group of 12 and 25 years. Research has found several important Internet user groups that are classified regarding their activities and lifestyles, such as the teens, executives, silver surfers, and digital moms (Treviño, 2017; Treviño & Morton, 2016; IAB México & Millward Brown, 2014). The teen segment is interesting as it is comprised young users between 13 and 18 years of age and who use the Internet daily for approximately two to five hours (IAB México & Millward Brown, 2014a). Executive users are employees, staff, and middle managers who surf the Internet on most mobile devices (IAB México & Millward Brown, 2014b).

The silver surfer's segment is Internet users older than 50 years of age, and despite their slow acceptance of new technologies, are progressively active online and enjoy informative websites, travel sites, and other e-commerce sites related to clothes, personal items, and luxury articles (Treviño & Morton, 2016).

Finally, a segment that is increasingly important today is the digital moms' group. This group comprises women who have children younger than 12 years (or older but still living at home), daily spend approximately six hours online, and own several digital devices such as smartphones, tablets, laptops, and desktops (Treviño & Morton, 2016, IAB México, Treviño & Pineda, 2017). Many companies and brands target this group of Internet users because they make frequent online purchases, is very active on social networking sites, search for information, and communicate online. Research has recognized that the digital moms' segment has important implications for online marketing strategies. For example, it is known that digital moms use the Internet to make online recommendations and reviews, as well as to follow brands on social media. This group of online users also enjoys making online purchases and searching for discounts coupons online (Treviño, 2017). Based on the above information, this chapter focuses on understanding the digital moms' segment regarding the symbolic meanings they attach to the technology they own and use. Furthermore, the author intends to shed light on how digital moms perceive the different digital marketing strategies commonly used by brands, in an attempt to obtain knowledge that helps companies implement more engaging strategies.

Technology and Its Symbolic Meaning

Defining technology is important for the understanding of this research. Technology can be defined in a broad sense as the objects, tools, or machines created and used by people to enhance life (Calvert & Terry, 2013). The knowledge behind creating those objects and designing them to perform specific functions can also be considered as technology (Brooks, 1973). However, a more contemporary approach to defining technology is one that considers the relationships between machines, users, and designers. For purposes of this research, technology will be addressed based on Calvert and Terry's (2013) view of considering technology as situated within networked social relations and its use and creative misuse by people. Through this approach, it is assumed that technology has to be understood based on its particular context of design and use.

Today, the rise of different ICTs has provided society with many new communication options. Specifically, the term ICT comprises different communication technologies, such as computer hardware and software, the Internet, wireless networks, cell phones, email, instant messaging, and video-conferencing (TechTerms.com, 2010). ICTs also compose many online tools and word-of-mouth forums such as discussion boards, blogs, consumer product rating websites, and social networking sites such as Facebook and Twitter (Mangold & Faulds, 2009). These ICTs affect the lives of consumers', as through its use they communicate with others, look for information, evaluate, and make various decisions. In general, this phenomenon includes people with the desire to connect, and therefore new interactive technologies and online economies grow and evolve at a fast pace. Considering that technological evolution has brought significant changes in consumers' lives, it becomes interesting to understand what it means to them and how they perceive such tools. By addressing these pointers from a marketing perspective, companies can obtain knowledge as to why people choose one medium over another, as well as why they react differently to digital marketing strategies.

For this purpose, the framework of symbolic interactionism can be relevant as it views society as a dynamic network of communication and understands interactions concerning the meanings people assign to things (Trevino, Lengel, & Daft, 1987). This theoretical approach focuses on understanding the relationship between shared meanings (i.e., symbols) and verbal and non-verbal actions and communications (i.e., interactions) (LaRossa & Reitzes, 1993). More specifically, Blumer (1969) identified three core principles that shed light on this theory: (a) people act toward things and each other based on the meanings they have assigned for them; (b) the meanings come from social interactions with others; and (c) these meanings are managed and transformed by an interpretative process that allows people to make sense of their social worlds. By expanding Blumer's initial principles, it is also relevant to recognize that the symbols and meanings that objects have are embedded in the existing cultural and organizational contexts (Snow, 2001).

When analyzing media choices, the symbolic interactionism approach may be useful in understanding why people use specific technological tools and communication mediums. If every object can be considered a symbol, and therefore, has a meaning, then it is possible to question whether the new technological tools carry symbolic cues (Trevino, Lengel, & Daft, 1987). In sum, it is known that people assign meanings to the objects they own. Therefore, we can expect something almost similar to occur for digital tools and technology itself. Understanding such meanings and roles in today's context can contribute to a better comprehension of the audiences of brands in the online environment as it is a prerequisite for a successful brand performance (Singh & Sonnenburg, 2012).

New Technologies and Digital Marketing Strategies

With the rise of ICTs, marketing practices have also been evolving, causing considerable changes in consumer behavior that require organizations to rethink their strategies. Previous literature has found that companies report several benefits of having digital marketing strategies. For example, it establishes a direct dialog with the customer, increases knowledge about customers, suppliers, and partners, as well as builds, consolidates, maintains brand awareness, and improves the overall communication process (Tiago & Veríssimo, 2014).

However, little is known about the attitudes and perceptions of consumers toward popular digital marketing tools that can be strategically used in an integrated digital marketing strategy. Particularly, it has been found that most investments for the total online marketing budget go into social networking strategies followed by email, paid search, and SEO in that order (Tiago & Veríssimo, 2014). For such reasons, the present chapter will address the following: (a) social networking sites; (b) website design and usability; (c) SEO; (d) SEM; and (e) email marketing. In the next section, these activities will be analyzed as a basis for the present research.

Social Networking Sites

Social networking sites (SNSs) are characterized as interactive media, enabling two-way communication rather than one-directional as in traditional media (Lee & Cho, 2011). These technologies have been designed to be socially oriented to share content, interests, and interact with other members. SNSs are not only used for entertainment; previous research has proven that consumers also take advantage of SNSs to discuss brand experiences and preferences (Araujo & Neijens, 2012).

Through the Internet messages in SNSs can be shared and exchanged at any time, resulting in important implications for marketing and consumer behavior research and practice. For example, people now use this technology to obtain information, evaluate products and services, make purchases, and recommend them to others. A consumer behavior survey on the topic found that 72% of participants had used information on Facebook to make retail and restaurant decisions, and 50% of respondents had tried a new brand because of a recommendation found in SNSs (Empathica, n.d.). It is evident that this online communication between consumers' influences organizations and the overall market. Previous research on this topic has suggested that consumers trust brand pages in SNSs, and more importantly, they consider these pages to influence their purchase decisions (Araujo & Neijens, 2012). As a result, companies are beginning to identify SNSs' tools as an opportunity to conduct several marketing activities. Specifically, this new channel of communication is being used to promote services and/or products. The different abilities of SNSs, such as the creation of groups of people who share the same interests, geolocation technologies, and the integration of applications, make them unique for marketing, advertising, and communication.

Considering the frequent use of SNSs, it becomes interesting to understand this mediums role in consumers' lives as a basis for implementing marketing strategies.

SEO

Search engines, such as Google and Bing, are very important information sources for customers, especially, when they need new products or services. They are useful to search for details, compare prices, analyze customer reviews, and even make purchases. It has been found that many customers use search engines as a starting point for surfing the Internet; therefore, search engines can be considered as a link between users and websites (Baye, De los Santos, & Wildenbeest, 2016).

Concerning marketing, being on top of the organic search engine results is relevant as it has been proven that higher ranking results and more frequent appearance of a website in the search result list can generate more clicks on a company's website (Park, Yu, Yu, & Liao, 2015). Particularly, it is known that users rarely click on links beyond the first search results page; therefore, increasing the search engine ranking is now essential to business success (Sen, 2005; Gudivada, Rao, & Paris, 2015).

The digital marketing technique that works to improve visibility in search engines is SEO. SEO's main objective is to optimize a website in a way that the company receives more organic traffic through searches on search engines as it is based on the premise that more clicks translate into more sales.

Appearing in the organic results in Google depends on several factors and the exact algorithm that Google uses to determine a website's ranking is not known completely; however, the website's relevance to the search query made by a user may be the starting point. In this way, keyword results are crucial for an SEO strategy. In other words, marketers should ensure that the website includes the relevant keywords on all elements of the site, such as the page title, the meta description, head tags, body text, anchor text in links, and alt text in images. Additionally, site quality and brand awareness also impact search engine rankings, since users tend to click on websites that are more trusted, recognized, and have an overall positive reputation (Baye, De los Santos, & Wildenbeest, 2016).

SEM

When a user visits a search engine, he or she enters a specific search query and receives results that are divided into organic and sponsored listings. The organic results are ranked according to relevance and other factors considered by a "secret" algorithm. As previously mentioned, organic rankings can be improved based on several factors and a well-planned SEO strategy. When firms do not have a good organic ranking on search engines, one alternative is to implement an SEM campaign to place ads on the sponsored results. SEM, also known as "paid search" or "pay-per-click" (PPC) advertising, targets customers by placing ads on search engines when users search for specific keywords. A paid search campaign is different from other traditional advertising campaigns because companies are charged only when users click on an ad and not on the number of impressions. Furthermore, when planning a new PPC campaign, companies must select keywords that users might search for when requiring their products or services. Next, advertisers bid on those selected keywords to have them appear alongside the organic search engine results.

SEM is a good option for online companies as it is very easy to set up and can generate important traffic to a company's website (Boughton, 2005). More importantly, this traffic is generally interested in a company's offering because SEM delivers ads to users who are already searching for the product or service (Boughton, 2005). Ad placement depends on several factors. First, search engines consider the bid for each keyword. In other words, the more a company is willing to pay per click, the higher the ad placement on the sponsored results. Just as in organic results, generally, higher rankings translate into greater traffic. Furthermore, Google also considers keyword relevance with the ad and ad relevance with the landing page to assign a quality score that will also determine ad placement. Therefore, Google provides an incentive for companies to bid only on relevant keywords, to write targeted ads, and to direct users to relevant landing pages (Boughton, 2005).

SEM is one of the fastest growing digital marketing tools in the industry as more companies are investing in this strategy to reach potential customers, as online search volume grows rapidly (Sen, 2005; Dou, Lim, Su, Zhou, & Cui, 2010).

Email Marketing

Email marketing can be defined as a form of direct marketing that uses electronic mail to communicate commercial messages to an audience (Fariborzi & Zahedifard, 2012). This digital marketing tool is one of the oldest, and it has proven to be beneficial for companies despite the high number of junk or spam emails, as it provides a direct communication channel with customers (Ryan, 2016). Email marketing has been considered the most cost-effective digital marketing tool for acquisition and retention due to the low cost of sending large numbers of emails and the high response rates obtained. In other words, email marketing has the highest return on investment among other marketing tools (Jenkins, 2008; Fariborzi & Zahedifard, 2012).

Among the benefits that email marketing affords to companies, the possibility of building a direct interaction with customers that work to establish a long-term relationship with them is one. Additionally, with email marketing, companies can easily measure the success of their marketing efforts by tracking information about the number of emails sent, open rates, click rates, best days, and times to send campaigns, among others (Fariborzi & Zahedifard, 2012).

Some of the disadvantages of email marketing relate to the volume of emails received by people each day; thus, there is the risk that a company's email could become lost in a full inbox or even get classified as spam. For these reasons, research has focused on determining the factors that can increase the open rate of emails. First, customers will welcome regular emails regarding of brands they recognize and from which they are expecting to receive communication. Second, if customers identify that a certain company will always provide valuable content, then there is more probability of having higher open rates (Ryan, 2016). Additionally, research has suggested the importance of personalization of emails, for example, adding consumer-specific information such as the recipient's name. It has been found that by personalizing emails, the probability of the recipient opening it increases by 20%, sales increase by 31%, and the number of users unsubscribing from the email newsletter reduces by 17% (Sahni, Wheeler, & Chintagunta, 2018).

In sum, email marketing has been regarded as a valuable marketing tool that delivers short messages with a clear value proposition and a call to action for users. Popular email marketing campaign objectives include attracting potential customers, persuading them to repurchase, building loyalty and preference, and announcing or reminding about special events or news (Carmen & Nicolae, 2010).

Website Design

Despite the increasing use of other online tools by companies—especially SNSs—having a well-planned website is still crucial for most organizations. In fact, all the digital marketing techniques we reviewed previously in this chapter are basically designed to drive traffic to the website. It is important to understand that the purpose of the website is to convert received traffic into leads or customers that will ultimately result in actual profits. These conversions will only be possible if the website serves the customer by enhancing the consumer's experience with the brand and does not only provide information about the company.

Website design is a digital marketing technique that should not be discounted, that is, when planning the content, structure, and "look and feel" of their website, companies should always bear in mind the conversion goals being pursued. For example, a conversion objective can be an actual transaction when the customer makes an online purchase or a subscription to the email newsletter, submits a question, or the download of a whitepaper from the website (Ryan, 2016).

Overall, the user experience that a company provides through their website is one of the main determinants to drive conversion. It is also crucial to design the company's website with the target market in mind to achieve a successful user experience. Identifying what customers will want while surfing the website can be the first step when starting the design or redesign process (Ryan, 2016). Furthermore, web usability also impacts user experience as it focuses on delivering a simple and easy-to-use design. The theory of web usability suggests that websites should be designed in a way that users can find the information they are looking for and accomplish their goals effortlessly.

Research on website design has suggested several factors that determine a successful website. Particularly, meta-analyses of papers related to website design have found that information quality/business content, ease-of-use /navigation efficiency, page loading speed/responsiveness, visual appearance, security, personalization, and marketing/customer focus are the major categories that make a website successful (Gehrke & Turban, 1999; Park & Gretzel, 2007). Furthermore, studies have also suggested that the design of a website can be divided into visual, navigational, and informational dimensions. If this is not planned sufficiently, it could lead to consumer irritation and feelings of discomfort (Hasan,

2016). Other research on this topic identified that the general content and appearance of the website are two factors that ranked as most important for users and significantly impact behavior. Interestingly, the overall evaluation of the website is influenced by the perceptions of web design quality. These results imply that the appearance of a website is highly important for users as it will determine their overall evaluations and lead to higher usage intentions (Al-Qeisi, Dennis, Alamanos, & Jayawardhena, 2014).

Taking this into consideration, website design can be regarded as an important technique for a successful digital marketing strategy. Considering that companies are investing in digital marketing strategies by implementing a mix of the different tools described above, it is important to understand how customers perceive such strategies and the attitudes they have toward them.

Methodology

The choice of method is a crucial step in any research project. Choosing a method depends on the goal of the investigation, the nature of the phenomenon, and the level of theoretical maturity (Smith, 1983; Bryman, 1984; Edmonson & McManus, 2007). Given that the phenomenon of interest requires a deep understanding of the meanings and perceptions that consumers give to digital marketing strategies, a qualitative methodology was used as it seemed appropriate. Furthermore, the digital marketing literature is scant and can be classified as "nascent-phase," particularly from the customer's perspective, for exploring perceptions and attitudes toward companies' online marketing strategies. Therefore, through qualitative methods researchers can discover the meanings of consumers' actions (Hudson & Ozzane, 1988; Healy et al., 2007).

Data Collection

The data collection process was divided into two phases (Figure 1). Phase one included four focus groups and five in-depth interviews conducted by the author in late 2014 and early 2015. Furthermore, Phase 2 included twenty in-depth interviews and two focus groups conducted by a group of four marketing students supervised by the author (Tables 1 and 2). The data of the second phase were collected in early 2018. The analysis of data collected at different periods allows the researcher to understand the phenomenon more deeply since the author contains five years' worth of data on the digital moms' segment and their online behavior. Furthermore, the triangulation of data derived using several methods is useful to ensure the validity and credibility of the research (Miles & Huberman, 1994).

Sample

Considering that research on digital marketing mainly focuses on teens and millennials as their subjects, this research intends to shed light on another relevant consumer group for the marketing literature: the digital moms. As previously discussed, these online users show notable implications for branding, consumer behavior, and marketing strategy. Therefore, to be included in this study, women must meet the following criteria: (a) have children who live at home; (b) use the Internet daily; (c) own at least one device with Internet access; and (d) maintain at least one active account on a social networking site, chat forum, blog, or any other communication forum on the web. Participants were chosen through convenience and snowball sampling (Miles & Huberman, 1994; Flick, 2009).

Figure 1. Research phases

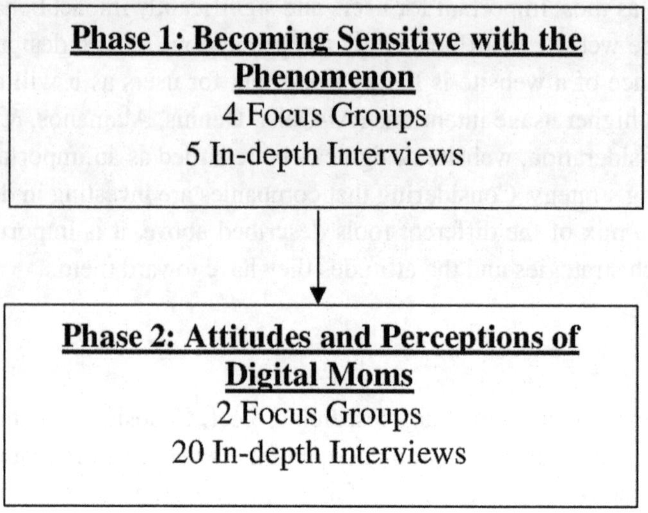

RESULTS

As women become mothers, they experience life differently. Being responsible for another individual who requires constant attention demands a considerable amount of time and effort. Participants of the present research take their "mom" role very seriously; therefore, they perform their activities and interests in their free time. Findings suggest that the Internet and the different tools used for accessing it represent an important part of their daily activities. It is known that consumers choose to use and buy products not only for the functional attributes but also for the meanings they convey (Belk, 1988). By considering these factors, several symbolic meanings of the digital technological tools were derived from the narratives of participants. This facilitated the researcher to understand the context of each mother (Table 3).

Symbolic Meanings of the Internet and Devices

Security: Being Available

One of the most recurrent themes that participants refer to when talking about technological tools and devices they use is security. Mothers reflected on the fact that possessing a smartphone helps them feel more secure when leaving home, as well as at other times because it allows them to be in touch with their family and friends. Older mothers find this issue paradoxical as the lack of such technology during their adolescence did not prevent them from feeling secure. However, nowadays, they find it difficult to leave the house without their smartphones. For example, two participants comment on how the smartphone helps them feel more secure in critical times and how they still believe they are safer if they can be reached:

Look, in 2009, when the city began to be unsafe, it is amazing how the cellphone helped you feel a little safer, then, it is something that remained. (It helped me) by being communicated... (Maricela, 40)

Table 1. Demographics of focus group participants

Name	Age	Occupation	Kids
Phase I			
Group 1			
Alejandra	46	Sales agent	3
Rosario	44	Sales agent	3
Sandra	47	Own business	3
Josefa	48	Insurance agent	3
Yolanda	33	Entrepreneur	2
Group 2			
Ana	41	Home keeper	3
Irene	42	Home keeper	3
Maruca	48	Student	2
Juliana	40	Home keeper	2
María	52	Home keeper	2
Group 3			
Carolina	30	Employee	2
Elisa	33	Home keeper	1
Mirna	29	Graphic designer	1
María del Rosario	26	Home keeper	1
Group 4			
Teresa	30	Home keeper	2
Karla	32	Teacher	2
Paula	33	Employee	1
Isabel	32	Home keeper	3
Gaby	29	Teacher	2
Phase II			
Group 1			
Susana	35	Home keeper	2
Saralicia	31	Home keeper	1
Ailin	31	Home keeper	2
Fernanda	34	Own business	5
CatalinaD	27	Own business	1
Group 2			
AnaGeorgina	32	Home keeper	2
Mislene	35	Home keeper	1
Michelle	35	Own business	4
Georgina	31	Artist	3
Lynette	42	Real estate	2
Lyu	38	Own business	2

Table 2. Demographics of in-depth interview participants

Name	Age	Occupation	Kids
Phase I			
Claudia	40	Home keeper	2
NancyM	36	Employee	2
Maricela	40	Teacher	3
Gina	32	Home keeper	3
NancyS	41	Home keeper	3
Phase II			
MarianaV	29	Own business	1
MarianaG	32	Own business	1
Catalina	33	Own business	3
RosaMaría	46	Architect	2
Liliana	45	Home keeper	3
Cynthia	44	Home keeper	2
DanielaD	30	Own business	1
Gabriela	35	Own business	2
Maridy	33	Lawyer	1
Myriam	32	Employee	1
Tatiana	32	Own business	1
AnaSofia	31	Home keeper	2
Ana	37	Own business	2
Alma	28	Home keeper	1
Verónica	46	Own business	2
MarianaM	37	Own business	4
DanielaF	40	Own business	2
Teresa	28	Employee	1
Mayerling	31	Employee	1
AnaSylvia	30	Own business	2

When I forget my cellphone... oh my God, what if something happens? So, I go back for it (the cell phone)... really, I see the telephone as a means for security... (Carolina, 30)

Maricela's and Carolina's narratives are examples of how the cellphone has become a security medium in their daily routine. Being available for others and knowing that they can communicate with their family at any given moment translates into a calming sense of security given the unsafe environment in which they feel they live.

Control: Parental Tool

Another implication of possessing devices with Internet access is family control. This is, in fact, related to the security feeling previously described, but is further directed toward other family members, especially the children. Mothers refer to IT devices, such as smartphones and tablets, as tools that help them with some childcare tasks. IT allows parents to monitor their children in different ways, which mothers translate into a control feeling that they like and need. This symbolic meaning was present for both mothers with young and older children. Younger mothers benefit from video calls to monitor their children when they are alone with the nanny. It serves as a good way to observe what the child is doing and how he or she is being treated:

When we have to go out (of the house), we leave them with our domestic employee, but we call them on FaceTime... 'how are you, are you going to bed now'? [...] So, everything is via FaceTime, 'let me see what you are doing, turn around the camera to see who is with you.' (Juliana, 40)

For older mothers, smartphones offer other ways to help them monitor their teenagers or young adults. For example, María reflects on how she sometimes needs to look for her son when he does not answer at night:

I have an application called Friends because I have a 23-year-old boy that likes to go out at night, so... most of the time he forgets to tell me where is he going, so I see the Friends app, and the GPS tells me where he is... 'oh, ok, he is at his friend's house.'(María, 52)

The sense of control that smartphones provide to mothers can be suggested by the previous examples provided by Juliana and María. It is interesting how IT devices have also translated into a parental tool that they find useful to keep track of their children, despite their age.

Dependence: Connected 24/7

A third meaning found within the participants' narratives was the need to be connected at all times and the dependence they have developed for these devices. Digital moms find it difficult to leave their devices and daily Internet access, even when on vacation. Additionally, this dependence is likened to specific behaviors, such as expecting them and other people to answer their messages and calls immediately and to assume that what is shared on SNSs is known by everyone. Even though they admit that this dependence on Internet access may sometimes stress them, it is something that they cannot live without.

It creates me a conflict, and I realize it now that I just went on vacation... It is sad...you are at the beach, which such a divine view, and you can see everyone sitting, with their iPhones... but, we are at the beach! [...] we went on vacations, and we were all with our iPhones, at morning, at evening, and night. In the past, when you went on vacations, you did not need it (the iPhone) that was the last thing you thought about... (Juliana, 40)

Juliana's example indicates how even on vacations she experiences dependence on her smartphones; however, a desperation feeling is also present when lacking an Internet connection:

It happens to me that when I go to the United States, they tell me at home, you have to turn off your Data Roaming, because it is very expensive, and so and so… When I am at McAllen or any other part of the USA, I am desperate looking for a place with Wi-Fi so I can communicate. (María, 52)

Mothers who participated in this study reflected on how they were aware that this dependence is sometimes not justified, particularly when they feel desperation and anxiety to find Internet access even if they are not expecting an important call. However, they accepted this form of communication as inevitable as it is now part of their daily lives.

Adaptation/Change: The Challenge to Keep Up With IT

The use of digital technology also symbolizes adaptation and change for digital moms. In their narratives, it is evident how, despite being active users of technology and devices with Internet access, they still struggle to keep up each new generation of IT and do not consider themselves to be tech-savvy. Hence, participants reflected on how they have to try to understand new technologies and how to use them to not become obsolete in this rapidly changing world.

For example, one participant reflects the struggle in adopting new technology:

We need to change with the technological advance, and that change is difficult to me… because I didn´t live it, I am not used to this change…and my kids are all the time with that (technology) […] they were born that way, in this new era… and I have a hard time accepting this, so this is a conflict between my kids and me. (Irene, 42)

Additionally, participants commented that this change has also influenced the tools they use in their homes. As technology becomes increasingly mobile, many devices in the home become obsolete. For example, traditional landline telephones are becoming less common as more people own personal mobile phone and can be reached in this manner. In the same manner, the home computer, or desktop, is also becoming obsolete as household members have access to a laptop, tablet, or smartphone.

In fact, I have nine months without a telephone in my home because it is no longer needed… everything is by cell phone. You do not use the cellphone that much actually to make calls. Everything is now via WhatsApp. (Sandra, 47)

The computer in my house is now obsolete because everything we do is in the iPad or iPhone. (Juliana, 40)

These examples suggest that mothers are also coping with technological advance. The home telephone, where all members of the family received phone calls to the same number, is practically obsolete as personal mobile devices allow direct contact at any time. Additionally, a similar phenomenon is occurring with the desktop computer, which was used as a family computer, and is now being replaced by laptops or tablets owned by individual members in the family. The symbolic meanings that these cultural and technological changes bring to mothers include the struggle to adapt and keep up with the latest generation of technology, even though they use and enjoy their current IT.

Table 3. Symbolic Meanings of Technological Tools

Meaning	Description
Technological Tools	
Security	Feeling secure by the possession of the device
Control	Family control by monitoring children's activities
Dependence	The necessity of being connected at all times
Adaptation/Change	Keeping pace with the new generation IT

Source: Author

Perception of Digital Marketing Tools

This research also attempts to understand how digital moms perceive companies' different online marketing efforts by analyzing the most common digital marketing tools: (a) advertising on SNSs; (b) SEO; (c) SEM; (d) email marketing; and (e) website design. In the next section, results about digital moms' perceptions are presented.

Advertising on SNSs

Digital moms reported as being active on Facebook, Instagram, Twitter, Pinterest, and YouTube. Particularly, Facebook is the platform where they search for information on new products, services, and brands in general. Furthermore, they trust Facebook's company pages because they can contact brands directly, look for reviews, and form communities with other customers. As some participants commented:

Nowadays, I believe it is an advertising medium [Facebook], I do not know if it is the strongest medium, but I believe so… I get to learn about things, like concerts and all that stuff, by social networks… or promotions, for example, HEB sometimes advertises in their social networks about the Halloween promotion…2X1…well, you take advantage of this, right? (Claudia, 40)

Some [Facebook brand pages] have helped me as a mother…For example, when I was breastfeeding […] I did not understand how (to breastfeed). So, I went to the Facebook page of the brand "Liga de la Leche." each time I had questions, I consulted this page. It was great. (Paula, 33)

Furthermore, Instagram is used by moms to be informed about news, products, and services. Participants reported following international accounts. Instagram was also reported as being useful in learning about small and local business, as many new companies use advertising on Instagram in the form of paid ads, as well as through local influencers.

[I use Instagram to learn about] more local things. I have learned about places (restaurants and stores), and I have tried them because of their advertising on Instagram.(Teresa, 28)

Digital moms have mixed attitudes toward social network advertising. For example, it was found that Facebook's right column advertising is perceived negatively and that participants rarely click or respond to such ads. On the contrary, Facebook's newsfeed ads and Instagram's paid ads and influencer marketing were found to have a positive overall perception among participants. As two moms commented:

The worst thing that they can do to me is that they show me the ads on the right [of the screen, in Facebook], I cannot stand it! (Maricela, 40)

I feel that sometimes [the advertising] gives me the opportunity to get to know new things that are related to my interests. I would say that what I see in the ads are things that I like.(Alma, 28)

SEO

True to expectations, organic results that appear in the top positions are given higher credibility by participants. Digital moms in this study reported that they preferred clicking on the first results on the organic section once they make a search query. As one participant mentioned:

I feel that the first result [on the search results page] is the only one correct.(Rosa María, 46)

Furthermore, results suggest that besides the position of the website on the results page, the content is also important for clicking a link. Participants reported that they first read the title of the link and then read the description about the website they intend to visit. With this information, they form a perception about the results and finally decide which website to visit. This highlights the importance of a good SEO strategy that includes using keywords with a relevant header, meta-descriptions, and a display URL. One participant reflected on the process through which she selects a link on the search results page:

I read the title first; then I read a little bit about what is under the title [the meta description]. (Mayerling, 31)

SEM

Interestingly, participants in this study recognized that the search results page is divided into two sections: the organic results and the sponsored results. They can identify whether a result link is an advertising link or not and, in general, they reported a negative attitude toward sponsored results. Digital moms are good users of technology and are frequent users of the Internet. For these reasons, even though they do not understand exactly how SEM works—as in who pays whom and when—they recognize that companies are paying to appear on the sponsored section of the results page of a search engine. As one participant mentioned:

I do not like to click on the sponsored results because those are the ones [companies] are paying for, so they are not necessarily the most popular results, so I do not trust them. (Myriam, 32)

Website Design

Digital moms use SNSs, such as Facebook and Instagram, almost as search engines to look for new products and services. However, they reported that when they find a company they are interested in through these SNSs, they sometimes visit their official website to look for further information. A company's website is rated by digital moms based on the design and overall look and feel. Consistent with previous research on the topic, a poor design can lead participants to abandon the website.

Furthermore, the usability is also important: digital moms reported that in general, they look for simple and easy-to-use sites. Additionally, if the website is an e-commerce site, meaning that users can purchase products, then digital moms look for good-quality images regarding size and zoom options to analyze the product, detailed descriptions, and reviews by other customers. As one participant mentioned:

When I visit a website, if I do not like what I see and inspire me, I close it and look for another one. (Teresa, 28)

Email Marketing

Finally, email marketing was also analyzed to understand participants' perceptions toward this digital media strategy. In general, it was found that digital moms believe that receiving too many emails from a company is annoying. If they receive many emails with advertising by brands every day in their inbox, they have mixed feelings toward this kind of digital marketing strategy. Participants reported to rarely open emails from companies and that this was only when they intended to make a purchase and they recall receiving an email from such brand.

When I have a specific need, when I am going to buy, let say kid's clothes, I open [the emails] from kids' brands. (Mariana M, 37)

You know, I do like it (to receive emails from brands) because, you can say, I received today something but I do not need it today, so I delete it (it does not matter)... but sometimes, there are things that I am looking for, and I go and check (the inbox)... Groupon, Kidzania, or others, I say, let me check what I have. (Then I decide.)(Irene, 42)

This finding suggests that email marketing can be good for brand awareness even though this customer segment does not open the received email regularly, they are aware of the brands in their inbox and return to them when needed (Table 4).

DISCUSSION AND CONCLUSION

There is evidence to suggest that consumers attach meanings to different IT tools and devices. On the one hand, devices have several attached meanings such as security, family control, dependence, and adaptation. Digital moms feel a sense of security by having a smartphone as it enables them to contact or be contacted by family and friends. The security feeling is also related to dependence on IT devices and technology itself. Results indicate that there is an urge to be connected at all times and people also

Table 4. Attitudes toward digital marketing tools

Digital Marketing Tool	Digital Moms' Attitude
Social networking site advertising	Participants generally have positive attitudes toward ads on social media except for Facebook right column ads.
Search engine optimization	Participants value and have positive attitudes toward the first organic results on search engines.
Search engine marketing	Participants show a negative attitude toward paid ads on the results page of search engines.
Website design and usability	Participants value and have positive attitudes toward a well-designed website that is easy to navigate.
Email marketing	Participants have a generally positive attitude toward emails received by brands, but only open them when they have a specific need for a product or brand.

Source: Author

expect to obtain an immediate response from others. This can lead to a vicious circle, starting with the fear of feeling insecure, which in turn increases the use of mobile devices to feel safe. Regular usage of these devices increases our abilities as well, and we get used to this easy and rapid form of communication. This phenomenon is common in today's society as the fear of not having access to our smartphone and devices can be found in other segments of the population as well.

Additionally, there is now a term that addresses this situation: "nomophobia." Nomophobia refers to "no-mobile-phone phobia" and describes extreme dependence on one's smartphone. For this research particularly, the dependence expressed by participants stems from the desire to achieve excellence in all mom-related activities throughout the day as well as being reachable and reaching others at any given moment. It is interesting to question whether women are more prone to developing dependence or addiction to mobile phones than men, as women have a greater propensity to communicate with others and to develop affective relationships.

New forms of communication are drastically different from the traditional ones. Consumers have now replaced telephone calls with instant messages. Therefore, some protocols, such as invitations, announcements, and notifications that once were sent via physical letters, have been replaced by WhatsApp messages and social networking messages and alerts. Additionally, IT devices also represent a means of family control by digital moms as they take advantage of the available technologies to monitor their children. Tools such as video calls and GPS (Global Positioning System) monitoring allow them to keep track of their children's activities throughout the day. Finally, despite digital moms being active users of technology, they still struggle to keep up with newer-generation IT. The use of IT devices represents a constant challenge to become knowledgeable and not be left behind. For older digital moms, the use of such technologies is not considered natural, as they grew up without digital technologies, and, for this reason, they feel a certain lag compared with younger mothers.

On the other hand, SNSs, especially Facebook, showed interesting meanings associated by consumers. One meaning commonly found on Facebook is a nostalgic feeling derived from the reconnection with old friends and family who are not physically close. Consumers find this SNS to be a tool that allows them to reunite with people they care about but have been distanced with for some or the other reason. Additionally, there is a strong sense of community attached to SNSs such as Facebook and WhatsApp. In fact, there are some characteristics consistent with Muñiz and O'Guinn (2001), such as shared consciousness, rituals and traditions, and a sense of moral responsibility.

Furthermore, as consumers display such symbolic meanings toward IT devices and SNSs, companies are now using digital marketing strategies to reach consumers online. This research particularly explored the generalized attitudes toward five of the most common digital marketing strategies used by organizations. It noteworthy that four out of the five strategies explored were positively perceived: SNSs advertising, SEO, website design and usability, and email marketing. However, ads on social media need to deliver a clear, unique value proposition to digital moms and, more importantly, should be placed in a natural, non-invasive manner. Participants reflected on how advertising that flows naturally with their consumption of social media content is useful and even enjoyable, such as ads on Facebook's newsfeed (as it appears along the content of their Facebook friends), as well as ads on their Instagram stories. However, ads on Facebook that are located on the right of the screen were clearly perceived as a desperate attempt to target customers and participants rejected them.

Furthermore, these negative attitudes for those particular ads on Facebook also stem from the fact that the ads are normally related to past searches and participants commented that they did not like to be exposed in that manner. Finally, an interesting finding of this research is related to SEM, considering the recent increase of the total digital marketing budget dedicated to this strategy by organizations. We can be certain on the fact that ads on search engines' results pages are: (a) identified by participants so they can clearly understand and locate results that are sponsored by a company; (b) not valued and often ignored; and (c) are not trusted by participants. These results demand further research to identify if other types of online users respond better to this specific digital marketing strategy.

Overall, these results shed light on the perceptions of digital moms toward technological tools and digital marketing strategies. Particularly, results contribute to the literature by (a) addressing the symbolic meanings that technological tools have in their lives and (b) providing insights of how digital moms perceive different digital marketing strategies commonly implemented by brands. In sum, managerial implications derived from these results as brands targeting this group of Internet users can use both symbolic meanings and perceptions to inspire a creative and holistic digital marketing strategy.

LIMITATIONS AND FUTURE RESEARCH

No research is without limitations. Particularly, this study focused on one segment of Internet users in Mexico and used a qualitative method to collect information; therefore, these results cannot be generalized to all consumers. Digital moms are characterized as frequent users of online technologies, and it can be assumed that they are more educated on digital marketing techniques that are applied by companies. As mentioned earlier, it becomes interesting to understand how different segments of online users react toward the same digital marketing strategies proposed in this study. This can have important managerial implications as companies seek knowledge regarding which digital marketing strategy to implement based on the target consumer group.

Furthermore, future research can also consider the timeline or sequence of the purchase decision process, which involves different digital marketing strategies or whether usage frequency makes any difference in the attitudes toward them. For example, considering that SEM is generally received negatively by participants in this study, it would be interesting to shed light on when online users' value and use paid results over organic one on the search engine results page. Hopefully, this research can serve as a basis and inspiration for further research on the topic.

REFERENCES

Al-Qeisi, K., Dennis, C., Alamanos, E., & Jayawardhena, C. (2014). Website design quality and usage behavior: Unified Theory of Acceptance and Use of Technology. *Journal of Business Research*, *67*(11), 2282–2290. doi:10.1016/j.jbusres.2014.06.016

Araujo, T., & Neijens, P. (2012). Friend me: Which factors influence top global brands participation in social network sites. *Internet Research*, *22*(5), 626–640. doi:10.1108/10662241211271581

Baye, M. R., De los Santos, B., & Wildenbeest, M. R. (2016). Search engine optimization: What drives organic traffic to retail sites? *Journal of Economics & Management Strategy*, *25*(1), 6–31. doi:10.1111/jems.12141

Belk, R. W. (1988). Possessions and the extended self. *The Journal of Consumer Research*, *15*(2), 139–168. doi:10.1086/209154

Blumler, J. G. (1979). The role of theory in uses and gratifications studies. *Communication Research*, *6*(1), 9–36. doi:10.1177/009365027900600102

Boughton, S.B. (2005). Search engine marketing. *Perspectives in Business, 2*(1), 29-33.

Brooks, H. (1973). The technology of zero growth. *Daedalus*, *102*(4), 139–152.

Bryman, A. (1984). The Debate about Quantitative and Qualitative Research: A Question of Method or Epistemology? *The British Journal of Sociology*, *35*(1), 75–92. doi:10.2307/590553

Calvert, M., & Terry, J. (Eds.). (2013). *Processed lives: gender and technology in everyday life*. Routledge.

Carmen, P., & Nicolae, P. A. (2010). Email marketing campaigns: The easiest path from organizations to consumers–an exploratory assessment. *Annals of Faculty of Economics*, *1*(1), 737–742.

Dou, W., Lim, K. H., Su, C., Zhou, N., & Cui, N. (2010). Brand positioning strategy using search engine marketing. *Management Information Systems Quarterly*, *34*(2), 261–279. doi:10.2307/20721427

Edmonson, A., & McManus, S. (2007). Methodological Fit in Management Field Research. *Academy of Management Review*, *32*(4), 1155–1179.

Empathica. (n.d.). *White paper: What is the Opportunity for "SoLoMo" (Social.Local.Mobile.) to Improve the Customer Experience?* Author.

Fariborzi, E., & Zahedifard, M. (2012). E-mail Marketing: Advantages, Disadvantages and Improving Techniques. *International Journal of e-Education, e-Business, e-. Management Learning*, *2*(3), 232.

Flick, U. (2002). An introduction to qualitative research. *Sage (Atlanta, Ga.).*

Gehrke, D., & Turban, E. (1999, January). Determinants of successful website design: relative importance and recommendations for effectiveness. In HICSS (p. 5042). IEEE. doi:10.1109/HICSS.1999.772943

Gudivada, V. N., Rao, D., & Paris, J. (2015). Understanding search-engine optimization. *Computer*, *48*(10), 43–52. doi:10.1109/MC.2015.297

Hasan, B. (2016). Perceived irritation in online shopping: The impact of website design characteristics. *Computers in Human Behavior*, *54*, 224–230. doi:10.1016/j.chb.2015.07.056

Healy, M. J., Beverland, M. B., Oppewal, H., & Sands, S. (2007). Understanding retail experiences-the case for ethnography. *International Journal of Market Research*, *49*(6), 751–778. doi:10.1177/147078530704900608

Hudson, L. A., & Ozanne, J. L. (1988). Alternative ways of seeking knowledge in consumer research. *The Journal of Consumer Research*, *14*(4), 508–521. doi:10.1086/209132

Jenkins, S. (2008). *The truth about email marketing*. FT Press.

LaRossa, R., & Reitzes, D. C. (1993). Symbolic interactionism and family studies. In Sourcebook of family theories and methods (pp. 135-166). Springer US. doi:10.1007/978-0-387-85764-0_6

Lee, S., & Cho, M. (2011). Social media use in a mobile broadband environment: Examination of determinants of Twitter and Facebook use. *International Journal of Mobile Marketing*, *6*(2), 71–87.

Mangold, W. G., & Faulds, D. J. (2009). Social media: The new hybrid element of the promotion mix. *Business Horizons*, *52*(4), 357–365. doi:10.1016/j.bushor.2009.03.002

IAB Mexico & Millward Brown. (2014). *Estudio de consumo de medios entre internautas mexicanos*. Author.

IAB Mexico & Millward Brown. (2014a). *Estudio de consumo de medios entre internautas mexicanos. Segmento Teens*. Author.

IAB Mexico & Millward Brown. (2014b). *Estudio de consumo de medios entre internautas mexicanos. Segmento Ejecutivos*. Author.

IAB Mexico & Millward Brown. (2014c). *Estudio de consumo de medios entre internautas mexicanos. Segmento Digital Moms*. Author.

Miles, M., & Huberman, M. (1994). *Qualitative Data Analysis: An Expanded Sourcebook* (2nd ed.). Thousand Oaks, CA: SAGE Publications, Inc.

Muniz, A. M. Jr, & O'Guinn, T. C. (2001). Brand community. *The Journal of Consumer Research*, *27*(4), 412–432. doi:10.1086/319618

Park, L. S., Yu, J., Yu, S., & Liao, L. (2015). *Search engine optimization for category specific search results*. U.S. Patent 9,116,994.

Park, Y. A., & Gretzel, U. (2007). Success factors for destination marketing websites: A qualitative meta-analysis. *Journal of Travel Research*, *46*(1), 46–63. doi:10.1177/0047287507302381

Ryan, D. (2016). *Understanding digital marketing: marketing strategies for engaging the digital generation*. Kogan Page Publishers.

Sahni, N. S., Wheeler, S. C., & Chintagunta, P. (2018). Personalization in Email Marketing: The Role of Non-informative Advertising Content. *Marketing Science*, *37*(2), 236–258. doi:10.1287/mksc.2017.1066

Sen, R. (2005). Optimal search engine marketing strategy. *International Journal of Electronic Commerce*, *10*(1), 9–25. doi:10.1080/10864415.2005.11043964

Singh, S., & Sonnenburg, S. (2012). Brand performances in social media. *Journal of Interactive Marketing*, *26*(4), 189–197. doi:10.1016/j.intmar.2012.04.001

Smith, J. K. (1983). Quantitative versus Qualitative Research: An Attempt to Clarify the Issue. *Educational Researcher*, *12*(3), 6–13. doi:10.3102/0013189X012003006

Snow, D. A. (2001). Extending and broadening Blumer's conceptualization of symbolic interactionism. *Symbolic Interaction*, *24*(3), 367–377. doi:10.1525i.2001.24.3.367

TechTerms.com. (2010, January 4). *ICT*. Retrieved Dec 11, 2018, from http://www.techterms.com/definition/ict

Tiago, M. T. P. M. B., & Veríssimo, J. M. C. (2014). Digital marketing and social media: Why bother? *Business Horizons*, *57*(6), 703–708. doi:10.1016/j.bushor.2014.07.002

Trevino, L. K., Lengel, R. H., & Daft, R. L. (1987). Media symbolism, media richness, and media choice in organizations a symbolic interactionism perspective. *Communication Research*, *14*(5), 553–574. doi:10.1177/009365087014005006

Treviño, T. (2017). Madres digitales en Monterrey, México: Estudio de hábitos, comportamientos y actitudes en Internet. *Revista Argentina de Investigación en Negocios*, *3*(2), 71–79.

Treviño, T., & Morton, F. (2016). Online Shopping in Mexico: Exploring the Promising and Challenging Panorama. In Mexican Business Culture: Essays on Tradition, Ethics, Entrepreneurship and Commerce and the State (pp. 166-182). McFarland & Company.

Treviño, T., & Pineda, J. L. (2017). *Mamás Digitales en México: ¿Por qué se conectan con las marcas en Internet?* El Financiero.

KEY TERMS AND DEFINITIONS

Bing: Originated from MSN Search, it is a search engine developed by Microsoft to provide standard web search, as well as specialized searches for news, shopping, images, videos, maps, and other categories.

Email Marketing: A valuable and digital marketing tool that delivers short messages with a clear value proposition and a call to action for users.

Global Positioning System (GPS): It is a satellite-based navigation system composed of 24 satellites put into orbit by the US Department of Defense.

Pay-per-Click (PPC): It is a digital advertising model where the advertiser pays an amount (fixed or determined by auction) when a user clicks on one ad.

Protocol: Formal description of message formats and rules that guide the exchange of messages between computers.

Silver Surfer: Internet user older than 50 years of age.

Social Networking Sites (SNSs): It is an interactive media enabling two-way communication rather than one-directional as in traditional media.

Usability: The extent to which a product can be used by specified users to achieve goals with efficiency and satisfaction.

Chapter 15
Google Trends Metadata as a Revenue Indicator for Digital Marketing Activities in Spanish Businesses

Jesús Manuel Palma-Ruiz
https://orcid.org/0000-0002-1039-6243
Universidad Autónoma de Chihuahua, Mexico

Raúl Gómez-Martínez
https://orcid.org/0000-0003-3575-7970
Universidad Rey Juan Carlos, Spain

ABSTRACT

The digital world is changing at an extraordinary phase. The never-ending advances in new information and communication technologies (ICT) have more than ever changed the way in which we live, communicate, and process information. This has reshaped our habits to cope with a world constantly demanding new daily virtual experiences. People of all ages are in need to grip these experiences in one way or another. Regarding the advances in ICT, the internet alongside digital and social media have created whole new possibilities to gather real-time data and store valuable information while being virtually connected at all times. This postulates an evident challenge for companies to capitalize on the possibilities of digital marketing media and an opportunity to reach customers effectively using metadata and other resources virtually available. In this chapter, the authors used OLS regressions using Google Trends query data from 2008 to 2016 to measure the growing interest in digital marketing and other related topics and the monetization of such interest in the Spanish media sector.

DOI: 10.4018/978-1-5225-8939-6.ch015

INTRODUCTION

The substantial advances in the information and communications technology (ICT) during the past decades and the highly competitive and globalized markets have paved the way for companies to adopt digital marketing activities increasingly. Nowadays, digital marketing efforts represent an essential activity for all businesses to remain visible for both customers and investors.

The development and innovation of ICTs as well as the explosion of the Internet and social media and networks represent a valuable opportunity and demand alternative methods to the use of traditional surveys to gather insightful information about users and consumers search for information and evaluate alternatives before purchases and investment decisions. This widespread of digital marketing practices and techniques, along with social networks and mobile technology, has contributed to the individualization of marketing where companies are increasingly communicating with users and customers, providing tailored solutions 24/7 (Wymbs, 2011; Brady, Fellenz, & Brookes, 2008; Simmons, 2008; Royle & Laing, 2014).

As a result of these changes in consumer behavior, firms are required to rethink their marketing strategies in the digital territory (Tiago & Veríssimo, 2014; Stephen, 2016). Companies must be eager to know, practice and invest in digital marketing activities to cope, remain visible and competitive in this challenging digital world (Stone & Woodcock, 2014). As better put by Stone and Woodcock (2014, p. 4), "digital marketing and its linked analytics, particularly real-time high-performance analytics, are opening up new marketing opportunities, leading to improved marketing return on investment, and then identify why so many companies fail to obtain the expected benefits."

Google Trends represents a relatively new approach to providing new techniques to study different economic values. Therefore, the primary objective of this chapter is to use Google Trends data as an indicator of the total or local interest for a specific topic closely linked to the term digital marketing, neuromarketing, and landing page in Spain and analyze if such interest has been monetized overtime by the Spanish marketing firms.

This chapter aims to deliver at least two main contributions. Firstly, to illustrate an actual case for using Google Trends as a tool for analysis and forecasting based on real-time customer metadata over a series of time. Secondly, to inform with alternative techniques to gather and analyze information, such as Google Trends, encouraging researchers to explore further attempts in this and additional lines of research. This chapter is organized into four main sections. The Background section offers an overview of Google Trends and a review of the current literature on this topic. The Methodology section presents the hypothesis of study and the examination of data. The section of Solutions and Recommendations offers discussion and future research directions. Finally, the conclusion section delivers a discussion of the overall coverage of this chapter and final remarks.

DIGITAL MARKETING CHALLENGES AND OPPORTUNITIES

The continuously growing ICT developments and innovations, including social, mobile, and the Internet of Things (IoT) provide emerging and alternative approaches to the use of new sources and forms of data, real-time metadata or big data. This availability of data provides researchers with unlimited possibilities. For example, how segmented users and consumers seek information and evaluate alternatives before purchase or investment decisions, such insights would provide valuable opportunities to predict behaviors, and more importantly to capitalize on these. Such new approaches to assess metadata information has provided innovative techniques to study different econometric variables.

IBM Marketing Cloud (2017) states that 2.5 quintillion bytes of data are created on a daily basis. In other words, 90% of the data in the world today has been created in the last two years alone, and this data growth rate is likely to keep accelerating due to continuous ICTs advancements. With such overwhelming information currently available, companies need to emphasize a clear strategy to access and interpret relevant metadata for better and faster business decision-making and useful in forecasting trends (Özköse, Arı, & Gencer, 2015; Järvinen & Karjaluoto, 2015).

Therefore, analytical and technical skills and useful performance metrics have become decisive in digital marketing, thus determinant for marketing strategy processes where digital technologies are having and will have a significant impact (Kannan & Li, 2017; Mulhern, 2009). Though, this challenging aspect of digital marketing skills is a result of the vitality of the field and the excess of data available and the existing number of analytical tools (Fisher, 2009). However, this data is useless without proper analysis and interpretation (Chaffey & Patron, 2012; Court, Gordon, & Perrey, 2012). As Valos, Ewing, & Powell (2010) discussed it, "decisions will be based on data-driven extrapolations and statistical heuristics" (p. 363).

As the digital world keeps advancing an excess of data is generated, metrics for such data are usually not used for strategic purposes, and the possibilities to capitalize on this usage remain unexplored (Järvinen & Karjaluoto, 2015; Järvinen, Töllinen, Karjaluoto, & Jayawardhena, 2012). Authors demonstrate that measuring and optimizing digital marketing performance measurement applying web analytics has improved the efficiency of marketing actions and successively increased revenues (Phippen, Sheppard, & Furnell, 2004; Weischedel & Huizingh, 2006; Wilson, 2010).

GOOGLE TRENDS

Google Trends is a public service offered by Google Inc., that shows how often one term or topic is entered in Google for searching information about it. Google Trends can be used to extract data for precise search terms and general topics, thus providing relevant information on topics of interest for users and customers. Therefore, the use of search queries and web analytics is an important developmental step toward measurable digital marketing. As stated by Choi and Varian (2012), queries can be useful leading indicators for subsequent and actual consumer purchase decision-making. In other words, data can be used to understand online customer behavior and provide actual benefits to the business outlining a product/service and marketing strategy (Nakatani & Chuang, 2011).

The information provided by Google Trends is taking a particular interest in several lines of research. In financial research, Gómez-Martínez (2013) developed a model where the evolution of stock indices is explained by the mood of investors measured as the Internet search activity for specific terms related to financial markets. Other studies also used Google data to explain the evolution of different financial values like the demand and volatility of securities listed on the NYSE and NASDAQ (Vlastakis & Markellos, 2012). Smith (2012) used Google Trends to explain the market volatility currency. Rose and Spiegel (2012) used information provided by Google Trends to explain the dollar liquidity during the financial crisis. Also, Chen, Ki So, Wu, and Ming Yan (2014) used Google search query data to improve the timeliness of business cycle turning point's identification. Others have used Google Trends data to identify attention shifts in search queries for companies listed in the Standard and Poor´s 100 index and changes in stock prices and market movements (Heiberger, 2015).

If focused on non-purely financial terms, Ettredge, Gerdes, and Karuga (2005) examined the unemployment rate in the U.S.A. using web search data, which proved useful in forecasting. Askitas and Zimmermann (2009) demonstrated the strong correlation of search terms as "unemployment office" or "unemployment rate" with the evolution of the German labor market. McLaren and Shanbhoge (2011), in the context of the UK market, used Google Trends to explain the evolution of the labor and housing markets, and as a predictor of house pricing and sales (Wu & Brynjolfsson, 2015). Guzman (2011) proposed a measure of real-time inflation expectations based on metadata raised from Google Internet search queries. Other studies have used Google Trends data to examine the determinants of interest in Bitcoin and construct customer profiles (Yelowitz & Wilson, 2015).

Other practical applications for Google Trends metadata include predicting the quality of Chinese universities and companies (Vaughan & Chen, 2015), and forecasting tourism in China (Yang, Pan, Evans, & Lv, 2015), South Korea (Park, Lee, & Song, 2017), Vienna (Önder & Ulrich, 2016), Hong Kong (Bangwayo-Skeete & Skeete, 2015), Puerto Rico (Rivera, 2015).

Google Trends has proven to be a good indicator to measure the interest in a certain topic, and how such interest is associated with higher consumption of that specific product or service. In other words, the higher the number of searches recorded for a particular topic, an increase in sales should then be registered. This has been demonstrated for entrepreneurship (Gómez, Prado, & Idoeta, 2015), museum visitors (Gómez, Rodríguez, & Pérez-Bustamente, 2016), wine cellar visitors, (Gómez, Prado, & Díez, 2016), and wine production (Gómez, Plaza, Prado, & Prado, 2016). In this chapter, the authors used the information given by Google Trends to measure the interest in digital marketing activities and determine the effect of such interest in the Spanish media sector.

Using Google Trends´ chart visualization, the horizontal axis of the main graph represents time, and the vertical is the relative numbers of searches made in a period, weekly for less than five years and monthly for the whole time series from 2004 to date. Below the main graph, the popularity is broken down by countries, regions, cities, language and more.

As stated by Yelowitz and Wilson (2014), Google Trends does not report raw search counts for a topic. Instead, Google computes the number of topic searches relative to all searches, normalizes the series, so the highest value is 100, scaling all other values relative to such highest. Figure 1 shows how Google Trends represents the time series of different topics related to digital marketing such as "*digital marketing*," "*landing page*" or "*neuromarketing*" in Spain, from 2008 to 2016.

Additionally, it is possible to refine the main graph by region and time period, and these historical series can be exported to a spreadsheet format to study it. The statistical metadata available in Google Trends is a clear indicator of the total or local interest for a specific topic over time closely linked to the term searched.

METHODOLOGY

As we have seen, Google Trends shows the interest of the population about one topic, in this case, we can observe clearly in Figure 1 that the interest in digital marketing in Spain has increased from 2008 to 2016, with records of maximum numbers of searches in 2016 of the topics selected, "digital marketing",

Figure 1. Google Trends search query data on digital marketing topics
Note: Numbers represent search interest relative to the highest point on the chart for the given region and time. A value of 100 is the peak popularity for the term. A value of 50 means that the term is half as popular. A score of 0 means there was not enough data for this term.

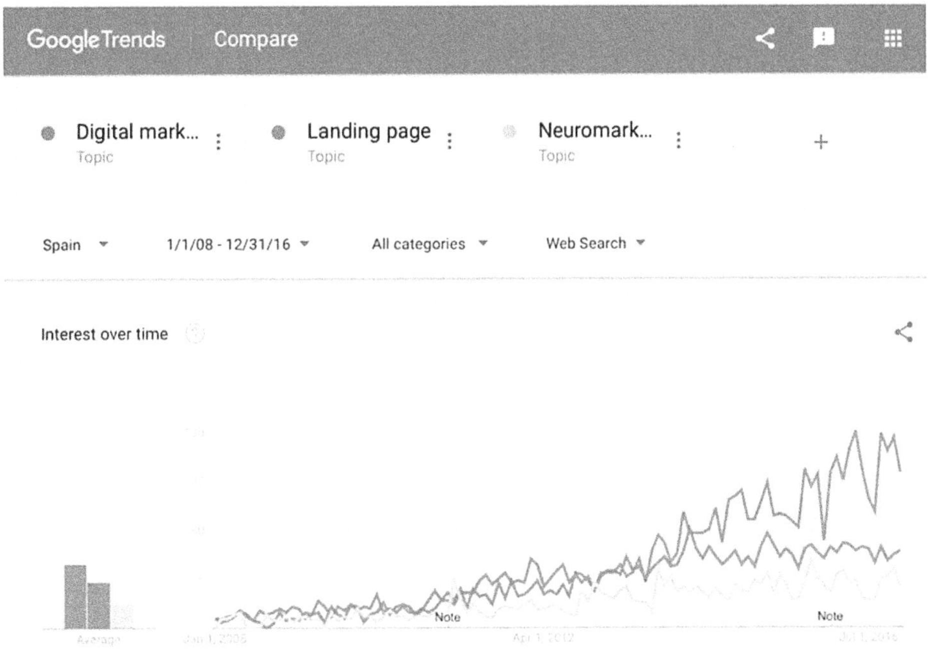

**For a more accurate representation see the electronic version.*

"neuromarketing" and "landing page". The research question for this study is if that specific increasing interest has represented a business opportunity to capitalize for the marketing firms that operate in Spain, thus increasing their revenues. So, the hypothesis to test is, therefore:

H_0: More interest in digital marketing activities means more revenues for Spanish marketing firms.

To validate this hypothesis, we will plot revenue of Spanish marketing firms versus Google Trends of each of those digital marketing related topics. If the slope of the regression line of the plot is positive, then we will validate H_0.

Data

The data for the exogenous variable has been collected directly from the web of Google Trends (http://www.google.es/trends/). We used only searches made using Google because it represents over 80% of the total searches that were made, considering highly representative. We collected Google Trends search query data from January 2008 to December 2016 for Spain related to digital marketing topics: "digital marketing," "neuromarketing" and "landing page."

The data of the endogenous variable has been collected directly from the National Statistics Institute of Spain (https://www.ine.es/). Revenue data of Spanish marketing firms are available from 2008 to 2016 on a yearly basis. We can observe in Figures 2 and 3 that the revenue of Spanish marketing firms is decreasing for the studied period.

Figure 2. Total revenue spanish marketing firms (data in thousands €)

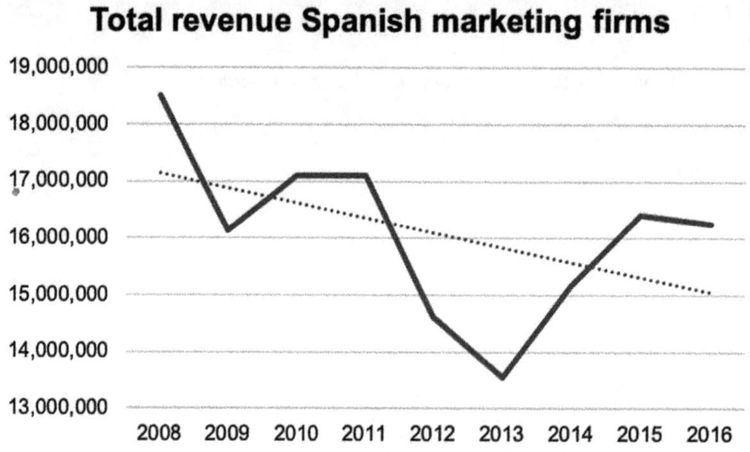

Figure 3. Total revenue spanish marketing firms by type (data in thousands €)

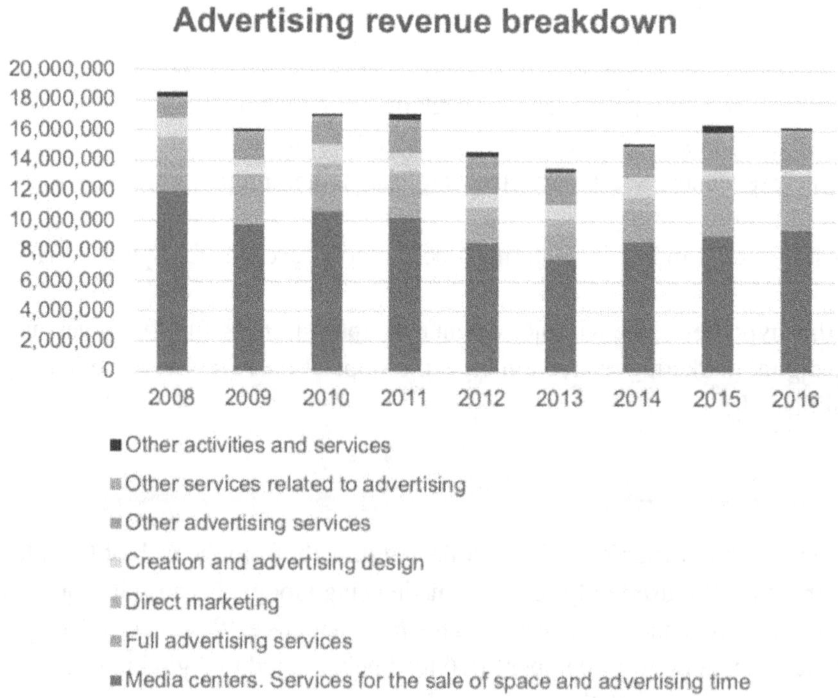

**For a more accurate representation see the electronic version.*

SOLUTIONS AND RECOMMENDATIONS

As we can observe in Figures 4, 5, and 6 the slope of the ordinary least squares (OLS) regression is negative in all the plotted graphs compared to Google Trends metadata related to "digital marketing," "neuromarketing" and "landing page." It appears that despite the opportunity derived from the increasing interest in digital marketing activities in Spain from the year 2008 to 2016, this has not been monetized by Spanish marketing firms.

This conceivably has an explanation while analyzing the macroeconomic context during this period. Spain has suffered one of the most profound structural crises starting in 2007. From 2008 to 2010, governmental policies took place to lessen the adverse effects of the recession, and expenditure cut measures began in 2010, signaling a period of austerity, which continued through 2014 (Banyuls & Recio, 2015). This difficult period has placed an important burden on companies to confront the realities of recession and austerity. As a result, adjustments and cuts in marketing budgets were set, and activities such as

Figure 4. Total revenue spanish marketing firms vs. "digital marketing" google trends

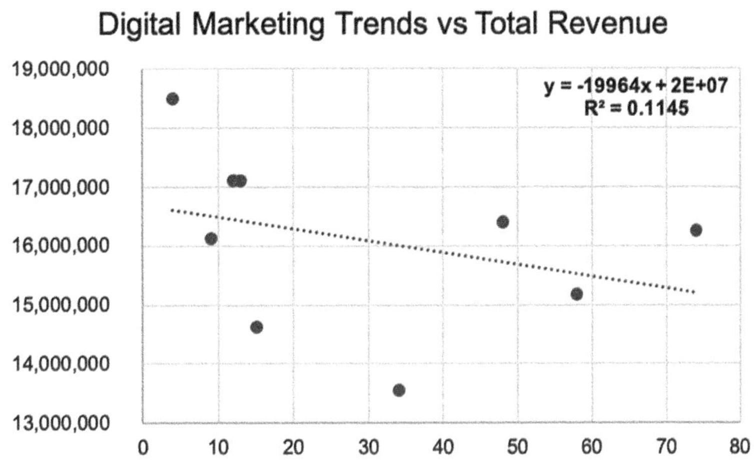

Figure 5. Total revenue spanish marketing firms vs. "landing page" google trends

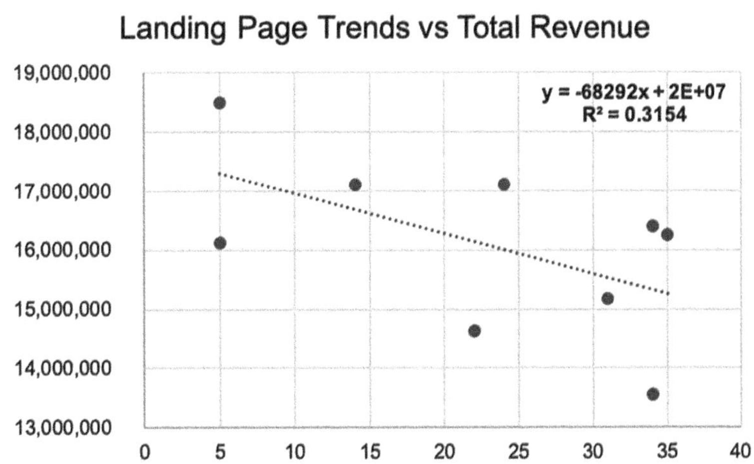

Figure 6. Total revenue spanish marketing firms vs. "neuromarketing" google trends

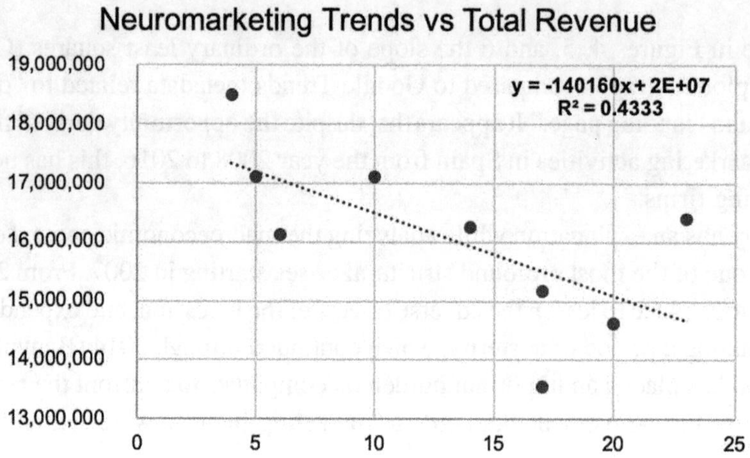

marketing innovations had to be placed on hold during the crisis, with priorities aimed at the company´s mere survival. For example, Medrano & Olarte-Pascual (2016) found that companies in Spain were less likely to implement marketing innovations in 2010 during the crisis.

Regardless of this situation, the interest in digital marketing is clearly shown, and it appears that marketing companies in one way or another have missed capitalizing on such trends which leads to another important reason to reconsider marketing strategies and related activities during difficult times. Besides, as other authors have emphasized, selected marketing metrics should comprise short and long-term as well as financial and non-financial performance measurements (Ambler & Roberts, 2008; O'Sullivan & Abela, 2007; O'Sullivan, Abela, & Hutchinson, 2009). In this study, we have only focused on financial indicators without considering other critical contextual variables. Also, a more in-depth analysis could be conducted while considering breaking down Google Trends data into smaller regions and reduced periods for a more comprehensive study. For these reasons, we believe that future studies should reproduce a similar analysis in different contexts while considering other relevant variables as a function of the equation.

CONCLUSION

The data analysis provided by Google Trends is representative of the exponential interest in both users and customers, given the relevance of digital marketing in Spain from 2008 to date added to the growth of social and digital media. Spain is just a case, and other relevant content analysis in different backgrounds can be conducted.

This chapter has fulfilled its purpose of illustrating the use of real-time metadata while using Google Trends as a tool for analysis over a series of time and in a specific context. Further approaches to disaggregate data can be explored as a way to inform of alternative techniques to gather and analyze information, encouraging researchers to undertake the challenges of using objective metadata and web analytics resources.

REFERENCES

Ambler, T., & Roberts, J. (2008). Assessing marketing performance: Don't settle for a silver metric. *Journal of Marketing Management*, *24*(7-8), 733–750. doi:10.1362/026725708X345498

Askitas, N., & Zimmermann, F. (2009). Google econometrics and unemployment forecasting. *Applied Economics Quarterly*, *55*(2), 107–120. doi:10.3790/aeq.55.2.107

Bangwayo-Skeete, P. F., & Skeete, R. W. (2015). Can Google data improve the forecasting performance of tourist arrivals? Mixed-data sampling approach. *Tourism Management*, *46*, 454–464. doi:10.1016/j.tourman.2014.07.014

Banyuls, J., & Recio, A. (2015). A crisis inside the crisis: Spain under a conservative neoliberalism. In S. Lehndorff (Ed.), *Divisive integration. The triumph of failed ideas in Europe* (pp. 39–68). Brussels, Belgium: European Trade Union Institute.

Brady, M., Fellenz, M. R., & Brookes, R. (2008). Researching the role of information and communications technology (ICT) in contemporary marketing practices. *Journal of Business and Industrial Marketing*, *23*(2), 108–114. doi:10.1108/08858620810850227

Chaffey, D., & Patron, M. (2012). From web analytics to digital marketing optimization: Increasing the commercial value of digital analytics. *Journal of Direct. Data and Digital Marketing Practice*, *14*(1), 30–45. doi:10.1057/dddmp.2012.20

Chen, T., Ki So, E. P., Wu, L., & Ming Yan, I. K. (2014). The 2007–2008 U.S. Recession: What Did the Real-Time Google Trends Data Tell the United States? *Contemporary Economic Policy*, *33*(2), 395–403. doi:10.1111/coep.12074

Choi, H., & Varian, H. (2012). Predicting the Present with Google Trends. *The Economic Record*, *88*(1), 2–9. doi:10.1111/j.1475-4932.2012.00809.x

Court, D., Gordon, J., & Perrey, J. (2012). Measuring marketing's worth. *The McKinsey Quarterly*, *3*, 113–118.

Ettredge, M., Gerdes, J., & Karuga, G. (2005). Using web-based search data to predict macroeconomic statistics. *Communications of the ACM*, *48*(11), 87–92. doi:10.1145/1096000.1096010

Fisher, T. (2009). ROI in social media: A look at the arguments. *Database Marketing & Customer Strategy Management*, *16*(3), 189–195. doi:10.1057/dbm.2009.16

Gómez-Martínez, R. (2013). Señales de inversión basadas en un índice de aversión al riesgo. *Investigaciones Europeas de Dirección y Economía de la Empresa*, *19*(3), 147–157. doi:10.1016/j.iedee.2012.12.001

Gómez-Martínez, R., Plaza-Casado, P., Prado-Román, C., & Prado-Román, M. (2016). Google Trends como indicador válido para los ingresos por la producción de vino. *Tourism and Hospitality International Journal*, *6*(2), 94–106.

Gómez-Martínez, R., Prado-Román, C., & Díez-Martín, F. (2016). Google Search Activity as Thermometer of Wine Cellar Visitors. In M. Peris-Ortiz, M. Del Río Rama, & C. Rueda-Armengot (Eds.), *Wine and Tourism*. Springer. doi:10.1007/978-3-319-18857-7_17

Gómez-Martínez, R., Prado-Román, M., & Mercado-Idoeta, C. (2015). Google Search Activity as Entrepreneurship Thermometer. In M. Peris-Ortiz & J. M. Sahut (Eds.), *New Challenges in Entrepreneurship and Finance*. Springer. doi:10.1007/978-3-319-08888-4_16

Gómez-Martínez, R., Rodríguez Herráez, B., & Pérez-Bustamante Yábar, D. C. (2016). Actividad de búsquedas en internet como variable para determinar la afluencia a museos. *Cuadernos de Turismo, 38*, 203–219.

Guzman, G. (2011). Internet search behavior as an economic forecasting tool: The case of inflation expectations. *Journal of Economic and Social Measurement, 36*(3), 119–167.

Heiberger, R. H. (2015). Collective Attention and Stock Prices: Evidence from Google Trends Data on Standard and Poor's 100. *PLoS One, 10*(8), e0135311. doi:10.1371/journal.pone.0135311 PMID:26258498

IBM Marketing Cloud. (2017). *10 Key Marketing Trends for 2017 and Ideas for Exceeding Customer Expectations*. Retrieved from https://www-01.ibm.com/common/ssi/cgi-bin/ssialias?htmlfid=WRL12345USEN

Järvinen, J., & Karjaluoto, H. (2015). The use of Web analytics for digital marketing performance measurement. *Industrial Marketing Management, 50*, 117–127. doi:10.1016/j.indmarman.2015.04.009

Järvinen, J., Töllinen, A., Karjaluoto, H., & Jayawardhena, C. (2012). Digital and social media marketing usage in B2B industrial section. *Marketing Management Journal, 22*(2), 102–117.

Kannan, P. K., & Li, H. (2017). Digital marketing: A framework, review, and research agenda. *International Journal of Research in Marketing, 34*(1), 22–45. doi:10.1016/j.ijresmar.2016.11.006

McLaren, N., & Shanbhogue, R. (2011). *Using Internet Search Data as Economic Indicators. Bank of England Quarterly Bulletin, 2011*, Q2.

Medrano, N., & Olarte-Pascual, C. (2016). The effects of the crisis on marketing innovation: An application for Spain. *Journal of Business and Industrial Marketing, 31*(3), 404–417. doi:10.1108/JBIM-02-2013-0048

Micu, A. C., Dedeker, K., Lewis, I., Moran, R., Netzer, O., Plummer, J., & Rubinson, J. (2011). Guest Editorial: The Shape of Marketing Research in 2021. *Journal of Advertising Research, 51*(1), 213–221. doi:10.2501/JAR-51-1-213-221

Mulhern, F. (2009). Integrated marketing communications: From media channels to digital connectivity. *Journal of Marketing Communications, 15*(2-3), 85–101. doi:10.1080/13527260902757506

Nakatani, K., & Chuang, T. T. (2011). A web analytics tool selection method: An analytical hierarchy process approach. *Internet Research, 21*(2), 171–186. doi:10.1108/10662241111123757

O'Sullivan, D., & Abela, A. (2007). Marketing performance measurement ability and firm performance. *Journal of Marketing, 71*(4), 79–93. doi:10.1509/jmkg.71.2.079

O'Sullivan, D., Abela, A., & Hutchinson, M. (2009). Marketing performance measurement and firm performance: Evidence from the European high-technology sector. *European Journal of Marketing*, *43*(5/6), 843–862. doi:10.1108/03090560910947070

Önder, I., & Ulrich, G. (2016). Forecasting Tourism Demand with Google Trends for a Major European City Destination. *Tourism Analysis*, *21*(2-3), 203–220. doi:10.3727/108354216X14559233984773

Özköse, H., Arı, E. S., & Gencer, C. (2015). Yesterday, today and tomorrow of big data. *Procedia: Social and Behavioral Sciences*, *195*, 1042–1050. doi:10.1016/j.sbspro.2015.06.147

Park, S., Lee, J., & Song, W. (2017). Short-term forecasting of Japanese tourist inflow to South Korea using Google trends data. *Journal of Travel & Tourism Marketing*, *34*(3), 357–368. doi:10.1080/10548408.2016.1170651

Phippen, A., Sheppard, L., & Furnell, S. (2004). A practical evaluation of Web analytics. *Internet Research*, *14*(4), 284–293. doi:10.1108/10662240410555306

Rivera, R. (2016). A dynamic linear model to forecast hotel registrations in Puerto Rico using Google Trends data. *Tourism Management*, *57*, 12–20. doi:10.1016/j.tourman.2016.04.008

Rose, A. K., & Spiegel, M. M. (2012). Dollar illiquidity and central bank swap arrangements during the global financial crisis. *Journal of International Economics*, *88*(2), 326–340. doi:10.1016/j.jinteco.2012.02.014

Royle, J., & Laing, A. (2014). The digital marketing skills gap: Developing a digital marketer model for the communication industries. *International Journal of Information Management*, *34*(2), 65–73. doi:10.1016/j.ijinfomgt.2013.11.008

Simmons, G. (2008). Marketing to postmodern consumers: Introducing the internet chameleon. *European Journal of Marketing*, *42*(3/4), 299–310. doi:10.1108/03090560810852940

Smith, G. P. (2012). Google Internet search activity and volatility prediction in the market for foreign currency. *Finance Research Letters*, *9*(2), 103–110. doi:10.1016/j.frl.2012.03.003

Stephen, A. T. (2016). The role of digital and social media marketing in consumer behavior. *Current Opinion in Psychology*, *10*, 17–21. doi:10.1016/j.copsyc.2015.10.016

Stone, M. D., & Woodcock, N. D. (2014). Interactive, direct and digital marketing: A future that depends on better use of business intelligence. *Journal of Research in Interactive Marketing*, *8*(1), 4–17. doi:10.1108/JRIM-07-2013-0046

Tiago, M. T. P. M. B., & Veríssimo, J. M. C. (2014). Digital marketing and social media: Why bother? *Business Horizons*, *57*(6), 703–708. doi:10.1016/j.bushor.2014.07.002

Valos, M. J., Ewing, M. T., & Powell, I. H. (2010). Practitioner prognostications on the future of online marketing. *Journal of Marketing Management*, *26*(3-4), 361–376. doi:10.1080/02672571003594762

Vaughan, L., & Chen, Y. (2015). Data mining from web search queries: A comparison of google trends and baidu index. *Journal of the Association for Information Science and Technology*, *66*(1), 13–22. doi:10.1002/asi.23201

Vlastakis, N., & Markellos, R. N. (2012). Information demand and stock market volatility. *Journal of Banking & Finance, 36*(6), 1808–1821. doi:10.1016/j.jbankfin.2012.02.007

Weischedel, B., & Huizingh, E. (2006). Website optimization with Web metrics: A case study. *Proceedings of the 8th International Conference on Electronic Commerce*, 463–470. 10.1145/1151454.1151525

Wilson, R. D. (2010). Using clickstream data to enhance business-to-business web site performance. *Journal of Business and Industrial Marketing, 25*(3), 177–187. doi:10.1108/08858621011027768

Wu, L., & Brynjolfsson, E. (2015). The Future of Prediction: How Google Searches Foreshadow Housing Prices and Sales. In *Economic Analysis of the Digital Economy* (pp. 89–118). University of Chicago Press.

Wymbs, C. (2011). Digital Marketing: The Time for a New "Academic Major" has Arrived. *Journal of Marketing Education, 33*(1), 93–106. doi:10.1177/0273475310392544

Yang, X., Pan, B., Evans, J., & Lv, B. (n.d.). Forecasting Chinese tourist volume with search engine data. *Tourism Management, 46*, 386-397.

Yelowitz, A., & Wilson, M. (2015). Characteristics of Bitcoin users: An analysis of Google search data. *Applied Economics Letters, 22*(13), 1030–1036. doi:10.1080/13504851.2014.995359

KEY TERMS AND DEFINITIONS

Digital Marketing: Refers to the use of digital technologies to create an integrated, directed and measurable communication to attain and secure customers while building deeper relationships.

Google Trends: It is a public service offered by Google Inc. that shows how often one term or tropic is entered in Google for searching information about it.

Internet of Things (IoT): Refers to the interconnection via the Internet of computing devices embedded in everyday objects, enabling them to send and receive data.

Landing Page: It is a single web page that appears in response to clicking on a search engine optimized search result (such as Google) or an online advertisement.

Metadata: A set of data that describes and gives information about other data, by helping to organize, find, and understand such data.

Neuromarketing: Refers to the application of alternative medical technologies to study the brain´s responses to marketing stimuli. This practice is used in marketing research by studying consumers´ affective, cognitive, and physical response to marketing stimuli.

Quintillion: A cardinal number represented in the USA by one followed by 18 zeros, and in Great Britain, France and Germany by one followed by 30 zeros.

Web Analytics: It is defined as the measurement, collection, analysis, and reporting of Internet data for understanding and optimizing usage.

Chapter 16
Corporate Social Responsibility and Digital Marketing

Usha Chauhan
BML Munjal University, India

Ruchi Garg
BML Munjal University, India

Ritu Chhikara
BML Munjal University, India

ABSTRACT

The purpose of this chapter is to make a combination of two concepts CSR and digital marketing and to find out the various challenges faced by practitioners for effective CSR communication. A total of 15 in-depth interviews were conducted in a leading automobile company. The interview transcripts were analyzed through thematic analysis. This chapter proposes different themes derived from the perceptions of the respondents and corporate reputation, public awareness, CSR efforts, profitability, CSR commitment, public image were found as the challenges faced by the practitioners. This chapter will provide insights to the practitioners on how to make effective CSR communication for further corporate reputation enhancement. It could also provide a platform for further debate between automobile controllers and significant stakeholders on how to tactically converse their CSR in the automobile concerns and enhance stakeholder commitment.

INTRODUCTION

Due to globalization, effective material information, ideas, and progression of unique threats for the universal communities, it upturns complexity get along futile to excerpt an understandable conceptualization of corporate social responsibility (CSR). Sethi (1975) initially invented the term ‘corporate social responsibility’, extended by Carroll (1979), then further classified by Wartick and Cochran (1985). Essentially, the thought behind the CSR is the identification that firms do have moral commitments and that they have also to reply practically to social forces. The CSR activities are going away on for old

DOI: 10.4018/978-1-5225-8939-6.ch016

time. The shifting times have posted the latest set of challenges and opportunities to individuals and organizations. The most significant facet of the shifting times is to predict the changes in advance to carry out in-depth research to inspect the pros and cons of the planned course of action. The organizations should have well-emerged means to disclose the CSR activities which are suggested after the complete examination of challenges and opportunities.

The economy is building a conversion towards becoming an extremely competing digital economy. The technological advancement is breaking innovative perspectives of opportunities in diverse fields of business and the CSR area as well. The major driving force of the CSR actions in the digital age should be to influence and incorporate the present and newest technologies in the practice of releasing CSR venture projects, agendas, and actions. The incorporation of technology in CSR is a mounting job and is pretty challenging. The shifting times are altering the outlook of people at a rapid rate. It is vital to be aware of the diverse prospect of every stakeholder in the CSR sphere.

The economy has to pass through a long and hard work to bring about the anticipated ideas of digitalization. The corporations should initiate building their assistance by focusing on a variety of digital actions to construct their most favorable involvement in the process of country development. The corporate houses should outline a short-lived, medium-lived, and long-lived business plan for the contributions which they plan to formulate in the region of digital technologies and its utilization in the domain of CSR. Researchers feel that there are a lot of possibilities for corporations to control the challenges and opportunities in the fields related to information technology (IT). The corporations can amalgamate their proficiency and IT expertise into the systems, actions, and operations, to donate to the holistic advancement of the world. The government can take part in the position of coordinator to diverse corporate houses in transferring their inputs working in the IT field.

The CSR conceived to advance communal prosperity through flexible business methods, and handouts of the corporate property has emerged noticeably in the preceding decade (Kotler & Lee, 2005). Enhancement of awareness headed for further tactical execution of CSR, relatively than limited, below encounter leadership, can be acknowledged as a viable number of organizations (McKinsey & Company, 2011). Exchanging information regarding CSR in the direction of stakeholders has reversed on account of the appearance of innovative digital technology in modern times. Web 2.0-based services, like as digital medium, award companies space to get in touch with their patrons on an entirely contrasting point earlier than. This endeavor many assistance, but also occur with jeopardy. Originations may exploit shared platforms to converse and talk about CSR notion and performances, but individuals and acts in groups moreover include to get the capability to utilize them as a podium to contact the corporation and dishonor them in public, possibly creating harm to the company's status.

Although corporations have initiated to widely embrace digital platform as a device for advertising, social dealings, and web care targets, the examination of practical online talk relating to the area of CSR has been underrated distantly (Heckadon, 2010; Nair, 2011).

BACKGROUND

The Concept of CSR

CSR has built up huge curiosity and has become one of the trendy affairs in management sciences. Undertakings have become indispensable players in social flowering, in which consumers are spotted not only as a market but also as an association, in which undertakings should chase the rules that assist in preserving the socioeconomic array, chase joint principles, and attempted not to damage the community while ensuring a profit. Although many researchers express their views on CSR, still there is not a single definition to elaborate the CSR concept at a single platform. However, the crux of all definitions is that organizations do CSR for the sake of increasing their reputation in society, that will be ultimately helpful in achieving the goal of profit maximization (Weber, 2008).

In the present scenario of the dynamic and conflicting environment, every business organization needs a competitive business model to meet out the objective of generating profit by making a balance with expectations of different stakeholders (Crane et al., 2000). The initial judgment on CSR was an exhibit by Bowen (1953) who characterizes CSR as a promise to chase a convenient approach, to frame suitable decisions, and to ensure those behaviors, acceptable in expressions of the ambitions and beliefs of our community (Elias, 2004). CSR is explained like a thought, through which companies merge, and share ecological affairs in their dealings and their interface with their stakeholders on an intentional footing, as they are gradually more alert to answerable conduct ahead to feasible trade sensation. Similar expressions for CSR are sustainability or sustainable augmentation (European Commission, 2007).

CSR concept generally comes into existence in early 1950 in the USA, when the objective of CSR was towards the fulfillment of business responsibilities. In the 1970s, the objective of business responsibilities came close to social welfare and move towards the fulfillment of stakeholder interest. In 2000, it became a strategic issue for business concerns for achieving sustainable development aim (Moura-Leite et al., 2011). In 2013, the CSR act was formulated, and the section 135 schedule VII of CSR Rules 2014 contains the essential provisions for companies to perform CSR. It becomes necessary for these organizations to allocate 2% of their net profit on CSR. As CSR is now under the law, it becomes beneficial to society, as those companies which are not hooked in social welfare will initiate CSR, and those who are already engaged can make a warm relationship with society.

Nowadays companies are doing CSR by engaging their employees in CSR programs. This will create a corporate reputation as companies own employees are highly motivated and actively participated in CSR initiatives. Although the public division account to be presently answerable for wellbeing, in further latest decagons corporations have turned into a new wake of their money-making, shared, green outcomes and have evoked to donate to immense collective improvement. European CSR first concerns encompass ecological security, physical condition and protection, balanced favorable circumstances, expertise, and proficiency creation, and novelty and headship, stakeholder commitment, control, and authority interactions, exposure and company links are an add up to designs for forwarding these concerns towards occupying the dominating of CSR in the association (Visser & Tolhurst, 2010).

The rationale for sign-in, in CSR, consists of ethical accountability, sustainability to make safe long lasting monetary discharge, accessing an authorization to act, and looking for company prestige increase (Porter, & Kramer, 2006). Corporate prestige is explained as the anticipated outlook of stakeholders on an association, which rely upon the amount to which the prospect of stakeholders collides (Fombrun & Shanley, 1990). Corporate reputation is frequently seen as an outcome of CSR used as a weapon (Fombrun, 1996); if shot favorably, can look after the corporation aligned with unconstructive advertising and jeopardy (Fombrun, Gardberg, & Barnett, 2000; Peloza, 2006). Corporate prestige was furthermore establishing positive belongings on product importance (Yang & Pai, 2010).

The Concept of Digital Marketing

The term digital marketing means marketing of goods and services by the company through digital channels. It is like an umbrella under which by applying digital marketing technologies, an organization targeting to construct brand consciousness for increasing sales, mounting customer choices and managing customers online (Financial Times, lexicon.ft.com) over and beyond conventional methods of communication like as radio, newspaper, and television. The latest ways to contact customers are by encouraging products and services through e-mails, display advertisements, and social media promotion supported by digital marketing.

Digital marketing is utilized as a platform for communicating and transferring ethics to stakeholders through diverse digital technologies. To put on a vision into the expansion of the Internet above the last fifteen years, it is sufficient to utter that 3.5 billion citizens used the Internet, while in 2000 that figure was only 400 million, which presents a growth rate of 875%. Besides with the enlargement of Internet practice, there was an expansion of associated actions such as digital marketing. The major distinction among conventional and digital marketing is that digital marketing targets on the consumer, presenting him a customized message and reply to his inquiry.

Numerous search engines can be utilized in two uniformly significant styles. The initial style is search engine optimization (SEO) that assists companies to display unpaid search outcomes. It is the method of advancing online information consequently that a search engine presents it as a top upshot of inquiries for a certain keyword. A different mode is search engine marketing (SEM) that permits marketers to purchase inventory in search decisions. When they are online, in addition to browsing, users can glimpse different themes. Besides to themes that substance, they can also glimpse ads in numerous ways, such as text, image, or video ads. That form of marketing is called display advertising. Further promotion opportunities on the Internet are social networks since they permit linking with the consumers by making a corporation profile on the social networks wherever consumers exist.

Globally, Facebook at present has more than 750 million representatives (Facebook, 2011), creating it the subsequent the majority of the well-liked website on the earth these days (Alexa, 2011). Social networking site in common sagacity that it permits its subscribers to united with associates, post status updates, exchange photos, and videos, share individual emails, make conversation openly with friends, construct a special outline and take part in games with associates, along with many others appearances is Facebook (Patterson, 2012). In distinction, at Twitter users can send up to 140-character response to the query "Finding's occurring?" because it is a microblogging aid. Twitter end users merely have inadequate space for the private drawing of outline, existing of the small manuscript the solitary story of your life with a profile photo. This restricted content-character describes Twitter as a micro-appeased digital social network that exploits a variety of contribution and yield channels (Krishnamurthy, Gill, & Arlitt, 2008).

As an enormous spring of data, for research and like a starting place for dealing feasibility such as pulling out statistics or people origin Twitter is very helpful (Savage, 2011; Pang, 201). Besides to the ways as mentioned earlier of advertising, personalized email promotion can be used, which indicates transferring facts and suggestions to society who have decided to accept that type of emails. So, in the current circumstances, customers are extra communally and environmentally conscious because of social media. At present customers perform spying job earlier than they are buying.

MAIN FOCUS OF STUDY

Communication of CSR

While companies may build up a far-reaching CSR plan of actions and commence numerous events to put into practice these plans. Communicating concerning CSR is essential to control its perspective finally. Alternatively, employing CSR the same as a wholesome advertising tool has its moral after effects. A business should barely exercise CSR for advertising objective on a genuine basis (Van de Ven, 2008). Stakeholders have a propensity towards reacting depressingly to bogus advertising actions (Forehand & Grier, 2003). Consequently, it is worthwhile for a business to come up to CSR communication with prudence, as for lots of companies impressive CSR message leftovers a confront (Clark, 2000).

Yearly CSR-reporting is a typical way for corporations to correspond in the turf of sustainable growth regarding their hard work. According to KMPG (2008), out of the 250 leading corporations endowed with global responsibility, corporate reports on social responsibility were available by 80 percent. So far, many types of research in this area has been managed. Attentiveness of a company's CSR actions between the exterior and interior stakeholders is normally short. This disbelief is a vital threat to defeat even as mounting the control of CSR communication (Du, Bhattacharya, & Sen, 2010). As soon as companies do not merely convey their fundamental, besides their gained achievements for appealing in CSR, inducing clients to be aware of that there is a triumph place of activity, messages are grasped as additionally believable (Forehand, & Grier, 2003) developing an understanding of a CSR as a major approach to shrink disbelief (Brønn & Vrioni, 2001).

On the other hand, communication has to not simply be covered in the ending stage of execution of a CSR plan. Clarkson (1995) states that CSR is a topic of making dealings with stakeholders. Conventionally, stakeholders are supposed to be as outsiders who encompass a communal bond with the concern. It is contended that in corporate dealings corporations be required to incorporate stakeholder affairs (Reynolds & Yuthas, 2008).

Concerning stakeholders' involvement, the practice of intensifying sustainability policy and describing fundamental ideas are significant components to facilitate forecast whether a policy is workable for the long duration. The latest way proposes many golden chances for the dissimilar phases concerning CSR.

Digital Social Media

Just as regards the commencement of the golden age, the Internet has advanced to a broad common practical background. The web 2.0 unlocked the concrete chunks and empowered users to partake online keenly. Social media as a cluster of online applications that sanction the configuration and change of user-generated information and put upon the intellectual and scientific groundwork of the web 2.0 (Kaplan & Heinlein, 2010). The two most significant social network sites in the present research are Facebook and Twitter. However, a social network site Twitter is doubtful owing to its restricted spotlight on private networking (Kwak et al., 2010). As a result, companies have keenly enforced the employing of social media as a device for bridging with prospective stakeholders.

Numerous scholars have highlighted the application of a social podium for business regarding the requisites of communal dealings (e.g., Burns, 2008; Mangold & Faulds, 2009; Fauser, Wiedenhofer, & Lorenz, 2011). User senses regarding the brand, and not as an originator for straight sales in which social media should be identified as donating towards the method that affects marketing strategies (Hoffman & Fodor, 2010). Frequently occupied justification of the impacts of social advertising is to discussions concerning brands on a collective platform serve as an electronic statement of mouth (Jansen, Zhang, Sobel, & Chowdhury, 2009). Downbeat word of mouth can move to smash up corporate fame. At this respect, Hennig-Thurau (2010) states that consequently, it is crucial that a concern reacts suitably to downbeat communication, to re-establish the confidence contained by the concern.

Embedding CSR and Digital Marketing

Even though definite study on CSR announcement through social ways is at a halt in its childhood, many types of research have ongoing analyzing the topic. By enhancing stakeholder dealings and structuring social assets, online contact additionally is characterized as its capability to fetch reputational profits and simplify social media exactly. Fieseler, Fleck, and Meckel (2010) examine CSR communication using blogs applying data accessed from the McDonald's CSR blog, they originate that the common elements of a blog displayed probably establish a channel of communication with stakeholders. However, the effects of a company blog on the network schedule remained minimal, promising of web 2.0 for CSR communication and wind up that an efficient exercising of these media form wants a swing from organization unilateral communication to shared CSR activities (Bittner & Leimeister, 2011).

Companies are upbeat in employing social platforms to connect consumers and revolve them addicted to their CSR handlers. Social media examination is anticipated as a means to recognize major players who possibly will be active like these agents (Sedereviciute, 2010). A novel approach of applying CSR entitles it "CSR 2.0". It operates the revolution of the online world from web 1.0 in the direction of web 2.0 as a figure of speech to express the elementary move to facilitate its senses to be prepared, consequently to form CSR accurately pertinent and valuable to create social platforms as a substitute of fixed, interrupted dealings with somewhat burdensome stakeholder board.

Moreover, the brand is promoting actions on CSR and its usage. The rationale to connect in social media might affect consumers' mindset towards concerns actions on the social platform. Somebody who is registered to Facebook only to reside within contact with getting on links possibly will recognize a marketable post on their information homepage differently than an individual who values Twitter as to stay up with the most recent information. Furthermore, observation hooked on the ambitions that force individuals to employ social podium is hence mandatory.

LITERATURE REVIEW AND RESEARCH PROPOSITIONS (RP)

1. **Ambiguity and Profitability**: As digital marketing is a cost consuming activity and CSR spending is controlled and directed by Government, it will be a challenge for organizations to justify the positive impact of Digital Marketing on CSR. And if any irregularity is found, it can give a negative impact on CSR spending of the organization as if governments exclude the amount spent on digital marketing for CSR.

RP1 – Unclear CSR laws about the cost of digital marketing will impact on the corporate image.

2. **Digital Media and CSR Efforts**: Social media is the very important tools for digital marketing, but nowadays the misuse of social media analytics (e.g., Facebook-Cambridge Analytica data breach) can lead to a sudden roadblock in digital marketing. As a result, any new CSR activity started by the organization can lead to delay or discontinuation of the same CSR activity.

RP2 – Wrong selection of digital marketing media can lead to delay or discontinuation of CSR efforts.

3. **CSR Consumer Education and Digital Resources**: In developing countries, like India, Bangladesh, and Sri-Lanka, the areas where CSR is needed, mostly lack basic facilities, so the selection of the mode of digital marketing for CSR can become an issue. The target segment can be out of reach from the fast media of digital marketing due to lack of infrastructure, e.g., Internet, mobile network reach and lack of equipment like mobiles, and computers.

The common community, like as customers or the narrow public, frequently execute not actively search for CSR knowledge regarding a concern, still with a hold to matters they regard as to exist mainly significant (Dawkins 2004). The common community regularly turn into attentive of a corporations CSR performance throughout self-sufficient platforms, such as perspective reporting on television and in the newspaper, associates phrase of entrance or business announcement mediums, like as higher-profile reason publicity programs, publicity or direct purchase announcement. Companies should employ a mixture of communication mediums or, otherwise centered on more than one extremely applicable channels to reach the all-purpose community successfully.

RP3 – Insufficient digital resources will impact on CSR consumer education.

4. **Corporate Reputation and Digital Marketing Expertise:** Digital marketing is a domain where subject matter expertise is a must for better and right results, and hiring a peak endowment is the biggest challenge managers report understanding. As a result, an organization and its CSR efforts can go away in an erroneous direction which can harm the brand reputation (Baden-Fuller & Ang, 2001; Balmer & Gray, 1999)

RP4 – Lack of expertise in digital marketing will lead to a negative impact on brand reputation.

5. **Digital Marketing and Corporate Reputation:** Marketing scholars have united some of the tactic narrative accesses in seeing at status and encompass comprehensive status to embrace the promotion of goods and services (Dowling, 1993; Herbig & Milewicz, 1995; Srivastava, Fahey, & Christensen 2001; Saurhaft & Atkins, 1989; Zimmerman, 2001). Company interactions with academics have looked the status to live a role in adversity supervision and the expansion of organizations' likeness (Alessandri et al. 2001). As a result, CSR communication is done through company websites. These websites need to be updated from time to time to meet out all type of stakeholders' expectations with changing the environment.

RP5 – Unorganized websites will impact negatively on corporate reputation.

6. **Digital Technology and Public Awareness:** In the course of promoting a firm curtail the information breach among companies and consumers, which, in revolve, composes it additional possible that clients will gaze out concerning the organizations CSR membership, and remunerate the firm for its CSR achievements. Customers seize addicted to examination firms' CSR activities when framing for actions (Brown & Dacin, 1997; Creyer & Ross, 1997; Sen & Bhattacharya, 2001; Bhattacharya & Sen, 2004; Penn, Schoen, & Berland, 2010.)

By using digital media, a company approaches to the target audience and conveys CSR initiatives, but choosing appropriate technology to satisfy diverse stakeholder is the biggest challenge.

RP6 – Inappropriate digital technology impact negatively on public awareness.

7. **Content and Public Image:** One exclusive feature of the CSR announcement is to facilitate frequent and numerous forthcoming associates, like administrators, company presses, shareholders and NGOs to local societies (Dawkins, 2004). Besides, these dissimilar associates disagree in stipulations of their outlooks of information requirements, and could consequently react differently to the diverse message means of CSR. Consequently, it is vital for a corporation to modify its CSR message to the particular requests of the diverse associates of the community. Confront of CSR announcement is how to decrease associates distrust. Whereas stakeholders argue they desire to be familiar with the excellent performance of the concerns they procure from or devote in, they as well rapidly become unconvinced of the CSR aims when organizations forcefully sponsor. The content of the CSR messages communicated through digital marketing should match the diverse audience needs; otherwise, it will be unable to hold maximum traffic and leadership.

RP7 – Mismatching of content with the audience will lead to poor public image.

8. **CSR Positioning and Digital Marketing:** CSR positioning is also expected to control the success of CSR communication. CSR positioning means the degree to which a corporation depends on its CSR actions to locate itself, relation to the contention, in the mindset of consumers. A corporation's CSR positioning is possible to achieve for strengthening the efficiency of CSR announcement as specified. As a result, the corporation has occupied the comparatively unusual and maybe dangerous attitude of positioning their own on CSR slightly than carelessly appealing in those actions. Consequently, stakeholders are expected not barely to disburse more awareness to its CSR communication, but also to imagine in the validity of its CSR efforts, arising in larger affiliation in support of the corporation.

RP8 – Digital marketing will directly be associated with CSR positioning.

9. **Profitability and Digital Marketing:** Firm's CSR achievements cannot constantly go collectively by way of prosperity, because the instigator trusts to carry out CSR with an advancing-profit intention in the brain is contracted and immoral (Kolstad, 2007). Although a wide number of organizations quiet follow building proceeds in their moral CSR job, and stakeholders in concern are not eager to sacrifice earnings to enlarge societal accountability achievement (Pava & Krausz, 1996). CSR needs a business knowing its societal obligations and subsequently transport out them, no issue

whether they be able to go ahead accumulating earnings or not for the business. The organization ought to have restricted reflection for increasing income, and income can be gained during satisfying former responsibilities (Kolstad, 2007). CSR and effectiveness can only set out mutually in a logical method. Some scholars also believe CSR is only an asset for the business and it will carry fewer donations on prosperity (Rainey, 2006). Several additional overheads, such as constituting ecological know-how, managing vegetation and educating workers, support the pecuniary load on behalf of the corporation and fetch monetary loss (Balabanis et al., 1998).

RP9 – Digital marketing will impact corporate profitability.

10. **Digital Marketing and CSR Commitment:** CSR communication, emphasizing on CSR commitment its CSR efforts is a helpful communication policy. CSR message is supposed to be truthful and evades the sense of boasting (Sen et al., 2009). Still, a corporations' CSR promise and its communal bang, as well offer like analytic suggestions by way of gaze at to its fundamental CSR purposes in diverse ways. As a substitute of focusing on the input face of its participation in a communal reason, a concern can center on the field part of CSR attempts, and to is the genuine gains that have gathered to the aimed audience of a societal reason.

RP10 – Digital marketing of CSR efforts will impact on CSR commitment.

Research Methodology

A research process in stroke to deal by way of the research purpose, researchers engaged in qualitative research, as it aids in admiring the significance individuals, allocate to collective experiences to clarify the intellectual processes essentially their actions (Weinreich, 1996).

Data Collection Technique

Semi-structured in detail interviews were organized to discover the questions as mentioned above by considering the respondents to be detailed on their knowledge which aided the researcher to take hold of the fundamental causes allied to the visions of the respondents on CSR and digital marketing combination. A semi-structured interview steer was employed and check out questions were too employed to explore in support for a rooted comeback. The interviews endured intended for an hour and were organized at a choice of sites since for each respondent's expediency and compliance.

Sampling Technique

The respondents were chosen to employ a determined sampling, which comprises seeking for entities whom there search criterion (Kuzel, 1992; Palys & Atchison, 2008). For the rationale of this consideration, a decisive covered factor was employed wherever respondents were directed to filled a questionnaire evaluating their basic knowledge on a combination of two terms CSR and digital marketing. Simply individual respondents were privileged who answered have the same opinion or robustly be dissimilar to the questions of the CSR and digital marketing questionnaire.

The interviews were conducted in December 2018, in a leading automobile company. Entirely 15 respondents from the National capital region (NCR) of India were contacted, and out of them, 13 respondents satisfied the stipulation to be preferred for further interviewed. Of the 13 respondents, 2 were female, and 10 were males. The range of the age was 25-45 years. The interviewers were selected from the CSR and digital marketing departments both.

DATA ANALYSIS

The interview translations were figured out throughout the thematic analysis. Thematic analysis is a technique for diagnosing, evaluating, and covering themes within statistics (Boyatzis, 1998; Braun & Clarke, 2006; Crabtree & Miller, 1999; Fereday & Muir-Cochrane, 2006). The thematic analysis supports in providing the constitutes recognized throughout literature reconsider.

Finding and Implications

1. **Public Image:** This theme explains image created in the mandate of the respondents when automobile company converses their CSR communication by changing the mode from Twitter to Facebook.

I think the challenge for marketers is how much CSR communication should be done through digital technologies. (F, 35)

Rationale to connect in social media might be affecting consumers' mindset in the direction of companies actions on social platforms. Somebody who is registered on Facebook only headed for residing in contact with getting on links possibly will recognize a marketable post on their information page in a different way than an individual who values Twitter as to stay up with the most recent information. Furthermore, observation addicted to the ambitions to force individuals to employed social platforms is for that reason mandatory. (M, 30)

2. **Public Awareness**: This subject explains respondents view on generating public awareness about corporation's CSR activities by using digital marketing.

According to me seeing is believing, whatever company communicate through digital technology positively will impact positively on audience also. (M, 45)

I have examined that CSR is attaining ripeness and that web-located medium proposes plentiful alternatives to cooperate with stakeholders. Consequently, concerns are searching the potential that social medium suggest as a podium to be in touch with stakeholders about the issues that take account of CSR (F, 25)

3. **CSR brand Positioning:** This theme covers respondent's views about how to create CSR brand positing through suitable digital marketing.

I found that unambiguous features are to be occupied, interested in the description at what time efficiently applying the channel to conquer budding returns, together with the increase of reputational worth. Consideration has also to be rewarded to shielding the concern from injurious dominations on social media, like as a harmful statement of the entrance, by answering in a suitable trend. (M,37)

I think digital marketing of CSR is cumbersome task rather than of goods and services because in exchange of goods and services company is expecting revenue, but for CSR digital marketing there is no such expectation. I think convincing people is a difficult task. (F,32)

4. **Corporate reputation**: This theme covers respondents view about companies how they make open discussion with stakeholders to attain corporate reputation.

I found huge difficulty in CSR is that companies be inclined to place the outline for the discussion, and still when organizations argue to discuss with stakeholders on the subject of CSR matters, they are just having communications regarding the stuff the companies have determined to have communities about. (M, 40)

I used to give my old/used stuff to my driver in the presence of numerous people.(M, 36)

I see my company is involved in girls' education then at least there will be thought in me that girl child should be educated, this is the motivation for other people also, so I believe doing this online is creating thoughts in other people mind. (F, 35)

More requirements to be identified regarding how innovative media have provided corporations with favorable circumstances to take on open dialogue. the bang of the online and digital media has focused resting on how the latest media have altered in the mode the social society collaborate with corporations. (M, 45)

5. **CSR Consumer Education**: This theme explains respondents view regarding how to overcome the challenge of being making consumers aware of CSR by using digital marketing.

I think all work was done by artificial intelligence, and once you like an advertisement, other related add were pop up simultaneously. (F, 32)

New-fangled digital mode of coordinating and discussion has allowed networks of activists to match CSR policies, importing institutional transform on CSR affairs; how Twitter has altered the manner message discharges and delivered dispute into CSR considerations; how blogging declining corporations' 'greenwashing' of their proceedings; and how social media provides to shifts in corporate society nationality dealings. (M, 26)

6. **CSR Commitment**: This theme describes respondents' views on how corporations become more committed towards stakeholders through digital technology.

I think if continuously company receiving likes and positive comments and more sharing of posts make CSR more committed in the digital world. (F, 32)

Everybody has there on philosophy somebody use CSR as a tool while somebody does it for humanity benefits, so it has nothing to do with the CSR the way you doing is a matter. (M,45)

In my opinion what leftovers unidentified is whether innovative media may have enlarged the frankness of corporate conversation about CSR. Because corporations' conversation about CSR still relics a black box, a spotlight on the level of frankness of discussion presents an exciting path for study. Modern scholarly concentration to the accurate conversation and corporate reflection has appeared in calls to reassess how companies might integrate conversation into their actions. (M,38)

7. **CSR Efforts:** This theme describes respondent's views on how corporations raise their CSR efforts more to face digital technology challenges.

I found that for communicating CSR efforts there is no the single best way, it depends on suitability. Like at my home there is the availability of AAJ TAK channel but not for NDTV news channel. (M,40)

I have found that people make comparisons of information available on websites like Company is giving cash back offers, discounts and what company is doing for social welfare (M,34)

8. **Corporate Profitability**: This theme explained the respondent's view of a corporation's profitability by using appropriate message content to make effective CSR communication for further corporate reputation enhancement.

I told you that it is not something we are doing for business agenda; we are doing it doing it for bringing that change in the mindset. (F,35)

I have noticed that if the company becomes failed in approaching the audience with a message in the same sense in which they want to approach, and a similar idea is copied by the competitor than it will impact previous company sale and profitability. For example, in our company initially, we manufactured a gearless bike soon it becomes obsolete from the market because of a scooter on same technology (GEARLESS) manufactured by a competitor and takes out the advantage of profitability (M,43)

SOLUTION AND RECOMMENDATIONS

This theoretical chapter has addressed the challenges faced by an automobile company by marrying two concepts, CSR and digital marketing, and exchanging CSR dealings to associates and wound up that there are various problems when demanding to converse CSR activities in the course of the similar social platforms for every concerned individual who has diverse outlooks and requirements. For CSR announcement to survive successfully, it has to be without doubt accessible, but not excessively present. Stakeholders clusters have diverse ambitions to discover this knowledge and, distinct level of commitments to operate on this knowledge.

Applicable on stakeholder theory, here are precise suggestions on behalf of automobile company which must be examined as soon as adopting a CSR communication arrangement. Beginning the examination in this chapter, planned CSR message must originally center on a combination of the stakeholder collectively, workers and customers. Select suitable contacting digital media for every group. For workers, inner communication of CSR events throughout the corporation's is online favorable whereas, simultaneously motivating them to make utilization of their social podiums to broaden CSR communication. For prospective workforce, applying the social podium LinkedIn could be a sensible selection since applicants will seek out for service promises through this avenue. For clients, communication through ought to be accessible in the course of the company website, Facebook, Twitter, YouTube, and Instagram. Within every case, social podiums are capable of flourishing the conversation it builds.

FUTURE RESEARCH DIRECTIONS

This theoretical paper was an effort to investigating communication through CSR and associates commitment in the automobile business. Since as a theoretical paper, this paper explains challenges by providing a suggestion. Besides, it possibly will provide a podium for additional debate between automobile operators and significant associates on how to tactically exchange CSR information in the automobile business and enhance individuals' commitment. One prospective research assignment could consist of a content study of the exchange of messages related to CSR which are appeared on automobile company websites' home page and digital medium to measure the quantity generated by conversation. Another perspective of research may well quantify stakeholder commitment in the course of a huge magnitude combined way, micro and macro level learning. Next prospective research could aim stakeholder clusters separately by dividing the unlike fields surrounded by the automobile sector. In the end, by making a novel digital podium possibly will be anticipated absolutely in favor of the automobile corporation headed for converse the CSR activities it holds.

CONCLUSION

CSR conveyance is a very intricate subject. It is very difficult to separate between CSR communication and efficient communication of CSR. Nevertheless, for increasing or enlarging stakeholder's commitment at the present scenario, a digital existence stands essentially. Corporations essentially examine how to select the right digital media with the most excellent capability aimed at the stakeholders, anything in the direction of circulation, as well as-as exactly how to promote genuine conversation. Through taking into account every stakeholder as a personage viewer, corporations may be capable to at last use digital media successfully. For instance, the workforce is significant stakeholders who are repeatedly not present since the study of online social media plus CSR communiqué regardless of the reality that everyone commitment moves to improve assurance as well as high confinement degrees (Park & Levy, 2014).

Indeed, higher involvement of internal stakeholders will be into the CSR actions, the extra they will pay attention in what outsiders believe regarding their company, recognized with its achievement, and sense individually disgraced when outsiders blamed their company. To connect workers, corporations should use an inside online existence through company websites, e-mail newsletters social media platforms, blogs, SEO as well as conventional print media. The message and channel must be selected carefully to make communication through CSR efficiently. CSR message can have a counterattack result if shareholders turn into doubtful then recognize principally extrinsic intentions in firm's societal wits. Henceforth, the major task of CSR communiqué stands to conquer shareholder disbelief, as well as to create constructive CSR adscriptions. This chapter ensures review of pertinent literature on CSR and digital marketing in all-purpose to show a theoretical structure of CSR message methods. Diverse features of CSR message being analyzed; since communication subject matter and communication mediums to society and shareholder, specific characteristics identified that have ascendancy for the success of CSR communiqué via digital marketing.

REFERENCES

Baden-Fuller, C., & Ang, S. W. (2001). Building reputations: The role of alliances in the European Business school scene. *Long Range Planning*, *34*(6), 741–755. doi:10.1016/S0024-6301(01)00088-7

Balabanis, G., Phillips, H. C., & Lyall, J. (1998). Corporate social responsibility and economic performance in the top British companies: Are they linked? *European Business Review*, *98*(1), 25–44. doi:10.1108/09555349810195529

Bittner, E., & Leimeister, J. M. (2011). Towards CSR 2.0. Potentials and challenges of Web 2.0 for corporate social responsibility communication. *Proceedings of the 11th Academy of Management Annual Meeting*.

Bowen, H. R. (1953). *Social responsibility of the businessman*. Harper & Row.

Boyatzis, R. E. (1998). *Transforming qualitative information: thematic analysis and code development*. London, UK: Sage.

Brown, R. M., Janney, J. J., & Paul, K. (2001). An empirical investigation of the relationship between change in corporate social performance and financial performance: A stakeholder theory perspective. *Journal of Business Ethics*, *32*(2), 143–156. doi:10.1023/A:1010786912118

Brown, T. J., & Dacin, P. A. (1997). The company and the product: Corporate associations and consumer product responses. *Journal of Marketing*, *61*(1), 68–84. doi:10.1177/002224299706100106

Burns, K. S. (2008). *A historical examination of the development of social media and its application to the public relations industry*. Paper presented at the 2008 ICA Preconference, Montreal, Quebec, Canada.

Carroll, A. B. (1979). A three-dimensional conceptual model of corporate performance. *Academy of Management Review*, *4*(4), 497–505. doi:10.5465/amr.1979.4498296

Clark, C. E. (2000). Differences between public relations and corporate social responsibility: An analysis. *Public Relations Review*, *26*(3), 363–380. doi:10.1016/S0363-8111(00)00053-9

Clarkson, M. E. (1995). A stakeholder framework for analyzing and evaluating corporate social performance. *Journal of Services Research*, *7*(1), 173–191.

Dawkins, J. (2004). Corporate responsibility: The communication challenge. *Journal of Communication Challenge*, *9*, 108–119.

Dowling, G. R. (1993). Developing your corporate image into a corporate asset. *Journal of Long Range Planning*, *26*(2), 101–109. doi:10.1016/0024-6301(93)90141-2

Du, S., Bhattacharya, C. B., & Sen, S. (2009). *Strengthening consumer relationships through corporate social responsibility.* Working paper, Simmons College School of Management.

Elias, R. Z. (2004). An examination of business students' perception of Corporate Social Responsibilities before and after bankruptcies. *Journal of Business Ethics*, *52*(3), 267–281. doi:10.1023/B:BUSI.0000037558.74693.d5

Fombrun, C., Gardberg, N. A., & Barnett, M. L. (2000). Opportunity platforms and safety nets: Corporate citizenship and reputational risk. *Business and Society Review*, *105*(1), 85–106. doi:10.1111/0045-3609.00066

Fombrun, C., & Shanley, M. (1990). What's in a name? Reputation building and corporate strategy. *Academy of Management Journal*, *33*, 233–258.

Forehand, M. R., & Grier, S. (2003). When is honesty the best policy? The effect of a stated company intent on consumer skepticism. *Journal of Consumer Psychology*, *13*(3), 349–356. doi:10.1207/S15327663JCP1303_15

Forehand, M. R., & Grier, S. (2003). When is honesty the best policy? The effect of a stated company intent on consumer skepticism. *Journal of Consumer Psychology*, *13*(3), 349–356. doi:10.1207/S15327663JCP1303_15

Friedman, M. (1970, September 13). The social responsibility of business is to increase its profits. *New York Times Magazine*.

Heckadon, D. A. (2010). *Critical success factors for creating and implementing effective social media marketing campaigns* (Master thesis). New York University.

Hennig-Thurau, T., Malthouse, E. C., Friege, C., Gensler, S., Lobschat, L., Rangaswamy, A., & Skiera, B. (2010). The impact of new media on customer relationships. *Journal of Service Research*, *13*(3), 311–330. doi:10.1177/1094670510375460

Hoffman, D. L., & Fodor, M. (2010). Can you measure the ROI of your social media marketing? *MIT Sloan Management Review*, *52*(1), 41–49.

Jansen, B. J., Zhang, M., Sobel, K., & Chowdury, A. (2009). Twitter power: Tweets as electronic word of mouth. *Journal of the American Society for Information Science and Technology*, *60*(11), 2169–2188. doi:10.1002/asi.21149

Kolstad, I. (2007). Why Firms Should Not Always Maximize Profits. *Journal of Business Ethics*, *76*(2), 137–145. doi:10.100710551-006-9262-7

Kotler, P., & Lee, N. (2005). *Corporate Social Responsibility: Doing the Most Good for our Company and our Cause*. Hoboken, NJ: John Wiley.

Kuzel, A. J. (1992). *Doing Qualitative Research*. Newbury Park, CA: Sage.

Kwak, H., Lee, C., Park, H., & Moon, S. (2010). What is Twitter, a social network or a news media? *Proceedings of the World Wide Web Conference in Raleigh, 19*, 591-600. 10.1145/1772690.1772751

McKinsey & Company (2011). *The business of sustainability: McKinsey global survey results*. Author.

Moura-Leite, R. C., & Padgett, R. C. (2011). Historical background of corporate social responsibility. *Social Responsibility Journal, 7*(4), 528–539. doi:10.1108/17471111111117511

Park, S.-Y., & Levy, S. E. (2014). Corporate social responsibility: Perspectives of hotel frontline employees. *International Journal of Contemporary Hospitality Management, 26*(3), 332–348. doi:10.1108/IJCHM-01-2013-0034

Patterson, A. (2012). Social-networkers of the world, unite and take over: A meta-introspective perspective on the Facebook brand. *Journal of Business Research, 65*(4), 527–534. doi:10.1016/j.jbusres.2011.02.032

Pava, M., & Krausz, J. (1996). The association between corporate social responsibility and financial performance: The paradox of social cost. *Journal of Business Ethics, 15*(3), 321–357. doi:10.1007/BF00382958

Porter, M. E., & Kramer, M. R. (2006). Strategy and society: The link between competitive advantage and corporate social responsibility. *Harvard Business Review, 84*, 78–92. PMID:17183795

Rainey, D. L. (2006). *Sustainable business development: inventing the future through strategy, innovation, and leadership*. Cambridge, UK: Cambridge University Press. doi:10.1017/CBO9780511617607

Reynolds, M., & Yuthas, K. (2008). Moral discourse and corporate social responsibility reporting. *Journal of Business Ethics, 78*(1-2), 47–64. doi:10.100710551-006-9316-x

Savage, N. (2011). Twitter as medium and message. *Communications of the ACM, 54*(3), 18–20. doi:10.1145/1897852.1897860

Sedereviciute, K. (2010). *Towards a more holistic stakeholder analysis approach. Mapping current and potential stakeholders from social media* (Master thesis). University of Aarhus, Denmark.

Sethi, S. P. (1975). Dimensions of corporate social performance: An analytical framework. *California Management Review, 17*(3), 58–64. doi:10.2307/41162149

Tuzzolino, F., & Armandi, B. R. (1981). A need-hierarchy framework for assessing corporate social responsibility. *Academy of Management Review, 6*(1), 21–28. doi:10.5465/amr.1981.4287982

van der Ven, B. (2008). An ethical framework for the marketing of corporate social responsibility. *Journal of Business Ethics, 82*(2), 339–352. doi:10.100710551-008-9890-1

Visser, W., & Tolhurst, N. (2010). *The world guide to CSR. A country-to-country analysis of corporate sustainability and responsibility*. Sheffield, UK: Greenleaf Publishing.

Wartick, S. L., & Cochran, P. L. (1985). The evolution of the corporate social performance model. *Academy of Management Review*, *10*(4), 758–769. doi:10.5465/amr.1985.4279099

Weber, M. (2008). The business case for corporate social responsibility: A company level measurement approach for CSR. *European Management Journal*, *26*(4), 247–261. doi:10.1016/j.emj.2008.01.006

Weinreich, N. K. (1996). A perfect union: Integrating quantitative and qualitative methods in social marketing research. *Social Marketing Quarterly*, *3*(1), 53–58. doi:10.1177/152450049600300106

KEY TERMS AND DEFINITIONS

Brand Positioning: The creation of a unique and positive impression on customers and marketplaces for being competitive in the market.

Corporate Reputation: It embraces the good image in the eyes of stakeholders for a company that is earned by satisfying the diverse needs of stakeholders in society.

CSR: Acronym of corporate social responsibility, that consists of fulfilling economic, social, discretionary and legal obligations towards society to increase corporate reputation and foster social change.

Digital Marketing: Techniques and strategies focused on reaching goods and services to a target audience by using online tools based on the internet and digital devices.

Facebook: Social media technique to get users together to socialize at a common shared platform for communication.

Search Engine Marketing (SEM): The use of tools and strategies to optimize the visibility and accessibility of sites and web pages with the use of search engines.

Search Engine Optimization (SEO): Optimization of a website to place it in the top positions of search engines.

Stakeholders: Formed by the combination of people and organizations (private and public) interested in the firm.

Chapter 17
Fundraising and Its Impact on Digital Marketing for NGOs

Ruth Sabrina Rojas Dávila
The Catholic University of Santiago de Guayaquil, Ecuador

ABSTRACT

The non-governmental organizations (NGOs) require human resources to carry out their activities. This includes both the professionals who are paid and the volunteers. The capture of this resource acquires as much importance as the implementation of the social goals that these organizations promote. It can be said then that just as the commercial or cultural sectors are approached from the field of communication and design, it is valid to make an academic approach to this social problem. Fundraising was born as a strategy applied in NGOs with the purpose of generating resources for them to be able to sustain themselves through time.

INTRODUCTION

The emergence of new forms of communication and the technological advances in which non-governmental organizations (NGOs) are immersed, make them seeking to be adapted to a new digital generation; these non-profit organizations share practices that apparently for years seemed to generate efficient links with potential volunteers or donors finally.

An NGO can produce a media strategy or communicate with clearly identifiable, predetermined and current results to become sustained for a longer time, and it can also promote other issues that they share with the target audience, such as good governance, strategies focused on solving socio-economic problems for economic growth and development by assuring public health and education, among others (Kumar, 2010). The creation of 4-helix helix schemes (University, NGOs, firms, and Government) contribute to achieving sustainable GDP (Gross Domestic Product) growth and socioeconomic wealth.

DOI: 10.4018/978-1-5225-8939-6.ch017

There is a major communication challenge for NGOs about whether the company seeks to establish a more effective communication when there is a problem that directly affects a segment or interest group, for example, the environment or through vulnerable groups. But effectiveness in NGOs depends mainly on the dissemination of information and, crucially, its amplification by the media (Couttenier & Hate, 2015). In this sense, the use of social networks has eased their real-time interaction with their stakeholders, which has mainly benefited the vulnerable groups helped.

Under this concept, the term "fundraising" was born aiming to increase the capacity of an entity to carry out and extend its mission in society through fundraising (Torres & de las Heras, 2017). What establishes this new strategic communication model for non-profit organizations is the increase in the number of loyal donors as an important part of the benefactors of the firms dedicated to this activity.

Due to this fact, fundraising needs a step-by-step evaluation to be a successful strategy within the market, as the fundraising plan must define how much money will be collected, in what period and what techniques will be used to achieve their goals. It must also include monitoring and detailed evaluation steps to modify the strategy, if necessary (Bonilla, 2013). However, the great disparity between first world countries and developing nations provokes that NGOs located in the most advanced economies on the planet have better (and cheaper) access to finance and donors. Donors located in a wealthy economic country does not seek any financial return after their contribution since what they seek is to help others, whether for philanthropic, ethical, moral or religious reasons.

Among the techniques for requesting funds considered more effective by the non-profit organizations are: large donations (69.7%), direct mail (66.7%), scheduled donation (61.4%), special events (54.7%), foundations (44.8%), telephone (34.8%), corporate donations (29.2%), Internet (28.4%) and email (21.3%), according to a study by the University of Indiana cited by Center on Philanthropy (Bonilla, 2013). The Internet becomes an effective tool to link strategies focused on NGOs especially in the change of generation that is lived in the world. Generation Y or Millennials is upsetting the current society since through digital means it is possible to reach this new generation and with it a new form of fundraising through the so-called digital volunteers. Also, thanks to ICTs, the impact of fundraising campaigns has a global impact, which maximizes their effectiveness.

The new proposals that are being generated as digital marketing strategies are opening a world of possibilities in the NGOs as they seek to segment the population and raise awareness with different social causes. Therefore, they will be people who are concerned about child malnutrition, especially in developing countries, among other factors affecting the population at risk of social exclusion. Digital marketing is enabling every injustice to have its individualized public to protect it. Social networks, moreover, can put a face to each cause when photographs and real stories are shown.

According to a survey conducted by the University of Massachusetts, 98% of charities have a presence on social networks. And of all the social networks, YouTube is the most used social tool, in 97% of cases, followed by Facebook with 92%, Twitter with 86% and Pinterest with 72%. It is also important to point out that the United Nations (UN) bases the entire strategy on humanitarian campaigns on the massive use of social networks appeared in the Internet and mobile phones since they are becoming more effective means of obtaining financial aid (ISDI, 2017).

This chapter aims to understand how fundraising-related concepts are applied in NGOs, as well as the steps to reach an effective strategy in digital media to establish mechanisms for measuring and monitoring the feasibility of the strategy chosen.

THEORETICAL FRAMEWORK

What Are NGOs?

According to Sckibick (2009)

The concept of the non-governmental organization was born in the UN during the post-war years, to catalog a special group of participants who did not have an official representation of their countries of origin but acted in some organization of that space of international concentration. (p. 2).

At this respect, Huertas (2015) recalls that the end of the Economic and Social Council of the UN considers that a nongovernmental organization is an international organization not established by intergovernmental agreement. Collaborative NGOs are defined and designed based on collaborations, based on a collaborative approach to making strategic decisions. Decision making is done by placing the mission in the foreground and taking the collaborative approach as the look from which to analyze reality and define the strategy and actions to be undertaken, which leads to overcoming the limits of the organization itself (Iglesias & Carreras, 2012).

These authors affirm that the characteristics of collaborative NGOs are as follows,

1. They are catalysts of alliances, networks, and ecosystems that favor the development of their mission. This team collaboration strengthens the organization and opens new perspectives to help beneficiaries in a growing number of places to have a greater impact. The union is a strength, and in the case of the third sector, the importance of being united towards a common goal is becoming increasingly important in a global environment.
2. They place collaborations at the center of their conception and identity. By definition, NGOs are characterized by collaboration among a group of people to solve a social problem. Social problems that determine the future of communities and countries, so they must be fixed to cope with the NGO's goals.
3. They place the mission at the center of their decisions and activities, not the organization. Although they focus their attention on the mission, values are also of fundamental importance, especially in NGOs guided by ethics, philanthropy, and charity towards the population at risk of social exclusion or located on the margins of society. Therefore, the mission and the values determine the central axis, in front of the vision, which has a secondary role in this type of organizations.
4. To analyze the strategies and ways of action have the resources and capabilities of the environment.
5. Build relationships from trust and not from control. An NGO must build on mutual trust to be fully operational. Without trust, there is no possibility to solve, or at least alleviate, a problem or social imbalance.

Therefore, NGOs must overcome fear, face the obstacles, search for finance, and address collaborations that are truly significant. We pointed earlier to the collaborative nature of the sector and the great multiplicity of collaborative experiences that take place in it. NGOs collaborate in many areas and with many actors defined by mutual trust and collaboration to solve a social issue. But many of these collaborations are not significant, neither are efficient nor effective (Noval, 2014).

Figure 1. Typology of NGOs.
Source: Adapted from Iglesias and Carreras (2012).

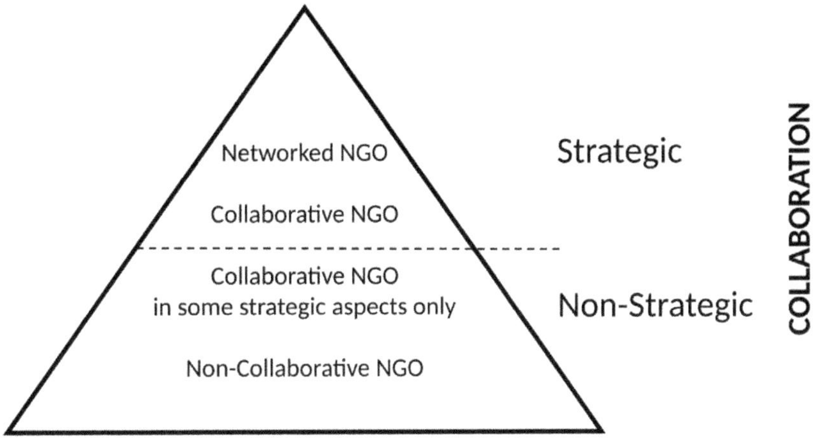

When trust in an organization fails, it runs the risk of disappearing. An aspect that is even more important in an NGO since, in many cases, they depend on the work of volunteers who do not receive any salary or help for carrying out their work. Therefore, since there is not even a contractual relationship between the NGO and the volunteers, this relationship is based solely on trust, so if it breaks down, the NGO is in danger of disappearing. As a result, significant collaborations with NGOs are needed.

As shown in Figure 2,

Figure 2. Classification of alliances for the NGO
Source: Adapted from Iglesias and Carreras (2012).

1. The first quadrant corresponds to strategic and efficient collaborations where resources must be invested and must be taken care of.
2. The second quadrant deals with collaborations with high strategic interest but not very efficient; in this case, the organization should consider how to improve this efficiency if that is possible (reducing the investment of resources or increasing the results obtained) or questioning their participation.
3. The third quadrant corresponds to non-strategic but efficient collaborations. In this case, the organization must monitor to maintain existing levels of efficiency, without increasing their participation or dedication, and finally
4. The fourth quadrant depicts to non-strategic or efficient collaborations. In this case, the organization's strategy seems clear: design an exit plan and end the collaboration.

Social Marketing in Digital Social Networks

Social Marketing, which according to Mendive (2008) "dates from July 1971 and was used by Kotler and Zaltmsn, to apply the postulates and techniques of commercial marketing, in good public campaigns or the dissemination of ideas that benefit the society" (p. 27).

These postulates suggest putting into practice the method of commercial thinking in social causes, to achieve a stated objective, which may not be economical as is the case of third sector organizations. Social Marketing then specializes in promoting the causes of the common good, so that NGOs use it to achieve a specifically defined goal: the increase in the number of volunteers. Mendive (2008) argues that "the methodology of marketing to detect and satisfy needs for consumption and use of goods and services is also useful to detect and meet social and charitable needs" (p. 28). In this way, this type of marketing allows to carry out actions that favor the organization, either by making it known, generating a good impression in the minds of those who visit it or causing a relationship with it so that it is preferred over other NGOs. (Rodríguez, 2014).

For Duque (2016) defining social marketing could be so complex that it would end up concluding that it is how the organization chooses activities and objectives to accomplish, according to its role in society and its corporate philosophy. In the search for the origins of this discipline, it is evident that it is a concept that has been evolving to the extent that the conditions of the time demand it.

Purpose of Social Marketing

It is considered within the social marketing that the concept of marketing is adopted, as a social discipline that has been strengthening as a dynamic of social exchanges between cooperating actors, individuals, organizations. These relationships are intertwined between social successes and failures, between social problems and, at the same time, solutions emanating from society itself seeking to establish new strategies to generate corporate social responsibility (Duque, 2016).

Some authors define the concept of marketing moving away from the position of a process in which only economic exchanges are made, to a broader conception of how the activity is implanted. Between 1969 and 1971, marketing evolved towards three new tasks based on social marketing: (a) the need to increase social awareness in companies and marketing (Shuptrine & Osmanski, 1975); (b) to assume that marketing has a certain social cost; and (c) to affirm that it is possible to apply marketing techniques to non-profit organizations (García, 2010).

Social Responsibility

The social responsibility of NGOs goes beyond the issues required in the social responsibility of the companies. Despite the absence of a legal framework, NGOs have elaborated other information of interest following the guidelines of monetary reporting mechanisms or accountability as the codes of conduct or certificates (Gálvez, Caba, & López, 2012). Traditional economic theories and the context where NGOs are developed determine 1) the question of NGOs' collective ownership; 2) the prohibition of the distribution of profit as an incentive to efficiency; and 3) NGOs' externalities and their public benefits, which also make them linked to social responsibility (Marcuello, 2007).

The term CSR is confused as it is related to paternalism, where the company has to cede part of its profits or performance to perform social tasks that benefit the community. With the passing of years, CSR has been taken into consideration by SMEs, since they reflect the level of commitment to the community where they carry out their commercial activities to position their brand and benefit society by offering an added value to the product or service offered in the market (Rojas & Torres Briones, 2017)

Perspectives Applied to the Marketing Within Social Responsibility

When combining marketing and social responsibility, this combination seeks to expand the concept of marketing with the support of social objectives that maintain traditional roles in the company. As a result, it is not intended that companies are transactional organizations, as they have a strong social and economic impact on society. This relationship between marketing and society determines the contribution of products and services carried out by firms, that from an economic point of view, it has a significant impact on society.

The importance and dimension of this social impact determine specific dimensions of social responsibility in marketing rooted in marketing ethics, retail, and CSR. At this respect, firms can have economic effects on social marketing, MRC (marketing related to the cause), fair trade, consumer responsibility, consumer vulnerability, philanthropy, green marketing, and responsible marketing. The social/environmental aspects link to the economic aspects of these factors and relate to their commercialization by applying the applicability of these products and services in the market to satisfy social needs, endowed with a specific scope for the construction of CSR. As a result, the CSR links to trustworthy business associations defined by having a good image, and reputation, and stakeholders. In short, social impact examines and measures the actions of CSR as a communication tool to increase consumer loyalty and reputation, with the use of corporate marketing to satisfy consumers and to identify and respond (perceptive associations) to companies based on their CSR actions.

The relationship between CSR and the overall performance of the company involves considering CSR as a corporate strategy, and a source of competitive advantage in organizations. Consequently, the performance of a company also links to actions undertaken in this regard.

Fundraising Models

Considering that the funds collected by NGOs must be validated by the activities carried out, two models can be mentioned, such as

The Model of Great Donors or The MG (Major Gift) Model

These donors are the most important with high incomes. This model analyzes the technical management systems used for identifying potential gift before, personal visits (senior level), elected campaigns promoting legacies, recognition donors by including their names in buildings, specific listings, and chairs. This model is especially used in the USA where billionaires donate for philanthropic or charity. A model based on large donors makes the NGO lose independence, so this type of model is not appreciated in other countries that seek democratization in obtaining funds and in the aid granted because a high permeability allows the aid to reach to the final beneficiary.

The Model of Foundation Directed to Research or The FR (Foundation Research) Model

The origin of these funds is from the promotion of research. The techniques are the identification of objectives and well-prepared study subjects. This model is widely used in Europe where, in addition to the public financing of the projects, there is also a private donation, especially in the countries of continental Europe, both in Central and Eastern European Countries (CEECs), Germany, and the Nordic countries (Denmark, Finland, Iceland, Norway, and Sweden). Once the results are obtained, and when the equilibrium point is reached, the donor can receive a counterpart, whether monetary or not.

These strategies are adapted and work best for certain institutions by including those who are responsible for attracting funds or diminishing operating costs by using outsourcing. Although for some authors the great risk of using this practice is that the organization loses control of the money collected, for many authors it is an optimal way to be financed while reducing risks. Internal human resources can understand the firm better and respond appropriately when internal problems arise, contrary to outsiders that can have a different point of view, vision, and working experience. The problem arises when there is a lack of control and little communication with the person who must carry out the parameters aligned with the organizational values. Consequently, the person must know the organization and know who and what companies are most interested in donating, as some companies only focus on some issues, being more sensitive to certain causes only.

Many charities, rightly or wrongly, are being criticized for their large expenditure. For example, in 2011, the American Breast Cancer Foundation (ABCF) spent $ 3.4 million in fundraising and $ 1.3 million in the programs and services it offers, so it was heavily criticized. And in 2010, the CEO of the American Cancer Society (ACS) received a salary and benefits of more than $ 2.2 million, as described by Charity Watch in 2012, which also was strongly criticized. While those numbers have caught the attention of critics, they have not necessarily deterred donors. In 2011, ABCF accumulated more than $ 5 million in contributions, while ACS received $ 883 million. From these donations, it can be inferred that donors prefer the set of characteristics that make up these charities, including their general expenses, but none of this would be possible if there were no campaign behind each of the foundations (Coffman, 2017, p. 410).

In figure 3 we propose a model to raise funds for NGOs as an effective strategy to fight poverty and reduce social imbalances. One of the keys to achieving this is to collaborate with public administrations given the crowding-in effect generated as a result of the public intervention. The model defines three consecutive stages, as follows,

Figure 3. A Fundraising model for Latin America
Source: Author

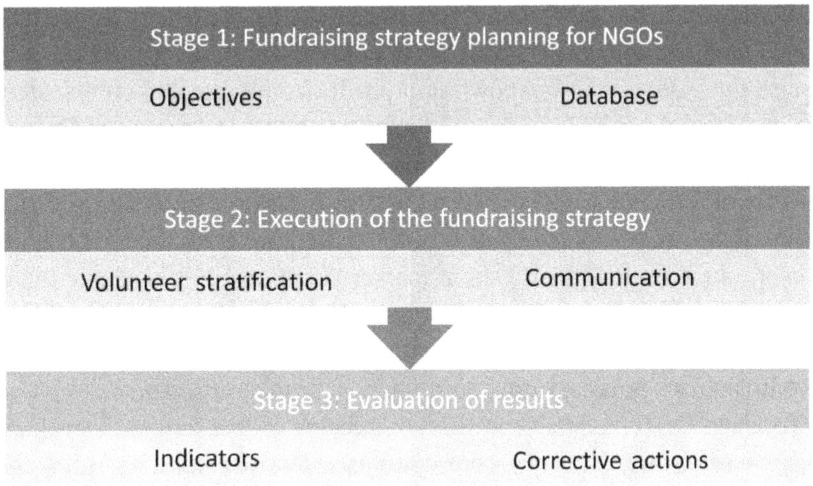

Stage 1: The NGO must carry out strategic planning to obtain financial resources by considering that objectives will be aligned with the mission, vision, and values of the organization. Goals set in conjunction with the volunteers' database who collaborate or not with the organization.
Stage 2: The fundraising strategy is executed, and the volunteers are stratified to carry out the assigned strategy. In this stage, the communication process is generated through digital media, where donations are being created.
Stage 3: In this stage, results are evaluated to make a diagnosis of the indicators achieved to propose, if necessary, corrective actions to change the strategy for moving the organization ahead.

Although complementary forms of alternative funding have existed for a long time, the combination of the 2008 First Global Crisis and the generalization in SMEs of incorporating technological advances have changed how to work and behave in highly-demanding markets with extensive social needs. So, many socioeconomic and cultural changes have influenced NGOs in the United States and Europe, but also in emerging markets, resulting in a challenge of the financial paradigm in the market. Consequently, this paradigm is now witnessing the emergence of new channels and alternative financial instruments out from the traditional banking sector (Tello, Romero, & Jaramillo, 2017) to include microcredits and crowdfunding.

CONCLUSION

Capturing private donations from non-profit organizations requires varied and complementary efforts and strategies to be applied. In Latin America, quite newcomers compared to what is done in the United States and Europe in the interest, and confidence in donating money, the interest in donating is increasing. One of the main problems in Latin America is the huge social imbalance between the rich and the poor, so by definition, the number of possible donors is quite reduced. Despite this fact, it has been an increasingly positive attitude to increase donations, especially in Latin American emerging countries (Brazil, Colombia, and Mexico).

Donors prefer traditional firms and certain NGOs only, linked to the Church and reputed organizations established in the country for a long time. That is why donors are more associated with a communication strategy to raise funds than with unknown non-profit institutions and civil society organizations. Many entities are in this group, which forces us to execute an increasingly specific job to raise money. For example, and according to Gonzalo Guzmán, director of the Chilean Fundraising Association, there are the cases in Chile of Telethon, that is very successful in per capita terms, and Hogar de Cristo, a case study. In Chile, there are about 15 thousand NGOs, ranging from a neighborhood council to the Red Cross. However, in the region, the donation market is not equal; it is adapted to each country. In Chile and Argentina, for example, there are differences. While the Chilean market is closer to a culture of giving, in Argentina the situation is different. At this respect, Ana Estenssoro, executive director of the ENI (Inclusive Businesses Spaces, from its acronym in Spanish, *Espacio de Negocios Inclusivos*) at the Universidad Torcuato Di Tella; as Diego Blasco, director of Institutional Development at the IAE Business School, agrees that Argentina is not a propitious scenario, at least regarding the given support. "Everything related to the civil society has just begun to take shape in the last 20 years since the crisis of 2001. But there are differences with other countries, in which taxes are favored," says Estenssoro (Torres & de Las Heras, 2017). These experts advise that the ideal approach is to have a mixed strategy, where efforts are not based solely on recruitment, but also on several formulas, at least taking into account the need and the context. This formula is better because if the organization wants to cover the operating expenses, it can be a good option to raise money individually.

A common example is that an aid organization collect money in the middle of a catastrophe collectively, but when the time passes and the event have been forgotten, the recruitment can follow through the affiliation of partners, and this manages a strategy within digital media.

There is also a term which now also maintains an extensive network of financial uptake and crowdfunding, also called crowdfunding, in which a group of people organized a network to raise money for their projects. It is a way to collect donations, as it is a mechanism that allows collecting small donations with a great impact. The success and, therefore, multiplication of this system has an increasing place in countries where the culture of online shopping, for example, is more advanced.

Finally, another system that is growing in popularity in Latin America and goes hand in hand with CSR is shared funding, that consists of companies aiming to have a mutually beneficial impact in social and environmental matters, although donations are separated, and the value of the company is evaluated by observing daily activities taking into account the value chain.

A future line of research on the topic analyzed in this chapter deals with how public relations works linked to digital marketing, based on the generation of fundraising strategies, and how it motivates fundraising through established and recurrent events.

ACKNOWLEDGMENT

The author thanks Prof. José Manuel Saiz Alvarez for his invitation to participate in this Handbook of Research.

REFERENCES

Bonilla, R. (2013). *Estrategia de comunicación para la captación de fondos en organizaciones sin fines de lucro. Estudio de caso hábitat para la humanidad El Salvador*. Universidad Centroamericana 'José Simeón Cañas'.

Coffman, L. C. (2017). Fundraising Intermediaries Inhibit Quality-Driven Charitable Donations. *Economic Inquiry*, *55*(1), 409–424. doi:10.1111/ecin.12379

Couttenier, M., & Hatte, S. (2015). *Mass Media Effects on Non-Governmental Organizations.* Working Paper, 13. Lausanne, Switzerland: University of Lausanne.

Duque, D. (2016). *El marketing social como metodología diferencial en la estrategia de negocio de las organizaciones (Master's Degree Project).* Manizales, Colombia: Universidad Nacional de Colombia.

Gálvez, M. M., Caba, M. C., & López, M. (2012). Responsabilidad social y transparencia on-line de las ONG: Análisis del caso español. *CIRIEC-España, Revista de Economía Pública. Social y Cooperativa*, *74*, 207–238.

García, J. S. (2010). El marketing y su origen a la orientación social : desde la perspectiva económica a la social. Los aspectos de organizavión y comunicación, 17(1), 61–77.

Huertas, R. (2015). *Organizaciones no gubernamentales y Social Media. Análisis de las Estrategias Comunicativas*. Malaga, Spain: University of Malaga.

Iglesias, M., & Carreras, I. (2012). *La colaboración efectiva en las ONG. Alianzas estratégicas y redes.* Barcelona, Spain: Instituto de Innovación Social.

ISDI. (2017). *Las ventajas que ofrece el marketing digital a las ONGs*. Retrieved October 15, 2018, from https://www.isdi.education/es/isdigital-now/ventajas-ofrece-marketing-digital-ongs

Kumar, S. (2010). Reviewing NGOs' media strategies: Possibilities for NGO-media collaboration. *International NGO Journal*, *5*(4), 84–87.

Marcuello, C. (2007). Responsabilidad social y organizaciones no lucrativas. *Ekonomiaz. Revista de Economía Vasca*, *65*, 208–227.

Mendive, D.E. (2008). *Marketing Social. Manual Práctico*. Buenos Aires: Editorial de los Cuatro Vientos.

Noval, L. (2014). *El fundraising como herramienta clave de captación de fondos de procedencia empresarial en las organizaciones no lucrativas. Aplicación práctica (Master's Degree Project).* University of Oviedo.

Rodríguez, L. (2014). Diseño de comunicaciones en redes sociales digitales para aumentar los voluntarios de dos ONGs en Argentina. Buenos Aires, Argentina: Academic Press.

Rojas, R., & Torres Briones, C. (2017). La Gestión del Conocimiento basado en la Teoría de Nonaka y Takeuchi. *INNOVA Research Journal*, *2*(4), 30–37.

Sckibick, M. (2009). *Las ONG como vía al desarrollo y a la transformación social: Un estilo de intervención y participación* (Ph.D. Thesis). Barcelona, Spain: Autonomous University of Barcelona.

Shuptrine, F. K., & Osmianski, F. A. (1975). Marketing's Changing Role: Expanding of Contracting. *Journal of Marketing*, *39*, 58–66.

Tello, A., Romero, A., & Jaramillo, C. (2017). The campaigns of crowdfunding and its impact on the financing of lucrative and non-profit projects in Ecuador. *Revista de Investigación Talentos*, *4*(2), 55–62.

Torres, R., & de las Heras, C. (2017). Fundraising, comunicación y relaciones públicas. Desarrollo cultural de una marca de ciudad: Málaga. *Chasqui. Revista Latinoamericana de Comunicación*, *136*(136), 375–394. doi:10.16921/chasqui.v0i136.2841

Chapter 18
The Use of Geolocalized Social Networks Information to Guide and Enhance the Design of Local Cultural and Tourist Policies

Víctor Temprano-García
University of Valladolid, Spain

Rebeca San José-Cabezudo
University of Valladolid, Spain

ABSTRACT

In recent years we have witnessed the upsurge in the use of social networks by companies and individuals, the latter being the real protagonists of its development. The diverse execution formats and the multiplicative effects on the reach and influence on equals have changed how organizations communicate with their users, but they have also become a valuable source of information. This chapter aims to understand the behavior of residents and tourists of a city to provide local decision makers insights and pioneer tools to help them design more effective action policies, which may have a positive impact on their cities. The methodological design used is based on the observation and collection of geolocalized data, provided spontaneously by residents and visitors to a town in a real context. Based on the analysis of the photographs that the subjects share about the city and the interactions that take place between the members of the social networks under study, the authors reach the main implications for decision makers to successfully design their policies.

DOI: 10.4018/978-1-5225-8939-6.ch018

INTRODUCTION

More than 3,300 million people, some 46% of the world's population, are connected to the Internet, a figure which increases to around 88% in North America and some 73% in Europe (Internet World Stats, 2015). The number of mobile device users is also growing fast. Globally, there are 3,790 billion mobile phone users, which meant 51% world mobile device penetration by January 2016 (Kemp, 2016). In Spain, according to the latest data published by the National Institute of Statistics (INE) for 2015, 78.7% of households in Spain had access to the internet, with the main type of Internet connection being through broadband established using a handheld device (smartphone or tablet). The mobile phone penetration rate in Spanish households was also reported to be 97%. According to the latest study published by the AIMC (AIMC, 2016), mobile phones are used by 93.9% of internet users to access the Internet, ahead of laptop computers (used by 76%) and desktop computers (71.4%). Moreover, 77.2% of users access social networks every day.

Social networks are still primarily used for friendship purposes (the option is chosen by 75.6% of users) and to keep up to date with current events (53.4%), family relations (49.2%), sharing hobbies (42.2%) and work relations (38.9%). Of the various social networks, Facebook, YouTube, and Twitter are, in that order, the most widely used (IAB, 2015).

Both the high penetration rates as well as the use of the Internet and the social networks, coupled with user willingness to create and share content, means that a huge amount of information is generated, in a wide variety of formats (written messages or texts, photographs, videos, etc.) and at breakneck speed. For example, according to an infographic published by the firm DOMO (James, 2012), by the time the Internet had reached 2,100 billion users, every minute over 680,000 items were shared, 100,000 tweets were sent, 48 hours of video were uploaded to YouTube and 3,125 new photographs were sent to Flickr, amongst the many other contents generated in other social networks and spaces on the Internet. The vast amount of information available coupled with the extraordinary speed at which is generated in a variety of formats (texts, photographs, videos, etc.). This fact provides the "seed" for the so-called Big Data, which has aroused so much interest today amongst scholars and practitioners. According to Gandomi and Haider (2015), *Volume*, *Variety*, and *Velocity* (or the *3Vs*) has emerged as a common framework to describe big data (Chen et al., 2012; Kwon et al., 2014)

In this new landscape, organizations face the challenge of harnessing, storing and analyzing all this information for decision-making purposes and generating greater value for all stakeholders. Although the situation could be applied to any other organization, our specific interest lies in ascertaining how local authorities can make the most of the potential offered by these new technologies and, particularly, social networks, in order to extract and examine the information generated by users with a view to devising more effective strategies and policies. More specifically, our goal is to analyze the information of tourist interest generated both by residents and visitors to the city of Valladolid (Spain). Over the last few years, scholars and professionals alike have shown great interest in the impact of social networks on the tourist industry. This interest is, particularly, on tourist behavior, due to the importance of the communities of travelers emerged on the Internet (e.g., TripAdvisor)(Miguéns et al., 2008), or how the information generated in social networks might have on the choice of tourist destinations (Di Pietro et al., 2010). In this research, we adopt a different approach and focus on examining the information from social networks which is used by public authorities to design more efficient tourist strategies and policies.

EXPERIMENTAL SECTION

Social Networks as a Source of Information

With developments in the Internet and Web 2.0, information has ceased to be the preserve of a privileged few and is now distributed and managed by many, thanks to the progress of information and communication technologies and, in particular, the Internet. Unlike conventional taxonomical or selective forms of distributing information, environment (reflected in phenomena such as blogs and, above all, social networks) said distribution is based on folksonomy or collaborative principles. In other words, all the members of the network participate and contribute towards distributing said information correctly, although not all do so equally, as there are veritable digital influencers (San José et al., 2012). Given such a context, beyond the actual information conveyed, it is individuals, acting as a node in these virtual networks, and their relations that are the real driving forces behind the scale and efficiency of the information's distribution.

Social networks are structures made up of people linked by one or more relations that may be friendship, work-related, hobbies or any other common interest they share. Social networks thus emerge as areas for social exchange or conversational networks composed of individuals who play an active part by spontaneously sharing experiences and opinions on issues of common interest (Wiertz & de Ruyter, 2007). As a result of this exchange of experiences, members of the network are likely to influence one another in their decisions and behaviors (Kozinets, 2002).

Social networks have expanded to embrace the phenomenon of user interaction, participation, and generated content. This fact engenders feelings of belonging and identification with the community, of sharing habits and traditions as well as a moral responsibility, thus leading to the creation of veritable communities (Muniz Jr & O'Guinn, 2001; Wiertz & de Ruyter, 2007)

Social networks, or areas of online exchange (e.g., Facebook, Twitter, YouTube, etc.), have provided the seed for virtual communities, distinguishing them from physical communities (Jones, 1995), also known as online communities (Kozinets, 2002). Virtual communities constitute an excellent research context to explore individual behavior and have attracted the interest of many marketing researchers (Dholakia et al., 2004; Porter, 2004). In these online spaces, individuals come together around some distinct interest to contact and interact with each other in order to exchange, share and pool resources, such as information, knowledge, experiences, entertainment, socio-emotional support, and friendship, through diverse computer-mediated communication systems, and in a number of different formats (texts, photographs, videos, etc.) (Jin et al., 2010). The communications which circulate the communities have a great capacity to influence the attitudes and behavior of the virtual community's members (Smith et al., 2005; Wangenheim & Bayón, 2004). This is particularly true in influencers or individuals whose messages might reach far and gain substantial credibility. In sum, for De Valck et al. (2009) a virtual brand community is, first and foremost, an online community based on social communications and relationships. Internet applications may supply the relational online space, but member-generated content and interpersonal communication are the essences of a virtual community (Wu & Fang, 2010). Thus, the value of a virtual community comes from the contents produced and shared during member interaction and conversation (Jin et al., 2010).

Ethnography is an anthropological method that has gained popularity in sociology, cultural studies, consumer research and a variety of other social science fields (Kozinets, 2002). This research method involves observing the practices of groups of people and even being able to take part in them, so as compare what people say and what they do. When applied to consumer behavior, "market-oriented ethnography" is an ethnographic focus on the behavior of people constituting a market for a product or a service (Arnould & Wallendorf, 1994). In line with Chong (2010), adopting this market research technique is supported by the value it provides vis-à-vis gathering and recording data systematically on individuals' behavior in a natural environment, thereby increasing the likelihood of spontaneously detecting moments or important answers in people's everyday lives. Moreover, being able to include multiple formats in the data observed (texts, photographs, etc.) can ensure the observer-researcher can enjoy greater reliability when interpreting behavior. Such content has become a valuable source of information for organizations to identify better and meet the customers´ needs.

"Netnography," or ethnography on the Internet (Kozinets, 1998), is a qualitative research methodology that adapts ethnographic research techniques to the study of cultures and communities emerging through computer-mediated communications. As the advent of networked computing opens up new opportunities for market-oriented consumer interaction, so it also opens up opportunities for marketing researchers to study the tastes, desires and other needs of consumers interacting in online communities (Kozinets, 2002).

Example of a Practical Application: The Case of Valladolid (Spain)

This study aims to understand the behavior of residents and tourists visiting the city of Valladolid based on the geolocalized photographs shared on social networks online, as well as estimating the impact on tourism promotion of the photographs taken by individuals of Valladolid. Information which the local authorities can employ to devise tourist policies that meet the needs of both groups of users. To achieve this goal, a process for observing and actively processing user-generated information was set up based on the criteria pre-established by the research team.

Measures

To accomplish our objective, the research team listed some variables to be measured. These variables related to user profiles (residents and tourists coming to the city of Valladolid), for example, their origin, number of photographs shared, visited, viewed, received, and when and where they were taken and shared, including the number of times they were visited and tags used to classify them. These variables would provide information concerning which areas have sparked the greatest interest and when, both in situ and on the Net, in addition to being able to pinpoint the influencers who help to create the image that the city of Valladolid has on the Net, amongst other matters.

Data Collection

Data were obtained on two photograph social networks: Flickr[1], a website for storing, organizing and sharing photographs and videos and including geolocation tools for the places where the photographs were taken, indicating the exact location coordinates, and Picasaweb[2] (Google), a digital platform for organizing photographs that also includes text editing and photo editing tools.

Table 1 provides a summary of the sources of information used and the key information taken from each for the present study.

The monitoring period for the two networks covered the whole of 2015, from 1 January to 31 December.

Data Processing

As pointed out by Kozinets (2002), once the online communities to be studied have been chosen, in order to gather data for their netnography two elements need to be taken into account: the data which the observer directly "copies" from the communications or interactions occurring between members and their personal remarks about the community, the members, the interactions and the interpretations. In order to copy, store and classify the online data, an *ad hoc*[3] platform for the Observatory of Culture and Tourism of the City of Valladolid was designed, through which it has been possible to label and define rectangles which allow us to collect geolocalized information from all categories of interest defined in the city of Valladolid. These categories are: Markets (2 items), Monuments (39 items), Ecclesiastic Monuments (33 items), Museums (22 items), Palaces (10 items), Parks (21 items), Squares (40 items), Bridges (4 items), Rivers of Light Walk[4] (36 items) and Theatres (3 items). These categories and the items included within[5] were built based on the official travel guide issued by the Valladolid's city council tourist resource center, and the interviews carried out by the city hall managers responsible for the culture and tourism policies. Image 1 shows an example of a geolocalized polygon - for the main square - built together by geolocalized photographs shared by users.

The observer's interpretations will be commented on following on from the results presented below.

Results

Having extracted and processed the data required for our study, we now present some of the results to emerge. Commencing with the information from users who shared images of the city of Valladolid in

Table 1. Syntax of the database used and the information obtained

Database	Fields	Information obtained
Flickr Picasa	Location	Visited place identification
	Position	User place of origin
	Distance between user and photograph	Type of user
	Views	Maximum, minimum and average views of a photograph taken in the city of Valladolid.
	Date a photograph was taken	Photographs filter based on the scope of time analyzed.
	Category	Category of the most often photographed places
	Title and Tags (word associated to the photograph)	Social group generation by affinities
	Longitude A	Valladolid tourist areas mapping through geolocalized polygons. Own design. Visualization through ArcGis
	Latitude A	
	Longitude B	
	Latitude B	

Figure 1. Main square of Valladolid geolocalized polygon

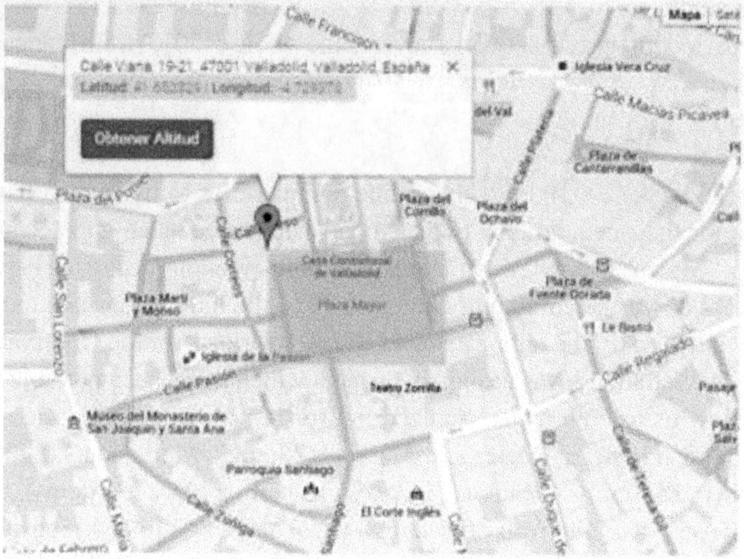

2015 through the previously identified social networks (Flickr and Picasa), the final sample came to 226 individuals.

Concerning users' country of origin, 56.19% did not state their country of origin[6]. Of those who did, 40.27% are Spanish, while users from other countries (Italy, the UK, Australia, Colombia, Russia, and Switzerland) accounted for a very small proportion, 3.54%.

As for the Spanish users, 99 users publicly declared their origin. In other words, we know where 43.80% of all users were from. Of these, 23.85% live in Valladolid (Spain), followed by users from Madrid (Spain), who account for 5.96%. The remainder comes from the various other provinces in Spain (Barcelona, León, Santander, etc.).

As far as activity in the chosen social networks is concerned, users took and shared 8,426 photographs over the study period, with each photo being seen an average of 546 times, with a standard deviation of 1.352. Put differently, just a few users account for most visits to the photographs, as can be seen in figure 2.

Focusing more closely on the photographs, of the 8,426 taken, the 20 which aroused the greatest interest, judging by the number of times they were viewed, generated 152,720 visits. Most photographs were taken in March and September (respectively, representing when Holy Week and the local festivities in honor of the patron saint took place,) and accounted for 40% of all the photographs of the city of Valladolid uploaded to said social networks in 2015.

As regards the interest shown in the various areas of the city in 2015 (see Table 2), prominent are the Monuments, both concerning the number of photographs taken of them as well as in the total number of visits to them. These are followed by the Squares and the Rivers of Light route. It should be pointed out that the Rivers of Light route feeds on and, in part, includes the other categories (Monuments, Squares, Church Monuments, Parks, Bridges, etc.). At the lower end of the Table are the markets, bridges, and theatres. There are two possible explanations for this: on the one hand, these categories contain fewer items than the rest and, on the other, because in part they again take in other categories such as the pre-

Figure 2. Distribution of users by the mean number of visits their photographs of the city of Valladolid received

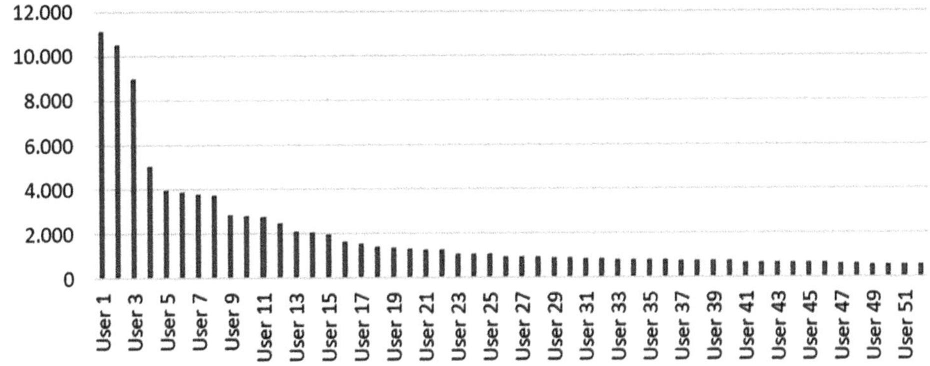

viously mentioned Rivers of Light. As for the markets, it should be highlighted that Valladolid's most emblematic market, the Mercado del Val, has been undergoing renovation work since October 2014.

Figure 3 shows the areas in the city that account for most of the geolocalized images. The tool used also allows us to analyze each area in greater detail. For instance, in one of the city's most emblematic spots, the Campo Grande park (Figure 4), it can be seen how the images are concentrated at the main entrance, through Plaza Zorrilla, and, to a lesser extent, at the Plaza de Colón, around the area of the Lake, the Bird House (Pajarera), Bandstand (Pérgola) with the Fountain of the Swan (Fuente del Cisne) and Fountain of Fame (Fuente de la Fama).

Table 2. Distribution of the tourist areas in Valladolid with geolocalized images in 2015

Category	Number of Photographs Frequency	Number of Photographs	Sum of views Frequency	Sum of views
Monuments	25,04 %	1.185	22,86 %	420.002
Squares	21,91 %	1.037	17,06 %	313.347
Rivers of Light	19,69 %	932	22,44 %	412.206
Parks	11,47 %	543	14,21 %	260.957
Ecclesiastic Monuments	8,92 %	422	10,22 %	187.728
Museums	7,71 %	365	8,08 %	148.417
Palaces	2,87 %	136	3,46 %	63.519
Theatres	1,80 %	85	0,87 %	16.037
Bridges	0,51 %	24	0,79 %	14.440
Markets	0,08 %	4	0,01 %	268
TOTAL		4.733		1.836.921

Figure 3. Distribution of the geolocalized images taken in the city of Valladolid in 2015

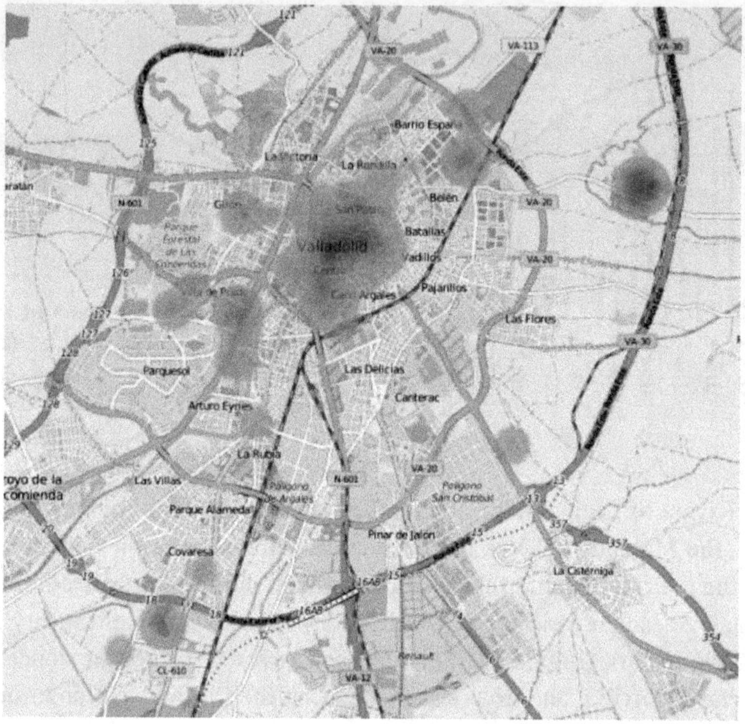

Figure 4. Distribution of the geolocalized images taken in the Campo Grande Park in the city of Valladolid in 2015

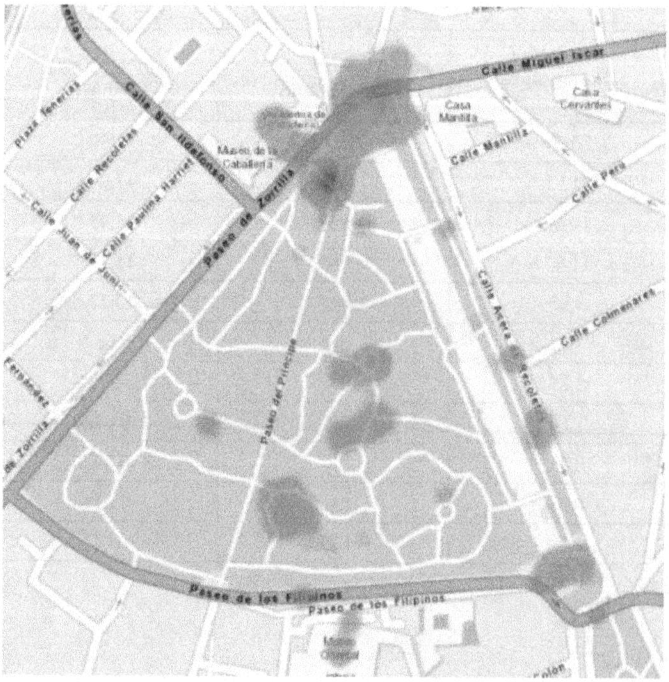

As regards the labels used by users to identify their photographs, as can be seen from figure 5, most common are the words Valladolid, Holy Week, Agility, Nikon, Sport, Dogs, Castilla y León. From the standpoint of tourism and this composition of words, the important number of photographs taken during Holy Week in Valladolid that is then shared spontaneously on the Internet may be inferred. There is also a large number related to sport and the meetings held by the Valladolid Agility Club, a sports association open to the practice of canine sports.

As follows, the results have been shown in a matrix, where the tourist categories performance in the city of Valladolid is ranked. We define tourist categories performance as the category awareness based on users and the likeliness to share the photograph among users. This ranking is built based on two variables: the abscissa axis (x-axis) represents the number of photographs taken and shared in the social networks, and the ordinate axis (y-axis) represents the number of views of these images. Thus, those categories (represented as circles) located in the 1st quadrant (bottom left), correspond to categories that are comprised of items with the number of pictures taken below the average, (i.e. little interest on the part of the tourists) and the number of views of the pictures shared by users also below the average. The 2nd quadrant (bottom right) correspond to categories comprising items with the number of pictures taken above the average, (i.e., some interest on the part of the tourists) and the number of views of the pictures shared by users, below the average. The 3rd quadrant (upper left) correspond to categories comprising items with the number of pictures taken below the average, (i.e., little interest on the part of the tourists) but with the number of views of pictures shared by users, above the average. Finally, the 4th quadrant (upper right) correspond to categories that are comprised of items with the number of pictures taken above the average, (i.e., some interest on the part of the tourists) and the number of views of the pictures shared by users, also above the average.

As can be seen from Figure 6, the monuments hold the greatest interest for tourists, followed by the Rivers of Light route (which overlaps with several other categories in which it is included) and the Squares of Valladolid. Fewer photographs are taken of the parks during the year, although the photographs are seen quite a large number of times. The quadrant containing the fewest number of photographs seen and having the least impact includes Church Monuments, Museums, Palaces and, finally, Theatres and Bridges of Valladolid.

Although few data are available concerning user origin, we were keen to ascertain whether there were any differences apparent in the level of interest which the various categories aroused. Residents showed a preference, in this order, for the Rivers of Light route, the Monuments, and the Squares. As far as the sample as a whole was concerned, greatest interest was shown for the Church Monuments. For their part, tourists evidenced a similar preference, albeit in a different order: Monuments, Squares and the Rivers of Light route, followed in this case by Parks (see figure 7 and 8).

Figure 5. Cloud of words of the labels linked to pictures taken in the city of Valladolid in 2015

Figure 6. Matrix of tourist categories in the city of Valladolid in terms of popularity in 2015

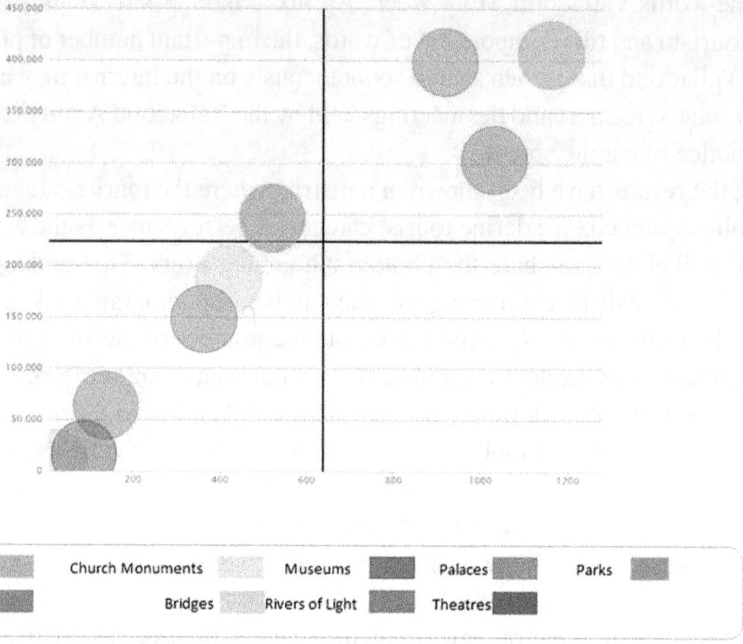

**For a more accurate representation see the electronic version.*

Figure 7. Matrix of tourist categories of the city of Valladolid in terms of popularity in 2015: Residents

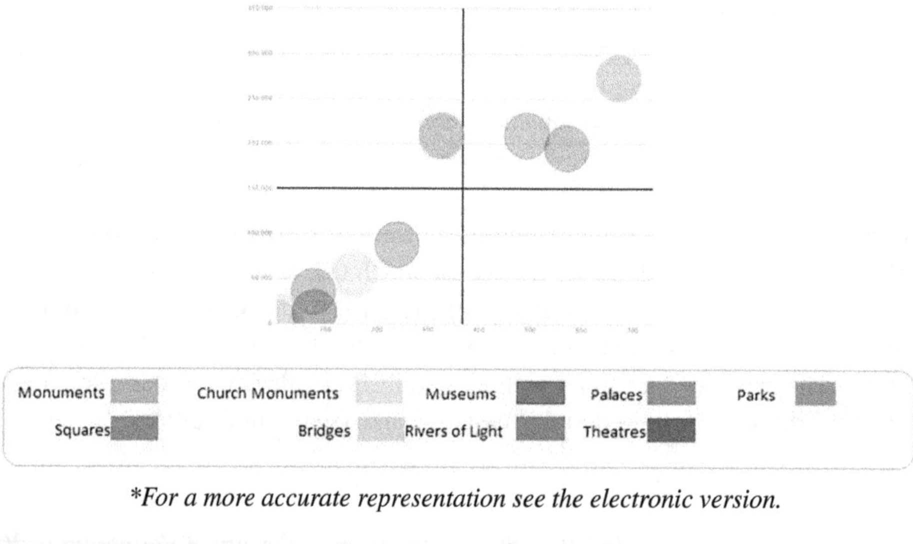

**For a more accurate representation see the electronic version.*

DISCUSSION OF RESULTS

It is an undeniable fact that the Internet and social networks have become an integral part of people's lives. It is also no less true that organizations must take advantage of the opportunities afforded to them by the new technologies when it comes to decision making. People speak on social networks and organizations must listen if they are to devise valuable proposals that will meet the demands of today. This fact is by no means an easy task. The information generated in real time is so vast and comes from so many sources

Figure 8. Matrix of tourist categories of the city of Valladolid in terms of popularity in 2015: Tourists

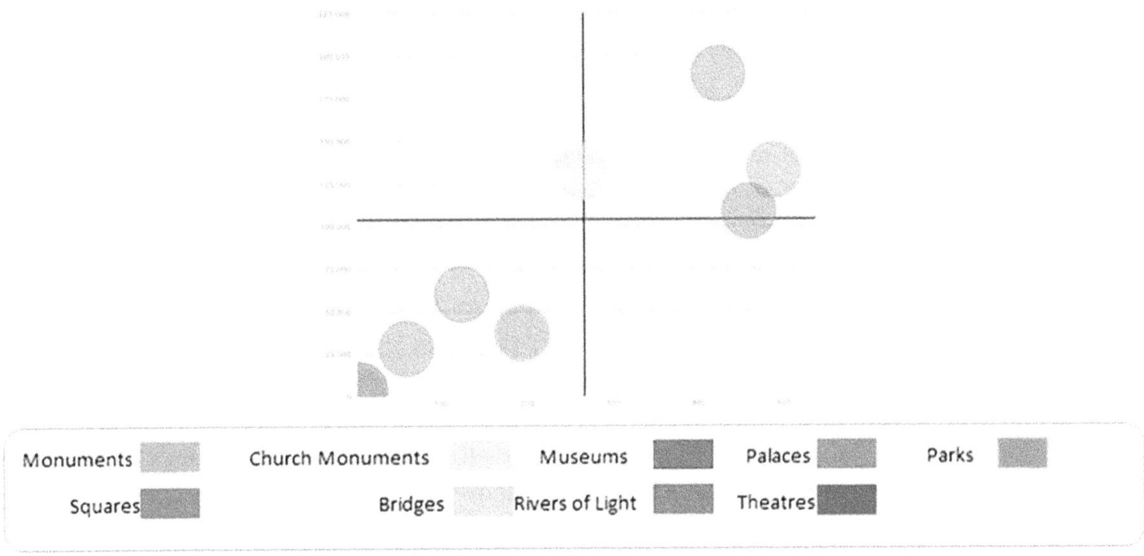

**For a more accurate representation see the electronic version.*

and in so many diverse formats (photographs, texts, etc.) that current data mining techniques prove insufficient. In this regard, the possibilities offered by ICT can help organizations to identify, capture, store, and process said data, although this should be complemented by analysis and interpretation from those professionals most suited to the goals of the particular research in question.

In the present research, based on the research team's prior knowledge and following a previously established procedure, a tool has been designed to obtain data and process it. After analysis, results have emerged which we feel to be of considerable importance for a city's tourism management and image. Based on the spontaneous actions of private users (in which the observer has not intervened) in social networks, we have been able to identify which areas have aroused the greatest interest amongst those visiting the city, on what dates and what influence the pictures of the city shared with other users might have had, amongst other aspects. We feel this information to be extremely valuable for local authority managers in that it helps them to pinpoint which areas need to be promoted further or exploited to a greater extent, or which need to be "improved." Implications for management are wide-ranging and diverse. The combination of new routes or tourist package deals, by using the most appealing areas when conducting publicity campaigns for the city, joint events between these areas and others. The use of geolocation based action (such as placing informative beacons that provide NFC (Near Field Communication signals) would enrich the visitor experience, all of which would help to forge enhanced brand capital for the city. In this regard, identifying digital influencers and cooperating with them is of prime importance in that their actions may have a great impact on the scope and veracity of communications, helping to attract new tourists to the city. Local managers should implement policies that foster active citizen involvement.

We must not overlook another of the main stakeholders involved in this study and which local managers equally seek to satisfy: residents. They should also be listened to and actively engaged to make them ambassadors for the city. In this sense, encouraging a feeling of identity and belonging to the city is key.

On a different note, the information obtained might also help managers to evaluate the efficacy of the funding dedicated to promoting tourism or conservation, improving and maintaining the city's heritage, in that these are measures which allow the efficacy of the action taken to be gauged regarding user satisfaction.

Such is the scale of the phenomena being explored in our research that the present analysis may be viewed merely as the first part of the study we intend to carry out and, as such, it is by no means free from limitations. Firstly, about how information has been gathered, the selection criteria followed to obtain information from one network or another is based on the possibility of extracting this information through the Application Programming Interface (API) and the users that make use of this social network. An API is a set of routines, protocols, and tools for building software applications used to communicate with an operating system, databases or communications protocols.

Facebook has an API available but does not allow query parameters-based information, events, terms, etc. Instagram has a very simple API, but the content is not based on tourism, therefore, is not acceptable for use in this study. Twitter allows queries and also has content, but the use of geolocation is decreasing. Flickr is a network specialized on photography with data geolocalized, and with an API for querying information based on content and geolocation, making it possible to analyze data used for the current research.

One further limitation is that the information accessed is public, in other words, it is the information which the user has authorized for open sharing. As a result, our tool fails to reflect data from users who have private profiles, that is to say, who share information with authorized users. Lastly, the final sample is made up of a large number of users who do not state where they are from. In future studies, we hope to be able to access larger and more representative samples that would enable us to conduct a more comprehensive and thorough statistical analysis.

About how information has been gathered, the observer has neither participated nor interacted with the users observed. Although this might endow the results with greater objectivity and less bias, directly participating in the communities might help us to obtain another kind of information. In future stages of the research, we intend to delve more deeply into this issue. Furthermore, we feel that it would be time to explore the possibility of cross-referencing the data obtained with that taken from other sources, whether primary or secondary (e.g., climate data) to gain a better understanding of the results to emerge and thus allow us to explore interesting new relations. It may also be interesting to analyze the economic and the reputational impact of cultural events in the city, by analyzing information from other social networks, such as Twitter, Facebook, Instagram, etc. and data related to tourists' expenditure data within a certain period.

REFERENCES

AIMC. (2016). *Navegantes en la Red – 18ª Encuesta AIMC a Usuarios de Internet*. Retrieved from: http://download.aimc.es/aimc/ROY76b/macro2015.pdf

Arnould, E. J., & Wallendorf, M. (1994). Market-oriented ethnography: Interpretation building and marketing strategy formulation. *JMR, Journal of Marketing Research*, *31*(4), 484–504. doi:10.1177/002224379403100404

Betters, E. (2016). *Google is shutting down Picasa: What'll happen to your photos and videos?* Pocket-lint Limited. Retrieved from: https://www.pocket-lint.com/apps/news/google/136712-google-is-shutting-down-picasa-what-ll-happen-to-your-photos-and-videos

Chen, H., Chiang, R. H., & Storey, V. C. (2012). Business Intelligence and Analytics: From Big Data to Big Impact. *Management Information Systems Quarterly*, *36*(4), 1165–1188. doi:10.2307/41703503

Chong, J. L. (2010). Evaluating the impact of Arnould and Wallendorf's (1994) market-oriented ethnography. *Journal of Business Research*, *63*(12), 1295–1300. doi:10.1016/j.jbusres.2009.08.001

De Valck, K., Van Bruggen, G. H., & Wierenga, B. (2009). Virtual communities: A marketing perspective. *Decision Support Systems*, *47*(3), 185–203. doi:10.1016/j.dss.2009.02.008

Dholakia, U. M., Bagozzi, R. P., & Pearo, L. K. (2004). A social influence model of consumer participation in network-and small-group-based virtual communities. *International Journal of Research in Marketing*, *21*(3), 241–263. doi:10.1016/j.ijresmar.2003.12.004

Di Pietro, L., Di Virgilio, F., & Pantano, E. (2012). Social network for the choice of tourist destination: Attitude and behavioural intention. *Journal of Hospitality and Tourism Technology*, *3*(1), 60–76. doi:10.1108/17579881211206543

Gandomi, A., & Haider, M. (2015). Beyond the hype: Big data concepts, methods, and analytics. *International Journal of Information Management*, *35*(2), 137–144. doi:10.1016/j.ijinfomgt.2014.10.007

Gibbs, S. (2018). Flickr bought by SmugMug as Yahoo breakup begins. *The Guardian*. Retrieved from: https://www.theguardian.com/technology/2018/apr/23/flickr-bought-by-smugmug-yahoo-breakup

IAB. (2015). *VI Estudio Redes Sociales de IAB Spain*. Retrieved from: http://www.iabspain.net/wp-content/uploads/downloads/2015/01/Estudio_Anual_Redes_Sociales_2015.pdf

INE. (2016). *Encuesta sobre Equipamiento y Uso de Tecnologías de Información y Comunicación en los hogares*. Retrieved from: http://www.ine.es/dyngs/INEbase/es/operacion.htm?c=Estadistica_C&cid=1254736176741&menu=resultados&idp=1254735976608

International World. (2015). *Usage and population statistics*. Retrieved from: http://www.internetworldstats.com/

James, J. (2012). *How Much Data is Created Every Minute?* Retrieved from: https://www.domo.com/blog/2012/06/how-much-data-is-created-every-minute/

Jin, X.-L., Lee, M. K., & Cheung, C. M. (2010). Predicting continuance in online communities: Model development and empirical test. *Behaviour & Information Technology*, *29*(4), 383–394. doi:10.1080/01449290903398190

Jones, S. (1995). *Understanding community in the information age*. Sage.

Kemp, S. (2016). *We Are Social* [Press release]. Retrieved from: http://wearesocial.com/specialreports/digital-in-2016

Kozinets, R. V. (1998). On netnography: Initial reflections on consumer research investigations of cyberculture. *Advances in Consumer Research. Association for Consumer Research (U. S.), 25*(1), 366–371.

Kozinets, R. V. (2002). The field behind the screen: Using netnography for marketing research in online communities. *JMR, Journal of Marketing Research, 39*(1), 61–72. doi:10.1509/jmkr.39.1.61.18935

Kwon, O., Lee, N., & Shin, B. (2014). Data quality management, data usage experience and acquisition intention of big data analytics. *International Journal of Information Management, 34*(3), 387–394. doi:10.1016/j.ijinfomgt.2014.02.002

Miguéns, J., Baggio, R., & Costa, C. (2008). Social media and tourism destinations: TripAdvisor case study. *Advances in Tourism Research, 26*(28), 1–6.

Muniz, A. M. Jr, & O'guinn, T. C. (2001). Brand community. *The Journal of Consumer Research, 27*(4), 412–432. doi:10.1086/319618

Porter, C. E. (2004). A typology of virtual communities: A multi-disciplinary foundation for future research. *Journal of Computer-Mediated Communication, 10*(1), 3.

San José, R., Camarero, C., & Rodríguez, J. (2012). Looking for online opinion leaders: Why companies must identify and take care of more active users of online opinion spaces. *Universia Business Review*, (35): 14–31.

Sigurbjörnsson, B., & Van Zwol, R. (2008). Flickr tag recommendation based on collective knowledge. *Proceedings of the 17th international conference on World Wide Web*, 327-336. 10.1145/1367497.1367542

Smith, D., Menon, S., & Sivakumar, K. (2005). Online peer and editorial recommendations, trust, and choice in virtual markets. *Journal of Interactive Marketing, 19*(3), 15–37. doi:10.1002/dir.20041

Wangenheim, F., & Bayón, T. (2004). The effect of word of mouth on services switching: Measurement and moderating variables. *European Journal of Marketing, 38*(9/10), 1173–1185. doi:10.1108/03090560410548924

Wiertz, C., & de Ruyter, K. (2007). Beyond the call of duty: Why customers contribute to firm-hosted commercial online communities. *Organization Studies, 28*(3), 347–376. doi:10.1177/0170840607076003

Wu, S.-C., & Fang, W. (2010). The effect of consumer-to-consumer interactions on idea generation in virtual brand community relationships. *Technovation, 30*(11), 570–581. doi:10.1016/j.technovation.2010.07.005

KEY TERMS AND DEFINITIONS

3Vs: Acronym of volume, variety, and velocity, this term deals with how to optimize big data.

Application Programming Interface (API): Set of routines, protocols, and tools for building software applications used to communicate with an operating system, databases, or communications protocols.

Ethnography: This is an anthropological method used in sociology, cultural studies, consumer research, and a variety of other social science fields to study people and cultures.

Flickr: Online photo-sharing service, which allows users to share their photos with the online community worldwide.

Google Photos: Launched on May 28, 2015, is a Google's smart home for photo-sharing and storage service.

Near Field Communication (NFC): Short-range wireless technology that allows you to connect two devices when sending (reading) and receiving (writing) a signal in both directions.

Netnography: The use of ethnography on the internet.

Reputational Capital: An asset that can be managed and accumulated and traded in for trust, the legitimization of a position of power and social recognition.

Valladolid: Medium-sized and Spanish industrial city of 300,000 inhabitants located in the region of Castile-Leon (Northwest of Spain).

ENDNOTES

1. Flickr is an online photo-sharing service, which allow users to share their photos with family, friends, and the online community at large (Sigurbjörnsson & Van Zwol, 2008). In 2018, it was sold to SmugMug, an independent image-hosting company (Gibbs, 2018)
2. Picasaweb is a website which allows to upload and share photos and videos. In 2016, Google decided to close Picasaweb to focus on Google Photos, their new photo-sharing and storage service (Betters, 2016).
3. The platform has been designed by the research team and the company GDP software, located in Valladolid.
4. The Rivers of Light walk flows through and connects different areas of the centre of Valladolid. The name stands for the Esgueva River, which once ran through the old city. The route uses a colour lighting code, green for the walk through the city, purple, white, red for ecclesiastic monuments depending on the catholic liturgical calendar, and institutional purple of the city of Valladolid is used in each of the buildings dedicated to offering an increased level of culture (e.g. theatres and museums).
5. A detailed description of the items and its coordinates, are available upon request to the authors.
6. User origin is taken from the field "origen_user", which users fill in freely when registering on the Flickr and Picasa platforms. In line with current legislation concerning protection of personal details, our algorithm is designed to gather public information from users, edited by them.

Chapter 19
Evolving Faster Than Lightning:
How Is Digital Marketing Changing the Brand? The Future for Digital Marketing Tools

Danny C. Barbery-Montoya
https://orcid.org/0000-0002-6005-4997
Universidad de Especialidades Espíritu Santo, Ecuador

ABSTRACT

This chapter aims to show the extent of digital marketing when using technological tools to create interaction between the company, customers, and stakeholders. The literature about the main tech tools used nowadays was extensively read to develop this chapter. Next, the authors delve into the digital behavior of the consumer when using these tools. Thus, they propose the OXS model to show the stages of eBehavior and connected with digital marketing tools (DMT) backed with security, which creates a new value string (digital) that results in a more powerful and effective eWOM. The proposal of this model explains the classification of brands within the digital context.

INTRODUCTION

Digital technologies and devices such as smartphones, smart products, the Internet of things (IoT), artificial intelligence and deep learning, show the changes, in the consumer´s life, for the near future; these digital technologies are changing the marketing approach and transforming research to what is known as digital marketing (Kannan & Li, 2017). Considering this, digital marketing is defined as a branch of marketing which uses digital devices and channels to promote products of a certain brand, and connect them with the consumer (Karatum, 2017); this is why digital marketing can also be seen as activities, institutions, and processes facilitated by the use of new technologies, communication, delivering value to customers and stakeholders while becoming an adaptive process (Kamman & Li, 2017).

DOI: 10.4018/978-1-5225-8939-6.ch019

Although digital marketing is growing fast, the progress in SMEs is slow (Pradhan, Nigam, & CK, 2018); however, digital channels are in great use by small businesses today, and it has proven to be more effective when connecting them with the consumer (Karatum, 2017). Thus, value must be created for the customer, and for this we must consider that creating digital value is not focused on developing marketing actions and sales only, but includes other edges where digital business operations, digital mindset and digital business models (in addition to marketing and sales) are of high importance for executives who work in this field (Seitz & Burosch, 2018).

Moreover, the digital consumer has evolved, with internet practices focused in fun, learning, feedback to a brand, and even talk about or work for a brand (Eigenraam, Eelen, van Lin, & Verlegh, 2018), making him a more participatory and collaborative consumer, it also depends on the age and therefore the generation to which he belongs, considering that digital tools are seeked according to speed, security and offered stimuli; such is the case, Baby Boomers are more skeptical and seek what they really consider useful for their lives; Generation X uses the internet as an additional practical channel; and Millennials are more prone to use the network to become acquainted with their environment, quicker and diversely considering their better skills for technology. (Barbery, Pástor, Idrobo & Sempértegui, 2018).

Nevertheless, not only the buyer's perspective must be taken into account, but also the employee's, the company´s, and additionally, the role of mobile technologies; each has a role which has been changing over time, and they must adapt to the technological developments of today (Shankar *et al.*, 2016). From any of these perspectives, we must consider that communication between company and customer is the key to the development of relations, sales support and brand building (Karjaluoto, Mustonen, & Ulkuniemi, 2015), taking into account that interactive marketing is a key skill in growth which needs the support of business intelligence (Stone & Woodcock, 2014). Although it is true that with a website these ties with the client can be created (Kriechbaumer & Christodoulidou, 2014), digital marketing must contemplate getting support from other hardware, and adapt itself to the tendencies of the market.

This is where the concept of brand community becomes important; it is built on four elements: product, brand, consumers, and marketers. Under this scheme, the social networks become facilitators in the exchange of information so that more robust brand communities are built, thus increasing consumer loyalty (Laroche, Habibi, & Richard, 2013); but we must still consider other elements linked to the construction of this community such as the stakeholders, content, channels, and results (Turner, 2017), in addition to those tools mentioned by Kannan and Li (2017) as an example.

The purpose of the chapter is to show the extent of digital marketing through a panorama which includes the interaction process between the company, customers, stakeholders and channels (devices) as major players, thus understanding how you can generate brand value with correct management of this scenario.

BACKGROUND

Interaction With the Consumer and the New Value Proposition

The value chain by Porter (1982) establishes a model where the raw material input must be transformed before being distributed and marketed, to finally provide services to customers who have purchased the product manufactured by the company. However, with the emergence of new technologies, digitalization has become a daily routine that is changing the traditional ways in which consumers and businesses interact with each other (Taiminen & Karjaluoto, 2015). With such a significant change, you can set a new value chain model where research, strategy and marketing activities play an important role in the development of the company. These strategies within a platform on the web, are oriented toward purposes such as newsgathering, relationship management, creative outlet, and entertainment, but they should also be managed as a consistent, personalized (customization), committed and secure multiplatform concept, generating impact on the company´s knowledge for development of new products, services or systems (Rojas & Torres, 2017); they should not be focused on e-purchase behavior only, in spite of this generating high costs for companies (Puto & Koscieniak, 2015).

Today, people are frequently more exposed to digital, assuming the role of consumer among so many purposes, seeking information about products, buying, consuming and exchanging experiences with other users (Stephen, 2016). This fast and open access to information generates reasons for interaction, which according to Velitchka and Andrew Rohm (2016), can be classified into ten groups: promotions and incentives, opportunities (timeliness), product information, commitment, buy, search, customer service, entertainment or fun, branded content, and customization / exclusivity, which shows that the existing consumer has evolved his rational purchase, has become smarter through meticulous investigative processes and higher standards. Thus, we find three types of consumers who interact with the brand: The first group interacts with all kinds of brands across all platforms; the second group of consumers, with a utilitarian mindset, is committed to the brand in his purchases and to the obtention of services, he seeks access to promotions and incentives; and finally a third group, who seeks timely content and hedonic interactions with the brand through the use of e-mail and social networks (Velitchka Rohm & Andrew, 2016).

This trend of digital studies focuses on five aspects: a) The digital consumer´s culture; b) Advertising; c) Impact of digital environments; d) Mobile: and e) The online WOM (eWOM) and comments (reviews) (Stephen, 2016). All these elements are involved and included as part of the interaction between company and customer, creating a doubt as to how to mix them to have a result that shows us the best way to build a brand of value.

Digital Environments

Digital environments are evolving, with some differences between total reality and 100% virtual environments. Farshid, Paschen, Eriksson, and Kietzmann (2018) define a continuum between the two environments by establishing a difference stressed by technologies (Figure 1)

- **Reality**: it refers to the physical, real world, which exists and in which people coexist and develop every day (Farshid *et al.*, 2018).
- **Augmented Reality (AR)**: generates an offline or online experience, it is different for the consumer taking into account that the spatial reality is transformed and works with additional elements which highlight the attributes of the product and the brand (De Ruyter, Isobel Keeling, & Ngo, 2018), in a nutshell, it is the integration of today's world with digital information on top (Farshid *et al.*, 2018); it can improve consumer engagement by creating a more intimate and personalized brand (Scholz & Duffy, 2018).
- **Virtual Reality (VR)**: generates a real-time interactive experience which emulates reality. The use of VR is wide: from connecting to traditional media and online media, to the generation of eWOM or presentation of virtual products, with the ability to see them realistically, and the op-

Figure 1. The current reality / virtual reality continuum
Source: Farshid, Paschen, Eriksson, and Kietzmann (2018)

Reality	Augmented Reality	Virtual Reality	Mixed Reality	Augmented Virtuality	Virtuality
The actual word that we experience with all of our senses.	Information and data overlaid on top of the actual world.	A complete digital representation of the actual world.	The introduction of possible elements into an actual world.	The introduction of actual elements into a possible world.	The introduction of actual elements into a possible world.
An actual house.	A realty app provides details of an actual house.	A 3D image of actual furniture. A virtual tour of an actual house.	Simulation of different furniture, virtual or new, in an actual house.	Staging of actual furniture in a new house.	A 3D model for a new house or new furniture.
Key concept: Physical co-presence of people and objects.	Key concept: Add utility to physical co-presence	Key concept: Enable perceived presence and full immersion.	Key concept: Adaption of actual scenarios.	Key concept: Participation in possible scenarios.	Key concept: Vision of a completely different world.
Real			Possible		
Actual Reality Continuum		Virtual Reality Continuum			

portunity of asking questions in real time, which can be answered, thus influencing the buying decision process (Martínez-Navarro, Bigné, Guixeres, Alcaniz, & Torrecilla, 2018). Virtual reality is shown as the 3-D representation of the current world or its elements (Farshid *et al.*, 2018).

- **Mixed Reality (MR)**: also known as hybrid reality, refers not only to the combination of real objects with virtual objects but with those which are possible (Farshid *et al.*, 2018.); it can also be defined as a mixture of augmented reality and augmented virtuality, where you can interact with both real and unreal objects (Flavián, Ibáñez-Sánchez, & Orús, 2018).
- **Augmented Virtuality (AV)**: unlike mixed reality, augmented virtuality shows a more virtual world; in short, it no longer introduces any virtual objects, but introduces real elements in a possible environment (Farshid *et al.*, 2018.); computers completely generate these environments, and a real person is inserted to interact with them (Flavián *et al.*, 2018).
- **Virtuality**: as opposed to reality, virtuality refers to a possible world or environment (Farshid *et al.*, 2018), i.e., a world where the virtual is amplified to 100%, it is created by computers and nothing is real (Flavián *et al.*, 2018).

An interesting feature about the subject of digital environments, is their use by means of mobile devices, facilitating their implementation, especially on trade issues, and generating benefits such as joy, perception of better aesthetics and customer service (Dacko, 2017), as well as establishing cognitive, emotional, behavioral, sensory and social responses toward the company; this will happen during the entire purchase process (Flavián *et al.*, 2018).

Internet of Things

The concept of the Internet of Things (IoT) refers to the use of smart objects inside a cyber-physical system, where using sensors, they play a specific role (Boyes, Hallaq, Cunningham, & Watson, 2018). Thus, the IoT is presented as an emerging technology which provides unsurpassed convenience for human life;

however, the nature of an open interaction such as IoT´s allows for a high number of intelligent devices to share their data with each other, allowing intruders to make improper use of this data exchange; communication dependence on wireless technologies renders IoT vulnerable to data theft (Yaqoob, Abaker, Hashem, & Ahmed, 2018) in untrusted environments. Paradoxically, IoT portrays this relation of trust with technology as an advantage, considering the use of monitoring and control applications, especially in corporate environments (Falkenreck & Wagner, 2017).

In business environments, companies can make use of IoT while exploring disruptive technologies focused on the human, gathering lots of information about behaviors in an easy and uncomplicated way, so that exchange solutions with consumers arise, facilitating their lives and creating a better relationship (Lo & Fields, 2018). The dilemma of buyers against the benefits presented by the IoT is the credibility they may have, in some cases, toward the product manufacturer (Falkenreck & Wagner, 2017).

User Experience

The User Experience (UX) has a broad definition that goes from design to product creation. The UX has become one of the most important factors for companies, so they are more competitive in the market (Park et al., 2018.); It manifests itself as an understanding of the individual in three phases: expectation, interaction, and experience in general, where there is an interaction that occurs within a system (Roto, 2007). This experience is ambiguous because it depends on the people´s perception of the world, where there are levels of objectivity and subjectivity, and where psychological and sociological components do exist (Anttonen & Jumisko-Pyykkö, 2008), which generate feelings and ratings toward the product (Galeano, 2008).

The design of user experience is connected to web design or with the design of devices that provide easiness for people, through the analysis of usability and aesthetics in products (Norman, 2004). Usability is presented as the way in which a product can be used to achieve a specific result, with effectiveness, efficiency, and satisfaction (Quiñones, Rusu, & Rusu, 2018). It is noted that the function of the UX is not only based on cognitive activities but also on the emotions awaken by the interaction with products (Filippi & Barattin, 2018), in such a way that perception is affected by the generated emotions.

Moreover, it is noted that the user experience can be anticipated by imagining positive or negative ideas from experience with a product (Jan & Proceedings, 2011); this is known as anticipated user experience (AUX), and it leads to seeking mechanisms for building more accurate ideas about the reality of the brand which the company wishes to show.

In no-physical interface designs, developed models are based on user-centered designs (UCD), where there should be easiness for interaction between machines and humans (Wong, Khong, & Thwaites, 2012); however, UX development is not based on the work of designers only, but involves the participation and collaboration of a team that includes communicators, users and technologies, and where constant testing is done in order to understand a way to achieve the best experience from the use of a product (Getto & Moore, 2017).

Digital, Social Media, and Mobile Marketing (DSMM)

Mobile marketing offers great advantages for businesses, such as creating offers based on weather conditions and natural disasters, adjustment of the price offer and promotions against those of the competitors or use short-term prices to reduce inventories. Besides, you can quickly evaluate the effectiveness of campaigns and provide special information when they are in a particular place or send relevant and personalized information according to purchase history, so that geolocation becomes highly relevant in social networks (Berman, 2016). Models of information exchange, products, services, and financiers are specifically influenced by social media displayed at the levels of cooperation and adaptation, which are present in this environment, seeking to maintain the communication with the consumers, support sales and build awareness in stakeholders as main objectives (Salo, 2017).

Generally speaking, mobile marketing eases the relations between company and consumers (Karjaluoto et al., 2015), and in any format or vehicle used for the socialization of content, the six phases in decision making and related to the evaluation of social media campaigns, should be taken into account: a) Establish assessment objectives, b) Identify the KPI's, c) Identify metrics for KPIs; d) Collect data; e) Generate reports; and f) Manage the decision making process (Brendan Keegan, & Rowley, 2017).

The relevance of data management should be noted in this section since this variable will be included as a high importance element for the development of actions focused on the consumer. In the same way, it is necessary to emphasize the participation of the stakeholders in the strategic process of the organization (Kull, Mena, & Korschun, 2016), since they will be involved with matters of brand awareness (Karjaluoto et al., 2015) generating eWom, and giving constant support to the popularity of the brand.

eWom: Comments and Reviews

The eWOM, or digital Word of mouth, has become the most influential communication channel today (Taken, 2012). It encompasses the knowledge of customers regarding the products, how to use them, their experience, recommendations and complaints (Kannan & Li, 2017), thus influencing the attitudes and behaviors in goods and services purchases by means of informal communication directed to consumers through Internet-based technologies (De Pelsmacker, van Tilburg, & Holthof, 2018), and so creating patterns of learning and knowledge based on the interaction between users who have experiences with them (Semerádová & Vávrová, 2016). eWOM is much more confident and richer in content than traditional Word of mouth due to its access to the digital world and easiness to be shared, (Kannan & Li, 2017).

It is proved that the request for information is strongly linked to the purchase frequency. However, we must consider the industry and the country home of the company (Müller, Pommeranz, Weisser, & Voigt, 2018). In this regard, comments and reviews are essential; there is also learning by companies about all the improvement opportunities that may arise, although, you should keep in mind the environment, where the reputation and positioning of the brand are at stake. Thus, the eWOM displays an increase in the monetary value of the brand due to viralization (Kannan & Li, 2017).

The eWOM also presents itself as a widely used way to generate digital engagement with consumers, creating online brand and advertising communities, this is done by the consumer himself (Eigenraam et al., 2018) while creating effects and attitudes in buying behaviors and therefore in commercial results (De Pelsmacker *et al.*, 2018).

Blockchain and Big Data

The blockchain is a distributed database with peer-to-peer technology, seeking a decentralization of systems and which can become the fifth revolutionary technology after mainframes, PCs, Internet, mobile and social communication media. (Parssinen, Kotila, Cuevas, Phansalkar, & Manner, 2018). It is used for business processes and serves as a "core infrastructure that runs the DNA connections (Data,

Network, AI)" (Kwak *et al.*, 2019, p. 121). As indicated by Kwak *et al.* (2019), it is the technology of the future business 4.0, seeking to provide security, reliability, flexibility, and transparency; even in high-risk environments, where IoT can be easily breached, blockchain becomes a highly credible, efficient and reliable tool.

Moreover, the use of BIG DATA becomes an essential tool not only for obtaining information from relevant customers or provide them with facilities but also as a way of analyzing processes to reduce weaknesses or risks that might affect them (Prokopowicz & Wielkopolski, 2017). Thus, companies and their digitalization processes underway, are adapting to the requirements from users, but they should also ensure data protection (Prokopowicz, Gwozdziewicz, Grzegorek, & Matosek, 2018), this is where technologies based on blockchain are shown as state-of-the-art options which fully meet such task.

ARE ALL TECHNOLOGIES APPLIED IN THE FIELD OF MARKETING?

One of the features that excel in technology, is its giant leaps while advancing, both in companies and households; however, while households (and people) are not aware of the scope of these tools, in terms of the information they receive through interaction and learning, companies keep on seeing them as tools of a technological nature where there is no closer look at the individual as consumer.

In the best case, the thought about benefits or improvements in experience among businesses lacks a clear definition of how the consumer behaves when presented with these facilities. Dynamic technological fluctuations in the market give the digital transformation of some organizations, but without conscience or systematic understanding focused on the person as a consumer-user of what is being offered. The following steps should be taken for this digital transformation to be executed systematically, a) A clearly defined marketing strategy; b) Identify the best practices of the current digital capabilities; c) Define flows and processes; d) Define the requirements for implementation; e) Review the hindrances in change generation; f) Manage the changes for a digital transformation while taking advantage of digital agility and efficiency in the performance of the integrated system channels (Gutiérrez & Nava, 2016).

As long as there are acceptability and acceptance in the process of adoption of new technologies (Barera, Sylvain, & Sutter, 2019), their proper use will adjust them to the marketing processes; similarly, if the consumer is not the focus, companies will not have a clear perception of your brand or the perspective of those who use it. While certification and authentication of brands are important to determine their value (Starr & Brodie, 2016), we should pay attention to brand value and consumer value (Tasci, 2016), where it is important to create functionality, psychological meaning and cultural relevance (Schmitt, 2012). Technological tools are shown as the best way to promote the brand through the facilities they provide, and thus achieve positive noise through the eWOM; safety levels must be observed when used, to protect the information that the user, consciously or unconsciously, provides, especially in environments with system vulnerabilities.

SOLUTIONS AND RECOMMENDATIONS

It is well known that the development of technologies has generated a high impact on marketing, inducing changes in the ways of research, analysis, and delivery of value to the customer. There are new ways to stimulate and interact with consumers in the development of marketing as a science, and where the use of technology has become a major component which generates a closeness with brands and may even improve the contact and communication with the customer (Anato, 2006).

Given that there is an increase in power by the customer, and due to the openness in information and the wide range of products to choose from, organizations seek to become more competitive to ensure sustainability in the long term; for this reason, they adopt information and communication technologies which contribute to the generation of value (Prada, 2016), which from a digital perspective, make an impact on the brand.

It is necessary that we know how the technology users behave in their role as consumers, identifying their expectations, experiences, and requirements in this interactive process; thus, the perception of the brand in such process and how it gains value can be determined.

Behavior Phases and OSX Model

eBehavior translates into electronic behavior, and it is based on how the consumer has migrated from his traditional behavior toward digital interaction. Thus, the tools above operate in three phases of e-Behavior, wherein each one shows the consumer behavior from a more realistic perspective, focused on creating brand value:

Phase One: Command behavior or behavior to give commands. Establishes a behavior focused on people generating commands (spoken or written) to receive a service. Brand value increases when there are utilitarian benefits or, when they perform as expected (Mohan, Jiménez, Brown, & Cantrell, 2017).

Phase Two: Interaction behavior. Defines a behavior where there is the interaction between the user, devices, and interfaces, thus generating a sensory experience. Brand value increases not only by function but also through the experience created using the technologies (Risitano, Romano, Sorrentino, & Quintano, 2016).

Phase Three: Socialization behavior or behavior of social exchange. Explains the social behaviors that generate brand value according to comments, reviews or recommendations. This behavior connects humans who express their self (Solomon, 2013) through brands (Schmitt, 2013), they may be charged with high doses of emotion (Stephen, 2016).

In sequential order, the phases of eBehavior translate into an experiential system in which the individual shows mastery over technology, and social influence to achieve a functional and self-expression result. Each interaction involves a learning process whose data is stored to transform it into information owned by the user, and which will be used again to improve his experience. This BIG DATA is relevant to acknowledge insights and behaviors, in such a way that market research is now migrated to modern digital systems, where it is not intrusive and flows like a normal behavioral process of the individual. This information system is known as OXS, and it is the fundamental basis for eBehavior, being predictive and anticipating through algorithmic models and logical sequences according to the user´s behavior.

Digital Tools Applied to the OXS Model

The eBehaviors based on the OXS model must be understood using contact points with the consumer, to detect how interaction and experience are created. These contact points determine the tools that should be considered as part of the marketing process, which seeks to understand people and generate benefits

Figure 2. The OXS eBehavior model for data collection
Source: Author

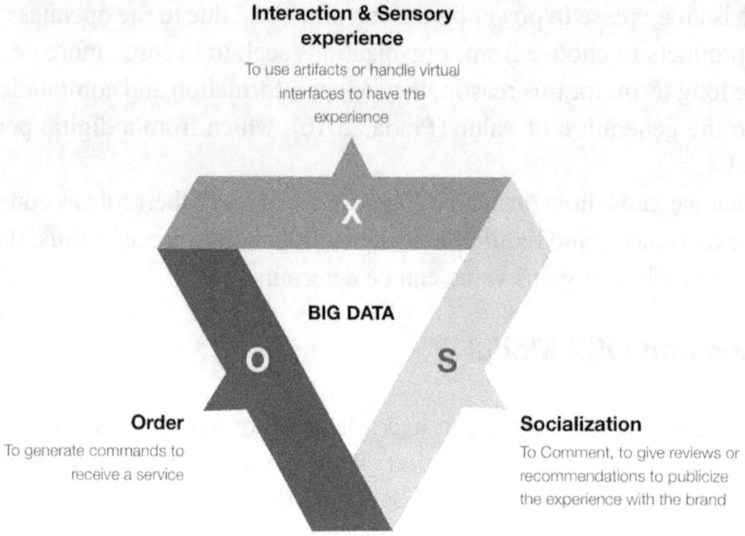

that are then communicated to other individuals. Thus, these digital marketing tools (DMT) line up with each phase of the OXS system, creating the first group of tools based on commands, a second group based on interaction and sensory experience; and finally, the third group of tools of a social nature.

- **DMT for Commands**: The first group has two technological tools. On the one hand, bots become a technological tool able to sort information and exchange content; the most important are those responsible for understanding algorithms to generate a better response to a command. On the other hand, the AI is shown as a predictive service adjusted to the requirements of the individual, either by voice or text command, to execute a particular command; being predictive, AI can have high value as it can decrease the efforts of people to generate some search. AI becomes a facilitator and personal assistant who knows the individual steps before they are taken.
- **DMT for Interaction and Experience**: With these tools, people may have a closer experience with artifacts (IoT) to create a more comfortable physical world. This comfort is also reflected on their experience in using these devices or virtual interfaces, converting the user experience (UX) into a basic tool. Moreover, virtual reality (VR) and augmented reality (AR) are elements which while do not modify the physical world of the individual, they establish a modified reality for the senses. With these tools, a more powerful sensory scar is built, and mental associations are tied to the user experience.
- **DMT for Socialization**: Socialization tools complete people´s understanding by generating content from their questions, comments, reviews and shared experiences with the brand. Here comes social media playing a viralization role in the content, before and after the experience, a subject previously reviewed in literature as was eWOM, which creates greater brand value through its notoriety, besides being the best resource optimization method, since the media do not propagate it but expands through the network when it is attractive to people. Beyond that, eWOM significantly helps to create new ideas about brand experiences so that negative prejudices disappear.

Backup and Data Usage

As explained in the literature review, technology behaviors allow us to detect the use, interaction and socialization moments of an individual according to the information generated as a result of these actions. This information obtained from BIG DATA must be protected and backed up to provide reassurance to the user and ensure the confidentiality of the information, which justifies the use of blockchain technology as a safety mechanism for the client; this technology works as a secure data repository and projects confidence to the user, who as a customer, looks for safety and confidence in every experience with the brand, while his information continues to go into storage.

Thus, a value chain model based on a technology to strengthen the relationship with the brand and establish a loyalty behavior is proposed. Interactions at each stage of eBehavior are reflected in the use of different types of technology and generates two data types: one to feed the database for each individual according to his experiences (Experience big data or XBD) and one generated in accordance to comments, reviews and criticisms on the web or social networking sites (Social big data or SBD). In both cases, the information that goes beyond the behavior of people and reaches consumer insights (Stone & Woodcock, 2014) is collected

The Digital Brand and the Road to Its "Humanization"

Long ago, Norman (2004) expressed his approach when talking about users rather than customers. This approach has led companies to generate a human-centered view rather than a transactional view. While the basis of the marketing, in its early days as a discipline, arose as the search for the satisfaction of needs, it has gradually evolved to end up generating value through interaction with consumers, through more friendly experiences which anticipate their requirements. In this way, humanization is sought through technology, which is a deal of understanding, interaction and socialization. Booking, Netflix,

Figure 3. Value chain for the brand using DMT
Source: Author

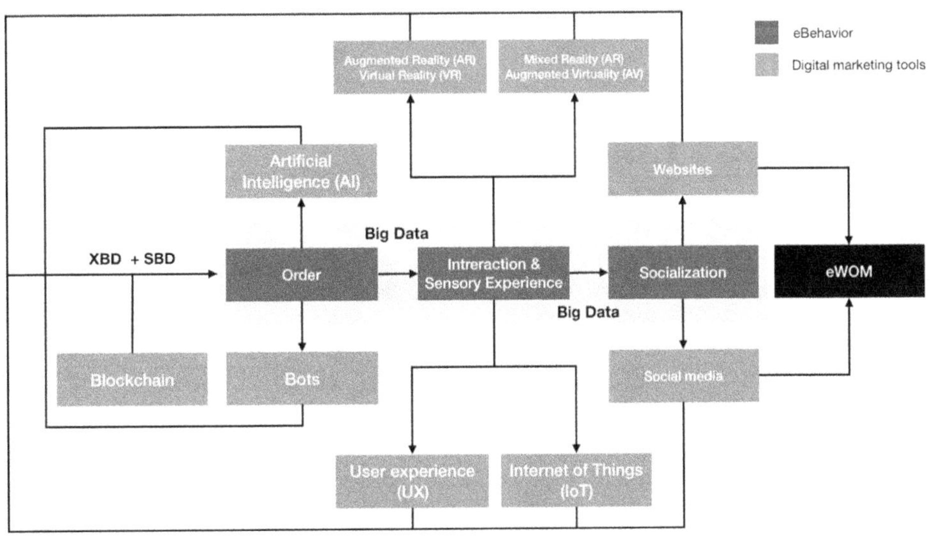

Spotify and other similar business models are examples where the digital brand has been built based on understanding and purveyance to the user, with associations given by the three phases of eBehavior.

Thus, building a digital brand is based on the dutiful brand, interactive brand, and friendly brand. However, there is a fourth kind based on safety and proactivity for the user and is to be called emphatic brand; this type of brand is closest to the user, created by him through loyalty and constant relationship. Digital brands become more human when they use MDT while having the participation of both companies and stakeholders in the construction process, through artifacts ranging from mobile devices to desktop computers. In other words, the emphatic brand is a product of user loyalty reflecting his personality with great accuracy.

FUTURE RESEARCH DIRECTIONS

The presented models aim to establish a guide for new and deeper studies on consumer behavior within technological environments. The constant technological evolution drives new researches, which should include the newest technology to recognize the workings of their interaction with people, as well as understand how to generate a better experience for the user. You cannot isolate the technological dynamics of companies and their efforts to be closer to the customer. Therefore it is also recommended that further studies establish how every business effort can generate an impact on the value of the brand, and affectivity degrees on the proposed digital brands.

Finally, it is recommended to apply the models proposed in the independent study for different DMTs, for example, understanding how each DMT generates contributions to a company or a brand; in this way, we can understand what are the DMTs which provide better results for a certain business, and how brands are perceived internally.

Figure 4. Digital brand construction
Source: Author

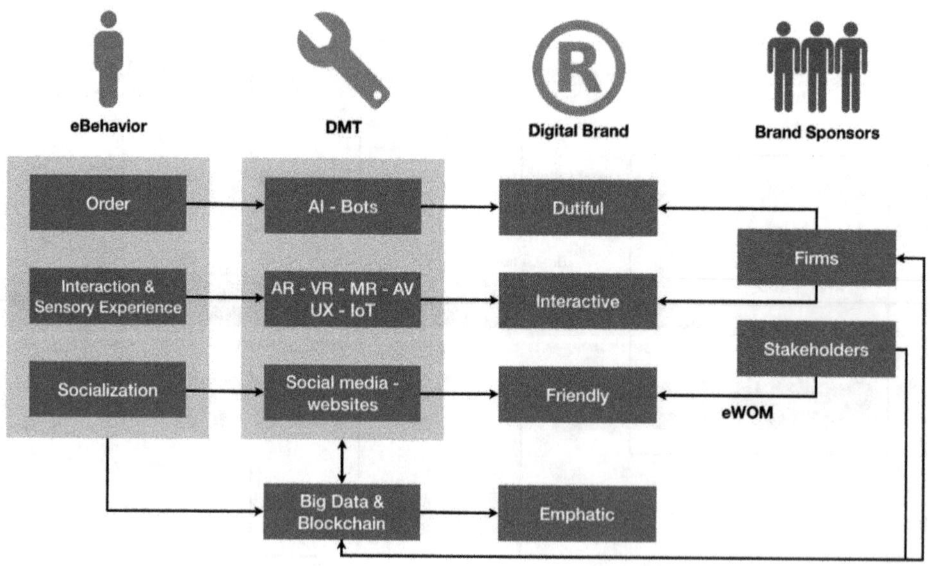

CONCLUSION

After some literature review, it is clear how customers show interaction behaviors with technology; as a starting point, we propose a classification of these behaviors through the eBehavior model known as OXS. With this model, the use of technological tools of marketing (DMT) that serve to achieve closeness and connection, arises in three phases: the first in which commands are given to achieve a result; the second in which there is interaction, and sensory experiences are created; and the third in which it is shared, and comments, opinions or reviews are expressed. These stages are based on the OXS model using different DMTs, thus generating the digital brand classified into four types: dutiful brand, interactive brand, friendly brand and emphatic brand, this last one created by value generation through the loyalty behaviors of the individual, who, by constant use of devices, generates relevant information for the companies, which in turn builds a brand closer to the consumer expectations.

The models presented in this theoretical study allow us a better view of the use of technologies in two particular situations: 1) The creation of better physical and virtual experiences to ease people´s lives and establish better ties with the benefits provided, so that there are a greater commitment and brand awareness; 2) Data collection and the guarantee of their safety, with the purpose of a better understanding of the user and the anticipation of his needs and desires, thus leading to brand loyalty.

Through the use of the technologies analyzed above, the interaction with customers grows every day while providing services and benefits by means of interconnected devices which show benefits in a physical environment (IoT); but we can also work with the virtual services which toy with the imagination or a possible world (AR, MR, VR), or real-time interaction with other users (Social media).

REFERENCES

Anato, M. (2006). El uso de los instrumentos clásicos del marketing y la tecnología digital en turismo. *Estudios y Perspectivas en Turismo*, *15*, 19–44.

Anttonen, J., & Jumisko-Pyykkö, S. (2008). Understanding the meaning of experiences with technology. *Workshop on Research Goals and Strategies for Studying User Experience and Emotion during NordiCHI08 Conference*, 1-4.

Barbery, D., Pástor, B., Idrobo, D., & Sempértegui, L. C. (2018). Análisis comparativo generacional del comportamiento de compra online. *Revista Espacios*, *39*(34), 16–29.

Barera, N., Sylvain, L., & Sutter, S. (2019). *Proceedings of the 20th Congress of the International Ergonomics Association (IEA 2018)*, *827*, 533-538. 10.1007/978-3-319-96098-2

Berman, B. (2016). Planning and implementing effective mobile marketing programs. *Business Horizons*, *59*(4), 431–439. doi:10.1016/j.bushor.2016.03.006

Boyes, H., Hallaq, B., Cunningham, J., & Watson, T. (2018). The industrial internet of things (IIoT): An analysis framework. *Computers in Industry*, *101*, 1–12. doi:10.1016/j.compind.2018.04.015

Brendan, K. J., & Rowley, J. (2017). Evaluation and Decision Making in Social Media Marketing. *Management Decision*, *55*(1), 1–28. doi:10.1108/IJBM-07-2013-0069

Dacko, S. G. (2017). Enabling smart retail settings via mobile augmented reality shopping apps. *Technological Forecasting and Social Change*, *124*, 243–256. doi:10.1016/j.techfore.2016.09.032

De Pelsmacker, P., van Tilburg, S., & Holthof, C. (2018). Digital marketing strategies, online reviews, and hotel performance. *International Journal of Hospitality Management*, *72*, 47–55. doi:10.1016/j.ijhm.2018.01.003

De Ruyter, K., Isobel Keeling, D., & Ngo, L. V. (2018). When nothing is what it seems: A digital marketing research agenda. *Australasian Marketing Journal*, *10*, 1–4. doi:10.1016/j.ausmj.2018.07.003

Eigenraam, A. W., Eelen, J., van Lin, A., & Verlegh, P. W. J. (2018). A Consumer-Based Taxonomy of Digital Customer Engagement Practices. *Journal of Interactive Marketing*, *44*, 102–121. doi:10.1016/j.intmar.2018.07.002

Falkenreck, C., & Wagner, R. (2017). The Internet of Things – Chance and challenge in industrial business relationships. *Industrial Marketing Management*, *66*, 181–195. doi:10.1016/j.indmarman.2017.08.007

Farshid, M., Paschen, J., Eriksson, T., & Kietzmann, J. (2018). Go boldly!: Explore augmented reality (AR), virtual reality (VR), and mixed reality (MR) for business. *Business Horizons*, *61*(5), 657–663. doi:10.1016/j.bushor.2018.05.009

Filippi, S., & Barattin, D. (2018).. . *Advances in Usability and User Experience*, *607*. doi:10.1007/978-3-319-60492-3

Flavián, C., Ibáñez-Sánchez, S., & Orús, C. (2018). The impact of virtual, augmented and mixed reality technologies on the customer experience. *Journal of Business Research*, *10*, 1–14. doi:10.1016/j.jbusres.2018.10.050

Galeano, A. R. (2008). Diseño centrado en el usuario. *Revista Educación Comunicación Tecnología*, *2*(4), 1–5.

Getto, G., & Moore, C. (2017). Mapping Personas: Designing UX Relationships for an Online Coastal Atlas. *Computers and Composition*, *43*, 15–34. doi:10.1016/j.compcom.2016.11.008

Gutierrez, C., & Nava Rogel, R. M. (2016). Mercadotecnia digital y las pequeñas y medianas empresas: revisión de la literatura. *Enlace, 13*, 45-61.

Jan, P., & Proceedings, E. (2011). General Characteristics of Anticipated User. *Diversity (Basel)*, 1–11.

Kannan, P. K., & Li, H. (2017). Digital marketing: A framework, review, and research agenda. *International Journal of Research in Marketing*, *34*(1), 22–45. doi:10.1016/j.ijresmar.2016.11.006

Karatum, S. (2017). The place of digital marketing on Turkish small businesses. *Journal of International Trade, Logistics, and Law*, *3*(2), 36–43.

Karjaluoto, H., Mustonen, N., & Ulkuniemi, P. (2015). The role of digital channels in industrial marketing communications. *Journal of Business and Industrial Marketing*, *30*(6), 703–710. doi:10.1108/JBIM-04-2013-0092

Killian, G., & McManus, K. (2015). A marketing communications approach for the digital era: Managerial guidelines for social media integration. *Business Horizons, 58*(5), 539–549. doi:10.1016/j.bushor.2015.05.006

Kriechbaumer, F., & Christodoulidou, N. (2014). SME website implementation factors in the hospitality industry: Groundwork for a digital marketing roadmap. *Worldwide Hospitality and Tourism Themes, 6*(4), 328–351. doi:10.1108/WHATT-01-2014-0006

Kull, A. J., Mena, J. A., & Korschun, D. (2016). A resource-based view of stakeholder marketing. *Journal of Business Research, 69*(12), 5553–5560. doi:10.1016/j.jbusres.2016.03.063

Kwak, K. H., Kong, J. T., Cho, S. I., Phuong, H. T., & Gim, G. Y. (2019). *Computational Science/Intelligence & Applied Informatics, 787*. Springer International Publishing. doi:10.1007/978-3-319-96806-3

Laroche, M., Habibi, M. R., & Richard, M. O. (2013). To be or not to be on social media: How brand loyalty is affected by social media? *International Journal of Information Management, 33*(1), 76–82. doi:10.1016/j.ijinfomgt.2012.07.003

Lo, F.-Y., & Campos, N. (2018). Blending Internet-of-Things (IoT) solutions into relationship marketing strategies. *Technological Forecasting and Social Change, 137*(9), 10–18. doi:10.1016/j.techfore.2018.09.029

Martínez-Navarro, J., Bigné, E., Guixeres, J., Alcañiz, M., & Torrecilla, C. (2018). (in press). The influence of virtual reality in e-commerce. *Journal of Business Research*. doi:10.1016/j.jbusres.2018.10.054

Mohan, M., Jiménez, F., Brown, B., & Cantrell, C. (2017). Brand skill: Linking brand functionality with consumer-based brand equity. *Journal of Product and Brand Management, 26*(5), 477–491. doi:10.1108/JPBM-06-2016-1247

Müller, J. M., Pommeranz, B., Weisser, J., & Voigt, K. I. (2018). Digital, Social Media, and Mobile Marketing in industrial buying: Still in need of customer segmentation? Empirical evidence from Poland and Germany. *Industrial Marketing Management, 73*(1), 70–83. doi:10.1016/j.indmarman.2018.01.033

Norman, D. A. (2004). *Emotional Design - Why we love (or hate) everyday things*. New York: B-Books.

Park, J., Han, S. H., Park, J., Park, J., Kwahk, J., Lee, M., & Jeong, D. Y. (2018). Development of a web-based user experience evaluation system for home appliances. *International Journal of Industrial Ergonomics, 67*(7), 216–228. doi:10.1016/j.ergon.2018.05.017

Parssinen, M., Kotila, M., Cuevas, R., Phansalkar, A., & Manner, J. (2018). Is Blockchain Ready to Revolutionize Online Advertising? *IEEE Access: Practical Innovations, Open Solutions, 6*, 1–1. doi:10.1109/ACCESS.2018.2872694

Prada, R. (2016). Las TIC, factor de efectividad en la aplicación del mercadeo digital en negocios de retail. *Revista Escuela de Administración de Negocios, 80*, 105-116.

Pradhan, P., Nigam, D., & Tiwari, C. K. (2018). Digital marketing and SMEs : An identification of the research gap via archives of past research. *Journal of Internet Banking and Commerce, 23*(1), 1–15.

Prokopowicz, D., Gwoździewicz, S., Grzegorek, J., & Matosek, M. (2018). Determinants of the Safety of the Electronic Daily Transfer in the Context of Global Trends on the Internet Development of the Mobile Banking. *International Journal of New Economics and Social Sciences, 7*(1), 188–201. doi:10.5604/01.3001.0012.2694

Prokopowicz, D., & Wielkopolski, G. (2017). The Big Data technologies as an important factor of electronic data processing and the development of computerized analytical platforms, Business Intelligence. *International Journal of Small and Medium Enterprises and Business Sustainability, 2*(4), 27–42.

Puto, A., & Kośćielniak, H. (2015). Analysis of Purchasing Behaviour of Polish e-customers. *Procedia Computer Science, 65*, 996–1005. doi:10.1016/j.procs.2015.09.060

Quiñones, D., Rusu, C., & Rusu, V. (2018). A methodology to develop usability/user experience heuristics. *Computer Standards & Interfaces, 59*, 109–129. doi:10.1016/j.csi.2018.03.002

Risitano, M., Romano, R., Sorrentino, A., & Quintano, M. (2017). The impact of consumer-brand engagement on brand experience and behavioural intentions: An Italian empirical study. *British Food Journal, 119*(8), 1884–1896. doi:10.1108/BFJ-11-2016-0579

Rojas, R. S., & Torres, C. L. (2017). La Gestión del Conocimiento basado en la Teoría de Nonaka y Takeuchi. *INNOVA Research Journal, 2*(4), 30–37.

Roto, V. (2007). User experience from a product creation perspective. In E. Law, A. Vermeeren, M. Hassenzahl, & M. Blythe (Eds.), Towards a UX Manifesto, COST294-MAUSE affiliated workshop. Lancaster, UK: Academic Press.

Salo, J. (2017). Social media research in the industrial marketing field: Review of literature and future research directions. *Industrial Marketing Management, 66*(7), 115–129. doi:10.1016/j.indmarman.2017.07.013

Schmitt, B. (2012). The consumer psychology of brands. *Journal of Consumer Psychology, 22*(1), 7–17. doi:10.1016/j.jcps.2011.09.005

Schmitt, B. (2013). The consumer psychology of customer-brand relationships: Extending the AA Relationship model. *Journal of Consumer Psychology, 23*(2), 249–252. doi:10.1016/j.jcps.2013.01.003

Scholz, J., & Duffy, K. (2018). We ARe at home: How augmented reality reshapes mobile marketing and consumer-brand relationships. *Journal of Retailing and Consumer Services, 44*(5), 11–23. doi:10.1016/j.jretconser.2018.05.004

Seitz, J., & Burosch, A. (2018). Digital Value Creation. In *2018 IEEE International Conference on Engineering, Technology, and Innovation (ICE/ITMC)* (pp. 1-5). IEEE. 10.1109/ICE.2018.8436380

Semerádová, T., & Vávrová, J. N. (2016). Using a systemic approach to assess Internet marketing communication within the hospitality industry. *Tourism Management Perspectives, 20*, 276–289. doi:10.1016/j.tmp.2016.09.007

Shankar, V., Kleijnen, M., Ramanathan, S., Rizley, R., Holland, S., & Morrissey, S. (2016). ScienceDirect Mobile Shopper Marketing : Key Issues, Current Insights, and Future Research Avenues. *Journal of Interactive Marketing*, *34*, 37–48. doi:10.1016/j.intmar.2016.03.002

Solomon, M. (2013). *Comportamiento del Consumidor*. Pearson.

Starr, R. G., & Brodie, R. J. (2016). Certification and authentication of brand value propositions. *Journal of Brand Management*, *23*(6), 716–731. doi:10.105741262-016-0012-6

Stephen, A. T. (2016). The role of digital and social media marketing in consumer behavior. *Current Opinion in Psychology*, *10*, 17–21. doi:10.1016/j.copsyc.2015.10.016

Stone, M. D., & Woodcock, N. D. (2014). Interactive, direct and digital marketing: A future that depends on better use of business intelligence. *Journal of Research in Interactive Marketing*, *8*(1), 4–17. doi:10.1108/JRIM-07-2013-0046

Taiminen, H. M., & Karjaluoto, H. (2015). The usage of digital marketing channels in SMEs. *Journal of Small Business and Enterprise Development*, *22*(4), 633–651. doi:10.1108/JSBED-05-2013-0073

Taken-Smith, K. (2012). Longitudinal study of digital marketing strategies targeting Millennials. *Journal of Consumer Marketing*, *29*(2), 86–92. doi:10.1108/07363761211206339

Tasci, A. D. A. (2016). Consumer Value and Brand Value: Rivals or Allies in Consumer-Based Brand Equity? *Tourism Analysis*, *21*(5), 481–496. doi:10.3727/108354216X14653218477561

Turner, P. (2017). Implementing Integrated Marketing Communications (IMC) through major event ambassadors. *European Journal of Marketing*, *51*(3), 605–626. doi:10.1108/EJM-09-2015-0631

Velitchka, M.H., & Rohm, A. (2016). *Article information: Hashtags and Handshakes*. Academic Press.

Wong, M.L., Khong, C.W., & Thwaites, H. (2012). Applied UX and UCD Design Process in Interface Design. *Procedia-Social and Behavioral Sciences, 51*(2000), 703-708. doi:10.1016/j.sbspro.2012.08.228

Yaqoob, I., Abaker, I., Hashem, T., & Ahmed, A. (2018). Internet of things forensics: Recent advances, taxonomy, requirements, and open challenges. *Future Generation Computer Systems*, *79*(1), 1003–1025.

ADDITIONAL READING

Cluley, R. (2018). The construction of marketing measures. *Marketing Theory*, *18*(3), 287–305. doi:10.1177/1470593117753981

Ditoiu, M.-C., & Platon, O.-E. (2012). Aspects Regarding the Romanian Social Network User's Profile and its Implications in Marketing Destination Pages. *Procedia Economics and Finance*, *3*(12), 182–187. doi:10.1016/S2212-5671(12)00137-2

García Mirón, S. (2011). La comunicación de experiencias de marca a través de las redes sociales: Análisis de caso de los patrocinadores del Mundial de Fútbol 2010. *Pensar la Publicidad*, *5*(2), 93–118. doi:10.5209/rev_PEPU.2011.v5.n2.37865

Hudson, S., Matson-Barkat, S., Pallamin, N., & Jegou, G. (2018). With or without you? Interaction and immersion in a virtual reality experience. *Journal of Business Research, 11*, 1–18.

Ivanov, A. E. (2012). The Internet's Impact on Integrated Marketing Communication. *Procedia Economics and Finance, 3*(12), 536–542. doi:10.1016/S2212-5671(12)00192-X

Romero-Calmache, M., & Fanjul-Peyró, C. (2010). La publicidad en la era digital: El microsite como factor estrat??gico de las campa??as publicitarias on-line. *Comunicar, 17*(34), 125–134. doi:10.3916/C34-2010-03-12

Shankar, V., Venkatesh, A., & Naik, P. (2010). Mobile Marketing in the Retailing Environment : Current Insights and Future Research Avenues. *INTMAR, 24*(2), 111–120. doi:10.1016/j.intmar.2010.02.006

Ueda, T., & Ban, H. (2018). Active Learning on Digital Marketing for Advertising A University Museum Exhibition. *Procedia Computer Science, 126*, 2097–2106. doi:10.1016/j.procs.2018.07.242

Varadarajan, R., & Yadav, M. S. (2009). Marketing Strategy in an Internet-Enabled Environment: A Retrospective on the First Ten Years of JIM and a Prospective on the Next Ten Years. *Journal of Interactive Marketing, 23*(1), 11–22. doi:10.1016/j.intmar.2008.10.002

Wafa, S. N., & Hashim, E. (2016). Adoption of Mobile Augmented Reality Advertisements by Brands in Malaysia. *Procedia: Social and Behavioral Sciences, 219*, 762–768. doi:10.1016/j.sbspro.2016.05.077

KEY TERMS AND DEFINITIONS

DMT: The acronym is referring to digital marketing tools. Under the context of the study, DMT relates to the use of specific technologies for marketing purposes (i.e., creating experiences, service and user support, and data collection for market research of behavioral type).

eBehavior: Term used to define the behaviors of purchase and use within digital environments.

eWOM: It refers to the digital word of mouth (i.e., comments or reviews included in social networking or web pages about a brand).

IoT: Acronym of the internet of things defined by devices or artifacts that can be used on the network.

OXS Model: A comprehensive model that is showing different types of eBehavior according to the objectives of the user: order, have the experience, and socialize.

UX (User Experience): It relates to the perception generated in the previous phase, during and after the use and interaction with a product.

Virtual: Term used to indicate the creation of possible elements or environments using a computer.

Chapter 20
Digital Marketing as a Communication Tool in Emerging Businesses

Carlos Luis Torres Briones
https://orcid.org/0000-0002-9891-3574
Universidad de Guayaquil, Ecuador

ABSTRACT

Emerging businesses face the daily challenge of competing in a world where major brands use their complete artillery to communicate and attract customers, and where small businesses are the most affected, so they should be more intelligent and daring to compete in the daily market. Here, the authors study the theory of digital marketing as a communication tool for emerging businesses and its benefits according to different authors. As a result, they propose the EComPymes model, where the appropriate basic tools for these type of companies are shown; thus, content generation through social media, mobile marketing, and email are the main options, not only for starting a business but competing with low budgets.

INTRODUCTION

According to GEM (Global Entrepreneurship Monitor) data for 2017, Ecuador has the highest rate of entrepreneurial activity (TEA) in Latin America (29.6%), being the highest in Latin America for the sixth consecutive year. Therefore, it is important to take into account this reality and the importance of good management and effective communication to benefit entrepreneurs.

In this context, the adequate design of marketing combinations involves the four Ps (Product, Price, Place, and Promotion). In the marketing communication's field, efforts should be coordinated towards the last P of the marketing combination: Promotion (Todorova, 2015). Among these promotional tools, we find advertising and direct marketing, where digital marketing shows significant importance. At this respect, Carniani (2006) mentions that the digital marketing communication is aimed towards achieving outlined objectives, which are active in the communication process, as each communication flow may request an information response from the market. This opportunity returns immediate feedback, so that digital communication can be easily measured at a low cost.

DOI: 10.4018/978-1-5225-8939-6.ch020

Many emerging business ventures are born with small capital, with the intention of becoming a big brand; therefore, seeking the best means that digital media must turned out to be as the most common and effective as possible. According to Cizmezi and Ercan (2015), the creation of brand awareness is the first and most important stage of marketing communication; thus digital marketing tools have become the most important asset for the interactivity between consumers and businesses.

Reviewing social networking makes us realize the huge amount of products or services offered by this mean, and here we notice that many small businesses or entrepreneurs are just beginning, especially in Latin America and the Caribbean. For Harris and Rae (2009), social networks play a key role in the future of marketing, as they are externally replacing the annoyance of the client with commitment, and internally they allow the transformation from the traditional approach of controlling to an open and collaborative approach. As a result, social networks are more conducive to success in the modern business environment.

Also, blogs are a fascinating interactive media for online communication, which has led many Internet users to post their opinions and share knowledge on various topics of interest (Pal & Kapur, 2010). At this respect, Insights (2018) presents an analysis of the digital state of Ecuador in a study carried out by 'We Are Social and Hootsuite' called "Digital in 2018", in which states that with a population of over 16 million, of whom 13.5 million are Internet users (80% of the population), 11 million (66%) are active users of Social Media.

The goal of this chapter is to study the importance of digital marketing as a communication tool for emerging businesses, and also the commitment of each business to use it properly. We will also try to identify the types of businesses that use this type of communication tool more often, and their results obtained, not only as a brand, but the effect on sales and business growth.

A major concern is to find the degree of knowledge for the correct use of digital marketing tools, is the proper use possible? When stakeholders meet business objectives, they contribute not only to research and academia, but also to the economic sector with query tools for entrepreneurs and business owners.

BACKGROUND

Emerging Businesses

Most countries in Latin America are considered emerging economies, and one can notice how people seek to face desperate situations arising from new businesses. Emerging economies are characterized by: first, they manage large fiscal deficits, usually financed from abroad. Second, financial systems tend to be repressed, which also affects the availability of credit for private sector companies. And third, they tend to have a crisis in their balance of payments, usually associated with the effects of political decisions affecting foreign trade (Guerrero, 2018).

Only the private sector can counterbalance these problems. Small and medium enterprises (SMEs) have an important role in the productive development of Latin America; however, due to their size, they have a small share of their country's GDP (gross domestic product). As a result, their production is mostly linked to domestic markets only. Therefore, a significant part of the population and the economy of the region depend on their activities. Moreover, the participation of PYMEs according to Ferraro Carlo (CEPAL, 2010), quoted by Pico and Coello (2017), "exports are quite small as a result of a scarce performance regarding competitiveness, which is also expressed in the notorious productivity gap concerning large companies." (p. 23).

Today´s SMEs are looking for ways to generate profits and grow fast, but above all, look for a strategic partner to save costs and allow them to continue growing. In Ecuador, "68% of Ecuadorian SMEs have computers, 82% Internet, and 99% access the Web through broadband" (El Universo Newspaper, 2018) But it is important to affirm that 40% of SMEs die within 5 years, 2/3 go to the second generation, and only 12% survive to the third generation (Crespo, 2013).

Thus, SMEs and startups should worry about competing in the market, often against the big budgets managed by large companies. That is why the optimization of resources linked to digital strategies is crucial for success reinforced with creativity, efficiency, and the good allocation of resources.

From Traditional Marketing to Digital Marketing

New technologies have introduced a new challenge for all sectors, especially for emerging businesses, forcing marketers to rethink the most appropriate ways to reach an ever younger audience, more accustomed to the use of digital devices and interaction with brands (González & Plaza, 2017). Marketing has evolved, from traditional or transactional marketing to the modern concepts of today's digital marketing.

Transactional Marketing

A course of transactional type characterizes the traditional marketing paradigm. The central thesis is that it circumscribes the marketing combination through a blend of four variables to convince the consumer to buy a certain product (Gummesson, 2002). The transactional approach to the traditional paradigm involves a market orientation in the short term, with appointed beginning and end, which are defined by the same exchange (Bagozzi, 1975), as opposed to a continuous process of customer relationship (Dwyer, Schurr, & Oh, 1987). For Kotler and Armstrong (2008), marketing is managing profitable customer relations which aim to create value for customers and capture their value to attract them. At this respect, Tuñez, Garcia, and Guevara (2011) define transactional marketing as focused on individual activities, highlighted on the features of the products, have a short-term plan only, give little emphasis on customer service and satisfaction, have a low level of commitment to the user, and dispose of a moderate contact level with consumers.

Marketing for Services

When talking about marketing for services, it is imperative to mention the quality of service and management thereof. Groonross (1994) mentions a general framework for quality management of services. There are three groups of actors: A, executives; B, employees, and C customers.

The policy to be pursued is established at the managerial level. The analysis of the market demands, requirements related to quality (1) and internal perceptions of the level of quality and performance of employees (2) is initiated. This knowledge is necessary to decide on the specifications of quality (3) and to carry out internal marketing of these specifications and the expected performance by employees. Furthermore, external marketing programs are planned at this level, and also the mechanisms for measuring quality in the future. Torres and Guzmán (2017) state that if an employer should keep staff who strives to serve well, with a smile, attentive to customers' needs, courteous, and above all, knows the product and is always ready to advise clients, fulfill promises and projects confidence, he or she would have 68% of the sales in the pocket.

Relationship Marketing

According to López (2009), in recent decades we have witnessed a dynamic change like relationships. Transactional marketing, where individual interests of the parties take precedence over joint profits, has given way to relationship marketing, which aims to maximize the value obtained by both parties from the relationship in which they are immersed. The establishment, development, and maintenance of long-term oriented relations represent a decisive step to achieve a competitive advantage. Loyal customers are one of the main sources of corporate profitability and become their most valuable asset. The evolution of the competitive scenario justifies that the nature of relations among distribution channel members is the subject of an ongoing process of change. Increased competition and changes in the behaviors of final consumers are factors which are changing the traditional situation of distribution channels.

For Tuñez, Garcia, and Guevara (2011), relationship marketing considers users as the most important asset of the organization, highlights the benefits of the product, has a long-term vision, gives emphasis on retaining and satisfying customers, disposes of a high level of engagement and contact with users, and affirms that the quality is inherent throughout the organization.

The predominance of activities of relational marketing, which highlight the relations with the different stakeholders (members of the cooperative, employees, customers, suppliers and leaders of local institutions), may surprise, given the low level of self-organization marketing processes and poor training of those responsible for the area. However, in our opinion, these facts alone brought a surprise to those who see cooperatives as if they were equal to any other company in the capitalist private sector. (De Sá, 2012).

Digital Marketing

Global communication experts place digital marketing as a discipline within marketing; this logic suggests that marketing adapts to contexts and industrial sector, and interact in the national and global market. The web is critical in developing a network of interconnected customers in real time, which enables an exchange of information and creates relationships between the customer and the company. (Molina, 2014).

For Moreno, Ruiz, and Peñaherrera (2017), many companies have assimilated the importance of social networks because it allows positioning through their consumers or users, and may economically represent knowledge and development of a brand or company. In Ecuador, some companies have clearly understood the role of digital media in their marketing strategy. Consequently, it is easy to see that social networks already occupy an important place in their communication plan, especially in marketing.

According to Fleming and Alberdiu (2000), digital marketing is based on the 4F (flow, functionality, feedback, and loyalty), which are the variables that make up an effective marketing strategy.

1. **Flow:** The user must feel attracted by the interactivity generated in the site to catch his attention and not to leave on the first page.
2. **Functionality:** Navigability has to be intuitive and user-friendly; In this way, we prevent the user to leave the page because he is lost.

3. **Feedback:** There must be an interaction with the Internet user to build a relationship with him. His perception and the consequent reputation achieved are keys to trust and bidirectionality.
4. **Loyalty:** Once there is a relationship with the Internet user, do not let him escape. A commitment must be developed, and we need to provide topics of interest for him.

Digital marketing is defined as a series of tasks aimed to meet the customer´s satisfaction, so that through these activities brand loyalty by consumers is generated, thus achieving benefits for the organization (Sainz, 2015). Digital marketing is also considered the refining of strategies which are known as traditional, to generate a positioning in the mind of the customer, and lead to the purchase of the product through Tic support, boosting sales for the company (Del Olmo & Fondevila, 2014).

Among the characteristics of digital marketing (Del Olmo & Fondevila, 2014) we find: (1) The communication is more interactive and personalized, developing closer links with each user (customer); (2) The information shared by digital media is more creative and dynamic for the client; (3) The scope of digital marketing allows encompassing a wide group of users from around the world; (4) Different types of digital advertisements are adaptable to various mobile devices; (5) Customers can get information more quickly, and companies can meet the concerns and disagreements of users immediately.

Online Business

Different types of online media controlled by a company, including websites, blogs, email lists, and social media presence. It is also known as "own media." (Chadwick & Chaffey, 2014, p. 10). Digital strategies and online marketing are having a major effect, allowing knowledge to spread almost instantly, and making it accessible to everyone, given the ease, speed, and economy with which information travels. But they do not generate the loyalty of its users, because when implementing tactics, the cultural characteristics to whom they are addressed are not very clear, especially when they are mass consumer' products. If a company fails to retain loyalty, it is more difficult to understand which reasons determine customer satisfaction.

A diversity of products is marketed through online marketing, using the Internet, and this generates the relations with existing customers; it facilitates to serve customers more effectively and to obtain a buying efficiency with better prices for new corporate customers. E-commerce leads to online exchanges where consumers can look for sellers, find out about their deals, initiate acquisitions, and sometimes even determine the conditions of the transaction.

Tuñez, Garcia, and Guevara (2011) demonstrate how the establishment of consolidated relationships among users participating in virtual social contexts, and practices associated with viral marketing, can disrupt the traditional process of information production. At this respect, the media agenda had been built with the participation of the media and their sources, but currently, the active participation of many of these users on the network builds an impact on the content creation they produce and disseminate through viral techniques. In most cases, these contents are not journalistic information, but when they reach a certain repercussion, they end up becoming news and surely access the agendas of traditional and digital media, being the users who promote the content selected by the media to create agendas delivered to citizens.

Figure 1. What should be done for an online marketing strategy?
Source: Elaborated from Quevedo (2017).

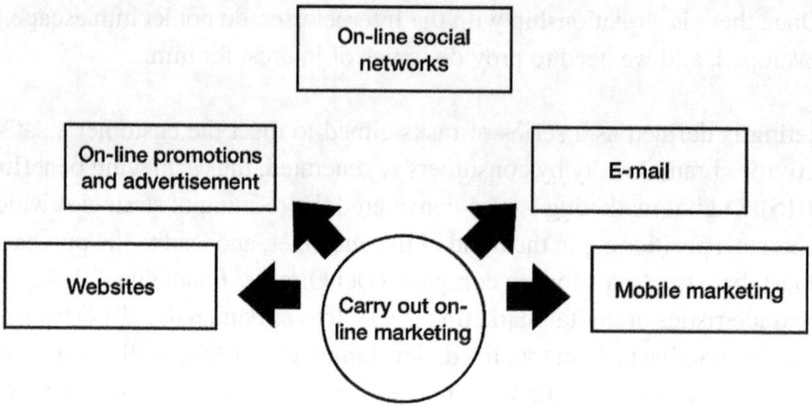

Digital Marketing Strategy

Today´s organizations have tremendous opportunities in digital media, from TIC-based companies to traditional businesses. This opportunity lies in the strengthening of the brands. Using a digital strategy allows the transformation of data into market intelligence, both in customers and competition, and it is clear that information is needed to compete in the market (Andrade, 2016). Digital strategies allow the company to improve the relationship with customers and find ways to interact with the brand.

Today´s customer is more trained and informed on the use of digital media, and the TIC market grows steadily. Just having a digital product is not enough, you also need to know how to aim it for it to be bought. Marketing is nowadays one of the company functions which is more dependent on technology. In 2012, Gartner research firm predicted that by 2017 marketing managers would spend more on digital technologies than tech managers. This forecast is more plausible as time passes, as a matter of fact in some companies it could be real before the prediction (Day, 2017).

Approaches thorough market analysis and interaction with customers, which were state of the art for the last few years, become obsolete at full speed, and it seems that every week there are new methods. The general nature of these new approaches is widely known, less known is the way in which they are changing the practice of marketing.

New marketing departments are turning to customer analysis (also called big data), predictive analysis and measurements of customer experiences, to create integrated engaging experiences, personalized and consistent at all points of contact between company and customers.

There are many ways to connect with these (video, SMS, social networks, websites, mobile devices, and other more traditional like direct advertising and sponsorship through media like television). Many delegate advisors say that investment in digital marketing is the strongest bet a company can make, as this rewires relations with customers, but also allows competition to gain an advantage if the company responds too slowly.

Barbery et al. (2018) explain the different digital tools marketing can use to generate stimuli depending on the target market, classifying them as follows: (1) *Baby Boomers*: email, website, e-branding, and e-marketing; (2) *Generation X*: email, social networks, search engines, website, search engine marketing, e-branding, web 2.0, and e-communication; (3) *Millennials*: Social media, online advertising, search engines, websites, search engine marketing, e.branding, corporate blogs, web 2.0, e.communication, and e-advertisement.

Franco et al. (2018) agree with those above, claiming that management of social networks and use of digital platforms such as Netflix are the preferred media for men between 25 and 55 years old.

According to Moschini (2012), a digital marketing strategy in social networks should be planned so that steps can be defined, results evaluated and performance optimized, for which one should follow the next protocol:

1. Define objectives: measurable goals should be propounded, which subsequently allow an accurate assessment of results.
2. Outline a strategy on content: commercial novelties, promotions, and contests should be scheduled, generate content with added value, all this must be properly planned over time.
3. Select criteria and measurement tools: define tracking parameters based on the proposed objectives, with tools like Google Analytics, Crowdbooster, and Klout.
4. Establish evaluation and optimization points: one of the main advantages of conducting Internet marketing is that we can get full transparency regarding the performance of our actions. It is possible to accurately assess what type of actions or content attract more of the selected audience, what are the right times for each task, and what channels generate better results.

Social Networks

For Garcia (2011), advertising agencies are being affected in their daily planning and the creation of campaigns, due to major changes brought by TIC implementation, thus modifying the strategies and objectives, and even the work routine of the advertisers. Social networks offer the most possibilities, not only to any user but to the media and, of course, to any advertiser, to achieve greater proximity to consumers, and obtain more accurate information regarding their attitudes, likes, and interests. Thus, we can see how advertisers use these social networks in the pursuit of greater complicity and loyalty from specific segments of their target.

Social networks continue to grow and, according to some accounts, they have become the main channel for customers to experience and interact with the world. People join general or more specialized networks and search, share, participate, consume and play to get support for achieving their goals, (Bolton et al., 2013).

Kaplan and Haenlein (2010) classify social networks according to their level of wealth (from static blogs to virtual social worlds or games like Second Life) and self-disclosure (from collaborative projects of anonymous content). Wikipedia for personal presentations on social networking sites like Facebook. The authors emphasize that companies must carefully choose their social networking platforms, develop their applications where necessary, involve employees and integrate or align their online activity.

Mobile Marketing

The intersection of mobile marketing and shopper marketing, known as mobile buyer marketing, is a rapidly evolving area. We formally define the mobile buyer marketing as the planning and execution of all marketing activities based on a mobile influence over a buyer, throughout and beyond the purchasing process: from the activator for an initial purchase through all the stages of purchase, consumption, repurchase, and recommendation. (Shankar, Kleijnen, Ramanathan, Rizley, Holland & Morrissey, 2016).

E-Commerce

In an e-commerce site, e-marketing should help consumers in their purchase; this requires a precise knowledge of customer preferences. For this reason, the owners of virtual stores should find out who, what, how and when to engage the customer, ergo, to know the "consumer´s decision process. And strengthen his commitment." (Gerrikagoitia et al., 2015). E-commerce as the development of cheap activities through telecommunications networks (Del Agila, 2000).

According to Santamaría and Escobar (2011), e-commerce can be considered a special case of a more general strategy such as the web, through which the company can establish multiple relationships, at the workplace any commercial activity generated by a web strategy is considered e-commerce, although the commercial transaction takes place outside the network.

Kenneth and Jane (2002) stated that "electronic commerce is the process of buying and selling goods and services electronically, through transactions via the Internet, networks and other digital technologies." (p. 25). For McLeod (2000) e-Commerce is the use of computers to facilitate all operations of the company. Many operations are internal: performed within the company, in the functional areas of financial, human resources, information services, manufacturing, and marketing. Other operations involve the company interfaces with the eight elements of the environment.

Focusing on marketing, Martín-Moreno and Sáez (2004) mention that e-commerce is not just a tool for business, but also comprises all steps of the transaction, such as supporting the marketing of the company in each of the following aspects: (a) electronic buying and selling of goods; (b) business information search; (c) negotiations between buyers and sellers; (d) online advertising; (e) management of collection and payments through the network, and (f) customer services.

This fact indicates the importance of electronic commerce within the business strategy, for which (Murillo, 2009) also mentions some of its main advantages:

- The distribution of the product or service can be improved, since through the Web, companies, and customers can directly interact, therefore eliminating the intermediaries and making immediate deliveries. Regarding time, this fact represents a big saving.
- Cost reduction in the transactions; ordering, quoting and others forms are eliminated, and this affects many procedures, which in some cases disappear. In this context, the costs of buy/sell transactions are considerably lower, not having to process all the information on the forms, and also avoiding order duplication.
- Easy access to information, since you can access databases which allow you to find deals, place bids, create markets, enter new markets, and gain some advantages in sales, etc.
- Improvement of relations between the company and customers, since you can engage in communications that can increase awareness of the product or service, meet consumer preferences, reach agreements for the benefit of both parties, and others.
- Better business communication; the company keeps its customers constantly updated about their products or services, and gives them the possibility of accessing business information 24 hours a day, no matter where they are.

INTERACTION OF STUDY VARIABLES

Issues and Controversies

The need for organizational development has led companies to rethink their business and find ways to redesign many aspects to face competition and remain in the market. The rapid growth of organizations is accompanied by the expansion of their functional structure, coupled with increased volume in their activities. Insofar as situations change, companies are transformed to assimilate new challenges promptly. Digital marketing is today, an important alternative for the development of sales. (Prada, 2016).

In an article of the journal Chasqui (Costales, 2013) stated: "In Ecuador, the first attempt at digital media or online media was a newsletter in Hoy newspaper which appeared in 1995. At that time, it was the only link for hundreds of Ecuadorians abroad. Likewise, the page for digital and advertising studies (iab Ecuador, 2017) stated: "The digital consumption in Ecuador for 2017 shows substantial changes, both regarding the increment in digital media consumption and social networks, and the behavior of Ecuadorians of different ages while consuming these media."

Digital popularization impacted on the way companies find, compete for and captivate customers, with a lower need for investment and greater openness to alternative and proximal ways of communication. These are several ways to increase approach and organizational memory, as well as to provide more awareness regarding the user and the strategic exploitation of information for the best results (Melo & Romero, 2016).

Due to the novelty of the phenomenon and its popularity, many companies have begun to use digital marketing as a tool to generate an interaction with brands within a market, some even without any strategy.

It is still unclear whether digital marketing can help businesses to get better results, some studies, carried out in Spanish companies which use digital social networks as a marketing tool, confirmed the findings of other studies about the direct and positive relation between market orientation and business performance, as well as the market and entrepreneurial orientations. Likewise, the results are consistent with previous studies which found no empirical evidence to support the direct effect of entrepreneurial orientation over performance.

Second, results show that companies should use digital social networks as a marketing tool in an intensive way, to strengthen the relationship between market orientation and business results. Only if companies are actively involved with these new technology platforms, and they develop a marketing strategy in digital social networks and have a community manager or specialized digital marketing agency, they could take advantage of the potential.

Uribe, Scepter, and Llonch (2013) concur with the aforementioned, and they state that the impact of online social networks as a marketing tool in the performance of companies is still unclear. However, the results show that a strong and decisive social media marketing strategy can enhance customer relationships and improve performance.

Another author stresses that digital marketing has similarities with the term electronic marketing, as both describe the operation and execution of marketing using electronic media such as web, email, interactive television, IPTV, and wireless media along with digital information regarding the characteristics and behavior of customers (Chadwick & Chaffey, 2014, p.10).

Figure 2. The intersection of the three main types of online media
Source: Adapted from Chadwick and Chaffey (2014, p.11).

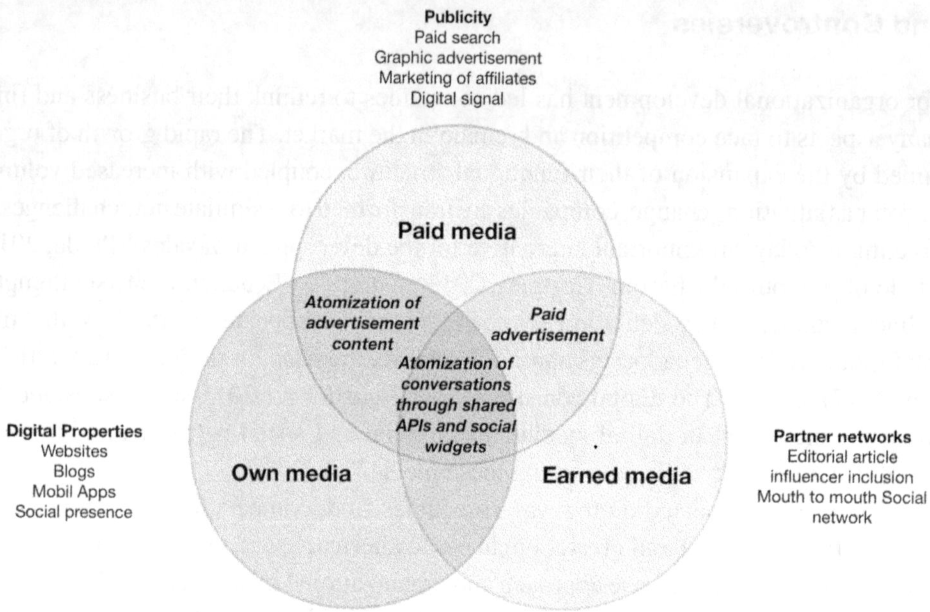

As can be seen, you can choose three types of media in digital marketing: (1) Advertising, all the digital media paid by the company in order to spread its message; (2) Partner networks, establish connections that can generate mouth to mouth, or dissemination through social networks or influencers; (3) Digital properties, which emphasize websites, blogs and mobile applications. Consequently, "marketing has been integrated into the businesses strategy to become an indissoluble part of their DNA, as organizations competing in the market to provide with value to their customers" (Andrade, 2016, p. 62).

SOLUTIONS AND RECOMMENDATIONS

Consumers are increasingly using social networks for many consumer-related issues, such as complaining about a brand or share shopping experiences. The growth of digital media represents an opportunity for businesses based on the exchange of information but also complicates the work of marketing managers who need to be ready to deal with current issues in the field (Hofacker & Belanche, 2016).

With the prospect of e-commerce and its benefits through technology, and as an implementation factor for electronic commerce in the PYMEs, the EComPymes model has been generated, as shown in Figure 3.

The EComPymes model proposes that any company which decides to venture into e-commerce should take into account the generation of safe, reliable and trustworthy contents to satisfy customers or target market. These contents must be adapted in at least three basic e-commerce tools for emerging businesses: social networks, mobile marketing, and email. The model proposes these three tools to lower costs, and probably no cost appears in the early stages, and basically obtain support from the ICTs (Information and Communication Technologies).

Figure 3. Model EComPymes
Source: Author

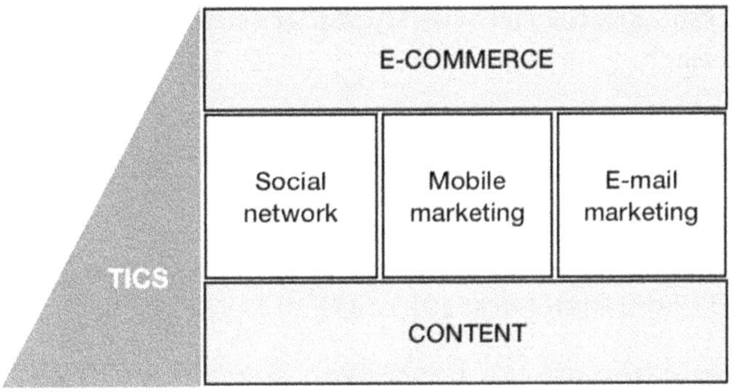

Regarding social networks; the most important are Facebook, Twitter, Instagram, LinkedIn, and YouTube. The use of each depends on the target market or the type of clients for each brand or company. Besides, mobile marketing is a rapid development area which relies primarily on the use of electronic media through a cellphone, such as instant messaging platforms and mobile applications. Finally, e-mail is probably one of the most widely used digital media, which allows direct engagement with the customer and the construction of a relationship through the information. Having the appropriate strategy must be taken into account, as the consumer inboxes are usually filled with information.

FUTURE DIRECTIONS RESEARCH

The digital marketing field is constantly changing; it is enough to see the evolution that marketing has had throughout history. Consumer behavior also changes as we evolve; therefore, business strategies must line up with these changes to offer their products or services. Among new and future research we find constant research over consumer trends about the consumption of digital media, so strategies must adapt to these changes.

Another area which generates research opportunities is the field of mobile applications or the Internet communications media, as media seems to migrate to digital platforms with dynamic and updated information which give a twist to communications.

CONCLUSION

Emerging businesses are always in a constant dilemma, grow and innovate lacking the resources of large companies; therefore, they have found an option to communicate and be known within the market, and also have better conditions to compete in the digital marketing. Literature research has helped us understand the reality of business and the significant addition of each digital media, which allowed the development of the EComPymes model to provide with the appropriate digital marketing tools, as a contribution for this field of study.

ACKNOWLEDGMENT

The author is grateful to Prof. José Manuel Saiz-Álvarez for his management and invitation to participate in this Handbook of Research.

REFERENCES

Andrade, D. (2016). Estrategias de marketing digital en la promoción de Marca Ciudad. *Revista EAN*, *51*(51), 59–72. doi:10.21158/01208160.n80.2016.1457

Bagozzi, R. (1975). Marketing as Exchange. *Journal of Marketing*, *39*(4), 32–39. doi:10.1177/002224297503900405

Bolton, R., Parasuraman, A., Hoefnagels, A., Migchels, N., Kabadayi, S., & Gruber, T. (2013). Entendiendo la generación Y y su uso de las redes sociales: Una agenda de revisión e investigación. *Journal of Service Management*, *24*(3), 245–267. doi:10.1108/09564231311326987

Chadwick, F., & Chaffey, D. (2014). *Marketing Digital, estrategia, implementación y práctica*. D.F., Mexico: Pearson.

Costales, J. R. (2013). Medios digitales en Ecuador, cuántos son y qué hacen. *Chasqui. Revista Latinoamericana de Comunicación*, *122*, 111–117.

Crespo, A. (2013). *El uso de las TICS como herramientas para la internacionalización de las PYMES, caso de estudio Empresa Rafael Paredes. Azuay*. Universidad del Azuay.

Day, G. S. (2017). *Reinventar el marketing en la era digital, OpenMind*. Madrid, Spain: BBVA Group.

De Sá, J. (2012). Las prácticas de gestión de marketing en las cooperativas portuguesas. *CIRIEC-España. C.I.R.I.E.C. España*, *76*, 199–227.

Del Águila, A. (2000). *Comercio electrónico y estrategia empresarial*. Madrid, Spain: RA-MA.

Del Olmo, J., & Fondevila, J. (2014). *Marketing digital en la moda*. Madrid, Spain: Ediciones Universidad de Navarra.

Diario El Universo. (2018). *Estrategias para que la pequeña y mediana empresa mantengan su posición*. Author.

Dwyer, F., Schurr, P., & Oh, S. (1987). Developing buyer-seller relationships. *Journal of Marketing*, *51*(2), 11–27. doi:10.1177/002224298705100202

Fleming, P., & Alberdiu, M. J. (2000). *Hablemos de marketing*. Madrid, Spain: ESIC Editorial.

Gerrikogoitia, J., Castander, I., Rebón, F., & Alzua-Sorzabal, A. (2015). New trends in smart electronic marketing based on web mining for electronic stores. *Procedia Ciencias Sociales y del Comportamiento.*, *175*, 75–83.

González, Z., & Plaza, N. (2017). Estrategias de marketing digital en el sector de la mode de lujo. Interacción y redes sociales como herramienta necesaria. *Revista Académica sobre Documentación Digital y Comunicación Interactiva, 15*, 17–27.

Grönross, C. (1994). *Marketing y gestión de servicios*. Madrid, Spain: Díaz de Santos S.A.

Guerrero, M. (2018). La importancia de las empresas de servicios en el desarrollo de los países de economías emergentes. *INNOVA*, *3*, 1–5.

Gummesson, E. (2002). *Total Relationship Marketing* (2nd ed.). Oxford, UK: Butterworth-Heinemann.

Hofacker, C., & Belanche, D. (2016). Eight challenges in social networks for marketing managers. *Revista Española de Marketing*, *20*(2), 73–80.

iab Ecuador. (2017). *Consumo Digital Ecuador 2017*. Quito.

Insights. (2018, Feb 8). Retrieved from https://insights.la/2018/02/08/luce-panorama-digital-ecuador/

Kaplan, A., & Haenlein, M. (2010). ¡Usuarios del mundo, únanse! Los retos y oportunidades de las redes sociales. *Business Horizons*, *53*(1), 59–68. doi:10.1016/j.bushor.2009.09.003

Kenneth, L., & Jane, L. (2002). *Sistemas de información*. D.F., Mexico: Pearson Educación.

Kotler, P., & Armstrong, G. (2008). *Fundamentos de Marketing*. D.F., Mexico: Pearson Educación.

López, J. (2009). Del Marketing Transaccional Al Marketing Relacional. *Entramado*, *5*(1), 6–13.

Martín-Moreno, M., & Sáez, F. (2004). Análisis preliminar del comercio electrónico. In M. Martín-Moreno & F. Sáez (Eds.), *Aplicaciones y abusos de Internet como canal de comunicación del correo electrónico* (pp. 1–32). Madrid, Spain: Politechnic University of Madrid.

McLeod, R. (2000). *Sistemas de información gerencial*. D.F., Mexico: Pearson Educación.

Melo, A., & Romero, H. R. (2016). *Digital Marketing for Small and Medium Enterprises*. Revista Observatorio de la Economía Latinoamericana.

Mirón, G. (2011). La comunicación de experiencias de marca a través de las redes sociales: Análisis de caso de los patrocinadores del Mundial de Fútbol 2010. *Pensar la Publicidad*, *5*(2), 93–118.

Molina, G. (2014). *Marketing deportivo digital*. Madrid, Spain: Librerías Deportivas Esteban Sanz.

Moreno, G. R., Ruíz, D. C., & Peñaherrera, L. V. (2017). Influencia del marketing digital en el uso de las redes sociales para la gestión empresarial de las PYMES. *Arjé. Revista de Postgrado FaCE-UC*, *11*(21), 271–279.

Pico, L., & Coello, R. (2017). Relación entre el ciclo de vida de las Pymes en redes sociales y el emprendimiento en la ciudad de Guayaquil. *INNOVA*, *2*(5), 125–136.

Prada, R. (2016). Las TICs, factor de efectividad en la aplicación del mercadeo digital en negocios de retail. *Revista EAN*, *80*(80), 105–116. doi:10.21158/01208160.n80.2016.1460

Quevedo, P. (2017). *Influencia del marketing digital y online en la fidelización de los clientes de consumo masivo en las redes sociales: categoría chocolatinas*. Manizales, Colombia: Universidad de Manizales.

Sainz, J. (2015). *El plan de marketing digital en la práctica*. Madrid, Spain: ESIC.

Santamaría, F., & Escobar, M. (2011). Estrategias empresariales ante el comercio electrónico. *Información Comercial Española. ICE. Revista de economía, 813*, 187–196.

Shankar, V., Kleijnen, M., Ramanathan, S., Rizley, R., Holland, S., & Morrissey, S. (2016). Mobile Shopper Marketing: Key issues, current insights, and future research avenues. *Journal of Interactive Marketing, 34*, 37–48. doi:10.1016/j.intmar.2016.03.002

Torres, C., & Guzmán, E. (2017). Modelo de evaluación de la calidad de servicio aplicado al retail de ropa en centros comerciales. *Revista Espacios, 38*(23), 28–38.

Túnez, M., García, J., & Guevara-Castillo, M. (2011). Redes sociales y marketing viral: Repercusión e incidencia en la construcción de la agenda mediática. *Palabra Clave (La Plata), 14*(1), 53–65.

KEY TERMS AND DEFINITIONS

Crowdbooster: It is a tool for monitoring and focusing our actions on Twitter and Facebook. It offers many tools to measure the results and draw conclusions from an online strategy.

eCommerce: It is the use of computers to facilitate all operations of firms and clients around the world.

EComPymes Model: Based on social networks, mobile marketing, and email, it has the goal of generation safe, reliable and trustworthy contents to satisfy stakeholders.

Google Analytics: Web analytics tool which belongs to Google company. It provides clustered information about the traffic reaching websites according to audience, acquisition, behavior, and conversions carried out on the website.

Klout: Website and mobile application which used social networking to qualify its users according to online social influence through the "Klout Score," which is a numerical value between 1 and 100.

LinkedIn: Business-oriented professional social network founded on December 14, 2002 and launched on May 5, 2003. It has more than 500 million users.

Mobile Marketing: Set of actions and techniques of online marketing aimed at mobile devices to attract and retain customers with the use of the internet.

Twitter: Social network that allows users to send and read short messages of 140 characters known as tweets. You can access Twitter through a web interface, SMS, or a mobile device application.

Compilation of References

Abbink, K., Irlenbusch, B., & Renner, E. (2006). Group Size and Social Ties in Microfinance Institutions. *Economic Inquiry*, *44*(4), 614–628. doi:10.1093/ei/cbl001

Abor, J., & Quartey, P. (2010). Issues in SME development in Ghana and South Africa, international research. *Journal of Financial Economics*, *39*, 218–228.

Abu-Saifan, S. (2012). Social Entrepreneurship: Definition and Boundaries. *Technology Innovation Management Review*, *2*(2), 22–27. doi:10.22215/timreview/523

Acs, Z. J., & Plummer, L. A. (2005). Penetrating the 'knowledge filter' in regional economies. *The Annals of Regional Science*, *39*(3), 439–456. doi:10.100700168-005-0245-x

Acs, Z. J., & Varga, A. (2005). Entrepreneurship, agglomeration and technological change. *Small Business Economics*, *24*(3), 323–334. doi:10.100711187-005-1998-4

Adomavičiūtė, E., Janiunaite, B., & Stuopyte, E. (2012). The Profile of Social Entrepreneurs Working for Non-governmental Organizations. *Social Sciences*, *77*(3), 17–29. doi:10.5755/j01.ss.77.3.2766

Ahlers, O., Hack, A., Madison, K., Wright, M., & Kellermanns, F. W. (2017). Is it all about money? Affective commitment and the difference between family and non-family sellers in buyouts. *British Journal of Management*, *28*(2), 159–179. doi:10.1111/1467-8551.12178

Ahlin, C. R., & Townsend, R. M. (2002). *Using repayment data to test across models of joint liability lending.* Working Paper No. 02-W27, Department of Economics, Vanderbilt University.

Ahlin, C. R., & Townsend, R. M. (2007). Using Repayment Data to Test across Models of Joint Liability Lending. *Economic Journal (London)*, *117*(517), F11–F51. doi:10.1111/j.1468-0297.2007.02014.x

AIMC. (2016). *Navegantes en la Red – 18ª Encuesta AIMC a Usuarios de Internet.* Retrieved from: http://download.aimc.es/aimc/ROY76b/macro2015.pdf

Alam, M. S. (2010). Transición Cultural y Emprendimiento Innovador. *5th International Conference on Product Innovation Management*, 1-2, 757-761.

Alemán, F., & Coronado, C. I. (2014). Emprendimiento social innovador: el caso de Biored Colombia SAS. *Global Conference on Business & Finance Proceedings*, *9*(2), 508-516.

Allen, N. J., & Meyer, J. P. (1990). The measurement and antecedents of affective, continuance and normative commitment to the organization. *Journal of Occupational Psychology*, *63*(1), 1–18. doi:10.1111/j.2044-8325.1990.tb00506.x

Alperovitz, G. (2011). The New-Economy Movement. *The Nation.* Retrieved from http://www.thenation.com/article/160949/new-economy-movement

Al-Qeisi, K., Dennis, C., Alamanos, E., & Jayawardhena, C. (2014). Website design quality and usage behavior: Unified Theory of Acceptance and Use of Technology. *Journal of Business Research, 67*(11), 2282–2290. doi:10.1016/j.jbusres.2014.06.016

Altinay, L., Madanoglu, M., De Vita, G., Arasli, H., & Ekinci, Y. (2016). The interface between organizational learning capability, entrepreneurial orientation, and SME growth. *Journal of Small Business Management, 54*(3), 871–891. doi:10.1111/jsbm.12219

Álvarez-Figueroa, O. (2014). Competitiveness in International Economy Present Conditions. *Economia y Desarrollo, 151*(1), 56–70.

Alvord, S., Brown, D., & Letts, C. (2004). Social entrepreneurship and societal transformation. *The Journal of Applied Behavioral Science, 40*(3), 260–282. doi:10.1177/0021886304266847

Ambler, T., & Roberts, J. (2008). Assessing marketing performance: Don't settle for a silver metric. *Journal of Marketing Management, 24*(7-8), 733–750. doi:10.1362/026725708X345498

Amit, R., & Zott, C. (2001). Value creation in e-business. *Strategic Management Journal, 22*(6-7), 493–520. doi:10.1002mj.187

Anato, M. (2006). El uso de los instrumentos clásicos del marketing y la tecnología digital en turismo. *Estudios y Perspectivas en Turismo, 15*, 19–44.

Andersen, T. L. (2006). Perspectives on Strategic Risk Management. Copenhagen Business School Press.

Andrade, D. (2016). Estrategias de marketing digital en la promoción de Marca Ciudad. *Revista EAN, 51*(51), 59–72. doi:10.21158/01208160.n80.2016.1457

Andrews, K. (1971). *The Concept of Corporate Strategy*. Homewood, IL: Dow Jones-Irwin.

Annamária, I. (2004). The evolution of university-industry-government relationships during the transition. *Research Policy, 33*(6–7), 975–995.

Anttonen, J., & Jumisko-Pyykkö, S. (2008). Understanding the meaning of experiences with technology. *Workshop on Research Goals and Strategies for Studying User Experience and Emotion during NordiCHI08 Conference*, 1-4.

Aparicio, G., Basco, R., Iturralde, T., & Maseda, A. (2017). An exploratory study of firm goals in the context of family firms, An institutional logics perspective. *Journal of Family Business Strategy, 8*(3), 157–169. doi:10.1016/j.jfbs.2017.08.002

Araujo, T., & Neijens, P. (2012). Friend me: Which factors influence top global brands participation in social network sites. *Internet Research, 22*(5), 626–640. doi:10.1108/10662241211271581

Argandoña, A. (2011). *The Common Good.* Working Paper, 937, Barcelona: IESE.

Argote, L., & Greve, H. R. (2007). A behavioral theory of the firm—40 years and counting, Introduction and impact. *Organization Science, 18*(3), 337–349. doi:10.1287/orsc.1070.0280

Aristotle. (1973). *Politics*. Grolier Jackson.

Armendariz de Aghion, B., & Gollier, C. (2000). Peer Group Formation in an Adverse Selection Model. *Economic Journal (London), 110*(465), 632–643. doi:10.1111/1468-0297.00557

Arnould, E. J., & Wallendorf, M. (1994). Market-oriented ethnography: Interpretation building and marketing strategy formulation. *JMR, Journal of Marketing Research, 31*(4), 484–504. doi:10.1177/002224379403100404

Askitas, N., & Zimmermann, F. (2009). Google econometrics and unemployment forecasting. *Applied Economics Quarterly*, *55*(2), 107–120. doi:10.3790/aeq.55.2.107

Astrachan, J. H., Klein, S., & Smyrnios, K. (2002). The F-PEC scale of family influence: A proposal for solving the family business definition problem. *Family Business Review*, *15*(1), 45–57. doi:10.1111/j.1741-6248.2002.00045.x

Astrachan, J. H., & Shanker, M. C. (2003). Family businesses' contribution to the US economy, A closer look. *Family Business Review*, *16*(3), 211–219. doi:10.1177/08944865030160030601

Astrachan, J. H., Zahra, S. A., & Sharma, P. (2003). *Family-sponsored ventures*. Kansas City, MO: Kauffman Foundation.

Atún, J.P. (2004). Logística Verde: Estrategias para implantarla y casos exitosos en Latinoamérica. *Revista Zona Logística*, *1*, 12–19.

Audretsch, D. B. (2009). The entrepreneurial society. *The Journal of Technology Transfer*, *34*(3), 245–254. doi:10.100710961-008-9101-3

Audretsch, D. B., & Belitski, M. (2017). Entrepreneurial ecosystems in cities: Establishing the framework conditions. *The Journal of Technology Transfer*, *42*(5), 1030–1051. doi:10.100710961-016-9473-8

Audretsch, D. B., & Keilbach, M. (2004a). Does entrepreneurship capital matter? *Entrepreneurship Theory and Practice*, *28*(5), 419–429. doi:10.1111/j.1540-6520.2004.00055.x

Audretsch, D. B., & Keilbach, M. (2004b). Entrepreneurship and regional growth: An evolutionary interpretation. *Journal of Evolutionary Economics*, *14*(5), 605–616. doi:10.100700191-004-0228-6

Audretsch, D. B., & Keilbach, M. (2007). The theory of knowledge spillover entrepreneurship. *Journal of Management Studies*, *44*(7), 1242–1254. doi:10.1111/j.1467-6486.2007.00722.x

Audretsch, D. B., Lehmann, E. E., & Paleari, S. (2014). Academic policy and entrepreneurship: A European perspective. *The Journal of Technology Transfer*, *40*(3), 363–368. doi:10.100710961-014-9359-6

Auletta, N., & Rivera, C. (2011). An ecosystem for entrepreneurship. *Debates IESA*, *16*(4), 12–17.

Austin, Stevenson, H., & Wei-Skillern, J. (2006). Social and Commercial Entrepreneurship: Same, different or both? *Entrepreneurship Theory and Practice*, *30*(1), 1–22. doi:10.1111/j.1540-6520.2006.00107.x

Avelino, F., Wittmayer, J., Haxeltine, A., Kemp, R., O'Riordan, T., Weaver, P., … Rotmans, J. (2014). *Game Changers and Transformative Social Innovation. The Case of the Economic Crisis and the New Economy*. TRANSIT Working Paper.

Ayanda, M. A., & Laraba, S. A. (2011). Small and medium scale enterprises as a survival strategy for employment generation in Nigeria. *Journal of Sustainable Development*, *4*(1), 200–206.

Ayyagari, M., Beck, T., & Demirguc-Kunt, A. (2007). Small and medium enterprises across the globe. *Small Business Economics*, *29*(4), 415–434. doi:10.100711187-006-9002-5

Azemikhah, H. (2006). The 21st Century, the Competency Era and Competency Theory, In Open Learning Institute of TAFE. In *AVETRA 9th Annual Conference*. University of Wollongong.

Baaken, T. (1989). *Bewertung technologieorientierter Unternehmensgründungen, Kriterien und Methoden zur Bewertung von Gründerpersönlichkeit, Technologie und Markt für Banken und Venture-Capital-Gesellschaften sowie für die staatliche Wirtschafts- und Technologieförderung*. Berlin, Germany: Erich Schmidt.

Baaken, T. (2002). Soft Skills und Schlüsselqualifikationen als integraler Ausbildungsbestandteil an Hochschulen. In F. Isenbart (Ed.), *Organisation und Management* (Vol. 25, pp. 4–18). Münster, Germany: Berichte aus der Hochschule.

Baaken, T., & Gosejohann, S. (2009). Higher Education in International Marketing by Integration of Industry Projects. *EDULEARN09 Proceedings, International Conference on Education and New Learning Technologies*, 5185-5195.

Baaken, T., Kiel, B., & Kliewe, T. (2015). Real World Projects with Companies Supporting Competence Development in Higher Education. *International Journal of Higher Education*, *4*(3), 129–139. doi:10.5430/ijhe.v4n3p129

Baaken, T., Kiel, B., Rossano, S., Baaken, M., & Maas, G. (2016). Competences in Entrepreneurship – Teaching Entrepreneurship in Higher Education from a new angle. In J. M. Saiz-Álvarez (Ed.), *Handbook of Research on Social Entrepreneurship and Solidarity Economics* (pp. 154–173). Hershey, PA: IGI. doi:10.4018/978-1-5225-0097-1.ch009

Baden-Fuller, C., & Ang, S. W. (2001). Building reputations: The role of alliances in the European Business school scene. *Long Range Planning*, *34*(6), 741–755. doi:10.1016/S0024-6301(01)00088-7

Bagozzi, R. (1975). Marketing as Exchange. *Journal of Marketing*, *39*(4), 32–39. doi:10.1177/002224297503900405

Baker, J. (2000). *Evaluating the impact of development projects on poverty: a handbook for practitioners (Spanish)*. Washington, DC: World Bank. doi:10.1596/0-8213-4697-0

Balabanis, G., Phillips, H. C., & Lyall, J. (1998). Corporate social responsibility and economic performance in the top British companies: Are they linked? *European Business Review*, *98*(1), 25–44. doi:10.1108/09555349810195529

Bamberger, I. (1994) *Product/Market Strategies of Small and Medium-Sized Enterprises*. Aldershot, UK: Ashgate Publishing Group.

Bamberger, I., & Weir, A. (1990). Strategic orientations of small European businesses, The STRATOS group. Aldershot, UK: Gower Publishing Company.

Banerjee, R. (2014). *SMEs financial constraints and growth*. BIS Working Papers, Bank for International Settlements.

Banerjee, A. V., Timothy, B., & Timothy, W. G. (1994). The neighbor's keeper: Design of a credit cooperative with theory and a test. *The Quarterly Journal of Economics*, *102*(9), 491–515. doi:10.2307/2118471

Bangwayo-Skeete, P. F., & Skeete, R. W. (2015). Can Google data improve the forecasting performance of tourist arrivals? Mixed-data sampling approach. *Tourism Management*, *46*, 454–464. doi:10.1016/j.tourman.2014.07.014

Banyuls, J., & Recio, A. (2015). A crisis inside the crisis: Spain under a conservative neoliberalism. In S. Lehndorff (Ed.), *Divisive integration. The triumph of failed ideas in Europe* (pp. 39–68). Brussels, Belgium: European Trade Union Institute.

Baporikar, N. (2014b). Innovation in the 21st Century Organization. In B. Christiansen, S. Yildiz, & E. Yildiz (Eds.), Transcultural Marketing for Incremental and Radical Innovation (pp. 339–365). Hershey, PA: IGI Global. doi:10.4018/978-1-4666-4749-7.ch016

Baporikar, N. (2014a). Strategic Management Overview and SME in Globalized World. In K. Todorov & D. Smallbone (Eds.), *Handbook of Research on Strategic Management in Small and Medium Enterprises* (pp. 22–39). Hershey, PA: Business Science Reference. doi:10.4018/978-1-4666-5962-9.ch002

Baporikar, N. (2015a). Role of Entrepreneurship in Networked Indian Economy. In P. Ordóñez de Pablos (Ed.), *Technological Solutions for Sustainable Business Practice in Asia* (pp. 36–59). Hershey, PA: Business Science Reference; doi:10.4018/978-1-4666-8462-1.ch003

Baporikar, N. (2015b). Distinctiveness of Techno-Entrepreneurship. *International Journal of Strategic Information Technology and Applications*, *6*(1), 15–25. doi:10.4018/IJSITA.2015010102

Baporikar, N. (2016). Understanding Knowledge Management Spectrum for SMEs in Global Scenario. *International Journal of Social and Organizational Dynamics in IT*, *5*(1), 1–15. doi:10.4018/IJSODIT.2016010101

Baporikar, N. (2017). Business Excellence Strategies for SME Sustainability in India. In P. Ordóñez de Pablos (Ed.), *Managerial Strategies and Solutions for Business Success in Asia* (pp. 61–78). Hershey, PA: IGI Global; doi:10.4018/978-1-5225-1886-0.ch004

Baporikar, N. (2018). Critical Success Factors for Executives in Global Economy. In A. Presenza & L. Sheehan (Eds.), *Geopolitics and Strategic Management in the Global Economy* (pp. 40–56). Hershey, PA: IGI Global; doi:10.4018/978-1-5225-2673-5.ch003

Baporikar, N., & Deshpande, M. (2017). SMEs and Branding Strategies. *International Journal of Applied Management Sciences and Engineering*, *4*(1), 43–55. doi:10.4018/IJAMSE.2017010104

Barba, V., & Atienza, C. (2012). Entrepreneurial behavior: Impact of motivation factors on the decision to create a new venture. *Investigaciones Europeas de Dirección y Economía de la Empresa*, *18*(12), 132–138. doi:10.1016/S1135-2523(12)70003-5

Barbery, D., Pástor, B., Idrobo, D., & Sempértegui, L. C. (2018). Análisis comparativo generacional del comportamiento de compra online. *Revista Espacios*, *39*(34), 16–29.

Barera, N., Sylvain, L., & Sutter, S. (2019). *Proceedings of the 20th Congress of the International Ergonomics Association (IEA 2018)*, *827*, 533-538. 10.1007/978-3-319-96098-2

Barney, J. (1991). Firm resources and sustained competitive advantage. *Journal of Management*, *17*(1), 99–120. doi:10.1177/014920639101700108

Barney, J. B. (2007). *Gaining and Sustaining Competitive Advantage*. Upper Saddle River, NJ: Prentice Hall.

Barney, J. B., Ketchen, D. J. Jr, & Wright, M. (2011). The future of resource-based theory: Revitalization or decline? *Journal of Management*, *37*(5), 1299–1315. doi:10.1177/0149206310391805

Baron, R. A. (2008). The role of affect in the entrepreneurial process. *Academy of Management Review*, *33*(2), 328–340. doi:10.5465/amr.2008.31193166

Barrero, A., Fuentes, M., & Mena, J. (2018). Formality and income gaps in the Chilean labor market. *Economía Chilena (Santiago)*, *21*(2), 108–127.

Barros, I., Hernández-Gómez, J., & Martín-Cruz, N. (2017). Familiness and socioemotional wealth in Spanish family firms, An empirical examination. *European Journal of Family Business*, *7*(1-2), 14–24. doi:10.1016/j.ejfb.2017.06.004

Barr, R. B., & Tagg, J. (1995). From Teaching to Learning – A new paradigm for undergraduate education. *Change*, *27*(6), 13–25. doi:10.1080/00091383.1995.10544672

Basco, R., & Pérez, M. J. (2011). Ideal types of family business management, Horizontal fit between family and business decisions and the relationship with family business performance. *Journal of Family Business Strategy*, *2*(3), 151–165. doi:10.1016/j.jfbs.2011.07.004

Baumol, W. J. (1968). Entrepreneurship in Economic Theory. *The American Economic Review*, *58*(2), 64–71.

Baumol, W. J. (1970). *Introducción a la dinámica económica*. Barcelona, Spain: Marcombo.

Bauweraerts, J., & Colot, O. (2017). Exploring nonlinear effects of family involvement in the board on entrepreneurial orientation. *Journal of Business Research*, *70*(1), 185–192. doi:10.1016/j.jbusres.2016.08.020

Bayardo, R. (2016). From culture to creativity. Some reflections from Argentina. *Revista Uruguaya de Antropología y Etnografía*, *1*(1), 39–46.

Baye, M. R., De los Santos, B., & Wildenbeest, M. R. (2016). Search engine optimization: What drives organic traffic to retail sites? *Journal of Economics & Management Strategy*, *25*(1), 6–31. doi:10.1111/jems.12141

Becerra, M. (2009). *Theory of the Firm for Strategic Management*. Cambridge, UK: Cambridge University Press. doi:10.1017/CBO9780511626524

Béchard, J., & Toulouse, J. (1991). Entrepreneurship and education: A viewpoint from education. *Journal of Small Business and Entrepreneurship*, *9*(1), 3–13. doi:10.1080/08276331.1991.10600386

Belausteguigoitia, I. (2007). *¿Entrepre.... qué?* Available at cedef.itam.mx/PDF/Entrepreneurship.pdf

Belk, R. W. (1988). Possessions and the extended self. *The Journal of Consumer Research*, *15*(2), 139–168. doi:10.1086/209154

Bercovitz, J., & Feldman, M. (2008). Academic entrepreneurs: Organizational change at the individual level. *Organization Science*, *19*(1), 69–89. doi:10.1287/orsc.1070.0295

Beretta, S. (2002). Unleashing the integration potential of ERP systems. *Business Process Management Journal*, *8*(3), 254–277. doi:10.1108/14637150210428961

Berglund, K., & Johansson, A. W. (2007). Constructions of entrepreneurship: A discourse analysis of academic publications. *Journal of Enterprising Communities: People and Places in The Global Economy*, *1*(1), 77–102. doi:10.1108/17506200710736276

Berman, B. (2016). Planning and implementing effective mobile marketing programs. *Business Horizons*, *59*(4), 431–439. doi:10.1016/j.bushor.2016.03.006

Berrone, P., Cruz, C., & Gómez-Mejía, L. R. (2012). Socioemotional wealth in family firms, Theoretical dimensions, assessment approaches, and agenda for future research. *Family Business Review*, *25*(3), 258–279. doi:10.1177/0894486511435355

Besley, T., & Coate, S. (1995). Group lending, repayment incentives, and social collateral. *Journal of Development Economics*, *46*(1), 1–18. doi:10.1016/0304-3878(94)00045-E

Betters, E. (2016). *Google is shutting down Picasa: What'll happen to your photos and videos?* Pocket-lint Limited. Retrieved from: https://www.pocket-lint.com/apps/news/google/136712-google-is-shutting-down-picasa-what-ll-happen-to-your-photos-and-videos

Beugelsdijk, S., & Noorderhaven, N. (2002). *Entrepreneurial attitude and economic growth; A cross-section of 54 regions.* Paper presented at the 2002 Conference of the European Regional Science Association (ERSA), Dortmund, Germany.

Bhide, A. (2000). *The Origin and Evolution of New Businesses*. Oxford, UK: Oxford University Press.

Bilán, S. G., Kisenwether, E. C., Rzasa, S. E., & Wise, J. C. (2005). Developing and assessing students' entrepreneurial skills and mind-set. *Journal of Engineering Education*, *94*(2), 233–243. doi:10.1002/j.2168-9830.2005.tb00844.x

Bittner, E., & Leimeister, J. M. (2011). Towards CSR 2.0. Potentials and challenges of Web 2.0 for corporate social responsibility communication. *Proceedings of the 11th Academy of Management Annual Meeting*.

Blanco, M. (2011). Narrative research: A way of generating knowledge. *Argumentos (México, DF)*, *24*(67), 135–156.

Blanco-Valbuena, C. E., Bernal-Torres, C. A., Camacho, F., & Díaz-Olaya, M. (2018). Creative and Cultural Industries: Study from the Knowledge Management Approach. *Información Tecnológica*, *29*(3), 15–28. doi:10.4067/S0718-07642018000300015

Block, J. H. (2012). R&D investments in family and founder firms, An agency perspective. *Journal of Business Venturing*, *27*(2), 248–265. doi:10.1016/j.jbusvent.2010.09.003

Blumberg, D.F. (2004). *Introduction to Management of Reverse Logistics and Closed Loop Supply Chain Processes.* CRC Press.

Blumler, J. G. (1979). The role of theory in uses and gratifications studies. *Communication Research*, *6*(1), 9–36. doi:10.1177/009365027900600102

Boley, H., & Chang, E. (2007). *Digital ecosystems: Principles and semantics. In Inaugural IEEE-IES Digital EcoSystems and Technologies Conference*. Cairns, Australia: IEEE.

Bolton, R., Parasuraman, A., Hoefnagels, A., Migchels, N., Kabadayi, S., & Gruber, T. (2013). Entendiendo la generación Y y su uso de las redes sociales: Una agenda de revisión e investigación. *Journal of Service Management*, *24*(3), 245–267. doi:10.1108/09564231311326987

Bonilla, R. (2013). *Estrategia de comunicación para la captación de fondos en organizaciones sin fines de lucro. Estudio de caso hábitat para la humanidad El Salvador*. Universidad Centroamericana 'José Simeón Cañas'.

Borzaga, C., Bodini, R., Carini, C., Depedri, S., Galera, G., & Salvatori, G. (2014). *Europe in transition: The role of social cooperatives and social enterprises*. Academic Press.

Boughton, S.B. (2005). Search engine marketing. *Perspectives in Business, 2*(1), 29-33.

Boulding, W., & Christensen, M. (2001). First Mover Disadvantage. *Harvard Business Review*, *79*(9), 20–21.

Bourgignon, F. (2008). *Millennium Development Goals at Midpoint: Where do we stand and where do we need to go?* Brussels, Belgium: European Commission.

Bowen, H. (2018). *Investment in learning: The individual and social value of American higher education*. London, UK: Routledge. doi:10.4324/9781351309929

Bowen, H. R. (1953). *Social responsibility of the businessman*. Harper & Row.

Boyatzis, R. E. (1998). *Transforming qualitative information: thematic analysis and code development*. London, UK: Sage.

Boyes, H., Hallaq, B., Cunningham, J., & Watson, T. (2018). The industrial internet of things (IIoT): An analysis framework. *Computers in Industry*, *101*, 1–12. doi:10.1016/j.compind.2018.04.015

Brady, M., Fellenz, M. R., & Brookes, R. (2008). Researching the role of information and communications technology (ICT) in contemporary marketing practices. *Journal of Business and Industrial Marketing*, *23*(2), 108–114. doi:10.1108/08858620810850227

Braunerhjelm, P., & Stuart, U. (2012). *Social Entrepreneurship: A Survey of Current Research.* Swedish Entrepreneurship Forum Working Paper, 9.

Brazda, J., Dellinger, M., & Rößl, D. (2012). *Genossenschaften im Fokus einer neuen Wirtschaftspolitik. Bericht der XVII. Internationalen Genossenschaftswissenschaftlichen Tagung*. IGT.

Brendan, K. J., & Rowley, J. (2017). Evaluation and Decision Making in Social Media Marketing. *Management Decision*, *55*(1), 1–28. doi:10.1108/IJBM-07-2013-0069

Brockmann, M., Clarke, L., & Winch, C. (2009). Competence and competency in the EQF and in European VET systems. *Journal of European Industrial Training*, *33*(8/9), 787–799. doi:10.1108/03090590910993634

Brooks, H. (1973). The technology of zero growth. *Daedalus*, *102*(4), 139–152.

Brown, R. M., Janney, J. J., & Paul, K. (2001). An empirical investigation of the relationship between change in corporate social performance and financial performance: A stakeholder theory perspective. *Journal of Business Ethics*, *32*(2), 143–156. doi:10.1023/A:1010786912118

Brown, T. J., & Dacin, P. A. (1997). The company and the product: Corporate associations and consumer product responses. *Journal of Marketing*, *61*(1), 68–84. doi:10.1177/002224299706100106

Brunet, I. (2011). *Creación de Empresas. Emprendimiento e innovación*. Madrid, Spain: Ra-ma Editorial.

Bryman, A. (1984). The Debate about Quantitative and Qualitative Research: A Question of Method or Epistemology? *The British Journal of Sociology*, *35*(1), 75–92. doi:10.2307/590553

Buckland, H., Garmilla, A., Murillo, D., Leticia, M., & Flores, S. (2018). *The digital revolution is facing the great challenges of the world*. Barcelona, Spain: Social Innovation Institute of ESADE.

Buitrago, F., & Duque, I. (2013). *The Orange Economy: An infinite opportunity*. Washington, DC: Inter-American Development Bank.

Burke, A., Fitzroy, F., & Nolan, M. (2009). Is there a North-South divide in Self-employment in England? *Regional Studies*, *43*(4), 529–544. doi:10.1080/00343400701827360

Burns, K. S. (2008). *A historical examination of the development of social media and its application to the public relations industry*. Paper presented at the 2008 ICA Preconference, Montreal, Quebec, Canada.

Busenitz, L., & Álvarez, A. (2001). The entrepreneurship of resource-based theory. *Journal of Management*, *27*(6), 755–775. doi:10.1177/014920630102700609

Caligiuri, P. (2013). *Cultural Agility. Building a Pipeline of Successful Global Professionals*. San Francisco, USA: Wiley.

Calvert, M., & Terry, J. (Eds.). (2013). *Processed lives: gender and technology in everyday life*. Routledge.

Camelo-Ordaz, C., García-Cruz, J., Sousa-Ginel, E., & Valle-Cabrera, R. (2011). The influence of human resource management on knowledge sharing and innovation in Spain, The mediating role of affective commitment International. *Journal of Human Resource Management*, *22*(7), 1442–1463.

Camisón, C. (1997). *La competitividad de la PYME industrial española: estrategia y competencias distintivas*. Madrid: Civitas.

Cantillon, R. (1952). *Ensayo sobre la naturaleza del comercio en general*. D.F, Mexico: Fondo de Cultura Económica. (Original work published 1755)

Caravalo, B. (2011). *Desarrollo sostenible, ética, filantropía y responsabilidad social*. Bogota, Colombia: Ediciones Econ.

Carland, J., Hoy, F., Boulton, W., & Carland, J. A. (1984). Differentiating Entrepreneurs from Small Business Owners: A Conceptualization. *Academy of Management Review*, *9*(2), 354–359. doi:10.5465/amr.1984.4277721

Carmen, P., & Nicolae, P. A. (2010). Email marketing campaigns: The easiest path from organizations to consumers–an exploratory assessment. *Annals of Faculty of Economics*, *1*(1), 737–742.

Carney, M., van Essen, M., Gedajlovic, E. R., & Heugens, P. P. (2015). What do we know about private family firms? A meta-analytical review. *Entrepreneurship Theory and Practice*, *39*(3), 513–544. doi:10.1111/etap.12054

Carranza, C. (2013). Economía de la Reciprocidad: Una aproximación a la Economía Social y Solidaria desde el concepto del don, *Otra Economía. Revista Latinoamericana de Economía Social y Solidaria*, *7*(12), 14–25.

Carroll, A. B. (1979). A three-dimensional conceptual model of corporate performance. *Academy of Management Review*, *4*(4), 497–505. doi:10.5465/amr.1979.4498296

Carroll, A., & Buschholtz, A. (2006). *Business & Society: Ethics & Stakeholder Management* (6th ed.). Thompson.

Casillas, J. C., Moreno, A. M., & Barbero, J. L. (2010). A configurational approach of the relationship between entrepreneurial orientation and growth of family firms. *Family Business Review*, *23*(1), 27–44. doi:10.1177/0894486509345159

Casillas, J. C., & Moreno, M. (2010). The relationship between entrepreneurial orientation and growth, The moderating role of family involvement. *Entrepreneurship Theory and Practice*, *22*(3-4), 265–291.

Castañeda-Rivera, E., & Garduño-Bello, B. (2017). Map of the creative industries in Mexico. A projection for CENTRO. *Economía Creativa*, *7*, 118–166.

Central Intelligence Agency. (2018). *The World Factbook.* Washington, DC: CIA.

Certo, S. T., & Miller, T. (2008). Social Entrepreneurship: Key Issues and Concepts. *Business Horizons*, *51*(4), 267–271. doi:10.1016/j.bushor.2008.02.009

Céspedes, A. H. (2009). *Emprendimiento Social y su Sustentabilidad.* Bogota, Colombia: HCGlobal Group.

Chadwick, F., & Chaffey, D. (2014). *Marketing Digital, estrategia, implementación y práctica.* D.F., Mexico: Pearson.

Chaffey, D., & Patron, M. (2012). From web analytics to digital marketing optimization: Increasing the commercial value of digital analytics. *Journal of Direct. Data and Digital Marketing Practice*, *14*(1), 30–45. doi:10.1057/dddmp.2012.20

Chamber of Commerce. (2003). Bogotá – Cundinamarca. Bases del plan regional de competitividad. Bogota, Colombia: Author.

Chaves Avila, R., & Monzon, J. L. (2012). *The social economy in the European Union.* Retrieved from http://roderic.uv.es/handle/10550/39363

Chavez, V. A., Stinnett, R., Tierney, R., & Walsh, S. (2017). The importance of the technologically able social innovators and entrepreneurs: A US National Laboratory Perspective. *Technological Forecasting and Social Change*, *121*, 205–215. doi:10.1016/j.techfore.2016.09.002

Chell, E. (2007). Social enterprise and entrepreneurship: Towards a convergent theory of the entrepreneurial process. *International Small Business Journal*, *25*(1), 5–26. doi:10.1177/0266242607071779

Chell, E. (2007). Social Enterprise and Entrepreneurship: Towards a Convergent Theory of the Entrepreneurial Process. *International Small Business Journal*, *25*(5), 12–21.

Chell, E., Nicolopoulou, K., & Karatas-Özkan, M. (2010). Social entrepreneurship and enterprise: International and innovation perspectives. *Entrepreneurship and Regional Development*, *22*(6), 485–493. doi:10.1080/08985626.2010.488396

Chen, H., Chiang, R. H., & Storey, V. C. (2012). Business Intelligence and Analytics: From Big Data to Big Impact. *Management Information Systems Quarterly*, *36*(4), 1165–1188. doi:10.2307/41703503

Chen, T., Ki So, E. P., Wu, L., & Ming Yan, I. K. (2014). The 2007–2008 U.S. Recession: What Did the Real-Time Google Trends Data Tell the United States? *Contemporary Economic Policy*, *33*(2), 395–403. doi:10.1111/coep.12074

Chesbrough, H., & Rosenbaum, R. (2000). *The role of the business model in capturing value from innovation (working paper).* Boston: Harvard Business School.

Child, J. (1972). Organizational structure, environment and performance, The role of strategic choice. *Sociology*, *6*(1), 1–22. doi:10.1177/003803857200600101

Chirico, F., & Salvato, C. (2008). Knowledge integration and dynamic organizational adaptation in family firms. *Family Business Review*, *21*(2), 169–181. doi:10.1111/j.1741-6248.2008.00117.x

Chirico, F., & Salvato, C. (2016). Knowledge internalization and product development in family firms. When relational and affective factors matter. *Journal of Business Venturing*, *40*(1), 201–229.

Chirico, F., Sirmon, D. G., Sciascia, S., & Mazzola, P. (2011). Resource orchestration in family firms. Investigating how entrepreneurial orientation, generational involvement, and participative strategy affect performance. *Strategic Entrepreneurship Journal*, *5*(4), 307–326. doi:10.1002ej.121

Chittithaworn, C., Islam, M. A., Keawchana, T., & Yusuf, D. H. M. (2011). Factors Affecting Business Success of Small and Medium Enterprises (SMEs) in Thailand. *Asian Social Science*, *7*(5), 180–190. doi:10.5539/ass.v7n5p180

Chittoor, R., & Das, R. (2007). Professionalization of management and succession performance - A vital linkage. *Family Business Review*, *20*(1), 65–79. doi:10.1111/j.1741-6248.2007.00084.x

Choi, H., & Varian, H. (2012). Predicting the Present with Google Trends. *The Economic Record*, *88*(1), 2–9. doi:10.1111/j.1475-4932.2012.00809.x

Chong, H. (2008). Measuring the performance of small and medium-sized enterprises: The grounded theory approach. *Journal of Business and Public Affairs*, *2*(1), 1–10.

Chong, J. L. (2010). Evaluating the impact of Arnould and Wallendorf's (1994) market-oriented ethnography. *Journal of Business Research*, *63*(12), 1295–1300. doi:10.1016/j.jbusres.2009.08.001

Chowdhury, A., & Garonne, P. (2007). Effective Foreign Aid, Economic Integration and Subsidiarity: Lessons from Europe. In *CASE Network Studies and Analyses, 346*. Warsaw, Poland: CASE-Center for Social and Economic Research. doi:10.2139srn.1436909

Chrisman, J. J., Chua, J. H., Pearson, A. W., & Barnett, T. (2012). Family involvement, family influence, and family-centered non-economic goals in small firms. *Entrepreneurship Theory and Practice*, *36*(2), 267–293. doi:10.1111/j.1540-6520.2010.00407.x

Chrisman, J. J., Hynes, T., & Fraser, S. (1995). Faculty entrepreneurship and economic development: The case of the University of Calgary. *Journal of Business Venturing*, *10*(4), 267–281. doi:10.1016/0883-9026(95)00015-Z

Christensen, C. M., & Eyring, H. J. (2011). The Innovative University. Changing the DNA of Higher Education from the Inside Out. San Francisco, CA: Jossey-Bass (The Jossey-Bass Higher and Adult Education Series).

Chua, J. H., Chrisman, J. J., & Sharma, P. (1999). Defining the family business by behavior. *Entrepreneurship Theory and Practice*, *23*(4), 19–39. doi:10.1177/104225879902300402

Clark, C. E. (2000). Differences between public relations and corporate social responsibility: An analysis. *Public Relations Review*, *26*(3), 363–380. doi:10.1016/S0363-8111(00)00053-9

Clark, J., & Guy, K. (2010). Innovation and Competitiveness: A review. *Technology Analysis and Strategic Management*, *10*(3), 363–395. doi:10.1080/09537329808524322

Clarkson, M. E. (1995). A stakeholder framework for analyzing and evaluating corporate social performance. *Journal of Services Research*, *7*(1), 173–191.

Coduras, A., Levie, J., Kelley, D.J., & Sam. (2006). *Global Entrepreuneurship Monitor Special Report: Una perspectiva global sobre la educación y la formación emprendedora*. Madrid: Global Entrepreneurship Monitor.

Coffman, L. C. (2017). Fundraising Intermediaries Inhibit Quality-Driven Charitable Donations. *Economic Inquiry*, *55*(1), 409–424. doi:10.1111/ecin.12379

Comisión Europea. (2002). *Desvincular la ayuda en aras de la eficacia*. Comunicación de la Comisión al Parlamento y al Consejo Europeo, 18 de noviembre, COM (2002) 639 final, no publicada en Diario Oficial.

Comisión Europea. (2005a). *Estrategia de la UE para África: Hacia un pacto euroafricano para acelerar el desarrollo en África*. Comunicación de la Comisión al Consejo, el Parlamento Europeo y el Comité Económico Social Europeo, COM (2005) 489 final, 12 de octubre, no publicada en Diario Oficial.

Comisión Europea. (2005b). *Coherencia de las políticas en favor del desarrollo. Acelerar el avance para cumplir los Objetivos de Desarrollo del Milenio*. Comunicación de la Comisión al Consejo, al Parlamento Europeo y al Comité Económico y Social, COM (2005) 134 final, de 12 de abril de 2005, no publicada en el Diario Oficial.

Comisión Europea. (2006a). *Ayuda de la UE: realizar más, mejor y más rápido*. Comunicación de la Comisión, de 2 de marzo, COM (2006) 87 final, no publicada en el Diario Oficial.

Comisión Europea. (2006b). *Financiación del desarrollo y eficacia de la ayuda-Retos que plantea el incremento de la ayuda de la UE durante el período 2006-2010*. Comunicación de la Comisión al Consejo y al Parlamento Europeo, de 2 de marzo, COM (2006) 85 final-Diario Oficial C 130 de 3 de junio de 2006.

Comisión Europea. (2006c). *Cómo hacer más productiva la ayuda europea: un marco común para la elaboración de los documentos estratégicos nacionales y la programación plurianual común*. Comunicación de la Comisión al Consejo y al Parlamento Europeo, de 2 de marzo, COM (2006) 88 final, Diario Oficial C 130 de 3 de junio de 2006.

Comisión Europea. (2006d). *Cómo hacer más productiva la ayuda europea: un marco común para la elaboración de los documentos estratégicos nacionales y la programación plurianual común*. Comunicación de la Comisión al Consejo y al Parlamento Europeo, de 2 de marzo, COM (2006) 88 final, Diario Oficial C 130 de 3 de junio de 2006.

Comisión Europea. (2008). *La UE como socio global para el desarrollo-Acelerar los avances hacia los Objetivos de Desarrollo del Milenio*. Comunicación de la Comisión al Parlamento Europeo, al Consejo, al Comité Económico y Social Europeo, y al Comité de las Regiones, COM(2008) 177 final, de 9 de abril, no publicada en el Diario Oficial.

Commission of the European Communities. (2003). *Libro verde. El espíritu empresarial en Europa*. Brussels: Bruselas.

Commission of the European Communities. (2006a). *Report on the implementation of the Entrepreneurship Action Plan*. Commission Staff Working Paper. Brussels: Author.

Commission of the European Communities. (2006b). *Programas de Apoyo a las PYME de la Unión Europea. Presentación general de los principales planes comunitarios de financiación para PYME*. Brussels: Author.

Commission of the European Communities. (2007). *Communication from the Commission to the Council, the European Parliament, the European Economic and Social Committee, and the Committee of the Regions*. Brussels, Belgium: European Union.

CONACYT. (2008). *Informe General del Estado de la Ciencia y Tecnología*. CONACYT.

Confino, J. (2015). *Beyond capitalism and socialism: could a new economic approach save the planet?* Retrieved from http://www.theguardian.com/sustainable-business/2015/apr/21/regenerative-economy-holism-economy-climate-change-inequality

Conner, K. R. (1991). A Historical Comparison of Resource-based Theory and Five Schools of Thought Within Industrial Organisation Economics: Do We Have a New Theory of the Firm? *Journal of Management*, *17*(1), 121–154. doi:10.1177/014920639101700109

Conteras, E. D., Fraile, A. M., & Silva, J. D. (2013). Diseño de un sistema de logística inversa para la recolección de envases y empaques vacíos de plaguicidas. *Revista Ingeniería Industrial*, *2*, 29–42.

Contreras, E., Tordecilla, R., & Silva, J. (2013). Revisión de estudios de caso de carácter cualitativo y exploratorio en logística inversa. *Revista EIA*, *10*, 153–164.

Cooper, D., & Schindler, P. S. (2008). *Business Research Methods*. Boston: McGraw-Hill Irwin.

Cooper, M. J., Upton, N., & Seaman, S. (2005). Customer relationship management, A comparative analysis of family and nonfamily business practices. *Journal of Small Business Management*, *43*(3), 242–256. doi:10.1111/j.1540-627X.2005.00136.x

Corbetta, G., & Salvato, C. A. (2004). The board of directors in family firms, one size fits all? *Family Business Review*, *17*(2), 119–134. doi:10.1111/j.1741-6248.2004.00008.x

Cortese, C. G. (2005). Learning through Teaching. *Management Learning*, *36*(1), 87–115. doi:10.1177/1350507605049905

Costales, J. R. (2013). Medios digitales en Ecuador, cuántos son y qué hacen. *Chasqui. Revista Latinoamericana de Comunicación*, *122*, 111–117.

Costanza, R., Erickson, J., Fligger, K., Adams, A., Adams, C., Altschuler, B., ... Kelly, J. (2004). Estimates of the genuine progress indicator (GPI) for Vermont, Chittenden County, and Burlington, from 1950 to 2000. *Ecological Economics*, *51*(1), 139–155. doi:10.1016/j.ecolecon.2004.04.009

Court, D., Gordon, J., & Perrey, J. (2012). Measuring marketing's worth. *The McKinsey Quarterly*, *3*, 113–118.

Couttenier, M., & Hatte, S. (2015). *Mass Media Effects on Non-Governmental Organizations*. Working Paper, 13. Lausanne, Switzerland: University of Lausanne.

Covarrubias, I. (2003). Emprendedores y empresarios: un enfoque institucional. *Revista CE. Contribuciones a la Economía*. Retrieved from www.eumed.net/ce/icm-emp.htm

Covin, J. G., & Slevin, D. P. (1989). Strategic Management of Small Firms in Hostile and Benign Environments. *Strategic Management Journal*, *10*(1), 75–87. doi:10.1002mj.4250100107

Covin, J. G., & Slevin, D. P. (1990). New venture strategic posture, structure, and performance, An industry life cycle analysis. *Journal of Business Venturing*, *5*(2), 123–135. doi:10.1016/0883-9026(90)90004-D

Covin, J. G., & Slevin, D. P. (1991). A conceptual model of entrepreneurship as firm behavior. *Entrepreneurship Theory and Practice*, *16*(1), 7–25. doi:10.1177/104225879101600102

Covin, J. G., & Wales, W. J. (2012). The measurement of entrepreneurial orientation. *Entrepreneurship Theory and Practice*, *36*(4), 677–702. doi:10.1111/j.1540-6520.2010.00432.x

Crane, A., & Matten, M. (2006). *Business Ethics*. London, UK: Oxford University Press.

Crespo, A. (2013). *El uso de las TICS como herramientas para la internacionalización de las PYMES, caso de estudio Empresa Rafael Paredes. Azuay*. Universidad del Azuay.

Cruz, C. C., Gómez-Mejía, L. R., & Becerra, M. (2010). Perceptions of benevolence and the design of agency contracts, CEO-TMT relationships in family firms. *Academy of Management Journal*, *53*(1), 69–89. doi:10.5465/amj.2010.48036975

Cruz, C., Larraza-Kintana, M., Garcés-Galdeano, L., & Berrone, P. (2014). Are family firms really more socially responsible? *Entrepreneurship Theory and Practice*, *38*(6), 1295–1316.

Cruz, C., & Nordqvist, M. (2012). Entrepreneurial orientation in family firms, a generational perspective. *Small Business Economics*, *38*(1), 33–49. doi:10.100711187-010-9265-8

Cuevas, H. (2007). *La empresa y los empresarios en la teoría económica*. Bogota, Colombia: Universidad Externado de Colombia.

Cyert, R. M., & March, J. G. (1963). *A behavioral theory of the firm*. Englewood Cliffs, NJ: Prentice-Hall.

Dacko, S. G. (2017). Enabling smart retail settings via mobile augmented reality shopping apps. *Technological Forecasting and Social Change*, *124*, 243–256. doi:10.1016/j.techfore.2016.09.032

Daghbashyan, Z., & Harsman, B. (2014). Universidad Elección y Emprendimiento. *Pequeña Economía de la Empresa*, *42*(4), 729–746.

Daniels, K. (1998). Towards integrating emotions into strategic management research, trait affect and perceptions of the strategic environment. *British Journal of Management*, *9*(3), 163–168. doi:10.1111/1467-8551.00081

Dasgupta, P. (2008). Nature in economics. *Environmental and Resource Economics*, *39*(1), 1–7. doi:10.100710640-007-9178-4

Davenport, T. H. (1993). *The Process of Innovation*. Boston: Ernst & Young - Harvard Business School Press.

Davey, T. A. (2015). Entrepreneurship at Universities - Exploring the factors influencing the development of entrepreneurship at universities. Amsterdam: Academic Press.

Davidson, E., & Vaast, E. (2010). Digital entrepreneurship and its socio-material enactment. *Proceedings of the 43rd Annual Hawaii International Conference on System Sciences*, 1–10.

Dávila, C. (1996). *Empresa e historia en América Latina. Un balance historiográfico*. Bogota, Colombia: TM Editores y Colciencias.

Dávila, C. (1997). Los comienzos de la historia empresarial en Colombia. *America Latina en la Historia Economica*, *7*(07), 73–101. doi:10.18232/alhe.v4i07.203

Dávila, J. C. (2009). *Capacidades dinámicas: un acercamiento a las teorías contemporáneas de la firma. Evidencias de dos organizaciones que operan en Colombia*. Bogotá, Colombia: Universidad de los *Andes*.

Davis, J. B. (2013). *The theory of the individual in economics: Identity and value*. Routledge.

Davis, T. (2008). *The OECD-Eurostat Entrepreneurship Indicators Programme. Preliminary Indicators for Italy, Europe and Other OECD Countries*. Urbino, Italy: Urbino University.

Dawkins, J. (2004). Corporate responsibility: The communication challenge. *Journal of Communication Challenge*, *9*, 108–119.

Day, G. S. (2017). *Reinventar el marketing en la era digital, OpenMind*. Madrid, Spain: BBVA Group.

De Bono, E. (1994). *El pensamiento lateral. El poder del pensamiento lateral para la creación de nuevas ideas*. Barcelona, Spain: Paidós Empresa.

De Clerc, D., & Arenius, P. (2006). The Role of Knowledge in Business Start-up Activity. *International Small Business Journal*, *24*(4), 339–358. doi:10.1177/0266242606065507

De Clercq, D., Dimov, D., & Thongpapanl, N. T. (2013). Organizational social capital, formalization, and internal knowledge sharing in entrepreneurial orientation formation. *Entrepreneurship Theory and Practice*, *37*(3), 505–537. doi:10.1111/etap.12021

De Moraes, J., & Benvenutti De Andrade, E. (2015). Who are the citizens of the digital citizenship? *International Review of Information Ethics*, *23*, 4–19.

De Pablo López, I. (2005). *El emprendizaje social: motor de desarrollo y cohesión social. V Seminario de creación de empresas. Cantoblanco*. Madrid, Spain: Autonomous University of Madrid.

De Pelsmacker, P., van Tilburg, S., & Holthof, C. (2018). Digital marketing strategies, online reviews, and hotel performance. *International Journal of Hospitality Management*, *72*, 47–55. doi:10.1016/j.ijhm.2018.01.003

De Ruyter, K., Isobel Keeling, D., & Ngo, L. V. (2018). When nothing is what it seems: A digital marketing research agenda. *Australasian Marketing Journal*, *10*, 1–4. doi:10.1016/j.ausmj.2018.07.003

De Sá, J. (2012). Las prácticas de gestión de marketing en las cooperativas portuguesas. *CIRIEC-España. C.I.R.I.E.C. España*, *76*, 199–227.

De Soto, H. (2000). *El misterio del capital*. Bogota, Colombia: Planeta.

De Valck, K., Van Bruggen, G. H., & Wierenga, B. (2009). Virtual communities: A marketing perspective. *Decision Support Systems*, *47*(3), 185–203. doi:10.1016/j.dss.2009.02.008

De Vitoria, F. (1535). *De eo ad quod tenetur veniens ad usum rationis*. Universidad Pontificia de Salamanca.

Deb, P., & Wiklund, J. (2017). The effects of CEO founder status and stock ownership on entrepreneurial orientation in small firms. *Journal of Small Business Management*, *55*(1), 32–55. doi:10.1111/jsbm.12231

Dees, J. G., & Anderson, B. B. (2006). Framing a theory of social entrepreneurship: Building on two schools of practice and thought. In R. Mosher-Williams (Ed.), *Research on social entrepreneurship: Understanding and contributing to an emerging field* (pp. 39-66). ARNOVA Occasional Paper Series.

Dees, J.G. (2001). *The Meaning of Social Entrepreneurship*. Retrieved from http://www.caseatduke.org/documents/dees_sedef.pdf

Dees, G. E. (2001). *Strategic tools for social entrepreneurs*. John Wiley & Sons.

Dees, J. G. (2005). Social entrepreneurship and education. *Current Issues in Comparative Education*, *8*(1), 51–55.

Dees, J. G. (2007). Taking social entrepreneurship seriously. *Society*, *44*(3), 24–31. doi:10.1007/BF02819936

Dees, J. G. (2017). The Meaning of Social Entrepreneurship. In *Case Studies in Social Entrepreneurship and Sustainability* (pp. 34–42). London, UK: Routledge.

Dees, J. G., Anderson, B. B., & Wei-Skillern, J. (2004). Scaling social impact. *Stanford Social Innovation Review*, *1*(4), 24–33.

Defourny, J., Favreau, L., & Laville, J. L. (Eds.). (1998). Insertion et nouvelle économie sociale. Un bilan international. Paris: Desclée de Brouwer.

Defourny, J., Hulgård, L., & Pestoff, V. (2014). *Social Enterprise and the Third Sector: Changing European Landscapes in a Comparative Perspective*. Routledge. doi:10.4324/9780203487747

Defourny, J., & Nyssens, M. (2010). Conceptions of social enterprise and social entrepreneurship in Europe and the United States: Convergences and divergences. *Journal of Social Entrepreneurship*, *1*(1), 32–53. doi:10.1080/19420670903442053

Dejaeghere, J. (2013). La educación, las habilidades y la ciudadanía: Un modelo emergente de la iniciativa empresarial en Tanzania. *Education and Computing*, *49*(4), 503–519.

Del Águila, A. (2000). *Comercio electrónico y estrategia empresarial*. Madrid, Spain: RA-MA.

Del Olmo, J., & Fondevila, J. (2014). *Marketing digital en la moda*. Madrid, Spain: Ediciones Universidad de Navarra.

Delgado-García, J. B., & de La Fuente-Sabaté, J. M. (2010). How do CEO emotions matter? Impact of CEO affective traits on strategic and performance conformity in the Spanish banking industry. *Strategic Management Journal*, *31*(5), 562–574.

Delmar, F., Davidsson, P., & Gartner, W. (2003). Arriving at the high-growth firm. *Journal of Business Venturing*, *18*(2), 189–216. doi:10.1016/S0883-9026(02)00080-0

Déniz-Déniz, M. C., Cabrera-Suárez, M. K., & Martín-Santana, J. D. (2018). Family firms and the interests of non-family stakeholders, The influence of family managers' affective commitment and family salience in terms of power. *Business Ethics European Review*, *27*(1), 15–28. doi:10.1111/beer.12155

Dess, G., & Beard, D. (1984). Dimensions of organizational task environments. *Administrative Science Quarterly*, *29*(1), 52–73. doi:10.2307/2393080

Dholakia, U. M., Bagozzi, R. P., & Pearo, L. K. (2004). A social influence model of consumer participation in network-and small-group-based virtual communities. *International Journal of Research in Marketing*, *21*(3), 241–263. doi:10.1016/j.ijresmar.2003.12.004

Di Pietro, L., Di Virgilio, F., & Pantano, E. (2012). Social network for the choice of tourist destination: Attitude and behavioural intention. *Journal of Hospitality and Tourism Technology*, *3*(1), 60–76. doi:10.1108/17579881211206543

Diario El Universo. (2018). *Estrategias para que la pequeña y mediana empresa mantengan su posición*. Author.

Diéguez-Soto, J., & López-Delgado, P. (2018) Does family and lone founder involvement lead to similar indebtedness? *Journal of Small Business Management*. doi:10.1111/jsbm.12422

Diez-Olivan, A., Del Ser, J., Galar, D., & Sierra, B. (2019). Data fusion and machine learning for industrial prognosis: Trends and perspectives towards Industry 4.0. *Information Fusion*, *50*, 92–111. doi:10.1016/j.inffus.2018.10.005

Digilina, O. B., Teslenko, I. B., & Abdullaev, N. V. (2019). Industry 4.0: Contents, problems, and perspectives. *Advances in Intelligent Systems and Computing*, *726*, 32–38. doi:10.1007/978-3-319-90835-9_4

Di-Noia, T., Di Sciascio, E., Donini, F. M., & Mongiello, M. (2004). A System for Principled Matchmaking in an Electronic Marketplace. *International Journal of Electronic Commerce*, *8*(4), 9–37. doi:10.1080/10864415.2004.11044308

Distaso, A. (2007). Well-being and/or quality of life in EU countries through a multidimensional index of sustainability. *Ecological Economics*, *64*(1), 163–180. doi:10.1016/j.ecolecon.2007.02.025

Dobni, C. B. (2008). The DNA of innovation. *The Journal of Business Strategy*, *29*(2), 43–50. doi:10.1108/02756660810858143

Doherty, B., & Thompson, J. (2006). The diverse world of social enterprise. *International Journal of Social Economics*, *33*(5/6), 361–375. doi:10.1108/03068290610660643

Dolado, J. J., González-Páramo, J. M., & Roldán, J. M. (1994). Convergencia económica entre las regiones españolas: Evidencia empírica (1955-1989). *Moneda y Crédito*, *198*, 81–119.

Domínguez, M., Blancas, F. J., Guerrero, F. M., & González, M. (2011). Una revisión crítica para la construcción de indicadores sintéticos. *Revista de Métodos Cuantitativos para la Economía y la Empresa*, *11*, 41–70.

Dorado, S. (2006). Social entrepreneurial ventures: Different values so different process of creation? *Journal of Developmental Entrepreneurship*, *11*(4), 319–343. doi:10.1142/S1084946706000453

Dou, W., Lim, K. H., Su, C., Zhou, N., & Cui, N. (2010). Brand positioning strategy using search engine marketing. *Management Information Systems Quarterly*, *34*(2), 261–279. doi:10.2307/20721427

Dowlatshahi, S. (2000). Developing a Theory of Reverse Logistics. *Interfaces*, *30*(3), 143–155. doi:10.1287/inte.30.3.143.11670

Dowling, G. R. (1993). Developing your corporate image into a corporate asset. *Journal of Long Range Planning*, *26*(2), 101–109. doi:10.1016/0024-6301(93)90141-2

Doz, Y. L., & Kosonen, M. (2010). Embedding strategic agility. A leadership agenda for accelerating business model renewal. *Long Range Planning*, *43*(2), 370–382. doi:10.1016/j.lrp.2009.07.006

Drayton, B. (2015). *Social entrepreneurs are not content just to give a fish or teach how to fish Ashoka - USA*. Retrieved from http://usa.ashoka.org/social-entrepreneurs-are-not-content-just-give-fish-or-teach-how-fish

Drayton, B. (2002). The citizen sector: Becoming as entrepreneurial and competitive as a business. *California Management Review*, *44*(3), 120–132. doi:10.2307/41166136

Drexel, I. (2003). *Two Lectures. The Concept of Competence – an Instrument of Social and Political Change. Centrally Coordinated Decentralization – No Problem? Lessons from the Italian Case.* Stein Rokkan Centre for Social Studies, Working Paper 26. Bergen, Norway: Uni Research.

Drucker, P. (1984). *La innovación y el empresario innovador*. Bogota, Colombia: Editorial Norma.

Drucker, P. F. (1993). *Gerencia para el Futuro*. Bogota, Colombia: Editorial Norma.

Du, S., Bhattacharya, C. B., & Sen, S. (2009). *Strengthening consumer relationships through corporate social responsibility.* Working paper, Simmons College School of Management.

Duncan, R. (1972). Characteristics of organizational environments and perceived environmental uncertainty. *Administrative Science Quarterly*, *17*(3), 313–327. doi:10.2307/2392145

Duque, D. (2016). *El marketing social como metodología diferencial en la estrategia de negocio de las organizaciones (Master's Degree Project)*. Manizales, Colombia: Universidad Nacional de Colombia.

Duque-Escobar, G. (2015). The urban and economic development of Manizales. *The POT of Manizales: 'Collective Let's Get on the Bus of the POT' SMP of Manizales Conference.*

Du, W., Pan, S. L., Zhou, N., & Ouyang, T. (2018). From an electronics marketplace to a digital entrepreneurial ecosystem (DEE): The emergence of a meta-organization in Zhongguancun, China. *Information Systems Journal*, *28*(6), 1158–1175. doi:10.1111/isj.12176

Dwyer, F., Schurr, P., & Oh, S. (1987). Developing buyer-seller relationships. *Journal of Marketing*, *51*(2), 11–27. doi:10.1177/002224298705100202

Dyer, W. G. (2006). Examining the "family effect" on firm performance. *Family Business Review*, *19*(4), 253–273. doi:10.1111/j.1741-6248.2006.00074.x

Dyer, W. G. Jr, & Dyer, W. J. (2009). Putting the family into family business research. *Family Business Review*, *22*(3), 216–219. doi:10.1177/0894486509333042

Echecopar, G., Angelelli, P., Galleguillos, G., & Schorr, M. (2006). *Seed capital for the financing of new companies Advances and lessons learned in Latin America.* Washington, DC: Inter-American Development Bank.

ECOTEC. (2007). *Design and implementation of the pilot action ERASMUS for young entrepreneurs, enterprise and industry.* Working Paper, 2. Brussels: Author.

Eddleston, K. A., Kellermanns, F. W., Floyd, S. W., Crittenden, V. L., & Crittenden, W. F. (2013). Planning for growth, Life stage differences in family firms. *Entrepreneurship Theory and Practice*, *37*(5), 1177–1202. doi:10.1111/etap.12002

Eddleston, K. A., Kellermanns, F. W., & Sarathy, R. (2008). Resource configuration in family firms, Linking resources, strategic planning and technological opportunities to performance. *Journal of Management Studies*, *45*(1), 26–50.

Eddy, J. (2006). Learning through teaching model results in improved student learning. *Teaching Matters*, *10*(2), 1–31.

Edmonson, A., & McManus, S. (2007). Methodological Fit in Management Field Research. *Academy of Management Review*, *32*(4), 1155–1179.

Egbe-Okpenge, E. G., & Igbo, H. I. (2012). Relación entre la Consejería y Emprendimiento Desarrollo de Habilidades de Nigerianos Fin de Carrera de Pregrado. *III World Conference on Psychology, Counseling, and Orientation (WCPCG 2012)*, *84*, 120-127.

Eigenraam, A. W., Eelen, J., van Lin, A., & Verlegh, P. W. J. (2018). A Consumer-Based Taxonomy of Digital Customer Engagement Practices. *Journal of Interactive Marketing*, *44*, 102–121. doi:10.1016/j.intmar.2018.07.002

EIM. (2003). *Entrepreneurship in Europe Green Paper.* Zoetermeer, The Netherlands: EIM Business & Policy Research.

Eisenhardt, K., & Martin, J. (2000). Dynamic Capabilities. What are they? *Strategic Management Journal*, *21*(10/11), 1105–1121. doi:10.1002/1097-0266(200010/11)21:10/11<1105::AID-SMJ133>3.0.CO;2-E

Elias, R. Z. (2004). An examination of business students' perception of Corporate Social Responsibilities before and after bankruptcies. *Journal of Business Ethics*, *52*(3), 267–281. doi:10.1023/B:BUSI.0000037558.74693.d5

Empathica. (n.d.). *White paper: What is the Opportunity for "SoLoMo" (Social.Local.Mobile.) to Improve the Customer Experience?* Author.

Endemann, W. (1874). Studien in der romanisch-kanonistischen Wirtschafts und Rechtslehre bis gegen 16 Jahrhunderts [Studies Done in the Roman-Canonique Economics and Law until the Sixteenth Century]. Berlin: Academic Press.

Engelen, A., Kube, H., Schmidt, S., & Flatten, T. C. (2014). Entrepreneurial orientation in turbulent environments, The moderating role of absorptive capacity. *Research Policy*, *43*(8), 1353–1369. doi:10.1016/j.respol.2014.03.002

Ensley, M. D., & Pearson, A. W. (2005). An exploratory comparison of the behavioral dynamics of top management teams in family and non-family new ventures, Cohesion, conflict, potency, and consensus. *Entrepreneurship Theory and Practice*, *29*(3), 267–284. doi:10.1111/j.1540-6520.2005.00082.x

Eriksson, M., Einarsson, T., & Wijkström, F. (2014). Report on the European social innovation policy framework in light of the third sector and civil society actors. A deliverable of the project: 'Impact of the Third Sector as Social Innovation' (ITSSOIN), European Commission–7th Framework Programme, Brussels, Belgium.

Ernest, K., Matthew, S. K., & Samuel, A. K. (2015). Towards Entrepreneurial Learning Competences. The Perspective of Built Environment Students. *Higher Education Studies*, *5*(1), 20–30. doi:10.5539/hes.v5n1p20

Escalona-Orcao, A. I., & Escolano-Utrilla, S. (2016). The potential for the intelligent development of rural areas: The spatial clusters of creative activities in Spain. *Revista de Geografía Norte Grande*, *65*, 91–107. doi:10.4067/S0718-34022016000300005

Esping-Andersen, G. (2002). *Why we need a new welfare state.* Oxford University Press. doi:10.1093/0199256438.001.0001

Ettredge, M., Gerdes, J., & Karuga, G. (2005). Using web-based search data to predict macroeconomic statistics. *Communications of the ACM*, *48*(11), 87–92. doi:10.1145/1096000.1096010

Etzkowitz, H. (2003). Innovation in innovation: The triple helix of university-industry-government relations. *Social Sciences Information. Information Sur les Sciences Sociales*, *42*(3), 293–337. doi:10.1177/05390184030423002

Etzkowitz, H., & Klofsten, M. (2005). The innovating region: Toward a theory of knowledge-based regional development. *R & D Management*, *35*(3), 243–255. doi:10.1111/j.1467-9310.2005.00387.x

Etzkowitz, H., & Viale, R. (2010). Polyvalent knowledge and the entrepreneurial university: A third academic revolution? *Critical Sociology*, *36*(4), 595–609. doi:10.1177/0896920510365921

European Commission. (2013). *Social economy and social entrepreneurship. In Social Europe guide* (Vol. 4). Brussels, Belgium: European Commission, Directorate-General for Employment.

European Qualifications Framework (EQF). (2014). Online at http.//ec.europa.eu/eqf/terms_en.htm

Evans, D. S., & Schmalensee, R. (2016). *Matchmakers: the new economics of multi-sided platforms*. Boston: Harvard Business Review Press.

Falkenreck, C., & Wagner, R. (2017). The Internet of Things – Chance and challenge in industrial business relationships. *Industrial Marketing Management*, *66*, 181–195. doi:10.1016/j.indmarman.2017.08.007

Fargion, S., Gevorgianiene, V., & Lievens, P. (2011). Developing entrepreneurship in social work through international education. Reflections on a European intensive program. *The International Journal of Entrepreneurship Education*, *30*(8), 964–980.

Fariborzi, E., & Zahedifard, M. (2012). E-mail Marketing: Advantages, Disadvantages and Improving Techniques. *International Journal of e-Education, e-Business, e-. Management Learning*, *2*(3), 232.

Farshid, M., Paschen, J., Eriksson, T., & Kietzmann, J. (2018). Go boldly!: Explore augmented reality (AR), virtual reality (VR), and mixed reality (MR) for business. *Business Horizons*, *61*(5), 657–663. doi:10.1016/j.bushor.2018.05.009

Fayol, H. (2003). *Administración industrial y general*. Bogota, Colombia: Stilo Impresores.

Ferkolj, A. (2010). *Enterprise risk management analysis with suggestions for improvements for the selected company* (Master's thesis). University of Ljubljana Faculty of Economics, Ljubljana.

Fernández, A. D., Adenso, D. F., Gil, M. J. A., José, Á. G. M., Torre, P. G., & Pilar, G. T. (2004). *Logística inversa y medio ambiente: aspectos estratégicos y operativos*. Madrid, Spain: McGraw-Hill Interamericana de España S.L.

Fernández, J., & Hernández, F. (2018). *Measurement and Diagnosis of Digital Entrepreneurship Ecosystems (MIDE-Digital) – Metropolitana*. Santiago, Chile: Universidad del Desarrollo.

Fernández-Pérez, V., Alonso-Galicia, P. E., Del Mar Fuentes-Fuentes, M., & Rodriguez-Ariza, L. (2014). Business social networks and academics' entrepreneurial intentions. *Industrial Management & Data Systems*, *114*(2), 292–320. doi:10.1108/IMDS-02-2013-0076

Ferrajoli, L. (2013). *Dei diritti e delle garanzie. Conversazione con M. Barberis*. Il Mulino.

Feshina, S. S., Konovalova, O. V., & Sinyavsky, N. G. (2019). Industry 4.0—Transition to new economic reality. *Studies in Systems, Decision, and Control*, *169*, 111–120. doi:10.1007/978-3-319-94310-7_11

Filippi, S., & Barattin, D. (2018).. . *Advances in Usability and User Experience*, *607*. doi:10.1007/978-3-319-60492-3

Fini, R., Grimaldi, R., & Sobrero, M. (2009). Factors fostering academics to start up new ventures: An assessment of Italian founders' incentives. *The Journal of Technology Transfer*, *34*(4), 380–402. doi:10.100710961-008-9093-z

Finlev, T., Maguire, R., Oppenheim, B., & Skvirsky, S. (2017). *Future Landscapes of the Orange Economy: Creative Pathways for Improving Lives in Latin America and the Caribbean*. Washington, DC: Inter-American Development Bank.

Fisher, T. (2009). ROI in social media: A look at the arguments. *Database Marketing & Customer Strategy Management*, *16*(3), 189–195. doi:10.1057/dbm.2009.16

Flavián, C., Ibáñez-Sánchez, S., & Orús, C. (2018). The impact of virtual, augmented and mixed reality technologies on the customer experience. *Journal of Business Research*, *10*, 1–14. doi:10.1016/j.jbusres.2018.10.050

Fleit, C. (2013). *Direct marketing news. Core competences make the difference in marketing*. Online at http.//www.dmnews.com/marketing-leaders-must-get-results/article/275003

Fleming, P., & Alberdiu, M. J. (2000). *Hablemos de marketing*. Madrid, Spain: ESIC Editorial.

Flick, U. (2002). An introduction to qualitative research. *Sage (Atlanta, Ga.)*.

Fombrun, C., Gardberg, N. A., & Barnett, M. L. (2000). Opportunity platforms and safety nets: Corporate citizenship and reputational risk. *Business and Society Review*, *105*(1), 85–106. doi:10.1111/0045-3609.00066

Fombrun, C., & Shanley, M. (1990). What's in a name? Reputation building and corporate strategy. *Academy of Management Journal*, *33*, 233–258.

Fonseca-Reis, A. C. (2008). *Creative economy: as a development strategy: a view of developing countries*. São Paulo, Brazil: Itaú Cultural.

Fontela, E., Guzmán, J., Pérez, M., & Santos, F. (2006). The Art of Entrepreneurial Foresight. *Foresight*, *8*(6), 3–13. doi:10.1108/14636680610712496

Forehand, M. R., & Grier, S. (2003). When is honesty the best policy? The effect of a stated company intent on consumer skepticism. *Journal of Consumer Psychology*, *13*(3), 349–356. doi:10.1207/S15327663JCP1303_15

Forouharfar, A., Rowshan, S.A., & Salarzehi, H. (2018). An epistemological critique of social entrepreneurship definitions. *Journal of Global Entrepreneurship Research*, 1-40.

Fossen, F. M., & Bütner, T. J. M. (2013). The returns to education for opportunity entrepreneurs, necessity entrepreneurs, and paid employees. *Economics of Education Review*, *37*(1), 68–84.

Fox, J. (2012). *The Economics of Well-Being*. Retrieved from https://hbr.org/2012/01/the-economics-of-well-being

Friedman, M. (1970, September 13). The social responsibility of business is to increase its profits. *New York Times Magazine*.

Fujisawa, Y., Ishida, Y., Nagatomi, S., & Iwasaki, K. (2015). A Study of Social Innovation Concepts: A Japanese Perspective. *Japan Social Innovation Journal*, *5*(1), 1–13. doi:10.12668/jsij.5.1

Fujita, M., & Thisse. (2002). *Economics of agglomeration Cities, industrial location, and regional growth*. Cambridge University Press.

Fullerton, J. (2015). *Regenerative Capitalism - How Universal Principles And Patterns Will Shape Our New Economy*. Greenwich, CT: Capital Institute. Retrieved from http://capitalinstitute.org/wp-content/uploads/2015/04/2015-Regenerative-Capitalism-4-20-15-final.pdf

Furtado, C. (1970). *Teoría y política del desarrollo económico*. México, D.F.: Siglo Veintiuno editores.

Gaiger, L. I. (2004). Emprendimientos económicos solidarios. In A. Cattani (Ed.), *La Otra Economía*. Buenos Aires, Argentina: Altamira-UNGS.

Galbraith, J. (2004). *La sociedad opulenta*. Barcelona, Spain: Ariel.

Galeano, A. R. (2008). Diseño centrado en el usuario. *Revista Educación Comunicación Tecnología, 2*(4), 1–5.

Gallegos, L. (2008). *Economía Social de Mercado, Medio Ambiente y Responsabilidad Social Empresarial*. Lima, Peru: Impresiones de Tarea Asociación Gráfica Educativa.

Gallino, L. (2014). *Vita rinviate. Lo scandalo del lavoro precario*. Roma-Bari: Editori Laterza.

Gallo, M. A., & Sveen, J. (1991). Internationalizing the Family Business: Facilitating and Restraining Factors. *Family Business Review, 4*(2), 181–190. doi:10.1111/j.1741-6248.1991.00181.x

Galloway, L., Anderson, M., Brown, W., & Wilson, L. (2005). Enterprise skills for the economy. *Education + Training, 47*(1), 7–17. doi:10.1108/00400910510580593

Gallurt Plá, P. (2010). *Creación de Spin-Offs en las Universidades Españolas: Un modelo de Intenciones (Doctoral Theses)*. Sevilla, Spain: Pablo de Olavide University.

Gálvez, M. M., Caba, M. C., & López, M. (2012). Responsabilidad social y transparencia on-line de las ONG: Análisis del caso español. *CIRIEC-España, Revista de Economía Pública. Social y Cooperativa, 74*, 207–238.

Gámir, L., & … . (2007). *Innovación y productividad*. Madrid, Spain: LID Editores.

Gandomi, A., & Haider, M. (2015). Beyond the hype: Big data concepts, methods, and analytics. *International Journal of Information Management, 35*(2), 137–144. doi:10.1016/j.ijinfomgt.2014.10.007

Garcés-Galdeano, L., Larraza-Kintana, M., García-Olaverri, C., & Makri, M. (2016). Entrepreneurial orientation in family firms, The moderating role of technological intensity and performance. *The International Entrepreneurship and Management Journal, 12*(1), 27–45. doi:10.100711365-014-0335-2

García, J. S. (2010). El marketing y su origen a la orientación social : desde la perspectiva económica a la social. Los aspectos de organizavión y comunicación, 17(1), 61–77.

García, J., Vialop, J., & Xurinachs, L. M. (2006). *La dimensión cooperativa: economía solidaria y transformación social*. Barcelona, Spain: Icaria.

Gartner, W. (1985). A Conceptual Framework for Describing the Phenomenon of New Venture Creation. *Academy of Management Review, 10*(4), 696–706. doi:10.5465/amr.1985.4279094

Geels, F. W. (2010). Ontologies, socio-technical transitions (to sustainability), and the multi-level perspective. *Research Policy, 39*(4), 495–510. doi:10.1016/j.respol.2010.01.022

Gehrke, D., & Turban, E. (1999, January). Determinants of successful website design: relative importance and recommendations for effectiveness. In HICSS (p. 5042). IEEE. doi:10.1109/HICSS.1999.772943

GEM. (2013). *Global Entrepreneurship Monitor España, 2012 y 2013*. Madrid, Spain: GEM.

GEM. (2016). *México. Reporte Regional Querétaro*. Querétaro, Mexico: Global Entrepreneurship Monitor.

Genchev, S. E. (2009). Reverse logistics program design: A company study. *Business Horizons, 52*(2), 139–148. doi:10.1016/j.bushor.2008.09.005

George, G., & Bock, A. J. (2011). The Business Model in Practice and its Implications for Entrepreneurship Research. *Entrepreneurship Theory and Practice, 35*(1), 83–111. doi:10.1111/j.1540-6520.2010.00424.x

Geroski, P., Mata, J., & Portugal, P. (2007). *Founding Conditions and the Survival of New Firms*. Copenhagen, Denmark: Danish Research Unit for Industrial Dynamics.

Gerrikogoitia, J., Castander, I., Rebón, F., & Alzua-Sorzabal, A. (2015). New trends in smart electronic marketing based on web mining for electronic stores. *Procedia Ciencias Sociales y del Comportamiento., 175*, 75–83.

Getto, G., & Moore, C. (2017). Mapping Personas: Designing UX Relationships for an Online Coastal Atlas. *Computers and Composition, 43*, 15–34. doi:10.1016/j.compcom.2016.11.008

Ghatak, M. (1999). Group Lending, Local Information, and Peer Selection. *Journal of Development Economics, 60*(1), 27–50. doi:10.1016/S0304-3878(99)00035-8

Ghatak, M., & Guinnane, T. W. (1999). The economics of lending with joint liability: Theory and practice. *Journal of Development Economics, 60*(1), 195–228. doi:10.1016/S0304-3878(99)00041-3

Ghemawat. (1991). *Commitment, the Dynamics of Strategy*. Free Press.

Gibbs, S. (2018). Flickr bought by SmugMug as Yahoo breakup begins. *The Guardian*. Retrieved from: https://www.theguardian.com/technology/2018/apr/23/flickr-bought-by-smugmug-yahoo-breakup

Gilbert, C., Eyring, M., & Foster, R. N. (2012). Two Routes to Resiliency. Rebuild your core while you reinvent your business model. *Harvard Business Review, 90*(12), 66–73.

Giménez, D. A., Calabrò, A., Edelman, L. F., Minola, T., & Cassia, L. (2018) The impact of affective commitment and in-group-collectivism on daughters' succession intentions. *Academy of Management Proceedings, 18*(1). Available in https://journals.aom.org/doi/abs/10.5465/AMBPP.2018.223

Gintis, H. (2000). Beyond *Homo economicus*: Evidence from Experimental Economics. *Ecological Economics, 35*(3), 311–322. doi:10.1016/S0921-8009(00)00216-0

Giovanelli, F. (2014, September). Economia sociale di mercato. Una risposta alla crisi? *XIV International Conference on the Role of the Catholic Church in a Process of the European Integration.*

Global Entrepreneurship Monitor. (2006). *Global report summary*. London, UK: Author.

Goel, S., Voordeckers, W., Van Gils, A., & van den Heuvel, J. (2013). CEO's empathy and salience of socioemotional wealth in family SMEs–The moderating role of external directors. *Entrepreneurship and Regional Development, 25*(3-4), 111–134. doi:10.1080/08985626.2012.710262

Goldstein, H., & Drucker, J. (2006). The economic development impacts of universities on regions: Do size and distance matter? *Economic Development Quarterly, 20*(1), 22–43. doi:10.1177/0891242405283387

Gómez, F., & Robledo, R. (Eds.). (1998). El pensamiento económico de la Escuela de Salamanca. Salamanca, Spain: University of Salamanca.

Gomez, R., & Santor, R. (2003). *Do peer group members outperform individual borrowers? A test of peer group lending using Canadian micro-credit data.* Bank of Canada Working Paper, No. 33.

Gómez-Martínez, R. (2013). Señales de inversión basadas en un índice de aversión al riesgo. *Investigaciones Europeas de Dirección y Economía de la Empresa, 19*(3), 147–157. doi:10.1016/j.iedee.2012.12.001

Gómez-Martínez, R., Plaza-Casado, P., Prado-Román, C., & Prado-Román, M. (2016). Google Trends como indicador válido para los ingresos por la producción de vino. *Tourism and Hospitality International Journal*, *6*(2), 94–106.

Gómez-Martínez, R., Prado-Román, C., & Díez-Martín, F. (2016). Google Search Activity as Thermometer of Wine Cellar Visitors. In M. Peris-Ortiz, M. Del Río Rama, & C. Rueda-Armengot (Eds.), *Wine and Tourism*. Springer. doi:10.1007/978-3-319-18857-7_17

Gómez-Martínez, R., Prado-Román, M., & Mercado-Idoeta, C. (2015). Google Search Activity as Entrepreneurship Thermometer. In M. Peris-Ortiz & J. M. Sahut (Eds.), *New Challenges in Entrepreneurship and Finance*. Springer. doi:10.1007/978-3-319-08888-4_16

Gómez-Martínez, R., Rodríguez Herráez, B., & Pérez-Bustamante Yábar, D. C. (2016). Actividad de búsquedas en internet como variable para determinar la afluencia a museos. *Cuadernos de Turismo*, *38*, 203–219.

Gómez-Mejía, L. R., Cruz, C., Berrone, P., & De Castro, J. (2011). The bind that ties, Socioemotional wealth preservation in family firms. *The Academy of Management Annals*, *5*(1), 653–707. doi:10.5465/19416520.2011.593320

Gómez-Mejía, L. R., Haynes, K. T., Núñez-Nickel, M., Jacobson, K. J., & Moyano-Fuentes, J. (2007). Socioemotional wealth and business risks in family-controlled firms, Evidence from Spanish olive oil mills. *Administrative Science Quarterly*, *52*(1), 106–137. doi:10.2189/asqu.52.1.106

González, Z., & Plaza, N. (2017). Estrategias de marketing digital en el sector de la mode de lujo. Interacción y redes sociales como herramienta necesaria. *Revista Académica sobre Documentación Digital y Comunicación Interactiva, 15*, 17–27.

González, A. A., Linck, T., & Moguel, R. (2003). El comercio de valores éticos: Las reglas del juego de café solidario. *Revista Europea de Estudios Latinoamericanos y del Caribe*, *75*(75), 31–45. doi:10.18352/erlacs.9692

Gordon, I. R., & McCann, P. (2000). Innovation, agglomeration and regional development. *Journal of Economic Geography*, *5*(5), 523–543. doi:10.1093/jeg/lbh072

Gorosquieta, J. (1941). El sistema de ideas tributarias en los teólogos y moralistas principales de la «Escuela de Salamanca» (siglos XVI y XVII). Madrid: Academic Press.

Grahammer, J. C. D., & Grahammer, C. D. (2013). Lost in Theorization: On the Effectiveness of Policies to Promote Creative Industries in Peru. *Derecho & Sociedad*, *49*, 39–54.

Grant, R. (1991). The Resource-Based Theory of Competitive Advantage: Implications for Strategy Formulation. *California Management Review*, *33*(3), 114–135. doi:10.2307/41166664

Grant, R. M. (2010). *Contemporary Strategy Analysis*. Chichester, UK: John Wiley & Sons.

Green, C. J., Kirkpatrick, C. H., & Murinde, V. (2006). Finance for small enterprise growth and poverty reduction in developing countries. *Journal of International Development*, *18*(7), 1017–1030. doi:10.1002/jid.1334

Green, K. M., Covin, J. G., & Slevin, D. P. (2008). Exploring the relationship between strategic reactiveness and entrepreneurial orientation. The role of structure style fit. *Journal of Business Venturing*, *23*(3), 356–383. doi:10.1016/j.jbusvent.2007.01.002

Grice-Hutchinson, M. (1952). *The School of Salamanca: Readings in Spanish Monetary Theory*. Oxford University Press.

Grice-Hutchinson, M. (1982). *El pensamiento económico en España (1117-1740)*. Barcelona, Spain: Crítica.

Grice-Hutchinson, M. (1989). El concepto de la Escuela de Salamanca: Sus orígenes y su desarrollo. *Revista de Historia Económica*, *2*, 22–26.

Grönross, C. (1994). *Marketing y gestión de servicios*. Madrid, Spain: Díaz de Santos S.A.

Grundey, D., & .... (2008). El Papel de la Política Institucional de Desarrollo de Emprendimiento Innovador en Lituania. *Transformaciones en Negocios y Economía, 7*(2), 86–101.

Grzega, J. (2003). *LdL in universitären Kursen. Ein hochschuldidaktischer Weg zur Vorbereitung auf die Wissensgesellschaft*. Retrieved from http://www. ldl. de/material/berichte/uni/ldl

Grzega, J. (2005). *Learning By Teaching. The Didactic Model LdL in University Classes*. Retrieved from http://www. ldl. de/material/berichte/uni/uni. htm

Grzega, J., & Schöner, M. (2008). The didactic model (Lernen durch Lehren) as a way of preparing students for communication in a knowledge society. *Journal of Education for Teaching, 34*(3), 167–175. doi:10.1080/02607470802212157

Gudivada, V. N., Rao, D., & Paris, J. (2015). Understanding search-engine optimization. *Computer, 48*(10), 43–52. doi:10.1109/MC.2015.297

Guerin, K. (2002). *Subsidiarity. Implications for New Zealand.* Treasury Working Paper Series, 02/03. Wellington, New Zealand: New Zealand Treasury.

Guerra, L. (2006). La economía de la solidaridad. O la vuelta de los valores sociales a la economía. *Revista Umbrales, 168*, 1–7.

Guerrero, L. (2012, Sep 28). Obsolescencia programada y e-waste. *Revista Fortuna.*

Guerrero, M. (2018). La importancia de las empresas de servicios en el desarrollo de los países de economías emergentes. *INNOVA, 3*, 1–5.

Guerrero, M., & Urbano, D. (2014). Academics" start-up intentions and knowledge filters: An individual perspective of the knowledge spillover theory of entrepreneurship. *Small Business Economics, 43*(1), 57–74. doi:10.100711187-013-9526-4

Guerrero, M., Urbano, D., & Gajón, E. (2014). The internal pathways that condition university entrepreneurship in Latin America: An institutional approach. In *Innovative Pathways for University Entrepreneurship in the 21st Century* (pp. 89–118). Emerald Group Publishing Limited. doi:10.1108/S1048-473620140000024004

Gummesson, E. (2002). *Total Relationship Marketing* (2nd ed.). Oxford, UK: Butterworth-Heinemann.

Gundlach, G. T., Achrol, R. S., & Mentzer, J. T. (1995). The structure of commitment in exchange. *Journal of Marketing, 59*(1), 78–92. doi:10.1177/002224299505900107

Gundlach, M., & Zivnuska, S. (2010). An experiential learning approach to teaching social entrepreneurship, triple bottom line, and sustainability: Modifying and extending practical organizational behavior education. *American Journal of Business Education, 3*(1), 19–29. doi:10.19030/ajbe.v3i1.364

Gutierrez, C., & Nava Rogel, R. M. (2016). Mercadotecnia digital y las pequeñas y medianas empresas: revisión de la literatura. *Enlace, 13*, 45-61.

Gutiérrez, H., & Montemayor, E. (2015). *Academic Entrepreneurship in Mexico An analysis of the most significant resources influencing university researchers to create academic spinoffs.* Panel Session 3: Entrepreneurial University and Triple Helix's development, 77.

Guzman, G. (2011). Internet search behavior as an economic forecasting tool: The case of inflation expectations. *Journal of Economic and Social Measurement, 36*(3), 119–167.

Guzmán, J., & Liñán, F. (2005). *Perspectives on Entrepreneurial Education: A US-Europe Comparison*. Madrid, Spain: Jean Monnet European Studies Center-Nebrija University.

Guzmán-Vásquez, A., & Trujillo-Dávila, M. A. (2008). Emprendimiento social-revisión de literatura. *Estudios Gerenciales*, *24*(109), 105–125. doi:10.1016/S0123-5923(08)70055-X

H.H. Benedicto XVI. (2009). *Carta Encíclica "Caritas in Veritate" sobre el desarrollo humano integral en la caridad y en la verdad*. The Vatican City: Author.

H.H. Francisco. (2013). *Exhortación Apostólica "Evangelii Gaudium" sobre el anuncio del Evangelio en el mundo actual*. The Vatican City: Author.

H.H. León XIII. (1891). *Carta Encíclica Rerum Novarum sobre la situación de los obreros*. The Vatican City: Author.

H.H. Pablo VI. (1967). *Carta Encíclica Populorum Progressio sobre la necesidad de promover el desarrollo de los pueblos*. The Vatican City: Author.

H.H. Pío XI. (1931). *Carta Encíclica Quadragesimo Anno, sobre la restauración del orden social en perfecta conformidad con la ley evangélica*. The Vatican City: Author.

Ha-Brookshire, J. E. (2009). Does the firm size matter on firm entrepreneurship: US apparel import intermediary case. *Journal of Small Business and Enterprise Development*, *16*(1), 131–145. doi:10.1108/14626000910932926

Hair, J. F., Anderson, R. E., Tatham, R. L., & Black, W. C. (2007). *Análisis multivariante*. Madrid, Spain: Pearson-Prentice Hall.

Hall, J. (2010). Measuring what Matters to Make a Difference. *Journal of Futures Studies*, *15*(2), 151–154.

Harman, H. H. (1967). *Modern factor analysis*. Chicago: University of Chicago Press.

Harper, M., & Vogel, R. (2005). The Role of Savings as a form of MFI Funding: Debate. *MicroBanking Bulletin*, *11*, 5–9.

Hasan, B. (2016). Perceived irritation in online shopping: The impact of website design characteristics. *Computers in Human Behavior*, *54*, 224–230. doi:10.1016/j.chb.2015.07.056

Haugh, H. (2007). Community-led social venture creation. *Entrepreneurship Theory and Practice*, *31*(2), 161–182. doi:10.1111/j.1540-6520.2007.00168.x

Hayek, F. (2002). Competition as a discovery procedure. *The Quarterly Journal of Austrian Economics*, *5*(3), 9–23. doi:10.100712113-002-1029-0

Hayek, M., Randolph-Seng, B., Atinc, G., & Montalvo, D. (2018). The influence of political skill on career success in an Ecuadorian family firm, The mediating role of affective commitment. *International Journal of Cross Cultural Management*, *18*(2), 175–190. doi:10.1177/1470595818768347

Healy, M. J., Beverland, M. B., Oppewal, H., & Sands, S. (2007). Understanding retail experiences-the case for ethnography. *International Journal of Market Research*, *49*(6), 751–778. doi:10.1177/147078530704900608

Heckadon, D. A. (2010). *Critical success factors for creating and implementing effective social media marketing campaigns* (Master thesis). New York University.

Heiberger, R. H. (2015). Collective Attention and Stock Prices: Evidence from Google Trends Data on Standard and Poor's 100. *PLoS One*, *10*(8), e0135311. doi:10.1371/journal.pone.0135311 PMID:26258498

Hemmen, S. (2015). Leadership styles and innovative entrepreneurship: An international study. *Cybernetics and Systems*, *46*(3-4), 271–286. doi:10.1080/01969722.2015.1012896

Hennig-Thurau, T., Malthouse, E. C., Friege, C., Gensler, S., Lobschat, L., Rangaswamy, A., & Skiera, B. (2010). The impact of new media on customer relationships. *Journal of Service Research, 13*(3), 311–330. doi:10.1177/1094670510375460

Hernández, R., Fernández, C., & Baptista, P. (2014). Research Metodology (6th ed.). Mexico D.F., Mexico: McGraw-Hill.

Hernández, I. (2008). *Empresa, innovación y desarrollo.* Bogota, Colombia: Universidad Nacional de Colombia.

Hernández-Linares, R, López-Fernández, MC, & Fielden, L.V. (forthcoming). The moderating effect of the family firm status on the relationship between entrepreneurial orientation and SMEs performance. An empirical study in Portugal.

Hernández-Linares, R. (2017). *Análisis de la relación entre orientación emprendedora, orientación al mercado, orientación al aprendizaje y rendimiento de la organización. La influencia del contexto organizacional, empresa familiar versus empresa no familiar* (Unpublished doctoral dissertation). University of Cantabria, Spain.

Hernández-Linares, R., Kellermanns, F. W., & López-Fernández, M. C. (2018a). A note on the relationship between learning, market, and entrepreneurial orientations in family and nonfamily firms. *Journal of Family Business Strategy, 9*(3), 192–204. doi:10.1016/j.jfbs.2018.08.001

Hernández-Linares, R., Kellermanns, F. W., & López-Fernández, M. C. (2018b). Dynamic capabilities and SME performance, The moderating effect of market orientation. *Journal of Small Business Management.* doi:10.1111/jsbm.12474

Hernández-Linares, R., & López-Fernández, M. C. (2018). Entrepreneurial orientation and the family firm, Mapping the field and tracing a path for future research. *Family Business Review, 31*(3), 318–351. doi:10.1177/0894486518781940

Hernández-Linares, R., Sarkar, S., & Cobo, M. J. (2018b). Inspecting the Achilles heel, a quantitative analysis of 50 years of family business definitions. *Scientometrics, 115*(2), 929–951. doi:10.100711192-018-2702-1

Hernández-Linares, R., Sarkar, S., & López-Fernández, M. C. (2017). How has the family firm literature addressed its heterogeneity through classification systems? An integrated analysis. *European Journal of Family Business, 7*(1-2), 1–13. doi:10.1016/j.ejfb.2017.06.003

Herrerías, A. (2006). *Fundamentos para la historia del pensamiento económico.* D.F., Mexico: Limusa.

Herrmann, P., & Nadkarni, S. (2014). Managing strategic change. The duality of CEO personality. *Strategic Management Journal, 35*(9), 1318–1342. doi:10.1002mj.2156

Herscovitch, L., & Meyer, J. P. (2002). Commitment to organizational change, Extension of a three-component model. *The Journal of Applied Psychology, 87*(3), 474–487. doi:10.1037/0021-9010.87.3.474 PMID:12090605

Hesmondhalgh, D. (2002). *The cultural industries.* London, UK: Sage Publications.

Heyse, V. (2014). *Aufbruch in die Zukunft, Erfolgreiche Entwicklung von Schlüsselkompetenzen in Schulen und Hochschulen.* Münster, Germany: Waxmann.

Heyse, V. (Ed.). (2010). *Grundstrukturen menschlicher Kompetenzen. Praxiserprobte Konzepte und Instrumente.* Münster, Germany: Waxmann.

Heyse, V., & Erpenbeck, J. (2008). *Kompetenztraining. Informations- und Trainingsprogramme. 2., überarb. u. erg.* Stuttgart, Germany: Schäffer-Poeschel.

Hira, S. (2016). The long journey of decolonizing the mind in Latin America. *Tabula Rasa, 25,* 175–194. doi:10.25058/20112742.80

Hisrich, R. (2007). Entrepreneurship: Research and Practice. A Call to Action for Psychology. *Journal of the American Psychoanalytic Association, 62*(65), 575–589.

Hitt, M., Ireland, D., & Hoskisson. (1997). *Strategic management: Competitiveness and globalization*. West Publishing Company.

Hobijn, B., & Franses, P. H. (2001). Are living standards converging? *Structural Change and Economic Dynamics*, *12*(2), 171–200. doi:10.1016/S0954-349X(00)00034-5

Hofacker, C., & Belanche, D. (2016). Eight challenges in social networks for marketing managers. *Revista Española de Marketing*, *20*(2), 73–80.

Hoffman, D. L., & Fodor, M. (2010). Can you measure the ROI of your social media marketing? *MIT Sloan Management Review*, *52*(1), 41–49.

Honeycutt, J. (2001). *Así es la Gestión del Conocimiento*. Madrid, Spain: McGraw-Hill Interamericana.

Hoogendoorn, B., der Zwan, P., & Thurik, R. (2011). *Social entrepreneurship and performance: The role of perceived barriers and risk. ERIM Report Series Research in Management. ERS-2011-016-ORG*. Rotterdam: Erasmus Research Institute of Management.

Horga, I. (2010). The Multilevel Governance and the Request of the Subsidiarity Principle. *MPRA Paper, 44477*. Munich, Germany: University Library of Munich.

Horngren, C. T., & Foster, G. (1991). *Contabilidad de Costos. Un Enfoque Gerencial*. D.F., Mexico: Prentice Hall.

Hovne, A. S., Hovne, B. S., & Schott, T. (2014). Entrepreneurs' innovation benefitting from their education and training and from national policy and culture: A global study. *International Journal of Entrepreneurship and Small Business*, *23*(1-2), 127–144. doi:10.1504/IJESB.2014.065312

Hudson, L. A., & Ozanne, J. L. (1988). Alternative ways of seeking knowledge in consumer research. *The Journal of Consumer Research*, *14*(4), 508–521. doi:10.1086/209132

Huertas, R. (2015). *Organizaciones no gubernamentales y Social Media. Análisis de las Estrategias Comunicativas*. Malaga, Spain: University of Malaga.

Hughes, M., & Morgan, R. E. (2007). Deconstructing the relationship between entrepreneurial orientation and business performance at the embryonic stage of firm growth. *Industrial Marketing Management*, *36*(5), 651–661. doi:10.1016/j.indmarman.2006.04.003

Hurtado, J. (2004). 'Vicios privados, beneficios públicos' o la diestra administración del legislador utilitarista. *Lecturas de Economía*, *61*, 71–99.

iab Ecuador. (2017). *Consumo Digital Ecuador 2017*. Quito.

IAB Mexico & Millward Brown. (2014). *Estudio de consumo de medios entre internautas mexicanos*. Author.

IAB Mexico & Millward Brown. (2014a). *Estudio de consumo de medios entre internautas mexicanos. Segmento Teens*. Author.

IAB Mexico & Millward Brown. (2014b). *Estudio de consumo de medios entre internautas mexicanos. Segmento Ejecutivos*. Author.

IAB Mexico & Millward Brown. (2014c). *Estudio de consumo de medios entre internautas mexicanos. Segmento Digital Moms*. Author.

IAB. (2015). *VI Estudio Redes Sociales de IAB Spain*. Retrieved from: http://www.iabspain.net/wp-content/uploads/downloads/2015/01/Estudio_Anual_Redes_Sociales_2015.pdf

IBM Marketing Cloud. (2017). *10 Key Marketing Trends for 2017 and Ideas for Exceeding Customer Expectations.* Retrieved from https://www-01.ibm.com/common/ssi/cgi-bin/ssialias?htmlfid=WRL12345USEN

Iglesias, M., & Carreras, I. (2012). *La colaboración efectiva en las ONG. Alianzas estratégicas y redes.* Barcelona, Spain: Instituto de Innovación Social.

INE. (2016). *Encuesta sobre Equipamiento y Uso de Tecnologías de Información y Comunicación en los hogares.* Retrieved from: http://www.ine.es/dyngs/INEbase/es/operacion.htm?c=Estadistica_C&cid=1254736176741&menu=resultados&idp=1254735976608

Insights. (2018, Feb 8). Retrieved from https://insights.la/2018/02/08/luce-panorama-digital-ecuador/

Internal Revenue Service. (2018). *Taxpayers. Small Business.* Available in: http://www.sii.cl/contribuyentes/empresas_por_tamano/microempresas.pdf

Internal Revenue Service. (2018b). *Taxpayers: companies by size.* Available in: http://www.sii.cl/contribuyentes/contribuyentes.htm

International World. (2015). *Usage and population statistics.* Retrieved from: http://www.internetworldstats.com/

Iparraguirre, D. (1954). Las fuentes del pensamiento económico en España de los siglos XIII al XVI. *Estudios de Deusto, 2*(3), 79–113.

Irwin, R. (1978). New Business Ventures and the Entrepreneur. *American Journal of Small Business, 37*(1), 160–168.

ISDI. (2017). *Las ventajas que ofrece el marketing digital a las ONGs.* Retrieved October 15, 2018, from https://www.isdi.education/es/isdigital-now/ventajas-ofrece-marketing-digital-ongs

Jacobs, J. (1961). *The death and life of great American cities.* Vintage.

Jain, P. S. I. (1996). Managing Credit for the Rural Poor: Lessons from the Grameen Bank. *World Development, 24*(1), 79–89. doi:10.1016/0305-750X(95)00116-T

James, J. (2012). *How Much Data is Created Every Minute?* Retrieved from: https://www.domo.com/blog/2012/06/how-much-data-is-created-every-minute/

James, C. (2001). Social entrepreneurs. *Management., 10*, 58–67.

Jan, P., & Proceedings, E. (2011). General Characteristics of Anticipated User. *Diversity (Basel)*, 1–11.

Jansen, B. J., Zhang, M., Sobel, K., & Chowdury, A. (2009). Twitter power: Tweets as electronic word of mouth. *Journal of the American Society for Information Science and Technology, 60*(11), 2169–2188. doi:10.1002/asi.21149

Jansen, J. J., Van Den Bosch, F. A., & Volberda, H. W. (2005). Managing potential and realized absorptive capacity. How do organizational antecedents matter? *Academy of Management Journal, 48*(6), 999–1015. doi:10.5465/amj.2005.19573106

Järvinen, J., & Karjaluoto, H. (2015). The use of Web analytics for digital marketing performance measurement. *Industrial Marketing Management, 50*, 117–127. doi:10.1016/j.indmarman.2015.04.009

Järvinen, J., Töllinen, A., Karjaluoto, H., & Jayawardhena, C. (2012). Digital and social media marketing usage in B2B industrial section. *Marketing Management Journal, 22*(2), 102–117.

Javalgi, S. L., & Martin, R. (2018). Epistemological foundations of international entrepreneurship. *The International Entrepreneurship and Management Journal, 14*(3), 671–680. doi:10.100711365-018-0517-4

Jenkins, S. (2008). *The truth about email marketing.* FT Press.

Jiménez, I. F., Millán, M. F., & Suárez, D. F. (2018). Effect of the added value of cultural consumption: An approach to the orange economy in Colombia. *Ploutos*, *7*(2), 4–11.

Jin, X.-L., Lee, M. K., & Cheung, C. M. (2010). Predicting continuance in online communities: Model development and empirical test. *Behaviour & Information Technology*, *29*(4), 383–394. doi:10.1080/01449290903398190

Johansen, V. (2014). Educación Emprendimiento y Rendimiento Académico. *Scandinavian Journal of Educational Research*, *58*(3), 300–314. doi:10.1080/00313831.2012.726642

Johnson, M. W., Christensen, C. M., & Kagermann, H. (2010). Reinventing your Business Model. In *Harvard Business Review on Business Model Innovation* (pp. 47–70). Boston: Harvard University Press.

Jones, S. (1995). *Understanding community in the information age*. Sage.

Kaboom. (2015). *Play Matters*. Retrieved from http://kaboom.org/

Kagermann, H., Wahlster, W., & Helbig, J. (2013). Umsetzungsempfehlungen für das Zukunftsprojekt Industrie 4.0. In H. Kagermann, W. Wahlster, & J. Helbig (Eds.), *Abschlussbericht des Arbeitskreises Industrie 4.0*. Frankfurt am Main, Germany: Forchungsunion and Acatech.

Kallmuenzer, A., Strobl, A., & Peters, M. (2017). Tweaking the entrepreneurial orientation-performance relationship in family firms, The effect of control mechanisms and family-related goals. *Review of Managerial Science*, *12*(4), 855–883. doi:10.100711846-017-0231-6

Kalmanovitz, S. (2001). *Las instituciones colombianas en el siglo XX*. Bogota, Colombia: Alfaomega y Cambio.

Kannan, P. K., & Li, H. (2017). Digital marketing: A framework, review, and research agenda. *International Journal of Research in Marketing*, *34*(1), 22–45. doi:10.1016/j.ijresmar.2016.11.006

Kantis, H. (2002). *Desarrollo emprendedor: América Latina y la experiencia internacional*. Bogota, Colombia: Banco Interamericano de Desarrollo & Fundes Internacional.

Kantis, H., Federico, J., & Menéndez, C. (2012). *Policies to promote dynamic entrepreneurship in Latin America: trends and challenges. CAF Documento de Trabajo, 9*. Caracas, Venezuela: CAF.

Kapkiyai, C., Kimitei, E., Mutwol, P., & Kimaiyo, I. K. (2015). Effects of Group Lending on Accessibility of Micro Credit Facilities among Low-Income Households in Keiyo South District. *European Journal of Business and Management*, *7*(3), 39–46.

Kaplan, A., & Haenlein, M. (2010). ¡Usuarios del mundo, únanse! Los retos y oportunidades de las redes sociales. *Business Horizons*, *53*(1), 59–68. doi:10.1016/j.bushor.2009.09.003

Karatum, S. (2017). The place of digital marketing on Turkish small businesses. *Journal of International Trade, Logistics, and Law*, *3*(2), 36–43.

Karjaluoto, H., Mustonen, N., & Ulkuniemi, P. (2015). The role of digital channels in industrial marketing communications. *Journal of Business and Industrial Marketing*, *30*(6), 703–710. doi:10.1108/JBIM-04-2013-0092

Karlan, D. S. (2001). *Social Capital and Group Banking*. Boston: Boston University, Department of Economics.

Karlan, D. S. (2003). *Social Capital and Group Banking. Mimeo*. Princeton, NJ: Princeton University.

Kayasan, O. (2011). Papel del Estado en la innovación para estimular el espíritu empresarial: Países Emergentes Perspectivas. Actas de la VI Conferencia Europea sobre Innovación y Emprendimiento (ECIE), 1-2, 511-518.

Kellermanns, F. W., Dibrell, C., & Cruz, C. (2014). The role and impact of emotions in family business strategy. New approaches and paradigms. *Journal of Family Business Strategy*, *5*(3), 277–279. doi:10.1016/j.jfbs.2014.08.002

Kellermanns, F. W., & Eddleston, K. A. (2006). Corporate entrepreneurship in family firms, A family perspective. *Entrepreneurship Theory and Practice*, *30*(6), 809–830. doi:10.1111/j.1540-6520.2006.00153.x

Kellermanns, F. W., Eddleston, K. A., & Zellweger, T. M. (2012). Extending the socioemotional wealth perspective, A look at the dark side. *Entrepreneurship Theory and Practice*, *36*(6), 1175–1182. doi:10.1111/j.1540-6520.2012.00544.x

Kelly, K. (1999). *New rules for the new economy*. Penguin.

Kemp, S. (2016). *We Are Social* [Press release]. Retrieved from: http://wearesocial.com/specialreports/digital-in-2016

Kennedy, D., Hyland, A., & Ryan, N. (2006). Writing and using Learning Outcomes: A Practical Guide. In *Bologna Handbook: Implementing Bologna*. Berlin, Germany: European University Association.

Kennedy, E. J., Lawton, L., & Walker, E. (2001). The case for using live cases. Shifting the paradigm in marketing education. *Journal of Marketing Education*, *23*(2), 145–151. doi:10.1177/0273475301232008

Kenneth, L., & Jane, L. (2002). *Sistemas de información*. D.F., Mexico: Pearson Educación.

Kenney, M., & Goe, W. R. (2004). The role of social embeddedness in professorial entrepreneurship: A comparison of electrical engineering and computer science at UC Berkeley and Stanford. *Research Policy*, *33*(5), 691–707. doi:10.1016/j.respol.2003.11.001

Kets de Vries, M. F. R. (1985). Narcissism and Leadership: An Object Relations Perspective. *Human Relations*, *38*(6), 583–601. doi:10.1177/001872678503800606

Keynes, J. M. (1986). *Teoría general de la ocupación, el interés y el dinero*. D.F., Mexico: Fondo de Cultura Económica.

Kiel, B. (2014). Companies' Demand for Competences to Overcome Disruptive Changes. In T. Baaken & J. Teczke (Eds.), *Managing Disruption and Destabilisation* (pp. 91–108). Cracow, Poland: Cracow University of Economics.

Kiiru, M. J., & Kenia, M. (2007). *The Impact of Microfinance on Rural Poor Households' Income and Vulnerability to Poverty: Case Study of Makueni District, Kenya*. Bonn, Germany: University of Bonn.

Killian, G., & McManus, K. (2015). A marketing communications approach for the digital era: Managerial guidelines for social media integration. *Business Horizons*, *58*(5), 539–549. doi:10.1016/j.bushor.2015.05.006

Kim, H. (2014). Exploring and Emerging Field: The Implications of Global Social Entrepreneurship. *Management and Marketing Journal*, *1*, 14–30.

Kirzner, I. (1986). *The open-endedness of knowledge. Ideas on Liberty*. Academic Research Library.

Kirzner, I. (1997). Entrepreneurial Discovery and the Competitive Market Process: An Austrian Approach. *Journal of Economic Literature*, *35*(1), 60–85.

Kirzner, I. (2000). *Entrepreneurial discovery and the law of supply and demand. In Ideas on Liberty*. Academic Research Library.

Knight, F. (1942). Profit and Entrepreneurial Functions. *The Journal of Economic History*, *2*(S1), 126–132. doi:10.1017/S0022050700083479

Kolstad, I. (2007). Why Firms Should Not Always Maximize Profits. *Journal of Business Ethics*, *76*(2), 137–145. doi:10.100710551-006-9262-7

Kontinen, T., & Ojala, A. (2010). The internationalization of family businesses: A review of extant research. *Journal of Family Business Strategy*, *1/2*(2), 97–107. doi:10.1016/j.jfbs.2010.04.001

Kotler, P. (1999). *El Marketing según Kotler*. Buenos Aires, Argentina: Editorial Paidos SAICF.

Kotler, P., & Armstrong, G. (2008). *Fundamentos de Marketing*. D.F., Mexico: Pearson Educación.

Kotler, P., & Keller, K. L. (2007). *A Framework of Marketing Management*. London, UK: Pearson Education.

Kotler, P., & Lee, N. (2005). *Corporate Social Responsibility: Doing the Most Good for our Company and our Cause*. Hoboken, NJ: John Wiley.

Kotter, J. P. (2012). Accelerate! How the most innovative companies capitalize on today's rapid fire strategic challenges and still make their numbers. *Harvard Business Review*, *90*(11), 44–58. PMID:23155997

Kozinets, R. V. (1998). On netnography: Initial reflections on consumer research investigations of cyberculture. *Advances in Consumer Research. Association for Consumer Research (U. S.)*, *25*(1), 366–371.

Kozinets, R. V. (2002). The field behind the screen: Using netnography for marketing research in online communities. *JMR, Journal of Marketing Research*, *39*(1), 61–72. doi:10.1509/jmkr.39.1.61.18935

Kozlinska, I. (2011). Contemporary approaches to entrepreneurship education. *Journal of Business and Management*, *4*(1), 205–220.

Kraiczy, N. D., Hack, A., & Kellermanns, F. W. (2014). New product portfolio performance in family firms. *Journal of Business Research*, *67*(6), 1065–1073. doi:10.1016/j.jbusres.2013.06.005

Kriechbaumer, F., & Christodoulidou, N. (2014). SME website implementation factors in the hospitality industry: Groundwork for a digital marketing roadmap. *Worldwide Hospitality and Tourism Themes*, *6*(4), 328–351. doi:10.1108/WHATT-01-2014-0006

Krikke, H. R., van Harten, A., & Schuur, P. C. (1999). Business case Océ: Reverse logistic network re-design for copiers. *OR-Spektrum*, *21*(3), 381–409. doi:10.1007002910050095

Kuckertz, A., Kollmann, T., & Krell, P. (2012). *Opportunity Recognition Propensity and Actual Opportunity Exploitation–Two Validated Scales*. Paper presented at the 16 Forum Gründungsforschung, Potsdam, Germany.

Kuckertz, A. (2011). Entrepreneurship education. Status quo and prospective developments. *Journal of Entrepreneuship Education*, *16*(1), 59–71.

Kull, A. J., Mena, J. A., & Korschun, D. (2016). A resource-based view of stakeholder marketing. *Journal of Business Research*, *69*(12), 5553–5560. doi:10.1016/j.jbusres.2016.03.063

Kumar, A., Mangla, S. K., Luthra, S., Rana, N. P., & Dwivedi, Y. K. (2018). Predicting changing pattern: Building model for consumer decision making in the digital market. *Journal of Enterprise Information Management*, *31*(5), 674–703. doi:10.1108/JEIM-01-2018-0003

Kumar, S. (2010). Reviewing NGOs' media strategies: Possibilities for NGO-media collaboration. *International NGO Journal*, *5*(4), 84–87.

Kumar, S., & Putnam, V. (2008). Cradle to cradle: Reverse logistics strategies and opportunities across three industry sectors. *International Journal of Production Economics*, *115*(2), 305–315. doi:10.1016/j.ijpe.2007.11.015

Kuratko, D. F. (2003). *Entrepreneurship Education: Emerging Trends and Challenges for the 21st Century*. 2003 Coleman Foundation White Paper Series for the U.S. Association of Small Business & Entrepreneurship.

Kuratko, D. F. (2005). The emergence of entrepreneurship education: Development, trends, and challenges. *Entrepreneurship Theory and Practice*, *29*(5), 577–598. doi:10.1111/j.1540-6520.2005.00099.x

Kurtz, D. L. (2012). *Marketing Contemporáneo*. D.F., Mexico: Cengage Learning Editores.

Kuzel, A. J. (1992). *Doing Qualitative Research*. Newbury Park, CA: Sage.

Kuznets, S. (1973). Modern economic growth: Findings and reflections. *The American Economic Review*, 247–258.

Kuznets, S. S., & Murphy, J. T. (1966). *Modern economic growth: Rate, structure, and spread (C. 2)*. Yale University Press.

Kwak, H., Lee, C., Park, H., & Moon, S. (2010). What is Twitter, a social network or a news media? *Proceedings of the World Wide Web Conference in Raleigh*, *19*, 591-600. 10.1145/1772690.1772751

Kwak, K. H., Kong, J. T., Cho, S. I., Phuong, H. T., & Gim, G. Y. (2019). *Computational Science/Intelligence & Applied Informatics, 787*. Springer International Publishing. doi:10.1007/978-3-319-96806-3

Kwon, O., Lee, N., & Shin, B. (2014). Data quality management, data usage experience and acquisition intention of big data analytics. *International Journal of Information Management*, *34*(3), 387–394. doi:10.1016/j.ijinfomgt.2014.02.002

Lake, R. W. (2015). The Financialization of Urban Policy in the Age of Obama. *Journal of Urban Affairs*, *37*(1), 75–78. doi:10.1111/juaf.12167

Lamb, C. W., Hair, J. F., & McDaniel, C. (2006). *Marketing*. D.F., Mexico: Thomson.

Landsdale, D., Abad, C., & Vera, D. (2012). Key drivers to establish the dynamic ecosystem of entrepreneurship in Ecuador. *Polémika*, *9*(1), 18–25.

Lanero, A., Vázquez, J. L., Gutiérrez, P., & García, M. (2011). Evaluación de la conducta emprendedora en estudiantes universitarios. Implicaciones para el diseño de programas académicos. *Pecvnia. Universidad de León.*, *12*(1), 219–243.

Laroche, M., Habibi, M. R., & Richard, M. O. (2013). To be or not to be on social media: How brand loyalty is affected by social media? *International Journal of Information Management*, *33*(1), 76–82. doi:10.1016/j.ijinfomgt.2012.07.003

LaRossa, R., & Reitzes, D. C. (1993). Symbolic interactionism and family studies. In Sourcebook of family theories and methods (pp. 135-166). Springer US. doi:10.1007/978-0-387-85764-0_6

Larrañeta, B., Zahra, S. A., & González, J. L. G. (2012). Enriching strategic variety in new ventures through external knowledge. *Journal of Business Venturing*, *27*(4), 401–413. doi:10.1016/j.jbusvent.2011.11.004

Latouche, S. (2007). De-growth: An electoral stake? *The International Journal of Inclusive Democracy*, *3*(1), 14–18.

Latouche, S., & Harpages, D. (2010). *L'heure du décroissance*. Paris, France: Editions Thierry Magnier.

Lawrence, T., Phillips, N., & Tracey, P. (2012). Educating Social Entrepreneurs and Social Innovators. *Academy of Management Learning & Education*, *11*(3), 319–323. doi:10.5465/amle.2012.0224

Le Deist, F. (2009). Competence. Conceptual approach and practice in France. *Journal of European Industrial Training*, *33*(8/9), 718–735. doi:10.1108/03090590910993599

Leadbeater, C. (Ed.). (1997). *The Rise of the Social Entrepreneur*. London, UK: Demos.

Leask, G., & Parnell, J. A. (2005). Integrating Strategic Groups and the Resource-Based Perspective: Understanding the Competitive Process. *European Management Journal*, *23*(4), 458–470. doi:10.1016/j.emj.2005.06.003

Lederman, D., Messina, J., Pienknagura, S., & Rigolini, J. (2014). *El emprendimiento en América Latina: muchas empresas y poca innovación*. World Bank Publications. doi:10.1596/978-1-4648-0284-3

Lee, S., & Cho, M. (2011). Social media use in a mobile broadband environment: Examination of determinants of Twitter and Facebook use. *International Journal of Mobile Marketing*, *6*(2), 71–87.

Lele, A. (2019). Industry 4.0., *Smart Innovation. Systems and Technologies*, *132*, 205–215.

León, N. (2006). *Mecanismos para la regulación ambiental*. Bogota, Colombia: Universidad Nacional de Colombia.

Lepoutre, J., Justo, R., Terjesen, S., & Bosma, N. (2011). Designing a Global Standardized Methodology for Measuring Social Entrepreneurship: The Global Entrepreneurship Monitor Social Entrepreneurship Study. *Small Business Economics*, *40*(3), 693–714. doi:10.100711187-011-9398-4

Levy, J. P., & Varela, J. (2003). *Análisis multivariable para las ciencias sociales*. Madrid, Spain: Pearson-Prentice Hall.

Lewin, A., & Minton, J. (1986). Determining Organizational Effectiveness: Another Look, and an Agenda for Research. *Management Science*, *32*(5), 514–538. doi:10.1287/mnsc.32.5.514

Li, H., y Zuo, X. (2013). Investigación de Empleo del Colegio de Graduados y Emprendimiento - Tomando Estudiantes Formación Superior en especialidades como productor del sector servicios para un ejemplo. *Actas de la Conferencia Internacional sobre Educación de Tecnología y Sistema de Información (ICETIS 2013)*, 126-133.

Liles, P. R. (1977). New business ventures and the entrepreneur. *Harvard Business Review*, *5*(1), 184–193.

Lim, M., & Svensson, P. (2007). The Embedded Critic: Marketing in the Future of the University. In *5th Critical Management Studies Conference*. Manchester Business School.

Liñán, F., Rodriguez-Cohard, J. C., & Rueda-Cantuche, J. M. (2011). Factors affecting entrepreneurial intention levels: A role for education. *The International Entrepreneurship and Management Journal*, *7*(2), 195–218. doi:10.100711365-010-0154-z

Lin, L. M., & Hsia, T. L. (2011). Core capabilities for practitioners in achieving e-business innovation. *Computers in Human Behavior*, *27*(5), 1884–1891. doi:10.1016/j.chb.2011.04.012

Lipman, A. (1965). Social Backgrounds of the Bogota Entrepreneur. *Journal of Inter-American Studies*, *7*(2), 227–235. doi:10.2307/165147

Litz, R. A. (1995). The family business, Toward definitional clarity. *Family Business Review*, *8*(2), 71–81. doi:10.1111/j.1741-6248.1995.00071.x

Li, W., Badr, Y., & Biennier, F. (2012). Digital ecosystems: challenges and prospects. In *Proceedings of the international conference on management of Emergent Digital EcoSystems* (pp. 117-122). Addis Ababa, Ethiopia: ACM.

Lo, F.-Y., & Campos, N. (2018). Blending Internet-of-Things (IoT) solutions into relationship marketing strategies. *Technological Forecasting and Social Change*, *137*(9), 10–18. doi:10.1016/j.techfore.2018.09.029

Lonial, S. C., & Carter, R. E. (2015). The impact of organizational orientations on medium and small firm performance, A resource-based perspective. *Journal of Small Business Management*, *53*(1), 94–113. doi:10.1111/jsbm.12054

López, R. (1995). Desarrollos conceptuales y operacionales acerca de la creatividad. Cuadernos de trabajo, 1, 49-65.

López, A., Niembro, A., & Ramos, D. (2014). The competitiveness of Latin America in the trade of services based on knowledge. *Revista de la CEPAL*, *113*, 23–41.

López-Cardona, D., & Tabares-Hoyos, R. (2013). La obsolescencia programada y percibida en el sector de electrodomésticos de Manizales. Simposio ASPROMER.

López, J. (2009). Del Marketing Transaccional Al Marketing Relacional. *Entramado*, *5*(1), 6–13.

Lumpkin, G. T., & Dess, G. (1996). Clarifying the Entrepreneurial Orientation Construct and Linking It to Performance. *Academy of Management Review*, *21*(1), 135–172. doi:10.5465/amr.1996.9602161568

Lundström, A., & Zhou, C. (2014). Rethinking social entrepreneurship and social enterprises: A three-dimensional perspective. In *Social Entrepreneurship* (pp. 71–89). Cham: Springer. doi:10.1007/978-3-319-01396-1_4

Lusardi, A., & Mitchell, O. (2007). Financial literacy and retirement preparedness: Evidence and implications for financial education. The problems are serious, and the remedies are not simple. *Business Economics (Cleveland, Ohio)*, *1*(1), 35–44. doi:10.2145/20070104

Luzardo, A., De Jesús, D., & Pérez, M. (2017). *Orange Economy: Innovations you may not know were from Latin America and the Caribbean.* Washington, DC: Inter-American Development Bank.

Magretta, J. (2010). Why Business Model Matter. In Harvard Business Review on Business Model Innovation (pp. 1-18). Boston: Academic Press.

Mahecha, E., & Zambrano, C. (2013). La inviabilidad del capitalismo en el siglo XXI. *Educación y Desarrollo Social*, *8*(1), 10–47.

Mahoney, J., & Padian, J. R. (1992). The Resource-Based View within the Conversation of Strategic Management. *Strategic Management Journal*, *13*(5), 363–380. doi:10.1002mj.4250130505

Mair, J., & Martí, I. (2006). Social Entrepreneurship Research: A Source of Explanation, Prediction, and Delight. *Journal of World Business*, *41*(1), 36–44. doi:10.1016/j.jwb.2005.09.002

Mair, J., & Schoen, O. (2007). Successful Social Entrepreneurial Business Models in the Context of Developing Economies: An Explorative Study. *International Journal of Emerging Markets*, *2*(1), 54–68. doi:10.1108/17468800710718895

Makhija, M. (2003). Comparing the resource-based and market-based views of the firm: Empirical evidence from Czech privatization. *Strategic Management Journal*, *24*(5), 433–451. doi:10.1002mj.304

Mallard, B. (2012). Micro enterprises and alternative socioeconomic dynamics in the BioBío region, (Chile). *Revista Márgenes Espacio Arte y Sociedad*, *9*(11), 169–184.

Mandyoli, B., Gervase Iwu, C., & Magoda, Z. (2016). Determining the Nexus between Social Entrepreneurship and the Employability of Graduates. *Socioeconomica*, *5*(10), 279–298. doi:10.12803/SJSECO.51009

Mangold, W. G., & Faulds, D. J. (2009). Social media: The new hybrid element of the promotion mix. *Business Horizons*, *52*(4), 357–365. doi:10.1016/j.bushor.2009.03.002

Mansfield, B. (2004). Competence in transition. *Journal of European Industrial Training*, *28*(2/3/4), 296-309.

Mantzavinos, C., North, D., & Shariq, S. (2003). *Learning, Institutions, and Economic Performance.* Bonn, Germany: Max Plank Institute for Research on Collective Goods.

Manyika, J., Chui, M., Bughin, J., Dobbs, R., Bisson, P., & Marrs, A. (2013). *Disruptive technologies: Advances that will transform life, business, and the global economy.* New York: McKinsey Global Institute.

Marcotte, C. (2011). Country entrepreneurial profiles: Assessing the individual and Organizational levels of entrepreneurship across countries. *Journal of Enterprising Culture*, *19*(2), 169–200. doi:10.1142/S021849581100074X

Marcotte, C. (2012). Measuring entrepreneurship at the country level: A review and research agenda. *Entrepreneurship and Regional Development*, *25*(3/4), 174–194.

Marcotte, C., Sousse, S. A., Molz, R., Farashahi, M., & Hafsi, T. (2010). Strategy implementation in emerging countries: three theoretical approaches. In R. Molz & A. Taleb (Eds.), *The Multinational Enterprise in Developing Countries, Local versus Global Logic*. New York, NY: Routledge.

Marcuello, C. (2007). Responsabilidad social y organizaciones no lucrativas. *Ekonomiaz. Revista de Economía Vasca*, *65*, 208–227.

Marginean, S. (2009). Globalization, Technology, and Competitiveness: From Industrial Revolution to Knowledge Economy. *Revista Economica*, *47*(4-5), 114–119.

Maritain, J. (1951). *La persona y el bien común*. Bilbao, Spain: Desclée de Brouwer.

Markman, G. D., & Gartner, W. (2002). Is Extraordinary Growth Profitable? A Study of Inc. 500 High-Growth Companies. *Entrepreneurship Theory and Practice*, *23*(1), 65–75. doi:10.1111/1540-8520.t01-2-00004

Marques, A. P., & Couto, A. I. (2017). SMEs and family SMEs, Specificities from the Portuguese socio-business context. *European Journal of Economic Business Studies*, *3*(2), 190–199. doi:10.26417/ejes.v8i1.p190-199

Marshall, A. (1890). *Principles of Economics: An introductory volume*. Academic Press.

Martí Frías, B. (2014). *La logística inversa: Gestión de RAEEs*. Valencia, Spain: Polytechnic University of Valencia.

Martin, M. (2004). *Surveying Social Entrepreneurship: Toward an Empirical Analysis of the Performance Revolution in the Social Sector*. Available at SSRN: http://ssrn.com/abstract=1319499

Martin, B., McNally, J., & Kay, M. (2013). Examining the formation of human capital in entrepreneurship: A meta-analysis of entrepreneurship education outcomes. *Journal of Business Venturing*, *28*(2), 211–224. doi:10.1016/j.jbusvent.2012.03.002

Martínez, L. (2018). *Política pública de emprendimiento en Colombia 2006-2016: Un análisis cognitivo desde los instrumentos de la planificación* (Ph.D. Thesis). Bogota, Colombia: Universidad Externado de Colombia.

Martínez, H. (2005). *El marco ético de la Responsabilidad Social Empresarial*. Bogota, Colombia: Pontificia Universidad Javeriana.

Martínez-Navarro, J., Bigné, E., Guixeres, J., Alcañiz, M., & Torrecilla, C. (2018). (in press). The influence of virtual reality in e-commerce. *Journal of Business Research*. doi:10.1016/j.jbusres.2018.10.054

Martín-Moreno, M., & Sáez, F. (2004). Análisis preliminar del comercio electrónico. In M. Martín-Moreno & F. Sáez (Eds.), *Aplicaciones y abusos de Internet como canal de comunicación del correo electrónico* (pp. 1–32). Madrid, Spain: Politechnic University of Madrid.

Martin, R. L., & Osberg, S. (2007). Social Entrepreneurship: The Case for Definition. *Stanford Social Innovation Review*, *18*(1), 1–16.

Max-Neef, M., Elizalde, A., & Hoppenhayn, M. (2006). *Desarrollo a Escala Humana*. Available at www.ecoportal.net

Max-Neef, M. (1994). *Desarrollo a escala humana. Conceptos, aplicaciones y algunas reflexiones*. Montevideo, Uruguay: Nordan-Comunidad.

Max-Neef, M. (1997). *Economía Descalza. Señales desde el Mundo Invisible, Colección Pensamiento Descalzo, 1*. Montevideo, Uruguay: Nordan-Comunidad.

McCann, J., Selsky, J., & Lee, J. (2009). Building agility, resiliency, and performance in turbulent environments. *People & Strategy*, *32*(3), 44–52.

McClelland, D. (1989). *Estudio de la motivación humana*. Madrid, Spain: Narcea Ediciones.

McClelland, D., & Winter, D. (1970). *Cómo se motiva el éxito económico*. D.F., Mexico: Unión Tipográfica Editorial Hispanoamericana.

Mcdonough, W., & Braungart, M. (2005). *Cradle to Cradle: De la Cuna a la Cuna: Rediseñando la forma en que hacemos las cosas*. Madrid, Spain: McGraw-Hill Interamericana de España.

McGee, J., & Sammut-Bonnici, T. (2002). Network industries in the new economy. *European Business Journal*, *14*(5), 116–132.

McKernan, S. (2002). The Impact of Microcredit Programs on Self-Employment Profits: Do Noncredit Program Aspects Matter? *The Review of Economics and Statistics*, *84*(1), 93–115. doi:10.1162/003465302317331946

McKinsey & Company (2011). *The business of sustainability: McKinsey global survey results*. Author.

McLaren, N., & Shanbhogue, R. (2011). *Using Internet Search Data as Economic Indicators. Bank of England Quarterly Bulletin*, *2011*, Q2.

McLeod, R. (2000). *Sistemas de información gerencial*. D.F., Mexico: Pearson Educación.

McLuhan, M. (1964). Understanding Media. In The Extensions of Man. Berkeley, CA: Gingko Press.

McNelly, B., & Kevane, M. (2002). Improving Design and Performance of Group Lending: Suggestions from Burkina Faso. *World Development*, *30*(11), 2017–2032. doi:10.1016/S0305-750X(02)00119-5

Meadows, D. H., Meadows, D. L., Randers, J., & Behrens, W. W. (1972). *The limits to growth*. Retrieved from https://www.google.com/books?hl=tr&lr=&id=vb8_BAAAQBAJ&oi=fnd&pg=PA25&dq=%22limits+to+growth%22&ots=7pmu7LshCf&sig=ktZdt_jikOFMt7NCcgRJMSbVa0s

Medrano, N., & Olarte-Pascual, C. (2016). The effects of the crisis on marketing innovation: An application for Spain. *Journal of Business and Industrial Marketing*, *31*(3), 404–417. doi:10.1108/JBIM-02-2013-0048

Meier, R., & Pilgrim, M. (1994). Policy-induced constraints on small Enterprise development in Asian developing countries. *Small Enterprise Development*, *5*(2), 32–38. doi:10.3362/0957-1329.1994.017

Melo, A., & Romero, H. R. (2016). *Digital Marketing for Small and Medium Enterprises*. Revista Observatorio de la Economía Latinoamericana.

Memili, E., Zellweger, T. M., & Fang, H. (2013). The determinants of family owners-managers' affective organizational commitment. *Family Relations*, *62*(3), 443–456. doi:10.1111/fare.12015

Méndez, R., Michelini, J. J., Prada, J., & Tébar, J. (2012). Creative economy and urban development in Spain: An approach to its spatial logics. *EURE (Santiago)*, *38*(113), 5–32.

Mendive, D.E. (2008). *Marketing Social. Manual Práctico*. Buenos Aires: Editorial de los Cuatro Vientos.

Mercurio, Z. A. (2015). Affective commitment as a core essence of organizational commitment. An integrative literature review. *Human Resource Development Review*, *14*(4), 389–414. doi:10.1177/1534484315603612

Merschmann, U., & Thonemann, U. W. (2011). Supply chain flexibility, uncertainty and firm performance, An empirical analysis of German manufacturing firms. *International Journal of Production Economics*, *130*(1), 43–53. doi:10.1016/j.ijpe.2010.10.013

Meulman, J., & Heiser, W. (2012). *SPSS Categories 20.0.* Chicago, IL: SPSS.

Meyer, J. P., & Allen, N. J. (1991). A three-component conceptualization of organizational commitment. *Human Resource Management Review*, *1*(1), 61–89. doi:10.1016/1053-4822(91)90011-Z

Micu, A. C., Dedeker, K., Lewis, I., Moran, R., Netzer, O., Plummer, J., & Rubinson, J. (2011). Guest Editorial: The Shape of Marketing Research in 2021. *Journal of Advertising Research*, *51*(1), 213–221. doi:10.2501/JAR-51-1-213-221

Miguéns, J., Baggio, R., & Costa, C. (2008). Social media and tourism destinations: TripAdvisor case study. *Advances in Tourism Research*, *26*(28), 1–6.

Miles, M., & Huberman, M. (1994). *Qualitative Data Analysis: An Expanded Sourcebook* (2nd ed.). Thousand Oaks, CA: SAGE Publications, Inc.

Miller, D. (1983). The correlates of entrepreneurship in three types of firms. *Management Science*, *29*(7), 770–791. doi:10.1287/mnsc.29.7.770

Miller, D., & Le Breton-Miller, I. (2011). Governance, social identity, and entrepreneurial orientation in closely held public companies. *Entrepreneurship Theory and Practice*, *35*(5), 1051–1076. doi:10.1111/j.1540-6520.2011.00447.x

Miller, D., & Le Breton-Miller, I. (2014). Deconstructing socioemotional wealth. *Entrepreneurship Theory and Practice*, *38*(4), 713–720. doi:10.1111/etap.12111

Miller, T. L., Wesley, C. L. II, & Williams, D. E. (2012). Educating the Minds of Caring Hearts: Comparing the Views of Practitioners and Educators on the Importance of Social Entrepreneurship Competences. *Academy of Management Learning & Education*, *11*(3), 349–370. doi:10.5465/amle.2011.0017

Ministry of Culture. (2012). *Plan of the Creative Economy Secretary: Policies, Guidelines, and Actions 2011 to 2014.* Brazil, Ministry of Culture.

Ministry of Economy, Development, and Tourism. (2017). *Results report Companies in Chile, Fourth Longitudinal Survey of Companies.* Santiago de Chile: Division of Commercial and Industrial Policy of the Ministry of Economy, Development, and Tourism.

Ministry of Finance. (2001). *Law 19,749 Establishes Standards to Facilitate the Creation of Micro Family Business.* Available in: http://bcn.cl/1uxup

Ministry of Finance. (2002). *Decree 102. Regulates Law 19.749 That Establishes Standards to Facilitate the Creation of Family Micro Business.* Available in: http://bcn.cl/1v7mk

Ministry of Interior. (2018). *Decree 2385. Fixed and systematized text of Decree-Law number 3,063, of 1979, on Municipal Income.* Available in: http://bcn.cl/1v06x

Mintzberg, H. (1973). Strategy-making in three modes. *California Management Review*, *16*(2), 44–53. doi:10.2307/41164491

Mirón, G. (2011). La comunicación de experiencias de marca a través de las redes sociales: Análisis de caso de los patrocinadores del Mundial de Fútbol 2010. *Pensar la Publicidad*, *5*(2), 93–118.

Mises, L. (1998). Monopoly prices. The characteristic features of monopoly prices. *The Quarterly Journal of Austrian Economics*, *1*(2), 1–28.

Mittal, V., & Ross, W. T. Jr. (1998). The impact of positive and negative affect and issue framing on issue interpretation and risk-taking. *Organizational Behavior and Human Decision Processes*, *76*(3), 298–324. doi:10.1006/obhd.1998.2808 PMID:9878512

Mohan, M., Jiménez, F., Brown, B., & Cantrell, C. (2017). Brand skill: Linking brand functionality with consumer-based brand equity. *Journal of Product and Brand Management*, *26*(5), 477–491. doi:10.1108/JPBM-06-2016-1247

Molina, G. (2014). *Marketing deportivo digital*. Madrid, Spain: Librerías Deportivas Esteban Sanz.

Montero, C. (1997). State-business relations in a global economy. The case of Chile. *Nueva Sociedad*, *151*, 122–135.

Mora, G. L. A. (2008). *Gestión logística integral*. Bogota, Colombia: Ecoe Ediciones.

Morales-Astola, R. (2016). Border cultural management and the challenge of Latin America. In U. Bustamante-Lozano, J. L. Mariscal-Orozco, & C. Yáñez-Canal (Eds.), *Forms and configurations of cultural management in Latin America*. Universidad Nacional de Colombia.

Moravec, J. W. (2008). A new paradigm of knowledge production in higher education. *On the Horizon*, *16*(3), 123–136. doi:10.1108/10748120810901422

Morduch, J. (2008). *How can the poor afford microfinance? Financial Access Initiative. Wagner Graduate School*, New York University.

Morelos, C. (2004). La fe en la eucaristía: luces y sombras en Asia. *XLVIII Congreso Eucarístico Internacional*, Guadalajara, Mexico.

Moreno, G. R., Ruíz, D. C., & Peñaherrera, L. V. (2017). Influencia del marketing digital en el uso de las redes sociales para la gestión empresarial de las PYMES. *Arjé. Revista de Postgrado FaCE-UC*, *11*(21), 271–279.

Morgan, R. M., & Hunt, S. D. (1994). The commitment-trust theory of relationship marketing. *Journal of Marketing*, *58*(3), 20–38. doi:10.1177/002224299405800302

Morgan, T. J., & Gómez-Mejía, L. R. (2014). Hooked on a feeling, The affective component of socioemotional wealth in family firms. *Journal of Family Business Strategy*, *5*(3), 280–288. doi:10.1016/j.jfbs.2014.07.001

Moriano, J. (2005). El perfil psicosocial del emprendedor. *Consejo económico y social*, 263.

Moriano, J., Palací, F., & Morales, J. (2006). El perfil psicosocial del emprendedor universitario. *Revista de Psicología del Trabajo y de las Organizaciones*, *22*(1), 75–99.

Morris, M. H., & Kaplan, J. B. (2014). Entrepreneurial (versus managerial) competences as drivers of entrepreneurship education. Annals of Entrepreneurship Education and Pedagogy, 134-151.

Morris, M. H., Webb, J. W., & Franklin, R. (2011). Understanding the manifestation of entrepreneurial orientation in the nonprofit context. *Entrepreneurship Theory and Practice*, *35*(5), 947–971. doi:10.1111/j.1540-6520.2011.00453.x

Morris, M., Schindehutte, M., & Allen, J. (2005). The entrepreneur's business model: Toward a unified perspective. *Journal of Business Research*, *58*(6), 726–735. doi:10.1016/j.jbusres.2003.11.001

Morris, R. (2011). *High Impact Entrepreneurship*. London, UK: Global Report Center for High Impact Entrepreneurship Endeavor and GEM.

Mottner, S., & Wymer, W. (2011). Non-profit education: Course offering and perceptions in accredited US business schools. *Journal of Nonprofit & Public Sector Marketing*, *23*(1), 1–19. doi:10.1080/10495142.2010.508207

Moura-Leite, R. C., & Padgett, R. C. (2011). Historical background of corporate social responsibility. *Social Responsibility Journal*, *7*(4), 528–539. doi:10.1108/1747111111117511

Mowday, R. T., Steers, R. M., & Porter, L. W. (1979). The measurement of organizational commitment. *Journal of Vocational Behavior*, *14*(2), 224–247. doi:10.1016/0001-8791(79)90072-1

Moya, X., Guerrero, R., & Arregui, R. (2018). Chile: Create and sustain employment through a combination of technical assistance and financial inclusion. *MktDESCUBRE*, *1*(9), 84–94.

Moylan, W. A. (2008). Learning by project: Developing essential 21st-century skills using student team projects. *International Journal of Learning*, *15*(9), 287–292. doi:10.18848/1447-9494/CGP/v15i09/45935

Mozas-Moral, A. (2013). Emprendimiento y Economía Social. *C.I.R.I.E.C. España*, *78*, 7–9.

Mueller, S., Chambers, L., & Neck, H. (2014). The Distinctive Skills of Social Entrepreneurs. *Journal of Enterprising Culture*, *21*(3), 301–334. doi:10.1142/S0218495813500131

Mukerjee, S. (2014). Agility. A crucial capability for universities in times of disruptive change and innovation. *Australian Universities Review*, *56*(1), 56–60.

Mulder, M., Gulikers, J., Biemans, H., & Wesselink, R. (2009). The new competence concept in higher education. Error or enrichment? *Journal of European Industrial Training*, *33*(8/9), 755–770. doi:10.1108/03090590910993616

Mulgan, G. (2006). The process of social innovation. *Innovations*, *1*(2), 145–162. doi:10.1162/itgg.2006.1.2.145

Mulhern, F. (2009). Integrated marketing communications: From media channels to digital connectivity. *Journal of Marketing Communications*, *15*(2-3), 85–101. doi:10.1080/13527260902757506

Müller, J. M., Pommeranz, B., Weisser, J., & Voigt, K. I. (2018). Digital, Social Media, and Mobile Marketing in industrial buying: Still in need of customer segmentation? Empirical evidence from Poland and Germany. *Industrial Marketing Management*, *73*(1), 70–83. doi:10.1016/j.indmarman.2018.01.033

Muniz, A. M. Jr, & O'Guinn, T. C. (2001). Brand community. *The Journal of Consumer Research*, *27*(4), 412–432. doi:10.1086/319618

Muñoz, P. J. (2016). Italy launches to regulate the collaborative economy: About the Bill Discipline of digital platforms for sharing goods and services and provisions for promoting the sharing economy. *Revista Democracia Digital e Governo Eletrônico*, *1*(14), 83–95.

Munshi, N. V. (2010). Value creation, social innovation and entrepreneurship in global economies. *Journal of Asia-Pacific Business*, *11*(3), 160–165. doi:10.1080/10599231.2010.500569

Nadirkhanlou, S., Pourezzat, A. A., Gholipour, A., & Zehtabi, M. (2013). Requirements of Knowledge Commercialization in Universities and Academic Entrepreneurship. In *Innovation through Knowledge Transfer 2012* (pp. 179–194). Heidelberg, Germany: Springer. doi:10.1007/978-3-642-34219-6_20

Nagle, T. T., & Holden, R. K. (2002). *Estrategia y Tácticas de Precios*. Madrid, Spain: Pearson-Prentice Hall.

Nakatani, K., & Chuang, T. T. (2011). A web analytics tool selection method: An analytical hierarchy process approach. *Internet Research*, *21*(2), 171–186. doi:10.1108/10662241111123757

Naldi, L., Cennamo, C., Corbetta, G., & Gómez-Mejía, L. (2013). Preserving socioemotional wealth in family firms, Asset or liability? The moderating role of business context. *Entrepreneurship Theory and Practice*, *37*(6), 1341–1360. doi:10.1111/etap.12069

Naldi, L., Nordqvist, M., Sjöberg, K., & Wiklund, J. (2007). Entrepreneurial orientation, risk-taking, and performance in family firms. *Family Business Review*, *20*(1), 33–47. doi:10.1111/j.1741-6248.2007.00082.x

Nambisan, S. (2017). Digital Entrepreneurship: Toward a Digital Technology Perspective of Entrepreneurship. *Entrepreneurship Theory and Practice*, *41*(6), 1029–1055. doi:10.1111/etap.12254

National Statistics Institute. (2017a). *Final report Official Survey V Micro-Entrepreneurship Survey*. Chile: Author.

National Statistics Institute. (2017b). *Micro Entrepreneurship Survey. Full V database SPSS Micro Entrepreneurship Survey*. Chile: Author.

Ndou, V., & Del Vecchio, P. (2013). Fomento del espíritu empresarial innovador de desarrollo de activos de conocimiento: una evaluación de la situación en los países de los Balcanes Occidentales. In Quinta Conferencia Anual de la Asociación Euromediterránea de la Academia EUROMED de Negocios (pp. 1187–1197). Montreux, Switzerland: Academic Press.

NEF. (2015). *Wellbeing*. Retrieved from http://www.neweconomics.org/issues/entry/well-being

Nicholls, A. (2010). The legitimacy of social entrepreneurship: Reflexive isomorphism in a pre-paradigmatic field. *Entrepreneurship Theory and Practice*, *34*(4), 611–633. doi:10.1111/j.1540-6520.2010.00397.x

Nicholls, A., & Murdock, A. (2012). The nature of social innovation. In *Social innovation* (pp. 1–30). London: Palgrave Macmillan. doi:10.1057/9780230367098_1

Nieto-Antolín, M. (2003). Dynamic characteristics of the process of technological innovation in the company. *Investigaciones Europeas de Dirección y Economía de la Empresa*, *9*(3), 111–128.

Nightingale, P., & Coad, A. (2014). Muppets and gazelles: Political and methodological biases in entrepreneurship research. *Industrial and Corporate Change*, *23*(1), 113–143. doi:10.1093/icc/dtt057

Nordqvist, M., & Melin, L. (2010). Entrepreneurial families and family firms. *Entrepreneurship and Regional Development*, *22*(3-4), 211–239. doi:10.1080/08985621003726119

Norman, D. A. (2004). *Emotional Design - Why we love (or hate) everyday things*. New York: B-Books.

Norris, D., Brodnick, R., Lefrere, P., Gilmour, J., & Baer, L. (2013). Transforming in an age of disruptive change. Part 1. Back to the future, zooming to the present. *Planning for Higher Education*, *41*(2), 1–44.

North, D. (2003). The role of institutions in economic development. *United Nations Discussion Paper Series, 2003.2.*

North, D. (1993). Desempeño económico en el transcurso de los años. *Nobel Prize Conference*, Stockholm, Sweden.

Noruzi, M. R., Westover, J. R., & Rahimi, G. R. (2010). An exploration of social entrepreneurship in the entrepreneurship Era. *Asian Social Science*, *6*(6), 4–10. doi:10.5539/ass.v6n6p3

Nosella, A., & Grimaldi, R. (2009). University-level mechanisms supporting the creation of new companies: An analysis of Italian academic spin-offs. *Technology Analysis and Strategic Management*, *21*(6), 679–698. doi:10.1080/09537320903052657

Noval, L. (2014). *El fundraising como herramienta clave de captación de fondos de procedencia empresarial en las organizaciones no lucrativas. Aplicación práctica (Master's Degree Project)*. University of Oviedo.

O'Boyle, E. J. (2005). Homo Socio-Economicus: Foundational to social economics and the social economy*. *Review of Social Economy*, *63*(3), 483–507. doi:10.1080/00346760500255635

O'Sullivan, D., & Abela, A. (2007). Marketing performance measurement ability and firm performance. *Journal of Marketing*, *71*(4), 79–93. doi:10.1509/jmkg.71.2.079

O'Sullivan, D., Abela, A., & Hutchinson, M. (2009). Marketing performance measurement and firm performance: Evidence from the European high-technology sector. *European Journal of Marketing*, *43*(5/6), 843–862. doi:10.1108/03090560910947070

Ocaña, M. (1996). Francisco de Vitoria: vida, muerte y resurrección. *Anales del Seminario de Historia de la Filosofía*, *1*, 297-317.

OECD. (2002). *OECD Small and Medium Enterprise Outlook*. Paris, France: OECD.

OECD. (2004). *OECD Compendium II on SME and Entrepreneurship Related Activities Carried Out by International and Regional Bodies*. Paris, France: OECD.

Oliva, R., & Lázaro, I. (2018). *Creative economy in Latin America and the Caribbean: Measurements and challenges (No. IDB-TN-01488)*. Washington, DC: Inter-American Development Bank.

Olson, D. L., & Dash Wu, D. (2010a). A review of enterprise risk management in supply chain. *Kybernetes, 39*(5), 694–706. doi:10.1108/03684921011043198

Olson, D. L., & Dash Wu, D. (2010b). Enterprise risk management: A DEA VaR approach in vendor selection. *International Journal of Production Research, 48*(16), 4919–4932. doi:10.1080/00207540903051684

Omerzel, D. G., & Antoncic, B. (2008). Critical entrepreneur knowledge dimensions for the SME performance. *Industrial Management & Data Systems, 9*(108), 1182–1199. doi:10.1108/02635570810914883

Önder, I., & Ulrich, G. (2016). Forecasting Tourism Demand with Google Trends for a Major European City Destination. *Tourism Analysis, 21*(2-3), 203–220. doi:10.3727/108354216X14559233984773

Onphanhdala, P., & Suruga, T. (2010). Entrepreneurial human capital and micro and small business in Lao PDR. *The Developing Economies, 48*(2), 181–202. doi:10.1111/j.1746-1049.2010.00104.x

Orrego, C. (2009). La fenomenología y el emprendimiento. *Pensamiento y gestión, 27*, 235-252.

Osburg, T., & Schmidpeter, R. (2013). *Social Innovation: Solutions for a Sustainable Future*. Springer Science & Business Media. doi:10.1007/978-3-642-36540-9

Ossanna, J. A. (2008). Las misiones jesuitas en la región del Guayrá en las primeras décadas del siglo XVII. *Mundo Agrario, 8*(16), 1–12.

Osterwalder, A. (2004). *The Business Model Ontology - A Proposition in a Design Science Approach*. Lausanne, Switzerland: University of Lausanne, Ecole des Hautes Etudes Commerciales.

Osterwalder, A., & Pigneur, Y. (2010). *Business Model Generation*. Hoboken, NJ: John Wiley & Sons.

Otero-Gómez, M. C., & Giraldo-Pérez, W. (2018). Cultural Consumption as a means for International Tourist development. An analysis applied to Villavicencio–Colombia. *Encuentros, 16*(1), 64–77.

Özköse, H., Arı, E. S., & Gencer, C. (2015). Yesterday, today and tomorrow of big data. *Procedia: Social and Behavioral Sciences, 195*, 1042–1050. doi:10.1016/j.sbspro.2015.06.147

Páez, S. (2011). Acercamiento a las características del universitario emprendedor en la unidad de emprendimiento empresarial en la Universidad Nacional de Colombia. *Revista EAN, 71*, 52–69.

Park, L. S., Yu, J., Yu, S., & Liao, L. (2015). *Search engine optimization for category specific search results*. U.S. Patent 9,116,994.

Park, J., Han, S. H., Park, J., Park, J., Kwahk, J., Lee, M., & Jeong, D. Y. (2018). Development of a web-based user experience evaluation system for home appliances. *International Journal of Industrial Ergonomics, 67*(7), 216–228. doi:10.1016/j.ergon.2018.05.017

Park, S., Lee, J., & Song, W. (2017). Short-term forecasting of Japanese tourist inflow to South Korea using Google trends data. *Journal of Travel & Tourism Marketing, 34*(3), 357–368. doi:10.1080/10548408.2016.1170651

Park, S.-Y., & Levy, S. E. (2014). Corporate social responsibility: Perspectives of hotel frontline employees. *International Journal of Contemporary Hospitality Management*, *26*(3), 332–348. doi:10.1108/IJCHM-01-2013-0034

Park, Y. A., & Gretzel, U. (2007). Success factors for destination marketing websites: A qualitative meta-analysis. *Journal of Travel Research*, *46*(1), 46–63. doi:10.1177/0047287507302381

Parssinen, M., Kotila, M., Cuevas, R., Phansalkar, A., & Manner, J. (2018). Is Blockchain Ready to Revolutionize Online Advertising? *IEEE Access: Practical Innovations, Open Solutions*, *6*, 1–1. doi:10.1109/ACCESS.2018.2872694

Patterson, A. (2012). Social-networkers of the world, unite and take over: A meta-introspective perspective on the Facebook brand. *Journal of Business Research*, *65*(4), 527–534. doi:10.1016/j.jbusres.2011.02.032

Pava, M., & Krausz, J. (1996). The association between corporate social responsibility and financial performance: The paradox of social cost. *Journal of Business Ethics*, *15*(3), 321–357. doi:10.1007/BF00382958

Pavlin, S., Kesting, T., & Baaken, T. (2016). An Integrative View on Higher Education and University-Business Cooperation in the Light of Academic Entrepreneurship. *European Journal of Education*, *51*(1), 3–9. doi:10.1111/ejed.12168

Paxton, J., Graham, D., & Thraen, C. (2000). Modeling group loan repayment behavior: New insights from Burkina Faso. *Economic Development and Cultural Change*, *48*(3), 639–655. doi:10.1086/452613

Pena, M. A. (2009). *La Escuela de Salamanca. De la Monarquía hispánica al Orbe católico*. Madrid, Spain: Biblioteca de Autores Cristianos.

Pereira de Castro-Pacheco, A., Benini, E. G., & Pasquotto-Mariani, M. A. (2017). The creative economy in Brazil: The development of local tourism in the southern marsh of Mato Grosso. *Estudios y Perspectivas en Turismo*, *26*(3), 678–697.

Pereira, F. (2003). Reflexión sobre algunas características del espíritu emprendedor colombiano. *Revista Economía. Gestión y Desarrollo*, *1*, 9–26.

Pereira, F. (2007). *La evolución del espíritu empresarial como campo del conocimiento. Hacia una visión sistémica y humanista. Cuadernos de Administración*. Bogota, Colombia: Universidad Javeriana de Bogotá.

Pérez, C. (2009). *Técnica de Análisis de Datos con SPSS 15*. Madrid, Spain: Pearson Educación.

Perry, S. J., Hunter, E. M., & Currall, S. C. (2016). Managing the innovators, Organizational and professional commitment among scientists and engineers. *Research Policy*, *45*(6), 1247–1262. doi:10.1016/j.respol.2016.03.009

Peteraf, M. A., & Barney, J. B. (2003). Unraveling the Resource-based Tangle. *Managerial and Decision Economics*, *24*(4), 309–323. doi:10.1002/mde.1126

Peters, T., & Waterman, R. (1984). *En busca de la excelencia*. Bogota, Colombia: Editorial Norma.

Pfeffer, J. (1994). *Competitive advantage through people*. Boston: Harvard Business School Press. doi:10.2307/41165742

Phillips, W., Lee, H., Ghobadian, A., O'Regan, N., & James, P. (2015). Social Innovation and Social Entrepreneurship: A Systematic Review. *Group & Organization Management*, *40*(3), 428–461. doi:10.1177/1059601114560063

Phippen, A., Sheppard, L., & Furnell, S. (2004). A practical evaluation of Web analytics. *Internet Research*, *14*(4), 284–293. doi:10.1108/10662240410555306

Pico, L., & Coello, R. (2017). Relación entre el ciclo de vida de las Pymes en redes sociales y el emprendimiento en la ciudad de Guayaquil. *INNOVA*, *2*(5), 125–136.

Pikkety, T. (2014). *Capital in the 21st century*. Harvard University Press.

Pimentel, D., Couto, J. P., & Scholten, M. (2017). Entrepreneurial orientation in family firms, Looking at an outermost European region. *Journal of Enterprising Culture*, *25*(4), 441–460. doi:10.1142/S0218495817500169

Pinchot, G. (1985). Intrapreneuring. Bogota, Colombia: Norma.

Pindado, J., & Requejo, I. (2015). Family business performance from a governance perspective, a review of empirical research. *International Journal of Management Reviews*, *17*(3), 279–311. doi:10.1111/ijmr.12040

Pinillos, M., Reyes, L., & Soriano, I. (2007). *Actividad emprendedora en países de alto desarrollo*. Madrid, Spain: Universidad Rey Juan Carlos.

Pinto, L. (1999). Currículo por competencia: Necesidad de una nueva escuela. *Tarea: Revista de Educación y Cultura*, *43*, 10–17.

Pitt, M. M., & Khandker, S. R. (1998). The Impact of Group-Based Credit on Poor Households in Bangladesh: Does the Gender of Participants Matter? *Journal of Political Economy*, *106*(5), 958–996. doi:10.1086/250037

Ployhart, R. E., & Moliterno, T. P. (2011). Emergence of the Human Capital Resource: A Multilevel Model. *Academy of Management Review*, *36*(1), 127–150. doi:10.5465/amr.2009.0318

Podsakoff, P. M., MacKenzie, S. B., Lee, J. Y., & Podsakoff, N. P. (2003). Common method biases in behavioral research. A critical review of the literature and recommended remedies. *Applied Psychology*, *88*(5), 879–903. doi:10.1037/0021-9010.88.5.879 PMID:14516251

Podsakoff, P. M., & Organ, D. W. (1986). Self-reports in organizational research, Problems and prospects. *Journal of Management*, *12*(4), 531–544. doi:10.1177/014920638601200408

Pombo, C., Gupta, R., & Stankovic, M. (2018). *Social Services for Digital Citizens: Opportunities for Latin America and the Caribbean*. Washington, DC: Inter-American Development Bank.

Ponds, R., Van Oort, F., & Frenken, K. (2010). Innovation, spillovers, and university-industry collaboration: An extended knowledge production function approach. *Journal of Economic Geography*, *10*(2), 231–255. doi:10.1093/jeg/lbp036

Pongracz, E. (2014). Education as a key factor in the development of social entrepreneurship. In *13th. International Academic Conference, Antibes, Proceedings*. Prague: International Institute of Social and Economic Sciences.

Ponomariov, B., & Boardman, P. C. (2008). The effect of informal industry contacts on the time university scientists allocates to collaborative research with industry. *The Journal of Technology Transfer*, *33*(3), 301–313. doi:10.100710961-007-9029-z

Ponti, F., & Ferràs, X. (2008). Pasión por innovar. Un modelo novedoso que incentiva la creatividad empresarial. Bogota, Colombia: Norma.

Popkova, E. G., Ragulina, Y. V., & Bogoviz, A. V. (2019). Fundamental differences of transition to industry 4.0 from previous industrial revolutions, *Studies in Systems. Decision and Control*, *169*, 21–29.

Porter, C. E. (2004). A typology of virtual communities: A multi-disciplinary foundation for future research. *Journal of Computer-Mediated Communication*, *10*(1), 3.

Porter, L. W., Steers, R. M., Mowday, R. T., & Boulian, P. V. (1974). Organizational commitment, job satisfaction, and turnover among psychiatric technicians. *The Journal of Applied Psychology*, *59*(5), 603–609. doi:10.1037/h0037335

Porter, M. (2002). *Ventaja competitiva. Creación y sostenimiento de un desempeño superior*. CECSA.

Porter, M. E. (1980). *Competitive Strategy*. New York: Free Press.

Porter, M. E. (1980). *Competitive Strategy: Techniques for analyzing industries and competitors*. New York: Free Press.

Porter, M. E. (1985). *Competitive advantage*. New York: Free Press.

Porter, M. E. (1985). *Competitive advantage: Creating and sustaining superior performance*. Free Press.

Porter, M. E. (1990). *Competitive Advantage of Nations*. New York: The Free Press. doi:10.1007/978-1-349-11336-1

Porter, M. E. (1991). Towards a dynamic theory of strategy. *Strategic Management Journal*, *12*(S2), 95–117. doi:10.1002mj.4250121008

Porter, M. E. (2001). *Strategy and the Internet*. Academic Press.

Porter, M. E. (2008). *On competition*. Harvard Business Press.

Porter, M. E., & Kramer, M. R. (2006). Strategy and society: The link between competitive advantage and corporate social responsibility. *Harvard Business Review*, *84*, 78–92. PMID:17183795

Porter, M. E., Schwab, K., & Sachs, J. (2004). *The global competitiveness report 2004-2005*. New York, NY: Palgrave Macmillan.

Powell, T. H., Thomas, H., & McGee, J. (2004). *Dynamic knowledge creation. Dynamics of Strategy*. University of Surrey.

Poza, E. J. (2005). *Empresas de Familia*. D.F., Mexico: Thomson.

Prada, R. (2016). Las TIC, factor de efectividad en la aplicación del mercadeo digital en negocios de retail. *Revista Escuela de Administración de Negocios*, *80*, 105-116.

Prada, R. (2016). Las TICs, factor de efectividad en la aplicación del mercadeo digital en negocios de retail. *Revista EAN*, *80*(80), 105–116. doi:10.21158/01208160.n80.2016.1460

Pradhan, P., Nigam, D., & Tiwari, C. K. (2018). Digital marketing and SMEs : An identification of the research gap via archives of past research. *Journal of Internet Banking and Commerce*, *23*(1), 1–15.

Prahalad, C.K., & Hart, S.L. (2002). The fortune at the bottom of the pyramid. *Strategy + Business, 26*, 1–14.

Prahalad, C. (2010). *The Fortune at the Bottom of the Pyramid: Eradicating Poverty Through Profits*. Upper Saddle River, NJ: Prentice Hall. doi:10.19177/reen.v1e220081-23

Prahalad, C. K., & Hamel, G. (1990). Core competency concept. *Harvard Business Review*, *64*, 56–64.

Prange, C., & Schlegelmilch, B. B. (2010). Heading for the next innovation archetype? *The Journal of Business Strategy*, *31*(1), 46–55. doi:10.1108/02756661011012778

Prats, J., & Agulles, R. (2009). Competencias que todo emprendedor debería desarrollar. Algo más que intuición para los negocios. *IESE Business Insight*, *2*, 50–57.

Priem, R., & Butler, J. (2001a). Is the resource-based "view" a useful perspective for strategic management research? *Academy of Management Review*, *26*(1), 22–40.

Priem, R., & Butler, J. (2001b). Tautology in the resource-based view and the implications of externally determined resource value: Further comments. *Academy of Management Review*, *26*(1), 57–66. doi:10.5465/amr.2001.4011946

Prokopowicz, D., Gwoździewicz, S., Grzegorek, J., & Matosek, M. (2018). Determinants of the Safety of the Electronic Daily Transfer in the Context of Global Trends on the Internet Development of the Mobile Banking. *International Journal of New Economics and Social Sciences*, *7*(1), 188–201. doi:10.5604/01.3001.0012.2694

Prokopowicz, D., & Wielkopolski, G. (2017). The Big Data technologies as an important factor of electronic data processing and the development of computerized analytical platforms, Business Intelligence. *International Journal of Small and Medium Enterprises and Business Sustainability*, *2*(4), 27–42.

Protogerou, A., Caloghirou, Y., & Lioukas, S. (2008). *Dynamic capabilities and their indirect impact on firm performance.* DRUID 25th Celebration Conference, Copenhagen, Denmark.

Puto, A., & Koŝcielniak, H. (2015). Analysis of Purchasing Behaviour of Polish e-customers. *Procedia Computer Science*, *65*, 996–1005. doi:10.1016/j.procs.2015.09.060

Quatraro, F., & Vivarelli, M. (2015). Drivers of entrepreneurship and post-entry performance of newborn firms in developing countries. *The World Bank Research Observer*, *30*(2), 277–305. doi:10.1093/wbro/lku012

Quevedo, P. (2017). *Influencia del marketing digital y online en la fidelización de los clientes de consumo masivo en las redes sociales: categoría chocolatinas.* Manizales, Colombia: Universidad de Manizales.

Quiñones, D., Rusu, C., & Rusu, V. (2018). A methodology to develop usability/user experience heuristics. *Computer Standards & Interfaces*, *59*, 109–129. doi:10.1016/j.csi.2018.03.002

Racic, D., & Viduka, Z. (2013). Desarrollo de Emprendimiento Innovador en Croacia: Análisis y Recomendaciones de Política. In Actas de la Conferencia Internacional de Innovación Valle-Beijing 2013 Suzhou-Silicio (SIIC): Innovación Tecnológica y Diásporas en una Era Global (pp. 56–60). Suzhou, China: Academic Press. doi:10.1109/SIIC.2013.6624166

RAE. (1992). *Diccionario de la Lengua Española*. Espasa Calpe.

RAEE Colombia, . (2014). *Cifras y estimativos para Colombia*. Electrodomésticos.

Rai, A. S., & Sjöström, T. (2004). Is Grameen lending efficient? Repayment incentives and insurance in village economies. *The Review of Economic Studies*, *71*(1), 217–234. doi:10.1111/0034-6527.00282

Rainey, D. L. (2006). *Sustainable business development: inventing the future through strategy, innovation, and leadership*. Cambridge, UK: Cambridge University Press. doi:10.1017/CBO9780511617607

Raisch, S., & Birkingshaw, J. (2008). Organizational ambidexterity. Antecedents, outcomes, and moderators. *Journal of Management*, *34*(3), 375–409. doi:10.1177/0149206308316058

Ramola, F. (1973). Economistas españoles de los siglos XVI y XVII. *Economics and Politics*, *63*, 159–165.

Ramos, C. A. (2015). The paradigms of scientific research. *Avances en Psicología: Revista de la Facultad de Psicología y Humanidades*, *23*(1), 9–17.

Randall, D. M., Fedor, D. B., & Longenecker, C. O. (1990). The behavioral expression of organizational commitment. *Journal of Vocational Behavior*, *36*(2), 210–224. doi:10.1016/0001-8791(90)90028-Z

Rao, A. (2007). Evaluation of enterprise risk management (ERM) in Dubai – an emerging economy. *Risk Management*, *9*(3), 167–187. doi:10.1057/palgrave.rm.8250031

Rauch, A., Wiklund, J., Lumpkin, G., & Frese, M. (2009). Entrepreneurial Orientation and Business Performance: An Assessment of Past Research and Suggestions for the Future. *Entrepreneurship Theory and Practice*, *33*(3), 761–787. doi:10.1111/j.1540-6520.2009.00308.x

Rausch, E., Sherman, H., & Washbush, J. B. (2002). Defining and assessing competences for competency-based, outcome-focused management development. *Journal of Management Development*, *21*(3), 184–200. doi:10.1108/02621710210420264

Ray, G., Barney, J. B., & Muhanna, W. A. (2004). Capabilities, business processes, and competitive advantage: Choosing the dependent variable in empirical tests of the resource-based view. *Strategic Management Journal, 25*(1), 23–37. doi:10.1002mj.366

Razeto, L. (1993). *Los caminos de la economía de solidaridad.* Santiago, Chile: Vivarium.

Razeto, L. (1998). El factor C y la economía de la solidaridad. In *Cuadernos de Educación, 1.* Montevideo, Uruguay: Cofac.

Red Senk. (2011). *Escala e Impacto en Negocios sociales en Iberoamérica.* Retrieved from http://www.sekn.org/cms/index.php/proyectos.html

Reggiani, T. (2005). *Grameen Bank II: a possible analysis with a relational perspective. MPRA (Munich Personal RePec Archive) Paper, 1526.* Munich, Germany: University Library of Munich.

Reinstaller, A. (2013). *An evolutionary view on social innovation and the process of economic change.* WWW for Europe.

Renaut, A. (2005). *La Responsabilidad Social de las empresas en Europa: ¿tiene el diálogo social alguna oportunidad?* International Labor Organization.

Revilla, A. J., Pérez-Luño, A., & Nieto, M. J. (2016). Does family involvement in management reduce the risk of business failure? The moderating role of entrepreneurial orientation. *Family Business Review, 29*(4), 365–379. doi:10.1177/0894486516671075

Reyes-Godínez, M. (2016). Economy and culture in Mexico. Notes of an agenda under construction. Periférica Internacional. *Revista para el análisis de la cultura y el territorio, 17,* 209-229.

Reynolds, M., & Yuthas, K. (2008). Moral discourse and corporate social responsibility reporting. *Journal of Business Ethics, 78*(1-2), 47–64. doi:10.100710551-006-9316-x

Ricardo, D. (1959). *Principios de Economía Política y Tributación.* Fondo de Cultura Económica.

Rifkin, J. (2011). *The Third Industrial Revolution: How Lateral Power Is Transforming Energy, the Economy, and the World.* New York: Palgrave Macmillan.

Risitano, M., Romano, R., Sorrentino, A., & Quintano, M. (2017). The impact of consumer-brand engagement on brand experience and behavioural intentions: An Italian empirical study. *British Food Journal, 119*(8), 1884–1896. doi:10.1108/BFJ-11-2016-0579

Rivera, R. (2016). A dynamic linear model to forecast hotel registrations in Puerto Rico using Google Trends data. *Tourism Management, 57,* 12–20. doi:10.1016/j.tourman.2016.04.008

Roberts, D., & Woods, C. (2005). Changing the world on a shoestring: The concept of social entrepreneurship. *University of Auckland Business Review, 23,* 45–51.

Robinson, M. A., Sparrow, P. R., Clegg, C., & Birdi, K. (2007). Forecasting future competency requirements. A three-phase methodology. *Personnel Review, 36*(1), 65–90. doi:10.1108/00483480710716722

Rodima-Taylor, D. (2012). Social innovation and climate adaptation: Local collective action in diversifying Tanzania. *Applied Geography (Sevenoaks, England), 33,* 128–134. doi:10.1016/j.apgeog.2011.10.005

Rodrigo-Alarcón, J., García-Villaverde, P. M., Ruiz-Ortega, M. J., & Parra-Requena, G. (2018). From social capital to entrepreneurial orientation, The mediating role of dynamic capabilities. *European Management Journal, 36*(2), 195–209. doi:10.1016/j.emj.2017.02.006

Rodríguez, L. (2014). Diseño de comunicaciones en redes sociales digitales para aumentar los voluntarios de dos ONGs en Argentina. Buenos Aires, Argentina: Academic Press.

Rodríguez, C., & Jiménez, M. (2007). Emprenderismo, acción gubernamental y academia. Revisión de la literatura. *Innovar (Universidad Nacional de Colombia), 15*(26), 73–89.

Rodríguez-Ramírez, A. (2009). New perspectives to understand business entrepreneurship. *Pensamiento & Gestión, 26*, 94–119.

Rogers, D. S., Duraiappah, A. K., Antons, D. C., Munoz, P., Bai, X., Fragkias, M., & Gutscher, H. (2012). A vision for human well-being: Transition to social sustainability. *Current Opinion in Environmental Sustainability, 4*(1), 61–73. doi:10.1016/j.cosust.2012.01.013

Rojas, R., & Torres Briones, C. (2017). La Gestión del Conocimiento basado en la Teoría de Nonaka y Takeuchi. *INNOVA Research Journal, 2*(4), 30–37.

Roman, S., & Loebl, E. (1979). *The Responsible Society. Alternative to Communism and Capitalism*. New Delhi, India: Abhinav Publications.

Roodman, D., & Qureshi, U. (2006). *Microfinance as Business*. Washington, DC: Center for Global Development.

Rosas-Baños, M. (2012). Economía Ecológica y Solidaria: Rumbo a una propuesta teórica integrada que visualice las rutas hacia la transición. *Revista de la Red Iberoamericana de Economía Ecológica, 18*, 89–103.

Rose, A. K., & Spiegel, M. M. (2012). Dollar illiquidity and central bank swap arrangements during the global financial crisis. *Journal of International Economics, 88*(2), 326–340. doi:10.1016/j.jinteco.2012.02.014

Rothaermel, F. T., Agung, S. D., & Jiang, L. (2007). University entrepreneurship: A taxonomy of the literature. *Industrial and Corporate Change, 16*(4), 691–791. doi:10.1093/icc/dtm023

Roto, V. (2007). User experience from a product creation perspective. In E. Law, A. Vermeeren, M. Hassenzahl, & M. Blythe (Eds.), Towards a UX Manifesto, COST294-MAUSE affiliated workshop. Lancaster, UK: Academic Press.

Royle, J., & Laing, A. (2014). The digital marketing skills gap: Developing a digital marketer model for the communication industries. *International Journal of Information Management, 34*(2), 65–73. doi:10.1016/j.ijinfomgt.2013.11.008

Rumelt, R. P. (1991). How much does Industry Matter? *Strategic Management Journal, 12*(3), 167–185. doi:10.1002mj.4250120302

Rumelt, R. P., Schendel, D., & Teece, D. (1994). *Fundamental Issues in Strategy*. Cambridge, MA: Harvard Business School Press.

Ryan, D. (2016). *Understanding digital marketing: marketing strategies for engaging the digital generation*. Kogan Page Publishers.

Sahni, N. S., Wheeler, S. C., & Chintagunta, P. (2018). Personalization in Email Marketing: The Role of Non-informative Advertising Content. *Marketing Science, 37*(2), 236–258. doi:10.1287/mksc.2017.1066

Sainz, J. (2015). *El plan de marketing digital en la práctica*. Madrid, Spain: ESIC.

Saiz-Álvarez, J. M. (2013b). ¿Constituye el ordoliberalismo social un nuevo paradigma socioeconómico ante la triple-C para el emprendimiento? In Cultura Emprendedora y Economía Social. Ávila, Spain: Universidad Católica de Ávila.

Saiz-Álvarez, J. M. (2018). Business Strategies and Advanced Techniques for Entrepreneurship 4.0. Hershey, PA: Information Science Reference (IGI Global).

Saiz-Álvarez, J. M. (2019). Managing Social Innovation Through CSR 2.0 and the Quadruple Helix: A Socially Inclusive Business Strategy for the Industry 4.0. In A. Guerra Guerra (Ed.), Organizational Transformation and Managing Innovation in the Fourth Industrial Revolution (pp. 228-244). Hershey, PA: IGI Global.

Saiz-Álvarez, J. M., Muñiz, E., & Huezo, L. (2016). Informational Competencies, Entrepreneurship, and Integral Values in Higher Education. In Innovation and Shifting Perspectives in Management Education. Hershey, PA: Information Science Reference (IGI Global).

Saiz-Álvarez, J. M. (2011). Factores clave de éxito en la internacionalización de la empresa familiar: Una aplicación a la pyme. *Economía Industrial*, *380*, 57–62.

Saiz-Álvarez, J. M. (2013a). Socioeconomía de la solidaridad, valores y justicia social: La necesidad de recristianizar la economía. *Revista Gestión y Sociedad*, *6*(2), 69–80.

Salas-Muñoz, R. (n.d.). A critical analysis of the conceptual framework of sustainable development and their measurement tools. *Revista En-Contexto, 6*(8), 171-184.

Salgado-Lévano, A. C. (2007). Qualitative research: Designs, evaluation of methodological rigor and challenges. *Liberabit*, *13*(13), 71–78.

Salo, J. (2017). Social media research in the industrial marketing field: Review of literature and future research directions. *Industrial Marketing Management*, *66*(7), 115–129. doi:10.1016/j.indmarman.2017.07.013

Sambamurthy, V., Bharadwaj, A., & Grover, V. (2003). Shaping agility through digital options. Reconceptualizing the role of information technology in contemporary firms. *Management Information Systems Quarterly*, *27*(2), 237–263. doi:10.2307/30036530

San José, R., Camarero, C., & Rodríguez, J. (2012). Looking for online opinion leaders: Why companies must identify and take care of more active users of online opinion spaces. *Universia Business Review*, (35): 14–31.

San Juan Pablo II. (1991). *Enciclical Letter Centesimus Annus en el centenario de la Rerum Novarum*. The Vatican City: Author.

San Juan Pablo, I. I. (1989). Enciclical Letter Sollicitudo rei socialis. The Vatican City: Author.

San Juan XXIII. (1961). *Enciclical Letter Mater et Magistra, sobre el reciente desarrollo de la cuestión social*. The Vatican City: Author.

Sánchez-Serra, D. (2016). Location determinants of creative industries' firms in Spain. *Journal of Regional Research*, *34*, 23–48.

Sánchez-Trujillo, M. G., Molina-Ruiz, H. D., & García-Vargas, M. L. (2018). The economic dimension of the creative economy. *TEPEXI Boletín Científico de la Escuela Superior Tepeji del Río*, *5*(9). doi:10.29057/estr.v5i9.2971

Santamaría, F., & Escobar, M. (2011). Estrategias empresariales ante el comercio electrónico. *Información Comercial Española. ICE. Revista de economía*, *813*, 187–196.

Santos del Cerro, J. (1998). El pensamiento económico de la Escuela de Salamanca. *VI Congreso de Economía Regional de Castilla y León*, 1829-1837.

Santos, A., Neto, P., & Serrano, M. M. (2016). A long-term mortality analysis of subsidized firms in rural areas: An empirical study in the Portuguese Alentejo region. *Eurasian Economic Review*, *6*(1), 125–151. doi:10.100740822-015-0035-4

Santos, F. J. (2004). Crecimiento, desarrollo y empresarialidad en el proceso de globalizacion economica. *Revista de Economía Mundial*, *10/11*, 171–202.

Santos, F. J., Barroso, M., & Guzmán, C. (2013). La economía global y los emprendimientos sociales. *Revista de Economía Mundial*, *35*, 21–45.

Sastre-Castillo, M. A., Peris-Ortiz, M., & Danvila-Del Valle, I. (2015). What Is Different about the Profile of the Social Entrepreneur? *Nonprofit Management & Leadership*, *25*(4), 349–369. doi:10.1002/nml.21138

Savage, N. (2011). Twitter as medium and message. *Communications of the ACM*, *54*(3), 18–20. doi:10.1145/1897852.1897860

Say, J. B. (1821). *Letters to Thomas Robert Malthus on Political Economy and Stagnation of Commerce*. London, UK: Academic Press.

Scharmer, C. O., & Käufer, K. (2010). In front of the blank canvas. Sensing emerging futures. *The Journal of Business Strategy*, *31*(4), 21–29. doi:10.1108/02756661011055159

Schepers, J., Voordeckers, W., Steijvers, T., & Laveren, E. (2014). The entrepreneurial orientation-performance relationship in private family firms, the moderating role of socioemotional wealth. *Small Business Economics*, *43*(1), 39–55. doi:10.100711187-013-9533-5

Schmalensee, R. (1985). Do markets differ much? *The American Economic Review*, *75*, 341–351.

Schmitt, B. (2012). The consumer psychology of brands. *Journal of Consumer Psychology*, *22*(1), 7–17. doi:10.1016/j.jcps.2011.09.005

Schmitt, B. (2013). The consumer psychology of customer-brand relationships: Extending the AA Relationship model. *Journal of Consumer Psychology*, *23*(2), 249–252. doi:10.1016/j.jcps.2013.01.003

Scholars, E. (2010). *From words to action: supporting cooperative and social enterprises to achieve a more inclusive, sustainable and prosperous Europe | Euricse*. Retrieved from http://www.euricse.eu/publications/from-words-to-action-supporting-cooperative-and-social-enterprises-to-achieve-a-more-inclusive-sustainable-and-prosperous-europe/

Scholz, J., & Duffy, K. (2018). We ARe at home: How augmented reality reshapes mobile marketing and consumer-brand relationships. *Journal of Retailing and Consumer Services*, *44*(5), 11–23. doi:10.1016/j.jretconser.2018.05.004

Schreiner, M. (2003). A cost-effectiveness analysis of the Grameen Bank of Bangladesh. *Development Policy Review*, *21*(3), 357–382. doi:10.1111/1467-7679.00215

Schumacher, E. F. (1973). *Small is beautiful: Economics as if people really mattered.* London: Abacus.

Schumpeter, J.A. (1978). *Teoría del desenvolvimiento económico*. Fondo de cultura económica.

Schumpeter, J. (2008). *Historia del Análisis Económico*. Barcelona: Ariel Economía. (Original work published 1954)

Schumpeter, J. A. (1939). *Ciclos económicos*. Buenos Aires, Argentina: Claridad.

Schumpeter, J. A. (1946). *Capitalismo, socialismo y democracia*. Buenos Aires, Argentina: Claridad.

Schumpeter, J. A. (1947). Theoretical Problems: Theoretical Problems of Economic Growth. *The Journal of Economic History*, *7*(S1), 1–9. doi:10.1017/S0022050700065189

Schumpeter, J. A. (1947a). The creative response in economic history. *The Journal of Economic History*, *7*(2), 149–159. doi:10.1017/S0022050700054279

Schwab, C. (2015). *Are you ready for the technological revolution?* Retrieved from https://agenda.weforum.org/2015/02/are-you-ready-for-the-technological-revolution/

Schwab, K. (2010). *The global competitiveness report 2010-2011*. Geneva: World Economic Forum.

Sciascia, S., Mazzola, P., & Chirico, F. (2013). Generational involvement in the top management team of family firms, Exploring nonlinear effects on entrepreneurial orientation. *Entrepreneurship Theory and Practice*, *37*(1), 69–85. doi:10.1111/j.1540-6520.2012.00528.x

Sciascia, S., Mazzola, P., & Kellermanns, F. W. (2014). Family management and profitability in private family-owned firms, Introducing generational stage and the socioemotional wealth perspective. *Journal of Family Business Strategy*, *5*(2), 131–137. doi:10.1016/j.jfbs.2014.03.001

Sckibick, M. (2009). *Las ONG como vía al desarrollo y a la transformación social: Un estilo de intervención y participación* (Ph.D. Thesis). Barcelona, Spain: Autonomous University of Barcelona.

Sedereviciute, K. (2010). *Towards a more holistic stakeholder analysis approach. Mapping current and potential stakeholders from social media* (Master thesis). University of Aarhus, Denmark.

Seelosa, C., & Mair, J. (2005). Social entrepreneurship: Creating new business models to serve the poor. *Business Horizons*, *48*(3), 241–246. doi:10.1016/j.bushor.2004.11.006

Seitz, J., & Burosch, A. (2018). Digital Value Creation. In *2018 IEEE International Conference on Engineering, Technology, and Innovation (ICE/ITMC)* (pp. 1-5). IEEE. 10.1109/ICE.2018.8436380

Semerádová, T., & Vávrová, J. N. (2016). Using a systemic approach to assess Internet marketing communication within the hospitality industry. *Tourism Management Perspectives*, *20*, 276–289. doi:10.1016/j.tmp.2016.09.007

Senger, J. (1971). Managers' Perceptions of Subordinates' Competence as a Function of Personal Value. *Academy of Management Journal*, *14*(4), 415–423.

Sen, R. (2005). Optimal search engine marketing strategy. *International Journal of Electronic Commerce*, *10*(1), 9–25. doi:10.1080/10864415.2005.11043964

Sethi, S. P. (1975). Dimensions of corporate social performance: An analytical framework. *California Management Review*, *17*(3), 58–64. doi:10.2307/41162149

Sexton, D., Pricer, R., & Nenide, B. (2002). Measuring performance in high growth firms. *Babson Entrepreneurship Research Conference*, Wellesley, MA.

Seyfang, G., Hielscher, S., Hargreaves, T., Martiskainen, M., & Smith, A. (2014). A grassroots sustainable energy niche? Reflections on community energy in the UK. *Environmental Innovation and Societal Transitions*, *13*, 21–44. doi:10.1016/j.eist.2014.04.004

Seyfang, G., & Smith, A. (2007). Grassroots innovations for sustainable development: Towards a new research and policy agenda. *Environmental Politics*, *16*(4), 584–603. doi:10.1080/09644010701419121

Shafer, S., Smith, H., & Linder, J. (2005). The power of the business model. *Business Horizons*, *48*(3), 199–207. doi:10.1016/j.bushor.2004.10.014

Shane, S., & Venkataraman, S. (2000). The Promise of Entrepreneurship as a Field of Research. *Academy of Management Review*, *25*(1), 217–226.

Shankar, V., Kleijnen, M., Ramanathan, S., Rizley, R., Holland, S., & Morrissey, S. (2016). ScienceDirect Mobile Shopper Marketing : Key Issues, Current Insights, and Future Research Avenues. *Journal of Interactive Marketing*, *34*, 37–48. doi:10.1016/j.intmar.2016.03.002

Shanker, M. C., & Astrachan, J. H. (1996). Myths, and realities, Family businesses' contribution to the US Economy. A framework for assessing family business statistics. *Family Business Review*, *9*(2), 107–123. doi:10.1111/j.1741-6248.1996.00107.x

Shan, P., Song, M., & Ju, X. (2016). Entrepreneurial orientation and performance. Is innovation speed a missing link? *Journal of Business Research*, *69*(2), 683–690. doi:10.1016/j.jbusres.2015.08.032

Sharir, M., & Lerner, M. (2006). Gauging the success of social ventures initiated by individual social entrepreneurs. *Journal of World Business*, *41*(1), 6–20. doi:10.1016/j.jwb.2005.09.004

Sharma, S. (2006, August). Are micro-finance institutions exploiting the poor? *InfoChange News & Features*.

Sharma, P. (2004). On overview of the field of family business studies, Current status and directions for the future. *Family Business Review*, *17*(1), 1–36. doi:10.1111/j.1741-6248.2004.00001.x

Sharma, P., Chrisman, J. J., & Gersick, K. E. (2012). 25 years of family business review, Reflections on the past and perspectives for the future. *Family Business Review*, *25*(1), 5–15. doi:10.1177/0894486512437626

Shaw, E., & de Bruin, A. (2013). Reconsidering capitalism: The promise of social innovation and social entrepreneurship? *International Small Business Journal*, *31*(7), 737–746. doi:10.1177/0266242613497494

Shek, D. T., & Lin, L. (2015). Nurturing university students to be social entrepreneurs: Relevance of service leadership education. *International Journal on Disability and Human Development: IJDHD*, *14*(3), 285–293.

Shen, K. N., Lindsay, V., & Xu, Y. (2018). Digital entrepreneurship. *Information Systems Journal*, *28*(6), 1125–1128. doi:10.1111/isj.12219

Shinnar, R. S., Giacomin, O., & Janssen, F. (2012). Entrepreneurial perceptions and intentions: The role of gender and culture. *Entrepreneurship Theory and Practice*, *36*(3), 465–493. doi:10.1111/j.1540-6520.2012.00509.x

Short, J. C., Moss, T. W., & Lumpkin, G. T. (2009). Research in social entrepreneurship: Past contributions and future opportunities. *Strategic Entrepreneurship Journal*, *3*(2), 161–194. doi:10.1002ej.69

Shortreed, J. (2010). Enterprise risk management and ISO 31000. *Journal of Policy Engagement*, *2*(3), 8–10.

Shuptrine, F. K., & Osmianski, F. A. (1975). Marketing's Changing Role: Expanding of Contracting. *Journal of Marketing*, *39*, 58–66.

Sieger, P., Bernhard, F., & Frey, U. (2011). Affective commitment and job satisfaction among non-family employees, Investigating the roles of justice perceptions and psychological ownership. *Journal of Family Business Strategy*, *2*(2), 78–89. doi:10.1016/j.jfbs.2011.03.003

Sigurbjörnsson, B., & Van Zwol, R. (2008). Flickr tag recommendation based on collective knowledge. *Proceedings of the 17th international conference on World Wide Web*, 327-336. 10.1145/1367497.1367542

Silakalne-Araja, D., & Arajs, R. (2012). Promoción de la Educación de Adultos en el negocio innovador. *Scientific International Conference on Society, Integration, and Education 2012*, 429-440.

Simmel, G. (1900). A chapter in the Philosophy of value. *American Journal of Sociology*, *5*, 16.

Simmel, G. (1910). How is society possible? *American Journal of Sociology*, *16*(3), 13–23. doi:10.1086/211904

Simmons, G. (2008). Marketing to postmodern consumers: Introducing the internet chameleon. *European Journal of Marketing*, *42*(3/4), 299–310. doi:10.1108/03090560810852940

Simtowe, F., & Zeller, M. (2006). *Determinants of Moral Hazards in Microfinance: Empirical Evidence from Joint Liability Lending Programs in Malawi. MPRA (Munich Personal RePec Archive) Paper, 461*. Munich, Germany: University Library of Munich.

Singer, P. (2002). *Introdução à Economia Solidária*. São Paulo, Brasil: Fundação Perseu Abramo.

Singh, S., & Sonnenburg, S. (2012). Brand performances in social media. *Journal of Interactive Marketing*, *26*(4), 189–197. doi:10.1016/j.intmar.2012.04.001

Skinner, J.D. (1994). Learning by Teaching. *Zielsprache Englisch*, *2*(94), 38-39.

Slade, G. (2006). *Made to break: technology and obsolescence in America*. Boston: Harvard University Press.

Smelser, N. (1965). *Sociología de la vida económica*. Uteha.

Smelser, N., & Swedberg, R. (2005). *Introducing Economic Sociology*. Princeton University Press.

Smilor, R. W., Gibson, D. V., & Dietrich, G. B. (1990). University spin-out companies: Technology start-ups from UT-Austin. *Journal of Business Venturing*, *5*(1), 63–76. doi:10.1016/0883-9026(90)90027-Q

Smith, A. (1776). *La riqueza de las naciones*. Madrid, Spain: Alianza Editorial.

Smith, A. (1958). *Investigación sobre la naturaleza y causas de la riqueza de las naciones*. Fondo de Cultura Económica. (Original work published 1776)

Smith, D., Menon, S., & Sivakumar, K. (2005). Online peer and editorial recommendations, trust, and choice in virtual markets. *Journal of Interactive Marketing*, *19*(3), 15–37. doi:10.1002/dir.20041

Smith, G. P. (2012). Google Internet search activity and volatility prediction in the market for foreign currency. *Finance Research Letters*, *9*(2), 103–110. doi:10.1016/j.frl.2012.03.003

Smith, I. H., & Woodworth, W. P. (2012). Developing Social Entrepreneurs and Social Innovators: A Social Identity and Self-Efficacy Approach. *Academy of Management Learning & Education*, *11*(3), 390–407. doi:10.5465/amle.2011.0016

Smith, J. K. (1983). Quantitative versus Qualitative Research: An Attempt to Clarify the Issue. *Educational Researcher*, *12*(3), 6–13. doi:10.3102/0013189X012003006

Snow, D. A. (2001). Extending and broadening Blumer's conceptualization of symbolic interactionism. *Symbolic Interaction*, *24*(3), 367–377. doi:10.1525i.2001.24.3.367

Soini, E., & Veseli, L. (2011). Factors influencing SMEs growth in Kosovo. *International Business Management*, *75*, 8–64.

Solomon, M. (2013). *Comportamiento del Consumidor*. Pearson.

Somers, M. J. (2010). Patterns of attachment to organizations, commitment profiles and work outcomes. *Journal of Occupational and Organizational Psychology*, *83*(2), 443–453. doi:10.1348/096317909X424060

Soubbotina, T. P. (2004). *Beyond economic growth: An introduction to sustainable development*. World Bank Publications. doi:10.1596/0-8213-5933-9

Soubbotina, T. P., & Sheram, K. (2000). *Beyond economic growth: Meeting the challenges of global development*. World Bank Publications.

Spear, R., Aiken, M., Noya, A., & Clarence, E. (2013). *Boosting social entrepreneurship and social enterprise creation*. Paris, France: OECD.

Spector, P. E. (2006). Method variance in organizational research, Truth or urban legend? *Organizational Research Methods, 9*(2), 221–232. doi:10.1177/1094428105284955

Spulber, D. F. (2012). El conocimiento tácito con el emprendimiento innovador. *Revista Internacional de Organización Industrial, 30*(6), 641–653.

Stachová, K., Papula, J., Stacho, Z., & Kohnová, L. (2019). External partnerships in employee education and development as the key to facing industry 4.0 challenges. *Sustainability, 11*(2), 345. doi:10.3390u11020345

Stajano, A. (2010). *Research, Quality, Competitiveness. EU Technology Policy for the Knowledge-based Society*. Springer.

Stanley, L. (2010) Emotions and family business creation, an extension and implications. *Entrep Theor Pract, 34*(6), 1085–1092.

Stanley, L., Hernández-Linares, R., López-Fernández, M. C., & Kellermanns, F. (2019). (forthcoming). A typology of family firms, An investigation of entrepreneurial orientation and performance. *Family Business Review*.

Starr, R. G., & Brodie, R. J. (2016). Certification and authentication of brand value propositions. *Journal of Brand Management, 23*(6), 716–731. doi:10.105741262-016-0012-6

Stenholm, P., Pukkinen, T., & Heinonen, J. (2016). Firm growth in family businesses, The role of entrepreneurial orientation and the entrepreneurial activity. *Journal of Small Business Management, 54*(3), 691–713.

Stephen, A. T. (2016). The role of digital and social media marketing in consumer behavior. *Current Opinion in Psychology, 10*, 17–21. doi:10.1016/j.copsyc.2015.10.016

Stevenson, H., & Jarillo, C. (1990). A paradigm of entrepreneurship: Entrepreneurial management. *Strategic Management Journal, 11*, 17–27.

Stiglitz, J. E. (1990). Peer Monitoring and Credit Markets. *The World Bank Economic Review, 4*(3), 197–203. doi:10.1093/wber/4.3.351

Stiglitz, J. E. (2011). Rethinking Development Economics. *The World Bank Research Observer, 26*(2), 230–236. doi:10.1093/wbro/lkr011

StiglitzJ. E. (2018). *Beyond GDP*. Retrieved from https://www.project-syndicate.org/commentary/new-metrics-of-wellbeing-not-just-gdp-by-joseph-e-stiglitz-2018-12

Stiglitz, J. E., Sen, A., & Fitoussi, J.-P. (2010). *Report by the commission on the measurement of economic performance and social progress*. Paris: Commission on the Measurement of Economic Performance and Social Progress.

Stojanova, H., Lietavcova, B., & Raguž, I. V. (2019). The dependence of unemployment of the senior workforce upon explanatory variables in the European Union in the context of Industry 4.0. *Social Sciences, 8*(1), 29. doi:10.3390ocsci8010029

Stone, M. D., & Woodcock, N. D. (2014). Interactive, direct and digital marketing: A future that depends on better use of business intelligence. *Journal of Research in Interactive Marketing, 8*(1), 4–17. doi:10.1108/JRIM-07-2013-0046

Storey, D. (1994). *Understanding the Small Business Sector*. New York: Routledge.

Stuart, R. W., & Abetti, P. A. (1987). Start-up ventures towards the prediction of initial success. *Journal of Business Venturing, 2*(3), 215–230. doi:10.1016/0883-9026(87)90010-3

Subhan, Q. A., Mian Rahat Mehmood, M. R., & Sattar, A. (2013). Innovation in small and medium enterprises (SME's) and its impact on economic development in Pakistan. *Proceedings of 6th International Business and Social Sciences Research Conference*.

Sudharson, K., Ali, A. M., & Sermakani, A. M. (2012). Una perspectiva organizativa de Comunicación del Conocimiento en Desarrollo de Emprendimiento Educación para Estudiantes de Ingeniería. In *Actas de la Segunda Conferencia Internacional de Información Integrado* (Vol. 73, pp. 590–597). Budapest, Hungary: IC-ININFO.

Sullivan Mort, G., Weerawardena, J., & Carnegie, K. (2003). Social entrepreneurship: Towards conceptualization. *International Journal of Nonprofit and Voluntary Sector Marketing*, *8*(1), 76–88. doi:10.1002/nvsm.202

Sussan, F., Autio, E., & Kosturik, J. (2016). *Leveraging ICTs for Better Lives: The Introduction of an Index on Digital Life. CPRLATAM Conference*, Mexico.

Swedberg, R. (2003). *The economic sociology of capitalism: an introduction and agenda.* Cornell University.

Szpilbarg, D., & Saferstein, E. (2014). From 'culture industry' to creative industries: An analysis of the mutation of the concept and its contemporary uses. *Estudios de Filosofía Práctica e Historia de las Ideas*, *16*(2), 99–112.

Taiminen, H. M., & Karjaluoto, H. (2015). The usage of digital marketing channels in SMEs. *Journal of Small Business and Enterprise Development*, *22*(4), 633–651. doi:10.1108/JSBED-05-2013-0073

Taiwo, M. A., Awolaja, M. A., & Yusuf, A. B. (2012). Impact of small and medium enterprises on economic growth and development. *American Journal of Business and Management*, *1*(1), 18–22. doi:10.11634/21679606170644

Taken-Smith, K. (2012). Longitudinal study of digital marketing strategies targeting Millennials. *Journal of Consumer Marketing*, *29*(2), 86–92. doi:10.1108/07363761211206339

Tapscott, D., & Williams, A. (2010). Innovating the 21st-Century University: It's Time! *EDUCAUSE Review*, *45*(1), 16–29.

Tarapuez, E., & Botero, J. (2007). Algunos aportes de los neoclásicos a la teoría del emprendedor. *Cuadernos Americanos*, *23*, 39–63.

Tasci, A. D. A. (2016). Consumer Value and Brand Value: Rivals or Allies in Consumer-Based Brand Equity? *Tourism Analysis*, *21*(5), 481–496. doi:10.3727/108354216X14653218477561

Tavakol, M., & Dennick, R. (2011). Making sense of Cronbach's Alpha. *International Journal of Medical Education*, *2*, 53–55. doi:10.5116/ijme.4dfb.8dfd PMID:28029643

Taylor, F. (2003). *Principios de la administración científica.* Bogota, Colombia: Stilo impresores.

Technical Cooperation Service. (2016). *Results evaluation of the Technical Cooperation Service programs.* Report No. 3 Final Results. Santiago of Chile: Technical Cooperation Service.

Technical Cooperation Service. (2018). *Small Business Development Center in Chile.* Technical Cooperation Service.

Technical Cooperation Service. (2018b). *Grocery stores of Chile. Fund.* Technical Cooperation Service.

TechTerms.com. (2010, January 4). *ICT.* Retrieved Dec 11, 2018, from http://www.techterms.com/definition/ict

Teece, D. (2010). Business models, business strategy and innovation. *Long Range Planning*, *43*(2-3), 172–194. doi:10.1016/j.lrp.2009.07.003

Teece, D. J. (2007). Explicating Dynamic Capabilities: The Nature and Microfoundations of (Sustainable) Enterprise Performance. *Strategic Management Journal*, *28*(13), 1319–1350. doi:10.1002mj.640

Teece, D. J. (2009). *Dynamic Capabilities and Strategy Management.* New York: Oxford University Press Inc.

Teece, D. J., Pisano, G., & Shuen, A. (1997). Dynamic Capabilities and Strategy Management. *Strategic Management Journal*, *18*(7), 509–533. doi:10.1002/(SICI)1097-0266(199708)18:7<509::AID-SMJ882>3.0.CO;2-Z

Tehseen, S., & Ramayah, T. (2015). Entrepreneurial Competences and SMEs Business Success. The Contingent Role of External Integration. *Mediterranean Journal of Social Sciences*, *6*(1), 50–61.

Teichler, U. (2003). Hochschule und Arbeitswelt: Konzeptionen, Diskussionen, Trends (Vol. 873). Frankfurt/M: Campus Verlag.

Tello, A., Romero, A., & Jaramillo, C. (2017). The campaigns of crowdfunding and its impact on the financing of lucrative and non-profit projects in Ecuador. *Revista de Investigación Talentos*, *4*(2), 55–62.

Thackara, J. (2006). *In the bubble. Designing in a complex world.* Boston: MIT Press.

Thake, S., & Zadek, S. (1997). *Practical people, noble causes: How to support community social entrepreneurs*. London, UK: New Economics Foundation.

Thompson, J., Alvy, G., & Lees, A. (2000). Social entrepreneurship – a new look at the people and the potential. *Management Decision*, *38*(5), 328–338. doi:10.1108/00251740010340517

Thorgren, S., & Omorede, A. (2015). Passionate Leaders in Social Entrepreneurship. Exploring an African Context. *Business & Society*, *57*(3), 525–561.

Thornton, P. (1999). The Sociology of Entrepreneurship. *Annual Review of Sociology*, *25*(1), 19–46. doi:10.1146/annurev.soc.25.1.19

Tiago, M. T. P. M. B., & Veríssimo, J. M. C. (2014). Digital marketing and social media: Why bother? *Business Horizons*, *57*(6), 703–708. doi:10.1016/j.bushor.2014.07.002

Ticlau, T. C. (2014). Contemporary business education: A solution for global leadership challenges. *Anfiteatur Economic*, *16*(37), 885–901.

Tironi-Rodó, M. (2010). What is a cluster? Geographies and practices of the experimental music scene in Santiago, Chile. *EURE. Revista Latinoamericana de Estudios Urbano Regionales*, *36*(109), 161–187.

Toca, C. (2010). Consideraciones para la formación en emprendimiento: Explorando nuevos ámbitos y posibilidades. *Estudios Gerenciales*, *26*(4), 41–60.

Torres, C., & Guzmán, E. (2017). Modelo de evaluación de la calidad de servicio aplicado al retail de ropa en centros comerciales. *Revista Espacios*, *38*(23), 28–38.

Torres, R., & de las Heras, C. (2017). Fundraising, comunicación y relaciones públicas. Desarrollo cultural de una marca de ciudad: Málaga. *Chasqui. Revista Latinoamericana de Comunicación*, *136*(136), 375–394. doi:10.16921/chasqui.v0i136.2841

Tracey, P., & Phillips, N. (2007). The distinctive challenge of educating social entrepreneurs: A postscript and rejoinder to the special issue on entrepreneurship education. *Computers in Human Behavior*, *16*(2), 264–271.

Treviño, T., & Morton, F. (2016). Online Shopping in Mexico: Exploring the Promising and Challenging Panorama. In Mexican Business Culture: Essays on Tradition, Ethics, Entrepreneurship and Commerce and the State (pp. 166-182). McFarland & Company.

Trevino, L. K., Lengel, R. H., & Daft, R. L. (1987). Media symbolism, media richness, and media choice in organizations a symbolic interactionism perspective. *Communication Research*, *14*(5), 553–574. doi:10.1177/009365087014005006

Treviño, T. (2017). Madres digitales en Monterrey, México: Estudio de hábitos, comportamientos y actitudes en Internet. *Revista Argentina de Investigación en Negocios*, *3*(2), 71–79.

Treviño, T., & Pineda, J. L. (2017). *Mamás Digitales en México: ¿Por qué se conectan con las marcas en Internet?* El Financiero.

Túnez, M., García, J., & Guevara-Castillo, M. (2011). Redes sociales y marketing viral: Repercusión e incidencia en la construcción de la agenda mediática. *Palabra Clave (La Plata)*, *14*(1), 53–65.

Turgot, J. (1776). *Reflections on the Formation and Distribution of Wealth*. London, UK: E. Spragg.

Turner, P. (2017). Implementing Integrated Marketing Communications (IMC) through major event ambassadors. *European Journal of Marketing*, *51*(3), 605–626. doi:10.1108/EJM-09-2015-0631

Turriago, Á. (2002). *Gerencia de la innovación tecnológica*. Bogota, Colombia: Alfaomega y Cambio.

Tuzzolino, F., & Armandi, B. R. (1981). A need-hierarchy framework for assessing corporate social responsibility. *Academy of Management Review*, *6*(1), 21–28. doi:10.5465/amr.1981.4287982

Tynan, B., Lee, M. J. W., & Barnes, C. (Eds.). (2008). Polar bears, black gold and light bulbs. Creating stable futures for tertiary education through instructor training and support in the use of ICTs. *Proceedings of World Conference on Educational Multimedia, Hypermedia and Telecommunications.*

Tynan, B., & Lee, M. J. W. (2009). Tales of adventure and change. Academic staff members' future visions of higher education and their professional development needs. *On the Horizon*, *17*(2), 98–108. doi:10.1108/10748120910965485

Urama, Ke., & Acheampong, E. (2013). Social Innovation Creates Prosperous Societies. *Stanford Social Innovation Review*. Retrieved from http://www.ssireview.org/articles/entry/social_innovation_creates_prosperous_societies

Uribe, B. (2017). La enseñanza de la ciencia. *Perfiles Educativos*, *39*(158), 226–230.

Valdivia-López, M., & Cuadrado-Roura, J. M. (Eds.). (2017). The economics of creative activities: a perspective from Spain and Mexico. Ciudad de Mexico, Mexico: Regional Center for Multidisciplinary Research, Universidad Nacional Autónoma de México.

Valencia, A., & Darío, G. (2012). Self-employment and entrepreneurship. A working hypothesis to explain one of the strategies adopted by governments to face the progress of the market. *Semestre Económico*, *15*(32), 103–127.

Valenzuela, M., Di Meglio, R., & Reinecke, G. (Eds.). (2006). *From the house to the formality. Experiences of the Micro Family Business Law in Chile*. Chile: International Labor Organization.

Valos, M. J., Ewing, M. T., & Powell, I. H. (2010). Practitioner prognostications on the future of online marketing. *Journal of Marketing Management*, *26*(3-4), 361–376. doi:10.1080/02672571003594762

Valquíria, B., & Renata, C.A. (2013). *Historia secreta de la obsolescencia programada*. Academic Press.

Van der Sijde, P. (2012). Profiting from knowledge circulation. The gains from university-industry interaction. *Industry and Higher Education*, *26*(1), 15–19. doi:10.5367/ihe.2012.0082

van der Ven, B. (2008). An ethical framework for the marketing of corporate social responsibility. *Journal of Business Ethics*, *82*(2), 339–352. doi:10.100710551-008-9890-1

Van Praag, C. M., & Van der Sluis, J. (2004). Economic returns to education for entrepreneurs: The development of a neglected child in the family of the economics of education? *Swedish Economic Policy Review*, *11*(2), 183–225.

Vandekerkhof, P., Steijvers, T., Hendriks, W., & Voordeckers, W. (2018). Socioemotional wealth separation and decision-making quality in family firm TMTs, The moderating role of psychological safety. *Journal of Management Studies*, *55*(4), 648–676. doi:10.1111/joms.12277

Vardaman, J. M., & Gondo, M. B. (2014). Socioemotional wealth conflict in family firms. *Entrepreneurship Theory and Practice*, *38*(6), 1317–1322.

Varela, R. (2001). *Innovación empresarial. Arte y ciencia en la creación de empresas.* Pearson.

Varga, A., & Schalk, H. (2004). Knowledge spillovers, agglomeration, and macroeconomic growth: An empirical approach. *Regional Studies*, *38*(8), 977–989. doi:10.1080/0034340042000280974

Varian, H. (1990). Monitoring agents with other agents. *Journal of Institutional and Theoretical Economics*, *146*, 155–174.

Vaughan, L., & Chen, Y. (2015). Data mining from web search queries: A comparison of google trends and baidu index. *Journal of the Association for Information Science and Technology*, *66*(1), 13–22. doi:10.1002/asi.23201

Veciana, J. (2001). Creación de empresas como campo de estudio y salida profesional: Evolución, estado actual y tendencias de desarrollo. *RGE-Revista de Gestão e Economia*, *12*(3), 2–9.

Vega, A., Rojas, M.J., & Salazar, G. (2018). University Social Responsibility: Recent contributions to the Small Companies Development in Chile. *Revista Venezolana de Gerencia, 23*(1), 328-345.

Vega, A., & Rodríguez, P. (2015). Regionalisms in South America and their effects on intraregional development from an economic, scientific and technological perspective. *Espaciotiempo. Revista Latinoamericana de Ciencias Sociales y Humanidades*, *8*(9), 7–16.

Velamuri, S. R., & Venkataraman, S. (2004). An empirical study of the transition from paid work to self-employment. *The Journal of Entrepreneurial Finance*, *10*(1), 1–16.

Velasco, R., & Saiz, M. (2007). Business creation policies and their evaluation. *Working Papers, 118*, 1-70.

Velitchka, M.H., & Rohm, A. (2016). *Article information: Hashtags and Handshakes.* Academic Press.

Venkatraman, N. (1989). Strategic orientation of business enterprises, The construct, dimensionality, and measurement. *Management Science*, *35*(8), 942–962. doi:10.1287/mnsc.35.8.942

Venkatraman, N., & Henderson, J. C. (1998). Real strategies for virtual organizing. *Sloan Management Review*, *40*, 33–48.

Vera-Oyarzún, M. B., & Moreira-López, V. H. (2009). Characterization of Small Agricultural Enterprises in Southern Chile. *Idesia*, *27*(3), 89–99.

Vera, P. (2017). Processes of urban requalification and innovation imaginaries. The Rosario case, Argentina. *EURE. Revista Latinoamericana de Estudios Urbano Regionales*, *43*(129), 209–234. doi:10.4067/S0250-71612017000200010

Vesper, K. (1979). Growing concerns. *Harvard Business Review*, *2*, 164–170.

Virtanen, M. (1997). The Role of Different Theories in Explaining Entrepreneurship. *Journal of Best Papers of the 42nd World Conference "International Council for Small Business 1997"*.

Visser, W., & Tolhurst, N. (2010). *The world guide to CSR. A country-to-country analysis of corporate sustainability and responsibility.* Sheffield, UK: Greenleaf Publishing.

Vives, A., & Peinado-Vara, E. (2011). *La Responsabilidad Social de la Empresa en América Latina. Manual de gestión.* Montevideo, Uruguay: Inter-American Development Bank.

Vlastakis, N., & Markellos, R. N. (2012). Information demand and stock market volatility. *Journal of Banking & Finance*, *36*(6), 1808–1821. doi:10.1016/j.jbankfin.2012.02.007

Wales, W. J., Gupta, V. K., & Mousa, F. T. (2013). Empirical research on entrepreneurial orientation, An assessment and suggestions for future research. *International Small Business Journal*, *31*(4), 357–383. doi:10.1177/0266242611418261

Wales, W., Monsen, E., & McKelvie, A. (2011). The organizational pervasiveness of entrepreneurial orientation. *Entrepreneurship Theory and Practice*, *35*(5), 895–923. doi:10.1111/j.1540-6520.2011.00451.x

Wang, C. L., & Ahmed, P. K. (2007). Dynamic capabilities: A review and research agenda. *International Journal of Management Reviews*, *9*(1), 31–51. doi:10.1111/j.1468-2370.2007.00201.x

Wangenheim, F., & Bayón, T. (2004). The effect of word of mouth on services switching: Measurement and moderating variables. *European Journal of Marketing*, *38*(9/10), 1173–1185. doi:10.1108/03090560410548924

Waring, M. (2018). *Social pressures and curriculum innovation: A study of the Nuffield Foundation Science Teaching Project*. London, UK: Routledge. doi:10.4324/9780429453922

Wartick, S. L., & Cochran, P. L. (1985). The evolution of the corporate social performance model. *Academy of Management Review*, *10*(4), 758–769. doi:10.5465/amr.1985.4279099

Weber, M. (1942). *Historia económica general*. Fondo de Cultura Económica.

Weber, M. (1964). *Economía y sociedad. Esbozo de sociología comprensiva*. Fondo de Cultura Económica.

Weber, M. (1984). *La ética protestante y el espíritu del capitalismo*. Madrid, Spain: Sarpe.

Weber, M. (2008). The business case for corporate social responsibility: A company level measurement approach for CSR. *European Management Journal*, *26*(4), 247–261. doi:10.1016/j.emj.2008.01.006

Weerawardena, J., & Mort, G. S. (2006). Investigating Social Entrepreneurship: A Multidimensional Model. *Journal of World Business*, *41*(1), 21–35. doi:10.1016/j.jwb.2005.09.001

Weinreich, N. K. (1996). A perfect union: Integrating quantitative and qualitative methods in social marketing research. *Social Marketing Quarterly*, *3*(1), 53–58. doi:10.1177/152450049600300106

Weischedel, B., & Huizingh, E. (2006). Website optimization with Web metrics: A case study. *Proceedings of the 8th International Conference on Electronic Commerce*, 463–470. 10.1145/1151454.1151525

Wennberg, K. (2009). Knowledge combinations and the survival of financial services ventures. *Journal of Evolutionary Economics*, *19*(2), 259–276. doi:10.100700191-008-0124-6

Wenner, M. D. (1995). Group Credit: A Means to Improve Transfer and Loan Repayment Performance. *The Journal of Development Studies*, *32*(2), 263–281. doi:10.1080/00220389508422414

Wernerfelt, B. (1984). A resource-based view of the firm. *Strategic Management Journal*, *5*(2), 171–180. doi:10.1002mj.4250050207

West, M., & Posner, A. (2013). Defining Your Competitive Advantage. *Stanford Social Innovation Review*. Available from: http://www.ssireview.org/blog/entry/defining_your_competitive_advantage

Westhead, P., & Howorth, C. (2007). 'Types' of private family firms. An exploratory conceptual and empirical analysis. *Entrepreneurship and Regional Development*, *19*(5), 405–431. doi:10.1080/08985620701552405

White Paper on Entrepreneurship in Spain. (2011). Barcelona, Spain: ESADE Business School.

Wiertz, C., & de Ruyter, K. (2007). Beyond the call of duty: Why customers contribute to firm-hosted commercial online communities. *Organization Studies*, *28*(3), 347–376. doi:10.1177/0170840607076003

Wiklund, J., & Shepherd, D. (2005). Entrepreneurial orientation and small business performance, A configurational approach. *Journal of Business Venturing*, *20*(1), 71–91. doi:10.1016/j.jbusvent.2004.01.001

Williams, D. L., Beard, J. D., & Rymer, J. (1991). Team Projects: Achieving their Full Potential. *Journal of Marketing Education*, *13*(2), 45–53. doi:10.1177/027347539101300208

Wilson, F., Kickul, J., & Marlino, D. (2007). Gender, Entrepreneurial Self-Efficacy, and Entrepreneurial Career Intentions: Implications for Entrepreneurship Education 1. *Entrepreneurship Theory and Practice*, *31*(3), 387–406. doi:10.1111/j.1540-6520.2007.00179.x

Wilson, R. D. (2010). Using clickstream data to enhance business-to-business web site performance. *Journal of Business and Industrial Marketing*, *25*(3), 177–187. doi:10.1108/08858621011027768

Winter, S. G. (2003). Understanding dynamic capabilities. *Strategic Management Journal*, *24*(10), 991–995. doi:10.1002mj.318

Winterton, J. (2009). Competence across Europe. Highest common factor or lowest common denominator? *Journal of European Industrial Training*, *33*(8/9), 681–700. doi:10.1108/03090590910993571

Wiseman, R. M., & Gómez-Mejía, L. R. (1998). A behavioural agency model of managerial risk taking. *Academy of Management Review*, *23*(1), 133–153. doi:10.5465/amr.1998.192967

Wompner, F. H. (2012). El emprendimiento como factor de movilización social. *Nómadas*, *36*, 58–69.

Wong, M.L., Khong, C.W., & Thwaites, H. (2012). Applied UX and UCD Design Process in Interface Design. *Procedia-Social and Behavioral Sciences, 51*(2000), 703-708. doi:10.1016/j.sbspro.2012.08.228

Wong, Y.-J., Chang, S.-C., & Chen, L.-Y. (2010). Does a family-controlled firm perform better in corporate venturing? *Corporate Governance*, *18*(3), 175–192. doi:10.1111/j.1467-8683.2010.00792.x

Wu, L., & Brynjolfsson, E. (2015). The Future of Prediction: How Google Searches Foreshadow Housing Prices and Sales. In *Economic Analysis of the Digital Economy* (pp. 89–118). University of Chicago Press.

Wu, S.-C., & Fang, W. (2010). The effect of consumer-to-consumer interactions on idea generation in virtual brand community relationships. *Technovation*, *30*(11), 570–581. doi:10.1016/j.technovation.2010.07.005

Wu, Y. C., Kuo, T., & Shen, J. P. (2013). Exploring social entrepreneurship education from a web-based pedagogical perspective. *Computers in Human Behavior*, *29*(2), 329–334. doi:10.1016/j.chb.2012.08.012

Wydick, B. (1999). Can Social Cohesion Be Harnessed to Repair Market Failures? Evidence from Group Lending in Guatemala. *Economic Journal (London)*, *109*(457), 463–475. doi:10.1111/1468-0297.00457

Wymbs, C. (2011). Digital Marketing: The Time for a New "Academic Major" has Arrived. *Journal of Marketing Education*, *33*(1), 93–106. doi:10.1177/0273475310392544

Yang, X., Pan, B., Evans, J., & Lv, B. (n.d.). Forecasting Chinese tourist volume with search engine data. *Tourism Management, 46*, 386-397.

Yaqoob, I., Abaker, I., Hashem, T., & Ahmed, A. (2018). Internet of things forensics: Recent advances, taxonomy, requirements, and open challenges. *Future Generation Computer Systems*, *79*(1), 1003–1025.

Yelowitz, A., & Wilson, M. (2015). Characteristics of Bitcoin users: An analysis of Google search data. *Applied Economics Letters*, *22*(13), 1030–1036. doi:10.1080/13504851.2014.995359

Yin, L., & Li, J. (2013). Estudio sobre la situación actual de la educación empresarial. III Conferencia Internacional de Educación y Gestión de la Educación (EEM), 188-191.

Yunus, M. (2006). *El banquero de los pobres: los microcréditos y la batalla contra la pobreza en el mundo*. Barcelona, Spain: Paidós.

Yunus, M., Moingeon, B., & Lehmann, L. (2010). Building Social Business Models: Lessons from the Grameen Experience. *Long Range Planning*, *43*(2-3), 308–325. doi:10.1016/j.lrp.2009.12.005

Yusuf, M., Adams, C., & Dingley, K. (2016). Digital citizen participation within schools in the United Kingdom and Indonesia: An Actor-Network Theory (ANT) perspective. *Information*, *7*(4), 69–81. doi:10.3390/info7040069

Zabludovsky, G. (2007). Las mujeres en México: Trabajo, educación superior y esferas de poder. *Política y Cultura*, *28*, 9–41.

Zabludovsky, G., & de Avelar, S. (2001). *Empresarias y ejecutivas en México y Brasil*. D.F., Mexico: UNAM.

Zahra, S. A. (1996). Technology strategy and financial performance: Examining the of the firm's competitive environment. *Journal of Business Venturing*, *11*(3), 189–219. doi:10.1016/0883-9026(96)00001-8

Zahra, S. A. (2012). Organizational learning and entrepreneurship in family firms, Exploring the moderating effect of ownership and cohesion. *Small Business Economics*, *38*(1), 51–65. doi:10.100711187-010-9266-7

Zahra, S. A., Hayton, J. C., & Salvato, C. (2004). Entrepreneurship in family vs. non-family firms, A resource-based analysis of the effect of organizational culture. *Entrepreneurship Theory and Practice*, *28*(4), 363–381. doi:10.1111/j.1540-6520.2004.00051.x

Zahra, S. A., & Nielsen, A. P. (2002). Sources of capabilities, integration and technology commercialization. *Strategic Management Journal*, *23*(5), 377–398. doi:10.1002mj.229

Zahra, S. A., Rawhouser, H. N., Bhawe, N., Neubaumm, D. O., & Hayton, J. C. (2008). Globalization of social entrepreneurship opportunities. *Strategic Entrepreneurship Journal*, *2*(2), 117–131. doi:10.1002ej.43

Zain, S. M. (2013). Educación Sostenible y Emprendimiento disparadores Innovación Cultura en 3R. VI Foro Internacional sobre la Enseñanza de la Ingeniería (IFEE), 128-133.

Zaratiegui, J. R. (1999). La Gestión por Procesos: Su papel e importancia en la empresa. *Economía Industrial*, *330*, 81–88.

Zellweger, T. M., Nason, R. S., Nordqvist, M., & Brush, C. G. (2013). Why do family firms strive for nonfinancial goals? An organizational identity perspective. *Entrepreneurship Theory and Practice*, *37*(2), 229–248. doi:10.1111/j.1540-6520.2011.00466.x

Zhuang, J., Gunatilake, H. M., Niimi, Y., Khan, M. E., Jiang, Y., Hasan, R., . . . Huang, B. (2009). *Financial Sector Development, Economic Growth, and Poverty Reduction: A Literature Review*. Asian Development Bank Economics Working Paper Series, No. 173, 1-46.

Zott, C., Amit, R., & Massa, L. (2011). The business model: Recent developments and future research. *Journal of Management*, *37*(4), 1019–1042. doi:10.1177/0149206311406265

About the Contributors

Jose Manuel Saiz-Alvarez, Ph.D. (with Hons.) in Economics & Business Administration, Autonomous University of Madrid (Spain); Ph.D. (with Hons.) in Sociology, Pontifical University of Salamanca (Spain), is a member of the National System of Researchers of the National Council for Science and Technology (CONACYT) in Mexico, and a regular member of the Mexican Academy of Sciences. Research Professor, EGADE Business School-Tecnologico de Monterrey (Mexico), and visiting professor, the Catholic University of Santiago de Guayaquil (Ecuador) and Autonomous University of Manizales (Colombia). Honorary Professor, Autonomous University of Madrid (Spain). Certificate of Recognition, Capitol House of Representatives of Puerto Rico. Diploma of Honor, Valahia University of Targoviste (Romania). He has given more than one hundred lectures in Europe and America and is the author of more than three hundred publications in his specialty. To date, he has supervised 74 doctoral theses and is a member of Editorial Boards and referee of numerous national and international journals. He is in the Who's Who in the World, from the 2011 Edition.

* * *

Patricia Alonso-Galicia has a Ph.D. in Administration from the University of Cantabria, Spain, and a member of the Santander Chair in Family Business at the University of Granada, Spain. Currently a professor of entrepreneurship at Tecnológico de Monterrey, Querétaro Campus, she develops research in entrepreneurial cognition, academic entrepreneurship, the impact of training in the entrepreneurial spirit and emotional intelligence. He has published his work in high impact scientific journals such as European Management Journal and Journal of Managerial Psychology. In addition, she has been Director of the Entrepreneur Institute of San Luis (IESL) of the Economic Development Department of the City Hall of San Luis Potosí (2012-2015). She has teaching experience in subjects related to strategy, costs, creativity, sources of financing for entrepreneurs and acceleration of family businesses, as well as more than ten years of work experience in the food industry, especially in marketing project management. She has co-authored the book "Startup U: Entrepreneurs of High Impact", published in Mexico and Spain and currently directs the Educational Innovation Project: "Effect of the development of emotional competences in students of entrepreneurship subjects".

Marieke C. Baaken (BA), born in Germany, has completed her studies in economics and cultural anthropology at the Georg-August-University in Göttingen, Germany. Actually she is completing her double degree Master Program in International Economics at Georg-August-University in Göttingen and RUG Rijksuniversiteit Groningen, NL. Before Marieke worked at TecMinho, the Technology Transfer

Branch of Minho University in Braga/Guimarães Portugal as a Market Researcher and Analyst in a Horizon2020 project in European Nanomedicine after she was six months working at Centro de Transferencia Tecnológica y Educación Continua (CTEC), Costa Rica, establishing events on University-Business Cooperation with SMEs as well as creating and launching a Student Entrepreneurship Contest.

Thomas Baaken (Dr. rer. pol., Dr. habil.) holds a position as Tenure Professor in Marketing at the Münster University of Applied Sciences MUAS (www.fh-muenster.de) since 1992. 1998-2003 Thomas Baaken held the position of the Vice President Research and TechTransfer at MUAS. In 2002 he founded the "Science-to-Business Marketing Research Centre" Marketing (www.science-marketing.com), which is creating Marketing Strategies for Research. Thomas was Visiting Professor at the ECIC Entrepreneurship Commercialisation and Innovation Centre of The University of Adelaide AUS in in 2003/2004. During that stay, he held the 1st Science-to-Business Conference which has since been replicated across the world. Thomas was appointed Adjunct Professor with the ECIC in 2008. Besides his Adjunct Position at ECIC, Thomas holds International Fellowships at VU Vrije Universiteit Amsterdam, The Netherlands, Guest Professorship at Christ University in Bangalore, India, PD at IHI Zittau of Technical University Dresden, Germany and Research Fellowship at Satakunta University of Applied Sciences in Finland.

Neeta Baporikar is currently Director/Professor (Business Management) at Harold Pupkewitz Graduate School of Business (HP-GSB), Namibia University of Science and Technology, Namibia. Prior to this, she was Head-Scientific Research, with Ministry of Higher Education CAS-Salalah, Sultanate of Oman, Professor (Strategic Management and Entrepreneurship) at IIIT Pune and BITS India. With more than a decade of experience in industry, consultancy, and training, she made a lateral switch to research and academics in 1995. Dr. Baporikar holds D.Sc. (Management Studies) USA, Ph.D. in Management, University of Pune INDIA with MBA (Distinction) and Law (Hons.) degrees. Apart from this, she is also an External Reviewer, Oman Academic Accreditation Authority, Accredited Management Teacher, Qualified Trainer, Doctoral Guide and Board Member of Academics and Advisory Committee in accredited B-Schools. Reviewer for international journals, she has to her credit several conferred doctorates, refereed research papers, and authored books in the area of Entrepreneurship, Strategy, Management and Higher Education.

Danny Barbery-Montoya is an Economist specialized in marketing graduated from Escuela Superior Politécnica del Litoral (Ecuador). Master in Business Administration, Escuela de Posgrados de Administración de Empresas (Ecuador), and Master in Creation and Business Management, Nebrija University (Spain). Ph.D. in Business Sciences, Nebrija University (Spain). Professor at Universidad de Especialidades Espíritu Santo (Ecuador).

Christopher Boachie is a lecturer of Central Business School, Central University College in Accra Ghana, an academic and a practicing Chartered Accountant (ACCA-UK) with specialization in corporate finance, international trade, auditing, financial statement fraud, and financial risk management. He was educated in Kwame Nkrumah University of Science and Technology in Kumasi Ghana, The Technical University of Freiberg in Germany and the London School of Accountancy (UK). He is currently reading his Ph.D. at the Open University of Malaysia. He has considerable, teaching, consulting and practice experience in the application of accountancy and finance theory and financing of international trade and risk management.H e is a Chartered Accountant with the Association of Certified Chartered Accountants of UK. He was an Investment Manager and in charge of oil and gas unit of International Energy Insurance. He has worked and consulted for Stephens and Co in London, LD and sons both in Ghana and Italy. He is a founding Director of Premia consulting firm in Ghana. His professional focus is on corporate financial analysis, financial accounting and reporting and has a strong passion for financial risk management.

Guillermo Bustamante-Pavez is a Ph.D. candidate in Communication, Universidad de Los Andes (Chile) M.A. in Communication and Digital Journalism, Universidad Mayor (Chile) M.A. in Marketing Direction, Universidad Diego Portales (Chile) M.A. in Digital Marketing, Universitat Pompeu Fabra (Barcelona, Spain) and B.Sc in Social Communication Universidad Católica de la Santísima Concepción. His research interests are focused on Transmedia Storytelling, News Game, and Quality Journalism. He currently works as Professor at the Journalism School in Universidad Finis Terrae (Chile). He is a member of the 'Cátedra Latinoamericana de Narrativas Transmedia, Instituto de Cooperación Latinoamericana (ICLA), Universidad Nacional de Rosario (Argentina), and a partner of the Association of Researchers in Communication of Chile, IncomChile. ORCID: https://orcid.org/0000-0001-6997-0353.

Usha Chauhan is a Ph.D. candidate in Corporate Social Responsibility, School of Management, BML Munjal University, Haryana (India). She has more than five years of experience in teaching at UG-PG College, Hodal Haryana (India).

Ritu Chhikara is an Assistant Professor at School of Management, BML Munjal University. She holds a PhD in Retail Management from Faculty of Management Studies, University of Delhi. Before Ph.D., she worked with Microsoft India, in Sales and Marketing domain. She was involved in their public sector education business. Dr. Ritu has a Master's in Business Administration with specialization in Marketing from FMS, Delhi. She is an engineer in Electronics and Communication and has worked with Birlasoft as a Software Engineer. Currently, she is working on a project titled "State of Retail Education in India: Identifying the Gaps between Industry and Academia" funded by the Indian Council for Social Science Research (ICSSR). She is a regular writer in business magazines, and her recent articles have featured in Business Today, SME World, SAR Economist, etc. Her current research interest is in the area of Retailing in Emerging Economies (particularly India), Consumer Behaviour, Relationship Marketing Strategies, and Customer Experience Management. Dr. Ritu has presented papers in National and International Conferences of repute. She has also published articles in peer-reviewed journals. Her other interests include reading history, swimming, and practicing yoga.

Laura Victoria Fielden Burns currently teaches at the English Philology Department in the Education Faculty of the University of Extremadura in Badajoz (Spain). Her Ph.D. was completed at the same university, and she holds an M.A. in Romance Languages from the University of North Carolina, Chapel Hill (USA). She has participated in numerous research projects, international conferences, and scientific publications, and is a member of the "Gexcall" research group. Her research focuses on motivation in language learning, as well as English for Specific Purposes.

Cynthia Franco-Rodriguez is currently regional director of the technology transfer office of Tecnologico de Monterrey campus Guadalajara. Full-time professor in the entrepreneurship Area (2008). Degree in Business Administration (1996), Master in business management for experienced executives (2005). PhD in Legal and Business Sciences (2017). The areas of specialization are: Intellectual Property management (advice to protect inventions, distinctive signs and copyrights). Management of research and technological development projects Sectoral Innovation Fund (SE and CONACYT), mixed fund (CONACYT and Government of the state of Jalisco) and program stimulus to innovation. Monitoring in the performance and development of consultancy projects related to the private sector. Collaboration with companies such as Nike in Mexico, Sinergit and Confivero in the development of new products, process analysis and implementation of ERP´s. Between 2008 and 2011, projects were carried out to identify business opportunities for some sectors in the states of León, Zacatecas, Sonora and Jalisco with the aim of promoting regional development and strategic planning. Specialization courses in technology transfer (Oxford University UK); Technology Marketing (University of Texas Austin); Competitive Intelligence (Steinbeis Mexico) and valuation of intangibles (Becerril Coca and Becerril). Teaching in technology management, technological entrepreneurs and training for the development of business leadership. Certification in Teacher Skills Development Program (PDHD).

Ruchi Garg is an assistant professor in the School of Management at the BML Munjal University. She is pursuing her fellowship programme in management (FPM) from Management Development Institute, Gurgaon. Her FPM topic is "An investigation into the concept of Brand Love and its proximal and distal co-variates: A mixed method research in India". Prior to this, she did her M.Phil in Management from C.D.L.U, Sirsa. She also qualified UGC- NET and JRF in Management. She has two years of experience in teaching. She did her MBA from Maharishi Dayanand University, Rohtak. She has expertise in several software tools like SPSS, AMOS, etc. In addition to this, she has published her research papers with national and international journals. She has also presented number of research papers in National and International conferences. She is a reviewer of Journal of relationship marketing. Her research interest includes Consumer-brand relationship, Brand love, Sustainability marketing, and Word-of-mouth communication.

Raúl Gómez-Martínez has a Ph.D. in Business Economics and Finance from the Universidad Rey Juan Carlos of Madrid with "outstanding cum laude." Since 2007 he teaches finance subjects in undergraduate and master programs. He has participated in research projects, national and international congresses, and seminars. Published several articles in scientific journals and book editorials. Currently, he coordinates the "Emotional Economy" line of study in the M&BE research group. Since 1997 he has worked as a consultant with the main national financial institutions (Santander Group, BBVA, Bankia, Caja Rural, etc.) both in Spain and abroad, mainly in projects related to Treasury, Financial Markets, Products of Investment, SW Quality Assurance and Big Data & Analytics. From June 2015 to December 2017 he was the general manager of Apara technology company and since January 2017 he has been a founding partner of InvestMood Fintech.

Remedios Hernández-Linares is an associate professor in the Department of Financial Economy and Accounting at the University of Extremadura (Spain). She received her Ph.D. from the University of Cantabria (Spain). Her primary research interests include family businesses, business strategy, entrepreneurship, and higher education learning. Her work has appeared in Scientometrics, Family Business

Review, Journal of Family Business Strategy, European Journal of Family Business, and the book entitled The Routledge Companion to Family Business.

Bert Kiel (Dr. rer. nat.) is professor of international marketing and sales at Münster University of Applied Sciences. He earned his diploma degree in physics from the University of Bonn, as well as a diploma degree Wirtschaftsphysiker from the Fernuniversität Hagen. He earned his doctoral degree in natural sciences in 1999 from the University of Erlangen Nürnberg. Prior to entering academia, Bert Kiel held various industry positions including chief commercial officer of Cotel, Bolivia and Managing Consultant of Detecon International Gmbh. He worked for 10 years as a consultant and manager on five continents. His research interests focus on competences in marketing and sales. His teaching interest includes international sales, international marketing, sustainable business administration, CRM, e-commerce and Negotiations.

Diego Lopez Cardona is Professor at the University of Manizales (Colombia), Associate Professor at the University of National University of Colombia headquarters Manizales. Ph.D. in Computing Sciences, Pontifical University of Salamanca (Spain). M.A. in Education, University of Manizales (Colombia). Some specialization courses at University of Cantabria (Spain), and Technological University of Pereira (Colombia). B.Sc. in Industrial Engineering, The National University of Colombia, Manizales (Colombia).

María Concepción López-Fernández has a Ph.D. and associate professor of Strategy and holds the Santander Chair in Family Business at the University of Cantabria (Spain). Her primary research interests include entrepreneurship, family business, strategy, innovation, flexibility, and tourism. Her articles have been published, among others, in Family Business Review, Journal of Family Business Strategy, Journal of Small Business Management, International Journal of Production Research, R&D Management, Journal of Manufacturing Systems, Cornell Hospitality Quarterly, and Tourism Management.

Gideon Maas Ph.D.), born in South Africa, is the Professor in Professional Practice at Coventry University in UK and the Director of the International Centre for Transformational Entrepreneurship at this University. Gideon serves also as President of the Institute for Small Business and Entrepreneurship (www.isbe.org.uk) He has extended international business and academic experiences in various countries such as China, Europe and Africa. Within the academic environment he has created various entrepreneurship centres at different universities over the past years, developed and implemented undergraduate and post-graduate modules and programmes focusing specifically on enterprise and entrepreneurship.

María Naranjo-Sánchez, B.A. in English Studies, and M.A. in Secondary Education and University Research, she is a substitute professor of English at the University Centre of Merida (Spain). As a member of the research group "GexCall," she has been involved as a researcher in European projects mostly in the field of education and language training. She is a Ph.D. candidate, and her primary research areas are languages for specific purposes, and ICT applied to language learning.

Balzhan Orazbayeva, affiliated with the Science-to-Business Marketing Research Centre at Münster University of Applied Sciences (MUAS) in Germany, researches university-business collaboration and social innovation. She was a senior analyst in the consulting project for the European Commission (DG Education and Culture), implementing the largest European study in the area of university-business cooperation. Balzhan is the co-editor of the Future Universities Thoughtbook. She leads creative research process as part of Erasmus+ project in the field of social innovation. In her role of educator, Balzhan is a lecturer in social innovation and entrepreneurship. She also coordinates industry projects executed by students as part of International Marketing and Strategic Marketing modules at MUAS. Balzhan is a doctoral candidate at VU Amsterdam and focuses in her Ph.D. on higher education in the context of university-business collaboration. She holds a Bachelor degree on International Relations in a field of political and social sciences from German-Kazakh University (DKU) in Almaty, Kazakhstan. In addition, she holds a Master degree on Integrative Project Management from International Institute (IHI) Zittau, a central academic unit of Dresden University of Technology (TUD) in Germany.

Jesús Manuel Palma-Ruiz is Associate Professor in the Faculty of International Economics, Universidad Autónoma de Chihuahua (UACH) in Mexico. He holds an International Ph.D. (Hons.) in Business and Entrepreneurial Management with application to SMEs, Entrepreneurship, and Family Firms, University of Cantabria (UC) in Spain. He is a member of the National System of Researchers of the National Council for Science and Technology (CONACYT) in Mexico. He is a former scholar for the Walton International Program in the USA, Carolina Foundation in Spain, and CONACYT in Mexico and Spain. With more than 15 years of professional experience in both private and public sectors, he has been a professor of business for graduate and undergraduate levels at Tecnológico de Monterrey and UACH. He is a collaborator in research groups in Mexico and Spain. He has been Visiting Professor and Santander´s Bank Chair of Family Business Coordinator at UC. He has published in scientific journals on topics related to entrepreneurship and family business, and co-edited books with IGI Global and Springer editorials.

Carlos Ricardo Rey-Campero is a professor at the Universidad Externado de Colombia in the areas of project management, financial evaluation, and financial mathematics. He is also a professor at the Pontificia Universidad Javeriana (Colombia) in the areas of project evaluation. Author of articles in academic journals on topics of entrepreneurship and the formulation and evaluation of projects. Project director of undergraduate and postgraduate degrees (masters) in issues of business creation, business plans, and feasibility studies. Professional experience in formulating and evaluating strategies for investment projects, structuring business models and preparing business plans. He has a degree in Civil Engineering from the Pontificia Universidad Javeriana, an MBA from the University of Los Andes and a Doctorate in Business Sciences with a specialization in family business and entrepreneurship from the Universidad Antonio de Nebrija.

Ruth Rojas Dávila, DBA (candidate) in Business Administration, The Catholic University of Peru-CENTRUM (Peru); M.Sc. in Business Administration, Salesian Polytechnic University (Ecuador); B.Sc. in Engineering with specialization in Business Administration, Marketing, and Advertising, has been teaching at the Catholic University of Santiago de Guayaquil (Ecuador) and Ecotec University (Ecuador) for more than 10 years and has more than 20 years of experience in public and private firms.

Sue Rossano Rivero, born in Mexico, is currently a Junior Professor in Entrepreneurship and International Business Development at the faculty of business at Münster University of Applied Sciences (MUAS) and a researcher at the Science-to-Business Marketing Research Centre in the same university, where she leads one out of three Research Lines, namely "Science-to-Business". Sue holds a Bachelor degree from Northwood University in Michigan (USA) on International business and economics. She holds a master's degree in Electronic Commerce from the Graduate School of Business from Tec de Monterrey (México) and completed her PhD on Academic Entrepreneurship at Vrije Universiteit Amsterdam at the faculty of social and organisational sciences. Her research focuses on "Entrepreneurial competences within the university."

Guido Salazar-Sepúlveda is a Ph.D. candidate in Law and Business Administration, Universidad de Lleida (Spain), M.Sc. in Industrial Engineering, Universidad de Concepción (Chile), Master of Business Administration, Universidad del Mar (Chile), and B.Sc. in Fishing Engineering, Universidad Católica de la Santísima Concepción (Chile). He currently works as Qualification Office Director, Universidad Católica de la Santísima Concepción (Chile). He has experience as Project Engineer on Entrepreneurship Training. He has carried out programs for the Chilean Technical Cooperation Service, Inter-American Development Bank, the Regional Agency for Innovation and Development of the Biobio Region, and the Foundation for Agrarian Innovation. He is also an Entrepreneurship and economic development studies research fellow in the Foundation 'School of International Affairs' (Chile). ORCID: https://orcid.org/0000-0002-4979-6869.

Rebeca San José-Cabezudo has a Ph.D. in Business Administration from the University of Valladolid (Spain) where she teaches courses related to Marketing and Management. Her primary research focuses on new technologies and e-marketing (e.g., online communities, mobile marketing, electronic commerce, omnichannel customer behavior, online loyalty programs, video games or internet advertising). She has participated in many scientific conferences, and her research has been published in internationally ranked journals, including Internet Research, Technovation, Computers in Human Behaviour, Electronic Commerce Research and Applications, Online Information Review, Telematics and Informatics, Psychology and Marketing, and Journal of Advertising, among others.

Víctor Temprano-García is Ph.D. and Lecturer in Marketing at the University of Valladolid (Spain). His research focuses on brand deletion decision-making, brand strategy, brand portfolio management, and strategic marketing. He has published several papers, book chapters, and conference papers on brand management. He has participated in over 40 research and consultancy projects. In 2016 he was awarded the AEMARK Best Work in Progress Award, and the Research Award of the Economic and Social Council of Castilla y León in 2004. He is a former member of the Board of Directors of the Valladolid Business School (Spain), a former advisor of the Spanish Federation of Marketing Presidency, and a former partner of MCV Network Team, Llc.

Carlos Torrejón Martín, Ph.D. in Business Sciences, Nebrija University (Spain); D.B.A., Complutense University of Madrid (Spain); MBA, Instituto de Empresa (Spain); PDD, IESE Business School-University of Navarre (Spain), is a member of the Royal Institution of Chartered Surveyors, specializing in Finances and Investment. He has more than 20 years of experience in financial management, financial analysis, investment, real estate, personal finance, management and business organization, entrepreneurship, and skills for entrepreneurs and managers. He teaches in Spain at Nebrija Business School, ENME, and EU-School.

Carlos Torres Briones, Ph.D. in Business Sciences, Nebrija University (Spain); M.Sc. in Creation and Business Management, Nebrija University (Spain); M.Sc. in Business Administration, Espiritu Santo University (Ecuador); B.Sc. in Engineering in Business Studies with concentration in Marketing, Espiritu Santo University (Ecuador) is a Research Professor, University of Guayaquil (Ecuador), and at Federico Santa Maria University Guayaquil Campus (Ecuador).

Teresa Treviño is currently Associate Professor of Marketing at Universidad de Monterrey. She holds a PhD. in Management Sciences and a Master's degree in Marketing from EGADE Business School, Tecnológico de Monterrey, Mexico. Her research interests focus on online consumer behavior and digital marketing, specifically consumer-brand relationships on the Internet, motivations and uses and gratifications of different online segments when using social media, e-WOM, and the impact of online marketing strategies on consumers. She is currently a member of Mexico's National Researchers System (CONACyT).

Alejandro Vega-Muñoz has a Ph.D. in Business Studies, Universidad Antonio de Nebrija (Spain), M.Sc. in Industrial Engineering, Universidad de Concepción (Chile), B.Sc. in Port Engineering, Universidad Católica de la Santísima Concepción (Chile), and B.Sc. in Education, Universidad de Antofagasta (Chile). His research interests are focused on sectoral economics, international relations, economic geography and their relationship with economic development studies. He currently works as a Researcher in Universidad Autónoma de Chile (Chile), Foundation 'School of International Affairs' (Chile), PIIE Corporation (Chile), and Universidad Nacional de la Patagonia San Juan Bosco (Argentina). Member of SOCHIGEO (Sociedad Chilena de Ciencias Geográficas), and Professor at HEIs in Chile, Spain, Argentina, and Peru. ORCID: http://orcid.org/0000-0002-9427-2044.

Murat Yulek is a professor of economics at Istanbul Commerce University (Turkey) and a partner at PGlobal Global Advisory and Training Services Ltd, an Ankara based international advisory company. Murat holds and has held high-level executive responsibilities in financial and non-financial corporations including as director and chairman. He has a project, corporate finance and economic development experience in various countries in Europe, Africa, North America and Asia with tenures at institutions including the International Monetary Fund, the Islamic Development Bank and the Turkish Prime Ministry. He has authored or managed financial, macroeconomic, sectoral studies, impact, feasibility, and financial valuation studies and related training in various countries. He has taught at Georgetown and Yale Universities. Previously, he also served as Dean of the Faculty of Business Administration at THK University in Turkey. He authored some books and articles in economics, development, and finance. His most recent books have been published by Springer, New York, covering economic planning, industrial policy and suitable design of public procurement policies aiming at increasing the technological level in emerging countries. Murat also writes columns at newspapers and financial journals and is a frequent speaker at various for a organized by institutions such as Global Economic Symposium, Yale University (USA), Duke University (USA), Prime Ministry of Turkey, COMCEC, Economic Cooperation Organization, Dubai Economic Council, CFO Forum-Vienna (Austria), Khazanah Megatrands Forum, The Economist Round Table, Ewha Women's University (Korea), Wirtshaftsrat, APU Ritsumeikan University (Japan), Korea Institute for International Economic Policy, Universita degli Studi di Parma (Italy) and Eurofinance Conferences. He is actively involved in the organization of Istanbul Finance Summit (Chairman of the Advisory Board) and Sarajevo Business Forum (Member of the Advisory Board). He sits in the advisory boards of various other national and international institutions, platforms and academic journals. He holds an MBA degree from Yale University (USA), Ph.D. and M.A. degrees from Bilkent University (Turkey), an MSM (Management) degree from Boston University (USA) and a B.Sc. degree from Bogazici University (Turkey).

Index

F

G

H

I

J

K

L

M

N

O

P

Q

R

S

T

U

V

W

Z

www.ingramcontent.com/pod-product-compliance
Lightning Source LLC
LaVergne TN
LVHW062108300926
849161LV00010B/2401